INDIAN PRIVATE INTERNATIONAL LAW

This book provides an authoritative account of the evolution and application of private international law principles in India in civil commercial and family matters. Through a structured evaluation of the legislative and judicial decisions, the authors examine private international law in the Republic and whether it conforms to international standards and best practices as adopted in major jurisdictions such as the European Union, the United Kingdom, the United States, India's BRICS partners – Brazil, Russia, China and South Africa – and other common law systems such as Australia, Canada, New Zealand and Nepal.

Divided into 13 chapters, the book provides a contextualised understanding of legal transformation on key aspects of the Indian conflict-of-law rules on jurisdiction, applicable law and the recognition and enforcement of foreign judgments or arbitral awards. Particularly fascinating in this regard is the discussion and focus on both traditional and contemporary areas of private international law, including marriage, divorce, contractual concerns, the fourth industrial revolution, product liability, e-commerce, intellectual property, child custody, surrogacy and the complicated interface of 'Sharia' in the conflict-of-law framework.

The book deliberates the nuanced perspective of endorsing the Hague Conference on Private International Law instruments favouring enhanced uniformity and predictability in matters of choice of court, applicable law and the recognition and enforcement of foreign judgments.

The book's international and comparative focus makes it eminently resourceful for legislators, the judges of Indian courts and other interested parties such as lawyers and litigants when they are confronted with cross-border disputes that involve an examination of India's private international law. The book also provides a comprehensive understanding of Indian private international law, which will be useful for academics and researchers looking for an in-depth discussion on the subject.

Volume 6 in the series Studies in Private International Law – Asia

Studies in Private International Law – Asia

Editor: Anselmo Reyes
Advisory Editor: Paul Beaumont

Much has been written about private international law in the EU and the US. Less is known about the conflict of laws in Asia. Thus, little attention has been paid so far to the modernisation of private international law codes and rules that has been taking place over the last decade all over Asia. That trend continues. Now is the time to take stock of those reforms that have already taken place and suggest further improvements for the future.

Published under the celebrated series *Studies in Private International Law*, this monograph sub-series provides a forum for discussion and analysis of private international law in Asia. The series is not solely a survey of jurisdictions for practitioners. Comprising in-depth thematic and country-specific studies, each volume considers the private international law of Asian countries from a variety of perspectives. An underlying assumption is that private international law in different jurisdictions follow broad discernible patterns. Each volume in this sub-series highlights those patterns and discusses how rules in different Asian jurisdictions are either converging with, or diverging from, the patterns identified. Such an analytical framework will assist academics, judges, lawyers and legislators to envisage ways in which laws affecting cross-border relationships can be harmonised across jurisdictions and be made more responsive to the needs of citizens in Asia and elsewhere.

Volume 1: Recognition and Enforcement of Judgments in Civil and Commercial Matters
Edited by Anselmo Reyes

Volume 2: Indonesian Private International Law
Afifah Kusumadara

Volume 3: Chinese Private International Law
Edited by Xiaohong Liu and Zhengyi Zhang

Volume 4: Direct Jurisdiction: Asian Perspectives
Edited by Anselmo Reyes and Wilson Lui

Volume 5: Japanese Private International Law
Kazuaki Nishioka and Yuko Nishitani

Volume 6: Indian Private International Law
Stellina Jolly and Saloni Khanderia

Indian Private International Law

Stellina Jolly
and
Saloni Khanderia

•HART•
OXFORD • LONDON • NEW YORK • NEW DELHI • SYDNEY

HART PUBLISHING

Bloomsbury Publishing Plc

Kemp House, Chawley Park, Cumnor Hill, Oxford, OX2 9PH, UK

1385 Broadway, New York, NY 10018, USA

29 Earlsfort Terrace, Dublin 2, Ireland

HART PUBLISHING, the Hart/Stag logo, BLOOMSBURY and the Diana logo are trademarks of Bloomsbury Publishing Plc

First published in Great Britain 2021

A catalogue record for this book is available from the British Library.

Library of Congress Cataloging-in-Publication data

Names: Jolly, Stellina, 1976- author. | Khanderia, Saloni, author.

Title: Indian private international law / Stellina Jolly and Saloni Khanderia.

Description: Oxford, UK ; New York, NY : Hart Publishing, an imprint of Bloomsbury Publishing, 2021. | Series: Studies in private international law – Asia ; volume 6 | Includes bibliographical references and index.

Identifiers: LCCN 2021033855 (print) | LCCN 2021033856 (ebook) | ISBN 9781509938186 (hardback) | ISBN 9781509938193 (pdf) | ISBN 9781509938209 (Epub)

Subjects: LCSH: Conflict of laws—India.

Classification: LCC KNS480 .J65 2021 (print) | LCC KNS480 (ebook) | DDC 340.90954—dc23

LC record available at https://lccn.loc.gov/2021033855

LC ebook record available at https://lccn.loc.gov/2021033856

ISBN: HB: 978-1-50993-818-6
ePDF: 978-1-50993-819-3
ePub: 978-1-50993-820-9

Typeset by Compuscript Ltd, Shannon
Printed and bound in Great Britain by TJ International Ltd, Padstow, Cornwall

To find out more about our authors and books visit www.hartpublishing.co.uk. Here you will find extracts, author information, details of forthcoming events and the option to sign up for our newsletters.

FOREWORD

India has become an important role player on the international (commercial) scene. The law of the Republic, therefore, now more than ever, needs a lively and sophisticated branch of conflicts law, or private international law, to provide for, and support, the ever-increasing entanglement of national, regional, and international affairs in the private sphere. Development of case law (and legislation) in this regard is naturally preceded by academic curiosity. The Indian academic tradition in private international law has already been established for some time. Recently, however, there seems to have been an upsurge in scholarly activity in the field, including this fine book by two distinguished conflicts authors. A commendable openness to international, regional, and supranational instruments and the comparative study of a wide variety of national legal systems are the hallmark of their academic endeavours. Nevertheless, their commentaries and suggestions are well integrated into the current framework of Indian private international law in a way that facilitates the reception of valuable and suitable ideas from other traditions. The authors, from South Asian University and Jindal Global Law School, respectively, are both also much-appreciated associates of the Research Centre for Private International Law in Emerging Countries at the University of Johannesburg. Together with other emerging conflicts lawyers, they constitute the embodiment of our hope for the future innovative development of Indian private international law along rigorous intellectual lines. The authors, the series editor, and the publisher deserve our heartfelt congratulations.

Jan L Neels
Professor of Private International Law, University of Johannesburg
Honorary Member of the Governing Council of UNIDROIT
March 2021

FOREWORD

This book closes a gap in the literature on private international law from a comparative perspective by exploring a legal system which, so far, has not been very present in the global private international law discourse: India – a legal system which covers a vast (and partly internationally most mobile) population of great cultural diversity. Tushar Kumar Biswas comes in the *Encyclopaedia of Private International Law* to conclude that legal practice in India mainly relies on English literature as in India 'there has not been much doctrinal development' in this area of law.

It is rather surprising that India is a blind spot of private international law doctrine. Although India clearly belongs to the common law world, it had to react to the fact that English private international law has for decades been influenced by the legislation of the European Union and the case-law of the European Court of Justice. Hence, India, as other common law jurisdictions had to find their own solutions and had to emancipate from the jurisprudence of the English courts. The Indian solutions could, after the exit of the United Kingdom from the European Union, even serve as an inspiration for the new role of the English common law in the area of private international law.

Against this background, this volume of the *Studies* will be an important source not only for academics and practitioners in India but also a valuable contribution to the private international law community worldwide. The authors do not restrict themselves to thoroughly document the current state of Indian private international law, covering all areas of this branch of law and gathering the relevant case-law of the Indian courts. They also explore a potential reform of the Indian rules defining jurisdiction, determining the applicable law and dealing with the recognition and enforcement of foreign decisions in the light of international developments.

The effort of both authors commands the most tremendous respect and should be rewarded by many interested readers.

Anatol Dutta
Professor of Private Law, Private International Law and Comparative Law,
Ludwig-Maximilians-University, München
March 2021

ACKNOWLEDGEMENTS

The beginning of this enriching knowledge collaboration began in the 8th Journal of Private International Law Conference room in Munich, 2019. Prof. Paul Beaumont, University of Stirling, introduced us to each other. Professor Beaumont proposed the idea of a book on Indian Private International Law.

We were excited about the idea, as it was a substantial opportunity to contribute to the research on Indian private international law, which remains a domain under-researched and underdeveloped. We also felt that a book showcasing the Indian private international law in the global context could significantly reduce the academic void and lack of material faced by the faculties and students all over India. As far as the content of the book is concerned, it emanated and emerged out of our experience of teaching the courses of Conflicts of laws / Private International law at South Asian University (SAU), New Delhi, and OP Jindal Global Law School (OPJGU), Haryana, India. The curious questions and the vibrant deliberation with the dynamic minds in and around the classroom gestated the content for this book.

After this initial stage of fruition, many rendered their assistance in putting together the current version. Reviewers of this volume deserve a special mention for their valuable suggestions and comments. We would also like to thank the entire Hart team, especially Prof. Anselmo Reyes, International Judge of the Singapore International Commercial Court and Series Editor, Prof. Paul Beaumont, University of Stirling, and Ms Roberta Bassi, Commissioning Editor (Hart Publications) and Ms Rosemarie Mearns, Editorial Assistant (Hart Publications), for their encouraging response to our project, the constant cooperation, and for ensuring an accelerated publication process.

We would also like to acknowledge the support of the Alexander von Humboldt Stiftung, Bonn, Germany. Half of the research for this book has been funded through the Alexander von Humboldt Fellowship that was granted to Saloni to pursue research as an Experienced Researcher at the Chair for Private Law, Private International Law and Comparative Law, Ludwig Maximilians University, Munich.

Special thanks are extended to Professor Jan Neels and Professor Anatol Dutta for contributing the foreword to this book. We are sure the endorsement and support provided by them will increase the credibility and visibility of our work. We also express our gratitude to our colleagues and University functionaries at SAU and OPJGU for their constant encouragement.

We take this opportunity to acknowledge the research assistance rendered by Nikita Mohapatra, Sayan Kumar Panda, students at Maharashtra MNLU, Aurangabad and Ms Upasna Agrawal, an alumnus of OPJGU. We thank Prakriti Malla, LLM student at South Asian University, who became the first reader of the manuscript. She provided valuable feedback and materials to incorporate references to Nepal, which otherwise would have been overlooked.

In particular, we would like to express our most sincere gratitude to the Lord for His constant grace in helping us with this auspicious book-project. We also want to express our appreciation to all the teachers who have shaped our careers. We are incredibly grateful to our parents for their love, blessings, caring, and sacrifices for making us what we are today.

I (Stellina) want to thank my husband and son Agastya (my lifeline), for supporting and encouraging me in this academic journey.

I (Saloni) would like to thank my mother and my friends at OPJGU and Ludwig Maximilians University, München for being my pillar of strength with their tireless words of encouragement. I am extremely grateful to the Alexander von Humboldt Foundation for awarding me a fellowship and Prof Anatol Dutta, Professor of Private Law, Private International Law and Comparative Law, Ludwig Maximilians University, Munich for hosting me as a Humboldt Fellow for the successful completion of this book.

CONTENTS

LIST OF ABBREVIATIONS

ACA	The Arbitration and Conciliation Act
APPIL	Asian Principles of Private International Law
ART	Assisted Reproductive Technology
BRICS	Brazil, Russia, India, China and South Africa
CA	The Competition Act 2002
CCA	Commercial Courts, Commercial Division and Commercial Appellate Division of High Courts Act 2015
CISG	United Nations Convention on Contracts for the International Sale of Goods
CPA	The Consumer Protection Act 1986
CPC	The Code of Civil Procedure 1908
CRC	Convention on the Rights of the Child
CAWC	Crime Against Women Cell
CGAP	Council on General Affairs and Policy
EU	European Union
HCCCA	Hague Principles of Choice of Court Agreements
HCCH	Hague Conference on Private International Law
ICA	Indian Council of Arbitration
ICA	The Indian Contract Act 1872
ICMR	Indian Council of Medical Research
IPC	Indian Penal Code
ICC	International Chamber of Commerce
ICARA	International Child Abduction Remedies Act
UNIDROIT	International Institute for the Unification of Private Law
ISA	International Surrogacy Agreements
KAC	Kuwait Airways Corporation
NSB	National Surrogacy Board

NTPC	National Thermal Power Corporation of India
NRI	Non- Resident Indians
MIC	Methyl Isocyanate
MWCD	Ministry of Women and Child Development
OPC	Overseas Projects Corporation
PKPA	Parental Kidnapping Prevention Act
PETL	Principles of European Tort Law
SSB	State Surrogacy Boards
SEBI	The Securities and Exchange Board of India
TMA	The Trade Marks Act 1999
UCCJA	Uniform Child Custody Jurisdiction Act
UCCJEA	Uniform Child Custody Jurisdiction and Enforcement Act
UCIL	Union Carbide, India, Ltd
UK	United Kingdom
USA	The United States of America
UNCITRAL	United Nations Commission on International Trade Law

TABLE OF CASES

TABLE OF CONVENTIONS

TABLE OF LEGISLATION

PART I

General Principles

1

Introduction

Conflict of Laws, also referred to as private international law, is premised on the assumption that human interactions across borders cannot be determined by reference to one set of laws. Global contracts, e-commerce transactions, cross border marriages, divorces, and insolvency are some of the glowing examples, the effects of which travels to more than one jurisdiction. If diverse municipal legal systems have contributed to the conflicts, the situation is further complicated by contrasting approaches to conflict of laws followed by jurisdictions. The challenges presented by the various national laws and conflict of laws have sought to be remedied by active, broad, and reinvigorated international legal responses aimed at codifying and harmonising the process and principles of private international law. Simultaneously, the increased interactions aided by globalisation, migrations, and the internet in the personal and commercial domain have given it a new boost and fillip. However, the scenario has presented new challenges to private international law with its role and character undergoing rapid transformations. Moving away from its exclusive focus on jurisdictional concerns, the applicable law, and the enforcement of foreign court orders, today, the subject navigates through a strenuous and ongoing determination to produce legal responses in areas much beyond the contracts and family matters. As a result, the harmonisation effort is likely to increase in the coming times to embrace new domains and challenges, including issues of intellectual property, the internet, etc. Despite the many codification attempts furthered by international cooperation, mainly under the aegis of the Hague Conference of Private International Law, the discipline has not attained the desirable certainty and predictability.

India is no exception to this legal predicament. India provides an exponentially expanding yet unripe territory for the study of this subject. Under the forces of globalisation, there is an expansion of economic interaction between India and other countries. The increased financial business is reflected in the number of bilateral commercial agreements and investment treaties signed between India and other countries. Further, the ever-growing Indian diaspora settled mostly in America, Europe, and Australia has thrown innumerable challenges to the operation of private international law in India. Questions frequently arise whether western nations would recognise a marriage celebrated in India. There have been similar questions on the validity of a divorce or a custody order obtained in jurisdictions outside India. Where should the enforcement of such orders be sought?

A matured private international law principle is crucial for the legal infrastructure to facilitate international transactions. Nevertheless, unfortunately, private international law is still in its infancy in India, despite increasingly being called upon to address new legal challenges. Further, though a party to some of the Hague Codification Conventions, India has steadfastly opposed the accession to most of the Hague Conventions, which has furthered complications and uncertainty in transactions having a foreign element. Research into India's state practice is still developing, and judicial statements are evolving the jurisprudence of private international law. There has been no systematic attempt done to present an Indian perspective on private international law. Several reasons are attributed to the underdeveloped state of private international law in the country.

In most civil law jurisdictions, matters of foreign law are treated as a question of law which obligates the judges to take cognizance of the presence of the foreign law. In contrast, under the Indian legal framework, foreign law is treated as a question of fact, which needs to be proved by expert evidence. There is no judicial obligation to take cognizance of the application of foreign law. For this reason, even in those cases with a definite presence of a foreign element, parties to the case prefer to rely on domestic law, and the court inevitably applies domestic laws. For instance, in the *Union Carbide and Others v Union of India and Others*,[1] which is popularly referred to as the Bhopal Gas Case, the most significant industrial tragedy in the country, the parties argued the case according to the principles of domestic law – despite the fact that the company and its principal office was located in the US.

Though labelled as the Federal Republic, the Indian legal system is governed by a single unified system of law, with a unified system of judicial administration, notwithstanding the constitutional distribution of legislative powers between the centre and the states. Thus, there has been no scope for developing private international law principles even when matters span across state borders within the Federal set-up. However, the ever-increasing diaspora and the growing commercial interdependence and transactions have provided a platform for expanding the doctrines and principles of private international law. Further, the innumerable cross-border subjects raised before the domestic courts and the inevitability of evaluating foreign judgments have created a compulsion for increased attention to the subject.

The Indian legal system, with its fledgling and highly insufficient apparatus on private international law, has on many occasions presented an ad hoc response towards the three primordial conflict of laws questions – jurisdictional, choice of law, and enforcement concerns – within the dispute domains of commercial law as well as family law. The pattern is often seen as evolving, where the legal system has attempted to read in a few features that were otherwise the prevalent methodology adopted in the English, US, and European systems for disputes with a foreign element. In *Lalji Raja and Sons v Hansraj Nathuram*[2] reliance was placed on private international law to support the contention that in a personal action, a decree pronounced *in absentia* by a foreign court, to the jurisdiction of which the defendant had not in any way submitted himself, was an absolute nullity. The courts also differed from other South Asian jurisdictions in interpreting an exclusive jurisdiction clause. They stressed that the validity of such agreements was not violative of public policy and the notion of national sovereignty. In the seminal case of *Modi Entertainment Network and Another v WSG Cricket PTE. Ltd*,[3] the Supreme Court of India espoused the principle of a 'sliding scale' developed in the internet jurisdiction case of *Zippo Manufacturing* by the courts in the US. Simultaneously, Indian legal systems also developed their unique practices, founded within domestic law. In *Y Narasimha Rao and Ors. v Y Venkata Lakshmi and Anr*,[4] the Supreme Court observed that 'the marriages which take place in this country can only be under either the customary or the statutory law in force in this country.

[1] [1991] 4 SCC 584.
[2] [1971] AIR 974.
[3] [2003] 4 SCC 341.
[4] [1991] 3 SCC 451.

Hence, the only law that can be applicable to the matrimonial disputes is the one under which the parties are married and no other law.'[5] In *Sondur Rajini v Sondur Gopal*, the court further observed that

> the time at which the domicile is to be determined is when the parties tie the nuptial knot under the Hindu Marriage Act and not the date when an application is made for matrimonial reliefs. As a natural corollary thereof, even if a party to the matrimonial petition establishes that after marriage he acquired domicile of some other country, it would not take away the jurisdiction of the court in India if on the date of the marriage he was domiciled in India. It is unjust that a party to the marriage can change his entire system of personal law by his or her unilateral decision.[6]

In a related vein, in cases of intercountry child abduction, judicial statements have relied on the concept of 'intimate contact' as the basis of jurisdiction.[7] Judicial opinion on the applicable law on contractual issues has demonstrated a well-defined shift from its former position, which obligated commercial contracts, enforceable in India, to choose an applicable law with a close relation to the facts of the case. This book presents the unique features of Indian States' practice in disputes with the foreign element being addressed within the country's legal system.

Thus, this book is an effort to infuse and sustain research in the domain of private international law in India. It provides a critical analysis of India's legislative and judicial practice and the development of private international law. Traversing through the historical evolution of private international law in India, the book highlights the unique features meticulously and systematically evolved by the legislative and judicial approaches. The book addresses the three major pillars of private international law – jurisdiction, choice of law, and enforcement as they are applied and developed by the Indian courts in the domain areas of family law and commercial law. The research in the family law domain addresses the traditional research areas of the institution of marriage, divorce, and some of the contemporary concerns affecting the nations at large – inter-country child retrieval and the country statement on accession to the Hague Conventions related to this domain. In commercial law, the book addresses the concerns raised regarding the choice of law issues in transnational contracts and enforcement of foreign judgment/arbitral awards in the country. The work evaluates India's engagement and disengagements with international instruments and conventions, especially the Hague Conference on private international law.

This book is divided into six parts.

Part I consist of four chapters and provides an overview of the structure and functioning of the Indian legal framework. Chapter two discusses the historical imperatives and evolution of the basic principles of private international law with a focus on the sources of private international law. Chapter three discusses the foundational concepts of domicile, nationality and residence as a connecting factor. Navigating through the statutory provisions, judicial statements, and juristic narratives, concepts such as characterisation, connecting factors, and *renvoi* are elaborated. Chapter four delves into India's statutory position of pleading and proving foreign law and explores the exclusion of foreign law while emphasising the judicial approach towards developing an international public policy.

[5] ibid [17].

[6] *Sondur Rajini v Sondur Gopal* [2005] [4] MhLj 688.

[7] *Surindar Kaur Sandhu v Harbax Singh Sandhu & Anr* AIR [1984] 1224; *Sarita Sharma v Sushil Sharma* [2000] 1 SCR 915; *V Ravi Chandran v Union of India* [2010] 1 SCC 174.

Part II of the book focuses on the rules of jurisdiction in cross-border civil and commercial disputes before Indian courts. Chapter five discusses the private international law of jurisdiction in India. In particular, this chapter examines the statutory provisions concerning: (1) the persons who may file a suit before the Indian courts; (2) the rules on immunity from suits; and (3) the circumstances in which the courts in India will assume jurisdiction in transnational disputes – and, in particular, those relating to civil and commercial matters. The chapter also examines certain contemporary issues that have compelled the Indian courts to re-visit traditional rules on jurisdiction while adjudicating transnational disputes. Of particular relevance in this respect has been the regulation of choice of court agreements (also referred to as exclusive forum-selection clauses) concluded in favour of a foreign court. While scrutinising the prevailing case-law, the chapter additionally provides a comparative analysis of the rules in this regard in some major jurisdictions such as the EU, the UK, Canada and Australia. The chapter also discusses the provisions of the Hague Convention on Choice of Court Agreements, 2005 (the HCCCA) and whether India would benefit from its endorsement.

Part III of the book is divided into four chapters. This part explores the private international law concerns of marriage and divorce. Chapter six traces the statutory position and judicial statements applicable to marriage with its exposition of formal and essential validity of a marriage. The chapter also addresses the conflicts of law concerns of same-sex marriages and critically evaluates the Indian legal response concerning the recognition of foreign same-sex marriage. Chapter seven investigates the rules on jurisdiction, applicable law, and the complexity surrounding the recognition of foreign divorce, nullity, and ancillary financial orders. Both chapters examine the reception and acceptance of the Indian legal systems in western jurisdictions with particular reference to polygamous marriages and extrajudicial divorce, mainly in the form of *talaq*. One may wonder why incorporating the response of other jurisdictions to Indian marriages and divorce is in a book dealing with Indian private international law. It is partly influenced by the author's experience of teaching private international law at the South Asian University and the growing significance of the topic at the global level in private international law disputes. Considering the large Muslim population, the issue is of utmost importance. The chapters also provide an overview of India's position and its engagement with Hague Conventions on family law matters. Chapter eight evaluates the judicial pattern in dealing with intercountry child abduction, focusing on its compatibility with the 1980 Hague Child Abduction Convention. Unlike the other domains of private international law, the area of child abduction has received significant legislative attention with the draft Bills prepared by the Ministry of Women and Child Welfare and Law Commission of India. The chapter critically analyses the provisions of the Bills while evaluating India's reasons concerning its decision to refrain from accession. The chapter draws parallels with India's neighbouring countries Pakistan and Sri Lanka, which have acceded to 1980 Hague Child Abduction Convention. Chapter nine focuses on the private international law concerns surrounding cross-border surrogacy since India occupies a core position in the global landscape of surrogacy.

Part IV of the book contains two chapters and focuses on the principles of Indian private international law vis-à-vis the applicable law in contractual and non-contractual matters. Accordingly, chapter ten examines the mechanism to decipher the applicable law in cross-border disputes in matters of contract under the principles of Indian private international law. It provides an in-depth discussion on judicial dicta on the subject, considering the absence of the codification of the rules in this regard. The chapter, thus, analyses the diverging interpretations given by the Indian judiciary to the common law doctrine of the 'proper law of contract', which is employed to ascertain the governing law in such disputes. The chapter draws parallels with the practice adopted in some other jurisdictions such as the EU, the UK, China, Russia,

Australia, Canada and Nepal to provide the readers with an insight into how the application of the proper law of contract theory is problematic. The chapter also explores possible uses of the Hague Principles on the Choice of Law in International Commercial Contracts to develop and supplement the Indian conflict-of-law rules on the applicable law in contractual matters. Chapter eleven examines the principles of Indian private international law in non-contractual matters. Reminiscent of the approach in contractual obligations, the mechanism to ascertain the applicable law in non-contractual obligations, namely those involving tortious claims, has not been codified. This chapter accordingly analyses judicial trends in this regard. In particular, the chapter examines the various facets of non-contractual disputes such as product liability, unjust enrichment, defamation, unfair competition and the infringement of intellectual property, to name a few and the mechanism to identify the applicable law in such matters. In doing so, it highlights the excessive influence of English common law on the subject in India and the predicaments that it creates. The chapter analyses global trends to demonstrate the apparent flaws in the Indian rules in this regard.

Part V of this book focuses on the last pillar of private international law, viz., the recognition and enforcement of foreign judgments and arbitral awards. It is divided into two chapters. Chapter twelve examines the grounds on which a foreign judgment is eligible for recognition and enforcement in an Indian court. The chapter discusses the relevant provisions of the Code of Civil Procedure 1908, which regulate the procedural rules in this regard. In this respect, the chapter discusses the relevance of the 'doctrine of obligation' in determining the extraterritorial effect of foreign judgments in India. Like the approach of the previous chapters, this chapter, too, analyses the global trends as regards the law on the recognition and enforcement of foreign judgments in jurisdictions such as the EU, UK, Australia and Canada. Further, the chapter discusses the provisions of the HCCCA and the 2019 Hague Judgments Convention on the Recognition and Enforcement of Foreign Judgments in Civil and Commercial Matters (the Judgments Convention), which stipulate the rules on the recognition and enforcement of foreign judgments, and deliberates whether India should endorse them. Chapter thirteen examines the principles of Indian private international law on the recognition and enforcement of foreign arbitral awards. In doing so, it highlights the statutory requirements in the Arbitration and Conciliation Act 1996 on the subject which give effect to the provisions of the 1927 Geneva Convention on the Execution of Foreign Arbitral Awards 1927 (the 1927 Geneva Convention) and the 1958 Convention Recognition and Enforcement of Foreign Arbitral Awards (popularly known as the New York Convention).

Part VI (comprising) Chapter fourteen offers concluding observations.

In short, this book focuses on delineating the principles of the Indian private international law and examining whether these conform to the internationally accepted standards. In doing so, and as aforementioned, each of the chapters in the book delves in detail into the present private international law rules of some other major jurisdictions and, in particular, the EU, but also other common law jurisdictions such as the UK, Australia, and Canada. In addition to the fact that the Indian rules on the subject remain uncodified, the Republic has expressed certain skepticism in ratifying treaties and conventions aimed at harmonisation to foster predictability and certainty vis-à-vis its private international law, the book chiefly intends to make a case for the development of its principles in this regard. However, it needs to be pointed out that the authors do not advocate for the country's accession to all Hague Conventions but advocate for the evolution and development of a transparent and robust system of private international law to suit the sensibilities of Indian legal systems and social reality. This book is an earnest attempt on the authors' part to contribute to a systematic study of Indian private international law and place it in the global context and hopefully it will be a significant contribution.

2

Basic Concepts and Status of Private International Law in India

I. Introduction

A and B, domiciled Indian citizens, were married in Delhi, India, according to the Hindu rites. Two children were born of the marriage. Later, the husband left for the US. The wife continued to live in India with her minor children. The wife moved an application under section 488 of the Criminal Procedure Code 1973, India alleging that the husband had neglected to maintain her and the two minor children. The husband contended that his marriage with the petitioner (wife) was dissolved by a decree of divorce granted by the Second Judicial District Court of Nevada in the US. The case raised several legal questions, including the competence of the US courts in entertaining a divorce petition of a marriage solemnised in India and the broader question of recognition of foreign divorce decrees.

A dispute involving a well-defined foreign element cannot be resolved by exclusively relying on the domestic legal framework. In scenarios where the matters before the judiciary have a strong foreign element, the disputes must be resolved by reference to private international law. This chapter explores the historical and conceptual foundation of the subject.

This chapter is divided into six parts (including the Introduction). Section II provides a brief synopsis of the Indian legal framework. Section III explores the nature and scope of the subject, focusing on the subject's core fundamentals, namely: jurisdiction, recognition, and enforcement of foreign judgments, and choice of law. Section IV discusses the legal sources and framework of private international law in India. Section V explains the meaning and application of fundamental concepts embedded in private international law focusing on characterisation, connecting factors, and *renvoi*.

II. Overview of Indian Legal Framework

In India, private international law has evolved gradually responding to the varied social, political and legal structures in operation. The country's legal infrastructure is primarily shaped by the common law system and carries the influence of British colonial rule.[1] India became an independent nation along with other South Asian countries in 1947 and adopted a

[1] KM Sharma, 'Civil Law in India' (1969) 1(1) *Washington University Law Quarterly*, 1–39, 2.

Constitution profoundly centred on the Government of India Act 1935 passed by the British Parliament.[2] The Constitution of India declares India to be a Socialist, Secular, and Democratic Republic.[3] Though Article 1 of the Constitution describes India as a 'Union of States', the country has adopted a quasi-federal structure.[4] A catena of cases have provided precision on the specificities of the quasi-federalist structure of India. The Supreme Court in *State of West Bengal v Union of India* has observed that the Constitution of India does not fit into the traditional prototype of the federation.[5] An analogous view was echoed in *State of Rajasthan and others v Union of India*.[6] In the seminal case of *SR Bommai v Union of India*, the court observed that 'democracy and federalism are the essential features of the Indian Constitution and part of its Basic Structure'.[7] The Constitution of India encompasses the following classical features of federalism: a division between federal and state governments, the supremacy of the Constitution, an independent judiciary, and bicameralism.[8] However, unlike a classical federation, the Indian federal structure is not the outcome of a compact between several sovereign units, but a product of the transformation of a unitary system into a federal system.[9] Article 3 of the Constitution not only allows the union government to change the boundaries of a State but even to extinguish a State.[10] The fact that India is not a federation in the traditional sense of the term is of paramount importance to private international law as there is no existence of a separate legal system among States in the Indian framework. Private international law treats the Indian legal system as a single entity.

The fundamental postulate under the Indian Constitution enjoins that power has been strewn on the legislature to make the law, the executive to implement the law, and the judiciary to interpret the law within the limits set down by the Constitution.[11] The President is the head of the union executive.[12] Article 74(1) of the Constitution of India provides that there shall be a Council of Ministers, with the Prime Minister as its head to aid and advise the President.[13] The country has a bicameral Parliament whose upper house is the Council of States (Rajya Sabha), and the lower house is the House of People (Lok Sabha).[14] State legislatures elect Rajya Sabha members, and Lok Sabha members are elected directly by the people in general elections.[15] As far as the legislative division of power between the union government and state governments are concerned, Seventh Schedule of the Constitution contains three lists on which the central and the state governments can make the laws.[16] On the Union List, Parliament has exclusive powers to legislate.[17] While the state has exclusive powers to legislate on the State List, Parliament can also do so in certain situations.[18] On matters in the Concurrent List, both the union and States are

[2] A Glendhill, *The Republic of India: The Development of Its Laws and Constitution* (Greenwood, 2013) 15.
[3] Constitution of India 1950, Preamble.
[4] ibid, Art 1.
[5] *State of West Bengal v Union of India* [1964] SCR [1] 371.
[6] *State of Rajasthan and others v Union of India etc.* AIR [1963] 1241.
[7] *SR Bommai v Union of India* AIR [1994] SC 1918 [90].
[8] BN Schoenfeld, 'Federalism in India' (1959) 20(1) *The Indian Journal of Political Science* 52–62, 52.
[9] AK Ghosal, 'Federalism in the Indian Constitution' (1953) 14(4) *The Indian Journal of Political Science* 317–332, 318.
[10] Constitution of India (n 3) Art 3.
[11] ibid: See AK Thiruvengadam, *The Constitution of India: A Contextual Analysis* (Bloomsbury Publishers, 2017) 77.
[12] Constitution of India (n 3) Art 52.
[13] ibid, Art 74(1).
[14] ibid, (n 3) Art 79.
[15] ibid, Arts 80, 81.
[16] ibid, seventh schedule.
[17] ibid, Art 246.
[18] ibid, Arts 249, 250, 252, 253.

competent to enact legislation. In case of a conflict between a State and central legislation on a subject matter under the Concurrent List, the parliamentary legislation shall prevail. In addition, residuary powers of legislation are vested in the union, and that provides a protuberant unitary feature to the federalism in India.[19] In the judicial sphere, the Supreme Court of India is the guardian and interpreter of the Constitution,[20] and is followed by High Courts at the state level.[21] The Supreme Court and High Courts exercise extraordinary constitutional powers to issue prerogative writs in cases of infringements of the fundamental rights guaranteed by the Constitution.[22] The judicial decisions of the Supreme Court are legally binding on the lower courts and tribunals of India underlining the operation of the doctrine of *stare decisis*.[23] India's legal system follows the adversary system of legal procedure wherein the judge acts as a neutral arbiter safeguarding the balance between the contending rivals without actively taking part in the forensic debate in the court.

Though the Indian Constitution is based on a secular framework, in matters of concerns such as marriage, divorce, etc, the legal system is intensely influenced by the cultural and religious norms of the population.[24] The existence of personal laws based on religious beliefs impacts the private international law practices of India and in its reception in other jurisdictions. The succeeding section provides an overview of nature; scope and conceptual foundations of private international law in general and then discusses the subject in the context of India.

III. Conceptual Foundations of Private International Law

A. Nature of Private International Law

Private international law is that part of the domestic legal system which comes into operation whenever the court is confronted with a dispute that comprises a specific and clear foreign element.[25] The manifestation of a foreign element is a *sine qua non* for the invocation of private international law, and the primary function of private international law is to indicate how a dispute needs to be addressed in the presence of foreign elements. Foreign elements in a dispute can be presented in numerous ways, ranging from the parties' different nationalities or domicile, to the cause of action originating in more than one jurisdiction. For example, A domiciled in India files a suit against B domiciled in Britain for breach of an employment contract to be performed in France. The scenario presents foreign elements in the form of the domicile of B and the contract's place of performance. In such situations, exclusive reliance on domestic legal systems results in the prospect of the forum's laws coming into conflict with the legal system with which the case's facts are intimately connected. Correspondingly, in a case

[19] ibid, Art 248.

[20] ibid, Art 124.

[21] AK Thiruvengadam (n11) 118; see also MP Jain, *Indian Constitutional law* 8th edn (Lexis Nexis, 2018).

[22] Constitution of India (n 3) Arts 32, 139, 226.

[23] ibid, Art 141.

[24] The Hindu Marriage Act 1955, India; The Hindu Adoption & Maintenance Act 1956, India; The Hindu Succession Act 1956, India; The Hindu Minority and Guardianship Act 1956, India; See F Ahmad, 'The Problem with Personal Laws in India' in S Choudhry and J Herring (eds), *The Cambridge Companion to Comparative Family Law* (Cambridge University Press, 2019) 225–253.

[25] K Trimmings, P Torremans, A Mills, U Grusic, C Heinze, *Cheshire, North, and Fawcett: Private International Law* 15th edn (Oxford University Press, 2017) 3; JO Brien, *Conflict of Laws* (Cavendish Publishing, 1989) 3; See also RH Graveson, *Conflict of Laws* 7th edn (Sweet and Maxwell, 1974).

involving the determination of the validity of a marriage between two domiciled French citizens before the Indian court, the application of Indian laws would result in flagrant injustice as the facts underlying the case are substantially connected to the French legal system. However, it is critical to note that the presence of foreign elements must be real and specific.

In *Dell Computer Corp v Union Des Consummateurs*[26] the Dell company sold computer equipment retail over the internet. It had its Canadian head office in Toronto and a place of business in Montreal. On 4 April 2003, the order pages on its English-language website indicated incorrect prices for two models of handheld computers.[27] On being informed of the errors, Dell blocked access to the erroneous order pages through the usual address. D, circumventing Dell's measures by using a deep link that enabled him to access the order pages without following the usual route, ordered a computer at the incorrect price indicated there.[28] When Dell refused to honour D's order at the lower price, the *Union des consommateurs* and D filed a motion for authorisation to institute a class action against Dell. Dell applied for referral of D's claim to arbitration pursuant to an arbitration clause in the terms and conditions of sale, and dismissal of the motion for authorisation to institute a class action.[29] The Superior Court and the Court of Appeal in Quebec held, that

> the foreign element must be a point of contact that is legally relevant to a foreign country, which means that the contact must be certain and clear to play a role in determining whether the dispute comes under the category of private international law.[30]

The court refused to accept an arbitration clause as automatically indicating the presence of a foreign element warranting the application of the rules of private international law.

The raison d'être of private international law is the existence of a number of municipal systems of law that differ critically from each other in the rules by which they regulate the legal relations.[31] The point has been elaborated by Savigny when he stated

> it is the diversity of positive laws [in different territorial units] which makes it necessary to mark off for each in sharp outline, to fix the area of its authority, to fix the limits of different positive laws in respect to one another.[32]

Savigny traced the foundation of the private international law obligations to the law of nations and believed that private international law disputes need to be adjudicated in the same way irrespective of the state where a suit is filed.[33] Civilised nations constitute one unit, and private international law matters must be adjudicated in the same way everywhere.[34] Though some continental scholars took up the idea, the overriding view of jurists and the practice of the states imply that private international law is treated as part of domestic legal systems, and a sizeable variation in approaches is found in legislations of nations. Franz Khan attributed that the dispute in private international law starts from the title page itself.[35]

[26] *Dell Computer Corp v Union Des Consummators* [2007] SCC 34.
[27] ibid [4].
[28] ibid.
[29] ibid [5].
[30] ibid [3], [26], [50]–[53], [56]–[58].
[31] *Cheshire, North and Fawcett* (n 25) 3 See also AK Kuhn, 'Doctrines of Private International Law in England and America Contrasted with those of Continental Europe' (1912) 12(1) *Columbia Law Review* 44–57.
[32] FKV Savigny, *Private International Law and the Retrospective Operation of Statutes: A Treatise on the Conflict of Laws and the Limits of Their Operation in Respect of Place and Time* cited in *Cheshire, North and Fawcett* (n 25) 5.
[33] FKV Savigny, *System of Modern Roman Law* (Hyperion Press 1867) 23, 27. This proposition appeared in the final volume of his System of Modern Roman Law published in German. W Guthrie translated it into English in 1869; see also *Cheshire, North, and Fawcett* (n 25) 23.
[34] ibid (Mancini followed this theory in Italy).
[35] Quoted by Supreme Court of India in *Indian and General Investment Trust, Ltd. v Sri Ramchandra Mardaraja Deo, Raja of Khalikote* AIR [1952] Cal 508 [20].

Private international law is primarily a procedural law that identifies which legal system possesses jurisdiction and which laws would apply to a particular dispute.[36] In that sense, private international law is not a specific branch of a legal system such as contract or criminal law. However, it has a distinct flavour of its own since the subject, through specifically identified legal mechanisms, guides the ascertainment of the legal system applicable to a case.[37] It needs to be highlighted that the reference to a foreign system of law with a federal legal structure is not to be understood in the sense of 'state' in international law but to specific federal units. For instance, a reference to the law of the US indicates relevant laws of California, Texas, etc.[38] The hybrid nature of the subject involving international elements and the domestic legal system has given rise to several narratives on the subject's nomenclature.[39] Despite the presence of a large diaspora spread across jurisdictions and the enlarged cross border economic transactions, India has not enacted precise legislation to deal with private international law. The subject matter of private international law is addressed through statutory provisions scattered in numerous legislations. Judicial statements also constitute a significant source of private international law. The courts have elaborated on the nature of the subject in numerous conflict of law cases.

In *Mrs. Santi Singh v Governor of Punjab and Anr*[40] it was held that 'the rules of conflict of laws or private international law are adumbrated by various writers not to have any statutory force of universal application in all countries'. The court traced the development of the subject to the judicial decisions determined from time to time in different countries. The judgment emphasised the domestic nature of the subject. The nature of the subject was also discussed in the case of *Indian and General Investment Trust, Ltd. v Sri Ramchandra Mardaraja Deo.*[41] The subject matter of the dispute concerned the recognition and execution of foreign judgment. The court observed that 'the peculiar difficulties of this case arise from the fact that it is not entirely governed by the municipal law of any particular country; it is also governed by that branch of law called "private international law"'.[42] The court quoting from Hibbert's work observed that

> the name 'private international law' is rather unfortunate because it is difficult to conceive of a law that is both international and, at the same time, private.[43] It is called 'private' inasmuch as it deals with the legal relations of individuals and not of states; it is 'international', in as much as it deals with conflicts of laws of different nations. It is properly called law, inasmuch as its rules are enforced by courts, and in that respect, it is a branch of the ordinary law of the land.[44]

The judgment highlighted the complexities of the subject involving both an international and a private character.

B. Private International Law or Conflicts of Laws

The three different nomenclatures – conflict of laws, private international law, and international private law – are employed interchangeably, although none are wholly accurate or adequately

[36] JG Castel, 'Procedure and the Conflict of Laws' (1970) 16(4) *McGill Law Journal* 603–632, 604; J P George and AK Teller, 'Conflict of Laws' (2004) 57 *SMU Law Review* 719–758.
[37] JG Collier, *Conflict of Laws* 3rd edn (Cambridge University Press, 2001) 7.
[38] ibid.
[39] WE Beckett, 'What is Private International Law' (1926) 7 *British Year Book of International law* 73–96.
[40] *Mrs. Santi Singh v Governor of Punjab and Anr* AIR [1959] P H 375 [3].
[41] *Indian and General Investment Trust, Ltd* (n 35).
[42] ibid [20].
[43] ibid citing WN Hibbert, *International Private Law or Conflict of Laws* (University of London Press, 1918).
[44] ibid.

descriptive of the domain's scope and nuance.[45] The term 'private international law' was first employed by Story in his formative work of *Commentaries on the Conflict of Laws*.[46] The term private international law is followed in civil law jurisdictions, including France, Italy, Greece, etc.[47] Jurisdictions and juristic opinions employ the term 'private international law' to highlight the subject's cross border and international character.[48] Despite its name, private international law is not international in the real sense as every country has its own domestic system of conflict of laws rules and its sources are the same as other municipal law subjects.[49] The existence of a distinct domestic system of private international law distinguishes it from public international law, which regulates the sovereign relationship between nations and has its sources in treaties, customs, and general principles of law recognised by civilised nations[50] The phrase 'conflict of laws' originated from the work of Ulrich Huber[51] and is employed to highlight the divergent and competing nature of municipal laws and the core interrelationship with domestic legal systems. This is comprehensible since most of federal countries like the US and Australia are characterised by the presence of different legal systems within their federal set-up. In such scenarios, a reference to the term conflict of laws is desirable as the subject matter does not have an international connection; instead, the issue is about applying conflicting legal systems.[52] However, the term is misleading as the subject aims to avoid or minimise conflicts between legal systems.[53] AV Dicey, who wrote the first treatise on the subject from an English perspective, employed the term conflict of laws, and common law countries have largely preferred to use the term conflict of laws.[54] The term 'international private law' is applied in selected jurisdictions to emphasise the private nature of legal relations in contrast to the public relations regulated by public international law.[55] Judicial statements in India do not reveal a specific preference of nomenclature either in favour of private international law or conflict of laws. For clarity and alignment with the title, this book will employ the term 'private international law'.

C. Scope of Private International Law

Identification of a foreign element in a dispute indicates the supplication of private international law and the need to ascertain the applicable law. The function of private international law is primarily to pinpoint the system of applicable law, and this function has been compared to an office at a railway station where the passenger can learn the specific platform in which

[45] FK Juenger, 'Private International Law or International Private Law' (1994) 5 *Kings College Law Journal* 45–64, 45.

[46] J Story, *Commentaries on the Conflict of Laws* 2nd edn (Little Brown, 1841) 11; J Westlake, *A Treatise on Private International Law* 7th edn (Maxwell & Sons, 1925) 5.

[47] TK Saha, *Textbook on Legal Methods, Legal Systems and Research* (Universal Law Publishers, 2010) 54.

[48] Juenger (n 45) 46.

[49] Collier (n 37) 6.

[50] ibid 5; JR Stevenson, 'The Relationship of Private International Law to Public International Law' (1952) 52 *Columbia Law Review* 561–588; A Nussbaum, 'Rise and Decline of the Law-of-Nations Doctrine in the Conflict of Laws' (1942) 42 *Columbia Law Review* 189–192.

[51] Quoted in EG Lorenzen, 'Huber's De Conflictu Legum' (1919) 13 *Illinois Law Review* 375, 401–418; DE Childress III, 'Comity as Conflict: Resituating International Comity as Conflict of Laws' (2010) 44 *University of California Davis Law Review* 12, 18.

[52] L Weinburg, 'The Federal-State Conflict of Laws: Actual Conflicts' (1992) 70 *Texas Law Review* 1743–1796, 1753.

[53] Collier (n 37) 5.

[54] AV Dicey, *A Digest of the Law of England with Reference to the Conflict of Laws* (Stevens and Sons Limited, 1896); Brien (n 25) 3–4.

[55] Germany, Austria, Switzerland, etc employ this nomenclature; see A Nussbaum, *Principles of Private International Law* (Oxford University Press, 1945).

the train is arriving. The court, in the case of *Indian and General Investment v Sri Ramchandra Mardaraja Deo*, observed that 'the function of private international law is complete when it has chosen the appropriate system of law'.[56] In the process of identifying the applicable law to a dispute, what exactly comes under the domain of and scope of private international law is still a debatable topic.[57] Some jurisdictions provide prominence to the question of choice of law as constituting the major subject matter.[58] Jurisdictions like Afghanistan include issues of nationality and domicile as part of its private international law,[59] whereas, many jurisdictions provide for issues of domicile and nationality as part of administrative law or constitutional law. For some jurisdictions, all three areas – jurisdiction, choice of law, and enforcement of judgments – remain at the heart of most private international law endeavours in one way or another.[60] The authors of this book have approached the scope of the subject as covering issues of jurisdiction, choice of law and enforcement of foreign judgments.

i. Jurisdiction

Private international law confronts issues of jurisdiction in two scenarios. First, to determine whether the court before which a matter is filed possesses personal and subject matter jurisdiction to entertain the case.[61] Second, in deciding whether to recognise a foreign judgment, a court will be called on to address whether the foreign court that rendered the judgment was a court of competent jurisdiction.[62] It is the common practice among nations that jurisdictional matters are determined by reference to domestic statutory provisions except in situations where there has been the codification of rules on jurisdiction.[63] In India, the subject matter of jurisdiction is detailed under the general statute of Civil Procedure Code 1908,[64] and specific issues under the Hindu Marriage Act 1955,[65] the Hindu Succession Act,[66] the Indian Succession Act 1925,[67] the Transfer of Property Act 1882, etc.[68] The courts in India have supplemented and clarified the contours of jurisdiction principles. In *Ct A Ct. Nachiappa Chettiar v Ct ACt. Subramama Chettiar*[69] concerning the division of certain immovable properties situated in Myanmar, it was pointed out that courts in India have no jurisdiction to determine questions of title in respect of immovable properties in foreign countries or to direct division thereof.[70] The Supreme Court relied on Dicey's opinion to highlight that the courts of a country have no jurisdiction to adjudicate upon the title or the right to the possession of any immovable property not situated in such country.[71] The courts have unswervingly ruled that jurisdictional

[56] ibid.

[57] ibid.

[58] M Martinek, 'The Seven Pillars of Wisdom in Private International Law – The German and the Swiss Experience with the Codification of Conflicts Law Rule' (2001) *Chinese Yearbook of Private International Law and Comparative Law* 15–54.

[59] WM Naseh, 'Conflicts of Laws: State Practice in Afghanistan' in in SR Garimella and S Jolly (eds), *Private International Law* (Springer, 2017) 63–88.

[60] *Cheshire, North, and Fawcett* (n 25) 7.

[61] Brien (n 25) 175.

[62] ibid 181.

[63] A Mayss, *Principles of Conflicts of Laws* 3rd edn (Cavendish Publishing Ltd, 1999) 13.

[64] The Code of Civil Procedure 1908.

[65] The Hindu Marriage Act (n 24).

[66] ibid.

[67] The Indian Succession Act 1925, India.

[68] The Transfer of Property Act 1882, India.

[69] *Ct A.Ct. Nachiappa Chettiar v Ct A.Ct. Subramama Chettiar* AIR [1960] SC 307.

[70] ibid [44].

[71] ibid [17] citing AV Dicey and JHC Morris, *Conflict of Laws* 6th edn (Sweet and Maxwell, 1949) 141, 348.

issues in personal law matters are largely based upon *lex domicilii*.[72] In cases involving child custody, the courts have relied on the child's habitual residence and the indigenous innovation of 'most intimate contact' as the bases of jurisdiction.[73] The rules and practice on jurisdictions will be dealt with in detail in chapter five of this book.

ii. Choice of Law

Choice of law arises in the second stage of disputes encompassing a foreign element, once the court has pronounced on jurisdictional matters. Legal systems have developed a system of rules and principles, and codification work has been undertaken by the Hague Conference on Private International Law (HCCH)[74] and other international bodies,[75] to guide the courts in selecting the applicable law. The underlying rationale underscoring choice of law is the interest of justice[76] and the principle of comity[77] in maintaining harmonious relations between nations. Besides the reference to comity and justice, scholars have propounded several other rationales for private international law.[78] Specific rules on choice of law governing family, contractual and non- contractual matters are dealt with in detail in chapters six to eleven of this book respectively.

iii. Recognition and Enforcement of Foreign Judgment

This question is concerned with whether and in what scenarios a country is bound to give effect and recognise the laws of another country. Similar to the issue of jurisdiction, the recognition and enforcement of foreign judgments are roughly determined by the domestic legal system. However, meaningful efforts on codifying jurisdictional rules have been undertaken by the HCCH[79] and other international bodies.[80] Prominent among the regional codification efforts

[72] L Jhambolkar, 'Conflict of laws' in SK Varma and K Kusum (eds), *Fifty Years of the Supreme Court of India: Its Grasp and Reach* (Indian Law Institute 2000) 651–684, 654.

[73] *Surinder Kaur Sandhu v Harbax Singh Sandhu & Anr* AIR [1984] 1224.

[74] Hague Conference on Private International Law has been established with the aim of progressive unification of Private international law. for more information can be accessed at www.hcch.net/en/instruments/conventions.

[75] United Nations Commission on International Trade Law (UNCITRAL); The International Institute for the Unification of Private Law in Rome (UNIDROIT). The codification attempts of these bodies have been elaborated in the chapters dealing with contractual matters.

[76] P Diwan and P Diwan, *Private International Law: Indian and English* 4th edn (Deep Publishers, 1998) 45.

[77] JK Bleimaier, 'The Doctrine of Comity in Private International Law' (1979) 24(4) *Catholic Lawyer* 327–332.

[78] WW Cook propounded the local law theory see WW Cook, 'The Logical and Legal Bases of the Conflict of Laws' (1924) 33(5) *Yale Law Journal* 457–488; U Huber propounded vested rights theory see L Davies, 'The Influence of Huber's De Conflictu Legum on English Private International Law' (1937) 18 *British Yearbook of International Law* 49, 59; FE Noronha, *Private International Law in India* 2nd edn (Universal Law Publishing, 2013) 22–26.

[79] Some of the notable conventions include Convention on the Recognition and Enforcement of Foreign Judgments in Civil and Commercial Matters 1971; Convention on the Recognition and Enforcement of Decisions Relating to Maintenance Obligations 1973 (hereinafter Maintenance Convention 1973); Convention on Jurisdiction, Applicable Law, Recognition, Enforcement, and Co-operation in Respect of Parental Responsibility and Measures for the Protection of Children 1996) (hereinafter 1996 Protection Convention); The Convention on Choice of Court Agreements 2005); Convention on the Recognition and Enforcement of Foreign Judgments in Civil or Commercial Matters 2019) (hereinafter Convention Recognition and Enforcement of Judgments 2019), available at www.hcch.net/en/instruments/conventions.

[80] Foremost among the legal instruments initiated by the UNCITRAL include the United Nations Convention on Contracts for the International Sale of Goods (January 1988) U.N. Doc A/CONF 97/18, (hereinafter cited as CISG); Convention on the Recognition and Enforcement of Foreign Arbitral Awards (adopted 10 June 1958, entered into force 7 June 1959) 330 UNTS 3(hereinafter cited as New York Convention); Among the effort of the UNIDRIOT, Principles on International Commercial Contracts (first published 1994, revised in 2004, 2010 and 2016) is significant.

are the conventions and regulations passed by the EU enforceable in the member countries.[81] The Civil Procedure Code under sections 13, 14 and 44A lay down the core provisions relating to recognising foreign judgment in India.[82] Comity and reciprocity form the foundation of Indian statutory provisions.[83] In *Bhagwan Shankar v Rajaram Bapu Vithal*[84] the applicant obtained a money decree in the Joint Second-Class Subordinate Judge's Court at Sholapur. The decree was transferred to the Court of Nyayadhish, Akalkot for execution.[85] The respondent contended that he was a foreigner and had not submitted to the jurisdiction of the Court at Sholapur. Hence the Court at Sholapur was not competent, and therefore the Akalkot Court could not execute a foreign judgment within the meaning of section 13 Civil Procedure Code.[86] The judgment espoused the general principle that a court's jurisdiction is not attracted against a foreign defendant unless the defendant has submitted to its jurisdiction.[87] The recognition and enforcement of foreign judgments and arbitral awards are dealt in detail in chapters twelve and thirteen of this book.

IV. Genesis of Private International Law in India

A. Gradual Evolution Beginning with the British Rule

Compared with other branches of municipal law, a systematic body of rules of private international law is comparatively absent in India.[88] Since the country's legal system is solidly built on common law foundations, the court's decisions are the primary source of private international law.[89] During British times, the presence of various personal laws gave rise to an interpersonal conflict of laws. Since India was a federation between British India and princely States with distinct legal systems, a princely State's judgment was considered a foreign judgment. Thus, the genesis of private international law in the country was mainly the English law narrative applied to conflict of law cases.[90]

Professor Baxi notes that most private international law disputes in India relate to peripheral conflicts decisions concerning mainly the recognition and enforcement of foreign judgments.[91]

Panchapakesa Iyer and Ors. v KM Hussain Muhammad Rowther and Ors. was one of the first cases decided on private international law.[92] The case was concerned with the validity of a judgment passed at Penang, Malaysia, regarding the execution of a will. The facts showed that Kawana Nayana Noor Muhammad died in Penang on 16 October 1918.[93] The bulk of Noor

[81] Council Regulation (EC) 1215/2012 of 12 December 2012, on Jurisdiction and the Recognition and Enforcement of Judgments in Civil and Commercial Matters OJ L351/1; Council Regulation (EC) 2201/2003 of 27 November 2003, concerning Jurisdiction and the Recognition and Enforcement of Judgments in Matrimonial Matters and the matters of Parental Responsibility repealing Regulation (EC) No 1347/2000.

[82] Code of Civil Procedure 1908 (n 64).

[83] ibid, s 13.

[84] *Bhagwan Shankar v Rajaram Bapu Vithal* AIR [1951] Bom 125.

[85] ibid [1].

[86] ibid [2].

[87] ibid [6].

[88] Noronha (n 78) 26–27; Diwan and Diwan (n 76) 59–60.

[89] Noronha, ibid.

[90] ibid 26–27.

[91] U Baxi, 'Conflict of Laws' in *Annual Survey of Indian Law* 1967 *and 1968* (Indian Law Institute) 227–285, 227.

[92] *Panchapakesa Iyer and Ors. v KM Hussain Muhammad Rowther and Ors* AIR [1934] Mad 145.

[93] ibid [1].

Muhammad's property was in Penang, but a part of it consisted of immovable property in the Tanjore District. In October 1919, Noor Muhammad's widow started proceedings in the Supreme Court at Penang to administer her husband's estate claiming an account against the defendants.[94] The Registrar of the Supreme Court inquired into the assets and liabilities of the estate and, after taking into account immovable property in Tanjore District and property in Penang, concluded that the widow was entitled to a one-third share.[95] The Madras High Court observed that the court in Penang had adopted an incoreect interpretation of international law regarding a court's jurisdiction over immovable property situated in another country. The High Court further observed that the applicable law in the case should have been based on the place where the property was situated.[96]

While grappling with private international law cases, courts in India have deliberated on the rationality of applying private international law and their positions have oscillated between 'comity' and 'justice'.

In *United Arab Republic And Anr. v Mirza Ali Akbar Kashani*,[97] the plaintiff instituted a suit for recovery of damages against the defendant United Arab Republic for breach of a contract for the supply of tea by the plaintiff.[98] The defendant entered an appearance in the suit through the Vice-Consul in charge of the Consulate General of the United Arab Republic in Calcutta and took out a Master's Summons for an order, inter alia, that the plaint be rejected.[99] At the time of the hearing, it was admitted that the defendant was a sovereign state recognised by the Central Government of India.[100] The Calcutta High Court relying on Oppenheim observed that the doctrine of immunity was based on the comity of nations which recognises the equality of all states.[101] The Court further stated that the general rule of *par in parem non habet imperium* prevents a state from claiming jurisdiction over another. Hence, although states can sue in a foreign court, they cannot as a rule be sued unless they voluntarily submit to the jurisdiction of the court concerned.[102]

Legislation has also referred to comity as a reason for invoking foreign law. The Foreign Marriages Act 1969 empowers diplomatic and consular offices to perform the marriages of persons, one of whom is a citizen of India, abroad but provides that no such marriage can be performed if such a marriage is prohibited in the country where it is to be performed.[103] The case of *Viswanathan v Abdul Wajid* involved the question of recognition of foreign judgments. The court not only traced the foundation of private international law to comity but also highlighted the domestic nature of the subject by clarifying that private international law is not a law governing relations between independent states.[104]

The court's position gravitated to consideration of justice in *Satya v Teja*, also involving the question of recognition of a foreign judgment. The court opined that the Indian conflict of laws may require that the law of a foreign country be applied in a given case which contains a foreign element based on considerations of justice.[105]

[94] ibid [3].
[95] ibid [3].
[96] ibid [9].
[97] *United Arab Republic and Anr. v Mirza Ali Akbar Kashani* AIR [1962] Cal 387.
[98] ibid [1].
[99] ibid.
[100] ibid.
[101] ibid [12] see also R Higgins and others, *Oppenheim's International Law* 8th edn (Green and Co. Ltd, 1955) 264.
[102] ibid [12].
[103] Foreign Marriages Act 1969, India s 11.
[104] *Viswanathan v Abdul Wajid* AIR [1963] SC 1 (SC) 14–15.
[105] *Satya v Teja* AIR [1975] SC 105 [8].

B. Underdeveloped Status of Private International Law in India

As stated earlier, compared to other branches of municipal law, the subject of private international law has been sluggish to evolve. An archetypal example was seen in the legal battle, which followed the ghastly Bhopal gas tragedy. On 2 December 1984, a massive leak of toxic methyl isocyanate (MIC) occurred from the plant of Union Carbide India Ltd (UCIL), a subsidiary of Union Carbide Corporation, a New York corporation with headquarters in Danbury, Connecticut.[106] Immediately after the incident, the Government of India filed a suit against Union Carbide in the US, mainly due to the possibility of being awarded a massive sum of damages.[107] However, the Southern District Court of New York dismissed the case based on *forum non conveniens*.[108] Subsequently, a case was filed against Union Carbide in Bhopal, India. From the point of legal perspective, the case saw the application of the rule of 'absolute liability'[109] developed in *MC Mehta v Union of India*[110] which modified the strict liability rule developed in the historical case of *Rylands v Fletcher*.[111] In comparison to the principle of strict liability, the invocation of absolute liability entails no defence for the torts committed. Following the incident, India enacted several statutes including, the Environmental Protection Act 1986, Public Liability Insurance Act 1991, etc.[112] Even though the defendant company was headquartered in a foreign country, no discussion or arguments were raised about the possibility of invoking the law of the place of the company's headquarters based on the doctrine of control. All the evidence suggested that it was a decision to shut down a refrigeration unit designed to keep the methyl isocyanate cool and inhibit chemical reactions that led to the catastrophic incident.[113] The decision to shut down the coolant was taken by the company's headquarters based in Connecticut.[114] Indian courts that have frequently borrowed from the practices of international jurisprudence could have relied on the Rome II Regulation provisions which enable parties seeking compensation to rely on the law of the place which gave rise to the incident causing the damage.[115] The central reason for the lack of investigation into the application of foreign law in the Bhopal case and other cases involving foreign elements lies in the country's legal structure. An Indian court is not obliged to look into foreign law unless proved by the parties.[116] Foreign law needs to be proved by expert evidence as a question of fact.[117] The complexity involved in establishing the content of foreign law dissuades parties from pleading foreign law and consequently leads to the application of and reliance on domestic law.

[106] S Rajagopalan, 'Bhopal Gas Tragedy: Paternalism and Filicide' (2014) 5 *Journal of Indian law and Society* 201, 205–206.

[107] ibid.

[108] ibid; S Rajagopalan, R Schwadron, 'The Bhopal Incident: How the Courts Have Faced Complex International Litigation' (1987) 5(2) *Boston University International Law Journal* 445, 451–454.

[109] *Union Carbide Corporation v Union of India Etc* AIR [1992] 248 [82]–[83] see also MK Sinha, 'The Bhopal Gas Leak Disaster Case: Union Carbide Corporation, etc. v Union of India, etc.' (1992) 1 (1) *Asia Pacific Law Review* 118–125.

[110] 1987 SCR [1] 819.

[111] [1868] UKHL 1.

[112] The Environmental Protection Act 1986, India; The Public Liability Insurance Act 1991, India.

[113] VP Nanda, 'For Whom the Bell Tolls in the Aftermath of the Bhopal Tragedy: Reflections on Forum Non Conveniens and Alternative Methods of Resolving the Bhopal Dispute' (1987) 15(2) *Denver Journal of International Law and Policy* 235–254.

[114] ibid, Nanda, 236–237.

[115] Council Regulation (EC) No 864/2007 on the law applicable to Non-Contractual obligations (Rome II) Art7.

[116] Indian Evidence Act 1872, s 101.

[117] ibid, s 45.

Professor Baxi points out that matters become further convoluted because the Indian legal system combines private international law principles with substantive law, thus obscuring private international law's remit.[118] He cites examples from Indian statutes, including provisions of capacity and limitations under the Indian Contract Act 1872[119] and *lex domicilii* principles under the Indian Succession Act 1925.[120] He further elaborates that matters of domicile are addressed as part of constitutional matters leading to the overlooking of private international law concerns.[121] The fact that the country lacks specific legislation in the field acts as a strong deterrent to the development of private international law in India. Professor Baxi cites the non-existence of academic engagement in the subject as a major causative factor leading to the starvation of the subject.[122] Academic and juristic work detailing Indian private international law was virtually absent until the late twentieth century. As part of course curriculums at law schools, great treatises of Dicey, Cheshire, and Graveson were prescribed and taught to students without contextualising the socio-political-legal scenario.[123] Paras Diwan undertook the first methodical attempt to present an Indian perspective on the subject for law students and his book has profoundly borrowed from the common law tradition.[124] Due to the stimulus afforded by increased cross-border transactions and an enormous and widespread Indian diaspora, the subject has been enduring concrete transformations. These impetuses have provided a foundation for a renewed academic interest in the subject with endeavours to deliberate on the Indian practice of private international law. However, a general framework and a robust theoretical foundation for the subject have not been investigated much.[125]

C. Sources of Private International Law in India

The existence of private international law owes much to the presence of divergent municipal systems of law that differ significantly from each other in regulating cross-border legal relations. The conflicts between these laws are steadily increasing and as a consequence several codification attempts have been made at the international level through conventions and regulations.[126] India has been engaging with attempts at codification and unification of private international law. India has ratified the 1993 Hague Convention on Inter-Country Adoption of Children.[127] The country has enacted the Arbitration and Conciliation Act to implement the 1958 New York Convention.[128] However, the country has steadfastly opposed and has refused to accede to the 1980 Hague Inter-county Child Abduction Convention and the 1980 UN Convention on Contracts for the International Sale of Goods (CISG).[129] Besides these international conventions, national laws and domestic judicial decisions are the primary sources of private international law.

[118] Baxi (n 91) 227.
[119] ibid 227; Indian Contract Act 1872, ss 1, 28.
[120] Indian Succession Act (n 67) s 5.
[121] Baxi (n 91) 229; Domicile provisions are also covered under Part XI of the Constitution of India 1950, Arts 5–11.
[122] Baxi (n 91) 227, 228.
[123] ibid 228.
[124] Diwan and Diwan (n 76).
[125] Baxi (n 91) 228.
[126] The Conventions and legal instruments adopted by the Hague Conference of the Private International Law can be accessed at www.hcch.net/en/instruments/conventions.
[127] Convention on Protection of Children and Co-operation in Respect of Intercountry Adoption (29 May 1993) (hereinafter cited as Adoption Convention).
[128] The Arbitration and Conciliation Act 1996, India Part II Chapter 1 deals with enforcement of foreign arbitral awards under the New York Convention 1958.
[129] S Jolly, 'International Parental Child Abduction: An Explorative Analysis of Legal Standards and Judicial Interpretation in India' (2007) 31 *International Journal of Law, Policy and the Family* 20–40.

i. Statutes

A lack of legislative interference historically characterises Indian private international law. The point was highlighted by the court in *Y Narasimha Rao and Ors v Y Venkata Lakshmi* which observed that

> the rules of private international law in this country are not codified and are scattered in different enactments such as the Civil Procedure Code, the Contract Act, the Indian Succession Act, the Indian Divorce Act the Special Marriage Act, etc. In addition, some rules have also been evolved by judicial decisions in matters of status, legal capacity of natural persons, matrimonial disputes, custody of children, adoption, testamentary and intestate succession, etc.[130]

The Civil Procedure Code 1908, passed during the British period, codified the rules on jurisdiction and recognition and enforcement of foreign judgments. However, the Civil Procedure Code did not provide any guidance on choice of law rules. Reference to jurisdiction, but an absence of provisions on choice of law, is also characteristic of statutes dealing with specific subjects such as marriage and divorce. The Hindu Marriage Act 1954,[131] the Special Marriage Act 1954,[132] and the Indian Divorce Act 1869[133] have only provided for rules on jurisdiction. The sole exception seems to be in the commercial field. The Arbitration and Conciliation Act 1996 has detailed provisions on jurisdiction, choice of law, and the enforcement of arbitral awards.[134] The incorporation of choice of law and jurisdiction clauses in arbitration was done in the context of the country's international obligations under the New York Convention.[135] In this regard, India can learn valuable lessons from its neighbouring country Nepal. Nepal has drafted its new Code of Civil Procedure that has a specific chapter dealing with private international law concerns. It provides for rules on jurisdiction, choice of law and the recognition of judgment, thereby providing much-needed clarity in legal disputes.[136]

ii. Domestic and International Judicial Decisions

In the absence of a specific legislative mandate, most of the evolution of private international law in the country was achieved through judicial decisions. The judicial decisions bear strong inspiration from international conventions[137] and juridical statements of other jurisdictions. An analysis of private international law decisions shows the strong indefinable impression of common law in the country's legal practice.[138] Reference to common law was unavoidable, with the Privy Council being the country's highest appellate authority until independence. A more or less similar approach of reading common law provisions into the domestic arena continued even

[130] *Y Narasimha Rao and Ors v Y Venkata Lakshmi And Anr* [1991] SCR (2) 821 [3].
[131] Hindu Marriage Act (n 24) s 19.
[132] The Special Marriage Act 1954, India s 31.
[133] The Indian Divorce Act 1869, India s 4.
[134] The Arbitration and Conciliation Act (n128).
[135] India ratified the New York Convention on 13 July 1960. Status available at https://uncitral.un.org/en/texts/arbitration/conventions/foreign_arbitral_awards/status2.
[136] The National Civil (Code) Act 2017 (Nepal) ss 692–721.
[137] *Satya v Teja* (n 105) the Supreme Court referred to the Convention on the Recognition of Divorces and Legal Separations (adopted 1 June 1970, entered into force 24 August 1975) (hereinafter Divorce and Separation Convention 1970); in *Narasimha Rao* (n 130), the Supreme Court referred to the Brussels Convention on jurisdiction and the enforcement of judgments in civil and commercial matters (27 September 1968) OJ L388/1.
[138] Noronha (n 78) 7.

after independence.[139] In *Indian and General Investment v Sri Ramchandra Mardaraja Deo*[140] the court expressly referred to the common law principle which conferred jurisdiction on the English courts from the mere transient presence of a defendant on English soil and held that such principle could not be considered adequate and 'foreign courts can scarcely be expected to recognise a jurisdiction based upon mere transient presence'.[141] The court explicitly stated that the courts in India are at liberty to lay down and follow their own rules with regard to private international law. Such liberty to lay down rules equips the judiciary not only to adopt the best practices of other jurisdictions based on a sense of justice, equity, and good conscience, but also to build up an indigenous jurisprudence.[142] Similar observations were made in *Satya v Teja*, involving the recognition of foreign divorce. The court ruled against the mechanical adoption of the rules of private international law as they have evolved in other countries.[143] Consequently, while judicial decisions reveal strong traces of common law influence, courts are gradually developing a body of Indian private international law.

iii. Juristic Writings

Judicial statements have referred to and engaged with scholastic writings by Dicey, Morris and Cheshire, to name a few.[144] However, indigenous writings on the subject have been far less in number and theoretical engagements or a broader private international law framework have not been focused.[145] Many reasons can be attributed to this underdeveloped status. The legal structure of India is based on strong unitary features. Hence, unlike federal jurisdictions like the US, Canada, and Australia, no opportunity exists to develop private international principles as between Indian States. Compared to other jurisdictions, until the 1980s the number of private international law disputes that had come up before the judiciary has been far less in number. However, the opening up of the economy and the increased Indian diaspora has facilitated a growth in cross border transactions. As a result, the number and magnitude of disputes having foreign elements began to swell prompting the judiciary into making private international law more operational.[146]

V. Operationalisation of Private International Law: Classic Concepts

The following sections will deliberate on the three essential stages of selecting applicable law, including the characterisation, connecting factors, and *renvoi*.

[139] ibid.
[140] *Indian and General Investment Trust, Ltd* (n 35) [21].
[141] ibid.
[142] ibid [22].
[143] *Satya v Teja* (n 105) [9].
[144] In *Laxmichand and Ors. v Mst. Tipuri* AIR [1956] Raj 81 [7] involving the recognition of a foreign judgment; in *Sankaran Govindan v Lakshmi Bharathi* AIR [1974] 1764, and *Dr. Yogesh Bhardwaj v State of UP* AIR [1991] 356, involving the question of domicile, the court referred to the writings of Dicey and Morris and Cheshire.
[145] Some of the early writings on the subject include Justice PV Rajamannar, 'The Future of Private International Law in India' (1952) 1 *Indian Yearbook of International Affairs* 20; TS R Rao, 'Private International Law in India' (1955) 3 *Indian Yearbook of International Affairs* 219; YS Chittale, 'First Decision of Supreme Court Involving Conflict of Law' (1956) 5(4) *American Journal of Comparative Law* 629; TSR Rao, 'Conflict of Laws in the Indian Tax System' (1959) 8 *Indian Yearbook of International Affairs* 215; VC Govindraj, 'Foreign Arbitral Awards and Foreign Judgments Based on Such Awards' (1964) 13(4) *International Comparative Law Quarterly* 1465.
[146] Baxi (n 91) 228.

A. Characterisation

Characterisation denotes the method through which the court assigns the nature and legal category of claims.[147] Characterisation is technically not unique to private international law, but is an inherent feature of all domestic and international judicial processes.[148] However, in private international disputes, the scenario can become complicated as jurisdictions differ in their approaches to legal concepts and issues.[149] For example, A from Pakistan, boarded a bus at Lahore, Pakistan. The bus is scheduled to go to Delhi, India. A is injured on the way in Amritsar, India. If a case is filed in Pakistan or India, the court must determine whether the subject matter should be considered part of contract or tort. Similarly, if the question before the Indian court concerns the succession to the specific property of a person domiciled in India but a national of the UK, the court should first determine the nature of the relevant properties as movable or immovable. The determination and assignment of specific categories become vital as the connecting factor applied in choosing the relevant law depends on the precise characterisation. If characterisation leads to a determination that the property is movable, the applicable law will depend on the connecting factor of domicile. Whereas, if the property is immovable, the applicable law will depend on the location of the property.

Numerous approaches have been developed by jurists and followed by different jurisdictions:

- Characterisation by the *lex fori*.
- Characterisation by the *lex causae*.
- Two-stage characterisation: primary characterisation following the *lex fori* and secondary characterisation the *lex causae*.
- Characterisation based on comparative law and analytical jurisprudence.[150]

i. Characterisation based on the lex fori

The first generalised proposition on characterisation was formulated by Bartin, who propounded that, in the absence of a unified approach among jurisdictions, the law of the forum should determine the nature of relationship.[151] Cheshire supported the idea in England,[152] Falconbridge in Canada, and Lorenzen in the US.[153] The proposition dealt a severe blow to the internationalisation of private international law. Bartin admitted two exceptions to the characterisation theory based on *lex fori*. First, determining whether the property is movable or immovable is to be determined by the *lex situs* (location of the property).[154] Second, the formation of a contract by

[147] CMV Clarkson and J Hill, *The Conflict of Laws* 4th edn (Oxford Press, 2011) 20.

[148] V Allarousse, 'A Comparative Approach to the Conflict of Characterization in Private International Law' (1991) 23(3) *Case Western Reserve Journal of International Law* 479–516, 479.

[149] D Falconbridge, 'Characterization in the Conflict of Laws' (1937) 53(2) *Law Quarterly Review* 235–258.

[150] J Unger, 'The Place of Classification in Private International Law' (1937) 19 *Bell Yard Journal of the Law Society's School of Law* 3–21.

[151] Bartin, 'De l'Impossibilite d'Arriver d'la Suppression Definitive des Conflits de Lois (1897) 24 *Clunet* 255, 255–68, 466–95, 720–60 quoted in V Allarousse (n 148) 482; Kahn supported this proposition.

[152] GC Cheshire, *Private International Law* 2nd edn (Oxford University Press, 1938) 24–45.

[153] EG Lorenzen, 'The Theory of Qualifications and the Conflict of Laws' (1920) 20 (3) *Columbia Law Review* 246–282; EG Lorenzen, 'The Characterisation, Classification, or Characterisation Problem in the Conflict of Laws' (1941) 50(5) *Yale Law Journal* 743–761; RA Pascal, 'Characterization as an Approach to the Conflict of Laws' (1940) 2(4) *Louisiana Law Review* 715–728.

[154] Bartin (n 151).

correspondence (not face-to-face) should be determined by reference to the law which postpones its formation for the longest period.[155] The theory is supported on the basis that otherwise the law of the forum would lose all control on a case. The application of the *lex fori* is also supported based on sovereign necessity.[156] However, the theory fails to articulate the accurate nature of private international law, as the choice of characterisation is innate in private international law and a mechanical application of the *lex fori* in most cases gives rise to legal isolation.[157] It is also criticised as a flagrant contradiction to use the forum's characterisation and to validate that it in accordance with conflict of laws principles.[158]

ii. Characterisation based on the lex causae

Despagnet and Wolff advocated the application of *lex causae* in opposition to Bartin's theory of *lex fori*.[159] According to Wolff, 'every legal rule takes its classification from the legal system to which it belongs'.[160] Despagnet proposed that the applicable law governing the legal facts determine their characterisation. He stated that reliance on the law of the forum was against the spirit of private international law. However, the theory suffers from a vicious circle issue.[161] In the words of Cheshire, 'If the law which is finally to regulate the matter (i.e., the *lex causae*) depends upon classification, how can classification be made according to that law.'[162] The point is that if the applicable law is to be selected based on characterisation, how the applicable law cannot govern characterisation.

iii. Characterisation based on Comparative Law

Rabel and Beckett advanced the outlook that analytical jurisprudence based on the comparative study of laws should govern characterisation.[163] Though the theory appears to be comprehensive, it has been criticised for being impractical as it imposes a heavy burden on a court to assess and evaluate different legal systems. Morris observed 'this view is superficially attractive because the judicial technique in conflict cases should be more cosmopolitan and less insular than in domestic cases'.[164] However, this approach puts a heavy burden and responsibility on the judicial system.

iv. Two-stage Characterisation

Falconbridge popularised the idea.[165] It was suggested that, in the first stage of the dispute, the legal category of the dispute should be determined by reference to the *lex fori*. In the second stage, the function of the courts would be to examine a relevant foreign law and its applicability to the facts.

[155] ibid.

[156] WE Beckett, 'The Question of Classification ("Qualification") in Private International Law' (1934) 15 *British Year Book of International Law* 46–81, 51; EG Lorenzen (n 153) 281.

[157] V Allarousse (n 148) 484.

[158] ibid. See generally Beckett (n 156) 55.

[159] M Wolff, *Private International Law* 2nd edn (Clarendon Press, 1950) 154.

[160] ibid.

[161] cited in Pascal (n 153) 719.

[162] Diwan and Diwan (n 76) 79.

[163] Beckett (n 156) 58–60; See also T Remus, 'Revival of Rabel's Transnational Characterisation for Rules of Conflict: Some Answers in a European Convention' (2017) *International Business Law Journal* 439–460.

[164] Dicey, Morris & Collins, *Conflict of Laws*, 15th edn (3rd Supp, Sweet & Maxwell, 2016) 40.

[165] Falconbridge (n 149) 236; see JM Cormack, 'Renvoi, Characterization, Localization and Preliminary Question in the Conflict of Laws: A Study of Problems Involved in Determining Whether or Not the Forum Should Follow Its Own Choice of a Conflict-of-Laws Principle' (1940) 14 *Southern California Law Review* 221–275.

An assessment of the practice of jurisdictions reveals that initially both the *lex fori* and the *lex causae* have been followed in the process of characterisation.

v. *Judicial Statements on Characterisation*

Ogden v Ogden[166] is a classic case illustrative of the complexities of the characterisation process. The facts of the case are recapitulated here. A ceremony of marriage in English form was celebrated in England without the knowledge of the parents between a domiciled Englishwoman and a Frenchman domiciled in France.[167] A French court annulled the marriage on the ground that the parental consent required under the French law had not been obtained.[168] Subsequently, the Frenchman contracted another marriage in France. The Englishwoman petitioned in England to dissolve her marriage on the ground of her husband's desertion and adultery. The petition was dismissed for want of jurisdiction as her domicile had changed to France after the marriage. The woman subsequently married an Englishman named William Ogden. Ogden filed a suit asking for a decree of nullity on the ground that, at the time of marriage, she was already a married woman. The English court held that the second marriage was bigamous and void, as the court would not recognise the nullity decree pronounced by the French court. The English court characterised parental consent based on the *lex fori* as a matter relating to formality and the law of the place of marriage (*lex loci celebrationis*) (England) applied to formalities of marriage.[169] As a practical consequence, the Englishwoman was considered married under the English law, but unmarried under French law.[170]

In *Re Cohn*, a mother and her daughter domiciled in Germany and residing in London died there during an air bombing raid. According to the mother's will, the daughter would inherit the mother's movables if the daughter survived her.[171] According to English conflict rules, succession to movables is governed by the law of the domicile, but procedural matters are governed by the *lex fori*.[172] According to the English statute, the legal presumption was that the elder died first, but according to the German one both died simultaneously. Though the method of proof was a matter of procedure, that was of no use as it was impossible to resolve who died first.[173] The judge decided that the *lex causae* was German and under German law the issue was substantive.[174] An analogous perspective was adopted in the case of *Re Maldonado*.[175] The fact that there are no universal criteria for characterisation might result in judgments being contingent on how the characterisation is achieved and this might embolden forum shopping. Savigny proposed that, in order to sidestep forum shopping, courts need to find the 'natural seat' or 'centre of gravity' by distinguishing the cluster of connecting factors for characterisation.[176] Categorising the centre of gravity would result in the same choice of law, no matter where the case was filed. However, the solution has not found much support owing to differing national approaches and as a result

[166] *Ogden v Ogden* (1908) 1 P 46 [Eng CA].

[167] ibid; JDI Hughes, 'Judicial Method and the Problem in Ogden v Ogden' (1928) 44 *Law Quarterly Review* 217–226.

[168] Collier (n 37) 14; A Reed, 'Essential Validity of Marriage: The Application of Interest Analysis and Depecage to Anglo-American Choice of Law Rules' (2000) 20(3) *New York Law School Journal of International and Comparative Law* 387–450, 392.

[169] T Baty, 'Capacity and Form of Marriage in the Conflict of Laws' (1917) 26(6) *Yale Law Journal* 444–463, 456.

[170] PK Agarwal, 'The Theory of Characterization: A Critical Legal Study Perspective' (2015) 4(3) *Voice of Research* 45.

[171] *Re Cohn* [1945] 1 ch 5; see V Allarousse (n 148) 494.

[172] ibid.

[173] ibid.

[174] Collier (n 37) 18.

[175] *Re Maldonadao* [1954] P 223.

[176] Savigny (n 33) 67–68.

forum shopping continues unabated. Generally, the process of characterisation following the *lex fori* and recognising the inescapable conceptual nature of the forum law has been adopted by most courts around the world.[177] Cormack, who supports the *lex fori* approach, writes that it may sound absurd to advocate that the forum apply the domestic law of another jurisdiction to a case when a court of that jurisdiction would not do so because it would characterise the question differently.[178] On practical grounds, the reliance of *lex fori* is supported as there is a burden placed on the judicial system when there is a reliance on foreign law.[179]

The classical debate regarding which law characterises the matters submitted – *lex fori* or *lex causae* – has hardly ever been examined under Indian case law. However, selected elements of characterisation were seen in the first case of the *Delhi Cloth and General Mills and Ors. v Harnam Singh and Others* decided by the Supreme Court of India.[180] The plaintiffs were the partners of a firm known as Harnam Singh Jagat Singh. The firm carried on the business of producing cotton cloth at Lyallpur, which became part of Pakistan after the partition. The defendants, Delhi Cloth and General Mills Ltd, with headquarters at Delhi, carried on business at Lyallpur before partition.[181] The plaintiffs purchased cloth from the defendants from time to time and made advance lump-sum payments against their purchases. After the partition, the plaintiffs fled from Pakistan to India and became evacuees from Pakistan.[182] The Pakistan Government froze all evacuee assets and transferred the assets to a custodian of evacuee property. The plaintiffs sued the defendants in India to recover the balance amount and the Punjab High Court delivered a judgment in their favour against which the defendants appealed to the Supreme Court.[183] The plaintiffs took the position that the custodian did not pay them in Pakistan and that Pakistani law did not apply to the debt because of the plaintiff's presence in India and, if it did apply, it was confiscatory and therefore against the public policy of the forum.[184] The Court characterised the claim as one for debt involving contractual questions. Based on the test of real and substantial connection, the Court invoked Pakistani law as the applicable law. The applicable law would be living and changing even though Lyallpur was part of India when the transaction took place.[185] This sole judgment is, however, no indication of trends of Indian courts towards characterisation.

B. Connecting Factors

Once the court has characterised the legal dispute under consideration, the next concern is identifying the applicable law to the dispute.[186] For instance, A and B domiciled in India and of Indian nationality marry in England. The court is called upon to determine the validity of their marriage. Private international law postulates that the applicable law concerning the validity of a

[177] R Baratta, 'The Process of Characterisation in the EC Conflict of Laws: Suggesting a Flexible Approach' (2015) 6 *Yearbook of Private International Law* 155–170.
[178] Cormack (n 165) 227.
[179] ibid.
[180] *The Delhi Cloth and General Mills & Co Ltd. v Harnam Singh and Others* AIR [1955] 590.
[181] ibid [3].
[182] ibid [8].
[183] ibid [7]. YS Chitale, 'India: First Decision of Supreme Court Involving Conflict of Laws; Law Applicable to Debt' (1956) 5(4) *The American Journal of Comparative Law* 629, 631.
[184] ibid [41].
[185] ibid [46].
[186] S Szászy, 'The Basic Connecting Factor in International Cases in the Domain of Civil Procedure' (1966) 15(2) *International and Comparative Law Quarterly* 436–456, 436.

marriage is determined by the place of closest connection based on a factual assessment of each case. In terms of the validity of a marriage, two questions are identified; the formal and material aspects. The law of the place of the celebration determines the formal validity of a marriage. In the example cited above, since the marriage was contracted in London, the connecting factor being the place of celebration, the applicable law for formal validity would be English law.

Some of the commonly identified connecting factors are listed below.

- The law of the place of celebration determines the formal validity of the marriage.[187]
- The *lex situs* governs succession to immovable property.[188]
- Procedural matters are governed by the *lex fori*.[189]

The function of connecting factors is to link legal categories to the applicable law. Though the number of connecting factors under private international law is small, a consensus on connecting factors has materialised between civil law systems and common law jurisdictions only regarding specific factors. The unanimity on connecting factors have evolved through the historical development as evidenced through judicial statements and have subsequently been codified by international conventions and regulations.[190] As a result, conflict and indeterminacy associated with private international law persist at multiple levels. First, the approaches of the common law and civil law differ on connecting factors. According to common law countries, the law of the parties' domicile at the time of marriage or the law of the intended matrimonial home determines the material aspects of the marriage.[191] For civil law countries, the law of the parties' nationality at the time of marriage determines the material aspects of their marriage.[192] Similarly, for common law countries, succession to movable property is governed by the law of the last domicile of the deceased, but for civil law countries the same is determined by the law of nationality of the parties.[193] Second, specific issues are associated with more than one connecting factor, even under one legal system. A contract's formal validity is either governed by the law of the place of contracting or by the proper law of the contract.[194] Lastly, the understanding of connecting factors varies among jurisdictions. For instance, if an Indian court identifies the connecting factor as domicile, the question persists as to the meaning of domicile, whether it needs to be understood based on the forum's law or foreign law.[195]

In the case of *Re Annesley*, A died domiciled in France according to English law and in England according to French law. Russell J held that A died domiciled in France according to

[187] Clarkson & Hill (n 147) 33.

[188] ibid.

[189] ibid.

[190] Convention on Celebration and Recognition of the Validity of Marriages provided a place of marriage as the connecting factor to determine the formal aspect of marriage (hereinafter 1978 Validity of Marriages Convention 1978); Maintenance Convention 1973 (n 79) provides internal law of the habitual residence of the maintenance creditor shall govern the maintenance obligations; Divorce and Separation Convention 1970 (n 137) and Convention on the Law Applicable to Matrimonial Property Regimes 1978 (hereinafter Matrimonial Property Convention 1978) provides, habitual residence and nationality as the connecting factor; Convention of 25 October 1980 on the Civil Aspects of International Child Abduction adopts habitual residence as the connecting factor.

[191] Clarkson & Hill (n 147) 356–357.

[192] M Raiteri, 'Citizenship as a Connecting Factor in Private International Law for Family Matters' (2014) 10(2) *Journal of Private International Law* 309, 312; see also V Gaertner, 'European Choice of Law Rules in Divorce (Rome III): An Examination of the Possible Connecting Factors in Divorce Matters against the Backgrounds of Private International Law Developments' (2006) 2(1) *Journal of Private International Law* 99–136.

[193] Clarkson & Hill (n147) 506.

[194] ibid 33.

[195] Diwan and Diwan (n 76) 95.

the law of the forum.[196] Under Indian private international law, judicial statements and statutory provisions have elaborated on few connecting factors. In *Delhi Cloth Mills v Harnam Singh*, the court observed that the applicable law in the case of a contract is the place with which the transaction has its closest and most real connection and can be based on the parties' choice, which is restrictive in nature.[197] However, restrictive party autonomy has been modified in subsequent cases.[198] Under the Indian Succession Act 1925, section 5(1) provides that succession to immovable property in India of a deceased shall be regulated by the law of India wherever such person may have had his domicile at the time of his death.[199] Further, succession to movable property of a deceased is regulated by the law of the country in which such person was domiciled at the time of death.[200]

C. *Renvoi*

Renvoi, as a vexed legal question, has puzzled academics and practitioners of private international law.[201] The application of *renvoi* comes into operation in the last stages of the conflict of law process, once the law of the forum court identifies a foreign law as the applicable law in the dispute.[202] Beaumont and McEleavy define *renvoi* thus:

> [A] question of *renvoi* arises where the choice-of-law rules of the forum refer an issue to the courts of another country which, under its rules of choice of law, in turn, refers the issue back to the law of the forum or on to the law of a third country.[203]

For instance, consider a legal dispute before an Indian court relating to the validity of a marriage celebrated in India between two Indian nationals domiciled in France. The Indian court, based on domicile as the connecting factor on issues concerning capacity to marry, will identify French law as the applicable law. The question then would be the meaning and scope of the applicable French law. The term 'French law' can be given either a narrow or a broader interpretation. In the narrow interpretation, the reference to French law indicates the country's internal law referring to French domestic substantive laws on marriage. In the broader sense, a reference to French law indicates the whole of French law, including its conflict of laws. It could be that both Indian law (*lex fori*) and French law (*lex causae*) identify 'domicile' as the connecting factor but interpret 'domicile' to mean different things. It could also be that Indian law (*lex fori*) and French law (*lex causae*) differ on the applicable connecting factor – domicile and nationality, respectively.[204] In such a scenario, the Indian court may apply Indian law on the ground that a French court would apply Indian law.[205] This process is known as *renvoi* by remission. *Renvoi* can also arise

[196] *Re Annesley* [1926] ch 692.

[197] *British India Steam Navigation Co Ltd v Shanmughavilas Cashew Industries* [1990] 3 SCC 481, *Rabindra N Maitra v Life Insurance Corporation of India* AIR [1964] Cal 141 (CHC) [16]–[18].

[198] *National Thermal Power Corporation v Singer Company* [1992] 3 SCC 551 [14].

[199] Indian Succession Act (n 67) s 5(1).

[200] ibid.

[201] LT Bates, 'Remission and Transmission in American Conflict of Laws' (1931) 16(3) *Cornell Law Quarterly* 311–319, 313; AEV Overbeck, 'Renvoi in the Institute of International Law' (1963) 12(4) *American Journal of Comparative Law* 544–548; W Raeburn, 'The Open Offer Formula and the Renvoi in Private International Law' (1948) 25 *British Year Book of International Law* 211–235.

[202] M Shava, 'Choice of Law and the Doctrine of Renvoi in Israeli Law – A Comparative Commentary' (2000) 15 *Tel Aviv University Studies in Law* 123–146.

[203] PR Beaumont and PE McEleavy, *Antons Private International law* 3rd edn (W Green, 2011) 105.

[204] Collier (n 37) 20.

[205] ibid.

through transmission, if instead of referring the matter back to Indian law, French conflict law rules point to the application of the law of a third country.[206]

The concept of *renvoi* was employed in the classic case of *Forgo*.[207] Forgo was a Bavarian national who lived his life mostly in France. He died, leaving substantial movable property in France. The French court resolved the succession to movables based on the law of the nationality and referred to Bavarian law. Bavarian law provided for inheritance by collateral relatives of the maternal lineage. However, under Bavarian conflict of law rules, the applicable law was the law of the deceased's domicile. Consequently, the Bavarian legal system remitted the matter back to the French legal system. Accepting the *renvoi*, the French court applied French law to the case and, as a result, the entire of the deceased's property passed to the state to the detriment of his collateral relatives.[208]

i. Types of Renvoi

Scholars have discussed many scenarios of *renvoi*, which can be presented through an illustration. A, a British subject (UK citizen) domiciled in France, dies without a will. The English court has to decide on the distribution of A's movable property. In the first scenario, the English court (*lex fori*) applying its choice of law rules, decides that the law of the domicile governs intestate succession to movables and hence the applicable law is the French law. The English court would interpret French law to mean the substantive law of France, excluding its private international law rules. In this scenario, there would be no application of *renvoi*.[209] In the second scenario, the English court interprets the applicable French law (*lex causae*) to include its conflict of laws and applies the law that would be chosen under French law's conflict process. The French choice of law process refers the matter back to the law of nationality and the English court would accept the remission back and apply English law in a process known as single *renvoi* or partial *renvoi*.[210] Single *renvoi* was followed in *Forgo* but repudiated in *Re Askew*.[211] In the third scenario, the English court interprets the *lex causae* to include its conflicts of laws and rules of *renvoi*. English court would attempt to evaluate the situation from a French judge's perspective. The French court would refer the issue to English law as the law of nationality. While English law would refer the issue back to French law as the legal system of the deceased's domicile. France's legal system would accept the English remission. The English court would then apply French internal law. This is known as double or total *renvoi*.[212] Double *renvoi* was followed in the case of *Re Annesley*[213] and *Re Ross*.[214]

[206] EW Briggs, '"Renvoi" in the Succession of Tangibles: A False Issue Based on Faulty Analysis' (1954) 64 *Yale Law Journal* 195–219, 219; EG Lorenzon, 'Renvoi Theory and the Application of Foreign Law: Renvoi in General (1910) 10(3) *Columbia Law Review* 190–207.

[207] *L'Affaire Forgo* [1932] 59 Clunet 281.

[208] A Frederick, 'The Problem of Renvoi in Private International Law' (1926) 12 *Transactions of the Grotius Society* 63–79, 65.

[209] SB Stein, 'Choice of Law and the Doctrine of Renvoi' (1971) 17 *Mc Gill Law journal* 582, 584.

[210] ibid 585.

[211] [1930] 2 ch 259.

[212] Stein (n 209) 586.

[213] [1926] ch 692.

[214] [1930] 1 ch 377.

ii. Reflections from Other jurisdictions

Besides judicial practice, the idea is supported by voluminous literature, which has developed a strong theoretical foundation and an excessive academic obsession with the doctrine of *renvoi*.[215] The idea has been invoked, primarily in matters concerning title to foreign land,[216] formalities of a will,[217] and the status of marriage.[218] Along with the fervent academic obsession, the doctrine has also been criticised as impractical and imposing a high threshold on the judiciary. Notably, a substantial part of criticism has stemmed from American jurists who considered that *renvoi* was not part of American conflict of laws.[219] Falconbridge had expressed the fear that, if the court is misinformed as to foreign law or fails to interpret accurately the evidence of foreign law, the potential application of the doctrine of total *renvoi* may lead to a grotesque result or a miscarriage of justice.[220] Further, in addition to evidentiary problems and a high threshold, *renvoi* allows judges to interpret foreign law according to their personal view and circuitously bring in their public policy notions.[221] Because of these criticisms, the doctrine has not been invoked uniformly across jurisdictions.

The case of *Neilson v Overseas Projects Corporation of Victoria Ltd*[222] saw the revival of *renvoi* in international torts. The case involved a claim made by the appellant against Overseas Projects Corporation (OPC) for damages for personal injuries sustained due to OPC's negligence in China.[223] Under Australian choice of law rules, the law of the place of harm (*lex loci delicti*) governed the claim. The reference to the place of harm would have meant that Chinese law would apply, but a one-year statute of limitations barred that claim.[224] The High Court, however, found in favour of Neilson under the doctrine of total *renvoi*. The Court relied on Article 146 of the General Principles of Civil Law of the Peoples Republic of China (PRC), which states that, in a claim for compensation for damages resulting from any infringement of rights, the law of the place where the infringement occurred should be applied. Article 146 provides that where both parties are nationals of the same country, their own country's law may be applied.[225] The High Court referred back to the law of Australia, meaning that Australia's limitations period applied, and Neilson triumphed.[226]

In *Islamic Republic of Iran v Denyse Berend*,[227] Iran sought the return of a fragment of an Achaemenid limestone relief as a part of a national monument that was taken from its territory in 1932. A French citizen had purchased the property through an auction in New York.

[215] Several theories supporting *renvoi* have been propounded, including the mutual disclaimer theory, the theory or *renvoi* proper, and the foreign court theory. For a general discussion see generally E Lorentzen, 'The Renvoi Doctrine in the Conflict of Laws: Meaning of "the Law of the Country"' (1917) 27 *Yale Law Journal* 510–534; E Griswold 'Renvoi Revisited' (1938) 51(7) *Harvard Law Review* 1165–1208, 1183; A Briggs, 'In Praise and Defense of Renvoi' (1998) 47(4) *International and Comparative Law Quarterly* 877–884, 881.

[216] *Re Duke of Wellington* [1947] LR Ch 506.

[217] *Collier v Rivaz* (1841) 2 Curt. Ecc. 855 *Re Ross* [1930] 1 ch 377.

[218] *Re Askew* [1930] 2 Ch. 259; *R v Brentwood Superintendent Registrar of Marriages, ex parte Arias* [1968] 2 QB 956.

[219] Lorenzen (n 206); LT Bates, 'Remission and Transmission in American Conflict of Laws' (1931) 16(3) *Cornell Law Review* 311–319.

[220] JD Falconbridge, *Essays on the Conflicts of Laws* 2nd edn (Cambridge University Press, 2009) 51.

[221] Stein (n 209) 582; RA Leflar, 'Choice-Influencing Considerations in Conflicts Law' (1996) 41 *New York University Law Review* 267, 299.

[222] *Neilson v Overseas Projects Corporation of Victoria Ltd* [2005] HCA 54.

[223] ibid [20].

[224] ibid [4]–[7]; A Gray, 'The Rise of Renvoi in Australia: Creating the Theoretical Framework' (2007) 30(1) *University of New South Wales Law Journal* 103–126,106.

[225] ibid [277].

[226] ibid [278].

[227] *Iran v Berend* [2007] EWHC 132 (QB).

To overcome the *lex situs* rule in property matters, Iran relied on the invocation of *renvoi*, which would have meant the application of Iranian law to the dispute.[228] The court observed that the application of *renvoi* was a question of policy. The doctrine allows judges to further the public policy of a particular choice of law rule. Based on the fact that *renvoi* had never been invoked in the case of movable property in England, Eady J said: 'Millett J saw no room for the doctrine of *renvoi*, in the share context, and I see no room either as a matter of policy for its introduction in the context of a tangible object such as that in contention here.'[229]

One of the impetuses for the invocation of *renvoi* arose due to the divergent approaches of jurisdictions with respect to the application of the connecting factors of domicile and nationality. The 1955 Convention Relating to the Settlement of the Conflicts between the Law of Nationality and the Law of Domicile attempted to resolve the conflict. Article 1 of the Convention provides that when the state where the person concerned is domiciled requires the application of national law, but the state of which that person is a citizen requires the application of the law of domicile, all contracting states are to apply the provisions of the law of domicile. Article 2 states that when both the state where the person concerned is domiciled and the state of which that person is a citizen require the application of the law of domicile, all contracting states are to apply the provisions of the law of domicile.[230] Article 3 provides that when the state where the person concerned is domiciled and the state of which that person is a citizen both require the application of national law, all contracting states are to apply the provisions of national law.[231] The Convention has not come into force until now. Most of the international conventions which have attempted to codify the rules on private International law have excluded the application of *renvoi*.[232] However, the cases discussed above reveal that, despite voluminous criticism, the doctrine has endured and appears from time to time.[233]

iii. *Application of* Renvoi *under Indian Private International Law*

This section endeavours to identify the issues of *renvoi* in private international law that have been presented before the judiciary in India. An assessment of the Indian judicial scenario reveals that not many cases exist which have examined the concept of *renvoi*.

In *NTPC v Singer Co*,[234] the National Thermal Power Corporation of India (NTPC) entered into a contract with the Singer Company (Singer), a British entity, to supply equipment and erect certain projects in India. A dispute arose and Singer sought arbitration under the International Chamber of Commerce (ICC) rules in London, as provided in the contract. Singer won the arbitration and was granted an award by the ICC tribunal.[235] Singer then sought to enforce the award in India under the Indian Foreign Awards Act, limiting Indian courts' role in recognising and enforcing

[228] D Fincham, 'Rejecting Renvoi for Movable Cultural Property: The Islamic Republic of Iran v Denyse Berend' (2007) 14(1) *International Journal of Cultural Property* 111–120, 113.

[229] *Iran v Berend* (n 227) [23]–[24].

[230] ibid, Art 2.

[231] ibid, Art 3.

[232] The Hague Principles on Choice of Law in International Commercial Contracts (adopted November 2012, entered into force 19 March 2015) Art 8: 'Exclusion *of* renvoi; A choice of law does not refer to rules of private international law of the law chosen by the parties unless the parties expressly provide otherwise'; Council Regulation (EC) 593/2008 of 17 June 2008, on the law applicable to contractual obligations (Rome I Regulation) OJ L177/6 Art 20: 'Exclusion of renvoi The application of the law of any country specified by this Regulation means the application of the rules of law in force in that country other than its rules of private international law unless provided otherwise in this Regulation.'

[233] L Kramer, 'Return of the Renvoi' (1991) 66 *New York University Law Review* 979, 1016.

[234] *National Thermal Power Corporation v Singer Company* (n 198).

[235] ibid [2].

the foreign arbitral award. NTPC argued against enforcement, claiming that since the contract was governed by Indian law it was not a 'foreign award' under the Act.[236] NTPC argued that as a result, despite the contract's explicit submission to ICC arbitration, the whole case should be retried in India under the Indian Arbitration Act. The Delhi High Court dismissed NTPC's application and NTPC appealed to the Supreme Court of India.[237] The Court held that the parties have the freedom to choose the law governing an international commercial arbitration agreement. They may choose the substantive law governing the arbitration agreement and the procedural law governing the conduct of the arbitration. Such choice is exercised either expressly or by implication.[238] Where there is no express choice of the law governing the contract as a whole or the arbitration agreement in particular, there is in the absence of any contrary indication a presumption that the parties have intended that the proper law of the contract, as well as the law governing the arbitration agreement, are the same as the law of the country in which the arbitration is agreed to be held. On the other hand, where the proper law of the contract is expressly chosen by the parties, as in the present case, such law must in the absence of an unmistakable intention to the contrary govern the arbitration agreement which, though collateral or ancillary to the main contract, is nevertheless part of such contract.[239] The Court relied on Dicey and observed that the 'proper law is thus the law which the parties have expressly or impliedly chosen, or which is imputed to them by reason of its closest and most intimate connection with the contract'. However, it must be clarified that the expression 'proper law' refers to the substantive principles of the domestic law of the chosen system and not to its conflict of laws rules. The law of contract is not affected by the doctrine of *renvoi*.[240]

In *Hindustan Copper Ltd. v Centrotrade Minerals and Metals Inc.*[241] the parties had entered into a contract for the sale of copper concentrate. A dispute between the parties arose regarding the dry weight of the goods and Centrotrade invoked the arbitration clause before the ICC. The arbitral tribunal upheld the validity of the arbitration clause and Centrotrade's claims. Centrotrade applied to enforce the foreign award under section 48 of the Arbitration and Conciliation Act 1996. The same was allowed by a single bench of the Calcutta High Court.[242] The High Court held that in the handful of cases where parties might choose and agree to apply Indian law to their contract and nonetheless confer jurisdiction on a foreign court to supervise the arbitral procedure (such as in matters like setting aside an award), only in that small number of cases will the award be a foreign award under Part II of the 1996 Act. However, it would not have been a foreign award under the now-repealed Foreign Awards Enforcement Act provisions.[243] These judgments reveal the exclusion of the doctrine of renvoi in commercial matters.

In *Bhanu Constructions Company v AP State Electricity Board and others*[244] the Government of India (the 'Borrower') entered into a loan agreement with the Overseas Economic Co-operation Fund (the 'Fund') for obtaining funds for the implementation of the Srisailam Power Transmission System Project.[245] The validity, interpretation, and performance of the loan agreement and the supporting guarantee were governed by the laws and regulations of Japan.[246] The Fund refused to award the contract to the Borrower on the ground that it had not satisfactorily met the bid specifications.

[236] ibid.
[237] ibid.
[238] ibid [24].
[239] ibid.
[240] ibid [18].
[241] *Hindustan Copper Ltd. v Centrotrade Minerals and Metals Inc* [2004] SCC OnLine Cal 446.
[242] ibid [4], [23].
[243] ibid.
[244] *Bhanu Constructions Company Ltd. and Ors. v AP State Electricity Board and Ors* [1997] (6) ALT 328.
[245] ibid [2].
[246] ibid [2].

The Borrower challenged the rejection and argued that it was arbitrary and denied its legitimate expectation of fair treatment when it was admittedly the lowest bidder.[247] The Borrower contended that the loan agreement must be tested under Indian law or the Indian Constitution. The court observed that the agreement was governed by general terms and conditions which provided that the laws and regulations of Japan were to govern it. The court stated that 'one of the clearest rejections of any *renvoi* doctrine is to be found in the field of contract, it being thought that no sane businessman or his lawyers would choose the application of *renvoi*'.[248] The court quoted the observations of Lord Diplock on *renvoi* and stated that the term 'proper law of contract' indicated the substantive law of the country which the parties had chosen or to which the facts were closely connected. The reference to proper law is taken as excluding any *renvoi*, whether of remission or transmission.[249] The court went on to provide scenarios which examined the exclusion of *renvoi*. For example, if a contract made in England were expressed to be governed by French law, the English court would apply French substantive law to it, notwithstanding that a French court applying its own conflict rules might accept a *renvoi* to English law as the *lex loci* contract if the matter were litigated before it.[250]

Thus, the existing Indian jurisprudence shows a clear rejection of *renvoi* in the commercial field and conforms with global conventions, which have rejected the application of *renvoi* in the commercial field. In *Jose Paulo Coutinho v Maria Luiza Valentina Pereira*,[251] the question of succession and applicability of the Portuguese Civil Code was under consideration. The question was whether succession to the property of a Goan situated outside Goa in India will be governed by the Portuguese Civil Code 1867 as applicable in the State of Goa or the Indian Succession Act 1925. The petitioner argued that, since Portuguese law was applicable, the principles of private international law should apply. He invoked the doctrine of *renvoi* to urge that, since the citizens of Goa were governed by foreign law, the court should apply foreign law to the citizens of Goa. However, the argument was not sustained by the court. Besides these judicial statements, no dispute has arisen before the Indian courts on the application of *renvoi* in the field of family law or non-contractual matters.

VI. Conclusion

Private international law in India has had a gradual evolution beginning from British rule, wherein disputes principally dealing with interpersonal conflicts came up for judicial resolution. After independence, the scattered and limited statutory provisions of the Civil Procedure Code, Indian Succession Act, Hindu Marriage Act, Guardians and wards Act, etc, and judicial statements provided the foundation for, and acted as a source of, private international law in the country. Thus, adequacy or inadequacy of the principles of private international law in India essentially turns out to involve a critical assessment of the law laid down by the courts. Judicial statements have traced the rationale of the subject to comity and the promotion of justice as founded on English notions of private international law. Despite an increased number of cases, private international law in India is not backed by explicit legislation and the principles of English law have traditionally guided the courts.

[247] ibid [5].
[248] ibid [10].
[249] ibid.
[250] ibid.
[251] *Jose Paulo Coutinho v Maria Luiza Valentina Pereira* [2019] (10) SCJ 158 [13]–[18].

3

Domicile, Nationality, and Residence

I. Introduction

Applicable law in private international law is determined by supplicating the connecting factor. In personal matters, this connecting factor is decided by a person's fundamental relationship with a specific state or nation. Conflicts of law scholars have struggled to understand what that legal system should be. Two options were available: nationality *(lex patriae)* and the law of domicile *(lex domicili)*. Classically, domicile acted as the primary connecting factor in questions of status in matters of family law issues for common law jurisdictions, and nationality for civil law jurisdictions.[1] For instance, under the Indian Succession Act, the law of a person's domicile at the time of death would govern succession to movable and immovable property in India.[2] In recent times, codification attempts aimed at harmonising private international law rules have shown a preference for the invocation of habitual residence as a connecting factor. The connecting factors of domicile, nationality, and habitual residence also act as the bases of jurisdiction, which is the first stage of the conflicts of law process.[3]

This chapter deals with the conceptual foundations of the connecting factors of domicile, nationality and residence. The chapter is divided into five parts (including this Introduction). Section II discusses the concept, categorisation, and requirements of proving domicile. Section III addresses the connecting factors of nationality and residence. Section IV explores the statutory framework and judicial statements on ascertaining domicile under Indian private international law rules. While scrutinising the prevailing Indian legal position, this chapter provides a comparative analysis of relevant rules with the harmonised regimes developed by other jurisdictions. For the sake of clarity, this chapter first explores conceptual foundations as evolved by juristic opinion and other jurisdictions and then goes on to analyse the Indian legal scenario.

[1] GC Cheshire, 'Nationality and Domicile in Swedish Private International Law' (1951) 4 *International Law Quarterly* 39–59.

[2] Indian Succession Act 1925, ss 5–6.

[3] See A Iyer, 'Domicile and Habitual Residence' (1985) 6 *Singapore Law Review* 115; Council Regulation (EC) 1215/2012 of 12 December 2012, on Jurisdiction and the Recognition and Enforcement of Judgments in Civil and Commercial Matters OJ L351/1 Art 4 (ascribes domicile as the primary base of jurisdiction). However the regulation does not define the domicile and leaves it to the domestic jurisdictions to define the same; Convention on the Recognition of Divorces and Legal Separations (adopted 1 June 1970, entered into force 24 August 1975) (Art 2 provides for habitual residence and nationality as the basis of jurisdiction); Convention on the Law Applicable to Matrimonial Property Regimes 1978) Art 3 (provides for habitual residence and nationality as the applicable law).

II. Domicile

In 1858, Lord Cranworth famously articulated the meaning of domicile as indicating a permanent home and observed: '[I]f you do not understand your permanent home, I am afraid that no illustration drawn from foreign writers or cases will be of help.'[4] However, this formulation has been objected to as too simplistic. Morris observed that a person may be domiciled in a country that is not his home, and may even be homeless, while still possessing domicile.[5] Subsequent cases have clarified the contours and application of the principle of domicile. The fundamental principles of domicile include the following:

- No person can be without a domicile.[6]
- No person can, at the same time, have more than one domicile.[7]
- An existing domicile is presumed to continue until it is proven that a new domicile has been acquired.

A. Types of Domicile

Case jurisprudence and statutes have identified several types of domicile.

i. Domicile of Origin

Every person is born with a domicile that is ascribed by law as the domicile of origin. For this purpose, the law attributes to every individual at birth, the domicile of the father if the child is legitimate[8] and the domicile of the mother if the child is illegitimate.[9] Domicile of origin is presumed to endure until a new domicile known as 'domicile of choice' is acquired.[10] The persistence of the domicile of origin is seen in the case of *Bell v Kennedy*.[11] Bell had a Jamaican domicile of origin, but he was uncertain whether to settle in Scotland or England after leaving Jamaica. Therefore the House of Lords held that he had not lost his Jamaican domicile of origin. Since, the domicile of origin is a creation of law, the domicile of origin is never permanently lost but can be abandoned. The domicile of origin remains in abeyance or lies dormant until a domicile of choice is lost. The moment a domicile of choice is lost, the domicile of origin revives unless the domicile of choice is replaced by another domicile of choice.[12]

[4] *Whicker v Hume* [1858] 7HLC 124 [160].

[5] JHC Morris, *The Conflict of Laws* 2nd edn (Stevens and Sons, 1980) 18.

[6] *Bell v Kennedy* [1868] LR 1 Se & Div 307 (HL); S Symeneoids, *American Private International law* (Kluwer Law International Law 2008) 88.

[7] *Udny v Udny* [1869] LR 1 Sc & Div 441 (HL) 448.

[8] A Hutchinson, 'Domicile of Origin and Domicile of Choice' (1977) *New Law Journal* 879; DM Stone, 'The English Concept of Domicile' (1954) 17 *Modern Law Review* 244. See also Indian Succession Act (n 2) s 7.

[9] ibid, s 7. See K Trimmings, P Torremans, A Mills, U Grusic and C Heinze, *Cheshire, North, and Fawcett: Private International Law* 15th edn (Oxford University Press, 2017) 147.

[10] Indian Succession Act (n 2) s 9.

[11] *Bell v Kennedy* (n 6).

[12] *Udny v Udny* (n 7); *Harrison v Harrison* [1953] 1 WLR 865.

ii. Domicile of Choice

The two basic elements for obtaining a domicile of choice are the fact of residence *(corpus)* and the intention of remaining *(animus manendi et revertendi)*.[13] Domicile of choice is acquired by free will when one resides in a particular place with the intention of making it a permanent home.[14] The question of who has the capacity to acquire a domicile of choice is determined by the law of a person's existing domicile.[15]

Unlike the domicile of origin, which is ascribed by law, the domicile of choice is a question of fact, not of law, and it requires the co-existence of residence in a country and a bona fide intention to make a home in that country permanently. An initial line of cases has given preference to the fact of stay over the intention.[16] However, later decisions have tilted more in favour of assessing intention and have taken the position that, although length of residence is essential, even a short stay at a place coupled with an intention to make that place a permanent home may confer a domicile of choice.

In *Ramsay v Liverpool Royal Infirmary*[17] the House of Lords held that even though a man of Scottish origin spent 36 years of his life in Liverpool he had not acquired a domicile of choice in England and retained his Scottish domicile of origin. In *Puttick v Attorney General*,[18] it was held that a domicile of choice could not be acquired by illegal residence. Though residence and intentions are to be proved by evidence, intention is difficult to prove. Cheshire and North state that: '[N]othing must be neglected that can possibly indicate the bent of the residents mind. His aspirations, whims, amours, prejudices, health, religion, financial expectations.'[19] In *Winans v AG*,[20] the court stated that the burden of proving the acquisition of a new domicile of choice lies upon those who assert that the domicile of origin has been lost.[21] The domicile of origin continues until a fixed and settled intention of abandoning the first domicile and acquiring another as sole domicile is clearly shown. In *Munro v Munro*,[22] Lord Cottenham made it clear that the domicile of origin will prevail until a party manifestly intends to abandon one's former domicile and acquire another as one's sole domicile. However long, residence alone may not confer a new domicile, though it may be the most important ground from which to infer intention.[23] In *White v Tenant*,[24] White moved his home from West Virginia to Pennsylvania, but on the same day crossed back to take care of his wife who was sick with typhoid. He then caught the disease and died in West Virginia. The question arose as to which state should be considered to have been his domicile for purposes of intestate succession. The court held that White had left his West Virginia residence with no plans to return and with the intent and purpose of making his permanent home in Pennsylvania.Therefore, when he and his wife arrived at their new home, their domicile became Pennsylvania.

[13] ibid.

[14] D Hill, *Private International law* (Edinburgh University Press, 2014) 14–15.

[15] JG Collier, *Conflict of Laws* 3rd edn (Cambridge University Press, 2001) 40.

[16] ibid 5; *Bruce v Bruce* [1790] 2 Bos & P 229, 231; *Bempde v Johnstone* [1796] 3. Ves. 198, 201; *Hodgson v De Beauchesne* (1858) 12 Moo PCC 285, 329.

[17] *Ramsay v Liverpool Royal Infirmary* [1930] SC (HL) 8.

[18] *Puttick v Attorney-General* [1979] 3 All E R 463, 469.

[19] *Cheshire, North, and Fawcett* (n 9) 155.

[20] *Winans v Attorney-General* [1904] AC 287.

[21] ibid.

[22] *Munro v Munro* [1840] 7 Cl & Fin 842.

[23] ibid.

[24] *White v Tenant* [1888] 31 West Virginia 790.

a. Doctrine of Revival

The domicile of choice is less tenacious; as soon as the domicile of choice is abandoned, the domicile of origin revives under the English legal system.[25] The stringent requirement of the revival of domicile of origin has led to many unfortunate scenarios, as depicted by case jurisprudence.[26] It needs to be stressed that the US (in contrast to England) does not subscribe to the presumption of the continuance of a domicile of origin as a domicile of revival. Under the US legal system, a domicile of choice continues until a new one is acquired.[27] Collier explains that the differences of both legal systems can be attributed to the fact that the US was a country of immigration, whereas the UK has been a country of emigration.[28] Hence, it was easy for US courts to presume an intention on the part of persons who immigrated there to intend to make that country their permanent home. Similarly, Collier explains that, where a person having an English domicile of origin acquires a domicile of choice in another country and then decides to leave that country, it makes sense to presume that the person decided to return home. By contrast, Collier explains in the case of an Italian who acquired a domicile in Iowa and then died in the course of moving home to California, it would be preposterous to presume that the person dies domiciled in Italy.[29] *Animus non revertendi* (the intention of not returning), which plays a significant role in acquiring a domicile of choice, also influences the displacement of a domicile of choice.[30] However, the standard of proof is much less intense than in the situation of acquiring a domicile of choice by displacing the domicile of origin.[31]

iii. Domicile of Dependency

A domicile of dependency generally operates in three cases:[32]

(1) Infants.
(2) Married women.
(3) Mentally incapacitated persons.

Infants. Children below the age of majority are incapable of acquiring a domicile of choice and follow the domicile of their parents on whom they are legally dependent.[33] The law dictates that a legitimate child has a domicile of origin in the state of the father's domicile at the time of the child's birth. An illegitimate child has a domicile of origin in the state of the mother's domicile at the time of the child's birth.[34] Moreover, an orphan child has a domicile of origin in the state in which the orphan is found.

[25] R Fentiman, 'Domicile Revisited' (1991) 50(3) *The Cambridge Law Journal* 445–463, 450; *Cheshire, North and Fawcett* (n 9) 163.

[26] *Ramsay v Liverpool* (n 17).

[27] *Winans v Attorney-General* (n 20); *In re Estate of Jones* [1921] 192 Iowa 78.

[28] Collier (n 15) 51.

[29] ibid 52; see J Wade, 'The English Concept of Domicile: A Re-evaluation' (1974) 21(3) *Netherlands International Law Review* 265–288.

[30] P Diwan, *Indian and English Private International Laws* 4th edn (Deep & Deep Publications, 1998) 142.

[31] VC Govindaraj, *The Conflict of Laws in India: Inter-Territorial and Inter-Personal Conflict* 2nd edn (Oxford University Press India, 2019).

[32] L Collins, CGJ Morse and D McClean, *Dicey, Morris & Collins on the Conflict of Laws* 14th edn (Sweet and Maxwell, 2006) 153.

[33] Indian Succession Act (n 2) s 14.

[34] *In re Beaumont* [1902] 1 Ch 889; See 'The Power to Change the Domicile of Infants and of Persons Non Compos Mentis' (1930) 30(5) *Columbia Law Review* 703–714.

Married women. Traditionally, the domicile of a married woman followed that of her husband.[35] This notion was primarily due to the legal conception of a married couple as one person. However, legal reforms have altered most jurisdictions' position.[36] A married woman now has the capacity to acquire a domicile of choice. For instance, if we analyse the legal position in Nepal as revealed through the *Sabina Pandey* case, the court took the position that the wife's domicile was not dependent on that of her husband. The court used Sabina Pandey's residence and intention to assess her domicile independently of her husband's domicile. It held that, although the husband Puskar Raj Pandey may be considered to have a domicile in the US, since Sabina Pandey's actual residence and intention to reside in the US had not been proven, Sabina Pandey could not be said to be domiciled in the US.[37] However, jurisdictions such as Afghanistan still do not grant a woman the right to choose a domicile. Article 82 of the Afghan Civil Procedure Code states: 'If the defendant is a married woman, the hearing of the case shall be within the jurisdiction of the court located in the place of residence of the husband.'[38] Article 83 states:

> If the defendant is an unmarried woman and has attained the age of marriage (age of majority) or who possesses the full legal capacity, the court which is located in the place of residence of her father or her close relatives i.e. whoever is responsible for her feeding and upbringing shall have jurisdiction to hear the claim.[39]

Similarly, section 15 of the Indian Succession Act specifically discusses the mode of acquisition of a new domicile by a woman on her marriage. It provides that by marriage a woman acquires the domicile of her husband if she had not the same domicile before.[40] Section 16 is an explanation to section 15 and provides that a wife's domicile during her marriage follows the domicile of her husband.[41] However, an exception to section 16 stipulates that the wife's domicile no longer follows that of her husband if the sentence of a competent court separates them or if the husband is undergoing a sentence of transportation.[42] The principles set out under sections 15 and 16 have limited application as they only apply to the succession of movables possessed by Parsis and Christians. Section 2 of the Indian Divorce Act applicable to Christians provides that the courts in India will be able to entertain the proceedings for dissolution of a marriage only where the parties to the marriage are domiciled in India at the time when the petition is presented.[43] This created hardships for wives whose husbands migrated to another country, permanently leaving behind their wives in India. The problem is that, in determining the domiciles of the parties to proceedings for the dissolution of marriage, it is the domicile of the husband alone which is to be considered since a wife takes the domicile of her husband upon marriage.

While recommending a suitable amendment to section 2 of the Indian Divorce Act, the Law Commission of India recommended a change in the rule of private international law regarding a wife's domicile, that is, to abolish the wife's dependent domicile, as has been done in England.[44] Indian decisions have followed the common law principle of domicile of dependency

[35] *Warrender v Warrender* [1835] 6 ER 1239.

[36] Domicile and Matrimonial Proceedings Act 1973 (UK).

[37] S Regmi, 'Foreign Judgments in Matrimonial Disputes: Recognition in Nepal and Public Policy Considerations,' in SR Garimella, S Jolly (eds), *Private International Law: South Asian State Practice* (Springer 2017) 133–151.

[38] Civil Procedure Code 1990, Art 82 (Afghanisthan); N Abdullah, *Private International Law of Afghanistan* 6th edn (Saed, 2016) 62–67.

[39] ibid, Art 83 (Afghanistan).

[40] Indian Succession Act (n 2) s 15.

[41] ibid, s 16.

[42] ibid.

[43] Indian Divorce Act 1869, s 2.

[44] Law Commission of India, *Amendment of Section 2 of the Divorce Act 1869 Enabling Non-domiciled Estranged Christian Wives to Seek Divorce* (Report No 224, 2009).

in determining a wife's domicile. In *State of Bihar v Kumar Amar Singh*,[45] the court held that the domicile of the wife remained in India, even though she had migrated to Pakistan, because her husband remained in India. In *Kashiba Bin Narsapa v Shripat Narhiv*,[46] the Bombay High Court held that the domicile of a widow remained that of her husband, unless she acquired a domicile of choice. Most of these cases are related to the determination of citizenship and can be distinguished from typical conflict of law scenarios.

Mentally incapacitated persons. A mentally disabled person cannot acquire a domicile of choice. The person's domicile continues to be the same and follows the domicile of the individual on whom the person is dependent.[47] This position is different from the English position where the law says that a mentally disables person continues to have the same domicile prior to becoming incapacitated.[48]

iv. Domicile of Corporations

Under the English legal system, the domicile and nationality of a company are determined by the place of its incorporation, and that law determines the capacity to contract and the law applicable to the company's dissolution.[49] In comparison, the residence of a company is attributed to its main centre of business, where management and control are exercised.[50] The theory of incorporation was revised during the First World War in *Daimler Co Ltd v Continental Tyre and Rubber Co*, where all the shares of a company were held by German nationals, though the company had been incorporated in Britain. The court applied the effective control test and concluded that the company possessed German nationality.[51] In *McLeod &Co. Ltd. v State of Orissa*,[52] the court, relying on *Palmer's Company Law*, reiterated the same principle of English law with regard to a corporation's domicile, nationality, and residence.[53] However, in *TDM Infrastructure (P) Ltd. v UE Development India Pvt. Ltd.*,[54] it was held that, a company being an artificial person, its domicile would depend on the nature and purpose of the statute. The place of registration determines the nationality of a company. Indian cases have also taken the position that any corporation doing business in India has its residence in India, which need not be the place of its central management.[55] Since corporations are artificial entities, they may be considered domiciled or residents in a country for one purpose and not for another.[56] This position also means that a company can have multiple residences. It should be mentioned that international conventions that have codified private international principles have taken a broader approach when ascribing domicile, nationality, and residence to companies. Brussels Regulation I (Recast), which has

[45] AIR [1955] SC 282.

[46] [1891] ILR 19 Bom 697.

[47] Indian Succession Act (n 2) s 18.

[48] *Cheshire, North and Fawcett* (n 9) 156.

[49] Collier (n 15) 57. See generally Civil Code of Nepal. Section 697 states that questions as to the nature of the company is determined by the law of the country of incorporation, if that cannot be ascertained it shall be decided by the law of the country where the company is of registered or headquartered.

[50] ibid 58.

[51] *Daimler Co Ltd v Continental Tyre and Rubber Co* [1916] 2 AC 307.

[52] *McLeod & Co. Ltd. v State of Orissa* [1984] 1 SCC 434 [7].

[53] *State Trading Corporation v CIT* AIR [1963] SC 1811. Reiterated in *Technip SA v SMS Holding (Pvt) Ltd* (2005) 5 SCC 465.

[54] *TDM Infrastructure (P) Ltd. v UE Development India Pvt. Ltd* [2008] 14 SCC 271 [35].

[55] *Turner Morrison & Co. v Hunaerford Investment Trust Ltd* AIR [1972] AIR 1311.

[56] ibid.

codified rules on jurisdiction on civil and commercial matters, has provided for domicile as the main connecting factor. Unlike the classical approach, the Regulation has not equated the domicile of a company solely with its place of registration, but has also ascribed the domicile of a company to either its statutory seat, central administration, or principal place of business.[57] Similarly, the recently concluded 2019 Hague Convention on the Recognition and Enforcement of Foreign judgments in Civil or Commercial Matters elevates habitual residence as the main connecting factor.[58] The 2019 Convention defines the habitual residence of a company broadly to include either its statutory seat (under the law of which it was incorporated or formed), its central administration, or the state where it has its principal place of business.[59]

Domicile plays an essential role in determining the substantive validity of a marriage, divorce, and family matters. Domicile is also used to define jurisdiction.[60] The connecting factor of domicile is useful in countries where multiculturalism persists, as it helps the adoption of law close to the parties.[61] Though an essential connecting factor, the concept has been profoundly criticised. The criticisms mainly stem from the two parameters of domicile. The difficulty of proving an intention permanently to reside despite a long stay is evident in multiple cases. Second, there is the persistence of the domicile of origin and its revival. England, where the dominant connecting factor in choice of law is domicile, has attempted major reforms mainly concentrating on the domicile of origin. From the 1950s onwards in England, there have been several proposals for abolishing the doctrine of the revival of the domicile of origin and replacing it with the doctrine of the continuance of a domicile of choice until a new one is acquired (as in the US).[62] Nevertheless, the proposals have been rejected by Parliament and have not become a part of legislation.

III. Nationality and Residence

Cheshire and North observed that 'nationality is a possible alternative to domicile as the criterion of the personal law'.[63] Nationality represents a person's political status, by virtue of which one owes allegiance to some particular country.[64] As a connecting factor, nationality has dominated the scene in the private international law of Continental Europe. Virtually all choice-of-law rules concerning personal and family affairs are determined by reference to the law of nationality. Nationality is determined by birth, parentage, registration, and naturalisation, whereas domicile is acquired by residence in a particular country with the intention of residing there permanently. It follows that a person may be a national of one country, but be domiciled in another.

[57] Council Regulation (EC) 1215/2012 of 12 December 2012, on Jurisdiction and the Recognition and Enforcement of Judgments in Civil and Commercial Matters OJ L351/1 (recast) Art 63.

[58] ibid.

[59] ibid, Art 3(2).

[60] A Dutta, 'Domicile, Habitual Residence and Establishment' in J Basedow and others (eds) *Encyclopaedia of Private International Law* (Edward Elgar Publishing, 2017) 556.

[61] RH Graveson, *Conflict of Laws* 7th edn (Sweet and Maxwell, 1974)185; WLM Reese, 'Does Domicile Bear a Single Meaning?' (1955) 55(5) *Columbia Law Review* 589–597.

[62] The Law Commission had recommended against the revival of domicile of origin and proposed replacing the domicile by the concept of habitual residence or nationality. See The Law Commission, *The Law of Domicile* (Report No 88, 1986) and Scottish Law Commission, *Private International Law: The Law of Domicile* (Scot Law Com No 63, 1985); JJ Fawcett, 'Law Commission Working Paper No. 88: The Law of Domicile' (1986) 49(2) *Modern Law Review* 225–234; P McEleavy, 'Regression and Reform in the Law of Domicile' (2007) 56(2) *International and Comparative Law Quarterly* 453–462.

[63] *Cheshire, North and Fawcett* (n 9) 170.

[64] ibid.

Nationality is a more stable concept than domicile as it cannot be changed without the formal consent of states.[65] However, the concept is not much used in genuinely federal states where the legal system differs between states. Further, the fundamental principle of domicile dictates that no person can be without a domicile and that no person can have more than one domicile at the same time. But a person may be stateless or simultaneously be a citizen of more than one country.[66] The difficulties associated with the application of nationality and domicile as connecting factors have prompted a shift to habitual residence as a connecting factor in recent years. Alternatively, while retaining the connecting factor of nationality, states may provide that, in the case of dual nationality, the law of the country of habitual residence is to be applied.[67]

Habitual residence is employed as a connecting factor in many international conventions.[68] The application of habitual residence is advantageous as it is easier to establish than the complex intention associated with domicile. Habitual residence is a question of fact and does not need to be established through the legal presumptions associated with a domicile of dependency. For instance, unlike the domicile of children, who follow that of their legal guardians, a child's habitual residence is determined by the fact of a child's stay.[69] However, the concept has also been criticised as a weak link to determine a person's civil status. Hence, the practice of jurisdictions and codifications reveals the co-existence of all three connecting factors.

Brussels Regulation I (Recast), in dealing with jurisdictional regimes, retains the domicile of a defendant as the primary basis of jurisdiction.[70] Whereas, the 2019 Hague Convention on the Recognition and Enforcement of Foreign Judgments in Civil or Commercial Matters provides for habitual residence as the basis of recognition.[71]

IV. Ascertaining Domicile under Indian Private International Law Rules

A. Statutory Framework

The legal framework of domicile in India can be located in statutory provisions and judicial statements. Article 5 of the Constitution of India makes domicile an essential requirement for

[65] Hill (n 14) 16.

[66] ibid.

[67] See The National Civil (Code) Act 2017, Nepal (2074) part 6 Provisions relating to Private International Law, s 715. In case of double nationality, law of country of habitual residence to be applied: (1) If this Part contains a provision to the effect that any matter is determined according to the law of the country of nationality and a person is having nationality of two or more countries at the same time, his or her nationality shall be determined according to the law of the country of his or her nationality, where he or she habitually reside. (2) If such matter cannot be determined according to the law of the country referred to in sub-section (1), it shall be determined according to the law of the country of his or her nationality, to which he or she has the closest connection.

[68] G Zohar, 'Habitual Residence: An Alternative to the Common Law Concept of Domicile' (2009) 9 *Whittier Journal of Child and Family Advocacy* 169–204; P Rogerson, 'Habitual Residence: The New Domicile' (2000) 49 *International law and Comparative Law Quarterly* 86–107; P Stone, 'The Concept of Habitual Residence in Private International Law' Hague Convention on the Recognition and Enforcement of Foreign Judgments in Civil or Commercial Matters (2000) 29(3) *Anglo-American Law Review* 342–367.

[69] Convention of 25 October 1980 on the Civil Aspects of International Child Abduction Art 4 (adopts habitual residence as a connecting factor) Convention on the Law Applicable to Succession to the Estates of Deceased Persons 1989, Art 3 (provides habitual residence as the applicable law). See also E Gallagher, 'A House is Not (Necessarily) a Home: A Discussion of the Common Law Approach to Habitual Residence,' (2015) 47(2) *New York University Journal of International Law and* Politics 463–500.

[70] Brussles Regulation 1(recast) (n 57) Art 4.

[71] Convention on the Recognition and Enforcement of Foreign Judgments in Civil or Commercial Matters 2019 Art 5.

acquiring citizenship.[72] Along with the provisions in the Constitution, the Indian Succession Act gives detailed provisions on the determination of domicile in the case of succession to the movables of Parsis and Christians. The Act mainly borrows the principles of domicile developed under English jurisprudence. Section 6 of the Succession Act provides that a person can have only one domicile for the purpose of succession to movable property.[73] Section 7 prescribes that the domicile of origin of every person of legitimate birth is the country in which at the time of birth the person's father was domiciled or, if the person is a posthumous child, in the country in which the child's father was domiciled at the time of the father's death.[74] The domicile of origin of an illegitimate child is the country in which, at the time of birth, the child's mother was domiciled.[75] Section 9 espouses that the domicile of origin prevails until a new domicile has been acquired.[76] A new domicile can be acquired by taking up a habitation in a country which is not that of the domicile of origin.[77] Although these provisions do not apply to Hindus, Buddhists, Jains, Sikhs or Muslims,[78] the principles have often been applied by courts as a part of the common law. There are references to domicile in other statutes as well.[79] However, none of these legislative provisions provide a clear definition of the concept of domicile. In the absence of an explicit definition of the concept, successive judicial statements have clarified the meaning and contours of the application of domicile in the domestic context and private international law. Most judicial statements on domicile have arisen under cases involving citizenship laws and constitutional matters, with only a few private international law issues. The cases show an unflinching loyalty to English jurisprudence.

B. Judicial Statements on Domicile

i. Meaning of Domicile

In *DP Joshi v State of Madhya Bharat*,[80] the term domicile was interpreted to indicate a permanent home. In *Central Bank of India v Ram Narain*[81] the court referred to *Craignish v Craignish* wherein Chitty J stated that 'a place is properly the domicile of a person in which his habitation is fixed without any present intention of removing therefrom'.[82] Residence need not be continuous. However, there must be an intention to reside forever in the country where residence has been taken up. An intention of never returning to the country of origin leads to a change in domicile. Post-independence, an initial question addressed by the judiciary was on the nature of domicile

[72] Constitution of India 1950, Art 5 – 'At the commencement of this Constitution, every person who has his domicile in the territory of India and – (*a*) who was born in the territory of India; or (*b*) either of whose parents was born in the territory of India; or (*c*) who has been ordinarily resident in the territory of India for not less than five years immediately preceding such commencement, shall be a citizen of India.'

[73] Indian Succession Act (n 2) s 6. It is to be mentioned that Bangladesh and Pakistan neighbouring countries of India has also retained the same pre-independence legislation on succession. The Succession Act (Bangladesh) 1925 retains the same provisions as the Indian Act.

[74] ibid, s 7.

[75] ibid, s 8.

[76] ibid, s 9.

[77] ibid, s 10.

[78] ibid, s 4.

[79] Hindu Marriage Act 1955, s 1(2) – 'It extends to the whole of India except the State of Jammu and Kashmir, and also applies to Hindus domiciled in the territories to which this Act extends who are outside the said territories.'

[80] *DP Joshi v State of Madhya Bharat* AIR [1955] 334.

[81] *Central Bank of India v Ram Narain* AIR [1955] 36.

[82] ibid [13].

in a federal jurisdiction like India. In *Pradeep Jain v Union of India*,[83] the court held that the word 'domicile' identifies the personal law by which an individual is governed in respect of various matters. The court noted that Article 5 of the Constitution is clear and explicit on this point. It only refers to one domicile, namely, 'domicile in the territory of India'.[84] In comparison, the legal position during the pre-Independence period was different. Princely States enjoyed legal personality under international law. As a consequence, numerous domiciles existed. The court further observed that there are two main categories of domicile, namely, domicile of origin and domicile of choice. While the former attaches to a person by birth, the latter is acquired by residence in a territory with the intention to settle there permanently.[85]

ii. Criteria for Acquiring Domicile

Judicial statements have clarified the intentional and residential requirements of domicile. In *Michael Antony Rodrigues v State of Bombay*,[86] Michael's father was of Goan nationality and had been carrying on business as a tailor in Bombay. Michael was born in Goa in 1918 and came to Bombay in 1927.[87] He was educated in Bombay and completed his school education there.[88] In 1942 when war broke out, he served in the Royal Indian Force and in 1948 reverted to his father's business. He appears on the municipal roll as a voter. On these facts, the Bombay High Court ruled that he had acquired a domicile of choice in Bombay.[89] The Court, in the instant case, differentiated between the concepts of domicile and nationality. The Court observed that 'in private International law a man may have one nationality and different domicile'.[90] In *SP Ghosh v Deputy Collector*, ten years of residence in England was not considered enough to confer a domicile of choice.[91] The court held:

> nationality depends, apart from naturalisation, on the place of birth or on parentage; domicile, as' we have seen, is constituted by residence in a particular country *animo manendi*. It follows that a man may be a national of one country but domiciled in another.[92]

In *Mandal v Mandal*, in the wake of the Nazi invasion in 1937, an Austrian-domiciled couple fled to India and lived in India from then on. The Panjab and Haryana High Court held that long residence and an intention to stay in India permanently were reflected in the facts and the couple had acquired domiciles of choice in India.[93] Applying the same standard, *in State of Maharashtra v Ghoreishi (Qureshi) Sayed Mahomed Sayed Hasan*, the court observed that, in the absence of evidence of long residence and a positive and absolute intention of making India a permanent home with the further intention never to leave, an inference of acquisition of domicile from the mere fact of long residence could not follow.[94]

[83] *Pradeep Jain v Union of India* AIR [1984] 1420.
[84] ibid. See also *Yogesh Bharadwaj v State of U.P.* AIR [1991] 356 [9], [12].
[85] ibid [7].
[86] *Michael Antony Rodrigues v State of Bombay* AIR [1956] Bombay 729.
[87] ibid [2].
[88] ibid.
[89] ibid [11].
[90] ibid.
[91] *SP Ghosh v Deputy Collector, Reserve Bank of India* AIR [1964] Cal 422.
[92] ibid [5].
[93] *Mandal v Mandal* [1956] ILR Punj. 215.
[94] *State of Maharashtra v Ghoreishi (Qureshi) Sayed Mahomed Sayed Hasan* AIR [1964] Bom 235 [11].

iii. Characteristic Features of Domicile

Kedar Pandey v Narain Bikran Shah is a vital judgment for clarifying the contours of domicile.[95] The appellant Kedar Pandey and respondent Narain Bikram were candidates for the Bihar State Legislative Assembly elections in 1962. The respondent was declared elected. The appellant filed a petition challenging the election on the ground that the respondent was not duly qualified under Article 173 of the Constitution as he was a citizen of Nepal and not a citizen of India.[96] The High Court found that the respondent had been born in Banaras on 10 October 1918, had been living in India from 1939 to 1949 and had acquired an Indian domicile.[97] While upholding the High Court decision, the Supreme Court succinctly summarised the principles of domicile as developed in England through caselaw and held applicable in India:

(1) The law attributes to every person at birth a domicile, which is called a domicile of origin.[98] A legitimate child born in wedlock to a living father receives the father's domicile at the time of birth; a legitimate posthumous child receives that of the mother.[99]
(2) This domicile may be changed, and a new domicile, called a domicile of choice, can be acquired. The domicile of origin is received by operation of law at birth; the domicile of choice is acquired by the residence of an individual in another country accompanied by an *animus manendi* [intention of remaining].[100] For this purpose, residence is a mere physical fact. If the required state of mind accompanies this physical fact, neither its character nor its duration is material. The state of mind, which is required, demands that the person should have formed a fixed and settled purpose of making a principal or sole permanent home in the country of residence.[101]
(3) The onus of proving that domicile has been chosen in substitution for the domicile of origin lies upon those who assert that the domicile of origin has been lost. The court relied on the decision in *Udny v Udny*[102] and held that what is required to be established is that the person alleged to have changed domicile of origin has voluntarily fixed one's habitation and that of one's family in a new country, not for merely special or temporary purposes, but with the intention of making it one's permanent home.[103]
(4) The domicile of origin continues unless a fixed and settled intention of abandoning the first domicile[104] and acquiring another as sole domicile is clearly shown. The tenacity and revival of the domicile of origin were reiterated in *Louis De Raedt v Union of India.*[105]

India's position on determining domicile of choice is well illustrated in the case of *Sankaran Govindan v Lakshmi Bharathi & Others.*[106] This case dealt with succession to the sale of the movable property of Dr Krishnan, who had been born in India. Dr Krishnan went to England for higher studies in 1920, became a doctor there, and was employed there by the National Health Service (NHS). He died in England.[107] The English High Court declared that Dr Krishnan had

[95] *Kedar Pandey v Narain Bikram Shah* AIR [1966] 160.
[96] ibid [2].
[97] ibid [3].
[98] ibid [10]; See also *Hari Narayanan v Meenakshi Narayanan* [2007] SCC On Line Mad 1525.
[99] ibid.
[100] ibid.
[101] ibid.
[102] ibid [12].
[103] ibid [10], [14].
[104] ibid [10].
[105] *Louis De Raedt v Union of India* [1991] 3 SCC 554.
[106] AIR [1974] SC 1764.
[107] *Sankaran Govindan v Lakshmi Bharathi & Others* AIR [1974] SC 1764 [2]–[3].

been domiciled in England and accordingly English law applied in matters of his succession. Only the next of kin were eligible to succession and thus the proceeds from the sale of his movables were given to his two brothers, who were the appellants.[108] The defendants, who were the children of the appellants, filed a partition suit in Kerala and prayed for distribution of the sale proceeds among all the parties. The trial court held that Dr Krishnan had been domiciled in India, and hence partitioned the amount to be distributed according to the Travancore Ezhava Act.[109] The Kerala High Court partially modified the order, but also held that Dr Krishna had been domiciled in India.[110] The appellants appealed to the Supreme Court. The latter Court referred to the case of *Bell v Kennedy*[111] and stated that domicile is a mixed question of law and fact. To establish domicile, there needs to be an intention of permanent residence at the appropriate time. The appropriate time varies with the nature of an inquiry. It could be past or present. If the person is deceased, it has to be ascertained as if one had formed and retained a permanent intention of residence in a given country at some point in one's life.[112] The key factors to be considered in determining intention include a person's tastes, conduct, actions, ambitions, health, hopes, and projects.[113] Accordingly, although until 1939 Dr Krishnan had an intention to return to India, his intention changed when he had a comfortable practice in England. He therefore died domiciled in England as he was a resident in England and his acts and conduct were only consistent with the intention to make England his permanent home.[114]

iv. Differentiating Domicile, Nationality and Residence

Judicial statements have further clarified and differentiated the concept of domicile, nationality, and residence. In *Yogesh Bharadwaj v State of UP*,[115] the court differentiated between domicile and residence and held that 'a residence is a fact'. Unlike the acquisition of a domicile of choice, intention is not necessary for acquiring residence. In *Union of India v Dudh Nath Prasad*,[116] the court held that etymologically both 'residence' and 'domicile' mean the same thing. However, there is a slight difference between them under private international law. 'Domicile' serves as a basis for jurisdiction in cases involving private laws, whereas 'residence' serves as a basis for jurisdiction in relation to taxation, voting rights, etc.[117] In *Hari Narayanan v Meenakshi Narayanan*, the court interpreted nationality to denote allegiance to a country and domicile to owe allegiance to the place of one's permanent home.[118]

v. Domicile and Migration

The Indian judiciary has often been faced with the issue of migration and its relevance in ascertaining domicile. In *Shanno Devi v Mangal Sain*,[119] the respondent was a successful candidate at the general election held in March 1957 for the Punjab Legislative Assembly. The election was

[108] ibid [6].
[109] ibid [9].
[110] ibid [12].
[111] *Bell v Kennedy* (n 6) 322.
[112] ibid [20].
[113] ibid [19].
[114] ibid [32]–[35], [53].
[115] *Yogesh Bharadwaj* (n 84) [11].
[116] *Union of India v Dudh Nath Prasad* (2000) 2 SCC 20.
[117] ibid [26]–[27].
[118] *Hari Narayanan* (n 98) [11], [13].
[119] *Shanno Devi v Mangal Sain* AIR [1961] 58.

challenged on the ground that the latter was not a citizen of India and therefore not qualified to stand for election.[120] It was found that he had been born sometime in 1927 to Indian parents in India (as defined in the Government of India Act 1935). However, the village in which he was born became part of Pakistan on 15 August 1947. In 1944 he had moved from his home district to Jullunder in what is now part of India.[121] The question was whether the respondent could be deemed to be a citizen of India within Article 6 of the Constitution of India.[122] The court imported a narrow definition to the term 'migrate' and held that 'migration' by itself could give rise to a new domicile.[123] However, the dictum was overruled in *Kulathil Mammu v State of Kerala*,[124] where the word 'migrate' was interpreted to include both intention and fact. Hence, if migration is to give rise to a new domicile, an intention to reside permanently must be established. Thus, most judicial decisions on domicile have been adjudication in connection with citizenship and constitutional rules. Disputes concerning direct conflict of law questions have been absent. That perhaps explains the absence of any judicial discussion on Hague Conventions which codify the connecting factors applicable to specific areas. In addition, due to the strong undercurrent of English jurisprudence, inadequate attention has been paid to the concepts of nationality and residence.

V. Conclusion

This chapter has examined the concepts, characteristics, and challenges surrounding the operationalisation of the principles of domicile, nationality, and residence. Particular focus has been paid to the concept of domicile as it constitutes the singular most used connecting factor in Indian private international law. For the sake of clarity, the chapter adopted an approach wherein it first explained the characteristics and operationalisation of the concept of domicile as developed in English jurisprudence and then went on to explore the Indian legal position. The chapter highlighted the 'doctrine of revival' which forms the backbone of the English concept of domicile. The principle is based on the need to attach a domicile to every individual in all circumstances and reflects the strong premise of the domicile of origin, its tenacity and persistence. However, the operationalisation of the doctrine of revival has often resulted in decisions defying logic, as seen in *Ramsay* in England and in the *Shankaran Bharati* case at the High Court stage in India. This chapter demonstrated that Indian decisions have followed the common law principle of the domicile of dependency in determining a wife's domicile. This position is unfortunate. Even after legal reforms have been undertaken in England to abolish the unity of domicile principle, Indian courts have sadly adhered to the archaic legal principle causing hardship to the women involved. This chapter evaluated the statutory framework and judicial decisions on the operationalisation of domicile in India. The case jurisprudence reflects an unflinching loyalty to English jurisprudence and the adoption of the entire English jurisprudence as seen in the *Kedar Nath* case.

[120] ibid [1].
[121] ibid.
[122] Constitution of India (n 72) Art 6.
[123] *Shanno Devi v Mangal Sain* (n 119) [13]–[18].
[124] *Kulathil Mammu v The State of Kerala* AIR [1966] 1614.

4

Proving, Pleading, and Excluding the Foreign Laws

I. Introduction

A, an Indian-domiciled citizen, entered into a contract with B, a Bangladesh-domiciled citizen, for the performance of a music show in Dhaka. The contract, which was concluded in Dhaka on 1 December 2017, stipulated that all payments had to be made in *taka*, the Bangladeshi currency. A refused to perform his side of the contract and B filed a suit against A for specific performance before the court in Delhi.

The dispute involves a foreign element and attracts the invocation of private international law. The case raises several questions. Which matters in this dispute can be considered as procedural and which as substantive? What are the principles guiding the selection of applicable law? What are the mechanisms of pleading and proving the content of foreign law? Are there circumstances in which the application of foreign law can be excluded? The issues of pleading, proving, and excluding foreign law are largely treated as peripheral areas of private international law and academic focus on them has been less. Nevertheless, these matters play a pivotal part in influencing the outcome of a dispute and the overall operation and development of private international law. This chapter examines issues of pleading, proof and the exclusion of foreign law. This chapter is divided into five parts, including the Introduction. Section II discusses the issues involved in characterising matters as substantive or procedural. Section III explores global and Indian approaches to the proof and pleading of foreign law. Section IV examines global and Indian judicial practice on the exclusion of foreign law, focusing on the application of public policy.

II. Substantive and Procedural Law

In legal disputes, matters are classified as substantive or procedural. The *lex causae* decides substantive matters. Procedural matters are determined by the *lex fori*.[1] This distinction between substance and procedure is crucial in private international law. Without identifying issues as substantial, the applicable law to a particular issue cannot be determined.[2] However, the difficulty is determining what questions are procedural matters and how the law of the forum characterises issues as substantive or procedural in nature.[3] There is a general understanding that it is the law

[1] RGarnett, *Substance and Procedure in Private International Law* (Oxford University Press, 2012) 1, 5–6; *Poyser v Minors* [1881] 7 QBD 329, 333; *Huber v Steiner* [1835] Bing NC 202.

[2] J M Carruthers, 'Substance and Procedure in the Conflict of Laws: A Continuing Debate in Relation to Damages' (2004) 53(3) *International and Comparative Law Quarterly* 691–711.

[3] RH Graveson, *Conflict of Laws* 7th edn (Sweet and Maxwell, 1974) 590.

of the forum (*lex fori*) that characterises issues as procedural or substantive. The power of the law of the forum to characterise an issue as substantive or procedural has been justified based on necessity, convenience,[4] justice, and equality.[5] The categorisation of substance and procedure and the wide variation followed by different jurisdictions have attracted criticism from scholars as encouraging forum shopping and undermining the choice of law process by favouring the application of the law of the forum in which a dispute is being heard.[6] Judicial dicta have laid down specific criteria to differentiate between substance and procedure. In *Pfeiffer v Rogerson*, the court stated that matters that affect the existence and extent of the parties' rights should be categorised as substance and the method and means of enforcing a right should be treated as procedural.[7] However, this differentiation based on a right-remedy[8] paradigm has been criticised for being artificial. In the place of a right-remedy approach, some jurists have suggested an outcome-determinative method where matters that might affect the outcome of litigation are classified as substantive.[9] But it would be wrong to assume that only substantive issues can affect the outcome of a case. Procedural issues, such as methods of proof and what constitutes admissible evidence, can also affect outcome.[10] Based on judicial statements, certain identified categories fall under procedural matters.

A. Categorising Substance and Procedure

i. Rights and Remedies

Matters affecting the rights of parties are classified as substantive and matters relating to their remedies are categorised as procedural.[11] Thus, a party can only obtain a remedy available under the law of the forum and not under the *lex causae*. For instance, A (an Indian national) enters into a contract with B (a Brazilian national) for a dance performance in Brazil. The parties have chosen Brazilian law as the applicable law of their agreement. A refuses to perform his part of the contract and B sues A before the Indian court. Assume that under the contract law of Brazil, there is no provision for specific performance, whereas specific performance is allowed under Indian law. Even though the applicable law is Brazilian law, a decree of specific performance can be granted by the Indian court. In respect of damages, heads of damage and remoteness of damage are considered substantive[12] and the arithmetical calculation of damages is treated as procedural.[13] At the same time, complexities surround the categorisation of damages, especially

[4] L Collins, CGJ Morse, D McClean, *Dicey, Morris & Collins on the Conflict of Laws* 14th edn (Sweet and Maxwell, 2006) [7-002].

[5] M Wolff, *Private International Law* 2nd edn (Clarendon Press,1950) 232.

[6] B Currie, 'Notes on Methods and Objectives in the Conflict of Laws' in *Selected Essays on the Conflict of Laws* (Duke University Press, 1963) 181; JD Falconbridge, *Essays on the Conflicts of Laws* 2nd edn (Cambridge University Press, 2009); RA Leflar, *American Conflicts Law* 3rd edn (Indiana Polis, 1977) 252–9; EG Lorenzen, *Selected Articles on the Conflict of Laws* (Yale University Press, 1947); WE Beckett, 'The Question of Classification ("Qualification") in Private International Law' (1934) 15 *British Year Book of International Law* 46–81.

[7] *Harding v Wealands* [2006] UKH. 24; see EB Crawford 'The Adjective and the Noun: Title and Right to Sue in International Private Law' (2000) *Judicial Review* 347, 348.

[8] S Peari, *The Foundation of Choice of Law: Choice and Equality* (Oxford University Press, 2018) 216.

[9] Garnett (n 1) 20–24.

[10] ibid.

[11] ibid.

[12] Carruthers(n 2) 697.

[13] JG Collier, *Conflict of Laws* 3rd edn (Cambridge University Press, 2001) 60; *Kohnke v Karger* [1951] 2 KB 67; *Henderson v Jaouen* [2002] 2 All ER 705.

in tort. The complications were evident in the case of *Boys v Chaplin*,[14] a case of negligence that happened in Malta between two British soldiers stationed there. It was held that the law relating to damages was partly procedural and partly substantive.[15] Questions of what constitutes evidence and the method, quality, and burden of proof are procedural.[16] Presumptions of law are treated as substantive, while presumptions of fact are treated as procedural.[17]

ii. Law of Limitation

Traditionally, common law jurisdictions characterise limitation as procedural, whereas in civil law jurisdictions it is treated as substantive.[18] When limitation is treated as procedural, the legal remedy is barred while the right remains. However, the treatment of limitation as substantive has the effect of extinguishing the right itself. Statutory reform[19] and judicial decisions[20] have clarified the discrepancy in the approaches of common and civil law jurisdictions concerning limitation.[21] Despite writers' eloquent criticism and statutory reforms in other jurisdictions, India still treats limitation as procedural under section 11 of the Limitation Act of 1963.[22] In its report, the Law Commission of India clearly stated that the law in India encourages forum shopping and recommended that the country make limitation substantive for contractual and non-contractual matters.[23] It is to be noted that all other South Asian countries consider limitation as a procedural matter.[24] In *Tung Sumser JBR v Indian Airline Corporation*[25] which came before the Nepalese court, there was a chance to address the issue of limitation. In this case, the plaintiff, who lost six of his family members in a plane crash, filed a petition against Indian Airlines for compensation. The matter was held to be inadmissible under the law of Nepal due to the expiry of the statutory period of limitation and the absence of a specific domestic law governing compensation in the specific circumstances. The case was a lost opportunity for the Nepalese court to evaluate the issue from the lens of private international law. It should be emphasised that there are no Indian judicial statements that have deliberated on the categorisation of matters as substantive and procedural under private international law.

III. Pleading Foreign Law

A. General Practice in Other Jurisdictions

Once the court has selected the application of foreign substantive law as the applicable law, a question arises as to the manner of proving the content of foreign law. The issue of foreign law is

[14] *Boys v Chaplin* [1971] AC 356.
[15] ibid.
[16] Collier (n 13) 61–62.
[17] ibid 61.
[18] E Rabel, *The Conflict of Laws: A Comparative Study* 2nd edn (Ann Arbor: University of Michigan Press, 964) 512.
[19] See Foreign Limitation Periods Act 1984 (UK); Limitation Act 1950 (NZ); Uniform Conflict of Laws Limitation Act 1982 (US).
[20] *Mc Kain v R.W. Miller & Co (South Australia) Pty Ltd* [1992] 174 CLR 1; *Tolofson v Jenson* [1994] 3 SCR 1022.
[21] G Panagopoulos, 'Substance and Procedure in Private International Law' (2005) 1(1) *Journal of Private International Law* 69–92.
[22] Limitation Act 1963, (India) s 11.
[23] Law Commission of India, *The Limitation Act, 1963* (Report No 89, 1983).
[24] See The Limitation Act (Bangldesh) 1908, s 11; The Limitation Act (Pakistan) 1908, s 11.
[25] *Tung Sumser JBR v Indian Airline Corporation* [NKP 2024 BS] decision No 389 [SC].

pivotal in private international law. Without understanding and applying the content of foreign law, the very concept of private international law becomes meaningless. The *lex fori* has to determine whether foreign law is to be treated as a question of fact or law. If it is a question of fact, what are the rules through which the relevant facts are to be ascertained? Similarly, if the *lex fori* considers foreign law to be a question of law, the issue arises whether judges are required apply foreign law *ex officio* and (if so) how do they ascertain the content of the *lex causae*.[26] A differentiation between questions of fact and questions of law is significant in legal proceedings. Questions of law are governed by the principle *iura novit curia* (the court knows the law). Questions of fact have to be proven by the parties.[27] In common law jurisdictions (such as England and the US),[28] foreign law is treated as a question of fact. Thus, courts will not take judicial notice of foreign laws.[29] The pleading and proof of foreign law are matters of procedure. If the parties fail to establish the content of foreign law, the law of the forum will apply by default. The rationale for the rule seems to be a general notion that, since the only law applied is domestic law, every other element has to be considered as a fact.[30] In civil law jurisdictions, the general position is that foreign law is a question of law[31] and has to be applied by the judge *ex officio*.[32] This is based on the notion of equality of nationals and foreigners and justifies the imposition of foreign law as a matter of obligation.[33]

Whether treated as a question of 'law' or 'fact', foreign law is of a peculiar kind.[34] The courts across jurisdictions have thrown light into the specificities of proof of foreign law. In jury trials, questions of foreign law are decided by the judge. In common law countries, even though foreign law is treated as a fact, appellate courts are allowed to overrule a judgment on the ground that foreign law has not been applied correctly.[35] In civil law countries, even though foreign law is treated as a question of law, an appeal on points of law is allowed based on the reason that the contested decision is a violation of the law. Despite codification reforms favouring party autonomy in the choice of law, nations differ on whether precedent may be used in determining the content of foreign law. As a result, a lack of certainty persists and has resulted in conflicting decisions.

B. Proof and Application of Foreign Law in India

Very little has been written on the subject of proof of foreign law in India from the point of view of private international law. The materials are primarily reliant on the literature on the

[26] R Hausmann, 'Pleading and Proof of Foreign Law – a Comparative Analysis' (2008) *The European Legal Forum* 1–13.

[27] ibid 1–2.

[28] *Carey v Bahama Cruise Lines* [1988] 864 F.2d 201 (1st Cir.) 205; *Trenwick Am. Reinsurance Corp. v IRC., Inc* [2011] 764 F. Supp. 2d 274, 302–03.

[29] R Fentiman, *Foreign Law in English Courts* (Oxford University Press, 1998) A Nussbaum, 'The Problem of Proving Foreign Law' (1941) 50(6) *Yale Law Journal* 1018–1044; WB Stern, 'Foreign Law in the Courts: Judicial Notice and Proof' (1957) 45(1) *California Law Review* 23–48; JG Sprinkling and GR Lanyi, 'Pleading and Proof of Foreign Law in American Courts' (1983) 19 *Stanford Journal of International law* 3–98.

[30] J H Beale, *A Treatise on the Conflict of Laws* (Baker Woorhis &Co 1935) 53; OC Sommerich and B Busch, 'Expert Witness and the Proof of Foreign Law' (1953) 38(2) *Cornell Law Review* 125–160, 127.

[31] German Code of Civil Procedure 2005, s 293 states that the laws applicable in another state, customary laws, and statutes must be proven only insofar as the court is not aware of them. In making inquiries regarding these rules of law, the court is not restricted to the proof produced by the parties in the form of supporting documents; it has the authority to use other sources of reference and issue the required orders for such use.

[32] Sommerich and Busch (n 30) 128.

[33] Hausmann (n 26) 1, 3.

[34] P Hay, 'The Use and Determination of Foreign Law in Civil Litigation in the United States', (2014) 62 *American Journal of Comparative Law* 213, 240, 223.

[35] ibid.

law of evidence.[36] Statutory provisions on pleading and proof of foreign law are contained in section 45 of the Evidence Act. Section 45 states that when the court has to form an opinion upon a point of foreign law, science, art or as to handwriting, the opinions on that point of persons specially skilled are relevant facts. Such persons are called experts.[37] Further, section 84 contains a presumption of the genuineness of documents, laws, and decisions printed under the government's authority.[38] Under section 38, when forming an opinion on the law of a country: (1) any statement of such law contained in a book purporting to be printed or published under the authority of the government of that country and to contain any such law; and (2) any report of a ruling of the courts of that country contained in a book purporting to be a report of such rulings are relevant.[39] Official copies of British parliamentary statutes are presumed genuine.[40]

It can also be mentioned that the 1961 Hague Convention Abolishing the Requirement of Legalisation of Foreign Public Documents removes the requirement of diplomatic agents (of the country where the public document is produced) to certify the provenance of public documents.[41] It provides for certification of a document by the attachment of an apostille. India acceded to the 1961 Convention in 2005.[42] However, its provisions have not been incorporated into the Indian Evidence Act 1872, and section 78 still requires certification by diplomatic agents which increases the procedural burden with regard to the certification of documents.

Concerning the proof of foreign law, India's position follows the general practice of other South Asian nations that consider it as a question of fact proved by adducing expert evidence.[43] For instance, section 23 of the Evidence Act 1974 (2031BS) of Nepal[44] states: 'If the court has to reach to a conclusion of any opinion, regarding law of a foreign country, science, art, signature or finger impression, opinion of the expert may be taken as evidence.'

Case jurisprudence has clarified the rules on pleading and proof of foreign law. In *Harishanker Jain v Sonia Gandhi*,[45] the petitioner challenged the election of the respondent on the ground that the respondent was not an Indian citizen at the date of the election. The petitioner made averments relating to Italian law to build a case that the respondent could not have renounced Italian citizenship and become a citizen of India when she applied for and was issued a certificate of citizenship under the Citizenship Act. The court observed that Italian law is a foreign law so far as India's courts are concerned. A point of foreign law is a matter of fact and a plea based on foreign law must satisfy the requirement of pleading a material fact.[46] Under section 57(1) of the Indian Evidence Act 1872, the court shall take judicial notice of, inter alia, all laws in force in India's territory.[47] This does not apply to foreign law. The court reiterated that sections 45 and 84 of the Evidence Act permit evidence of foreign law to be being tendered and the opinion of an expert to be adduced in proof of foreign law.[48] Under Order VI Rule 2 of the Code of Civil Procedure 1908, every pleading shall contain a statement in a concise form of the material facts relied on by a party, but not the evidence nor the law of which a court may take judicial notice.

[36] A Nussbaum, *Principles of Private International Law* (Oxford University Press, 1943) 248.
[37] Indian Evidence Act 1872, s 43.
[38] ibid, s 84.
[39] ibid, s 38.
[40] ibid, s 81.
[41] Convention Abolishing the Requirement of Legalisation for Foreign Public Documents (5 October 1961).
[42] ibid, Status Table.
[43] Bangladesh and Pakistan inherit the same Evidence Act – See The Evidence Act (Bangladesh) 1872; The Evidence Act (Pakistan) 1872. See also Evidence Act (Nepal) 1974 (2031 BS), ss 23, 6(f), 6(g), 52; Evidence Ordinance (Sri Lanka) ss 45, 38, 84.
[44] Evidence Act 1974 (2031 BS), s 23.
[45] *Harishanker Jain v Sonia Gandhi* [2001] 8 SCC 233.
[46] MN Venkatachalaih, *Halsbury's Laws of India- Evidence* 2nd edn (Lexis Nexis, 2019) 97.
[47] *Harishanker Jain* (n 45) [27]; Indian Evidence Act (n 37) s 57(1).
[48] *Harishanker Jain* (n 45) [28]; Indian Evidence Act (n 37) ss 45 and 84.

However, the rule against pleading law is restricted to the law of which a court is bound to take judicial notice. As the court does not take judicial notice of foreign law, it should be pleaded like any other fact if a party wants to rely on the same. In *Shin-Etsu Chemical Co. Ltd. v Aksh Optifibre Ltd*,[49] it was held that foreign law cannot be proved by affidavit and requires evidence to be led in a trial. The matter was regarding section 45 of the Arbitration and Conciliation Act 1996, in which the Supreme Court had to look at an arbitration clause governed by Japanese law. The courts accepted expert evidence over a treatise on foreign law.[50] In contrast, in *Pulaniappa Chetty v Nagappa Chettiar*[51] the court interpreted the Code of Civil Procedure of Ceylon without calling for expert evidence. Once foreign law is proved, the interpretation of the law is left for the Indian courts to determine.[52]

The burden of proving foreign law and its application lies on the party contending its application.[53] If the party fails, the court applies the *lex fori*.[54] In *Tamil Nadu Electricity Board v St CMS Electricity Co Ltd*, foreign law was not applied as the party contending foreign law did not explain foreign law or lead expert evidence on foreign law.[55] There are no Indian cases on failure in proving foreign law. However, as the Indian rule of burden of proof is similar to English law, a similar approach might be taken.[56] In *Rhodia Ltd. v Neon Laboratories Ltd*,[57] the plaintiff was a company incorporated under the provisions of the Indian Companies Act 1956 with its registered office in Mumbai. The defendants were an English public limited company incorporated under English law and an Indian company having its office in Mumbai.[58] The parties agreed to give the plaintiff an exclusive right to market and distribute the products Isoflurane, and Halothane in India, Sri Lanka, Bangladesh, and Nepal for an initial period of three years from 1997. The agreement dictated English law as the applicable law and provided for the English court to settle disputes.[59] The court noted that the parties had pleaded that the English law governed their agreement and the English court had exclusive jurisdiction. However, no evidence was adduced to prove what the settled legal position in England was in relation to exclusive jurisdiction.[60] In other words, the question of foreign law, which ought to have been proved as a fact, has not been properly addressed in the case. There being no evidence of the effect of an exclusive jurisdiction clause under English, the jurisdiction of the Indian court could not be ruled out.[61] The court placed reliance on the following passage from *Halsbury's Laws of India*:[62]

> Mode of proof: In general, an Indian court will not research into foreign law or the concepts which have a foreign origin. The foreign law or the concepts must be proved in civil proceedings by properly qualified witnesses, that is a person who is suitably qualified to do so on account of his knowledge or experience and who is competent to give expert evidence as to the law of any country, irrespective of whether he has acted or is entitled to act as a legal practitioner there. If his evidence is not contradicted, the court will typically accept it unless unreliable or extravagant.[63] Because foreign law or concepts of a

[49] *Shin-Etsu Chemical Co. Ltd. v Aksh Optifibre Ltd* AIR [2005] SC 3766.
[50] *Re Goods of D McIntyre* [1918] ILR. 41 All 248; *Rhodia Ltd v Neon Laboratories Ltd* AIR [2002] Bom 502.
[51] AIR [1930] Mad 146.
[52] *De Beeche v South American stores Ltd and Chilean Stores Ld* [1935] AC 148, *Technip* (n 308).
[53] *Guaranty Trust Co of New York v Hannay & Co* [1918] 2 KB 623.
[54] *Ertel Beiber & Co v Rio Tinto Co Ltd* [1918] AC 260.
[55] *Tamil Nadu Electricity Board v St C.M.S. Electricity Co Ltd* [2007] EWHC 1713 (Comm).
[56] A Setalavad, *Conflict of Laws* 2nd edn (Lexis Nexis Butterworths Wadhwa, 2011) 100.
[57] *Rhodia Ltd. v Neon Laboratories Ltd* [2002] SCC OnLine Bom 626.
[58] ibid [1].
[59] ibid.
[60] ibid [5].
[61] ibid [12] see *Harishanker Jain* (n 45).
[62] ibid.
[63] ibid, 75.238.

foreign origin are questions of fact, courts may not generally at common law rely upon a previous Indian decision on foreign law.

Thus judicial decisions reveal overwhelming support for proving the content of foreign law by adducing evidence.

i. Problem of Proving Foreign Law

The application of foreign law constitutes a central element of private international law. However, there are inherent problems associated with the pleading and proof of foreign law. The meaning and spirit of the content of the foreign law may not be apparent to judges and their understanding may be characterised by differences in an alien legal system. For instance, if a German court has to decide on the validity of a marriage based on an unfamiliar Afghan law, it will impose a heavy burden on the German judge to gather material on the content and context of the applicable law. A bare reading of a statute may not always present a comprehensive picture.[64] The problems become attenuated when we consider the existence of translated texts and whether the translations convey the real intention of statutory provision. The issue was raised in *Neilson v Overseas Projects Corporation of Victoria Ltd*.[65] before the Australian courts (the case has been discussed earlier in the chapter on *renvoi*). The case raised a cross-border tort claim. Chinese law barred the petitioners' claim where the cause of action arose, whereas the action was permitted by the law of the forum – Australian law. The Australian courts, relying on the translated text of the General Principles of the Civil Law of the People's Republic of China, ruled that the provision of Chinese law allow the court to apply the law of Australia. However, jurists have criticised the method and understanding of the Australian court in interpreting Chinese law, which many have felt wrongly decided.[66]

The process of proving foreign law through expert opinion is time-consuming and expensive.[67] The burden placed on the parties to adduce expert evidence adversely affects the parties who rely on the invocation of foreign law. Further, since parties must adduce evidence through experts, the evidence adduced may be partisan and will need to be tested by cross-examination. The situation calls for increased judicial cooperation. Under the European Convention on Information of Foreign Law, when issues of foreign law arise in legal proceedings, the Parties undertake to supply information concerning the applicable civil law and procedure and the relevant judicial system.[68] Each Party is to set up or appoint a 'receiving agency' to receive (and take action on) requests for information from the other party and a 'transmitting agency' to receive requests for information from judicial authorities and transmit them to a competent foreign receiving agency.[69] The names and addresses of these bodies are communicated by the Contracting Parties to the Secretary-General of the Council of Europe.[70] The Mutual Legal Assistance Act 2014 (2070BS) of Nepal provides mechanisms of mutual legal assistance between Nepal and foreign states in legal proceedings based on reciprocity and bilateral treaties.[71] The subject matter of legal assistance

[64] GS Alexander, 'The Application and Avoidance of Foreign Law in the Law of Conflicts: Variations on a Theme of Alexander Nekam' (1975) 70(4) *North Western University Law Review* 602–638, 604.

[65] *Neilson v Overseas Projects Corporation of Victoria Ltd* [2005] HCA 54.

[66] M Davies, 'Renvoi and Presumptions about Foreign Law: Neilson v Overseas Projects Corporation of Victoria Ltd' (2006) 30(1) *Melbourne University Law Review* 244.

[67] J Mc Comish, 'Pleading and Proving Foreign Law in Australia' (2007) 31(2) *Melbourne University Law Review* 400.

[68] European Convention on Information of Foreign Law [1968] ETS No 062 Art 1.

[69] ibid, Art 2.

[70] ibid.

[71] Mutual Legal Assistance Act 2070 (2014), (Nepal).

includes providing documents and evidence, freezing property, and enforcement of a foreign judgment.[72] Such mechanisms help courts with easy access to foreign law.

IV. Exclusion of Foreign Law

A. Categories of Exclusion

A central element of private international law is determining when foreign law is to be applied. However, most legal systems have specific rules, which exclude the application of foreign law in certain circumstances.[73] Dicey, Morris & Collins observes that 'courts have no jurisdiction to entertain an action … for the enforcement, either directly or indirectly, of a penal, revenue or other public law of a foreign State'.[74]

i. Penal Laws

Penal laws represent the act of a sovereign and as such can have no effect on the territory of others. The principle was stated in *The Antelope* in 1825 when Chief Justice Marshall held that the courts of no country enforce the penal laws of another.[75] Since then, writers[76] and case jurisprudence has painstakingly attempted to define the term 'penal', but no consensus has emerged. The general understanding is that the term 'penal' is not to be understood in the sense of being criminal laws.[77] In the seminal case of *Huntington v Attrill*,[78] Huntington sued in Maryland to enforce a New York judgment obtained under a statute making directors liable for corporate debts. The court refused to enforce the judgment as being penal. The court stated that the question of whether a statute of one state which in some aspects may be called penal is in actuality a penal law in the international sense, so as not to be enforceable in the courts of another state, depends upon the question whether its purpose is to punish an offence against the public justice of the state or to afford a private remedy to a person injured by the wrongful act.[79] In *Lynch v Government of Paraguay*,[80] the English court held that Paraguayan law, which vested the property of the deceased in the government, was a penal law and hence inapplicable to property left in England. In *Banco De Vizcaya v Don Alfonso de Borbon Y Austria*,[81] the petitioner bank claimed the property of the king of Spain based on Spanish law, which had classified the king as a traitor and directed the seizure of his property by the state. The English court classified the Spanish law as penal. Hence, the petitioner's claim failed. In *Attorney General of New Zealand v Oritz*,

[72] ibid, s 5.

[73] WW Yee, 'The Exclusion of Foreign Law: Public Policy in Choice of Law Process' (1995)16 *Singapore Law Review* 286–318.

[74] *Dicey, Morris & Collins on the Conflict of Laws* (n 4) 5R-01.

[75] *The Antelope* [1825] 23 US (10 Wheat.).

[76] MW Janis, 'The Recognition and Enforcement of Foreign Law: The Antelope's Penal Law Exception' (1986) 20(1) *The International Lawyer* 303 308; RA Leflar, 'Extra State Enforcement of Penal and Governmental Claims' (1932) 46(2) *Harvard Law Review* 193–225.

[77] *Attorney-General of New Zealand v Ortiz* [1984] AC 1 (HL).

[78] *Huntington v Attrill* [1892] 146 U.S. 657; PB Kutner, 'Judicial Identification of Penal Laws in the Conflict of Laws' (1978) 31(3) *Oklahoma Law Review* 590–634.

[79] ibid 602.

[80] [1871] LR 2 P&D 268.

[81] [1935] 1 KB 140.

the petitioner sought to apply New Zealand law, which sought seizure of an article and penal consequences for the illegal export of a Maori carving.[82] The Court of Appeal classified the law as penal and thus unenforceable. The House of Lords affirmed the decision on the ground that New Zealand had acquired no title to the carving and the conclusions of the Court of Appeal were held to be merely *obiter*.[83]

ii. Revenue and Public Laws

In *Government of India v Taylor*,[84] the Government of India sought to prove in the voluntary liquidation of a company registered in the UK but trading in India, for a sum due in respect of Indian income tax, including capital gains tax, which arose on the sale of the company's undertaking in India. The claim was not maintainable because it was a claim by the Government of India to recover Indian tax. English law generally does not permit the direct or indirect enforcement of foreign revenue laws. Lord Keith explained the position by stating that the enforcement of taxes would be an assertion of sovereignty by one state in the territory of another.[85] An expansionist interpretation has been followed in the field of public law, so as to include the enforcement of security laws[86] and matters vindicating the governmental interest of a state.[87] Cases from Australia and New Zealand provide illustrations. The UK Government attempted to prevent the publication of the book *Spycatcher* written by a former member of British secret intelligence. The Australian High Court held that the UK Government was trying to protect its sovereign interest in the defence of the nation, which the Australian court could not enforce.[88] In New Zealand, the publication was not prohibited as the book's material was in the public domain and the restriction on publication would be opposed to the public interest.[89]

B. Indian Judicial Decisions on Exclusion of Foreign Law

In the Indian context, no judicial statements have clarified the criteria for excluding foreign penal laws. The Supreme Court has observed that, in general, foreign revenue laws will not be enforced.[90] In *Dhondiram Chatrabhuj Marwadi v Sadasuk Sawattram Marwadi*,[91] a pre-Independence case, the Bombay High Court admitted a promissory note executed in the state of Hyderabad as evidence, despite it being inadmissible under the law in Hyderabad because foreign revenue law cannot be enforced. In another case, the court suggested that an Indian court will not entertain a suit to recover a toll on exports as it would imply the application of foreign

[82] *Attorney-General of New Zealand v Ortiz* (n 77).
[83] ibid [46].
[84] *Government of India v Taylor* [1955] AC 491; WE Holder, 'Public Policy and National Preferences: The Exclusion of Foreign Law in English Private International Law' (1968) 17(4) *International Law and Comparative Law Quarterly* 926–952, 931.
[85] Approved in *re State of Norway's application* (Nos 1 and 2) HL [1990] 1 AC 723; *Iran v The Barakat Galleries Ltd* [2007] EWHC 705 (QB).
[86] *Schemmer v Property Resources Ltd* [1975] Ch. 273; FD Strebel, 'The Enforcement of Foreign Judgments and Foreign Public Law' (1999) 21 *Loyola Los Angeles International Law and Comparative Law Journal* 55–129, 69.
[87] *Spycatcher* case, *Att-Gen (UK) v Heinemann Publishers Australia Pty. Ltd* [1988] 165 CLR 30.
[88] *Attorney General (UK) v Heinemann Publishers Australia Pty Ltd* [1988] 165 CLR 30.
[89] *Attorney General (UK) v Wellington Publishers Ltd* [1988] 1 NZLR 129.
[90] *Viswanathan R v Rukn-ul-Mulk Syed Abdul Wajid* AIR [1963] SC 1.
[91] [1918] ILR 42 Bom 522.

revenue law.[92] Similarly, in the *Government of India, Ministry of Finance v Taylor & another*,[93] the court stated that the enforcement of a claim for taxes is an extension of a state's sovereign power which imposed the taxes, and that an assertion of sovereign authority by one state within the territory of another … is (treaty or convention apart) contrary to all concepts of independent sovereignties. In comparison to the lack of jurisprudence on the exclusion of foreign laws, Indian courts have elaborated on the public policy exception underlying the application of foreign law.

V. Overriding Mandatory Norms and Public Policy (*Ordre Public*)

A. Public Policy and *Ordre Public*: Conceptual Dimension

The doctrine on the basis of which otherwise applicable foreign law is excluded is known as *ordre public* in civil law jurisdictions and 'public policy' in common law countries. The concept is of historical origin and one of the fundamental elements of the operationalisation of private international law. The doctrine is mandated by local exigencies[94] and is applied in the case of choice of law and the enforcement of foreign judgments.[95] Although the doctrine is part of all codified conventions of private international law, formal definitions of public policy are elusive, and lack of consensus persists as far as the definition and contours of public policy are concerned.[96]

Ordre public is based on statutory developments. Being of statutory origin, the judicial discretion enjoyed by the judges in determining the contours of *ordre public* is limited.[97] At common law, judicial discretion has led judges to interpret public policy in a variety of ways, leading in some cases to concerns of parochialism undermining the entire private international law system.[98] The current conceptualisation of public policy demands that it is not enough to show that foreign law differs from domestic law, but it is also necessary to show that applying foreign law would be wholly alien to fundamental notions of local justice.[99] It follows that the application of public policy in private international law cannot be extended to all situations where the foreign law conflicts with the domestic law.[100] It has also been argued that public policy is an exception as it affirmatively directs the application of the law of the forum and has to be narrowly constructed.[101] Public policy has been invoked in situations of violations of human rights.[102]

[92] *Krishnaji Panduran Sathe v Gajanan Balvant Kulkarni* [1909] ILR 373.

[93] *Government of India, Ministry of Finance v Taylor & Anr* [1955] 2 WLR 303.

[94] A Mills, 'The Dimensions of Public Policy in Private International Law' (2008) 4(2) *Journal of Private International Law* 201–236.

[95] A Briggs, 'Foreign Judgments and Human Rights; Note on USA v Montgomery' (2005) 121 *Law Quarterly Review* 185.

[96] K Chng, 'A Theoretical Perspective of the Public Policy Doctrine in the Conflict of Laws' (2018) 14(1) *Journal of Private International Law* 130–159.

[97] H Meidanis, 'Public Policy and Ordre Public in the Private International Law of the E.U.: Traditional Positions and Modern Trends' (2005) 30(1) *European Law Review* 95.

[98] O Kahn-Freund, RH Graveson, W Raeburn et al., 'Reflections on Public Policy in the English Conflict of Laws' (1953) 39 *Transactions of the Grotius Society* 39–83.

[99] *New Zealand Basing Ltd v Brown* [2016] NZCA 525, [65]; K Murphy, 'The Traditional View of Public Policy and Ordre Public in Private International Law' (1981) 11(3) *Georgia Journal of International and Comparative Law* 591–615, 591.

[100] Chng (n 96) 133.

[101] PB Carter, 'The Role of Public Policy in English Private International Law' (1993) 42 *International and Comparative Law Quarterly* 1–10, 9.

[102] *Empresa Nacional de Telecommunicaciones S A v Deutsche Bank AG* [2010] 1 All ER (Comm) 649, [22].

B. Approach of Indian Courts in Clarifying the Public Policy of India

The jurisprudence evolved by the Indian courts has broadly followed the restrictive approach to public policy followed by other jurisdictions. A majority of the cases where the public policy has been defined deal with the enforcement of foreign arbitral awards in India. In the landmark case, *Renusager Power Co Ltd v General Electric Co*,[103] the court held that foreign arbitral awards under the Foreign Awards Act 1961 can be refused enforcement only if it is against the fundamental principles of public policy, the interests of India, or morality.[104] Blatant illegality was used as a ground within the purview of public policy in *ONGC Ltd. v Saw Pipes*.[105] In explanation, the court stated that a violation of statutory laws could not be in the public interest. In *ONGC v Western Geco*,[106] the court went into a further analysis of what constitutes public policy in Indian law and added some new components to it, such as judicial approach,[107] respect for the rights of the parties, principles of natural justice, and avoiding perverse and irrational decisions. The fundamental policy of Indian law was held not to amount to every Indian statutory enactment, but only breaches of foundational principles of Indian law like the principles of natural justice and *Wednesbury* reasonableness principles.[108] In *Technip SA v SMS Holding (Pvt) Ltd*,[109] Technip (a French company) acquired Coflexip (another French firm that had acquired control of a listed Indian company, Seamec, through a convoluted route) in April 2000. Issues arose as to the date on which Technip acquired control of Seamec and the applicable law to the dispute. The Supreme Court decided the matter in favour of the application of the French law.[110] It was contended that such applicability was contrary to the Indian takeover code and against public policy. The court held that, since French law differed only marginally from the Indian law, the differences did not make the French provisions opposed to public policy. Accordingly, French law was applied.[111] The court observed that the power to discard a provision of foreign law must be exercised exceptionally and with great circumspection. Otherwise, the purpose of private international law would stand defeated. Recently, in *Vijay Karia and Ors v Prysmian Cavi E Sistemi Srl and Ors*,[112] the Supreme Court reiterated the judgment in *Cruz City*[113] and the definition given in the *Renusagar*[114] judgment to state that fundamental policy refers to legislation so basic to Indian law that it cannot be compromised.

[103] AIR [1994] SC 860; Reiterated in *Cruz City 1 Mauritius Holdings v Unitech Limited* [2017] 239 DLT 649.

[104] *British India Steam Navigation Co Ltd v Shanmughavilas Cashew Industries* [1990] 3 SCC 481; *National Thermal Power Corporation v Singer Company* [1992] 3 SCC 551 [14]; *Renusagar Power Co. Ltd v General Electric Co* AIR [1994] 860.

[105] [2003] 5 SCC 705.

[106] [2014] 9 SCC 263.

[107] ibid [27] the court explained judicial approach as an approach that ensures that the authority acts bonafide and deals with the subject in a fair, reasonable and objective manner and that its decision is not actuated by any extraneous consideration. Judicial approach in that sense acts as a check against flaws and faults that can render the decision of a court, Tribunal or Authority vulnerable to challenge.

[108] GL Peiris, 'Wednesbury Unreasonableness: The Expanding Canvas' (1987) 46 *Cambridge Law Journal* 53–82. The '*Wednesbury*' principle is a standard of unreasonableness. It is attracted if a reasoning or decision is so unreasonable that no reasonable person acting reasonably could have made it. The test was down in the case of *Associated Provincial Picture Houses Ltd v Wednesbury Corporation* (1948) 1 KB 223). The case espoused the standard of reasonableness.

[109] [2005] 5 SCC 465.

[110] ibid.

[111] ibid.

[112] 2020 S.C.C. OnLine SC 177. See C Jayaraj, 'Conflict of Laws' (2005) XLI *Annual Survey of Indian Law Indian Law Institute* 71–87, 83.

[113] *Cruz City* (n 103).

[114] *Renusagar* (n 103).

The Indian courts' approach to the interpretation of the public policy is broadly aligned with the approach of other jurisdictions. Most of the cases decided by the Indian judiciary have addressed the interpretation of foreign domestic law. No deliberation has taken on the interaction between international law and public policy. In this regard a reference to the case of *Kuwait Airways Corp v Iraqi Airways Co* provides an interesting illustration of how public policy is linked to international law. In 1990, Iraq invaded Kuwait[115] and seized aircraft belonging to Kuwait Airways Corporation (KAC). The Iraqi Government passed a resolution transferring all of KAC's property to Iraq Airways Corporation (IAC). The UN Security Council passed a resolution, based on which military action was taken against Iraq. The aircraft were damaged during the air strike.[116] After the liberation of Kuwait, KAC commenced legal proceedings against the Republic of Iraq and IAC, claiming the return of its ten aircraft or payment of their value and damages. Because the alleged wrongs were committed in Iraq and also given the absence of any particular connection with another country, it was held that the applicable law in the case would be the law of Iraq.[117] However, the Iraqi Government's action in nationalising Kuwait property was justified and legal under the applicable Iraqi law. Nonetheless, the House of Lords held that the invasion of Kuwait and the subsequent nationalisation constituted a 'gross violation of established rules of international law' and enforcement of Iraqi law would be 'manifestly contrary to the public policy of English law'.[118]

Along with the operation of public policy, currently jurisdictions are emphasising the overriding mandatory rules exception. Mandatory rules touch on the core economic, social, and political policies of a nation. Mandatory rules can be of the *lex fori*, the *lex cause* or the law of a third country (for example, where a contract is to be performed).[119] The best categorisation of mandatory rules is contained in Article 9(1) of the EU's Rome I Regulation on the law applicable to contractual obligations. That defines overriding mandatory rules as:

> provisions the respect for which is regarded as crucial by a country for safeguarding its public interests, such as its political, social, or economic organisation, to such an extent that they are applicable to any situation falling within their scope, irrespective of the law otherwise applicable.[120]

Some prominent examples of mandatory policies are concerning foreign exchange, the environment, and defence, which require absolute compliance. Invoking overriding mandatory rules would lead to the absolute application of the law of the forum. Whereas, in the case of public policy, whether the foreign law will prevail or it will lead to applying the law of the forum depends on the effect of public policy on the forum.[121]

VI. Conclusion

This chapter has examined the general principles governing categorisation of substantive and procedural matters in private international law. For the sake of clarity, this chapter has adopted

[115] *Kuwait Airways Corp v Iraqi Airways Co* [1995] 1 Lloyd's Rep 25, [1]; M Davies, The Effect in Private International Law of a Breach of Public International Law by a State Actor' (2001) 2(2) *Melbourne Journal of International Law* 523–534.

[116] *Kuwait Airways Corp v Iraqi Airways Co* (ibid).

[117] ibid [1].

[118] ibid [29].

[119] A Chong, 'The Public Policy and Mandatory Rules of Third Countries in International Contracts' (2006) 2(1) *Journal of Private International law* 27–70.

[120] Council Regulation (EC) 593/2008 of 17 June 2008, on the law applicable to contractual obligations (Rome I Regulation) OJ L177/6 Art 9(1).

[121] JJ Fawcett, 'Evasion of Law and Mandatory Rules in Private International Law' (1990) 49(1) *The Cambridge Law Journal* 44–62.

an approach wherein it first explains the characteristics and operationalisation of the concepts and principles as evolved in other jurisdictions and then goes on to explore the Indian legal position. The categorisation of issues as substantive and procedural has a direct consequence on the invocation of applicable law in private international law. This chapter illustrates that the Indian position treating limitation as procedural is not in conformity with the practice of other jurisdictions, undermines the objectives of private international law, and encourages forum shopping. This chapter highlighted that ostensible statutory reliance on proving the content of foreign law as a question of fact and the burden placed on the parties to plead foreign law have had the effect of hampering the growth of the subject by forcing parties in a dispute to rely on domestic law. Where the content of foreign law has not been proved, foreign law is presumed to be the same as the *lex fori* and the latter is applied. Case jurisprudence has been sparse as to the meaning of penal and revenue laws; However, cases have richly deliberated on public policy and have laid down the broad contours of its application. The cases have insisted on public policy as excluding foreign law only if the latter is contrary to the fundamental principles of Indian law, the interests of India, or morality.

PART II

Jurisdiction

5

Jurisdiction: Which Court will Adjudicate a Matter?

I. Introduction

According to the Latin maxim *ubi ius ibi remedium*, every right must be accompanied with a corresponding remedy. A legal right must be vindicated by initiating proceedings before an appropriate court which has jurisdiction to hear and adjudicate on the matter. The term 'jurisdiction' is derived from the Latin words *ius* (right) and *dicere* (to say or pronounce).[1] It refers to the power and authority of a court to administer (pronounce) justice (right) in a litigant's case[2] and denotes the competence of a court to hear a matter before it and pass requisite orders.[3] In other words, jurisdiction includes every act of the court from inquiring into the facts to applying legal principles, pronouncing judgment, and ensuring the execution of its decision.[4] In private international law, determination of a court's jurisdiction is the chief pillar and a pivotal factor from which flow all other aspects in the adjudication of a dispute with a foreign element in a civil or commercial matter. A dispute may involve a foreign element in numerous circumstances. This may be the position when immovable property is located within the territory of the court but is sold to a foreign national; when the performance of a contract occurred overseas; or when persons who were residing or domiciled within the territorial limits of the court were injured overseas. Once its jurisdiction has been established, a court will determine the mechanism that will be employed to identify the applicable law governing a dispute. The competence of a court in adjudicating on a matter will also determine whether its judgment is capable of being recognised and enforced abroad.

This chapter deals with Indian conflict of law rules on jurisdiction in civil and commercial matters. Suits of a civil nature which arise in family matters are subject to special rules which will be discussed in the next chapter. Section II examines rules on who may sue and be sued before an Indian court in civil and commercial matters. It discusses the provisions of the Code of Civil Procedure 1908[5] (CPC), the UN (Privileges and Immunity) Act 1947 (UN Privileges Act),[6] and

[1] Halsbury's Laws of India, *Civil Procedure* Vol 5, 2nd edn (Lexis Nexis, 2008) 65.042.

[2] ibid.

[3] ibid; CK Takwani, *Civil Procedure with Limitation Act 1963* 8th edn (Eastern Book Company) 40; JG Collier, *The Conflict Of Laws* 3rd edn (CUP, 2001) 71; and A Briggs, *The Conflict of Laws* 4th edn (OUP, 2019) 44 [Briggs, *Conflict of Laws*].

[4] ibid and the decision the Supreme Court in *Official Trustee v Sachindra Nath* AIR [1969] SC 823.

[5] Act No 5 of 1908.

[6] Act No 46 of 1947.

the Diplomatic Relations (Vienna Convention) Act 1972 (Diplomatic Relations Act).[7] Section III discusses the Indian court's jurisdiction in actions *in personam*. This part contains four sub-sections. Section A discusses the scope and meaning of suits of a civil and commercial nature. Section B examines the grounds on which an Indian court can exercise its jurisdiction in such matters. Section C discusses the procedure for the service of summonses. Section D highlights the factors which limit the jurisdiction of a court. In so doing, it examines Indian law provisions: (1) to prevent concurrent proceedings and inconsistent judgments; and (2) the circumstances in which a court may stay proceedings under the doctrine of *forum non-conveniens* or pursuant to a choice of court or arbitration agreement. Section IV focuses on the jurisdiction of an Indian court in *in rem* actions, primarily concerning disputes arising from a maritime claim against a ship or a vessel. Section V reflects on the position of Indian law vis-à-vis global trends to gauge the level of legal development in the country. In doing so, this part analyses the laws of countries such as Australia, Canada and the EU. The provisions of the Hague Convention on Choice of Court Agreements[8] (HCCCA) which harmonises the law on choice of court agreements among contracting states are also analysed. Section VI offers concluding remarks.

II. Persons who may File a Suit before an Indian Court

In general, every person – whether natural or juristic – may sue or be sued in a court in India, regardless of whether the person is a resident or a foreigner, provided the grounds on which the court may assume jurisdiction have been satisfied. Suits by or against a minor must, however, be instituted by the minor's guardian.[9] Suits by or against artificial (juristic) persons such as companies may be initiated by its secretary, director or principal officer in the name of the corporation.[10] Suits by or against a partnership must be initiated by two or more partners carrying on business in India – provided that they were partners at the time when the cause of action occurred.[11] At the same time, Indian law imposes restrictions on the right of the persons to sue and be sued before a court. These restrictions are discussed below.

A. Suits by Alien Enemies

Section 83 of the CPC prohibits the initiation of suits by alien enemies. There is no prohibition on the initiation of lawsuits against such persons. An alien enemy is a person who is a national of a country at war with India and residing in the Republic without the permission of the Indian Government. Therefore, nationals of an enemy country residing in India with the consent of the Indian Government may commence suit. The limitation under section 83 is not extended to foreign corporations which enjoy legal personality under the law in which they were

[7] Act No 43 of 1972.

[8] Hague Conference on Private International Law, Convention on Choice of Court Agreements, 30 June 2005, 44 I.L.M. 1294 [hereinafter the HCCCA]. The text of the HCCCA is reproduced in (2006) 2 *Journal of Private International Law* 270.

[9] Order 32 of the CPC.

[10] ibid, Order 29.

[11] ibid, Order 30, Rule 1.

incorporated.[12] Accordingly, the secretary, director or principal officer of such company may initiate a suit in India in the name of the corporation.

B. Suits by a Foreign State

Section 84 prohibits a foreign state[13] from initiating a suit before a civil court in India unless it is for the enforcement of a private right vested in its rulers, ambassadors, envoys or, in the case of a Commonwealth country, a High Commissioner acting in a private capacity.

C. Sovereign Immunity

Besides the restrictions on the filing of suits by alien enemies and foreign states, there are also limitations on the initiation of proceedings against foreign states and the former Indian Princely States due to the principle of sovereign immunity. The doctrine of sovereign immunity was developed during an era of laissez-faire when state entry into trading was not envisaged.[14] According to this principle, sovereign states are immune from the jurisdiction of the courts in another country. The doctrine of sovereign immunity, therefore, prohibits a sovereign state from being made a defendant in the courts of another country without the sovereign state's consent.[15] The principle is predicated on the policy consideration that the 'national interest will be better served if the wrongs to suitors involving relations with a foreign power are righted through diplomatic negotiations rather than by compulsions to judicial proceedings'.[16] In Indian law, the doctrine of sovereign immunity is imbibed from the provisions of the CPC, the UN Privileges Act and the Diplomatic Relations Act.

i. Section 86 of the CPC

Section 86 incorporates the doctrine of sovereign immunity and prohibits the initiation of suits against a foreign state without the consent of the Central Government. Section 86 thus gives effect to the concept of sovereign immunity, albeit in a limited manner, by requiring the permission of the central government before suing a foreign state in any court in India to prevent frivolous and unjustified litigation.[17] The consent of the Central Government is not required if the plaintiff initiates the proceedings in its capacity as a tenant of an immovable property which it claims to hold though the foreign state.[18]

[12] See, *Shamrao Krishnaji Honnali v United Home Building & Engineering Society (India) Ltd of Bangalore* [1935] 38 Bom LR 1092.

[13] See s 87A(a) of the CPC, which states that a foreign state refers to a country which is outside India and has been recognised by the Central Government.

[14] JP Ball, 'Sovereign Immunity of Governmental Trading Entities' (1959) *Sydney Law Review* 143, 143.

[15] See, J Hogan, 'International Law – Sovereign Immunity' (1961) *University of Miami Law Review* 450, 451.

[16] ibid.

[17] See, *Mirza Ali Akbar Kasani v United Arab Republic* AIR [1966] SC 230, 231-232; *Harbhajan Singh Dhalla v Union of India*, AIR [1987] SC 9; *Veb Deutfract Sccieederei Rostock v New Central Jute Mills Co Ltd* AIR [1994] SC 516 [5]; *Consulate General of Islamic Republic of Iran, Mumbai v Baldota Brothers* [2013] 3 Mh. L.J [37, 38] and *Rita Solomon & Ors v Republic of Italy & Anr* [2019] 260 DLT 331 [3].

[18] See, s 86(1) of the CPC.

The decision of the Supreme Court in *Veb Deutfract Sccieederei Rostock v New Central Jute Mills Co Ltd*[19] illustrates this point. The court was exercising its appellate jurisdiction in a dispute which arose from a suit against a company incorporated in Germany for allegedly delivering damaged goods. The company was an agent of the Government of Germany which has been recognised as a foreign state in India. The court reversed the decision of the Calcutta High Court which held that the suit against an organ of the German Government was not barred by section 86 of the CPC.[20] In doing so, the Supreme Court referred to the decision of the English court in *Baccus SRL v Servicio Nacional Del Trigo*,[21] which forms the genesis of the subject under English common law. The dispute arose between an Italian and a Spanish trading corporation for an alleged breach of contract by the latter. The parties had agreed on the jurisdiction of the High Court in London. The defendants claimed to be a department of the sovereign state of Spain which was headed by the Spanish Minister of Agriculture. In *Baccus*, the court per Jenkins LJ confirmed the extension of the principle of sovereign immunity to government-organised trading corporations.[22] It stated that the identification of a department as a government-organised trading corporation would depend on the nature of its activities and the interests of the foreign state.[23] Such corporations differ from ordinary trading corporations, insofar as the former's 'operations consist of purchasing and selling or importing and exporting staple commodities in the interest of the public for whom the foreign sovereign State is responsible'.[24] Accordingly, if a suit is initiated against a corporate body which is in truth a department of the sovereign state, the suit will in effect be considered as one between the plaintiff and a foreign state.[25] Further, the court in *Veb Deutfract*[26] referred to a dictum of the Calcutta High Court *Royal Nepal Airlines Corp v Manorama Meher Singh Legha*.[27] The court stated that the Nepal Airlines Corporation which had its office in Calcutta was eligible for limited sovereign immunity under section 86 insofar as it was a department of the Government of Nepal.[28] The Calcutta High Court stated:

> [O]ne of the principles of international law is that every sovereign State respects the independence of every other foreign State. This absolute independence and international comity underline the relationship between sovereign States.[29]

The limited sovereign immunity conferred by section 86 of the CPC thus extends to the different departments and organs through which a foreign state carries out business, whether incorporated or unincorporated bodies.[30] In other words, such departments must directly form part of the activities of the foreign state.[31] At the same time, the private activities of a foreign state would not benefit from the immunity granted under section 86.[32] The development of cultural activities or the facilitating of data centres in India is therefore not construed as a function of a foreign state in the performance of its sovereign obligations.[33] For this reason, disputes arising in such

[19] AIR [1994] SC 516.
[20] See, *New Central Jute Mills v VEB Deutr-Frachit Seerederai Rostock* AIR [1983] Cal 225.
[21] (1957) 1 QB 438 (C.A.).
[22] ibid 466.
[23] Ball (n 14) 143–144, referring to *Baccus* ibid.
[24] (n 21) 467; and Ball, (n 14) 144.
[25] Ball, (n 14) 143–144.
[26] (n 17).
[27] AIR [1966] Cal 319.
[28] (n 17) [8–9].
[29] ibid [5].
[30] ibid [8–9].
[31] ibid.
[32] See, *International Development Research Centre v Durgeshwarisahi* ILR [2007] 1 Delhi 640 [16].
[33] ibid.

matters would be subject to the jurisdiction of the Indian court without need for the Central Government's permission.

Section 86(2) prohibits the Central Government from consenting to suits against a foreign state unless the dispute falls within the ambit of clauses (a) to (d) of the provision.[34] The Central Government shall accordingly only consent to the initiation of the suit where the foreign state:

(a) initiated a suit against the person desiring to sue it;[35]
(b) trades within the local limits of the jurisdiction of the court where the proceedings have been initiated;[36]
(c) possesses immovable property within the local limits of the court and the dispute arises in relation to such property or the money charged thereon;[37]
(d) has expressly or impliedly waived the privilege of the immunity conferred.[38]

Section 86 obligates the Central Government to provide a hearing to the person who makes the request before refusing to permit the initiation of the suit.[39] The Central Government must thus follow the standards that are stipulated in section 86(2).[40] The consent letter of the Central Government which permits the initiation of the suits must therefore refer to a criterion indicated by section 86(2).[41] The law, however, prohibits the High Court from directing the Central Government to provide its consent even when the High Court finds the Central Government's refusal to have been arbitrary or contrary to law.[42] In this respect, the Supreme Court in *Union of India and Anr v Bilash Chand Jain and Anr* stressed that the High Court, insofar as it is exercising an administrative order of the Central Government, is not exercising an appellate jurisdiction over the matter.[43] Instead, the High Court is merely exercising a power of judicial review, which is much narrower than its appellate authority.[44] In such circumstances, the High Court may merely remand the matter to the Ministry of External Affairs with a direction to reconsider the case under section 86(2) of the CPC.[45] In a related vein, section 87-B prohibits suits by or against the rulers of the former Indian Princely States[46] unless a dispute has arisen wholly or partly from a cause of action which occurred before the commencement of the Constitution.[47] In such circumstances, the suit may be initiated by or against a former ruler in the same manner as against a ruler, ambassador or envoy of a foreign state.

ii. UN Privileges Act

The doctrine of sovereign immunity has also been incorporated in the provisions of the UN Privileges Act which gives effect to the 1946 UN Convention on Privileges and Immunity of the

[34] *Veb Deutfract* (n 17) [5–6]; and *Ram Naresh v Delhi Administration & Ors* ILR [2005] II Delhi 1041 [7].
[35] See, s 86(2)(a) of the CPC.
[36] ibid, s 86(2)(b).
[37] ibid, s 86(2)(c).
[38] ibid, s 86(2)(d).
[39] ibid, s 86(6) of the CPC; and *Rita Solomon* (n 17) [21].
[40] *Rita Solomon*, ibid [22].
[41] ibid [22].
[42] *Union of India and Anr v Bilash Chand Jain and Anr* [2009] 16 SCC 601 [4].
[43] ibid.
[44] ibid.
[45] ibid.
[46] See s 87(2)(a) of the CPC, which states that a former Indian State refers to an Indian State which has been notified as such by the Official Gazette of the Central Government. A list of former Indian States is available at: https://highcourtchd.gov.in/sub_pages/left_menu/Rules_orders/high_court_rules/vol-I-pdf/chap7V1.pdf.
[47] See s 87B(3)(b) of the CPC, which clarifies that the commencement of the Constitution refers to 26 January 1950.

United Nations to which India is a signatory. The statute confers immunity against legal proceedings against:

(a) the UN, its property and assets (wherever they are located) of the UN;[48]
(b) the officials of the UN for acts performed in their legal capacity;[49]
(c) the representatives of Members of the principal and subsidiary organs, conferences convened;[50]
(d) the experts that are performing missions for the Organisation.[51]

The legislation, however, permits the Secretary-General to waive the immunity expressly.[52] Further, it clarifies that such privileges and immunities shall not be exercised for the personal benefit of the individuals.[53] Accordingly, there is a duty on the Member to waive the immunity if it believes that not doing so is likely to impede the course of justice.[54]

iii. Diplomatic Relations Act

The provisions of the Diplomatic Relations Act give effect to the Vienna Convention on Diplomatic Relations 1961 (the 1961 Vienna Convention)[55] to which India is a signatory. According to the provisions of the legislation, diplomatic agents (heads of missions[56] and diplomatic staff[57]) are considered to be representatives of the sending state who perform sovereign functions of that country in the receiving state.[58] A court in India will not entertain civil or administrative proceedings against diplomatic agents[59] and members of the administrative and technical staff of missions and their families, who are not nationals of the Republic,[60] for acts in the performance of their official duties[61] unless the sending state has expressly waived the immunity conferred by the legislation.[62] In *PS Govindaswamy Naidu & Sons' Charities v V Prakash*, the Madras High Court clarified that the protection from the jurisdiction of the Indian courts under the Diplomatic Relations Act is also extended to consular offices of a sending State in India.[63] The legislation prohibits any public servant or agent from entering the premises of a foreign state's

[48] ibid, Art II: s 2 of the 1947 Act.
[49] ibid, Art V: s 18(a); and *Jyoti Sateeja v International Committee of the Red Cross & Ors* [2015] SCC OnLine Del 7996 [10].
[50] ibid, Art IV: ss 11(a) and 12.
[51] ibid, Art VI: s 22(a).
[52] ibid, Art VIII: s 29(a).
[53] ibid, Art IV: s 14; Art V: s 20; and Art VI: s 23.
[54] ibid.
[55] The text of the 1961 Vienna Convention is available at: https://legal.un.org/ilc/texts/instruments/english/conventions/9_1_1961.pdf.
[56] Art 1(a) of the 1961 Vienna Convention defines the head of the mission as the person charged by the sending State with the duty of acting in that capacity.
[57] ibid, Art 1(a) which defines the members of the staff of the mission as 'the members of the diplomatic staff, of the administrative and technical staff and of the service staff of the mission'.
[58] See, *Ram Naresh* (n 34) [17], [19].
[59] Art 31 of the 1972 Act; and *Eva Drdakova v M/s Khemka Exports Private Ltd* [2012] 114 (1) Bom LR 67 [6]. Also see Art 1(e) of the 1961 Vienna Convention defines a diplomatic agent a 'the head of the mission or a member of the diplomatic staff of the mission'.
[60] ibid, Art 37. Also see Art 1(f) of the 1961 Vienna Convention defines the members of the administrative and technical staff as 'the members of the staff of the mission employed in the administrative and technical service of the mission'.
[61] See, *PS Govindaswamy Naidu & Sons' Charities v V Prakash* [2019] 6 CTC 154 [28].
[62] ibid, Art 32 read along with Art 5.
[63] *PS Govindaswamy* (n 61) [48]–[51]. Also see, Art 3(2) of the 1961 Vienna Convention, which clarifies that the functions of the diplomatic mission include the consular functions by the mission.

diplomatic mission to serve legal process without permission.[64] However, the immunity under the legislation is from the jurisdiction of the Indian courts.[65] It does not negate the elements which form a cause of action.

The immunities conferred under the statute commence as soon as the persons indicated therein enter India to take up a post.[66] At the same time, the immunity granted to a diplomatic agent is based on the principle of reciprocity. The legislation endows the Central Government with the right to withdraw immunity if a state signatory to the Vienna Convention has breached its obligations by conferring lesser immunities than those stipulated under the Diplomatic Relations Act on the members of an Indian mission.[67] A person who claims to be protected under the provisions of the Act must provide proof to this effect.[68] A certificate issued by the Secretary to the Government of India in the Ministry of External Affairs is conclusive evidence of that fact.[69]

The principle of sovereign immunity under the Diplomatic Relations Act is not absolute and is restricted. In general, there will be no immunity from legal proceedings if a suit arises from a dispute in which the diplomatic agent was acting in its private (and not official) capacity. The Indian court will have jurisdiction over suits involving diplomatic agents or its members in the following circumstances.

(a) When the lawsuit concerns a real action for private immovable property situated in India, unless the diplomatic agent holds it on behalf of the sending state.[70] In *Syrian Arab Republic v AK Jajodia*, the Delhi High Court stated that the immunity available under Article 31 of the Diplomatic Relations Act does not extend to the renting or the leasing of immovable property by a representative of a sovereign state from a private individual or the citizen of India.[71] Such properties, having been rented for private purposes, are not considered as inviolable under Article 21 of the Diplomatic Relations Act.[72] They are not subject to immunity from search, seizure or arrest.[73] For this reason, the permission of the Central Government is not required for initiation of proceedings under section 86 of the CPC as the underlying transaction does constitute an act done by the mission or foreign state.[74] Such properties fall within the domain of a landlord-tenant relationship and the relevant property may be taken back after termination of the lease period or on bona fide requirement of the property by the landlord.[75]

(b) When the suit concerns an action relating to succession in which the diplomat is involved in a private capacity as executor, administrator, heir or legatee.[76] There is no reported case in which an Indian court has refused immunity to diplomatic agents on this ground. Nonetheless, a diplomatic agent is not eligible for immunity from civil proceedings before a court in India if the suit concerns succession matters in which the agent acts outside one's official capacity.

[64] ibid, Art 8; and *PS Govindaswamy* (n 61) [59], [60].

[65] See, R Oppong, *Private International Law in Commonwealth Africa* (CUP, 2013) 115, 116, referring to the application of the Vienna Convention 1961 in Nigeria.

[66] ibid, Art 39.

[67] ibid, Art 4.

[68] ibid, Art 9.

[69] ibid; and *Eva Drdakova*, (n 59) [4]–[5].

[70] ibid, Art 31(1)(a).

[71] ILR [2004] 2 Del 704 [14].

[72] ibid.

[73] ibid.

[74] ibid.

[75] ibid.

[76] Art 31(1)(b) of the 1972 Act.

(c) When the suit arises from a professional or commercial activity exercised by the diplomat in India outside of official functions.[77] As such, there is no general rule to ascertain whether a particular activity may be construed as commercial or not. In *Eva Drdakova v M/s Khemka Exports Private Ltd*, the Bombay High Court stated that an activity would not be considered as commercial (and would continue to be covered by immunity) if portions of premises held by employees of an embassy or consulate were leased to an outsider 'for the benefit of the principal activity of the Foreign Mission'.[78] Conversely, the Indian court would have jurisdiction over a dispute arising from the lease of a property to an outsider for conducting activities entirely unconnected with the sovereign functions of a foreign state.[79]

III. Jurisdiction *in personam*

A court is said to possess jurisdiction *in personam* if the dispute relates to a claim initiated to compel a defendant to do or refrain from doing something or to pay damages for the breach of law.[80] In other words, the dispute must relate to the determination of the rights and interests of the parties themselves vis-à-vis the subject-matter.[81] The effect of such an action is merely to bind the parties to the suit.[82] That said, a court in India possesses jurisdiction *in personam* whenever the dispute is of a civil or commercial nature.

A. When is a Suit Considered to be of a Civil or Commercial Nature?

i. Suits of a Civil Nature

A suit is considered to be of a civil nature if it involves the adjudication of private rights and remedies of persons and thus excludes criminal or political rights.[83] Therefore, the determination of the jurisdiction of an Indian court in a dispute initiated by the survivors of a person whose death was caused by murder does not fall within the scope of the CPC. Similarly, suits which primarily concern a person's religion or caste are outside the scope of the CPC, insofar as such disputes concern parties' political rights. Disputes arising in connection with contractual obligations, torts, the dissolution of marriage and immovable property are examples of suits of a civil nature.[84] The CPC generally regulates the jurisdiction of a court in a suit of a civil nature. The provisions of the statute are, however, inapplicable to disputes involving family matters. The latter are regulated by personal laws depending on the religion of a relevant person. The jurisdiction of an Indian court in family matters will be discussed in subsequent chapters.

ii. Suits of a Commercial Nature

The Commercial Courts, Commercial Division and Commercial Appellate Division of High Courts Act 2015 (CCA)[85] regulates the jurisdiction of a court in suits of a commercial nature.

[77] ibid, Art 31(1)(c).
[78] *Eva Drdakova* (n 59) [19].
[79] ibid.
[80] ibid.
[81] See the decision of the Supreme Court in *R. Viswanathan v Rukn-Ul-Mulk Syed Abdul Wajid* 1963 SCR (3) 22.
[82] ibid.
[83] See Takwani (n 3) 47, 50–51.
[84] ibid 51, 52.
[85] Act No 4 of 2016.

According to Section 2(c) of the statute, a suit is considered to be of a commercial nature if it arises out of any of the following matters – provided that the value of the subject matter is not less than Rupees 3,00,000 (INR three hundred thousand or more):[86]

(1) ordinary transactions of merchants, bankers, financiers and traders such as those relating to mercantile documents, including enforcement and interpretation of such documents;
(2) export or import of merchandise or services;
(3) issues relating to admiralty and maritime law;
(4) transactions relating to aircraft, aircraft engines, aircraft equipment and helicopters, including sales, leasing and financing of the same;
(5) carriage of goods;
(6) construction and infrastructure contracts, including tenders;
(7) agreements relating to immovable property used exclusively in trade or commerce;
(8) franchising agreements;
(8) distribution and licensing agreements;
(9) management and consultancy agreements;
(10) joint venture agreements;
(11) shareholders agreements;
(12) subscription and investment agreements pertaining to the services industry including outsourcing services and financial services;
(13) mercantile agency and mercantile usage;
(14) partnership agreements;
(15) technology development agreements;
(16) intellectual property rights relating to registered and unregistered trademarks, copyright, patent, design, domain names, geographical indications and semiconductor integrated circuits;
(17) agreements for sale of goods or provision of services;
(18) exploitation of oil and gas reserves or other natural resources including electromagnetic spectrum;
(19) insurance and re-insurance;
(20) contracts of agency relating to any of the above; and
(21) such other commercial disputes as may be notified by the Central Government
(22) the recovery of immovable property or the realisation of money from such property which was given as security; or
(23) contracts with a state or its agencies or a private body which carries out public functions.

B. Grounds on Which an Indian Court May Assume Jurisdiction in a Civil or Commercial Matter

In actions *in personam*, the jurisdiction of a court will depend on the existence of certain condition precedents which are the *sine qua non* for deciding a matter before it.[87] However, there is a presumption in favour of the jurisdiction of the court.[88] A suit of a civil nature must be instituted within the jurisdiction of the court within whose territorial limits the dispute arose.[89]

[86] See ss 2(c), 3A, 4, 7 and 10 of the CCA read along with s 47 of the Arbitration and Conciliation (Amendment) Act 2015 [2015 Arbitration Act].

[87] See Takwani (n 3) 46.

[88] ibid 54.

[89] ibid 47.

As a general rule, all commercial disputes, including those on international commercial arbitration[90] – where the value of the suit is more than Rs 3,00,000 – must be attempted to be resolved by mediation prior to seizing the jurisdiction of the court.[91] In situations where the resolution of the dispute by mediation is not feasible, for instance, because urgent interim relief is required, the plaintiff may directly initiate the proceedings before the appropriate court.[92] Such commercial disputes must be initiated before the Commercial Division of the High Court if it arises in Delhi, Bombay, Calcutta, Madras or Himachal Pradesh – which possess ordinary original civil jurisdiction and is, therefore, empowered to adjudicate new matters.[93] Commercial disputes above the aforementioned value in all other states in India must be initiated before the Commercial Courts that are created at the district level.[94]

All other civil and commercial matters (i.e. those in which the value of the subject matter is less than Rs 3,00,000) must be initiated in the court of the lowest grade which is competent to try the same.[95] Disputes arising in Delhi, Bombay, Calcutta, Madras or Himachal Pradesh must be initiated before the High Court (but not the commercial division) of that state, which possesses ordinary original civil jurisdiction and is, thus, empowered to hear new matters.[96] Disputes in civil and commercial (namely those where the value of the subject matter is below Rs 3,00,000) matters in all other states must be initiated before the District court of that state – before the Civil Judge or the Additional Civil Judge – depending on the pecuniary limits of the court.[97]

A court may assume jurisdiction for actions *in personam* in any civil and commercial matter according to the rules prescribed in Sections 16 to 20 of the CPC.[98] The court may hear the case and settle a dispute on the fulfilment of these prerequisites after the initial assumption of jurisdiction.[99] The jurisdiction of a court in civil and commercial matters may be divided into exclusive and permissive jurisdiction. The bases on which an Indian court may establish its jurisdiction are discussed below.

i. Exclusive Jurisdiction

Sections 16 to 18 of the CPC stipulate the circumstances in which the courts in India will possess exclusive jurisdiction over a matter. In particular, the provisions regulate the adjudication of disputes arising in relation to immovable property in India. The jurisdiction of the court will be mandatory. It will be unaffected by any choice of court agreement (also known as forum-selection clauses) between the parties which provide that a dispute must be adjudicated in a foreign forum.

[90] See s 2(f) of the Arbitration and Conciliation Act, 1996 (ACA) which defines an 'international commercial arbitration' as: 'an arbitration relating to disputes arising out of legal relationships, whether contractual or not, considered as commercial under the law in force in India and where at least one of the parties is – (i) an individual who is a national of, or habitually resident in, any country other than India; or (ii) a body corporate which is incorporated in any country other than India; or (iii) an association or a body of individuals whose central management and control is exercised in any country other than India; or (iv) the Government of a foreign country.'

[91] Section 12A of the CCA.

[92] ibid, s 12A(1) read along with Order XXXIX of the CPC that clarifies the circumstances in which the court may grant urgent interim relief in the form of a temporary injunction.

[93] Sections 4, 7 and 10(1) of the CCA. Also see, s 5(1) of the CCA for the procedure of appeals against the decisions of the Commercial Division.

[94] ibid, s 3. Also see, ss 3A and 13 of the CCA for the procedure of appeals against the decisions of the Commercial Court.

[95] Section 15 of the CPC.

[96] See ss 2(4) and 3 of the CPC. The procedure for appeals against the decisions may be found in ss 96–109 of the CPC read along with the rules of the High Court of the state.

[97] See s 2(4) of the CPC. The procedure for appeals against the decisions may be found in ss 96–109 of the CPC.

[98] See in this respect Explanation to s 6 of the CCA.

[99] See Takwani (n 3) 46.

Moreover, sections 16–18 prohibit recourse to any other ground, including that based on the defendant's residence or place of business (dealt with in sections 19 and 20 as discussed below). Section 16 of the CPC confers exclusive jurisdiction over a court in which immovable property is situated whenever the suit relates to the following matters:

(1) recovery of immovable property with or without rent;
(2) partition of immovable property;
(3) foreclosure, sale or redemption in the case of a mortgage or charge on immovable property;
(4) determination of any right or interest in immovable property;
(5) compensation of a wrong to immovable property; or
(6) recovery of movable property under restraint or attachment.

According to section 17 of the CPC, if the suit relates to relief or compensation for a wrong done to immovable property situated within the jurisdiction of different courts, the court within whose local limits a portion of the property is located will have exclusive jurisdiction over the matter, provided that the entire claim arose in its territory. In certain circumstances, however, the local limits of the jurisdiction of the court may be uncertain and cannot be identified. Section 18 permits any one of the courts which possess territorial and pecuniary jurisdiction to adjudicate on the matter, after recording a decree to that effect. The decree will have the same effect as if the property was situated within the court's jurisdiction.

ii. Permissive Jurisdiction

Sections 19 and 20 confer permissive jurisdiction on a court in India. Subject to certain limitations as indicated in section III.D of this chapter, a plaintiff may seise the jurisdiction of the court if the criteria below are met.

a. Residence

The term 'residence' refers to a natural and not juristic person.[100] In general, it is the residence of the defendant that is relevant in establishing the jurisdiction of a court in India. Section 19 of the CPC regulates the jurisdiction of a court for disputes arising in matters of tort or delict. It permits a court in India to assume jurisdiction in a dispute which arises from a wrong done to movable property or a person if the defendant was 'actually or voluntary' residing in its territory at the time of commencement of the suit.[101] Section 20 confers a similar right on the court for actions arising from residual matters which are not governed by the provisions of sections 16 to 19. In a suit against more than one defendant, the court may assume jurisdiction if each of such persons was actually or voluntarily residing in its territory at the time of commencement of the proceedings. A person is considered as 'actually and voluntarily' residing in the territory of a court if one has one's permanent abode in that place or has lived there for a considerable period.[102] The Supreme Court in *Yogesh Bharadwaj v State of U.P*[103] has clarified that in Indian private international law the term 'residence' connotes a physical fact and refers to a person's 'bodily presence as an inhabitant' of a place.[104] The Court added:

[100] See, *Halsbury's Laws of India* (n 1) [65.068].
[101] See s 19 of the CPC.
[102] See *Halsbury's Laws of India* (n 1) [65.068].
[103] (1990) 3 SCC 355 [17]–[21].
[104] ibid [11].

> [A]ny period of physical presence, however short, may constitute residence provided it is not transitory, fleeting or casual. The intention is not relevant to prove the physical fact of residence except to the extent of showing that it is not a mere fleeting or transitory existence.[105]

Accordingly, the mere presence of a defendant (or a plaintiff in suits arising from the infringement of a trademark or copyright) within the territorial limits of a court would not suffice in conferring the latter with jurisdiction. Further, the residence must be voluntary and must not be the result of imprisonment or the violation of immigration laws.[106] The Explanation to section 20 indicates that the CPC does not distinguish between habitual and ordinary residence of a defendant to establish the jurisdiction of a court in India.[107] Therefore, a court in India is considered to possess jurisdiction over tortious matters if the defendant has a permanent dwelling or a temporary residence in a place.[108] A defendant is deemed to be a resident of his or her place of permanent dwelling or temporary residence.[109] The provisions of the Copyright Act 1957[110] and the Trade Marks Act 1999 (TMA)[111] would additionally apply when the dispute concerns the infringement of a copyright or a trademark. In such circumstances, sections 62(2) of the Copyright Act 1957 and 134(2) of the TMA permit a court to assume jurisdiction if the plaintiff was 'actually and voluntarily' residing in its territory at the time of the commencement of the proceedings.

b. Place of Business

According to sections 19 and 20 of the CPC, a court may assume jurisdiction if the defendant was carrying on its business or personally working for gain in the court's territory at the time of the commencement of the proceedings.[112] The identification of the residence is irrelevant in suits against companies because such entities have no real existence in India.[113] In such circumstances, a court may assume jurisdiction when a corporation carries on business in its territory.[114] The term 'carry on business' refers to the place where a person carries out 'some real, substantial, and systematic or organised course of activity or conduct with a set purpose'.[115] In this respect, the Explanation to section 20 states that a corporation is deemed to carry on its business at the place of its sole or principal office in India.[116] In *Mayan (HK) Ltd. & Ors v Owners & Parties, Vessel MV Fortune Express & Ors* the Supreme Court clarified that the principal place of business of a corporation could be: (1) the place where the governing power of the corporation is exercised; (2) the place where the chief executive's offices are located; or (3) the place designated as such in its incorporation statutes and articles of association.[117] Likewise, a person who personally works for gain within the territorial limits of a court will also be subject to the latter's jurisdiction. There is no reported

[105] ibid [17].
[106] ibid [20]; and *Halsbury's Laws of India* (n 1) [65.068].
[107] See Explanation I to s 20 of the CPC.
[108] ibid.
[109] ibid.
[110] Act No 14 of 1957.
[111] Act No 47 of 1999.
[112] *Halsbury's Laws of India* (n 1) [65.070].
[113] See Collier (n 3) 82 (2001), referring to English common law on jurisdiction.
[114] ibid.
[115] See *Halsbury's Laws of India* (n 1) [65.069].
[116] See also, *Patel Roadways Ltd, Bombay v Prasad Trading Company*, [1991] 4 SCC 270 [9], [12]; and *Hakam Singh v Gammon (India) Ltd*, [1971] 1 SCC 286.
[117] [2006] 3 SCC 100 [32], referring to ss 4 and 10 of the Companies Act, 1956; and *ABC Laminart (P) Ltd v AP Agencies* [1989] 2 SCC 163.

case on the circumstances in which persons 'personally work for gain' in a place. However, the expression connotes the circumstances in which one performs work for a sum of money. By this principle, a solicitor is considered as 'personally working for gain' in Delhi if the solicitor represents clients in judicial proceedings for a sum of money in that state's courts. Likewise, a professor is considered as 'personally working for gain' in a Mumbai university if the educational institution that the professor is associated with is located in that state. However, the professor is not considered as 'personally working for gain' in Delhi if the professor was merely visiting Delhi to participate in a conference or seminar. Sections 62(2) of the Copyright Act and 134(2) of the TMA permit a court to assume jurisdiction if the plaintiff has carried on business or personally worked for gain in its territory at the time of commencement of proceedings.

The Supreme Court in *Dhodha House v SK Maingi & Patel Field Marshal Industries & Ors v PM Diesel Ltd*[118] has clarified the parameters of the expression 'carry on business' in the infringement of intellectual property. The proceedings arose in the form of an appeal from the decision of the High Court.[119] The appellant-defendant and the respondent-plaintiff were in the business of diesel engines in Rajkot, a state in Gujarat.[120] The plaintiff had filed a suit before the Delhi High Court seeking a perpetual injunction against the defendant which had allegedly infringed its trademark, copyright and trading style.[121] The plaintiff contended that the act of the defendant selling its goods in Delhi conferred jurisdiction upon that court for the reason that it violated the plaintiff's rights in that territory.[122] The Delhi High Court rejected the contention on the ground that it did not possess territorial jurisdiction to entertain the matter since the parties 'are resident and working for gain at Rajkot and no sale was effected by them within the territorial jurisdiction of the court'.[123] The question before the Supreme Court was whether the plaintiffs could be regarded as having carried on their business within the parameters of section 62(2) of the Copyright Act. Answering in the negative, the court stated that the expressions 'carry on business' and 'personally works for gain' 'connote two different meanings'.[124] The Court added that the presence of a person in a place is not necessary to establish that one is carrying on a business at that location.[125] Therefore, in certain circumstances, the jurisdiction of a court may be attracted under section 62(2) of the Copyright Act when a person is engaging in business through an agent in the territory.[126] This will be the position when the plaintiff in its capacity as a principal, is conducting business through a special (and not a general) agent who works exclusively for the former in that territory.[127]

The person who is 'acting as [an] agent, must be an agent in the strict sense of the term'.[128] Accordingly, a manager of a joint Hindu family will not be regarded as an 'agent' within the meaning of section 62(2) of the Copyright Act.[129] The agent must necessarily carry out an essential part of the business in that place and possess the power to conclude contracts and receive money on behalf of the principal in that territory.[130] As a result, the services of a

[118] 2006 (9) SCC 41.
[119] ibid [9].
[120] ibid.
[121] ibid [10]–[13].
[122] ibid.
[123] ibid [14].
[124] ibid [46].
[125] ibid.
[126] ibid.
[127] ibid.
[128] ibid.
[129] ibid.
[130] ibid.

commission agent to sell goods for the principal on a commission in that territory would not attract the provisions of section 62(2) of the Copyright Act for the reason that the person is not considered as 'carrying on business' in that place.[131]

In online transactions, it has been held that a plaintiff carries on business at every place from where it can conclude contracts with customers through a website. This was the position in *World Wrestling Entertainment v M/s Reshma Collection and Ors*[132] which concerned a dispute arising from the defendant's alleged infringement of the plaintiff's copyright and trademark. The plaintiff (a US company incorporated) was in the business of selling merchandise such as posters, calendars, and apparel to customers in Delhi through its website.[133] The defendants, on the other hand, were residents of Mumbai and were allegedly engaged in the business of manufacturing infringing goods.[134] The court per Badar Durrez Ahmed J rejected the defendant's contention that the court lacked jurisdiction because the defendant did not reside in its territory and that the plaintiff's hosting of a website to sell its products in Delhi would not amount to 'carrying on business' within the meaning of sections 62(2) of the Copyright Act and 134(2) of the TMA.[135] The court equated transactions which have been concluded in the physical realm with those which have been entered into online through a website.[136] It stated:

> [I]t is possible for an entity to have a virtual presence in a place which is located at a distance from the place where it has a physical presence. The availability of transactions through the website at a particular place is virtually the same thing as a seller having shops in that place in the physical world.[137]

In doing so, the court referred to a dictum of the Supreme Court in *Dhodha House*[138] to ascertain whether the act of sale done through another (in this case, a website) would indicate that the plaintiff was carrying on a business in the territory.[139] Answering in the affirmative, the court stated that the plaintiff's decision to host a website in Delhi through which it was able to sell its products would be regarded as carrying on business in that territory because the essential part of online transactions occurred in that place.[140]

c. Cause of Action

Judicial dicta clarify that 'cause of action' constitutes 'the bundle of facts which gives rise to the right or liability'.[141] It refers to the plaintiff's right to sue.[142] It is 'imperative for the suitor to allege and prove' the cause of action without which the plaint would be rejected summarily and the law would confer the defendant with an immediate right to judgment.[143] In *Kusum Ingots & Alloys Ltd v Union of India & Anr*, the Supreme Court clarified that a court might assume jurisdiction even when a small fraction of the cause of action has accrued in its territory.[144] CPC section 19

[131] ibid.
[132] 2014 SCC OnLine Del 2031.
[133] ibid [2]–[4].
[134] ibid [5].
[135] ibid [11], [12], [21].
[136] ibid [21].
[137] ibid [21].
[138] (n 118) [46].
[139] ibid [21].
[140] ibid [13], [14], [21].
[141] *ABC Laminart (P) Ltd v AP Agencies* [1989] 2 SCC 163 [11]. Also see *Union of India v Andani Exports Ltd* [2002] 1 SCC 567 [16]; and *Sonic Surgical v National Insurance Co. Ltd* [2010] 1 SCC 135, [3]–[6], referring to *IFB Automotive Seating and System Ltd v Union of India* AIR [2003] Cal 80; and *Dhodha House* (n 118) [19].
[142] *Kusum Ingots & Alloys Ltd v Union of India & Anr* [2004] 6 SCC 254, [12].
[143] ibid.
[144] ibid.

impliedly confers jurisdiction on a court which is in the place where the cause of action arose. The provision permits a court to assume jurisdiction in a suit for a wrong done to movables if the harmful act was committed in its territory.[145] However, if the harmful act consists of a series of acts and the act was committed at one place but its consequences were felt in another, the plaintiff may initiate the proceedings either of the two places.[146] Likewise, in a suit for tortious liability for a wrong done to a person, a court may assume jurisdiction when the act was committed in its territory.[147] In such circumstances, the plaintiff has a choice of initiating proceedings in the place where the defendant resides or the place where the wrongful act was committed.[148]

Section 20 of the CPC permits a court to assume jurisdiction when the cause of action occurred in its territory. The circumstances which constitute the cause of action have, however, not been defined by statute.[149] The Supreme Court in *ABC Laminart (Pvt) Ltd v AP Agencies, Salem* devised detailed guidelines to identify the place where the cause of action arises in disputes on contractual matters.[150] Suits for damages arising from the breach of a contract may be initiated at the place where the contract was made or at the place where it should have been performed, and the breach occurred.[151] A court in India may, therefore, assume jurisdiction if it is situated in the place where the cause of action occurred, if it was the *locus contractus* (the place where the agreement was concluded), or the *locus solutionis* (the place where the contract was performed by delivery or payment). According to section 4 of the ICA, as a general rule, a contract is considered to have been concluded at the place at which the offeror has received a communication of acceptance from the offeree.[152] The general rule is applicable to identify the place of the conclusion of a contract which has been using instantaneous communication, such as over the telephone or electronically (through e-mail).[153] In *Baroda Oil Cakes Traders v Parshottam Narayandas Bagulia*, the Bombay High Court stated that contracts concluded by post or telegram would not be subjected to the general rule stipulated under section 4 of the ICA.[154] This is because such agreements essentially depend on the intervention of a third party to transmit a message and are susceptible to being lost in transit.[155] The place of conclusion for such contracts will be the place from where 'the acceptance is put in the course of transmission by the offeree by posting a letter or dispatching a telegram'.[156] For example, the place of conclusion of a contract for the sale of goods between a seller in Delhi and a buyer in Sydney which has been negotiated telephonically will be Sydney if the latter makes an offer to the former to buy a certain product. Sydney is the place at which the offeror received the communication of the acceptance. However, suppose the (same) contract was negotiated by post. In that case, the place of conclusion of the contract will be Delhi which is the place from where the offeree (the Indian seller) communicated its acceptance to the Australian buyer. The court in *ABC Laminart*, however, stated that if the place of the conclusion and the performance coincide, then the suit cannot be initiated before any other forum in India. In such circumstances,

[145] Takwani (n 3) 143.
[146] ibid.
[147] Section 19 of the CPC.
[148] ibid; and *Globe Transport Corpn v Triveni Engineering Works* [1983] 4 SCC 707 [3].
[149] See *Kusum Ingots* (n 142) [12].
[150] AIR [1989] SC 1239.
[151] ibid [15]. Also see, *Halsbury's Laws of India* (n 1) [65.077].
[152] *ABC Laminart* ibid; and *Baroda Oil Cakes Traders v Parshottam Narayandas Bagulia* AIR [1954] Bom 41 [38]. See also N Bhadbhade (ed), *Pollock and Mulla on the Indian Contract and Specific Relief Acts: Volume 1* 14th edn (Lexis Nexis Publications 2014) 137.
[153] See in this respect, *ABC Laminart*, ibid; and *Baroda Oil Cakes*, ibid.
[154] (n 152) [47].
[155] ibid. Also see *World Wrestling Entertainment v M/s Reshma Collection and Ors* 2014 SCC OnLine Del 2031; and Bhadbhade (n 152) 137.
[156] ibid.

the plaintiff is precluded from filing a lawsuit before any other Indian court which may possess jurisdiction by being the place where the defendant resides or carries on business.[157] Similarly, in suits for agency, proceedings may be initiated at the place where the contract was made or at the place where the actions are rendered, and the payment is to be made by the agent.[158]

Suits for the termination of a contract should be initiated within the territorial limits of the court within whose jurisdiction the notice to repudiate the agreement is received.[159] In suits against corporations, a court may assume jurisdiction when a principal office is located within its territorial limits. The Explanation to section 20, however, clarifies that the court's jurisdiction would be ousted (and the location of the principal business of the corporation would be irrelevant) if the cause of action arose in another territory in India which coincides with the place where the subordinate office of the company is located. The decision of the Supreme Court in *Patel Roadways Ltd, Bombay v Prasad Trading Company*[160] succinctly illustrates this aspect. The dispute arose from the alleged breach of a contract which was concluded between the appellant (a corporation in the transport business) and the respondent (which had hired the services of the former).[161] The appellant had its principal place of business in Bombay and a subordinate office in Tamil Nadu.[162] The respondent hired the appellant to send consignments to Delhi from Tamil Nadu, the place where the latter's subordinate office was located.[163] The court stressed that:

> the linking together of the place where the cause of action arises with the place where a subordinate office is located clearly shows that in case of a corporation … the location of the subordinate office, within the local limits of which a cause of action arises is to be the relevant place for filing of a suit and not the principal place of business.[164]

The court added that the intention of the legislature in limiting the place of jurisdiction in the manner indicated above was to alleviate the hardship caused to the plaintiff who would be compelled to travel to the location where the company had its principal place of business.[165] The intention of the legislators, as expressed in section 20 is therefore to level the playing field between the plaintiff and the defendant.[166] This factor will remain an indispensable criterion, even in circumstances when the principal place of business of the plaintiff and the defendant are located in the same place but the cause of action arises in the place where the latter has a subordinate office.[167] The court will presume that the plaintiff had some nexus or connection with that place since the cause of action arose there.[168]

The identification of the place of the cause of action often involves several complexities in disputes arising from transactions which have been concluded online. Although the plaintiff may sue a defendant(s) at the place where the latter resides, carries on business or personally works for gain, the plaintiff may prefer to initiate proceedings at the place where the cause of action occurred to avoid the hardship involved in travelling to another place.

The Delhi High Court in *Banyan Tree Holding (P) Limited v A. Murali Krishna Reddy and Anr*[169] has stipulated guidelines to determine the circumstances in which a court in India may

[157] (n 150).
[158] ibid [15].
[159] ibid.
[160] (n 116).
[161] ibid.
[162] ibid.
[163] ibid.
[164] ibid [9]. See also, *New Moga Transport Co. v United India Insurance Co. Ltd & Ors* [2004] 4 SCC 677 [9]–[12].
[165] *Patel Roadways* (116) [13].
[166] ibid.
[167] ibid [14].
[168] ibid.
[169] 2009 SCC OnLine Del 3780.

possess jurisdiction by being the place of a cause of action under CPC section 20. The plaintiff was a corporation in the hospitality business that had adopted the mark 'Banyan Tree' to operate inter alia several spas under that name in India.[170] However, its registered office was in Singapore. The plaintiff alleged that the defendant was guilty of passing-off its trademark by creating a website which was deceptively similar to the one maintained by the plaintiff.[171] The defendants had their registered office in Hyderabad.[172] However, the plaintiff argued that the proceedings could be initiated in Delhi on the ground that the hosting of a universally accessible website (by the defendant) conferred the court with jurisdiction under section 20 of the CPC even though neither the plaintiff nor the defendant was residing in its territory.[173] The court per Murliadhar J referred to the legal position in the US,[174] Canada,[175] Australia[176] and the UK.[177] It stated that, in a dispute for the violation of a trademark through a universally accessible website, the cause of action is considered to have occurred within a court's territory if the conduct (in the case, the passing off) satisfied the 'tighter version of the effects test' which is also known as 'targeting'.[178] The court rejected an application of the 'effects test' which merely mandates the plaintiff to demonstrate an injurious effect on its goodwill and reputation as being too broad.[179]

Under the 'tighter version', the law imposes an onus on the plaintiff to demonstrate that the website 'specifically targeted' the viewers in that jurisdiction in addition to causing an injurious effect on the plaintiff's business, goodwill and reputation.[180] The fact that the defendant hosted a 'passive website' which lacked any interaction with consumers would not suffice to confer jurisdiction on an Indian court.[181] At the same time, 'the mere hosting of an interactive web-page without any commercial activity being shown as having being conducted within the forum-State, would not enable the court to assume jurisdiction'.[182] The plaintiff must show that the defendant had 'purposefully availed' of the jurisdiction of the forum state by specifically targeting customers to conclude a commercial transaction through the website.[183] The transaction must therefore not be in the form of a 'trap transaction' which has been set-up by the plaintiff.[184] In doing so, the court reversed its earlier decision in *Casio India Co. Ltd v Ashita Tele Systems Pvt. Ltd.*[185] It stated that the 'mere likelihood of deception, whereby an average person is likely to be deceived or confused, was sufficient to entertain an action for passing off'.[186] The dictum did not impose any onus on the plaintiff to prove that the act of the plaintiff had deceived the consumers.[187] The Delhi High Court's dictum in *Banyan Tree* represents the judicial position in India in identifying the place where the cause of action wholly or partially occurred under section 20 of the CPC for transactions concluded online. In subsequent decisions, the courts had the opportunity to demonstrate further that the defendant's mere intention to target the customers of the plaintiff

[170] ibid [3]–[5].
[171] ibid.
[172] ibid [7].
[173] ibid [7].
[174] ibid [11]–[28].
[175] ibid [29]–[31].
[176] ibid [33]–[34].
[177] ibid [32].
[178] Ibid [22], [26], [42]–[45], referring to the decision of the American courts in *Cybersell Inc v Cybersell Inc* 130 F.3d 41; and *Toys "R" Us v Step Two*, 310 F.3d 446 (2003).
[179] ibid.
[180] ibid [42].
[181] ibid [45].
[182] ibid [28].
[183] ibid [28], [40]–[44].
[184] ibid [43]–[57].
[185] 2003 (27) PTC 265 (Del).
[186] *Banyan Tree* (n 169) 34.
[187] ibid.

by hosting a universally accessible website would not suffice in conferring a court with jurisdiction under section 20 of the CPC. It is significant for the plaintiff to prove that the commercial transaction has been completed through the defendant's interactive page.

In *News Nation Networks Private v News Nation Gujarat & Ors*, the Delhi High Court referred to the principles espoused in *Banyan Tree*[188] to determine whether it possessed jurisdiction by being the place where the cause of action occurred while adjudicating a claim in a similar matter, namely, the violation of a trademark in a suit for passing off.[189] The plaintiff was a corporation which operated a Hindi news channel across India under the trade name 'News Nation' along with a website for the distribution of news.[190] It alleged that the defendants, who operated a newspaper with a deceptively similar name, had caused damage to it by operating a website with a similar domain name.[191] Besides the website, the defendants also maintained an interactive page on Facebook to distribute a newspaper.[192] The court relied on the 'tighter version of the effects test' established in the *Banyan Tree*[193] dictum to state that it had no jurisdiction on the matter since the cause of action did not occur in its territory.[194] It clarified that, although the maintenance of the Facebook page would be considered as interactive, it can 'at best be representative of the defendants issuing an advertisement of their product, i.e. the newspaper'.[195] The act did not result in the completion of a commercial transaction.[196] Therefore, the court would not possess jurisdiction regardless of whether the defendant's act of passing off had injured the plaintiff's business and reputation.[197]

Subsequently, in *Impresario Entertainment & Hospitality Pvt Ltd, v S & D Hospitality*,[198] the Delhi High Court examined whether the defendant's promotion and sale of goods and services which were allegedly infringing another person's trademark or copyright on a third-party website would confer jurisdiction under Indian law. The plaintiff alleged that the defendant who was operating a restaurant in Hyderabad under a similar trade name had targeted the former's customers in Delhi by advertising and promoting its services on websites such as Zomato, Facebook and Dine-Out.[199] The defendant's act had consequently led customers to believe that the restaurant in Hyderabad was a part of the plaintiff's brand.[200] The court referred to its earlier dictum in *Banyan Tree*[201] to determine whether the defendant had purposefully availed of the jurisdiction of the forum court.[202] Answering in the negative, the court stated that the allegation did not pass the test stipulated in *Banyan Tree*.[203] The act of the defendant of advertising its services on a website like Zomato was merely an invitation to offer.[204] The commercial transaction would be completed when customers made an offer by expressing their intention of dining in the restaurant, booking a table through the website, and going to Hyderabad for that purpose.[205] For this reason, the defendant's act did not confer jurisdiction upon the court since the maintenance of the webpage

[188] (n 169).
[189] C.S. (COMM) 334/2016, IA No 4525/2016 & 6625/2016, [9].
[190] ibid [4]–[5].
[191] ibid [6].
[192] ibid [11], [12].
[193] (n 169) [22], [26], [42]–[45].
[194] ibid [22].
[195] ibid [15].
[196] ibid.
[197] ibid [25].
[198] 2018 SCC OnLine Del 6392.
[199] ibid [7], [18].
[200] ibid.
[201] (n 169).
[202] *Impresario Entertainment* (n 198) [37]–[42].
[203] ibid [19].
[204] ibid.
[205] ibid.

on Zomato did not result in the culmination of a commercial transaction even though it may have targeted the plaintiff's customers and adversely impacted its reputation.[206]

However, in *Millennium & Copthorne International Limited v Aryans Plaza Services Private Limited & Ors*,[207] the Delhi High Court seemed to adopt a slightly different position when compared to its earlier dictum in *Impresario*.[208] The plaintiff (a corporation in the hotel business with a registered office in Singapore) had instituted proceedings on the ground that the defendant had passed-off the plaintiff's services as those of the defendant.[209] The defendant operated some hotels in Haryana under a deceptively similar trademark, which were listed on third party websites such as TripAdvisor, Goibibo and MakeMyTrip across India (including Delhi).[210] The defendants argued that the Court did not possess territorial jurisdiction over the matter and filed an application for the rejection of the plaint.[211] The court per Rajiv Sahai Endlaw J stated that the ability the customers to make a booking in the defendant's hotels in Haryana from Delhi was an act of carrying on business in Delhi, regardless of whether a reservation materialised.[212] It is irrelevant whether the hotel received payment for the booking considering that it would be 'unable to turn back a customer if [he or she] shows up in pursuance to such booking'.[213] The Court took judicial notice of the fact that in the present era a large volume of bookings and reservations for hotels, resorts and spas are conducted online through third party websites, as against directly or with the help of agents.[214] Therefore, the Court saw no reason to differentiate between the circumstances when a defendant had: (1) maintained an interactive webpage directly; and (2) employed the services of a third party to carry on its business in another place.[215] The dicta indicate that a court will not assume jurisdiction in circumstances where the advertisement merely promotes the defendant's business, which leads consumers to believe that it is the same as the plaintiff's, but does not culminate in any form of contract between the consumer and the defendant.

d. Submission

The provisions of the CPC implicitly indicate 'submission' as a valid base to confer the court with jurisdiction. The parties to a suit may confer jurisdiction on a court through submission. The submission may be express or implied (tacit), and may occur in several forms. CPC sections 19 and 20 delineate grounds on which a court may exercise permissive jurisdiction. The plaintiff may seize the jurisdiction of a court based on any of the factors identified. Judicial dicta clarify that sections 19 and 20 of the CPC do not compel the parties to adjudicate their dispute at any particular place, provided that the requisite factors in the provisions are satisfied.[216]

In *New Moga Transport*, the court illustrated that the law does not require a party to initiate legal proceedings before a court in India simply because the cause of action occurred within the court's territory.[217] Likewise, there is no obligation on a plaintiff to initiate proceedings before a court within whose territorial limits the defendant resides. Instead, the plaintiff may seize the jurisdiction of a court based on the place where the defendant personally works for gain. A plaintiff

[206] ibid.
[207] 2018 SCC OnLine Del 8260.
[208] (n 198).
[209] *Millennium* (n 207) [3].
[210] ibid [22].
[211] ibid [1], [9].
[212] ibid [24].
[213] ibid.
[214] ibid.
[215] ibid.
[216] ibid.
[217] (n 164) [9].

is said to have impliedly submitted to the jurisdiction of an eligible court by the act of filing a plaint and instituting proceedings before that forum. The plaintiff may institute the suit at the place where the defendant resides, carries on business, or works for gain.[218] In a dispute where there is more than one defendant, the CPC permits a court to assume jurisdiction if each of them resides, carries on business or personally work for gain at the commencement of proceedings within the court's territory. The plaintiff may institute a suit in a court where any of the defendants resides, carries on business, or works for gain at the time of the commencement of proceedings, if the others defendants who are outside the territorial limits of the forum have consented to the institution of the suit.[219] A defendant's acquiescence or submission for the purpose of conferring jurisdiction on a court under section 20 may be inferred from the acceptance of a summons. Likewise, the submission of a defendant may also be inferred through his or her voluntary and unconditional appearance before the court to argue a case on the merits.[220] An appearance solely to contest the jurisdiction or to request the stay or dismissal of the proceedings would not constitute voluntary submission on the part of a defendant.[221]

Express submission takes place when the parties to the dispute have concluded a choice of forum agreement to confer jurisdiction on any of the courts in a place where the cause of action occurred or where a defendant resides, carries on business, or personally works for gain.[222] Parties may explicitly opt-out of the jurisdiction of a court through an exclusion clause and instead initiate legal proceedings before another forum in India if it satisfies the prerequisites stipulated in sections 19 and 20 of the CPC.[223] The courts have held that such an agreement (to exclude the jurisdiction of one court and confer it on another eligible forum under sections 19 or 20 of the CPC) is not contrary to public policy or section 28 of the ICA which prohibits and declares null and void all agreements in restraint to legal proceedings.[224] It must be noted that the CPC prohibits parties from initiating legal proceedings before a court which would not otherwise have jurisdiction and the freedom within sections 19 and 20 to choose a forum must be strictly confined to the parameters stipulated therein. Judicial dicta confirm that 'it is not open to the parties by agreement to confer jurisdiction on any court which it does not otherwise possess' under the CPC.[225]

However, as provided in the Explanation to section 20 (discussed above), in suits against corporations, the jurisdiction of the court cannot be ousted in circumstances where the place of the cause of action coincides with the location of the company's subordinate office.[226] In such circumstances, such a court alone will possess jurisdiction to adjudicate the matter. The plaintiff cannot be expected to travel to the place where the company has its principal place of business when the corporation carries on business in the territory of the court where the cause of action arose. It is unclear whether this rule (that the jurisdiction of any other court will be ousted) applies if the place of the cause of action coincides with the place of the company's principal office and not the subordinate office. A close examination of the intention of Explanation 20 indicates

[218] See ss 19 and 20(a) and (b) of the CPC.

[219] ibid, s 20(b).

[220] See *Chormal Balchand Firm v Kasturi Chand Seraoji and Anr* [1936] 63 Cal 1033, 1043 [9], [10], [12]; and *Andhra Bank Ltd v R Srinivasan & Ors* [1962] 3 SCR 391 [9], [11] referring to submission of the defendant to establish the international jurisdiction of a court.

[221] ibid.

[222] See, *Patel Roadways* (n 116) [7], referring to *Hakam Singh* (n 116); *Hanil Era Ltd. v Puromatic Filters (P) Ltd* [2004] 4 SCC 671, [7]–[9]; *New Moga Transport* (n 164), [9], [14], [19]; and *Globe Transport* (n 148) [3].

[223] *Patel Roadways* ibid.

[224] ibid.

[225] ibid [7], referring to *Hakam Singh* (n 116).

[226] See also, *Patel Roadways* (n 116) [5].

that the principle will extend to situations where the place of the cause of action coincides with the location of the company's principal office in the interest of convenience to both the parties.

An express submission may also take place if the parties to a civil or commercial dispute have concluded a choice of court agreement through which they have agreed to confer jurisdiction on the courts in India. Whether or not the parties or their transaction have some nexus or connection with India would generally be irrelevant, provided that the principles of private international law to which the parties are subject permit the choice of any foreign court. There is, however, no reported case-law in which a court in India has adjudicated a dispute arising from an international contract in which jurisdiction was conferred upon the forum by a choice of court agreement and in which the Indian court would not otherwise have had jurisdiction under sections 19 or 20. Existing dicta chiefly concern the validity of choice of court agreements where the parties have opted out of the jurisdiction of an Indian court and instead conferred jurisdiction on a foreign forum. The parties' minimum preference for conferring jurisdiction on an Indian court when it does not otherwise possess the same (according to the principles indicated above) speaks volumes about the perceptions and public faith in the Indian judiciary.

C. Service of Summonses

Upon the determination of jurisdiction, the court will issue a summons on the defendant to appear and answer the claim of the plaintiff within 30 days from the date of service.[227] The service of a summons marks the foundation of the jurisdiction of the court. The process for issuing a summons to initiate a suit before an Indian court is regulated by sections 27–29 read along with Order 5 of the CPC. Although the CPC does not define the term 'summons', it refers to a document issued from the office of a court of justice calling upon the person to whom it is directed to attend before a judge or officer of the court for a certain purpose.[228] The summons must necessarily indicate whether the date fixed is for the settlement of issues or the final disposal of the proceedings.[229] The summons must be signed and sealed by the judge or an authorised officer[230] and shall be accompanied by the plaint.[231] Nonetheless, Indian law does not obligate the court to serve a defendant with the summons if the latter is present and admits to the plaintiff's claim as indicated in the plaint.[232]

i. Service of Summonses in India

The provisions of sections 27 and 28 of the CPC govern the procedure to serve a summons on a defendant who resides, carries on business, or personally works for gain within the local limits of a court's jurisdiction. The court may serve the summons employing any of the means discussed below.

a. Service by the Court

According to Order 5 of the CPC, a service of summons on a defendant who resides within the jurisdiction of the court must be effected through a court officer or by other means of

[227] See s 27, Order 5, Rule I(I) of the CPC.

[228] See Takwani (n 3) 244, referring to E Jowitt, *The Dictionary of English Law* (Sweet and Maxwell, 1972) 1700; and *Concise Oxford English Dictionary* (OUP, 2002) 1435, ff 134.

[229] ibid, Rule 5.

[230] ibid, Order 5, Rule I(3).

[231] ibid, Order 5, Rule 2.

[232] ibid, Order 5, Rule I(I): First Provisio.

communication such as by registered post, speedpost, approved courier service, telefax or e-mail.[233] Likewise, the service of a summons on a defendant who resides in another State in India must be effected by sending it to the court within that State.[234] The service of a summons on a defendant residing within the Presidency Towns of Bombay, Madras and Calcutta must, however, be effected through the Court of Small Causes in that jurisdiction.[235] The refusal of acceptance of the summons by the defendant or its authorised agent is treated as a valid acceptance under Indian law.[236]

b. Service by the Plaintiff

The court may at its discretion additionally permit the plaintiff to serve a summons on a defendant.[237]

c. Personal or Direct Service

In general, a summons must be served by delivering a copy of the same to the defendant.[238] In such circumstances, a court officer may, however, serve the summons on an authorised agent or on an adult family member of the defendant if the latter is absent from his or her residence at the time of service and there is no likelihood of being found.[239] Likewise, in a suit relating to the defendant's business, work or immovable property, a summons may similarly be served on an authorised agent if the defendant resides outside the jurisdiction of the court. In a suit against a corporation, the court must ordinarily serve a summons on the company's secretary, director or principal officer by leaving it at (or sending it by registered post, speedpost or electronic mail) to the company's registered office.[240] In the absence of a registered office, the summons may be served by sending it to the place where the corporation 'carries on its business' according to the criteria mentioned above.[241] In a suit against a partnership which carries on a business within the territorial limits of the court's jurisdiction, the summons must be served on any of the partners. In circumstances where the partnership has its principal place of business in India, the summons may be served on any person having control or management over the partnership.[242] The summons should, however, be served on each of the partners if the plaintiff is aware of the dissolution of the partnership at the time of the institution of a suit. In the case of suits concerning immovable property, the CPC authorises a court officer to serve the summons on an agent of the defendant who is in charge of the property in the absence of an agent authorised to accept service.[243]

[233] ibid, Order 5, Rule 9(3).
[234] ibid, s 28 read along with Order 5, Rules 21 and 23.
[235] ibid, Order 5, Rule 22.
[236] ibid, Order 5, Rule 9(5).
[237] ibid, Order 5, Rule 9A.
[238] ibid, Order 5, Rule 12.
[239] ibid, Order 5, Rules 12 and 15.
[240] ibid, Order 29, Rules 2(a) and (b) read along with s 20 of the Companies Act 2013 and Rule 35 of Companies (Incorporation) Rules, 2014.
[241] See section III.B.ii.b of this chapter.
[242] ibid, Order 30, Rules 3(a) and (b).
[243] ibid, Order 5, Rules 13 and 14.

d. Substituted Service

In exceptional circumstances, a summons may be served by affixing a copy on the door or other conspicuous part of the defendant's residence or place of business.[244] The CPC authorises a court officer to serve a summons in such a manner if the defendant or agent: (1) has refused to sign the acknowledgement of service; or (2) cannot be found within a reasonable period.[245]

ii. Special Rules for Service of Summonses in India

The CPC stipulates special rules for the service of summonses whenever a suit is initiated against certain persons as discussed below.

a. Soldiers, Sailors and Air Force Personnel

Service must be effected on the individual's commanding officer.[246] In such situations, the service may, however, be effected personally.[247]

b. Prisoners

The summons must be served on the officer in charge of the prison through post, fax, electronic mail, courier service or any other means authorised by the High Court.[248]

c. Public Officers (not Belonging to the Indian Military, Navy or Air Force) and Servants of a Railway or Local Authority

Service should be effected through the head of the office the person is employed.[249]

iii. Service of Summonses Abroad

In certain circumstances, the court may permit serve of a summons outside India provided that it possesses jurisdiction to adjudicate on the relevant matter. Section 29 read along with Order 5 of the CPC prescribes the procedure for service of a summons on a defendant residing outside India. The service of a summons outside India would be necessary whenever a dispute arises in relation to: (1) immovable property which has its *situs* within the territorial limits of the court's jurisdiction'; (2) the infringement of a trademark or copyright – where the court possesses jurisdiction under sections 62(2) of the Copyrights Act or 134(2) of the TMA, by being the place where the plaintiff resides; (3) a cause of action which occurred wholly or partly within its territory. There is no general rule for the service of a summons in such circumstances. Service must be effected depending on the peculiarities of each case. The court may cause the summons to be served abroad according to a number of means.

[244] ibid, Order 5, Rules 17 and 18.
[245] ibid.
[246] ibid, Order 5, Rule 28; and *Halsbury's Laws of India* (n 1) [65.301].
[247] *Halsbury's Laws of India*, ibid, referring to *Charan Singh v Dewan Singh* AIR [1972] Punj & Har 288, at ff 3.
[248] ibid, Order 5, Rule 24; and *Halsbury's Laws of India* ibid, [65.298].
[249] ibid, Order 5, Rule 27.

a. Service on a Defendant Residing in a Foreign Territory to which the Provisions of the CPC Apply or within the Jurisdiction of a Civil or Revenue Court Outside India Established with the Central Government's Authority

In such circumstances, service should be through the relevant court and effected as though the summons emanates from the latter.[250]

b. Service of Summons on a Defendant with No Agent

if the defendant has no authorised agent to accept service,[251] the summons should be sent to the defendant's residence by post, fax, email, approved courier service or other authorised manner.[252]

c. Service of Summons on a Defendant Residing in Pakistan or Bangladesh

For services on a defendant residing in Pakistan or Bangladesh, service of the summons or a copy thereof must be effected through a court in the latter countries.[253] However, service on a defendant who is a public officer (not belonging to the military, navy or air force) or a servant of a railway company or a local authority in either of those countries must be effected through an officer authorised by the Central Government of India.[254]

d. Service through a Political Agent or a Foreign Court

In some instances, the Central Government of India may, in the exercise of its foreign jurisdiction, appoint a political agent or establish a court in another country.[255] Service of a summons on a defendant who is actually or voluntarily residing, carrying on business or personally working for gain in the foreign country must be effected through that political agent, the court of that country, the Ministry of Foreign Affairs of that government, by post or any other means which has been authorised by the Central Government.[256]

D. Limitations to the Court's Jurisdiction

In general, there is a presumption in favour of the jurisdiction of the court.[257] Therefore, no court can refuse to exercise jurisdiction 'if it is of the description mentioned in the Section'.[258] Nonetheless, this right is not unlimited. The jurisdiction of an Indian court may be limited in certain circumstances.

i. When there is an Express or Implied Bar to Jurisdiction

Section 9 of the CPC and section 11 of the CCA prohibit a court from assuming jurisdiction in a matter if it has expressly or impliedly been barred to take cognisance of such issues by the law.

[250] ibid, s 29; and *Halsbury's Laws of India* (n 1) [65.299].
[251] ibid, Order 5, Rule 25; and *Halsbury's Laws of India* ibid, [65.299].
[252] ibid.
[253] ibid.
[254] ibid.
[255] ibid, Order 5, Rule 26; and *Halsbury's Laws of India* (n 1) [65.299].
[256] ibid.
[257] See, Takwani (n 3) 54.
[258] ibid 51, referring to the decision of the Supreme Court in *Most Rev. PMA Metropolitan v Moral Mar Marthoma* 1995 Supp (4) SCC 286, 318–319.

A decision of a court which lacks jurisdiction will be *male fide*, *ultra vires* and *dehors* the provisions of the CPC.[259]

a. Express Bar

A provision in a statute which prevents the court from taking cognisance is an express bar on its jurisdiction. Such provisions must, however, be strictly construed.[260] In this respect, section 10 of the CPC adopts the principle of *res sub judice* (a matter being under adjudication) and expressly prohibits a court from proceeding from the trial of a suit in the following circumstances:

(1) The subject-matter of the dispute before the court is also directly and substantially in issue in a previously instituted suit between the same parties who are litigating under the same title; and,
(2) Such suit is pending: (a) in the same or any other court in India having jurisdiction to grant the relief claimed; (b) any other court beyond the limits of India which has been established or constituted by the Central Government and which has like jurisdiction; or (c) before the Supreme Court.

The provision aims to prevent concurrent proceedings and inconsistent judgments in circumstances where two or more courts in India are eligible to adjudicate on the matter. To illustrate, in a suit for the infringement of a trademark, the plaintiff may initiate the proceedings at: (1) Delhi as the place where it carries on business under section 134(2) of the TMA; and (2) Calcutta as the place where the defendant carries on business under section 20 of the CPC. In such circumstances, the law imposes a duty on the court in Calcutta to stay the matter if the proceedings are already pending before a court in Delhi.[261] The Explanation to section 10 states that the provision is applicable only in situations when there are concurrent proceedings before two courts in India. As a result, there is no bar on an Indian court assuming concurrent jurisdiction if the previously instituted suit is before a foreign forum.

Judicial dicta demonstrate that the freedom available to an Indian court under section 10 to proceed to hear a matter which is pending before a foreign forum is inapplicable when the parties have concluded a choice of court agreement in favour of the foreign forum.[262] In such circumstances, the jurisdiction of the Indian court would be ousted, save in exceptional circumstances. A detailed discussion of this aspect is dealt with below. The provisions of section 10 are, therefore, restricted to circumstances in which a foreign court possesses jurisdiction in some other way according to the provisions of its private international law.

To illustrate: A (a plaintiff who is carrying on a business in Delhi) sues B (a defendant who is domiciled and residing in France) for the infringement of copyright owned by the former. Two courts would have concurrent jurisdiction in such matters. The court in Delhi would possess jurisdiction under section 134(2) of the TMA. The court in France would also be eligible to adjudicate the matter under Article 4 of the Brussels I *bis* Regulation[263] as the place where the

[259] ibid 56.
[260] ibid.
[261] See the decision of the Supreme Court in *Manohar Law Chopra v Seth Hiralal* AIR [1962] SC 527.
[262] See the decision of the Supreme Court in *Modi Entertainment Network and Another v W.S.G. Cricket PTE Ltd* [2003] 4 SCC 341.
[263] Brussels Convention on Jurisdiction and Enforcement of Judgments in Civil and Commercial Matters, 27 September 1968 [the Brussels Convention], which is now replaced by Regulation (EU) No 1215/2012 of The European Parliament and of the Council of 12 December 2012 on Jurisdiction and the Recognition and Enforcement of Judgments in Civil and Commercial Matters [the Brussels I *bis* Regulation].

defendant is domiciled.[264] There is no bar on the court in Delhi to stay the matter if it has been subsequently seised of the action. There is no reported case-law to clarify how the Indian court would deal with the predicament of inconsistent judgments when it is called upon to recognise and enforce the decision of a foreign court. Nonetheless, it is likely that the Indian court would give preference to its own judgment at the time of recognition and enforcement of a foreign judgment.

The jurisdiction of an Indian court will also be barred if the decision constitutes a *res judicata*. Section 11 of the CPC prohibits an Indian court from assuming jurisdiction if 'a matter directly or substantially in issue between the same parties' has already been decided in another suit.[265] It is irrelevant whether the case was initiated previously or subsequently. Section 11 accordingly rests on the principle of public policy that judicial decisions must be accepted as correct and that there must be an end to litigation.[266] Referring to the dictum of Sir William de Grey in *Duchess of Kingstone*,[267] the Supreme Court in *Daryao v State of UP* stressed two aspects for the principle of *res judicata* to be applicable. First,

> a judgment of a court of concurrent jurisdiction, directly upon the point is as a plea, a bar, or as evidence conclusive, between the same parties, upon the same parties, upon the same matter, directly in question in another court.[268]

Second,

> the judgment of a court of exclusive jurisdiction, directly on the point, is, in the like manner, conclusive upon the same matter, between the same parties, coming incidentally in question in another court, for a different purpose.[269]

Explanation IV to section 11 clarifies that the principle extends to 'every matter which might or ought to have been made a ground of defence or attack in the former suit'. In circumstances where the court has decided on several issues, each of the findings will operate as *res judicata* between all parties and bar the jurisdiction of all other courts from adjudicating on the matter.[270] Conversely, a question which has not constituted an issue in the previous suit will not operate as *res judicata* to bar the jurisdiction of a court in another hearing.[271]

b. Implied Bar

A court would be impliedly barred from exercising jurisdiction if it is prevented from taking cognisance according to the general principles of the law and the public policy of India.[272] The decision of the High Court of Punjab and Haryana in *Union of India v Ram Chand*[273] sheds light on this aspect. The court was seised of a dispute while exercising its appellate jurisdiction, which

[264] Art 4 of the Brussels I *bis* Regulation confers mandatory jurisdiction on the courts of the Members States. It provides that:

> subject to this Regulation, persons domiciled in a Member State shall, whatever their nationality, be sued in the courts of that Member State.

[265] See in this respect Explanations I and IV to s 11 of the CPC.

[266] Takwani (n 3) 68, 71.

[267] *Smith's Leading Cases* vol 2, 13th edn (Sweet and Maxwell, London 1929) 644, 645.

[268] AIR [1961] SC 1457 [10].

[269] ibid.

[270] Takwani (n 3) 87, 92–93.

[271] ibid.

[272] See Takwani (n 3) 53.

[273] AIR [1955] Punj 166.

arose from the alleged wrongful discharge of the respondent by an army commander under the Indian Army Act.[274] However, the court refused to adjudicate on the matter on the ground that such disputes are opposed to the public policy of India.[275] The court reasoned refusal that the Government of India Act 1935 provides for Crown servants (including soldiers) to hold office at pleasure and their services may be terminated at any time without notice.[276] Thus, although section 9 did not expressly bar civil courts from taking cognisance of such suits, 'public policy is a good ground which impliedly bars suits of a civil nature'.[277] It would be against the public policy of India for the court to assume jurisdiction in such circumstances by being 'injurious to and against the public weal'.[278]

The decision of the Supreme Court in *Dhulabhai v State of MP*[279] and *Raja Ram Kumar Bhargava v Union of India*[280] further illustrate the circumstances in which the jurisdiction of a civil court would be impliedly barred for being against the general principles of law. In *Dhulabhai*,[281] the court, while exercising its appellate jurisdiction, was seised of a dispute which arose from the State Government of Madhya Pradesh's alleged illegal levy of tax from the appellants who were tobacco dealers. The appellants sought a refund of the tax on the ground that the levy was constitutionally prohibited under the provisions of the Constitution of India 1950.[282] The provisions of the Madhya Bharat Sales Tax Act 1950, however, prohibited any court from questioning an assessment made or order passed under the statute.[283] The Supreme Court clarified that the jurisdiction of the civil courts would be impliedly barred in situations where a statute gives finality to the orders of special tribunals.[284] In such circumstances, the special tribunal will have exclusive jurisdiction on the dispute unless it has 'not acted in conformity with the fundamental principles of judicial procedure'.[285] The court added that the jurisdiction of a court would also be impliedly barred if a statute creates a special right and liability and further empowers a tribunal to adjudicate all questions concerning that right or liability.[286]

In *Raja Ram Kumar*, the court added that the jurisdiction of the civil court would be ousted if a statute creates a right which has not been recognised under common law and further provides a machinery for the enforcement of the right before some other competent authority.[287] In such cases, the right and the remedy are created at the same moment by legislation.[288] The situation would, however, be different when a statute specifies a right which pre-exists at common law, but stipulates a new remedy for its violation and does not expressly exclude the jurisdiction of the civil court.[289] In such cases, the civil court will possess concurrent jurisdiction and the parties may elect the forum in which to adjudicate their disputes.[290] A subsequent decision of the Madras

[274] ibid.
[275] ibid [53].
[276] ibid [40].
[277] ibid [53].
[278] ibid [31].
[279] AIR [1969] SC 78.
[280] 1988 171 ITR 254.
[281] (n 279).
[282] ibid referring to Art 301 of the Constitution of India 1950, which states that 'subject to the other provisions of this Part, trade, commerce and intercourse throughout the territory of India shall be free'.
[283] ibid [1], referring to s 17 of the Madya Bharat Sales Tax Act 1950, Act 30 of 1950.
[284] ibid 682 [A]–[C].
[285] ibid.
[286] ibid 89–90 [32].
[287] *Raja Ram Kumar* (n 280) [19].
[288] ibid.
[289] ibid.
[290] ibid.

High Court in *Chiranjeevi Rathnam v Ramesh*[291] illustrates this point. The dispute was initiated by the members of a private limited company alleging that indoor management was allegedly oppressive.[292] The question before the court was whether a civil court had jurisdiction to declare the appointment of some directors as void and grant a permanent injunction to restraint the company from conducting an extraordinary annual general meeting.[293] The court referred to the dicta of the Supreme Court in *Dhulabhai*[294] and *Raja Ram*.[295] It stated that the appointment of the directors of a company is a statutory right created by the Companies Act 2013.[296] Thus, it was not a common-law right.[297] Section 430 of the Companies Act 2013 bars the intervention of the civil court in proceedings in which jurisdiction has been conferred on a special tribunal or appellate tribunal[298] by sections 241 and 242 of the Companies Act 2013.[299] In such circumstances, the civil court will have no jurisdiction to adjudicate on the matter.[300]

Academic writings clarify that the jurisdiction of a court will be ousted if a statute confers the decision of the tribunal with finality and provides an 'adequate remedy to do what the civil courts would normally do in a suit'.[301] However, 'the mere conferment of special jurisdiction on a tribunal' in a matter has been held not to oust the jurisdiction of a civil court.[302] A court would continue to have jurisdiction if the tribunal had 'not acted in conformity with the fundamental principles of judicial procedure'.[303]

ii. Forum Non Conveniens

The doctrine of *forum non-conveniens* permits a court to stay proceedings on the ground that some other forum is more appropriate to adjudicate the matter in the interests of justice. The doctrine was developed by the courts in Scotland and was later adopted with minor modifications in the US.[304] The principle has also been adopted in Indian law.

The development of the principle of *forum non conveniens* can be traced back to the decision of the House of Lords in *The Atlantic Star*[305] in which the courts began to develop guidelines for invoking the doctrine and permitting a stay of the proceedings before them. In *The Atlantic Star*,[306] the dispute arose as a result of a collision of a Dutch vessel with a Dutch-owned barge anchored against a Belgian-owned barge in the territorial waters of Belgium. The owners of the Dutch barge initiated an action in the English Admiralty court. At the same time, the owners of the Belgian barge initiated proceedings before the Belgian court. In due course, the owners of the Dutch vessel also initiated proceedings before the Belgian court and sought a stay of the proceedings before the English court. The court refused to grant the stay and held that, although

[291] C.R.P(PD)(MD) No 870 of 2017.
[292] ibid [16].
[293] ibid [1].
[294] (n 279).
[295] (n 280).
[296] *Chiranjeevi Rathnam* (n 291) [14], [15], [18].
[297] ibid.
[298] ibid [18].
[299] ibid [20]–[24].
[300] ibid [28].
[301] See Takwani (n 3) 56–57, referring to *Dhulabhai* (n 279) 89–90.
[302] ibid 56, referring to *Firm Seth Radha Kishan v Administrator, Municipal Committee, Ludhiana* AIR [1963] SC 1547, 1551.
[303] ibid 55–56, referring to *Section y of State v Mask & Co* AIR [1940] PC 105, 110.
[304] See L Collins (ed) *Dicey, Morris and Collins on the Conflict of Laws Volume 1* (Sweet and Maxwell, London 2012) 538.
[305] [1974] AC 436.
[306] ibid.

the action before the English court could be construed as inconvenient, the plaintiff could not be denied the right to sue unless the proceedings were 'oppressive or vexatious'.[307] The court added that the terms 'vexatious' or 'oppressive' were not statutory but descriptive words to illustrate and indicate the boundaries of the court.[308] Thereafter, the House of Lords in the seminal case of *Spiliada Maritime Corporation v Cansulex Ltd*,[309] stated that, although the application of the doctrine of *forum non-conveniens* was a matter of judicial discretion, the stay could only be granted after the court has weighed all the relevant factors.[310] Thus, the court would stay the proceedings when:

(1) There is another forum which is clearly more appropriate for the trial of the suit and bears a real and substantial connection with the dispute, and
(2) It is more suitable to try the matter before the other forum in the interests of the parties and the ends of justice.[311]

The position of the English court in *Spiliada*[312] has also been accepted in Indian law. A court may stay a matter if there is another forum which is more appropriate to hear the case.[313] The application of the doctrine is limited to matters in which the court has discretionary or permissive jurisdiction under sections 19 or 20 of the CPC.[314] In such circumstances, the court may decline the matter when there is another court which also has jurisdiction under the provisions mentioned earlier, which may be more appropriate to adjudicate the matter. However, the principle is sparingly invoked and only when 'valid, sound and good reasons' permit the court to decline the matter before it.[315]

The decision of the Supreme Court in *Mayar (HK) Ltd. v Owners and Parties, Vessels MV Fortune Ltd*,[316] illustrates this point. The Court upheld the decision of the High Court, which had refused to decline jurisdiction on the ground that a forum in Singapore was more appropriate. The dispute arose as a result of an alleged breach of a contract between the plaintiff (a company incorporated in Hong Kong) and the defendant (a company incorporated and carrying on business in Singapore).[317] The defendant undertook to supply timber logs to the plaintiff at the port in Calcutta.[318] The plaintiff initiated the proceedings before the Calcutta High Court, which was the place where the cause of action arose, on the ground that the defendant breached the contract by supplying quantities which were less than those agreed under the contract.[319] The defendant, however, contended that the Singapore Court was more appropriate to adjudicate the dispute as its principal place of business was in Singapore.[320] The Court refused to stay the proceedings.

[307] ibid 468.
[308] ibid.
[309] [1987] AC 40 HL.
[310] C Schulze *On Jurisdiction and the Recognition and Enforcement of Foreign Money Judgements* (Edinburgh University Press 2005) 67 referring to *Spiliada* ibid.
[311] *Spiliada* ibid. For a detailed discussion on the applicability of the doctrine of *forum non conveniens* in English law, see Collier (n 4) 84–108; Briggs (n 4) 101–105.
[312] ibid.
[313] See *Moser Baer India Ltd. v Koninklijke Philips Electronics NV* 2008 (102) DRJ 713 [7].
[314] See *Kusum Ingots* (n 142); *Ansal Buildwell Ltd. v North Eastern Indira Gandhi Institute of Health and Medical Science* ILR [2005] 1 Del. 751 [25]; and *Glaxosmithkline Consumer Healthcare Ltd. & Ors. v Heinz India (P) Limited* 2019 SCC OnLine Del 9 [16].
[315] See *Sterling Agro Industries v Union of India* AIR [2011] Del 174 [29]; and *Glaxosmithkline Consumer Healthcare Ltd. & Ors. v Heinz India (P) Limited* 2019 SCC OnLine Del 9 [24].
[316] AIR [2006] SC 1828.
[317] ibid [3].
[318] ibid.
[319] ibid.
[320] ibid [32].

It referred to the dictum of the House of Lords in *Spiliada*.[321] It held that the burden was on the defendant who is seeking a stay to place relevant material before the court to demonstrate that there is another available forum which is 'clearly more appropriate'.[322] The defendant must prove two factors when requesting the court to decline its jurisdiction. First, that the proceedings before the court which has been seised would result in injustice by being vexatious or oppressive.[323] Second, that a stay would not deprive the other party of any 'legitimate personal or juridical advantage' otherwise available to it.[324] The Court did not clarify the factors that would be considered in analysing the 'legitimate personal or juridical advantage'. However, Collier, referring to the expression under English law, suggests that the Court will consider factors such as the damages that would be awarded to the other party, the limitation period, the interest-rate, the procedure for disclosing evidence, and other advantages such as the relative ease of enforcing a decision, before determining whether that party would be deprived of a 'legitimate personal or juridical advantage' if a stay is granted.[325]

The law, consequently, places an obligation on the court to balance the convenience of both the parties before declining jurisdiction.[326] In *Glaxosmithkline Consumer Healthcare Ltd. & Ors. v Heinz India (P) Limited*, the Delhi High Court commented that the principle must be invoked

> with caution when advantages and interest of justice clearly outweigh proceedings before a court which in law has jurisdiction but another court having concurrent jurisdiction is the more 'natural' and the plaintiff has deliberately avoided the said forum.[327]

In such circumstances, the court may refrain from assuming jurisdiction to prevent the proceedings from becoming oppressive or vexatious.[328] Although there are no fixed criteria, the courts have stated that they would assess connecting factors such as the existence of a more appropriate forum, the expenses involved, the law governing the transactions and other ancillary aspects.[329] In certain circumstances, the court may also examine the plausibility of multiple proceedings and conflicting judgments before invoking the principle.[330] Existing dicta demonstrate that the courts will decline to exercise jurisdiction if they have been seised of a matter by reason of their being in the place where the cause of action arose, if such place does not constitute a material, essential or integral part of the dispute.[331] It is irrelevant whether only a small fraction of the cause of action occurred within a court's territory provided that it constitutes a material part of the dispute.[332] Accordingly, only those facts which are necessary to adjudicate the *lis* would determine whether or not a court declines jurisdiction.[333]

[321] (n 309).
[322] *Mayar* (n 316) [29], [30], [32].
[323] ibid.
[324] ibid.
[325] Collier (n 4) 88, 89.
[326] *Sterling Agro* (n 315) [31].
[327] See *Glaxosmithkline Consumer Healthcare* (n 315) [30].
[328] ibid.
[329] See *Milk Food Ltd v Union Bank of India* 2007 (2) CTLJ 362 (Del) [28], [41]; *Sterling Agro* (n 315) [31]; *Glaxosmithkline Consumer Healthcare* (n 315) [21].
[330] *Glaxosmithkline Consumer Healthcare* ibid, [30].
[331] *Sterling Agro* (n 315) [16], [20], and [24]. Also see the decisions of the Supreme Court in *ONGC v Utpal Kumar Basu* [1994] 4 SCC 711; *National textile Corporation Ltd v Haribox Swalram* [2004] 9 SCC 786; and *Alchemist Ltd & Anr v State Bank of Sikkim & Ors* [2007] 11 SCC 335; and the decisions of the Delhi High Court in *Milk Food* (n 329) [28], [41]; and *Glaxosmithkline Consumer Healthcare* (n 315).
[332] ibid.
[333] See *Lohia Starlinger Ltd v Govt of NCT of Delhi* [2006] VAD (Del) 732.

iii. When the Parties have Concluded a Choice of Court Agreement in Favour of a Foreign Forum

The conclusion of a choice of court agreement or a forum selection clause through which the parties agree to adjudicate their disputes before a foreign forum may also oust the jurisdiction of the court. The CPC is silent on the operation of choice of court agreements in favour of a foreign forum. In such circumstances, the legal principles to govern forum selection clauses are developed by judicial dicta. Historically, parties to a contract were prohibited from ousting the jurisdiction of the courts in India. Such ouster clauses were construed as contradictory to the public policy of India. As indicated in the preceding section, the CPC merely permitted the parties to conclude a choice of court agreement through which they could confer jurisdiction on any forum under sections 19 and 20 to the exclusion of all others.[334] For instance, a dispute between A (the plaintiff, a resident of Rome) and B (the defendant, a resident of Mumbai) cannot be initiated before the courts in Delhi unless the cause of action which is material to the claim arose or the defendant carried on its business there. In this respect, the Supreme Court in *ABC Laminart (P) Ltd v AP Agencies* had stated:

> [S]o long as the parties to a contract do not oust the jurisdiction of all the courts which would otherwise have jurisdiction to decide the cause of action under the law, it cannot be said that the parties have by their contract ousted the jurisdiction of the court. Where there may be two or more competent courts which can entertain a suit consequent upon a part of the cause of action having arisen there within, if the parties agreed to vest jurisdiction in one such court to try the dispute which might arise as between themselves, the agreement would be valid.[335]

The Court further enunciated that:

> an agreement which purports to oust the jurisdiction of the court absolutely is contrary to public policy and, hence, void.[336]

However, under the present principles of private international law, the parties may oust the jurisdiction of the courts in India by concluding a choice of court agreement in favour of a foreign forum.

The Supreme Court's dictum in *British India Steam Navigation Co. Ltd. v Shanmughavilas Cashew Industries*[337] paved the way for the acceptance of choice of court agreements in international civil and commercial matters. The parties had concluded a choice of court agreement in favour of the English courts to adjudicate the disputes which might arise from their contract, which was evidenced by a bill of lading.[338] The Court stated:

> [T]he parties to a contract in international trade or commerce may agree in advance on the forum, which is to have jurisdiction to determine disputes which may arise between them. The chosen court may be a court in the country of one or both the parties, or it may be a neutral forum. The jurisdiction clause may provide for a submission to the courts of a particular country, or a court identified by a formula in a printed standard form, such as a bill of lading referring disputes to the courts of the carrier's principal place of business.[339]

[334] See the text accompanying notes 223–225.
[335] [1989] 2 SCC 163 [16].
[336] ibid [8].
[337] [1990] 3 SCC 481.
[338] ibid, 482.
[339] ibid [17].

In *Modi Entertainment Network and Another v. W.S.G. Cricket PTE Ltd*,[340] the Supreme Court enunciated the principles to grant an anti-suit injunction when the parties to an international contract had ousted the jurisdiction of an Indian court, which was the natural forum and instead conferred it on a foreign forum. The parties had concluded a contract which was evidenced by a licensing agreement through which the respondent granted the appellant an exclusive licence to telecast the ICC tournament, which was taking place in Kenya, on an Indian television channel.[341] As a part of the agreement, the appellant could sell advertising slots. The parties expressly agreed to confer non-exclusive jurisdiction on the English courts to adjudicate any disputes arising from the contract.[342] After the commencement of the telecast, the respondent complained to the television channel that the signals of the cricket tournament were being received in the Middle East.[343] The respondent requested the appellant to rectify the same, failing which it would discontinue the transmission.[344] The respondent sent the appellant a notice when the latter ignored the complaint.[345] The respondent initiated proceedings before the English court. In retaliation, the appellant filed a suit before the Bombay High Court to claim damages from the loss of advertising revenue.[346] The appellant also sought an anti-suit injunction against the respondents claiming that suit should be initiated before the Bombay High Court, which was the natural forum under section 20 of the CPC.[347] The Court granted an interim injunction on a prima facie finding that proceedings before the English court would be vexatious and oppressive.[348] The Supreme Court on appeal rejected the appellant's application for an anti-suit injunction to prevent the respondent from resolving the dispute before the English court as the chosen forum.[349] The Court stated that courts in India are courts of equity and exercise jurisdiction *in personam*. Therefore, they are empowered to grant an anti-suit injunction against a party over whom they have personal jurisdiction. Nonetheless,

> having regard to the rule of comity, this power will be exercised sparingly because such an injunction though directed against a person, in effect causes interference in the exercise of jurisdiction by another court.[350]

The Court clarified that the principles of Indian private international law permit parties to confer exclusive or non-exclusive jurisdiction over any foreign forum, including a neutral one, to adjudicate their international contracts.[351]

An exclusive jurisdiction agreement is one where the parties agree to adjudicate their disputes only before the court or courts indicated in the contract to the exclusion of all other forums. An agreement of this kind, therefore, precludes the parties from initiating actions arising out of their contract before another court.[352] For instance, a contractual clause which reads: 'Proceedings under this contract shall be initiated only before the District Court of Seoul or the District Court of Beijing' indicates that the parties have conferred exclusive

[340] (n 262).
[341] ibid [25].
[342] ibid 342.
[343] ibid.
[344] ibid.
[345] ibid.
[346] ibid.
[347] ibid.
[348] ibid.
[349] ibid [11].
[350] ibid [10].
[351] ibid [11].
[352] See T Hartley and M Dogauchi, 'Explanatory Report on the 2005 Hague Convention on Choice of Court Agreements' (HCCH Publications, 2007) [247] www.hcch.net/upload/expl37e.pdf [HCCCA, Hartley-Dogauchi Explanatory Report].

jurisdiction on the courts named in the agreement.[353] Conversely, a non-exclusive or permissive jurisdiction agreement is one where the parties agree to adjudicate the dispute before any one of the courts indicated in their contract.[354] Such clauses do not oust the jurisdiction of any of the courts indicated in the agreement.[355] For instance, a clause in the contract which reads: 'Proceedings under this contract may be initiated before the courts in London or any other court which has jurisdiction under the law of the state in which it is located' is an example of a non-exclusive jurisdiction agreement.[356] Whether a forum-selection clause confers exclusive or non-exclusive jurisdiction on a court will depend on the law which governs the clause. Judicial dicta suggest that the use of the words 'alone', 'only', 'solely' or 'exclusive' will generally lead to an inference that the parties intended to confer exclusive jurisdiction on the chosen forum.[357] The dictum of the Supreme Court in *Modi Entertainment*[358] demonstrates the extreme caution that the Indian judiciary will exercise before disregarding a forum-selection clause favouring a foreign court. In *Modi Entertainment*, the Court stated that it would not disregard the parties' forum selection clause because it would amount to a breach of contract and the court would not abet such a violation.[359] The mere fact that the dispute will be adjudicated before a foreign court which is neutral and does not otherwise possess jurisdiction would not of itself indicate that the foreign court is *forum non conveniens* or that its proceedings are vexatious or oppressive.[360] The Court rejected the contention of the appellant that the English court is *forum non conveniens* because the fact that the parties had concluded a forum-selection clause showed that they had thought about the matter and had foreseen the possible breach of the agreement.[361] The parties would have, accordingly, considered litigation expenses in England versus those in India before they agreed the jurisdiction clause.[362] The Court stated that whether proceedings before a foreign forum are to be regarded as vexatious and oppressive will depend on an assessment of the injustice that would be done to both parties.[363] The Court would assess the injustice to the defendant if it allowed the plaintiff to pursue the foreign proceedings; but also to the plaintiff if it was prohibited from doing so.[364]

The party that is applying for an anti-suit injunction must provide the court with 'good and sufficient reasons' to disregard a choice of court agreement and commence proceedings before another court.[365] The existence of strong reasons to displace the terms of the contract will depend on the facts and circumstances of each case.[366] In ordinary circumstances, a court in India will not grant an anti-suit injunction unless it is to prevent

> injustice in circumstances such as [those] which permit a contracting party to be relieved of the burden of the contract; or since the date of the contract the circumstances or subsequent events have made it impossible for the party seeking injunction to prosecute the case in the court of choice because the

[353] ibid [109], [246]. Also see generally J Fawcett 'Non-exclusive Jurisdiction Agreements in Private International Law' [2001] *Lloyd's Maritime & Commercial Law Quarterly* 234.

[354] ibid, HCCCA, Hartley-Dogauchi Explanatory Report.

[355] Collier (n 4) 96.

[356] HCCCA, Hartley-Dogauchi Explanatory Report (n 352) [109], [246].

[357] See for instance *ABC Laminart (P) Ltd v AP Agencies* [1989] 2 SCC 163 [20], [21]; *Moser Baer* (n 313) [11]; and *Times of Money Limited v Reminthome Corporation & Anr* [2012] 193 DLT 30 [33].

[358] (n 262).

[359] ibid [24].

[360] ibid.

[361] ibid.

[362] ibid.

[363] ibid [17] referring to the decision of the Privy Council in *SNI Aerospatiale v Lee Kui Jak* [1987] UKPC 12.

[364] ibid.

[365] ibid [27].

[366] ibid [26].

> essence of the jurisdiction of the court does not exist or because of a *vis major* or *force majeure* and the like.[367]

Consequently, a court in India may assume jurisdiction to prevent injustice if the chosen court lacks jurisdiction over the dispute under its law for some reason.[368] For instance, this may be the position when the choice of court agreement is null and void under the law of the foreign court – such as when one (or both) of the parties lacked the capacity to conclude the contract.

In certain circumstances, the pendency of a multi-party action before a court in India may qualify for the grant of an anti-suit injunction to prevent the opposite party from continuing the proceedings before the foreign forum and to avoid conflicting judgments.[369] Referring to the position in English common law, the court in *Modi Entertainment* accordingly stated that:

> where the dispute was between two contracting parties, one of which sued the other in a non-contractual forum, and the claims fell within the scope of the exclusive jurisdiction clause in their contract, and the interests of other parties were not involved, effect would in all probability be given to the clause. However, the court might well decline to grant an injunction or a stay where the interests of parties other than parties bound by the exclusive jurisdiction clause were involved, or grounds of claim not the subject of the clause were part of the relevant dispute so that there was a risk of parallel proceedings and inconsistent decisions.[370]

The decision in *Modi Entertainment*[371] represents the judicial position in India by the constitutional mandate under Article 141 which states that 'the law declared by the Supreme Court shall be binding on all courts within the territory of India'.[372] The decision has been adopted by courts across India whenever they have been presented with the opportunity to adjudicate a dispute in which the parties have conferred jurisdiction on another foreign forum.[373]

For instance, the Delhi High Court in *Moser Baer India Ltd. v Koninklijke Philips Electronics NV* refused to disregard the parties' forum-selection clause and adjudicate a dispute which arose from a contract evidenced by several Disc Patent License Agreements (DPLAs).[374] The parties had conferred exclusive jurisdiction over the courts of The Hague in the Netherlands.[375] The Court referred to the decision of the Supreme Court in *Modi Entertainment*.[376] It stated that although such agreements were not 'determinative', but a 'relevant factor' as to the nature of jurisdiction, it would not dismiss the proceedings before it 'save in an exceptional case for good and sufficient reasons'.[377] A party seeking an anti-suit suit injunction must, therefore, demonstrate that the conditions precedent stipulated in *Modi Entertainment*[378] have been satisfied. The Court added that the mere fact that proceedings in the foreign court would be expensive and inconvenient for the witnesses travelling from India would not in itself mean that they are oppressive

[367] ibid [24.4].
[368] ibid [24.1.a].
[369] ibid [22] referring to the decision of the English court in *Donohue v Armco Inc* [2002] 1 All ER 749 (HL).
[370] ibid.
[371] ibid.
[372] See Art 141 of the Constitution of India 1950.
[373] See for instance, the decisions of the Delhi High Court in *U. Can Migrate Consultants Pvt. Ltd v Canadian Connections Groups Ltd* [2007] 144 DLT 863; *Max India Ltd. v General Binding Corporation* FAO (OS) No 193/200; and *Swatch Ltd. v Priya Exhibitors Pvt. Ltd* 2008 (101) DRJ 99. See also, the decision of the Supreme Court in *Unique Pharmaceuticals Laboratories Ltd. v Stalco Freight International* 2005 SCC OnLine Bom 1082.
[374] 2008 (102) DRJ 713.
[375] ibid [2].
[376] (n 262).
[377] *Moser Baer* (n 313) [6], referring to the conditions precedent stipulated in the *Modi Entertainment Network* ibid, [24].
[378] (n 262).

or vexatious to the parties.[379] Likewise, in *Piramal Healthcare Ltd. v. Diasorin S.P.A.*,[380] the Delhi High Court refused to disregard the parties' forum-selection clause which conferred exclusive jurisdiction on the courts of Milan when it was called upon to adjudicate distributorship agreement for the sale of diagnostic products.[381]

It must be noted that the right to exclude the jurisdiction of a court in India is, however, limited to disputes which are governed by sections 19 and 20 of the CPC. The parties are prohibited from concluding a choice of court agreement which excludes the jurisdiction of the Indian court under section 16 to 18 of the CPC, which govern the adjudication of disputes arising in relation to immovable property in the Republic. This is for the reason that sections 16 to 18 confers exclusive jurisdiction on the Indian courts in such matters. Although there is no dictum to this effect, it is unlikely that a judgment of a foreign court which has assumed jurisdiction on a disputed regulated by sections 16 to 18 will be recognised or enforced in India.

A forum-selection clause in favour of a foreign (including a neutral) forum is not per se construed as opposed to the public policy of India under section 23 of the ICA. Such clauses are not agreements in restraint of legal proceedings and therefore do not fall within the scope and ambit of section 28 of the ICA, which declares such contracts as contrary to the public policy of India and so void. The decision of the Telecom Dispute Settlement and Appellate Tribunal (TDSAT) in *Kumarina Investment Ltd. v Digital Media Convergence Ltd & Anr* illustrates this.[382] In the case,[383] the TDSAT stated that the parties' choice of court agreement in favour of a foreign forum is not prohibited by the common law of India or any Parliamentary Act. The petitioner (a company incorporated in Cyprus and operating in Israel) and the respondent (a company incorporated in India) agreed to have disputes arising from their contract adjudicated by the English court.[384] The Indian company agreed to transmit specific television channels to the company in Israel, which would then re-transmit those channels throughout the world.[385] A dispute arose between the parties when the Indian company discontinued transmission of specific channels without prior notice.[386] The Israeli company initiated suit in India for the respondent's breach and challenged the validity of the choice of an unconnected forum.[387] The TDSAT referred to the Supreme Court's dictum in *Modi Entertainment*[388] and stated that the parties' choice of court agreement in favour of the English court was not prohibited by the common law of India or any Parliamentary Act.[389] Accordingly,

> agreements to refer any dispute that may arise to the courts of a country to which one of the parties belongs or on the courts of a third or 'neutral' country are valid as they do not violate either Sections 23 or 28 of the Indian Contract Act 1872; the rules of the Code of Civil Procedure 1908, and the principle that parties cannot by consent confer jurisdiction on a court which does not have jurisdiction do not apply to courts outside India.[390]

[379] *Moser Baer* (n 313) [6], [9].
[380] 172 [2010] DLT 131.
[381] ibid [2.6], [4].
[382] 2010 TDSAT 73 [28].
[383] ibid.
[384] ibid.
[385] ibid.
[386] ibid.
[387] ibid.
[388] (n 262).
[389] *Kumarina Investment* (n 382) 85.
[390] ibid [14].

Existing dicta do not clarify the circumstances in which a court in India will disregard a forum selection clause as opposed to the public policy. Nonetheless, it is likely that such clauses in favour of a foreign forum will not be given effect as they constitute agreements in restraint of trade. Section 27 of the ICA prohibits such contracts and declares them as void for being opposed to the public policy of India.[391] This would be analogous to the position where the parties designate a foreign law as the governing law of their contract and the application of such law in a matter would constitute a restraint of trade. The principles of Indian private international law disregard the parties' choice of law agreement in favour of foreign law if the application of the foreign law will contravene the provisions of section 27 of the ICA.[392]

iv. When the Parties have Concluded an Arbitration Agreement

The provisions of the Arbitration and Conciliation Act 1996[393] (ACA) prohibit a court from assuming jurisdiction in a dispute in relation to which the parties have concluded an arbitration agreement. It is irrelevant whether the dispute is of a civil or commercial nature.[394] Section 8 of the ACA regulates matters of a civil nature in respect to which the parties have concluded an arbitration agreement. A court is accordingly obligated upon being seized of a matter in a dispute between the same parties and the same subject matter to which the agreement relates, to refer the parties to arbitration unless it prima facie finds that the agreement is invalid. Judicial dicta clarify that section 8 of the ACA is a legislative command to the court to refer the parties to arbitration upon an application by the other party.[395] Such an application must, however, be made before the latter has submitted its first statement on the substance of the dispute.[396] The court would have no option but to refer the parties to arbitration if a party has made such application before filing its first statement.[397] The expression 'first statement on the substance of the dispute' must be distinguished from the filing of a written statement.[398] Instead, the phrase connotes a submission to judicial authority by the party making the application under section 8.[399] A party is not considered to have waived its right to invoke an arbitration clause or submitted itself to the jurisdiction of the court before it has filed its first statement on the substance of the dispute.[400] At the same time, the competence of the court will be unhindered, if the subject matter of the arbitration agreement relates to a dispute which the arbitrator is not competent or empowered to decide.[401]

[391] Section 27 of the ICA states:

> Every agreement by which any one is restrained from exercising a lawful profession, trade or business of any kind, is to that extent void. – Every agreement by which any one is restrained from exercising a lawful profession, trade or business of any kind, is to that extent void." Exception 1. – Saving of agreement not to carry on business of which goodwill is sold. – One who sells the goodwill of a business may agree with the buyer to refrain from carrying on a similar business, within specified local limits, so long as the buyer, or any person deriving title to the goodwill from him, carries on a like business therein, provided that such limits appear to the Court reasonable, regard being had to the nature of the business.

[392] See, the decisions of the Bombay High Court in *Taprogge Gesellschaft MBH v IAEC India Ltd* AIR [1988] Bom 157; and the TDSAT in *Kumarina Investment* (n 382) [11], [14], [16], [17].

[393] Act No 26 of 1996.

[394] *H Srinivas v HV Pai* [2010] 12 SCC 521 [6], [8].

[395] *Magma Leasing & Finance Ltd v Potluri* [2009] 10 SCC 103 [17], [18].

[396] ibid.

[397] ibid [17].

[398] See *Rashtriya Ispat Nigam Ltd v Verma Transport Co* [2006] 7 SCC 275 [36].

[399] ibid.

[400] ibid.

[401] See the decision of the Supreme Court in *Haryana Telecom Ltd v Sterlite Industries (India) Ltd* [1999] 5 SCC 688, [4], [5].

Likewise, the conclusion of an international commercial arbitration agreement[402] will oust the jurisdiction of the Commercial Division of the High Court or the Commercial Court (as the case may be).[403] An international arbitration agreement is regarded as 'commercial' if it satisfies the prerequisites of the CCA, as indicated in the preceding part of this chapter. Section 45 of the ACA obligates the court to refer the parties to arbitration at the request of any one of the parties or any person claiming though him, unless the arbitration agreement is 'null and void, inoperative or incapable of being performed'. The jurisdiction of an Indian court will not be precluded if consent to the arbitration agreement was obtained by fraud, coercion or misrepresentation; if the time limit to refer the matter to arbitration has passed; or if the agreement is vaguely worded and it is impossible to refer the matter to arbitration.[404]

The court's decision to retain jurisdiction in commercial matters is similarly based on a prima facie (as opposed to a final) finding as regards the validity of the arbitration agreement.[405] In *Shin-Etsu Chemical Co Ltd v Aksh Optifibre Ltd*, the court demonstrated a preference in favour of a prima facie finding to eliminate the need for elongated proceedings by recording necessary evidence, which is essential for a full-fledged hearing.[406] A court's refusal to refer parties to arbitration is appealable to 'a court authorised by law to hear appeals from such an order'.[407] If the appeal is successful, the court will lose jurisdiction over the matter, and the dispute will be decided by arbitration according to the agreement of the parties.[408] However, the court's decision that an arbitration agreement is valid is not appealable.[409] In such circumstances, the jurisdiction of the court in India would be ousted.

The provisions of the ACA prohibit the court from annulling a foreign award which has been conferred under a valid agreement, regardless of whether it is patently illegal or has not been given on the merits of a dispute.[410] A court in India may, in such scenarios, merely refuse to recognise and enforce foreign awards under the 1958 New York Convention on the Recognition and Enforcement of Foreign Arbitral Awards (New York Convention) or the 1927 Geneva Convention on the Execution of Foreign Arbitral Awards (1927 Geneva Protocol)[411] where one or more of the circumstances set out in sections 48 and 57 of the ACA is present.

IV. Jurisdiction in Actions *in rem*

A court is considered to possess jurisdiction *in rem* if it is called upon to adjudicate upon the status of a person or a thing, as opposed to merely determining the interest of a party to a suit in the subject matter.[412] In such circumstances, the decision of the court will be 'conclusive evidence for and against all persons whether parties, privies or strangers of the matter actually decided'.[413]

[402] See s 10(1) of the CCA read along with s 47 of the 2015 Arbitration Act.
[403] See s 10(1) of the CCA read along with s 47 of the 2015 Arbitration Act.
[404] *World Sport Group (Mauritius) Ltd. v MSM Satellite (Singapore) PTE Ltd* Civil Appeal No 895 of 2014 [26]–[29].
[405] Section 50(1)(a) of the ACA; and *Shin-Etsu Chemical Co Ltd v Aksh Optifibre Ltd* [2005] 7 SCC 234, 238.
[406] *Shin-Etsu* ibid, 240 et seq.
[407] Section 50(1)(a) of the ACA; and *Shin-Etsu* ibid, 238.
[408] ibid.
[409] ibid.
[410] See, *Bharat Aluminium Co. v Kaiser Aluminium Technical Service Inc* [2012] 9 SCC 552, [135]–[142] [*BALCO*], read along with s 48: Explanation 2 of the 2015 Arbitration Act.
[411] The official text of the 1927 Protocol may be accessed in the League of Nations, '*Treaty Series*' vol 92, 301, available at: http://treaties.un.org/doc/Publication/UNTS/LON/Volume%2092/v92.pdf.
[412] ibid.
[413] ibid.

The action *in rem* is intended to 'settle the destiny of the *res* itself'.[414] The judgment will affect not merely the parties to the dispute or those claiming through them, but the world at large.[415]

According to the provisions of the Admiralty (Jurisdiction and Settlement of Maritime Claims) Act 2017 (Admiralty Act),[416] a court in India possesses jurisdiction *in rem* when the dispute concerns a maritime claim against a vessel.[417] The statute, which came into force on 1 April 2018, repealed and replaced the Admiralty Courts Act 1840, the Admiralty Courts Act 1861, the Colonial Courts of Admiralty Act 1890, and the Colonial Court of Admiralty (India) Act 1891. The Admiralty Act confers exclusive jurisdiction on all maritime claims on the High Court within whose territorial waters[418] a vessel is found,[419] regardless of the residence or domicile of the owner of the ship.[420] According to section 5, the jurisdiction of the High Court extends to adjudicating on disputes arising inter alia in the following matters:

(1) the possession or ownership of the vessel or any share of the same;
(2) the employment or earnings of the vessel which arises between the co-owners;
(3) the mortgage or the charge on the vessel;
(4) loss or damage caused by the operation of the vessel;
(5) agreement concerning the carriage of goods or passengers or the hire or use of the vessel;
(6) construction, reconstruction or repair; dues in connection to any port, harbour, canal or dock;
(7) the contract for the sale of the vessel;
(8) damage or threat caused by the vessel to the environment or coastline;
(9) the cost that arose from the removal, recovery or destruction of a vessel which has sunk; maritime lien.

Sections 6 and 7, nonetheless, empower the High Court to exercise jurisdiction *in personam* over claims concerning the collision of vessels or related matters which have resulted in damage, loss of life or personal injury provided that:

(1) the cause of action arose wholly or in part within India;[421] or
(2) the defendant was actually and voluntarily residing, carrying on business or personally working for gain in India at the time of the commencement of the proceedings;[422] and
(3) proceedings which may have previously been initiated before a foreign court against the same defendant on the same subject matter have been discontinued or have come to an end.[423]

[414] ibid.
[415] Collier (n 4) 71–72.
[416] Act No 22 of 2017.
[417] See s 2(1) of the Admiralty Act which states that a 'vessel'

> includes any ship, boat, sailing vessel or other description of vessel used or constructed for use in navigation by water, whether it is propelled or not, and includes a barge, lighter or other floating vessel, a hovercraft, an off-shore industry mobile unit, a vessel that has sunk or is stranded or abandoned and the remains of such a vessel.
>
> Explanation. – A vessel shall not be deemed to be a vessel for the purposes of this clause, when it is broken up to such an extent that it cannot be put into use for navigation, as certified by a surveyor.

[418] ibid, s 2(k) which states that

> territorial waters shall have the same meaning as assigned to it in the Territorial Waters, Continental Shelf, Exclusive Economic Zone and Other Maritime Zones Act, 1976 (80 of 1976).

[419] ibid, s 4.
[420] ibid, s 1(2).
[421] ibid, s 7(iii)(a).
[422] ibid, s 7(iii)(b).
[423] ibid, s 7(2).

V. Reflections on Indian Law: Some Insights based on Global Trends

A. General Remarks on Indian Law

In general, Indian conflict of law rules on jurisdiction in an international civil or commercial matter resonates with the law on the subject in jurisdictions such as Australia, Canada and the EU. These jurisdictions similarly recognise factors such as the residence or the submission of the defendant, the place where a cause of action arose, the situs of immovable property, which has been recognised in Indian private international law as conferring jurisdiction on a court.[424] Under Australian law, the grounds on which a court may assume jurisdiction resonate with those prescribed in India. This can be explained by their common-law heritage. In Australia, the rules on the subject are 'defined by common law and partly by reference to statute'.[425] Although the rules on jurisdiction are not uniform between Australia and India, there are similarities in the grounds on which the courts in both countries may adjudicate a dispute on an international civil or commercial matter.[426]

An Australian court may assume jurisdiction in the following situations:

(1) When the defendant is domiciled or ordinarily resident in its territory.[427] A company which is incorporated or has its principal place of business in its territory is considered to be a 'resident' of that place.[428]

(2) When the cause of action which gave rise to the claim occurred in its territory.[429] Accordingly, the court will be eligible to adjudicate a dispute arising from the breach of a contract if it is the place where the contract was concluded.[430] As a general rule, a contract is considered to be concluded at the place where acceptance was communicated to the offeror.[431] However, the breach of a contract that is concluded by telephone would be the place where the words are spoken.[432] In a related vein, claims arising from tortious liability are subject to the jurisdiction of the court in the territory where the tort was committed or the where damage occurred wholly or in part.[433]

(3) When immovable property is situated in its territory.[434] Whether the *situs* of the property will confer exclusive jurisdiction on the court in whose territory it is situated remains unclear.

(4) When the defendant impliedly or expressly submitted to its jurisdiction.[435] The appearance of the defendant before the court to defend a case on its merits would result in an implied submission to the jurisdiction of that forum.[436] Likewise, the conclusion of a choice of court agreement would result in an express submission to the jurisdiction of that forum.[437]

[424] See for instance Oppong, (n 65) 47 et seq; Davies et al, *Nygh's Conflict of Laws in Australia* 9th edn (LexisNexis Butterworths, Australia 2020) 25 [*Nygh's Conflict of Laws*]; Walker *Halsbury's Laws of Canada: Conflict of Laws* (Lexis Nexis, 2011) 291 et seq; and C Tiburcio and J Dolinger, *Private International Law in Brazil* 2nd edn (Wolters Kluwer, 2017) 299 et seq.

[425] Nygh's *Conflict of Laws*, ibid 25.

[426] ibid 40.

[427] ibid 54.

[428] ibid 54.

[429] ibid 42.

[430] ibid 44–49.

[431] ibid.

[432] ibid 48.

[433] ibid 49–51.

[434] ibid 56–57.

[435] ibid 54.

[436] ibid 62–64.

[437] ibid 62.

In a related vein, the private international law of common law Canada also empowers its courts to adjudicate a civil or commercial matter if the defendant was residing,[438] domiciled[439] or carrying on business in its jurisdiction[440] or had otherwise expressly or impliedly submitted to its jurisdiction.[441] The jurisdiction of a Canadian court in a dispute arising from the breach of a contract is determined by looking at: (1) the place where the contract was made;[442] (2) the place where the contract was performed;[443] or (3) the law governing the contract.[444] Likewise, in matters of tort, the jurisdiction of the court will depend on the place of occurrence of the tort.[445] Disputes arising from an immovable property will be subject to the jurisdiction of a Canadian court if the property has its *situs* within the territory of that forum.[446]

Australian[447] and Canadian[448] law similarly permit an eligible forum to stay proceedings on account of *forum non conveniens* when it is 'clearly inappropriate' and there is another forum which should adjudicate the matter in the interests of justice.

In contrast, the principles of Nepalese private international law, which have been codified by the enactment of the National Civil Code Act 2017, do not seem to make room for party autonomy in the choice of courts.[449] The jurisdiction of a court in Nepal instead depends inter alia, on the residence of the defendant, the *situs* of movable or immovable property, the place of the conclusion or performance of a contract, and the place of payment on a financial transaction or dealing.[450] A court in Nepal will accordingly adjudicate a cross-border dispute in a civil or commercial matter if the defendant resides within its territory; the property is located within its jurisdiction; the contract was concluded or performed in Nepal; or if payment was made in Nepal.[451] In this manner, Nepalese private international law does not refer to the question of submission of the parties to the jurisdiction of the court. The provisions of the statute imply that a Nepalese court is empowered to exercise parallel jurisdiction regardless of whether the parties have conferred jurisdiction on a foreign forum in situations such as those where the contract was concluded or performed in Nepal. In this context, the principles of Indian private international law on jurisdiction, which are codified in the CPC, offer more clarity on the subject.

The conflict of law rules in the European Union (EU) stipulate similar grounds to those found under Indian private international law. The EU rules on the jurisdiction of a court in civil and commercial matters in the EU have been harmonised by the promulgation of Regulation (EU) No 1215/2012 of the European Parliament and of the Council of 12 December 2012 on Jurisdiction and the Recognition and Enforcement of Judgments in Civil and Commercial Matters (Brussels I *bis* Regulation).[452] The provisions of Brussels I *bis* Regulation extend to all

[438] *Halsbury's Laws of Canada* (n 424) 302.
[439] *Club Resorts Ltd v van Breda*, [2012] SCC 17 per LeBel J.
[440] ibid [120]; and *Halsbury's Laws of Canada* (n 424) 305.
[441] *Halsbury's Laws of Canada*, ibid, 299–300.
[442] ibid 317–320; and *Club Resorts* (n 439) [88].
[443] ibid 424.
[444] ibid 318.
[445] ibid 321–322; and *Club Resorts* (n 439).
[446] ibid 314.
[447] *Nygh's Conflict of Laws* (n 424) 33, 39.
[448] *Halsbury's Laws of Canada* (n 424) 341–351.
[449] See Art 718 of the National Civil Code Act 2017 [Nepalese PIL].
[450] ibid.
[451] ibid.
[452] See Recital 8 of the Brussels I *bis* Regulation. Also see the Recognition and Enforcement of Judgments in Civil and Commercial Matters (2007) www.ec.europa.eu/world/agreements/downloadFile.do?fullText=yes&treatyTransId=13041 [Lugano Convention]. The Lugano Convention facilitates closer cooperation in the European Economic Area and, thus, supplements the Brussels I *bis* Regulation.

the Member States (except Denmark), unless the subject-matter does not fall within the scope of its application.[453] The provisions of Brussels I *bis* Regulation were applicable to the UK until the transition period of Brexit, which came into effect on 31 January 2021. In the absence of any clarity at the moment regarding the conflict of law rules on jurisdiction that will be applicable in the UK, it is likely that traditional principles of English common law will come back into effect. Brussels I *bis* Regulation will likely continue to be applicable in the UK by its former membership to the EU, during the transition period of Brexit.

Unlike common law systems, the procedure to assume jurisdiction in civil law systems such as the EU may be described as a closed system.[454] This is because, unlike the conflict of law rules on jurisdiction in common law countries such as India, the grounds on which a court may assume jurisdiction are strictly defined in the civil law systems and the courts have little or no discretion on whether or not to hear a matter.[455] For this reason, the doctrine of *forum non conveniens* finds no place in a legal system such as the EU. In contrast, as has been shown above, in India the grounds on which a court may assume jurisdiction are broad, and the courts have the discretion to accept or decline jurisdiction if there is another more appropriate forum to adjudicate the matter.[456]

The Brussels I *bis* Regulation stipulates five grounds on which a court in a Member State shall possess exclusive jurisdiction. Thus, a court has exclusive jurisdiction over a dispute which concerns:

(1) a right *in rem* immovable property which has its *situs* in its territory;[457]
(2) the validity of the constitution, the nullity of the constitution or the dissolution of the company;[458]
(3) the validity of the entries in public registries;[459]
(4) the registration or validity of a patent, trademark, design or any other similar right;[460]
(5) the enforcement of a judgment of another court.[461]

In all other disputes of a civil or commercial nature, the Brussels I *bis* Regulation confers mandatory jurisdiction on the court of the Member State in which the defendant is domiciled.[462]

Although the residence of a defendant is irrelevant, the rules to determine the domicile of a defendant are akin to those which are applicable to identify residence. The domicile of a defendant who is a natural person is to be determined according to the provisions of the internal law of the forum.[463] On the other hand, a juristic person is considered to be domiciled at its principal place of business, statutory seat, or the place from which its central administration is conducted.[464] In certain circumstances, a court in another Member State (which is not the defendant's domicile) may, however, assume jurisdiction over the dispute if the cause of action occurred in its territory.[465] This will be the position when: (1) delivery of a product in a sale of

[453] see Arts 1 and 2 for a list of subject-matters which are excluded from the scope of the instrument; and Briggs (n 4) 52–53.
[454] See Schulz (n 310) 70 referring to the civil law rules on jurisdiction.
[455] ibid.
[456] ibid referring to the common law rules on jurisdiction.
[457] Art 24(1) of the Brussels I *bis* Regulation.
[458] ibid, Art 24(2).
[459] ibid, Art 24(3).
[460] ibid, Art 24(4).
[461] ibid, Art 24(5).
[462] ibid, Art 4. For a detailed discussion on the 'domicile' of the defendant under Art 4 see Briggs (n 4) 55–57.
[463] ibid, Art 62.
[464] ibid, Art 63.
[465] ibid, Art 7.

goods took place; or (2) services were rendered, within the territory of another Member State pursuant to the relevant contract.[466] Unlike Indian law, the Brussels I *bis* Regulation does not prescribe complicated rules to identify the place where the cause of action arose in claims for breach of contract. The place of the conclusion of the contract is irrelevant and performance is understood as delivery or the place where services were rendered for the purpose of determining the eligibility of an adjudicating forum. A court in a Member State which is not the defendant's domicile may assume jurisdiction over disputes concerning tortious liability if the harm occurred or may occur in the latter's territory.[467] In this respect, EU law is similar to Indian law. Likewise, the submission of a defendant is another ground which confers jurisdiction over the courts of a Member State. The defendant's appearance before a court impliedly confers jurisdiction on the court, unless the defendant's appearance is solely to contest the jurisdiction of that forum.[468]

The conclusion of a choice of court agreement in a civil or commercial matter in favour of a court in the EU will expressly confer jurisdiction on that forum.[469] In such circumstances, the chosen forum is obligated to adjudicate the dispute regardless of the domicile of the parties unless the agreement is null and void as regards its substantive validity under the law of the state in which the court is situated.[470] The parties may not, however, oust the jurisdiction of a court in matters which are subject to the exclusive jurisdiction of that forum, as indicated above.[471] The courts in a Member State may, nonetheless, stay the proceedings in certain exceptional circumstances to avoid concurrent jurisdiction over a matter and inconsistent judgments. This will be the position when the court has been seised of an action which falls within the exclusive jurisdiction of another Member State. A court in a Member State will also be obliged to stay proceedings when the parties have agreed to confer jurisdiction on another forum through a choice of court agreement, unless the chosen forum confirms that it does not possess jurisdiction in the matter.[472]

In all other circumstances (which do not fall within the exclusive jurisdiction of any court or when the parties have not concluded a choice of court agreement), a court is obligated to stay proceedings if a dispute between the same parties and the same cause of action is pending in a court of another Member State.[473] In this respect, EU law on the subject resonates with the principle of *res sub judice* which finds a place in Indian law.[474] The court which has been seised subsequently must wait for the other court to establish its jurisdiction before dismissing the proceedings before it. However, unlike Indian law, the Brussels I *bis* Regulation permits a court in a Member State to exercise its discretion and stay proceedings when a dispute between the same parties and the same cause of action is pending before a court in a non-Member State.[475] In contrast, the principle of *res sub judice* stipulated by section 10 of the CPC does not require Indian courts to stay proceedings when a dispute between the same parties concerning the same cause of action is pending before a foreign court.[476] In such circumstances, the Indian court is authorised to assume concurrent jurisdiction. The Brussels I *bis* Regulation instead authorises a court in a Member State to give 'reflexive effect' to Articles 24 and 25 of

[466] ibid, Art 7(1).
[467] ibid, Art 7(2).
[468] ibid, Art 26.
[469] ibid, Art 25.
[470] ibid.
[471] See Briggs (n 4) 61–62.
[472] See Art 31(2) of the Brussels I *bis* Regulation.
[473] ibid, Art 29.
[474] See s 10 of the CPC and text accompanying notes 260–265.
[475] Art 33 of the Brussels I *bis* Regulation.
[476] See Explanation to s 10 of the CPC.

the Brussels I *bis* Regulation[477] and stay proceedings if: (1) the court in a third country will render a judgment capable of recognition or enforcement in that Member State; and (2) it is necessary for the proper administration of justice.[478] The court in the Member State shall dismiss proceedings when the forum in the third country has pronounced its decision.[479] The Brussels I *bis* Regulation permits a court in a Member State to refuse to stay proceedings if a court in a non-Member State: (1) has (itself) stayed or dismissed the matter:[480] or (2) is unlikely to adjudicate the dispute within a reasonable period.[481] The EU law on the subject thus provides a valuable source of inspiration for the development of Indian law. Legislators should therefore consider an amendment of the CPC to authorise its courts to stay a matter when a dispute is pending before a foreign forum to prevent inconsistent judgments. In doing so, lawmakers may consider the factors prescribed under the Brussels I *bis* Regulation[482] permitting courts to stay matters in such circumstances.

B. Should India Ratify the HCCCA?

India has not ratified the HCCCA which came into effect on 1 October 2015.[483] In such circumstances, the principles on Indian private international law vis-à-vis the operation of choice of court agreements has been developed by case law, thereby rendering the law on the subject unpredictable and uncertain. As the name suggests, the HCCCA regulates the operation of exclusive choice of court agreements[484] in civil and commercial matters among its contracting parties.[485] To date, the HCCCA has been ratified by the EU,[486] Denmark, Mexico, Montenegro and Singapore.[487] China, the Republic of North Macedonia, the Ukraine, the US and Israel have signed the HCCCA, but have yet to ratify or accede to it.[488] In 2017 scholarly writings reported that Australia was likely to ratify the HCCCA,[489] but it is not yet a signatory to the convention.

The HCCCA stipulates the duties of the chosen and the non-chosen court in contracting states when called upon to adjudicate a dispute in respect of which the parties have concluded an exclusive choice of court agreement.[490] Article 5 of the HCCCA prohibits the chosen forum from declining to assume jurisdiction unless the agreement is null and void under the provisions of its substantive law.[491] A court in a Contracting State which has been chosen by the parties

[477] Briggs (n 4) 91–92; and P De Verneuil Smith et al. 'Reflections on *Owusu*: The Radical Decision in *Ferrexpo*' (2015) *Journal of Private International Law* 389, 397.
[478] Art 33(1)(b) of the Brussels I *bis* Regulation.
[479] ibid, Art 33(3).
[480] ibid, Art 33(2)(a).
[481] ibid, Art 33(2)(b).
[482] ibid, Art 33.
[483] See Art 31(1) of the HCCCA.
[484] See HCCCA, Hartley-Dogauchi Explanatory Report (n 352) [247].
[485] Art 1(1) of the HCCCA.
[486] The provisions of the Brussels I *bis* Regulation will govern the duties of the chosen and the non-chosen court when it is situated in a Member State. The provisions of the HCCCA will regulate the duties of the chosen and the non-chosen court when it is situated in one of its Contracting States.
[487] See www.hcch.net/en/instruments/conventions/status-table/?cid=98.
[488] ibid.
[489] See A Mills, 'The Hague Choice of Court Convention and Cross-Border Commercial Dispute Resolution in Australia and the Asia-Pacific' (2017) 18(1) *Melbourne Journal of International Law* 1; and BA Marshall and M Keyes, 'Australia's Accession to the Hague Convention on Choice of Court Agreements' (2017) 41 *Melbourne University Law Review* 246.
[490] See Arts 1(1), (2), 2(1)(a) and 3(a) of the HCCCA.
[491] ibid, Art 5; and P Beaumont and B Yüksel, 'The Validity of Choice of Court Agreements under the Brussels I Regulation and the Hague Choice of Court Agreements Convention' in K Boele-Woelki et al (eds), *Convergences and Divergences in Private International Law Liber Amicorum Kurt Siehr* (Eleven Publishers, 2010) 575–576.

by agreement may, therefore, decline jurisdiction if the contract has been concluded by fraud, duress, misrepresentation, or when the parties lacked capacity to conclude the same.[492] Article 6 imposes a corresponding duty on the courts of Contracting States which have not been chosen, to suspend or dismiss proceedings when seised of a matter to which the agreement relates, save in exceptional circumstances.[493] The non-chosen court is consequently prohibited from granting an anti-suit injunction to prevent the other party from commencing or proceedings before the chosen forum. A non-chosen court situated in a Contracting State may, nonetheless, assume jurisdiction if enforcement of the agreement is not feasible for any one or more of the following reasons:

(1) The choice of court agreement is null and void under the law of the chosen court and the latter has declined to adjudicate on the matter.[494]
(2) Any party to the choice of court agreement lacked the capacity to conclude the same.[495]
(3) Enforcement of the choice of court agreement it would lead to manifest injustice to a party.[496]
(4) Enforcement of the choice of court agreement would be manifestly contrary to the public policy of the state in which non-chosen court is situated;[497]
(5) The choice of court agreement is incapable of performance for a reason which is beyond the control of the parties (for instance, due to the occurrence of a *vis major* or *force majeure* event).[498]

Despite India' resistance to ratifying the HCCCA, its principles of private international law on choice of court agreements in favour of foreign forums corresponds with the instrument to a significant extent. Although there is no reported case in which a court in India has assumed jurisdiction in an international dispute on a civil or commercial matter because the parties have expressly chosen it, the Supreme Court's dicta in *British India Steam Navigation*[499] and *Modi Entertainment*[500] demonstrate the sanctity of choice of court agreements in Indian private international law. An Indian court would not assume jurisdiction when it has not been chosen. It is unlikely that an Indian court would decline to adjudicate a dispute in an international civil or commercial matter when it has been selected. Likewise, the grounds stipulated by the Supreme Court in *Modi Entertainment*[501] concerning the circumstances in which a court may disregard a forum selection clause resonate with those prescribed under the HCCCA. As has been shown above, the courts in India would not assume jurisdiction in a matter in respect to which the parties have concluded a choice of court agreement in favour of a foreign forum, unless it would result in injustice to the parties in some manner or when the contract is incapable of being performed for some reason such as the occurrence of force majeure or the like.[502]

[492] See, HCCCA Hartley-Dogauchi Report (n 352) 55 [125], [126].
[493] Art 6 of the HCCCA.
[494] ibid, Art 6(a).
[495] ibid, Art 6(b).
[496] ibid, Art 6(c).
[497] ibid.
[498] ibid, Art 6(d).
[499] (n 337).
[500] (n 262).
[501] ibid.
[502] ibid [24.4]. Also see generally S Khanderia, 'The Hague Judgments Project: Assessing its Plausible Benefits for the Development of the Indian Private International Law' (2019) *Commonwealth Law Bulletin* 452 [Khanderia, *The Hague Judgments Project*]; and S Khanderia, 'The Hague Convention on Choice of Court Agreements and the Enforcement of Forum-Selection Clauses in Indian Private International Law' (2019) 9(3) *International Journal of Private Law* 125. [Khanderia, *The Hague Convention*].

Although the HCCCA merely regulates the duty of a court in a Contracting State, India's ratification of the convention would play a significant role in augmenting the development of the Republic's private international law. First, the HCCCA would introduce certainty that the Indian courts would not decline jurisdiction when there is none under CPC sections 19 and 2, and when jurisdiction has been conferred through a choice of court agreement. At present, this factor is merely speculative. Second, India's ratification to the HCCCA would improve international trade in the country by introducing predictability concerning the duty of Indian courts to refrain from adjudicating on a matter when their jurisdiction has been ousted and conferred on another forum in a Contracting State, save on the satisfaction of the limited circumstances identified in the HCCCA. At present, in the absence of black letter law, interested parties are expected to peruse a jungle of judicial dicta to be apprised of the current legal position in India. Third, India's ratification to the HCCCA would provide certainty on the former's stance on choice of court agreements in favour of a foreign forum when it contravenes the public policy of the country. At present, there is no clear indication if the Indian courts will assume jurisdiction when the forum selection clause is contrary to the public policy of the Republic.[503] India's ratification of the HCCCA would, therefore, provide significant clarification to this effect.

VI. Conclusion

This chapter examined Indian conflict of law rules on jurisdiction in international civil and commercial matters. An analysis was made of the scope and ambit of the jurisdiction of the Indian courts. It was seen that in general Indian law permits every person to sue and initiate proceedings before the courts in civil or commercial matters. The right to sue is, however, not unrestricted and may be limited due to immunities from legal proceedings that may be conferred by the law on the defendant. This chapter explored the grounds on which an Indian court would assume jurisdiction in a civil or a commercial matter. In doing so, it differentiated between a claim of a civil and commercial nature under Indian law and the mechanism for determining the jurisdiction of the courts. It demonstrated the supremacy of the provisions of the CPC in determining the eligibility of an Indian court to adjudicate on a matter, regardless of whether it is of a civil or commercial nature. It was seen that, although Indian law does not explicitly categorise the jurisdiction of its courts as exclusive or permissive, these have implicitly been dealt with under the provisions of the CPC.

In matters concerning immovable property, the jurisdiction of the court will be exclusive. Thus, *all* disputes arising from immovable property (including those concerning the liability in tort for damage caused to immovable property) shall be mandatorily initiated before the court within whose territory the property has its *situs*. The jurisdiction of the court cannot be ousted through a choice of court or an arbitration agreement. The court may, if necessary, serve the defendant with a summons abroad. However, all other civil and commercial matters are subject to the permissive jurisdiction of the court. The court may, therefore, decline to exercise jurisdiction at its discretion by invoking the doctrine of *forum non conveniens* if there is another forum which is clearly more appropriate to adjudicate on the relevant matter in the interest of justice. The eligibility of the court, in matters which are subject to its permissive jurisdiction, will depend on the place where the defendant resides, carries on business, or works for gain. In suits arising from the infringement of a trademark or copyright, Indian law additionally permits its courts to assume

[503] See the text accompanying notes 382–392.

jurisdiction if the plaintiff resides, carries on business or works for gain within its territory. The occurrence of a cause of action within the territory of the court is another factor which confers jurisdiction on the courts. Thus, in disputes arising from a tortious matter, the court may assume jurisdiction if the damage to the person or movable property occurred in its territory. Likewise, in disputes concerning the breach of the contract, the court may assume jurisdiction if the contract was concluded or was performed in its territory. The place of the cause of action in online transactions will be every place from where the defendant was able successfully to conclude a contract with a customer, thereby causing loss to the plaintiff. At the same time, the chapter highlighted a tendency among Indian courts of staying proceedings by invoking the doctrine of *forum non conveniens* when the cause of action does not form an essential part of a claim.

Lastly, submission before the forum also forms a valid base of jurisdiction. Thus, the parties' express or implied submission to the jurisdiction of the court would suffice in conferring jurisdiction on an Indian forum in a civil or commercial matter. It was seen that the express submission of the parties to the jurisdiction of another Indian court is permitted within the parameters of the CPC. Put simply, the parties cannot oust the jurisdiction of a court and confer it on another Indian court when the latter does not otherwise possess jurisdiction through any of the means indicated above. At the same time, globalisation and the advent of international trade have prompted the development of the principles of Indian private international law. The parties may, under present principles, oust the jurisdiction of an Indian court in matters which are subject to its permissive jurisdiction and instead confer it on a foreign (including a neutral) forum. Likewise, the parties may also oust the jurisdiction of the Indian court by concluding an arbitration agreement. In such circumstances, the Indian court would not, save in exceptional circumstances, assume jurisdiction on the matter.

The chapter highlighted that Indian conflict of law rules on jurisdiction in civil and commercial matters substantially correspond with global practices. It, however, suggested that India should ratify the HCCCA in the interests of predictability and certainty and to improve international trade.

PART III

Family Law

6

Private International Law Practice in Marriage

I. Introduction

Having discussed the conceptual and theoretical dimensions of private international law in India and the rules regulating jurisdiction in Part II, the current chapter will focus on the matrimonial issues of private international law in India.

Marriage is the very foundation of civil society, and laws and definitions have been evolved in response to its religious, social, political, and cultural imperatives.[1] Religion, as a social institution, has profoundly impacted marriage and the laws regulating marriage.[2] The Christian concept of marriage has influenced many western jurisdictions.[3] In *Hyde v Hyde*, Lord Penzance described that marriage, as understood under by Christendom, may be defined as 'the voluntary union for life of one man to one woman to the exclusion of all others.'[4] Hindus consider marriage as a sacrament and union between men and women for seven lives.[5] Islam looks at the concept of marriage as a contract between men and women with permission to have more than one spouse.[6] Under the Indian legal framework, questions of marriage and divorce are strongly influenced by cultural and religious norms. The existence of personal laws based on religious beliefs impacts on private international law practices of India and their reception in other jurisdictions resulting in legal imbroglios.[7]

This chapter is divided into five parts including the Introduction. Section II traces the statutory position of marriage, as well as judicial statements on the subject, with an exposition on the formal and essential elements of a valid marriage. The chapter focuses on interreligious marriages and discusses the reception and acceptance of Indian legal systems in western jurisdictions with particular reference to polygamous marriages. Section III addresses conflict of law concerns arising out of same-sex marriages and critically evaluates the Indian legal response to recognition of foreign same-sex marriage. While scrutinising prevailing Indian legal positions, the chapter also analyses the rules codified by the EU and Hague Conventions on family law matters. Section IV deliberates on Indian engagements with Hague Conventions operating in matrimonial matters. Section V provides concluding remarks.

[1] *Shaw v Gould* [1868] LR 3 HLC [55].

[2] N Tebbe, 'Religion and Marriage Equality Statutes' (2015) 9(1) *Harvard Law & Policy Review* 25–62, 16.

[3] NA Joel, 'Religious and Legal Pluralism in Global Comparative Perspective' (2011) 25 *Emory International Law Review* 967–986.

[4] *Hyde v Hyde* 1 P & D 130; P Diwan, *Private International Law* (Deep and Deep Publications, 1993) 121.

[5] Diwan (n 4) 121.

[6] N Akhtar, *Family Law on Divorce and Judicial Separation* (Deep and Deep Publications, 2003) 192.

[7] AL Estin, 'Marriage and Divorce Conflicts in International Perspective' (2017) 27 *Duke Journal of Comparative and International Law* 485–517, 485.

II. Indian Legislative Framework on Marriage and its Religious Base

Marriages in India are governed by different sets of personal laws. This situation implies an absence of a uniform civil code on marriage applicable to all religious communities (except Goa and Pondicherry).[8] The reliance on personal laws has been in practice since the beginning of British rule in India which did not attempt to adopt uniform rules governing all religious communities.[9] In the post-Independence era, existing laws on personal laws were modified and transformative changes were brought into existence.

The Hindu Marriage Act was enacted in 1955 and applied to all Hindus as well as persons from other religious communities, namely, Sikhs, Jains and Buddhists.[10] In the Act, the conditions of a valid marriage between two individuals of the Hindu faith are given under section 5. These conditions are as follows:

- (i) Neither party has a spouse living at the time of the marriage.
- (ii) At the time of marriage, neither party is incapable of giving a valid consent as a result of unsound mind, a mental disorder making the person unfit for marriage or the procreation of children, or suffering from recurrent attacks of insanity or epilepsy.
- (iii) A minimum of 21 years of age for the bridegroom and 18 years of age for the bride.
- (iv) The parties are not within the prohibited degrees of relationship unless custom or usage permits such marriage.
- (v) The parties are not *sapindas*[11] of each other unless custom or usage permits such marriage[12]

The Indian Christian Marriage Act 1872 regulates marriages among Christians. The essential requirements in this Act are similar to those of the Hindu Marriage Act and, in addition, at least two witnesses must be present at the time of the marriage. The marriage has to be solemnised by a person licensed to grant a certificate of marriage.[13] Under Muslim law, marriage consists of an offer, a subsequent acceptance, and the provision of dower. Such a marriage is regulated by religious precepts and not by laws per se because there is no consolidated act to validate these marriages.[14] The Parsi Marriage and Divorce Act 1936 prescribes the conditions for a valid marriage among Parsis, such as the age of the groom and bride, the solemnisation of marriage by an Ashirvad ceremony performed by a Parsi priest, and the need for two witnesses.[15] The Special Marriage Act 1954 was enacted to give a choice to marry beyond one's religion or caste. The marriage can take place between Hindus, Muslims, Christians, Jains, Buddhists, and Sikhs. The Act extends not only to citizens in India but also to foreign nationals.[16] The Foreign Marriage Act 1969 governs marriages in which at least one of the parties is an Indian citizen and such marriage can be solemnised abroad and later registered under the Act.[17] Unlike the cross-border

[8] S Shetreet and HE Chodosh, *Uniform Civil Code for India: Proposed Blueprint for Scholarly Discourse* (Oxford University Press, 2015) 45.

[9] T Mahmood, 'Religion, Law, and Judiciary in Modern India' (2006) (3) *BYU Law Review* 755–776, 765.

[10] Hindu Marriage Act 1955 (India) s 2.

[11] ibid. The term *sapindas* is unique to Hindu law. Two persons are *sapindas* if they have a common ancestor.

[12] ibid, s 5; See PP Saxena, *Family Law Lectures: Family Law* 3rd edn (Lexis Nexis, 2011) 11.

[13] ibid, s 25; See K Sharma, *Family Law Lectures: Family Law* 4th edn (Lexis Nexis, 2015) 1.

[14] Mehr (dower) means money or property which the wife is entitled to receive from the husband in consideration of the marriage.

[15] Parsi Marriage and Divorce Act 1936, India s 3(b).

[16] Special Marriage Act 1954 (India) s 4.

[17] Foreign Marriage Act 1969 (India) s 4.

child abduction and adoption issues, where global conventions have attempted to establish a uniform approach, cross-border marriage and divorce are primarily left to the traditional conflict of laws approaches of each jurisdiction. Marriage regulation is thus a battleground over which conflicts between religious communities and states have been fought.

A. Determination of the Applicable Law in Marriage under the Principles of Indian Private International Law

i. Formal Aspects of Marriage

With respect to marriage, a fundamental distinction is followed in legal discussion regarding material and formal requirements.[18] Formal aspects include matters of less vital social interest, such as the length of public notice to be given before solemnisation of a marriage, the number of witnesses whose presence is required at a marriage ceremony, etc.[19] Formal matters are exclusively governed by the law of the place of celebration (*lex loci celebrationis*).[20] The 1978 Hague Convention on the Celebration and Recognition of the Validity of Marriages codified rules on formalities of marriage.[21] Article 2 of the 1978 Convention declares that formal requirements for marriages shall be governed by the law of the state where the marriage celebration took place.[22] The applicable law can be refused on the ground of public policy.[23] However, like many Hague instruments on family matters, the 1978 Convention has only been ratified by three countries and has not influenced the evolution of the law on a serious scale.

As far as Indian legislation is concerned, the statutes enumerated above, that is, the Hindu Marriage Act, the Special Marriage Act, and the Indian Marriage Act, do not have an explicit provision on the applicable law to regulate the formal aspects of marriage. However, the Foreign Marriage Act 1969 provides that the 'Central Government … may declare that marriages solemnised under the law in force in such foreign country shall be recognised by the courts in India as valid.'[24] Section 27 of the Foreign Marriage Act also states that the statute would not affect the validity of a marriage solemnised in a foreign country under a foreign law.[25] Section 11 of the Act authorises a marriage officer to refuse to solemnise a marriage if the marriage is prohibited by the law of the foreign country in which the marriage is to be solemnised.[26] This indicates that there is recognition of the principle of *lex loci celebrationis* in respect of formal validity. However, the statute also provides a general exception to the *lex loci celebrationis* rule on formal aspects of marriage. Section 13 of the Act permits the parties to choose the applicable form of marriage.[27] There are not many examples of cases wherein the court has decided questions regarding the

[18] Dicey Morris and Collins, *The Conflict of Laws* 14th edn (Sweet & Maxwell, 2006) 285; MH Hoffheimer, *Conflict of Laws* (Aspen Publishers, 2010) 56.

[19] ibid 285.

[20] RH Graveson, *Conflict of Laws* 7th edn (Sweet & Maxwell Ltd, 1974) 251; *Taczanowska v Taczanowski* [1957] CA 30; *Ogden v Ogden* [1908] CA [46].

[21] Convention on Celebration and Recognition of the Validity of Marriages (adopted on 25 March 1978 entered into force on 1 May 1991).

[22] ibid, Art 2.

[23] ibid, Art 5.

[24] Foreign Marriage Act 1969 (n 17) s 23.

[25] ibid, s 27.

[26] ibid, s 11(1).

[27] ibid, s 13(2).

validity of a marriage under foreign law. In *Noor Jahan Begum v Eugene Tiscenko,*[28] the main question was the validity of a marriage in the event of the religious conversion of one of the parties. The court stated that the English law position is usually adopted in private international law matters in India. Based on this, it can be presumed that the formal validity of marriages will be decided based on the *lex loci celebrationis.*

ii. Essential Aspects of Marriage

Material aspects are considered to be of considerable significance to a marriage and include capacity, consanguinity, religion, etc.[29] Several connecting factors have been advanced for the applicable law governing material aspects of marriage including the domicile of the parties,[30] the *lex loci celebrationis,*[31] and the intended matrimonial home.[32] According to the domicile approach, a valid marriage between persons domiciled in India and Nepal has to satisfy the material requirements of both legal systems.[33] The intended matrimonal home theory dictates that the material validity of the marriage is governed by the law of the matrimonial home of the parties. The intended matrimonial home approach has been criticised as it gives preference to the husband's domicile and has an uncertainty factor, as one has to follow a wait-and-see approach to ascertain the parties' matrimonial home.[34] Countries following the civil law system have adopted the law of nationality as the connecting factor in determining matters of essential validity.[35] In recent times there has been an attempt to consider the relevant factor as that of a real and substantive connection, in which both domicile and intended matrimonial home can play a part.[36] Under the *First Restatement*, the US does not distinguish between formal and essential elements of marriage. The general rule is that the validity of a marriage is determined by the law of the place where it is contracted or solemnised. If valid there, it is valid everywhere. The test of real and substantial connection is followed in the US in the *Second Restatement.*[37] The European approach towards matrimonial issues exhibits broad flexibility.

[28] *Noor Jahan Begum* v *Eugene Tiscenko* AIR [1941] Cal 582.

[29] Graveson (n 20) 251. Consanguinity and prohibited degrees of marriage comes under material validity in India.

[30] Convention on Celebration and Recognition of the Validity of Marriages (n 21) Art 2; See AJE Jaffey, 'The Essential Validity of Marriage in the English Conflict of Laws'(1978) 41 *Modern Law Review* 38–50; *Brook v Brook* [1861] 9 HL Cas 193; *Sottomayor v De Barros* (No 2) [1879] 5 PD 94; *Szecheter v Szecheter* [1970] 3 All ER 905; See also T Baty, 'Capacity and Form of Marriage in the Conflict of Laws' (1917) 26(6) *The Yale Law Journal* 444–463.

[31] R Fentiman, 'The Validity of Marriage and the Proper Law' (1985) 44(2) *Cambridge Law Journal* 256–279, 259; C M Schmitthoff, 'Validity of Marriage and the Conflict of Laws' (1940) 56 *Law Quarterly Review* 514–518.

[32] K Trimmings, P Torremans, A Mills, U Grusic and C Heinze, *Cheshire, North, and Fawcett: Private International Law* 15th edn (Oxford University Press, 2017) 910. Many cases have followed the dictum propounded by Cheshire. *Radwan v Radwan* (No2) [1972] 3AII ER1026.

[33] ibid 912.

[34] JD Falconbridge, *Essays on the Conflicts of Laws* (Canada Law Book, 1947) 641; EI Sykes, 'The Essential Validity of Marriage' (1955) 4(2) *International and Comparative Law Quarterly* 159–169.

[35] D Hill, *Private International Law* (Edinburgh University Press, 2014) 7.

[36] S Symeonides, *American Private International Law* (Kluwer Law International, 2008) 234.

[37] ibid 235–236; See also L Silberman, 'Same Sex Marriage: Refining the Conflict of Laws Analysis' (2005) 153(6) *University of Pennsylvania Law Review* 2195–2214; Restatement (Second) of Conflict of Laws (American Law Institute, 1971) s 283(1); s 6 of the Second Restatement states that when no statutory directive exists, the court should consider several factors to determine which state has the 'most significant relationship' to the marriage. Those factors include: (a) the needs of the interstate and international systems; (b) the relevant policies of the forum; (c) the relevant policies of other interested states and the relative interests of those states in the determination of the particular issues; (d) the protection of the parties' justified expectations; (e) the basic policies underlying the particular field of law; (f) certainty, predictability, and uniformity of result; and (g) ease in the determination and application of the law to be applied.

The 1978 Hague Convention lays down basic rules on the substantive requirements of marriage.[38] Article 3 lays down that a marriage shall be celebrated: (1) where the future spouses meet the substantive requirements of the internal laws of the state of celebration and one of them has the nationality of that state or habitually resides there; or (2) where each of the future spouses meets the substantive requirements of the internal law designated by the choice of law rules of the state of celebration.[39] Thus Article 3 provides alternative possibilities. If one of the future spouses is connected to the place of celebration, by nationality or residence, the law of the place of celebration will be the applicable law.[40] If the second alternative is used, substantive requirements for both the parties to the marriage would be different. The application of Article 3 can be illustrated through an example. The minimum age of marriage in England is 16. A (an English male aged 17) marries a French female aged 14 in England. The applicable law of marriage for both the parties would be English law as the parties meet the substantive requirements of the internal law of the state of celebration and one of them has the nationality of that state.[41] The applicable law can be refused where it is 'manifestly incompatible with the public policy' (*ordre public*) of the state of celebration.[42] The reference to 'manifestly incompatible' shows the drafter's intent that the exception should have a narrow application.[43] Article 13 specifies that contracting states may apply 'rules of law more favourable to the recognition of a foreign marriage'.[44] This provision allows the parties to adopt liberal rules concerning the recognition of foreign marriages.

Similar to the rules on the formal aspect of marriage, Indian matrimonial statutes do not contain rules governing essential aspects of marriage. A specific approach is also missing in judicial decisions concerning the material aspect of marriage. In *Parwatawwa v Channawwa*,[45] the plaintiff was the second wife of the defendant who was domiciled in Hyderabad. The parties married in Bombay and resided in Hyderabad. According to the then existing laws in Bombay, polygamous marriages were prohibited, whereas the same was allowed by laws in Hyderabad. The court summed up the theories of private international law and held:

> What emerges from this discussion is that on the question as to what law should govern capacity for marriage, there are at least three streams of thought. One view is that it is the law of the place of celebration which overlooks the distinction between formality and capacity. The second is that it is the law of the domicile of each party before the marriage which is demonstrated by the later pronouncements to be a conservative and orthodox view. The third is that the law of the intended matrimonial home is what governs capacity which has been explained as the best.[46]

Two factors favoured the application of the intended matrimonial home theory, namely, the desire to validate the marriage and the application of the doctrine of the wife's domicile of dependency

[38] WLM Reese, 'The Hague Convention on Celebration and Recognition of the Validity of Marriages' (1979) 20 *Virginia Journal of International Law* 25–36, 25.

[39] Convention on Celebration and Recognition of the Validity of Marriages (n 21) Art 3.

[40] Hague Conference on Private International Law, Explanatory Report on the 1978 Marriage Convention 291 (1978) Draft Convention adopted by the Thirteenth Session and Explanatory Report by A Malmström (hereinafter A Malmström Explanatory Report) https://assets.hcch.net/docs/af508de1-0674-4689-b127-cde2280dddf3.pdf.

[41] Law Commission and Scottish Law Commission, *Private International Law: Choice of Law Rules in Marriage* (Com No 165; Scot Law Com No 105, 1987) Part II, [2.1–2.11].

[42] Convention on Celebration and Recognition of the Validity of Marriages (n 21) Art 14.

[43] A Malmström Explanatory Report (n 40) 29.

[44] Convention on Celebration and Recognition of the Validity of Marriages (n 21) Art 13.

[45] *Parwatawwa v Channawwa* AIR [1966] Mys 100.

[46] ibid [63]; See also *Monica Variato* v *Thomas Variato* 2000[2] Goa LT 149[12]; *Saeesh Subhash Hegde v Darshana Saeesh Hegde* AIR [2008] KAR 142.

on the husband.[47] In *Lakshmi Sanyal v SK Dhar*,[48] the appellant Lakshmi filed a suit for a declaration that her marriage with the respondent was null and void. The parties were Roman Catholics.[49] The appellant claimed that she was a minor when the marriage was solemnised and her father or guardian's consent had not been obtained. Further, she contended that the marriage was void because the parties were within the prohibited degrees of consanguinity.[50] The High Court held that, from the standpoint of the canon law of the Roman Catholic Church, objection to the validity of the marriage on the ground of lack of consent could not be sustained.[51] On the question of the marriage being within the prohibited degrees of consanguinity, it was found that, since the consanguinity between the parties was of the second degree, it was undoubtedly an impediment in the way of the marriage under canon law. However, the impediment could be removed by a dispensation which had been granted by the competent authorities of the church. For that reason, the marriage could not be held null and void.[52] The Supreme Court held that the marital matters would have to be resolved by referring to the law of the parties' domiciles.[53]

The Indian courts' stand shows a preference towards the dual domicile rule in the case of material validity and the *lex loci celebrationis* rule in the case of the formal aspects of marriage. The approach is compatible with the broad standard followed in private international law. A reference to the legal position of Nepal illustrates a change from domicile to nationality as a connecting factor.

Unlike Indian personal law which is scattered among different statutes, Nepal has adopted two uniform codes to govern the personal matters of persons of all religious groups:[54] (1) *Muluki Dewani (Samhita) Ain* 2017 (Civil Code); and (2) *Muluki Dewani Kariyabidhi (Samhita) Ain* 2017 (Civil Procedure Code). While the first deals with substantive matters, the latter deals with procedural aspects. Nepal does not have different personal laws for different religious communities. Its laws on marriage, divorce, partition, adoption, and succession are uniform for all religious groups. Its new Civil Code provides that a citizen celebrating a marriage in a foreign country should comply with the rules on competence, qualification and the conditions for marriage specified by the law of Nepal. It further specifies that the law of the country where the marriage is concluded shall govern formal aspects of the marriage.[55] It prescribes that, in marriages between foreign nationals or between a foreign national and a citizen of Nepal celebrated in Nepal, each spouse shall comply with the rules on capacity, qualification and marriage conditions specified by the law of his or her nationality. Nepal being the place of marriage, its law would govern the formalities of marriage.[56] Such a clear position would alleviate judicial uncertainty and provide the foundation for a strong private international law.

[47] VC Govindaraj, *The Conflict of Laws in India: Inter-Territorial and Inter-Personal Conflict* 2nd edn (Oxford University Press, 2019); FE Noronha, *Private International Law in India: Adequacy of Principles in Comparison with Common Law and Civil Law Systems* (Universal Law Publishers, 2010) 110.

[48] *Lakshmi Sanyal v SK Dhar* AIR [1972] Goa 2667.

[49] ibid [12].

[50] ibid.

[51] ibid [11].

[52] ibid.

[53] ibid; KB Agarwal and V Singh, *Private International Law in India* (Kluwer Law International, 2010) 305.

[54] Muluki Dewani (Samhita) Ain (adopted 16 October 2017, entry into force on 17 August 2018) [hereinafter referred as[54] The National Civil (Code) Act, (Nepal) 2017) and Muluki Dewani Kariyabidhhi (Samhita) Ain (adopted 2017, entry into force 2018) [hereinafter referred as Civil Procedure Code].

[55] ibid, s 699; Similar provisions can be found in Afghanistan. See Afghanistan Civil Code, Official Gazette, Issue No 353, 1355/1977. Section 19 deals with essential aspects of marriage governed by the national law of the parties and s 23 regulates formal aspect of marriage as per the law of the place of celebration of marriage.

[56] ibid, s 700.

iii. Recognition of Foreign Marriages

India currently has no legislation governing the recognition and validity of foreign marriages. Section 23 of the Foreign Marriage Act 1969 provides that the 'Central Government may declare that marriages solemnised under the law in force in such foreign country shall be recognised by the courts in India as valid.'[57] Two points are noteworthy in this context. First, the term 'may' in section 23 denotes that recognition is discretionary. Second, the discretion is exercised only if the law enforced in a foreign country is similar to the laws under the Act for the solemnisation of marriages.[58] Further, the Foreign Marriage Act does not govern the validity of a marriage between two foreigners. It is expected that Indian courts would apply the *lex loci celebrationis* to determine formal validity and the *lex domicilii* to determine the material validity of marriages subject to the overriding rule of public policy. In the Indian context, most conflict of law questions have been about the validity of marriages between spouses of different religious communities and the practice of polygamy and its recognition in other jurisdictions.

B. Inter-Religious Marriages and Private International Law in India

In *Chetti v Chetti* a Hindu resident in England but with an Indian domicile, married an English lady with a domicile in London. Under the law of his domicile, as a Hindu, he could not contract a marriage with a non-Hindu. After the marriage, the husband returned to India and deserted his wife. She filed a case for judicial separation in England and the court granted the same.[59] Although the conventional rules of private international law dictated that the validity of the marriage has to be determined by the domicile of the parties, it was held that a Hindu who contracted a marriage with an English woman in England in due form according to the laws of England could not repudiate the marriage on the ground of an incapacity under his law that the courts of England refuse to recognise. It should be noted that the marriage would not have been recognised in India. In the instant case, the recognition of marriage was prompted more by the desire to do justice than by adherence to established principles of private international law.

The same dictum was followed by the Indian court in *Sainapatti v Sainapatti*[60] wherein a marriage between a Hindu and a Christian solemnised in England was held to be valid. The Indian court looked at the case from an English court's perspective. However, as pointed out by TS Rao, instead of analysing the case from an English perspective, the Indian court should have examined the laws of the parties' domiciles and assessed whether the courts in their respective domicilse would have recognised such a marriage.[61] This case shows the blind adherence to the English legal system of the Indian courts. The decision also suggests that the validity of cross-border and inter-religious marriages will be decided based on the *lex loci celebrationis* rather than by resorting to the laws of the parties' domiciles.

In *Sophy Auerbach v Shivaprosad Agarwalla*,[62] a Hindu male (who was domiciled in India and had a Hindu wife in India) married the plaintiff Sophie Auerbach (who was domiciled in

[57] Foreign Marriage Act 1969 (n 17) s 23.

[58] ibid.

[59] *Chetti v Chetti* (1909) 25(2) *Law Quarterly Review* 202–205.

[60] *Sainapatti v Sainapatti* AIR [1932] Lah 136; SS Singh, *Unification of Divorce Laws in India* (Deep and Deep Publishers, 1993) 57.

[61] TSR Rao, 'Conflicts of Laws in India' *Zeitschrift Für Ausländisches Und Internationales Privatrecht* (1958) 23(2) 259–279, 267.

[62] *Sophy Auerbach v Shivaprosad Agarwalla* AIR [1945] Cal 484; AM Setalvad, *Conflict of Laws* (Lexis Nexis, Butterworths, 2009) 384.

Britain and of the Jewish religion) in Paris under French law.[63] The plaintiff filed suit in the Calcutta High Court for a declaration that her marriage with the defendant was null and void as contrary to the *lex loci celebrationis*.[64] It was argued that the marriage in Paris was a nullity under French law because the defendant already had a wife living when he went through the marriage with the plaintiff and that the marriage was also a nullity under Indian marriage laws.[65] Two questions arose: (1) Was the marriage a nullity under French law? (2) If so, was the marriage a nullity under the Indian law applicable to the parties?[66] The court analysed the English case law and held that the French legal system would not recognise a potentially polygamous marriage as valid. Hence, French law would not have recognised the defendant's first marriage.[67] The court further pointed out that fundamental issues relevant to the case had not been argued by the parties. These included questions such as whether a domiciled Hindu male in India could contract a valid marriage of the Jewish faith and, if so, how was the marriage to be contracted and what forms and ceremonies were required.[68] The court found that English marriage law and cases threw no light on these questions. The court stated that marriage as recognised by the courts in India was not the monogamous relationship recognised by the courts in England, nor was marriage laws uniform for all persons in India. There was instead a heavy reliance on personal laws among the different religious communities in India.[69] In those circumstances, it was meaningless to speak of a *lex domicilii*, a *lex loci celebrationis* or a *lex loci contractus* in connection with Indian marriages in general.[70] The determining factor in most cases would be the personal law of the parties. However, the parties in the case had not attempted to show that a marriage in Paris between a Hindu domiciled in India and a foreign national, which was void under the French law, was also void under the Indian law applicable to the parties. Hence, the suit was dismissed.[71]

The effect of conversion on the law applicable to marriage was raised in *khambatta v Khambatta* (discussed in detail in the chapter 7 dealing with divorce).[72] The petitioner, a Scottish national married Gulam Ibrahim in Scotland, fulfilling Scottish law requirements. At the time of the marriage, the husband was a Muslim domiciled in British India and the wife was a Christian domiciled in Scotland.[73] After the marriage, the wife embraced Islam and she remained of that faith.[74] After some time, Gulam Ibrahim pronounced a *talaq* divorce pursuant to Islamic law. The court observed:

> [C]ertain principles of law relevant to the determination of this question are, in my opinion, firmly established in the realm of private international law: (1) the forms necessary to constitute a valid marriage and the construction of the marriage contract depend on the lex loci contractus, that is, the law of the place where the marriage ceremony is performed; (2) on marriage the wife automatically acquires the domicile of her husband; (3) the status of spouses and their rights and obligations arising under the marriage contract are governed by the lex domicilli, that is, by the law of the country in which for the

[63] ibid [2].
[64] ibid.
[65] ibid [11].
[66] ibid.
[67] ibid [13].
[68] ibid [24].
[69] ibid.
[70] ibid [26].
[71] ibid [28].
[72] *Jessie Grant Khambatta v Mancherji Cursetji Khambatta* [1934] 36 BOMLR 11.
[73] ibid [2].
[74] ibid.

> time being they are domiciled (4) the rights and obligations of the parties relating to the dissolution of the marriage do not form part of the marriage contract, but arise out of, and are incidental to, such contract, and are governed by the *lex domicilii*.[75]

The court held that, in the absence of an express contract, rights under the marriage are governed by the law of the parties' domicile at the time of divorce.[76]

In *Abdur Rahim Undre v Padma Adbur Rahim Undre*,[77] the plaintiff Abdur Rahim Undre married Smt. Padma in the UK in 1966 according to the formal rites prescribed by English marriage law. Later the parties came to India and the wife converted to Islam.[78] Thereafter relations between the parties became strained and the plaintiff alleged that he pronounced a *talaq* upon Padma in 1978. The court held that the parties' marriage was governed by the Special Marriage Act 1954 and the Foreign Marriage Act 1969. Hence the marriage could not be dissolved by the religious performance of *talaq*.[79] Thus, the decisions on the interreligious marriages illustrate uncertainty and divergent positions, ranging from the application of the *lex loci celebrationis* to the application of the *lex domicilii*.

C. Polygamous Marriages

Polygamous marriages were permitted for Hindus and Muslims during the British period.[80] The Hindu Marriage Act enacted in 1955 prohibited polygamous marriages among Hindus[81] but allowed them among Muslims. Case jurisprudence has thrown light into the position of legal systems concerning the validity and recognition of polygamous marriages.[82] Jurisdictions that follow monogamy have adopted a general prohibition on polygamous marriage in their territory.[83] For instance, England, Germany, the US and France do not allow polygamous marriages.[84] The interaction of these jurisdictions to polygamous marriage has arisen in two ways. First, a party to a marriage is domiciled or a national of these jurisdictions. Second, there has been the question of whether a polygamous marriage contracted in a foreign jurisdiction (such as India) should be recognised. Following the Christian concept of monogamy, English law initially rejected actual and potentially polygamous marriages, even when a spouse never contracted a second marriage.[85] In consequence, a party to a polygamous or potentially polygamous marriage was not allowed

[75] ibid [3].

[76] ibid [8].

[77] *Abdur Rahim Undre v Padma Adbur Rahim Undre* AIR [1982] Bom 341; V Saijwani, 'Personal Laws of Divorce in India with a Comment on Chaudry v Chaudry' (1989) 11 *Women's Rights Law Reporter* 41, 52.

[78] *Abdur Rahim Undre* (n 77) [1].

[79] ibid [3].

[80] W Menski, *Modern Indian Family law* (Routledge, 2013) 9, 144.

[81] ibid.

[82] GW Bartholomew, 'Polygamous Marriage' (1952) 15 (1) *Modern Law Review* 35–47; CA Esplugues, 'Legal Recognition of Polygamous Marriages' (1984) 17 (3) *Comparative and International Law Journal of Southern Africa* 302–321; W Kieran 'Polygamous Marriages and Potentially Polygamous Marriages in Irish Law: A Critical Reappraisal' (2013) 36 *Dublin University Law Journal* 249–276.

[83] In order to be recognised as legally valid, all marriages which take place in the UK must be monogamous and must be carried out in accordance with the requirements of the Marriage Act 1949.

[84] Bigamy is a crime in 49 states and the District of Columbia; See CA Smearman, 'Second Wives' Club: Mapping the Impact of Polygamy in US Immigration Law' (2009) 27(2) *Berkley Journal of International Law* 382, 429; MM Ertman, 'Race Treason: The Untold Story of America's Ban on Polygamy'(2010) 19(2) *Columbia Journal of Gender and Law* 287, 355–356; MD Costa, 'Polygamous Marriages in the Conflict of Laws' (1966) 44(2) *Canadian Bar Review* 293–335, 297.

[85] Esplugues (n 82) 303.

any relief or remedies in matrimonial proceedings before the English court.[86] However, countries like Germany did not follow this approach. A potentially polygamous marriage was recognised as valid in Germany based on the right to marriage in Article 6 of the Civil Code.[87]

i. Nature of Marriage

The positions of judges and jurists on the appropriate connecting factor for determining the nature and character of the polygamous marriage has vacillated among the *lex loci celebrationis*, the laws of the parties' domicile, and the law of the intended matrimonial home. According to *Dicey, Morris and Collins*, a marriage celebrated in monogamous form under the law of the place of celebration is monogamous regardless of the parties' personal law.[88] Thus, a Muslim or Hindu domiciled in India who marries in England following English formalities contracts a monogamous marriage.[89] In *Qureshi v Qureshi*, two Muslims respectively domiciled in Pakistan and India married in England. Even though the parties' *lex domicilii* allowed polygamy, the court applied the *lex loci celebrationis* and determined that their marriage was monogamous. In contrast, in *Lendrum v Chakravarti*[90] involving the marriage of an Indian male and a Scottish woman in Scotland, the court observed that a person domiciled in a monogamous country could not enter in a polygamous union. It is submitted that the *lex loci celebrationis* approach adopted in *Qureshi* is not only problematic but difficult to sustain rationally. If the argument is accepted, an English domiciled woman marrying an Indian Muslim male according to religious rights in India would be considered as giving rise to a potentially polygamous union based on the *lex loci celebrationis*. In the same vein, a marriage between an English domiciled woman and an Indian domiciled Muslim male in England would be considered as monogamous based on the *lex loci celebrationis*. The approach ignores a fundamental principle of the conflict of laws as matters of status in general and capacity to marry in particular should be governed by the law of the domicile or nationality and not by the *lex loci celebrationis*.[91] Cheshire, North and Fawcett have reasoned in favour of the application of the intended matrimonial home to determine whether a marriage is potentially polygamous.[92] In *Radwan v Radwan*, the capacity to contract a polygamous marriage was held to be determined by the intended matrimonial home and the domicile of the parties was said to be irrelevant. However, the approach was criticised for bringing uncertainty in the determination of the validity of a marriage. For instance, if an English domiciled woman marries a Hindu domiciled in India, the marriage takes place in India and the parties reside in England after the marriage, the marriage will be treated as valid, whereas if the parties settle down in India after the marriage, the marriage will be declared as polygamous.[93]

[86] *Khan v Khan* [1963] VR 203; See also Law Commission, *Polygamous marriages – Capacity to Contract a Polygamous Marriage and the Concept of the Potentially Polygamous Marriage* (Scotland Law Commission Working Paper No 83, 1982).

[87] Basic Law for the Federal Republic of Germany, Federal Law Gazette, Part 111 Classification number 100-1, Art 6(1) states that marriage and the family shall enjoy the special protection of the state.

[88] *Dicey, Morris and Collins* (n 18) 287.

[89] *Srini Vasan v Srini Vasan* [1946] P [6].

[90] *Lendrum v Chakravarti* [1929] SLT 416; L Paisson, *Marriage in Comparative Conflict of Laws: Substantive Conditions* (Brill, 1981) 174.

[91] PD Maddaugh, 'Validity of Marriage and the Conflict of Laws: A Critique of the Present Anglo-American Position' (1973) 23(2) The *University of Toronto Law Journal* 117–147, 120.

[92] *Cheshire, North, and Fawcett* (n 32) 757.

[93] JA Wade, 'Capacity to Marry: Choice of Law Rules and Polygamous Marriages' (1973) 22 (3) *International and Comparative Law Quarterly* 571–575; RD James, 'Polygamy and Capacity to Marry' (1979) 42(5) *Modern Law Review* 533–543, 535.

ii. Effect of a Change of Domicile on the Nature of a Polygamous Marriage

In *Hussain v Hussain*,[94] a British domiciled Muslim married a Pakistan domiciled Muslim in Pakistan. The parties resided in England after the marriage. The wife sought a judicial separation before the English courts. The husband argued that, following *Lee v Lau*,[95] the marriage was void as being potentially polygamous under the *lex loci celebrationis*. The court relied on section 11(d) of the Matrimonial Causes Act 1973, which prohibits an English domiciled person from contracting a polygamous marriage, and declared the marriage to be monogamous.[96] The case took the position that the parties' domiciles, based on the English statutory position, determined the capacity of the parties to contract a marriage.

Initially, the English courts adopted the position that the polygamous or monogamous character of a marriage must be determined at the time of marriage, so that a subsequent change of religion or domicile on the part of the spouses would not affect the nature of their marriage.[97] However the position underwent a change from the case of *The Sinha Peerage*.[98] This concerned a marriage between two Hindus domiciled in India which was at first potentially polygamous under Hindu law but which became monogamous when the spouses joined a religious sect practicing monogamy. The eldest son of the marriage, born after the parents' conversion, successfully claimed the right to succeed to his father's peerage as a lawfully begotten son. This formulation in respect of marriages that are potentially polygamous at the time of inception is supported by *Mehta v Mehta* where a marriage celebrated in India between an English woman and a Hindu male of the monogamous Arya Samaj sect was held to be monogamous.[99] In *Parkasho v Singh*,[100] confirming the previous position, the court ruled that a potentially polygamous marriage can be converted into a monogamous marriage by subsequent changes in the law. The wife filed a petition for maintenance, which was challenged because the marriage in India would not be recognised in England as potentially polygamous.[101] However, the court found that the Hindu Marriage Act 1955 prohibited polygamous marriages retrospectively and, as such, marriages were converted into monogamous unions. This validated the marriage for the purposes of maintenance.[102] Courts have a similar rationale to cases involving a change of the parties' domiciles. In *Ali v Ali*,[103] the marriage was contracted between two domiciled people in India. Subsequently, the couple migrated to England and the husband acquired a domicile in England. The husband filed a divorce petition and the court had to determine the validity of the marriage. The court observed that, even though the marriage had been potentially polygamous, the change of the parties' domicile converted the marriage into a monogamous marriage.[104] Judicial support can be found in the

[94] *Hussain v Hussain* [1982] 1All ER 369; A Briggs, 'Polygamous Marriages and English Domiciliaries' (1983) 32(3) *The International and Comparative Law Quarterly* 737–741.

[95] *Lee v Lau* [1967] P 14; Briggs (n 94) 737.

[96] ibid, Briggs.

[97] *Hyde v Hyde* (n 4); JHC Morris, 'The Recognition of Polygamous Marriages in English Law' (1953) 66 *Harvard Law Review* 961–1012, 962; L Carroll, 'Recognition of Polygamous Marriages in English Matrimonial Law: The Statutory Reversal *of* "Hyde v Hyde" in 1972' (1984) 5(1) *Institute of Muslim Minority Affairs Journal* 81–98.

[98] [1946] I All E R 348; *Dicey, Morris and Collins* (n 18) 972.

[99] [1945] 2 All E R 690; *Cheni v Cheni* [1962] 3 All E R 873.

[100] [1967] 1 All ER 737.

[101] ibid; See also P Shah, 'Attitudes to Polygamy in English Law' (2003) 52(2) *The International and Comparative Law Quarterly* 369–400, 372.

[102] P Shah, *Legal Pluralism in Conflict: Coping with Cultural Diversity in Law* (Routledge, 2016).

[103] *Ali v Ali* [1966] 2 WLR 620.

[104] T Dimitry 'The Conversion of a Polygamous Union into a Monogamous Marriage' [1968] 17(3) *The International and Comparative Law Quarterly* 721–729, 722; *Cheni v Cheni* [1962] 3 All ER 873; *Attorney General for Ceylon v Reid* [1965] 2WLR 671.

case of *Sara v Sara* where the potentially polygamous marriage of an Indian couple was held to have been converted into a monogamous marriage by the parties acquiring a domicile in British Columbia.[105]

iii. Recognition of Polygamous Marriages

Although many jurisdictions prohibit the celebration of polygamous marriages on their soil, a polygamous marriage concluded abroad between non-nationals under foreign law will generally be recognised as valid.[106] When the personal law and the *lex loci celebrationis* permit polygamy, there should be no impediment to recognition as a matter of principle.[107] However, in jurisdictions such as France and Germany which generally recognise foreign polygamous marriages not connected, reunification of the members of a polygamous family may be restricted. For example, the French Law Reform on the Right of Asylum 2015 states:

> [W]hen a polygamous foreigner resides in French territory with his/her first spouse, the benefit of family reunification cannot be granted to another spouse. Unless this other spouse is deceased or has lost her parental rights, her children cannot benefit from family reunification.[108]

In Ireland, the question of the recognition of a polygamous marriage was raised in *HAH v SAA*.[109] The husband, a refugee and naturalised Irish citizen, was originally from Lebanon. While domiciled there, he contracted two marriages, the first in 1975 and the second in 1988. Both were valid according to the parties' religious and domicile laws at the time of marriage. After he was recognised as a refugee, his second wife was admitted to Ireland.[110] In 2002, an application for the admission of his first wife to Ireland was rejected. The trial judge concluded that interpreting the word 'marriage' to include polygamous marriage was against Ireland's public policy based on culture, tradition, and the Irish Constitution.[111] The Supreme Court on appeal held that the second marriage could not be recognised, but that did not compel the state to 'deny all legal effect to polygamous marriages in all contexts'.[112] A similar position was taken by the US Board of Immigration of Appeal in the *Matter of H* where it was observed that the general rule is that the validity of a marriage is determined by the laws of the place where it is contracted or celebrated. If valid in those places, it is valid everywhere. An exception to the general rule, however, arises in the case of marriages opposed to public policy. The exception is ordinarily applied in cases where a marriage is repugnant to the public policy or laws of the parties' domicile, such as may be the situation with polygamous marriages.[113]

An increase in migration and the number of cross-border marriages has pushed jurisdictions to deal with polygamous marriages and has brought about changes in attitude as exemplified by statutory modifications and judicial statements. As stated by Kahn 'none of our laws, however

[105] Z Cowen, 'A Note on Potentially Polygamous Marriages' (1963) 12(4) *The International and Comparative Law Quarterly* 1407–1411, 1408.

[106] N Chigozie, 'Recognition of Polygamous Marriages under the English Law' (2014) 26 *Journal of Law, Policy and Globalization* 13–19, 16.

[107] Shah (n 102) 377.

[108] Law no 2015-925 of 29 July 2015 on the Reform of the Right of Asylum, www.legifrance.gouv.fr/jorf/id/JORFTEXT000030949483/; see Immigration Act (France) 1993, s 30.

[109] Ireland: Supreme Court, *HAH v SAA and Others*, 12 December 2017, www.refworld.org/docid/5a2fb7814.html.

[110] ibid.

[111] ibid.

[112] ibid; See also for Ireland's Position on Polygamous Marriages, K Walsh, 'Polygamous Marriages and Potentially Polygamous Marriages in Irish Law: A Critical Reappraisal' (2013) 36 *Dublin University Law Journal* 249–276.

[113] Matter of H –, 9I & N. Dec. 640, 641 (BIA 1962).

fundamental it may be, requires exclusive, absolute application. No foreign legal institution, however much we may disapprove of it, can be simply ignored.'[114]

Conflicts arising from polygamous marriages have been reduced in England with the statutory reforms adopted in 1973. Section 11(d) of the Matrimonial Causes Act 1973 provides that a polygamous marriage shall be void if either party was at the time of the marriage domiciled in England.[115] According to section 11, the avoidance of marriages pursuant to section 11(d) will only apply to marriages entered into after 31 July 1971.[116] The view at common law on marriages concluded up to 31 July 1971 is that a person domiciled in England cannot enter into a potential or actual polygamous marriage.[117] The position was further modified in respect of potentially polygamous marriages by the Private International Law (Miscellaneous Provisions) Act 1995. Section 5(1) of the 1995 Act expressly provides that a marriage contracted outside England and Wales is not void on the ground that it was entered into under a law which permits polygamy, where at the time of marriage either spouse was domiciled in England or Wales and both were single.[118] Similar changes in legislation were carried out in New Zealand and other jurisdictions. Section 2 of the New Zealand Family Proceedings Act 1980 defines 'marriage' to include a union that is: (1) entered into outside New Zealand; and (2) at any time polygamous, where the law of the country in which each spouse was domiciled at the time of union permitted polygamy.[119] The laws of other jurisdictions thus reveal a transformative change concerning polygamous marriages. Whereas global marriages and polygamous marriages dominated family law conflicts disputes in the twentieth century, the twenty-first century is faced with conflict arising out of same-sex marriages.

III. Same-Sex Marriage: Legal Analysis of Private International Law Principles

As a social institution, marriage has been a focal point of society's contemplation throughout history.[120] Though individuals are expected to be bound to each other within the contours of marriage, the institution of marriage has been observed to implement exclusionary treatment towards certain communities of people.[121] Traditionally, marriages have been understood to be the union of men and women, indicating a strictly heterosexual union.[122] However, with time, same-sex marriages have come to the forefront of sociopolitical discourse.[123] Varied and diverse

[114] Kahn, *Treatise on Private International Law* 1st edn (1898), cited in EGL, 'Polygamy and the Conflict of Laws' (1923) 32(5) *Yale Law Journal* 471–477, 473.

[115] Domicile and Matrimonial Causes Act 1973 (UK), s 11 (d).

[116] ibid, s 11.

[117] TC Hartley, IGF Karsten, 'The Domicile and Matrimonial Proceedings Act 1973' (1974) 37(2) *Modern Law Review* 179–186, 183.

[118] Private International Law (Miscellaneous Provisions) Act 1995 (UK), s 5.

[119] Family Proceedings Act 1980, New Zealand; PRH Webb and FM Auburn, 'New Zealand Conflicts of Laws: A Bird's Eye View: in Contemporary Problems in the Conflict of Laws' in KR Simmonds (ed), *Essays in Honour of John Humphrey Carlile Morris* (AW Sijthoff, 1978) 271–298.

[120] E Scott, 'A World Without Marriage' (2007) 41(3) *Family Law Quarterly* 537–566, 538; WD Manning, MA Longmore and PC Giordano, 'The Changing Institution of Marriage: Adolescents' Expectations to Cohabit and to Marry' (2007) 69(3) *Journal of Marriage and Family* 559–575, 562.

[121] Scott (n 120) 538.

[122] JA Redding, 'Dignity, Legal Pluralism, and Same-Sex Marriage' (2010) 75(3) *Brooklyn Law Review* 791–863, 795.

[123] ibid 801.

approaches characterise the legal response to same-sex relationships.[124] Some jurisdictions have exhibited a complete negation of same-sex relationships and the criminalisation of same-sex relationships, mainly due to religious and public policy perspectives.[125] Other jurisdictions have decriminalised same-sex relationships even though they have not legally permitted same-sex relationships.[126] Yet other jurisdictions have accorded different degrees of protection and acceptance to same-sex relationships, ranging from partnerships and civil unions to full-fledged marriages.[127]

In Asia, except for Nepal and Taiwan, no country recognises same-sex marriages.[128] Israel recognises same-sex marriages performed outside its borders.[129] The diverse approaches of jurisdictions to same-sex relationships presents challenges to traditional family laws and brings into conflict laws that relate to jurisdiction, choice of law, and the recognition of foreign same-sex marriages. No convention has been adopted at a global level to harmonise the rules on same-sex relationships, instead the issue has so far been left to be determined by the rules of private international law of different jurisdictions.

A. Legal Approach to Same-Sex Marriage in India

i. Statutory Framework

In Hinduism, many mythological stories pave the way for accepting same-sex relationships, but the same is fervently contested by religious texts that forbid such unions.[130] Nevertheless, in recent times, several scholars have acknowledged same-sex marriage as natural instead of immoral.[131] In Islam, same-sex relationships have been considered as a revolt against God's rules and, therefore, the death penalty is prescribed for the same.[132] From a Christian perspective, same-sex marriage is not acceptable as it is against the 'traditional' form of marriage, which is limited to the union of a man and a woman.[133] India's matrimonial statutes, including the Hindu

[124] JM Scherpe 'The Legal Recognition of Same Sex Couples in Europe and the Role of the European Court of Human Rights' (2010) 10 *Equal Rights Review* 83–96, 84.

[125] WN Eskridge Jr, 'A History of Same Sex Marriage'(1993) 79 *Virginia Law Review* 1419–1513, 1469; WS Johnson, *Time to Embrace: Same-Gender Relationships in Religion Law and Politics* 2nd edn (Wm. B. Eerdmans Publishing Co, 2006) 197; PD Young, *Religion Sex and Politics: Christian Churches and Same-Sex Marriage in Canada* (Fernwood Publishing & Co., 2012) 66; LD Wardle, 'Marriage and Religious Liberty: Comparative Law Problems and Conflict of Laws Solutions' (2010) 12 *Journal of Law and Family Studies* 315–364, 333.

[126] O Neill and R Allison, 'Recognition of Same-Sex Marriage in the European Community: The European Court of Justice's Ability to Dictate Social Policy' (2004) 37(1) *Cornell International Law Journal* 200, 212; J Gardiner, 'Same-sex Marriage – A Worldwide Trend?' in P Gerber and Safaris (eds), *Current Trends in the Regulation of Same-sex Relationships* (Federation Press, 2011) 28–42.

[127] *Obergefell v Hodges* [2015] 135 S Ct 2584 (2015) saw the pronouncement of the United States Supreme Court granting the right to marry same sex couples. Same Sex Couples Act (Marriage) UK 2013, Part 1 Extension of Marriage to the same-Sex Couple (1) The marriage of same sex couples is lawful www.legislation.gov.uk/ukpga/2013/30/contents/enacted.

[128] MS Hu, 'Taiwan's Road to Marriage Equality: Politics of Legalizing Same-Sex Marriage' (2019) 238 *The China Quarterly* 482–506.

[129] AB Pregat, 'Same Sex Relationships and Israeli Law', in M Saez (ed), *Same Sex Couples – Comparative Insights on Marriage and Cohabitation* (Springer, 2015) 131–162.

[130] N Bonvillain, *Women And Men: Cultural Constructs Of Gender* 3rd edn (Prentice Hall, 2001) 281.

[131] R Vanita, 'Same-Sex Weddings, Hindu Traditions, and Modern India' (2009) 91 *Feminist Review* 47–60.

[132] J Wafer, 'Muhammad And Male Homosexuality' in SO Murray and W Roscoe (eds), *Islamic Homosexualities: Culture, History, And Literature* (NYU Press, 1997) 89.

[133] R McVeigh and DD Maria-Elena, 'Voting to Ban Same-Sex Marriage: Interests, Values, and Communities' (2009) 74 (6) *American Sociological Review* 891–915.

Marriage Act 1955, the Special Marriage Act 1954, the Indian Christian Marriage Act 1872, the Parsi Marriage and Divorce Act 1936, and the Foreign Marriages Act 1969, have been drafted in a gender-neutral language. The legislative conditions have laid down age parameters for the solemnisation of a marriage. The important fact to be noted here is the usage of the word 'bride' and 'bridegroom' which has been interpreted to have a heterosexual approach. For instance, the Hindu Marriage Act prescribes 18 years for the bride and 21 years for the bridegroom which means that the marriage union has to be between a man and a woman.[134] It is essential to note that many consider marriage as an institution that contemplates procreation and the same has been mentioned under the Hindu Marriage Act and Special Marriage Act.[135] Owing to an impossibility of same-sex couples being able to engage in procreation due to physical constraints, the possibility under this Act is further reduced. Despite all the arguments against same-sex marriage, an important aspect should always be considered, which is the 'right to choose one's partner'.[136]

Further, the Hindu Marriage Act provides special grounds for divorce in the case of wives.[137] Section 2 of the Dissolution of Muslim Marriages Act 1939, sets out that, if the husband is suffering from a virulent venereal disease, a woman married under Muslim law to such a person shall be entitled to a decree for dissolution of her marriage.[138] Muslim personal laws governing marriages are largely based on *shariah*, which prescribes the death penalty for same-sex marriage.[139] Thus, considering the above scenarios, a bleak possibility of recognising same-sex marriages exists in Hindu, Christians, and Parsi personal laws, if the principles of statutory interpretation are applied and the need for allocation of civil rights to every individual is considered.

ii. Judicial Response to Same-Sex Marriages

A walk through case jurisprudence clarifies that the first breakthrough in same-sex relationships was the 2009 decision of the Delhi High Court in *Naz Foundation v Govt. of NCT of Delhi & Ors*,[140] where the Court interpreted the Constitution of India by reading down Section 377 of the Indian Penal Code (IPC), which termed same-sex activities as against the order of nature and thus a criminal offence.[141] Section 377 of the IPC is a residue of English criminal law and this relic of British rule was held to dictate same-sex conduct as acts of 'sexual perversity' where consent was immaterial.[142]

In *Naz Foundation v Govt of Delhi and Ors*,[143] Naz Foundation (NGO) working towards intervention and prevention of HIV/AIDS brought forward a petition in light of the public interest to safeguard the rights of homosexuals. Section 377 was challenged as violating Articles 14, 15, and 21 of the Constitution of India by interfering with the fundamental rights of homosexuals and obstructing the work of NGOs in curbing the spread of HIV/AIDS, since it drove homosexuals

[134] Hindu Marriage Act 1955 (n 10) s 5(iii); Section 4(c) of the Special Marriage Act (n 16); Section 3 of the Parsi Marriage and Divorce Act (n 15).

[135] ibid, s 12.

[136] *Shafin Jahan v Asokan K M* [2018] 5 SCALE 422. Many legal systems recognise the right of people to marry.

[137] Hindu Marriage Act 1955 (n 10) s 13(2).

[138] The Dissolution of Muslim Marriages Act 1939, s 2.

[139] Wafer (n 132).

[140] *Naz Foundation v Government of NCT of Delhi & Ors.* [2009] DLT 277 [160].

[141] Indian Penal Code 1860, s 377: 'Unnatural offenses: Whoever voluntarily has carnal intercourse against the order of nature with any man, woman or animal shall be punished with imprisonment for life, or with imprisonment of either description for the term which may extend to ten years, and shall also be liable to fine.'; See also SK Sarkaria, RA Nelson's *Indian Penal Code* 9th edn (Lexus Nexis, 2003) 3738.

[142] *Fazal Rab Choudhary v State of Bihar* AIR [1983] SC 323.

[143] *Naz Foundation* (n 140).

underground due to a fear of being persecuted or harassed.[144] A plain reading of the judgment strikes a chord of curiosity since the reply by the Union of India is peculiar. The reply provided by the Ministry of Home Affairs and the Ministry of Health and Family Welfare were strikingly different. The affidavit of the Ministry of Home Affairs was based on the premise that retention of section 377 was essential to curb child sexual abuse cases. The retention of section 377 was contended on the grounds of the morality of Indian society; for this purpose, reliance was placed on the 42nd Law Commission Report, where it was asserted that Indian society perceived such unnatural conduct as a criminal offence.[145] The affidavit of the Ministry of Health and Family Welfare reinforced the argument that, due to the lack of an enabling environment, homosexuals hide away after engaging in risky sexual practices.[146] Due to the fear of law enforcement mechanisms and systemic abuse and harassment, they mostly remained underground, posing a huge obstacle to tackling the spread of HIV/AIDS. Therefore, in order to do away with such precarious circumstances, it was submitted that decriminalisation was an important step forward. The Delhi High Court's judgment suggested reading down section 377 to uphold the Constitution's role in safeguarding the rights of the people. The Court relied on Indian and international human rights jurisprudence to conclude that section 377 hits at the core of an individual's identity by criminalising acts solely because of sexual orientation and therefore violates Article 15 of the Constitution.[147] It also held that popular morality could never be a weapon to dismantle the foundation of Article 21.[148] The Court referred to *Toonen v Australia*[149] and held that the interpretation of 'sex' under Article 15 included 'sexual orientation' since the terms were analogous. The decision of the Delhi High Court was appealed to the Supreme Court *in Suresh Kumar Koushal &Anr. v NAZ Foundation &others*.[150] The Supreme Court overturned the decision of the Delhi High Court and held that reading down section 377 of the IPC to permit homosexual activities was wrong and unsustainable.[151] It stated that decriminalising section 377 would instigate youth to engage in same-sex activities, thereby undermining society's morality.[152] On reading down section 377, the Court observed that the misuse of a law does not mandate unconstitutionality and is only a factor for Parliament to consider if the question of amending the provision arises.[153]

In the wake of the Aadhar dispute, a petition was filed by Justice KS Puttaswamy (Retd.) challenging the constitutionality of Aadhar on the grounds of inclusion of the right to privacy within the four walls of Article 21.[154] Though the case largely revolves around the implicit presence of

[144] ibid [6].

[145] ibid [12]; See also Law Commission of India, *Indian Penal Code*, (Report No 42, 1971) [16.124–16.127].

[146] ibid [15].

[147] ibid [144]; See also S Jolly and R Vohra, 'Recognition of Foreign Same Sex Marriage In India A Legal Exploratory Analysis' (2017) 59(3) *Journal of Indian law Institute* 302–326.

[148] ibid [79], see also N Ravichandran, 'Legal Recognition of Same-Sex Relationships in India' (2014) 5 *Journal of Indian Law and Society* 95–109.

[149] *Toonen v Australia* No 488/1992, CCPR/C/50/D/488/1992.

[150] *Suresh Kumar Koushal v Naz Foundation* AIR [2014] SC 563.

[151] ibid; T Khaitan, 'Koushal v Naz: Judges Vote to Recriminalise Homosexuality' (2015) 78(4) *Modern Law Review* 672–694; S Subramanian, 'The Indian Supreme Court Ruling in Koushal v Naz: Judicial Deference or Judicial Abdication' (2015) 47(4) *George Washington International Law Review* 711–762.

[152] Koushal (n 150) [10]; See S Narrain, 'Lost in Appeal: The Downward Spiral from Naz to Koushal' (2013) 6(4) *NUJS Law Review* 575–584, 582; U Baxi, 'Demosprudence versus Jurisprudence: The Indian Judicial Experience in the Context of Comparative Constitutional Studies' (2014) 14 *Macquarie Law Journal* 3–23, 22.

[153] Koushal (n 150) [47]. See N Brankle, 'Gay Rights in India: Matter of Naz Foundation Decision' (2015) 15 *Chicago-Kent Journal of International & Comparative Law* 1.

[154] *Justice KS Puttaswamy (Retd.) v Union of India* [2017] 10 SCC 1. Aadhar is a unique identification number for Indian citizens.

privacy in the constitutional mandate, the judgment also lays emphasis on sexual orientation being an indisputable part of privacy.[155] The Court revisited *Suresh Kumar Koushal & Anr v Naz Foundation & Others*[156] and held that sexual orientation forms an essential base of an individual's identity, life and liberty and thus should be protected at all times on an even platform.

In *Navtej Singh Johar & Others v Union of India & Others*,[157] the petitioner sought a declaration that the rights to sexuality, sexual autonomy, and choice of a sexual partner were a part of Article 21 of the Constitution of India and section 377 was inconsistent with the Constitution of India. The Court overruled the decision in *Suresh Kumar Koushal &Anr v Naz Foundation &Ors*[158] and held section 377 to be unconstitutional to the extent that it criminalised consensual sex between same-sex couples. The court relied on *Shafin Jahan v Asokan KM*[159] and *Shakti Vahini v Union of India*[160] to observe that the right to choose one's partner is intrinsic to every individual. It also emphasised that sexual orientation was within the ambit of the right to privacy under Article 21 by referring to *Justice KS Puttaswamy (Retd.) v Union of India*.[161] The Court also took into consideration the legislative history of section 377 and the principles of transformative constitutionalism and progressive realisation of rights to hold that archaic concepts of morality were long gone and thus with time it was important to safeguard fundamental rights.[162] But the judgment did not delve into the question of civil rights of same-sex couples. A review petition regarding civil rights of the same-sex couples was filed in April 2019 before the Supreme Court of India. This was later dismissed.[163]

Regardless of the dismissal, the Madras High Court struck a positive note when the Court allowed the marriage between a man and a transwoman in *Arun Kumar v The Inspector General of Registration &Ors*.[164] In its decision, the Court relied upon Justice GP Singh's *Principles of Statutory Interpretation*[165] to decode the meaning of 'bride' under section 5 of the Hindu Marriage Act 1955 and stated that every statute should be interpreted following the current legal system.[166] Further, in January 2020 the Kerala High Court requested the centre and state government to respond to a writ petition which demanded the recognition of same-sex marriages.[167] The decriminalisation of section 377 of the Indian Penal Code served as a turning point for this battle to secure the rights of homosexuals, as without the allocation of civil rights these relationships continue to go through nightmares every single day. Owing to the lack of recognition of same-sex marriage, these relationships are tormented with guilt, insult and indignity from the law itself, which is supposed to guarantee basic human rights, equality, and non-discrimination.

[155] P Thaorey, 'Informational Privacy: Legal Introspection In India' (2019) 2(Winter) *ILI Law Review* 160–179,167; See also RV Rao and S Rao (eds), *A Public Disclosure on Privacy – An Analysis of Justice KS Puttaswamyv. UOI* (NLSIU, Bangalore, 2018).

[156] *Koushal* (n 150).

[157] *Navtej Singh Johar &Ors v Union of India &Ors* AIR [2018] SC 4321.

[158] *Koushal* (n 150).

[159] *Shafin Jahan* (n 136).

[160] *Shakti Vahini v Union of India* [2018] 7 SCC 192.

[161] *Puttaswamy* (n 154).

[162] *Navtej Singh Johar* (n 157) [94].

[163] Press Trust of India, 'Supreme Court Dismisses Petition Seeking Civil Rights for Homosexuals', *Business Standard* (New Delhi, 15 April 2019) available at www.business-standard.com/article/pti-stories/sc-dismisses-plea-seeking-civil-rights-for-homosexuals-119041500965_1.html.

[164] *Arun Kumar v The Inspector General of Registration &Ors* WP (MD) No 4125 of 2019 and WMP (MD) No 3220 of 2019.

[165] Justice GP Singh, *Principles of Statutory Interpretation* (Lexis Nexis, 2016).

[166] *Arun Kumar* (n 164) [10].

[167] D Jyoti, 'Plea in Kerala High Court Seeks Recognition for Same-Sex Marriages', *Hindustan Times* (New Delhi, 28 January 2020) www.hindustantimes.com/india-news/plea-in-kerala-hc-seeks-recognition-for-same-sex-marriages/story-usG9x12oM4urkZPQK99aHP.html.

B. Recognition of Foreign Same-Sex Marriage and Application of Public Policy

Even though section 377 has been decriminalised, in the absence of an explicit verdict or statutory provisions, no same-sex marriage can be celebrated in India whether involving an Indian domiciled person or foreign nationals. Owing to the extraterritorial operation of the Hindu Marriage Act,[168] a marriage celebrated between an Indian domiciled and a Dutch domiciled gay couple in the Netherlands would not be recognised in India, even though the place of celebration permits same-sex marriages. Such an approach in extending statutory laws to out-of-state marriages of Indian domiciled persons resonates with the governmental interest analysis adopted by Currie.[169] Thus, the statutory framework in India would not recognise a same-sex marriage involving an Indian domiciled person regardless of the place of celebration. The real concern for the Indian legal system would be the recognition of foreign same-sex marriages involving foreign domiciled persons celebrated outside India. In the absence of specific legislation on recognising foreign marriages, the question would be whether the traditional principles of *lex domicilii* and *lex loci celebrationis* can be invoked to enable recognition to a foreign same-sex marriage.

The general rule as to the recognition of marriage is to validate marriages. However, it has been noted that when the domestic laws do not permit same-sex marriages, countries often invoke the concept of strong public policy based on which a forum can refuse to recognise foreign same-sex marriages even if the marriage fulfils accepted principles of dual domicile and the *lex loci* rule as far as the validity of marriages is concerned. The idea is that the invocation of a forum's public policy protects the interests of the forum with which the parties to the marriage have a significant connection. Almost all choice of law theories ranging from Currie's governmental interest analysis and Robert Leflar's choice-influencing considerations[170] favours the invocation of public policy. Leflar has identified numerous parameters influencing choice of law and public policy in the conflict process. These considerations include predictability of result, maintenance of international order, promotion of governmental interest, and promotion of the rule of law.[171] Public policy is invoked to exclude the application of foreign law when the application of foreign law violates the fundamental principles of the *lex fori*.[172] Public policy has played a prominent part in the conflict process involving marriage, recognition. However, the question is what is the yardstick for invoking public policy in the recognition or non-recognition of foreign marriages? An absolute preference for the law of the domicile of the parties over an application of foreign law will nullify comity among nations.[173] If Indian judicial statements are any indication, public policy has been interpreted in a divergent manner. Although there is no judicial decision directly on foreign marriages, an assessment in the contest of recognition of foreign divorces offers some guidelines.

[168] *Sondur Gopal v Sondur Rajini* [2013] 7 SCC 426.

[169] B Currie, *Selected Essays on the Conflict of Laws* (Duke University Press, 1963) 187.

[170] RA Leflar, 'Choice-Influencing Considerations In Conflicts of Law' (1996) 41 *New York Law Review*. 267, 282.

[171] ibid; See also B Cox, 'Same-Sex Marriage and the Public Policy Exception in Choice-of-Law: Does It Really Exist?' in Symposium Issue on 'Federalism Revisited: Extraterritorial Recognition of Same-Sex Marriage' (1996) 16 *Quinnipiac Law Review* 61–103, 65.

[172] ibid.

[173] B Cox, 'Same Sex Marriage and Choice of law: If we Marry in Hawai, Are we Still Married When we get Home' (1994) *Wisconsin Law Review* 1065; AC Adam and M Kuykendall 'Modernising Marriage' (2010) 44 *University of Michigan Journal of Law Reform* 765; L Kramer, 'Same-Sex Marriage, Conflict of Laws, and the Unconstitutional Public Policy Exception' (1997) 106 *Yale Law Journal* 1965.

In *Pires v Pires*,[174] in refusing to recognise a foreign divorce, the court stated that the foreign divorce would not be recognised as it was different from the forum law. By analogy, foreign same-sex marriages will not be recognised as the forum's laws do not permit same sex marriages. The 65th Report of the Law Commission of India has elaborated on public policy in the context of the recognition of foreign divorces and stated that public policy does not denote what the law ought to be. Instead, it focuses on what the current public perception of the law is.[175] The application of the current public perception as the yardstick of public policy brings uncertainty in the invocation of public policy, as it is difficult to assess the public sentiment of the majority. One could, for instance, argue for the recognition of foreign same-sex marriages as a matter of public policy, citing the decriminalisation of section 377 in support. When decriminalising section 377, the Supreme Court distinguished between social and constitutional morality.[176] The Court observed that *Suresh Kumar Koushal*[177] had been guided by the majority's perception based on social morality and therefore the case stood on a distinct platform from constitutional morality.[178] The fundamental facet of the rule of law in a democracy hinges on the fulcrum of constitutional provisions. Where constitutional supremacy prevails, contrary social principles should not be allowed to come in the way.[179] Public policy has to be interpreted not merely by looking into the social and moral perceptions of the majority. It also has to withstand constitutional scrutiny.

India's legal positions show a lack of clarity as far as the recognition of foreign same-sex marriages. The application of public policy to refuse a foreign same sex marriage would lead to a situation where a marriage that is recognised in one jurisdiction is considered invalid in another.[180] A possible solution could be to adopt a similar approach to that followed by jurisdictions recognising polygamous marriages. While rejecting the absolute rejection of polygamous marriages, such jurisdictions accord recognition to foreign polygamous marriages validly celebrated according to the laws of the parties' domiciles, while retaining a general prohibition on the contracting of polygamous marriages within their territories.[181]

IV. Hague Conference on Private International Law and Matrimonial Conventions

Since its inception, the HCCH has been attempting to harmonise private international rules. Marriage and divorce issues were one of the first focal areas of the HCCH's codification attempts. In 1978, the HCCH adopted the Convention on Celebration and Recognition of the Validity of Marriages.[182] Structurally, the 1978 Convention is divided into four chapters: (I) the celebration of marriages, (II) the recognition of the validity of marriages, (III) general clauses, and (IV) final clauses.

[174] *Joao Gloria Pires v Mrs. Ana Joaquina Rodrigues Pires* AIR [1967] Goa 113; See U Baxi, 'Conflict of Laws, Annual Survey of Indian Law' (1967–1968) Indian Law Institute 227–285.

[175] Law Commission of India, *The Recognition of Foreign Divorces* (Report No 65, 1976).

[176] *Navtej Singh Johar* (n 157) [10].

[177] *Koushal* (n 150).

[178] ibid [10].

[179] ibid [90].

[180] A Koppleman, 'Against Blanket Interstate Non-recognition of Same-Sex Marriage' (2005) 17(1) *Yale Law Journal and Feminism* 205–219, 217. See also A Koppleman, 'Same-Sex Marriage, Choice of Law, and Public Policy' (1997–1998) 76(5) *Texas Law Review* 921–1002, 987.

[181] Jolly &Vohra (n 147) 320.

[182] LD Wardle 'International Marriage and Divorce Regulation and Recognition: A Survey' (1995) 29(3) *Family Law Quarterly* 497–517, 507.

The acceptance of chapter II is mandatory for becoming a member of the Convention, whereas chapter I is optional.[183] The 1978 Convention does not define 'marriage' and instead applies in the broadest sense to unions in the form of marriage.[184] Article 1 states that chapter I shall apply to the requirements in a contracting state to celebrate marriages. Even though the term requirements cover formal and substantive aspects, separate rules are provided for formal and substantive requirements.[185] The 1978 Convention provides that the law of the place of celebration of marriage governs the formal aspect of marriage.[186] Article 3 deals with the substantive requirements of marriage and provides an obligation to celebrate a marriage where both spouses meet the substantive requirements of the internal law of the state of celebration, and one of them has the nationality of that state or habitually resides there or where the spouses meet the substantive requirements of the internal law designated by the choice of law rules of the state of celebration.[187] Article 4 provides a right to the state of celebration to require intending spouses to furnish any necessary evidence about the content of any foreign law which is applicable under the preceding Articles.[188] The 1978 Convention in chapter I (Article 5) and chapter II (Article 14) refers to overriding public policy as a ground for refusing foreign law application.[189] Article 6 was proposed by the Federal Republic of Germany and permits the possibility of not applying the internal law of a state to the substantive requirements for marriage in respect of a spouse who is neither a national of the state nor habitually resides there.[190]

The Convention's fundamental features are found in chapter II, which deals with the recognition of the validity of marriages and is based on the fundamental principle of *favor matrimonii*.[191] By adopting the *lex loci celebrationis*, the 1978 Convention provides under Article 9 a general rule on recognition.[192] The legal consequence of Article 9 would be the recognition of marriage in all Contracting States.[193] The 1978 Convention does not define the term 'recognition' but provides that the rules of chapter II will be applied even in situations where the question of the validity of marriage has arisen as an incidental matter.[194] The general obligation under Article 9 is qualified by a number of limited restrictions under Article 11.[195] Only three countries are party to the 1978 Convention.[196] The Law Commission of India has emphasised the need to examine the relevance and adaptability of the 1978 Hague Marriage Convention and has indicated that India should sign it.[197]

[183] Convention on Celebration and Recognition of the Validity of Marriages (n 21) Art 16.

[184] A Malmström Explanatory Report (n 40) 295.

[185] ibid, 295; see HP Glenn, 'Comment: The Conflict of Laws – the 1976 Hague Convention on Marriage and Matrimonial Property Regimes' (1977) 55 *Canadian Bar Review* 586, 600–603.

[186] Convention on Celebration and Recognition of the Validity of Marriages (n 21) Art 2.

[187] ibid, Art 3; See also U Tandon, 'Validity of Marriage under International Private Law with Special Reference to 1978 Hague Marriage Convention: Towards Harmonization and Unification of the Rules of International Private Law Relating to Marriage' (2013) 1 *Journal of Campus Law Centre* 32, 47.

[188] ibid, Art 4.

[189] ibid, Art 5, 14.

[190] ibid, Art 6, see also A Malmström Explanatory Report (n 40) 297.

[191] Reese (n 38) 25; A Malmström Explanatory Report (n 40) 289.

[192] Convention on Celebration and Recognition of the Validity of Marriages (n 21) Art 9.

[193] A Malmström Explanatory Report (n 40) 301.

[194] Convention on Celebration and Recognition of the Validity of Marriages (n 21) Art 12; see A Malmström Explanatory Report (n 40) 298.

[195] Convention on Celebration and Recognition of the Validity of Marriages (n 21) Art 11.

[196] Australia, Egypt and the Netherlands are the only three countries party to the Convention. www.hcch.net/en/instruments/conventions/status-table/?cid=88.

[197] Law Commission of India, *Need For Family Law Legislations For Non-Resident Indians* (Report No 219, 2009) 19.

V. Conclusion

In this era of globalisation, and movement of people, transnational marriages are on the rise. With the increasing number of foreign marriages, it is not unusual to come across cases involving connections with numerous jurisdictions. This chapter has evaluated Indian statutory provisions and judicial statements on the formal and essential validity of marriages and the recognition of foreign marriages. It observed that personal laws govern matrimonial relations among various religious communities. The analysis of matrimonial statutes noted that the Hindu Marriage Act, the Special Marriage Act, and the Indian Marriage Act do not have explicit provisions on the applicable law regulating formal and essential aspects of marriage. The limited case law suggests a preference towards the dual domicile rule in cases of material validity and the *lex loci celebrationis* rule in the case of formal aspects. The evaluation pointed out that India currently has no legislation governing the recognition and validity of foreign marriages. In the numerous cases which have come up concerning the validity of interreligious marriages, the position of the court has not been uniform and has deviated between application of the laws of the parties' domiciles and the *lex loci celebrationis*. This chapter also examined the problematic aspects of the recognition of polygamous marriage and the slow transformation of other jurisdictions towards the recognition of polygamous marriages. This chapter analysed the gradually evolving position of the Indian judiciary towards the recognition of same-sex marriage. However, uncertainty still surrounds the recognition of foreign same-sex marriage and the deployment of public policy as a basis for refusing recognition. India has not acceded to any Hague Conventions governing matrimonial matters The Law Commission of India has emphasised the need to examine the relevance and adaptability of the 1978 Hague Convention and has indicated that India should sign it.

7

Private International Practice in Divorce and Related Matters

I. Introduction

This chapter continues the deliberation on matrimonial subjects, this time engaging in divorce and interrelated topics. Marital disputes were among the initial concerns agitated under the domain of private international law in India. However, the force of globalisation, and the snowballing movement of people across borders have elevated matters of the family to a complex subject area of private international law. The scenario presents particular challenges to the Indian legal system, given the absence of uniform civil laws and the operation of the personal laws of each religious community.

This chapter is divided into six parts, including the Introduction. Section II explores rules on jurisdiction and applicable law guiding divorce cases in India. The Indian legal positions are analysed in the context of the legal practice adopted in other jurisdictions. Section III traces the judicial position and recommendations of the Law Commission of India concerning the recognition of foreign divorce decree. Emphasis is given to judicial narratives in respect of the recognition of foreign divorce decrees, given the absence of a statutory position of no-fault divorce and leading to scenarios of limping marriages. Section IV concentrates on conflicts of law issues concerning ancillary financial orders and the nullity of marriages. Section IV also examines the reception and acceptance of extrajudicial divorce in western jurisdictions with particular reference to *talaq*. The issue of recognition of *talaq* is significant, given the considerable Muslim population in India. While scrutinising the prevailing Indian legal positions, the chapter will provide an analysis of the rules developed in other jurisdictions, including the EU and in Hague Conventions on family law matters.

II. Conflict of Laws Issues in Divorce

In divorce disputes involving a foreign element, the following contours of private international law are to be addressed: jurisdiction, choice of law, and the recognition of foreign divorce decrees.

A. Statutory Framework and Judicial Statements on Jurisdiction

In the personal law sphere, we find the concurrent existence of personal laws applicable to various communities in India. For Hindus, divorce was not conceivable until the passing of the Hindu Marriage Act 1955.[1] The Indian Divorce Act 1869, heavily based on the English Matrimonial

[1] L Holden, '*Hindu Divorce: A Legal Anthropology* 1st edn (Routledge, 2016) 8.

Causes Act of 1857, regulates divorce among Indian Christians.[2] The Special Marriage Act 1954 governs divorce procedure for marriages contracted under the Act. Divorce for Muslims is governed by religious practice and not covered by any statute. However, the Dissolution of Muslim Marriage Act 1939 lays down procedures and grounds on which a Muslim wife can claim dissolution of marriage from the husband.[3]

The foregoing matrimonial statutes incorporate jurisdictional rules and illuminate the place and court in which a petition in a matrimonial cause is filed. According to section 19 of the Hindu Marriage Act, a divorce petition can be presented in the district court within the local limits of the place of the solemnisation of marriage, the marital residence, the residence of the respondent or, if the respondent resides outside India, the petitioner's residence.[4] In case the wife is the petitioner, the petition can be filed at the place of her residence.[5] A comparable jurisdictional mandate operates for the Parsis Marriage and Divorce Act 1936[6] and the Special Marriage Act 1954. The applicability of the Special Marriage Act is not restricted to Indians and the parties need not be domiciled in India to solemnise their marriage under the Special Marriage Act.[7] Under the Indian Divorce Act 1869, a petition in a matrimonial cause can be presented in the district court within the local limits where the parties reside or last resided together.[8] The Indian Divorce Act had also provided for the application of principles and rules, which conform with the rules for divorce and matrimonial cases in England.[9] The statutory provisions illustrate the supple jurisdictional rules for regulating divorce among the many religious communities.

In this background, an analysis of the practice of other legal systems and in Hague Conventions will help to appreciate and understand the Indian legal position vis-a-vis other countries.

Traditionally common law jurisdictions, including the US, have followed the connecting factor of the domicile or residence of the parties at the time of filing of proceedings as the basis of divorce jurisdiction.[10] At common law, the English courts only possessed jurisdiction to grant a divorce if the spouses were domiciled in England.[11] The rule caused hardship to wives whose husbands had deserted them and acquired a domicile abroad. Statutory reforms in 1973 abolished the concept of a unitary domicile for married women.[12] Currently, the Domicile and Matrimonial Proceedings Act 1973 postulates divorce jurisdiction based on either domicile or habitual residence of the parties for one year in England.[13] In the US, sections 70 and 71 of the Second Restatement specify jurisdiction to dissolve a marriage based on either spouse's domicile.[14] Section 72 provides an exception to the domicile rule when either spouse has a relationship with the state, making it reasonable for the state to dissolve the marriage.[15]

[2] Indian Divorce Act 1869 (India).
[3] The Dissolution of Muslim Marriage Act 1939 (India).
[4] Hindu Marriage Act 1955 (India) s 19.
[5] ibid, s 19(iii)(a).
[6] Parsi Marriage and Divorce Act 1936 (India) s 29.
[7] Special Marriage Act 1954 (India) s 4.
[8] Indian Divorce Act (n 2) ss 3(3), 4.
[9] ibid, s 7, the provision has now been omitted by the Indian Divorce (Amendment) Act 2001 (51 of 2001) s 4 (w.e.f. 3-10-2001).
[10] Dicey, Morris & Collins, *Conflict Of Laws* 15th edn (3rd Supp, Sweet & Maxwell, 2016) 46, 285, 291; HF Goodrich, 'Divorce Problems in the Conflict of Laws' (1923) 2(1) *Texas Law Review* 1–29, 1.
[11] JG Collier, *Conflict of Laws* 3rd edn (Cambridge University Press, 2001) 319.
[12] WR Duncan, 'The Domicile of Married Women' (1976–1977) 4 (1) *Dublin University Law Journal* 36–51, 38.
[13] Domicile and Matrimonial Proceedings Act 1973 (UK) s 5(2).
[14] Restatement (Second) of Conflict of Laws (American Law Institute, 1965) s 71.
[15] ibid, s 72. See HW Baade, 'Marriage and Divorce in American Conflicts Law: Governmental-Interests Analysis and the Restatement (Second)' (1972) 72(2) *Columbia Law Review* 329–381, 334.

This exception potentially confers jurisdiction based on residence, but leaves out other criteria, such as the place of marriage with only a negligible connection to the facts.[16]

For many nations with civil law traditions, the appropriate connecting factor in personal matters is nationality.[17] Article 3(1) of the Brussels II *bis* Regulation, which has codified jurisdictional rules on divorce and legal separations in the EU, provides for seven flexible alternative grounds of jurisdictions, including the common habitual residence of the spouses, the last common habitual residence of the spouses, the habitual residence of one of the spouses, as well as the common nationality of the spouses.[18] The grounds of jurisdiction provided in the Regulation reflect a genuine connection between a person and a Member State, but have been criticised as encouraging forum shopping.[19] The Regulation furthers the jurisdictional rule by stating that a divorce decree passed by a Member State shall be recognised in other Member States without any particular procedure being required.[20] The Regulation has been entirely superseded by the recast Brussels II Regulation, which will come into operation in the EU (except for Denmark) in 2022.[21]

Flexible bases of jurisdiction provided under the Indian matrimonial statutes broadly conform with other jurisdictions' current legislative practice. However, this has not been the historical position. A firm reliance on domicile may be seen in the few judicial statements that have been reported involving jurisdictional issues. In *Noor Jahan Begum* v *Eugene Tiscenko*,[22] the plaintiff, Noor Jehan Begum, was born in Poland. She married the defendant Eugene Tiscenko, a Russian subject, on 20 May 1931 in Berlin according to civil rights. The plaintiff and defendant last resided together in Rome. After that, the plaintiff came to Calcutta, while the defendant went to Edinburgh.[23] The plaintiff embraced Islam and took the name of Noor Jehan. The defendant refused to convert to Islam.[24] The plaintiff filed for dissolution of her marriage.[25] The court relying on *Le Mesurier v Le Mesurier*[26] held that the domicile of the married parties affords the only true test of jurisdiction to dissolve their marriage. The court observed that the wife's domicile was that of her husband and the husband had a Russian domicile.[27] In *Linton v Guderian*,[28] the petitioner was born in Poland. When he was very young, his family moved to Berlin and, when he was about 27, he went to London. In 1914 he was married the respondent.[29] For a brief period,

[16] AL Estin, 'Marriage and Divorce Conflicts in the International Perspective' (2017) 27 *Duke Journal of Comparative and International Law* 485–517, 502.

[17] P Franzina, 'The Evolving Role of Nationality in Private International Law' in S Forlati, A Annoni (eds), *The Changing Role of Nationality in International Law* (Routledge, 2013) 193–210.

[18] Council Regulation (EC) No 2201/2003 of 27 November 2003 concerning jurisdiction and the recognition and enforcement of judgments in matrimonial matters and the matters of parental responsibility, repealing Regulation (EC) No 1347/2000 Art 3(1).

[19] J Carruthers, 'Party Autonomy in the Legal Regulation of Adult Relationships: What Place For Party Choice In Private International Law?' (2012) 61 *The International and Comparative Law Quarterly*, 881–913, 893; L Clarkson, 'What Effect Does European Private International Law on Cross-border Divorce Have on National Family Laws and International Obligations of the Member States?' (2019) 5(4) *Athens Journal of Law* 435–456, 440.

[20] Brussels II *bis* Regulation (n 18) Art 21(2).

[21] B Musseva, 'The recast of the Brussels IIa Regulation: The Sweet and Sour Fruits of Unanimity,' (2020) 21 *ERA Forum*, 129–142 (with regard to divorce jurisdiction the recast retains the existing provisions).

[22] *Noor Jahan Begum v Eugene Tiscenko* AIR [1942] Cal 325.

[23] ibid [1].

[24] ibid.

[25] ibid.

[26] *Le Mesurier v Le Mesurier* [1895] AC 517. In the case, the core legal question was whether the Sri Lankan courts possessed jurisdiction to dissolve a marriage between a British national and a French lady. Privy Council accorded domicile as the sole basis of assuming jurisdiction to dissolve a marriage. The case was distinguished in the case of *Asokan Nee Kandasamy v Asokan* [1994] 1 SLR 413 by adopting residence of the petitioner wife also as the base of jurisdiction.

[27] *Noor Jahan* (n 22) [3]; See also TS Rao, 'Some Recent Developments And 'Non-Developments' In Indian Private International Law' (1985) 27(4) *Journal of Indian Law Institute* 555–563, 558.

[28] *Linton v Guderian* AIR [1929] Cal 599.

[29] ibid [1].

he was in New York and later in Honolulu. For the next ten years, he kept on moving to different places. In 1926, he decided to go to India and take his wife and two children with him.[30] As they were starting off from Europe, he learned of the possibility of business in Sweden and went to Stockholm, his wife and children going to India in the meanwhile.[31] He expected them to go to Colombo, but they went to Calcutta and the wife lived in the Grand Hotel. He followed soon after and arrived there towards the end of November 1926.[32] He filed a case for divorce in India. The question was whether the court in British India had the right to pronounce a decree for dissolution of the marriage. The court stated that there could be no doubt that the burden of proving that the petitioner had made up his mind to come to India and treat it as his ultimate and permanent home was on him. The court held that the power to grant a divorce rested with the court of the country in which the parties were domiciled at the date of the petition.[33] Compared to the current broad-based divorce jurisdiction, the judgments signal a historical reliance on domicile as the basis of divorce. The legal reforms in England influenced the shift to a broader base of divorce jurisdiction in India that are currently part of its matrimonial statutes. However, due to a strong allegiance to common law traditions, nationality has never been treated as a connecting factor historically or under the current statutory framework.

In *Vincent Joseph Konrath & Ors. v Jacintha Angela Vincent Konrath*,[34] the moot legal question was whether a Christian marriage solemnised outside India between Indian citizens domiciled in India could be dissolved in India. The court held that section 2 of the Indian Divorce Act 1869 provides that the court shall have jurisdiction to grant relief under the Act where the petitioner and the respondent profess the Christian religion and where the parties to the marriage are domiciled in India at the time when a petition is presented.[35]

B. Statutory Framework and Judicial Statements on Applicable Law

The Indian matrimonial statutes enumerated in section II.A do not include rules on the applicable law in a divorce. Besides, there are no judicial statements on the applicable law in divorces having a foreign element.

Khambatta v Khambatta[36] offers some guidance. The petitioner, a Scot, married Gulam Ibrahim in Scotland according to Scottish law. At the time of marriage, the husband was a Muslim domiciled in British India and the wife was a Christian domiciled in Scotland.[37] The wife embraced Islam, after she became domiciled in British India and she remained in that faith. The husband pronounced *talaq* under Islamic law.[38] The wife later married Khambatta under the Special Marriage Act. The wife petitioned for a divorce and the husband took the preliminary point that, at the date of the marriage, the petitioner was already married, so that the wife's second marriage was a nullity and could not be dissolved.[39] The main question was whether the

[30] ibid.
[31] ibid.
[32] ibid.
[33] ibid [3].
[34] *Vincent Joseph Konrath v Jacintha Angela Vincent Konath* AIR [1994] Bom 120.
[35] ibid [9].
[36] *khambatta v Khambatta* AIR [1994] Bom 120 [10].
[37] ibid [2]. See SVF Gerald, 'Indian and Far Eastern Cases on the Conflict of Laws' (1934) 17(4) *Journal of Comparative Legislation and International Law* 220–226.
[38] *Khambatta* (n 36) [2].
[39] ibid [2].

first marriage had been validly dissolved. The petitioner argued that the *lex domicilii* determines a husband's right to dissolve a marriage by *talaq* and Islamic law admits divorce by such method.[40] The respondent contended that, the marriage having been solemnised in Scotland, it must be recognised and treated as a Scottish marriage and, being monogamous, could not be terminated by the mere will of the husband.[41] The court held that in the absence of an express contract, rights under marriage are governed by the law of the domicile.[42] There was no matrimonial law in British India applicable to the inhabitants generally. The court stated:

> [A] Muhammadan husband might claim that by the law applicable to him, he is entitled to divorce his wife by *talaq*; the wife, being a Christian, may affirm that, though by marriage she acquired the domicile of her husband, she did not acquire his religion, and that by the law of his domicile applicable to Christians, she is not liable to be divorced by *talaq*. It is, however, not necessary in this case to determine what the position was while the wife remained a Christian because, at the time when the *talaq* was given, she had embraced the Muhammadan faith.[43]

The decision favours the application of the parties' *lex domicilii* at the time of divorce to determine their rights under a marriage.[44]

However, some judicial decisions favour the application of the *lex fori*. In *Giardano's* case, the husband (an Italian subject and domiciled in Italy) instituted divorce proceedings in India on the basis of residence. Based on the Indian Divorce Act, the divorce was granted on the ground of adultery committed by the wife. The court did not evaluate the position of Italian law as Italy had no provision for divorce.[45] In *Mandeep Kaur v Dharam Lingam*,[46] the respondent was a Canadian citizen. The wife petitioned to dissolve their marriage under the Hindu Marriage Act 1955. The court held that the Act would apply to a Hindu outside India only if the latter is domiciled in India. These decisions point to the application of the law of the domicile and the *lex fori* to divorces and illustrate the staunch influence of the English law.

Traditionally, English courts have preferred the application of the *lex fori*.[47] This approach is understandable and justified when domicile or nationality is the sole basis for the divorce jurisdiction and the inherent interest of the forum in regulating the life of the domiciliary. Similarly, section 285 of the Second Restatement provides that 'the local law of the domiciliary state in which the action is brought will be applied to determine the right to divorce'.[48] However, reliance on domicile or nationality does not offer autonomy to the parties. Slowly, statutes and case law in the US and England have begun to recognise some degree of party autonomy in marital relations.[49] A concept of party autonomy that allows parties to choose the law applicable to their divorce has been incorporated in the Rome III Regulation on the law applicable to divorce and legal separations.[50]

[40] ibid [5].

[41] ibid.

[42] ibid.

[43] ibid [9].

[44] JAC Smith, 'Eastern Marriages in English Law' (1952) 1(3) *International Comparative Law Quarterly* 301–312, 311.

[45] *Giardanos* case [1912] ILR 40 Cal 25 5; same dicta were followed in *Shireen Mall* AIR [1952] Pun 277 Quoted in Law Commission of India, *The Recognition of Foreign Divorces*, (Report No 65, 1976) ch 3.14, 29.

[46] *Mandeep Kaur v Dharam Lingam* 1 [2017] DMC 124 P&H.

[47] K Trimmings, P Torremans, A Mills, U Grusic and C Heinze, *Cheshire, North, and Fawcett: Private International Law* 15th edn (Oxford University Press, 2017) 967; Collier (n 11) 320.

[48] Second Restatement (n 14) s 285; PM North, *Essays in Private International Law* (Clarendon Press, 1993) 161.

[49] Estin (n 16) 487.

[50] Council Regulation (EU) No 1259/2010 on implementing enhanced cooperation in the area of separation the law applicable to Divorce and Legal Separations (EU Council Regulation) [2010] OJ L343/10, Art 1.

Article 5 of the Rome III Regulation provides the parties with the option to choose from the following connecting factors:

(a) The law of their common habitual residence at the time of the choice.
(b) The law of the last common habitual residence, if one of the spouses still resides there at the time of the choice.
(c) The law of the nationality of either of the spouses at the time of the choice or
(d) The law of the forum.[51]

The Rome III Regulation further provides that the choice needs to be in written form[52] and can be made at any time up to when the court is seised of the matter.[53] The application of *renvoi* is expressly excluded from the ambit of the chosen law.[54] Article 10 of the Rome III Regulation provides that, if the chosen law does not provide for divorce, the *lex fori* will apply.[55] This is consonant with a person's right to obtain a divorce. The Rome III Regulation incorporates the fundamental notion of public policy as a ground for excluding the application of chosen law.[56] The Regulation espouses habitual residence, last residence, common nationality, or the *lex fori* as the applicable law in the absence of choice by the parties.[57] Article 13 of the Rome III Regulation clarifies that parties can only choose a state law as the applicable law and there cannot be a choice of non-state law.[58] This means that parties cannot choose *sharia* or religious laws as the applicable law. However, they can refer to a religious law if it coincides with the law of their domicile.[59] Article 8 of the Rome III Regulation provides that in the absence of a choice of law by the parties, the courts are to choose the applicable law based on habitual residence, nationality, or the law of the forum.[60] Given the strong religious base of matrimonial laws in India, it is unlikely that the Indian legal system will incorporate provisions of party autonomy in the choice of law process in divorce.

III. Recognition of Foreign Divorce in India

A. Statutory Framework for Recognition of Foreign Divorce

There is no specific legislation addressing the grounds of recognition of foreign divorce decrees in India. Recognition of foreign divorce decrees is dealt with under section 13 of the Code of Civil Procedure 1908 (CPC) and section 41 of the Indian Evidence Act.[61] Section 13 of the CPC

[51] ibid, Art 5.
[52] ibid, Art 7.
[53] ibid, recital 20.
[54] ibid, Art 11.
[55] ibid, Art 10.
[56] ibid, Art 12.
[57] ibid, Art 8.
[58] ibid, Art 13.
[59] *Soha Sahyouni v Raja Mamisch* Judgment in Case C-372/16; See SL Gössl, 'Open Issues in European International Family Law: Sahyouni, Private Divorces and Islamic Law Under the Rome III Regulation' [2017] *The European Legal Forum* 68–74.
[60] Rome III Regulation (n 50) Art 8. See S Rutten, 'Recognition of Divorce by Repudiation (talaq) in France, Germany and the Netherlands' (2004) 11(3) *Maastricht Journal of European and Comparative Law* 263–285.
[61] Indian Evidence Act 1872, s 41 deals with the relevancy of certain judgments.

specifies that a foreign judgment shall be conclusive on any matter directly adjudicated between the same parties except in the following situations:

(a) where a court of competent jurisdiction has not pronounced judgment;
(b) where a decision has not been given on the merits of a case;
(c) where a decision was founded on an incorrect view of international law or a refusal to recognise the law of India;
(d) where the proceedings are opposed to natural justice;
(e) where a decision has been obtained by fraud;
(f) where a decision sustains a claim founded on a breach of any law in force in India.[62]

The High Courts and Supreme Court clarified the contours of the statutory provisions in a catena of cases. Among their judicial statements, the decision in *Y Narasimha Rao v Venkata Lakshmi*[63] marks a turning point in the approach of the Indian judiciary. Hence, the analysis below of the judicial position on recognition of foreign divorce decrees is divided into the that before and after *Y Narasimha Rao.*

B. Judicial Position on Recognition of Foreign Divorce

i. *Legal Position before Y Narasimha Rao*

In *Pires v Pires,*[64] the High Court of Goa clarified the principles applicable to a foreign divorce decree. The husband sought to enforce a divorce decree obtained from the High Court of Uganda. The petition was opposed because, the parties being Roman Catholic and the marriage having being solemnised in Goa, their marriage was said to be indissoluble. It was submitted that a divorce decree against existing legal provisions in India could not be recognised.[65] The Court refused to confirm the divorce because under existing laws in Goa a Roman Catholic marriage is not dissoluble. Hence, the divorce decree of the High Court of Uganda was against the public policy embodied in the Portuguese Civil Code applicable in Goa.[66] However, in *Marggarate v Chacko,* involving the validity of a divorce granted by the German court against the husband, the Kerala High Court recognised the German decree based on the real and substantial connection the petitioner wife with Germany.[67]

Satya v Teja Singh[68] was a landmark decision and instrumental in influencing the 65th Law Commission Report. The appellant and respondent, both Indian citizens, were married in India in 1955. The respondent husband left for the US in 1959 and from 1960 to 1964 lived in Utah as a student and later took on employment there.[69] In 1965 the appellant applied for a maintenance under section 488 of the Criminal Procedure Code.[70] The respondent relied on the divorce

[62] Code of Civil Procedure 1908 (India) s 13.
[63] *Y Narasimha Rao v Y Venkata Lakshmi* [1991] SCR (2) 821.
[64] *Pires v Pires* AIR [1967] GDD 113.
[65] ibid. See also TSR Rao, 'Some Recent Developments And 'Non-Developments' In Indian Private International Law' (1985) 27(4) *Journal of Indian Law Institute* 555–563, 558.
[66] ibid. See also KA Sharma 'Limping Marriages and Holidays Wives' in K Sharma, A Pal and T Chakrabarti (eds) *Critiquing, Nationalism, Transnationalism, and Indian Diaspora* (Creative Books, 2006).
[67] *Marggarate Maria Pulparampil Nee Feldman v Dr. Chacko Pulparampil And Ors* AIR [1970] Ker 1.
[68] *Satya v Teja Singh* AIR [1975] SC 105.
[69] ibid [2].
[70] ibid [3].

decree of the Nevada court as a complete answer to the appellant's claim.[71] The High Court held in favour of the respondent, applying the unity of domicile principle.[72] On appeal, the Supreme Court observed that in determining whether a divorce decree should be recognised in another jurisdiction as a matter of comity, public policy and good morals might be considered.[73] The court observed that the respondent had only gone to Nevada to establish a jurisdictional base for divorce. To confer jurisdiction on the ground of the respondent's residence and entitle a decree to extraterritorial recognition, the residence must be actual, genuine and accompanied by an intent to make the place of residence one's home.[74] Thus, the Nevada court lacked jurisdiction and its decree should not be recognised by the Indian court. The court held that the husband had perpetrated a fraud on the foreign court by claiming that he was domiciled within its jurisdiction.[75] The Supreme Court extended the meaning of 'fraud' in section 13(e) of the Code of Civil Procedure to cover not just fraud on the merits, but also as to jurisdiction.[76] The Court stated that the legislature ought to find a solution to the unsatisfactory situation in respect of the recognition of foreign divorces in Indian law. The Court noted that the British Parliament had, to a large extent, reformed English law by passing the Recognition of Divorces and Legal Separations Act 1971. The 1970 Hague Convention of 1970, which contains a comprehensive scheme for relieving the confusion caused by differing systems of laws, could serve as a model.[77] Even though the decision ultimately upheld the wife's prayer for maintenance, it was based on the factual scenario where the husband could not prove genuine residence or domicile in Nevada. The legal basis of the judgment otherwise adhered to the common law principle, according to which the wife's domicile follows that of the husband.[78]

In light of the court's observations about the utility of the 1970 Hague Convention, a brief overview of the main elements of the Convention is apposite.

a. 1970 Hague Convention on Recognition of Divorces and Legal Separations

The 1970 Hague Convention attempted to facilitate the recognition of divorces and legal separation obtained in states through officially recognised judicial or other proceedings.[79] The reference to other proceedings indicates that the scope of the 1970 Convention is broad enough to cover divorces or legal separations resulting from legislative, administrative, and even religious acts.[80]

[71] ibid [4].

[72] ibid [6]; See P Rana, 'Distant Silences and Default Judgments: Access to Justice for Transnationally Abandoned Women in India' (2014) 1(2) *Indian Journal of Law & Public Policy* 122–138, 137; see R Jagota 'Executability and Enforceability of Foreign Judgments and Decrees in India: An Analysis of Judicial Trends' (2015) 6(2) *Indian Journal of Law & Justice* 15–34, 24.

[73] ibid [22], see Jagota (n 72) 21.

[74] ibid [23].

[75] ibid [55]; A Malhotra and R Malhotra, 'Divorce Nullity and Related Matters under the Hindu Marriage Act 1955' [2005] *International Survey of Family Law* 275–310.

[76] See K Singh and Dr P Rajput, 'Laws Relating to NRI Marriages and their Impact on Women', (National Commission for Women) 25 http://ncwapps.nic.in/ExpertCommitteePDFFiles/EC_NRIMarriages.pdf; A Malhotra and R Malhotra, 'Marriage and Divorce-Complete Constitutional Justice' [2015] *International Survey of Family Law* 121, 149.

[77] ibid [57].

[78] L Jambholkar, 'Recognition of Foreign Divorce Decrees in India: A Case for Contextual Interpretation' (1991) 33(3) *Journal of Indian Law Institute* 432, 438.

[79] Hague Convention on the Recognition of Divorces and Legal Separations (adopted on 1 June 1970 effective from 24 August 1975) Art 1.

[80] P Bellet and B Goldman, 'Explanatory Report on the 1970 Hague Divorce Convention', 7 https://assets.hcch.net/docs/99ce43e1-b580-4009-9b75-5d88fa4e12f2.pdf; See also S Maidment, 'The Legal Effect of Religious Divorces' (1974) 37 *Modern Law Review* 611–626.

The possibility of religious divorce is significant, as the recognition of *talaq* has often presented difficulties in several jurisdictions. However, insistence on 'proceedings' and official recognition also allows enough leverage for nations to exclude the religious divorces based on lack of adherence to proceedings and official recognition.[81] Further, the 1970 Convention only applies between Contracting States. The 1970 convention insists on a sufficient claim and relation to jurisdiction by the connecting factor of habitual residence or nationality.[82] The reliance on habitual residence was added specially to protect the interest of abandoned wives who are allowed to file the petition for divorce in their habitual residence and enjoy the benefit of the 1970 Convention.[83] In order to accommodate the interest of the countries that relied on domicile, the 1970 Convention provides that the term habitual residence is deemed to include domicile as well.[84] Recognition of divorce can be refused on the ground of public policy[85] and in situations where the parties' common national law does not provide for divorce and do not recognise the divorce from other states.[86] Although the 1970 Convention allows for a public policy exception to the recognition of divorces, it does not attempt to explain or illustrate the possible essential components of this exception. It is feared that the application of this provision may lead to Member States avoiding recognition of a Muslim divorce pronounced in a third country. In line with the accepted principle of favouring recognition of foreign divorce decree, the 1970 Convention provides that Contracting States can adopt more favourable rules to recognise foreign divorces and legal separations[87] Twenty countries, including the UK, are parties to the 1970 Convention. India is not a party.[88] The 1970 Convention has inspired the Brussels II *bis* Regulation providing for recognition of foreign divorce decree.[89]

The large diaspora spread across jurisdictions has presented myriad challenges for the Indian legal system. At the Central Government's request, the Law Commission of India in its 65th Report examined the decision of the Supreme Court in *Satya v Teja* and recommended separate and self-contained legislation on foreign divorces and legal separation.[90] The Commission believed that such legislation should adopt a perspective of advancing substantial justice to both the parties. The Commission also considered ancillary orders passed by the foreign courts in matrimonial proceedings and recommended that such ancillary orders should not be treated as binding by Indian courts even though foreign decrees of divorce may be recognised.[91] The Commission also prepared a draft Recognition of Divorces and Legal Separations Bill. Section 4 of the draft Bill provided for recognition of a decree based on either spouse's habitual residence or nationality.[92] Section 6 provided that the court's jurisdiction should be treated as conclusive if both parties take part in the proceedings.[93] However, the recommendations of the Commission have not been implemented.

[81] ibid (Bellet & Goldman Explanatory Report).
[82] ibid 10.
[83] ibid 11.
[84] Hague Convention on the Recognition of Divorces and Legal Separations (n 79) Art 3.
[85] ibid, Art 10.
[86] ibid, Art 7.
[87] ibid, Art 17.
[88] Hague Convention on the Recognition of Divorces and Legal Separations www.hcch.net/en/instruments/conventions/status-table/?cid=80.
[89] Brussels II bis Regulation (n 18) Art 21, All EU members except Denmark are party to the Convention.
[90] Law Commission, 65th Report (n 45) 135.
[91] ibid, ch 19.27, 126.
[92] Recognition of Divorces and Legal Separations Bill 1976, Law Commission of India, s 4.
[93] ibid, s 6.

ii. Legal Position Post Y Narasimha Rao

The decision in *Y Narasimha Rao* deeply engaged with the private international rules on the recognition of foreign divorces in India.[94] The appellant (Narasimha) married the respondent (Venkata) in Tirupati in accordance with Hindu law as it was in 1975. The couple last resided together in New Orleans.[95] In 1978 the appellant filed a petition for dissolution of marriage in Missouri and obtained the decree on the ground of the irrevocable breakdown of the marriage by technically satisfying the 90-day residence requirement in Missouri.[96] The appellant married another women and the respondent filed a criminal complaint against the appellant for bigamy.[97] The Supreme Court observed that it could simply rely on *Satya v Teja* and decree on a narrow basis that the appellant fraudulently claimed residence in Missouri to obtain a divorce there. However, the Court instead proceeded on the assumption that the Missouri court rightly assumed jurisdiction and framed the real issue as whether, even in cases where a foreign court has properly assumed jurisdiction, an Indian court should recognise a foreign divorce decree.[98] The Court lamented the state of private international law in India and pointed out that, despite over 43 years of independence, no legislation has been passed dealing with private international law.[99] The Court put forward a fresh interpretation of section 13(a) to the effect that a foreign judgment should not be recognised if a court of competent jurisdiction has not pronounced it. The Court held that section 13(a) should be construed as meaning that a court will only be regarded as having competent jurisdiction, if the statute or law under which the parties were married recognises such court as competent to entertain the parties' matrimonial dispute. Any other court should be regarded as lacking competence in the dispute, unless both parties voluntarily and unconditionally subject themselves to the jurisdiction of that court.[100]

Section 13(b) was held to mean that: (1) the decision of the foreign court should be on a ground available under the law under which the parties were married; and (2) the decision should be the result of a judicial process where the respondent has voluntarily submitted to the jurisdiction and contested the claim.[101] For instance, where the parties were married in India, if a foreign divorce decree is granted based on the respondent's adultery, the decree would be accepted, since 'cruelty' is a ground under the Hindu Marriage Act 1955. On the other hand, a divorce on the ground of 'irretrievable breakdown of marriage' would not be accepted as this is not a ground under the Hindu Marriage Act 1955.[102]

The second part of section 13(c) was held to mean that marriages in India could only be contracted under either the customary or statutory law in force in India. Hence, the only law that can apply to matrimonial disputes is the one under which the parties were married and no other law.[103] While interpreting the requirement of natural justice under section 13(d), it was held that the principle of natural justice has to be extended to mean something more than mere compliance with the technical rules of procedure.[104] The Court espoused the final position as

[94] *Narasimha Rao* (n 63); See generally Jhambolkar (n 78).
[95] ibid [1].
[96] ibid.
[97] ibid [3].
[98] *Narasimha Rao* (n 63) [8]; See also Jhambholkar (n 78) 432.
[99] *Narasimha Rao* (n 63) [10].
[100] ibid [12]. See L Jhambolkar, 'Conflict of Laws' in SK Verma and Kusum (ed), *Fifty Years of the Supreme Court of India: Its Grasp*' (Indian Law Institute, New Delhi, 2000) 664.
[101] *Narasimha Rao* (n 63) [12].
[102] ibid.
[103] ibid.
[104] ibid.

'the jurisdiction assumed by the foreign court as well as the grounds on which the relief is granted must be in accordance with the matrimonial law under which the parties are married'. But the Supreme Court laid down three exceptions to this rule.

(1) The matrimonial action was filed in the forum where the respondent is domiciled or habitually reside and the relief was granted on a ground available in the matrimonial law under which the parties were married.
(2) The respondent voluntarily and effectively submitted to the jurisdiction of the forum and contested the claim on a ground available under the matrimonial law under which the parties were married.
(3) The respondent consented to the grant of the relief, although the jurisdiction of the forum was not in accordance with the provisions of the matrimonial law of the parties.[105]

The Court explained that its decision was founded on just and equitable principles. The parties are entitled to (and should) know in advance their rights and obligations when they marry under a particular law. Adherence to the parties' matrimonial law would rescue the institution of marriage from an uncertain maze of private international law rules.[106] The significance of the rules lies in their ability to protect women, the most vulnerable sector of Indian society, by removing strict adherence to domicile-based jurisdiction.[107]

Jhambolkar has remarked that the judgment attempted to provide a minimum standard for bringing certainty to the recognition of foreign judgments. She eloquently brings out the background of the judgment wherein previous decisions blindly relied on the common law principle of unity of domicile even after English law on the subject had changed.[108] Thus, the Supreme Court's judgment made a departure from a law of divorce based on domicile to the matrimonial law of the parties. A catena of decisions have followed *Narasimha Rao* and applied the matrimonial law of the parties.[109] In *Neeraja Saraph v Jayant V Saraph*,[110] the Supreme Court undertook an extensive assessment of problems introduced by an increased number of non-resident Indian marriages and a growing Indian diaspora. It recommended that the country enact legislation along the lines of the UK's Foreign Judgments (Reciprocal Enforcement) Act 1933.[111] In *Anubha v Vikas Aggarwal*,[112] the question concerned the enforceability of a foreign decree obtained on the ground of 'no fault' divorce in respect of parties whose marriage had been solemnised under the Hindu Marriage Act. Reviewing the precedents, the Court held that the ground on which the marriage had been dissolved was not available under the Hindu Marriage Act. The majority of judicial decisions after *Narasimha Rao* have insisted on recognising only those divorces, which was granted based on the matrimonial law of the parties. The position is not in conformity with the practice of major legal systems. The practice of selected jurisdictions as to the recognition of foreign divorce decree is discussed below.

[105] ibid [13]; See P Dommaraju, 'Divorce and Separation in India' (2016) 42(2) *Population and Development Review* 195, 223.
[106] *Narasimha Rao* (n 63) [13].
[107] ibid.
[108] Jhambholkar (n 78) 434.
[109] *V. Bhagat v Mrs. D. Bhagat* AIR [1994] 710; *Mrs. M. v Mr. A.* (1993) 1 DMC 384; *Mrs. Veena Kalia v Dr. Jatinder Nath Kalia* AIR [1996] Delhi 54; *Harmeeta Singh v. Rajat Taneja* 102 [2003] DLT 822; *Rajiv Tayal v Union of India And Ors* AIR [2006] Delhi 81; *Kashmira Kale v Mr.Kishorekumar Mohan Kale* AIR [2006] Delhi 81; *Hemavathi Shivashankar v Dr.Tumkur S Shivashankar* II [2010] DMC 854; *Sonder Gopal v Sondur Rajini* [2013] 7 SCC 426.
[110] *Neerja Saraph v Jayant V. Saraph* [1994] SCC (6) 461.
[111] ibid [4].
[112] *Anubha v Shri Vikas Aggarwal And Ors* AIR [2003] Delhi 175.

a. Reflections from Other Jurisdictions

Until 1953, English common law strictly adhered to domicile and recognised only divorce decrees granted by the country of the parties' domicile.[113] The condition of reciprocity as a ground for recognition of divorce was added in 1953.[114] It was supplemented by the *real* and substantial connection test in the famous case of *Indyka v Indyka*.[115] The current rules on recognition and enforcement of foreign divorce are codified under the Family Act 1986 and are based on numerous connecting factors, including domicile, nationality, and habitual residence.[116] Traditionally, the US courts recognised foreign divorces based on the principle of the comity of nations and recognised only those divorces granted by the parties' domicile.[117] In keeping with the due process clause of the US Constitution, the courts have also required that reasonable notice be given of proceedings.[118] Section 484 (1) of the *Restatement (Third) of Foreign Relations Law* suggests that the US is not bound to recognise a foreign divorce granted in a country that was not the domicile or habitual residence of both spouses at the time of divorce, even when one or both spouses are nationals of that country.[119] However, section 484(2) permits exceptions. Recognition may be granted on a broader basis than the parties' domicile, including where: (1) a divorce has been obtained in the country of domicile or residence of one of the parties; or (2) a divorce has been obtained from a court with personal jurisdiction over both parties and at least one spouse appeared in person before such court.[120] The Indian position does not conform with global practice. The disparity is leading to a situation of limping marriage where the divorce granted in one jurisdiction is not recognised in another jurisdiction. It is submitted that, based on the recommendations of the Law Commission, concrete legal reforms need to be undertaken urgently to bring justice to the parties. As proposed by the Supreme Court, the 1970 Hague Convention can be a template for the legal reforms.

C. Recommendations of the Law Commission

The increased number of legal disputes involving non-resident Indians highlighted in numerous judicial decisions has prompted the Law Commission of India to undertake a detailed analysis of the subject. The Commission in its 219th Report made a number of recommendations.[121] Relying on the earlier work of the Law Commission in its 211th Report,[122] it proposed the compulsory registration of marriages, especially in cases where one of the spouses is a non-resident Indian. This would ensure compliance with conditions of a valid marriage, provide proof of marriage, and deter bigamy.[123] The Commission repeated the proposal in its 217th Report to add the

[113] Collier (n 11) 322.

[114] ibid.

[115] [1969] 1 AC 33.

[116] Family Law Act 1986 (UK) s 46.

[117] *Basiouny v Basiouny* 445 So. 2d 916 (Ala. Civ. App. 1984); See also *Schwartz v Zik* 273 NJ. Super. 78, 640 A.2d 1212 (Ch. Div. 1993); *In re Marriage of Zadorozny* 70 Wash. App. 464, 853 P.2d 960 [1993].

[118] *Mullane v Central Hanover Trust Co* [1950] 339 US 306.

[119] Restatement of the Foreign Relations Law of the United States, (third) (American Law Institute Publishers, 1987) s 484.

[120] ibid, s 484(2). See also *Juma v Aomo* 68 A.3d 148 (2013); *Matter of Ramadan*, 891 A.2d 1186 (NH 2006); *Farag v Farag* 772 NYS.2d 368 (NYApp. Div. 2004); Estin (n 216) 505.

[121] Law Commission of India, *Need for Family Law Legislations for Non-resident Indians* (Report No 219, 2009).

[122] Law Commission of India, *Laws on Registration of Marriage and Divorce – A Proposal for Consolidation and Reform* (Report No 211, 2008).

[123] ibid [23]. See also, V Nimushakavi, 'Cross-Border Divorce Decrees – Recognition in India and Public Policy Considerations' in SR Garimella and S Jolly (eds), *Private International Law: South Asian State Practice* (Springer, 2017) 111.

irretrievable breakdown of marriage as a ground for divorce under the Hindu Marriage Act and Special Marriage Act.[124] The Commission felt that such a ground would provide non-resident Indians with an incentive to petition the Indian court for a divorce rather than seeking divorce on the ground of the irretrievable breakdown of marriage before a foreign court. This would enable Indian spouses to contest divorce petitions on just and equitable terms before Indian courts.[125] In the case of non-resident Indians, the Hindu Marriage Act 1955 and the Special Marriage Act 1954 should be amended to enable the court to make orders for maintenance and alimony, child custody, child support and the settlement of matrimonial property. This will ensure that a spouse and children on Indian soil are maintained and provided for in accordance with the income and living standard of a non-resident Indian spouse.[126] In matters of succession; the transfer of property; the making, execution and implementation of wills; the repatriation of funds by a non-resident Indian, state governments must simplify and streamline their procedures. Fast-track courts should be set up to deal with such cases expeditiously following a time-bound schedule.[127] Both judicial statements and Law Commission Reports have stressed the importance of updating India's laws in relation to the recognition of divorce in order to minimise the risk of limping marriages.

D. Gender in the Recognition of Foreign Divorce Decrees

An analysis of matrimonial disputes involving private international law concerns before the Indian courts reveals the hardships that Indian women face, including abandonment, desertion, lack of maintenance, etc. This situation is perpetuated by structural inequality and a lack of understanding of the impact on women of the differential treatment institutionalised by the legal system.[128] Few legal reforms and judicial statements have attempted to abolish discriminatory provisions on gender in the family law sphere.[129]

In *Githa Hariharan & Another v Reserve Bank of India & Another*,[130] the Supreme Court interpreted the provisions of the Hindu Minority and Guardianship Act 1956[131] and the Guardian and Wards Act 1890 that provide for the father to be the natural guardian of the child. The Court affirmed that the mother is also the natural guardian of the child. However, even after abolition of the concept of unity of domicile in England, Indian courts steadfastly adhered to the archaic principle and reiterated that the matrimonial domicile is the only reasonable option for assuming jurisdiction in a divorce suit.[132] In this scenario of prevalent discrimination, there has been a growing realisation of the need to examine private international law principles more closely.[133]

[124] Law Commission of India, *Irretrievable Breakdown of Marriage – Another Ground for Divorce* (Report No 217, 2009).

[125] ibid.

[126] ibid [25].

[127] ibid [25], [26].

[128] DL Bowen, VM Hudson and PL Nielsen, 'State Fragility and Structural Gender Inequality in Family Law: An Empirical Investigation' (2015) 4 *Laws* 654–672; D Rosenblum, 'Loving Gender Balance: Reframing Identity-Based Inequality Remedies' (2008) 76(6) *Fordham Law Review* 2873–2893, 2879.

[129] See N Subramanian, 'Legal Change and Gender Inequality: Changes in Muslim Family Law in India' (2008) 33(3) *Law & Social Inquiry* 631–672; Heaton Jacquelin, 'Striving for Substantive Gender Equality in Family Law: Selected Issues,' (2005) 21(4) *South African Journal on Human Rights* 547–574.

[130] *Githa Hariharan & Another v Reserve Bank of India & Another* AIR [1999] [2] SCC 22.

[131] Hindu Minority and Guardianship Act 1956 (India) s 6.

[132] *Satya v Teja* (n 68) [14]. See FE Noronha, *Private International Law in India: Adequacy of Principles in Comparison with Common Law and Civil Law Systems* (Universal Law Publishers, 2010) 110.

[133] K Knop, R Michaels and A Riles, 'From Multiculturalism to Technique: Feminism, Culture, and the Conflict of Laws Style' (2012) 64(3) *Cornell Law Faculty Publications* 589–656, 643.

It has been argued that a specific focus on public policy in connection with social, religious, and cultural practices may help address discrimination and inequality issues. Public policy has been invoked in relation to the recognition of foreign divorces. In *Satya v Teja*, the court observed that 'notions of a genuine divorce and substantial justice and the distinctive principles of our public policy must determine the rules of our private international law'.[134] The court questioned the validity of a foreign divorce obtained on the basis of a fraud on the foreign court and linked the issue with public policy, holding that such decrees 'offend against our notions of substantial justice'.[135] In *Y Narasimha Rao*, the court observed that family law is primarily determined and influenced by social, moral, and religious considerations and public policy plays a unique role in shaping the same.[136] Such interpretation was motivated by the desire to do justice to all parties, especially the wife in the case. The practical implication of the judgment was the incorporation of gender mainstreaming into the recognition of foreign divorce.

The linking of public policy with social considerations signals that social morals profoundly influence the definition of public policy in the matrimonial legislation. The 65th Report of the Law Commission of India has expounded on public policy in the context of the recognition of divorce and stated that public policy does not connote what the law ought to be. Instead, it focuses on what the current public perception of the law is.[137] The application of current public perception as a yardstick for public policy introduces ambiguity into the invocation of public policy, as it is difficult to gauge mainstream public sentiment. Public policy, as found in existing private international law conventions, can be adopted as a valuable tool in promoting gender mainstreaming in cross-border family law affairs. However, a word of caution needs to be added in terms of public policy. Public policy can be interpreted as a mechanism to promote gender equality and ameliorate the hardships faced by women concerning serious infringements of fundamental human rights. But public policy can also be a mechanism to prioritise local discriminatory domestic laws over the adoption of foreign legal systems. For instance, country A permits interfaith marriages and country B prohibits interfaith marriages. In a case involving the recognition of marriage between persons domiciled in country A, country B may invoke public policy to refuse recognition of the marriage.

E. Comparison with South Asian Jurisdictions

Indian judicial practice has influenced the legal evolution of private international law practice on the recognition of foreign divorces in other jurisdictions. *Sabina Pandey v Pushkar Pandey* laid down the rule for the recognition of foreign divorces in Nepal. Sabina Pandey and Pushkar Pandey married in Nepal. Sabina later filed a case in the Kathmandu District Court claiming her share in her husband's property.[138] Nepalese law requires property matters to be settled before proceeding under a divorce petition. Meanwhile, the Oklahoma Court granted a divorce on a petition filed by the husband. The Kathmandu District Court rejected Sabina Pandey's application on basis of the foreign divorce decree.[139] The Supreme Court of Nepal refused to recognise the divorce decree of the Oklahoma Court in light of a lack of connection between Sabina Pandey

[134] *Satya v Teja* (n 68) [38].
[135] ibid.
[136] *Narasimha Rao* (n 63) [9].
[137] Law Commission, 65th Report (n 45) ch 17.3 102.
[138] S Regmi, 'Foreign Judgments in Matrimonial Disputes: Recognition in Nepal and Public Policy Considerations,' in SR Garimella and S Jolly (eds), *Private International Law: South Asian State Practice* (Springer 2017) 133–151.
[139] ibid 143.

and Oklahoma. The court declared that Sabina Pandey was not domiciled in the US and had not submitted to the court's jurisdiction. It is pertinent to note that, unlike Indian judicial statements, the court in *Sabina Pandey* used residence and intention to assess her domicile independently of her husband's domicile. Relying on international human rights documents, the Supreme Court cited the violation of natural justice, as Sabina was not able to defend the judicial proceedings in the US, hence violating Nepal's public policy.[140] The Supreme Court also looked into the parties' matrimonial laws and held that the grounds of divorce under Oklahoma law were different from those recognised by Nepalese law. Two fundamental aspects of Nepalese public policy were invoked, a woman's right to property and access to justice.[141] The ratio of the decision closely follows the Indian decision in *Narasimha Rao*.

Unlike the Indian legal framework, the new Civil Code of Nepal has incorporated private international law principles. The Code prescribes that the law of the parties' nationality shall determine the capacity of the parties to marry and the *lex loci celebrations* determines the formal validity of a marriage.[142] The Code further states that legal separation shall be governed by the law of the country of the couple's habitual residence. The Code has limited provisions applicable to divorce. It states that divorce between Nepalese citizens or between a Nepali and a foreign national granted by a foreign court based on the *lex fori* will be recognised and enforced by Nepal's courts.[143]

IV. Ancillary Financial Orders and Nullity of Marriage

A. Rules on Recognition of Ancillary Orders

It is a common statutory provision that, when a court orders the dissolution of a marriage, the court also passes orders for maintenance, alimony, and similar matters. The question is whether and how far foreign ancillary orders are to be recognised. Under section 8(3) of the English Act of 1871, the courts were not required to recognise: (1) findings of fault made in divorce or separation proceedings; or (2) any maintenance, custody, or ancillary order made in any such proceedings.[144] The rationale was that a divorce decree determines status and the application of foreign law as to status does not involve the application of foreign law as to obligation.[145] American courts have also assumed that a court cannot adjudicate a personal claim unless it has jurisdiction over the defendant.[146] Similarly, the 1970 Hague Convention on the Recognition of Divorces and Legal Separations explicitly states that it does not apply to findings of fault or ancillary orders pronounced on the making of a decree of divorce or legal separation. In particular, it does not apply to orders relating to pecuniary obligations or the custody of children.[147]

The Law Commission of India in its 65th Report examined the practice of other jurisdictions concerning the recognition of ancillary orders. The Commission recommended that ancillary orders should not be treated as binding on Indian courts even when foreign decrees of divorce are recognised. The Commission noted that ancillary orders concern the custody of children and

[140] ibid.
[141] ibid 144.
[142] ibid 146. See also the National Civil (Code) Act 2017 (Nepal) (BS (Bikram Sambat) 2074) s 699.
[143] ibid, s 706 provides for divorce and s 705 deals with judicial separation.
[144] English Act of 1871, s 8(3) stated in Law Commission 65th Report (n 45) ch 19.4, 118.
[145] ibid.
[146] ibid, ch 19.7, 119.
[147] Hague Convention on Recognition of Divorce and Legal Separations (n 79) Art 1.

allied questions and it would be juristically imprudent to treat them as binding. The Commission recommended that, where a foreign divorce is recognised, regardless of whether the foreign court has also made ancillary orders, either party can apply to the competent court for ancillary orders.[148] No judicial statements have dealt with the recognition of foreign ancillary financial orders.

A discussion on the legal status of nuptial agreements is apposite in this context. Indian law concerning pre-and postnuptial agreements is not fully evolved. Such agreements may be characterised as contracts. If so, they would need satisfy the requirements for a valid contract in the Indian Contract Act 1872. However, judicial statements have found domestic prenuptial agreements to be contrary to public policy and therefore not binding.[149] In *Sandhya Chatterjee v Salil Chandra Chatterjee*, there was a possible deviation from an earlier trend of routinely rejecting pre- and post-nuptial agreements. There the court observed that, although the subject contract was found to be invalid for being contrary to public policy, when determining the enforceability of pre- and post-nuptial agreements, judges should take account of a paramount public policy of respecting contracts which have been freely and voluntarily entered into by two adults.[150] Nonetheless, it is doubtful whether Indian courts will recognise a foreign pre-nuptial agreement in the absence of a precise working out of the Indian position on the matter.

The Indian position has been influenced by traditional English law which regards pre-nuptial agreements as non-binding.[151] The idea was that the authority to decide on ancillary matters associated with matrimonial disputes should reside with the courts and any deviation from the court's authority[152] would encourage separation and be against public policy.[153] Thus the concept of a pre-nuptial agreement has not been fully incorporated into English law,[154] even though traditional reliance on public policy has undergone a transformation.[155] In comparison, the US has a favourable position in terms of the enforcement of pre- and post-nuptial agreements, including foreign pre-nuptial agreements, provided they are not violative of the public policy of the forum and are not against due process.[156] In *Stawski v Stawski*,[157] the New York court upheld the validity of a German pre-nuptial agreement considering it as fair and based on due process.

B. Enforcement of Dower

In discussions of pre- and post-nuptial agreements, dower (*mehr*) in Islamic law needs to be considered. *Mehr* refers to money or property which a bride is entitled to receive from a groom in consideration of their marriage.[158] This is an inherent component of a marriage contracted

[148] Law Commission 65th Report (n 45) ch 19.4, 122.

[149] *Tekait Mon Mohini Jemadai v Basanta Kumar Singh* (1901) ILR 28 Cal 751; *Krishna Aiyar v Balammal* [1911] ILR 34 Mad 398.

[150] *Sandhya Chatterjee v Salil Chandra Chatterjee* AIR [1980] Cal 244, [14].

[151] Law Commission, *Marital Property Agreements* (Law Com CP No 198, 2011) Part 4.

[152] Domicile Matrimonial Causes Act 1973 (n 13) ss 21–25.

[153] A Ghosh and P Kar, 'Prenuptial Agreements in India: An Analysis of Law and Society' (2019) 12(2) *NUJS Law Review* http://nujslawreview.org/2019/12/13/pre-nuptial-agreements-in-india-an-analysis-of-law-and-society/.

[154] Legislative initiatives are underway to provide proper financial settlement provisions under the law by amending the Matrimonial Causes Act 1973.

[155] *Radmacher v Granatino* [2010] UKSC 42; *Hopkins v Hopkins* [2015] EWHC 812.

[156] A Curry, 'The Uniform Premarital Agreement Act and its Variations throughout the States', (2010) 23 *Journal of The American Academy of Matrimonial Lawyers* 355; See also Uniform Premarital Agreement Act 1983.

[157] *Stawski v Stawski*, 843 NYS 2d 544 (App. Div. 2007). See also *Van Kipnis v Van Kipnis*, 872 NS2d 426 [2008].

[158] RK Singh, 'Law of Dower (Mahr) in India' [2010] 12(1) *Journal of Islamic Law and Culture* 58, 73; *Abdur Kadar v Salima* [1886] ILR 8 All 149; *Sayed Sabir Hussain v Farsand Hussain* AIR [1938] PC 80.

according to Islamic law and prescribed by the Quran.[159] *Mehr* becomes legally due to the wife immediately upon marriage. It is either payable on demand to the wife at the time of marriage (prompt *muajjal* dower) or deferred until the wife claims it (deferred *muajjal* dower).[160] The wife can claim deferred dower at the time of divorce, after the husband's death, or during the marriage itself.[161] Numerous conflict of law cases involving the recognition of dower have been reported and judicial treatment of the institution has been inconsistent. The issue is relevant for India, which has a sizeable Muslim population. The main question is as to the treatment by foreign jurisdictions of dower agreements entered in India.

In *Shenaz v Rizwan*,[162] the parties were married in India under Islamic law. The marriage contract provided that the wife was to have deferred *mehr*, payable in the event of the husband's death or divorce. The wife petitioned for dower after the dissolution of their marriage. The husband argued that the wife's claim was essentially one for matrimonial relief and thus unenforceable, since the contract of marriage and the dower provision were contrary to the policy and good morals of English law.[163] The court held that the wife was seeking to enforce a right *in personam*, arising not out of the relationship of husband and wife, but from a contract entered into in contemplation and consideration of marriage. It was therefore not a matrimonial right which the court would refuse to enforce.[164] The court taking a strict contractual interpretation, observed that the fact that the English courts had hitherto not recognised such a claim was insufficient reason for the court to decline jurisdiction.[165] In contrast, US practice suggests that dower is equated with pre-nuptial agreements[166] or contracts.[167] However, there is a fundamental fallacy in equating dower with pre-nuptial agreements as dower is an essential element of Islamic marriage and not intended as a settlement of the parties' assets.[168] The fallacy was exposed in *Chaudry v Chaudry*,[169] where the court equated a Pakistani dower of US$1,500 with a prenuptial agreement and decreed that the wife was only to receive the amount specified in the dower, even though she had been married to a doctor for 12 years and had no substantial assets of her own.[170]

Despite numerous cases where dower has been recognised, uncertainty and inconsistency still prevail, as seen in cases where dower has been unenforceable on grounds of vagueness, religion,[171] unfairness, or public policy.[172] The main reason for inconsistency has come from attempts in western jurisdictions to draw an analogy between dower on the one hand and prenuptial agreements or contractual provisions on the other. The point is that, even if the courts attempt to frame

[159] K Ali, 'Marriage in Classical Islamic Jurisprudence: A Survey of Doctrines' in F Vogel and A Quraishi (eds), *The Islamic Marriage Contract: Case Studies in Islamic Family Law* (HUP, 2008) 11–45.

[160] ibid.

[161] D Schawlowski 'The Islamic Mahr in German and in English Courts' (2010–11) 16 *Yearbook of Islamic and Middle Eastern Law* 147–166, 148.

[162] *Shenaz v Rizwan* [1965] 1 QB 390.

[163] ibid.

[164] ibid.

[165] *Qureshi v Qureshi* [1971] 1 WLR 518; See also *Uddin v Choudhury* [2009] EWCA Civ 1205.

[166] *Afghani v Ghafoorian*, Unpublished, No 1481-09-4, WL 1189383 (VA Ct. of Appeals 2010).

[167] P Fournier, 'Flirting with God in Western Secular Courts; Mahr in the West' (2010) 24(1) *International Journal of Law, Policy and the Family* 67–94.

[168] T Siddiqui, 'Interpretation of Islamic Marriage Contracts by American Courts' (2007) 41(3) *Family Law Quarterly* 639–658, 647.

[169] *Chaudry v Chaudry* 388 A.2d 1000 (N.J. Super. Ct. App. Div. 1978); see also *Ahmad v Ahmad*, No L-00-1391, 2001 WL 1518116.

[170] V Saijwani, 'Personal Laws of Divorce in India with a Comment on Chaudry v. Chaudry' (1989) 11(1) *Women's Rights Law Reporter* 41, 60.

[171] *Kaddoura v Hammoud* [1998] 168 DLR 503.

[172] K Spencer 'Mahar Contract: Internal Pluralism And External Perspectives' (2011) 1(2) *Onati Socio-Legal Series* 1–19, 1 http://opo.iisj.net/index.php/osls/article/view/70/0.

the contours of dower through secular contract law, the foundation of dower is based on religion and the institution was established for a purpose which mere recourse to contract law may not be able to meet.

V. Annulment and Nullity of Marriages

A. Statutory Provisions and Judicial Decisions on Nullity of Marriage in India

Unlike divorce, which terminates a lawful marriage, relieves parties from their future obligations as husband and wife and leads to consequences in the form of maintenance and joint custody of children, an annulment decree declares that a marriage never existed. Even in those legal systems and religious laws which do not permit divorce, annulment is permitted. The question is whether the rules of jurisdiction, choice of law, and recognition that apply to foreign divorces should also apply to annulment cases.

Indian statutes dealing with marriage contain special provisions on the annulment of marriages. Section 11 of the Hindu Marriage Act deals with the annulment of void marriages. It states that a marriage solemnised after commencement of the Act shall be null and void if it contravenes any of the conditions in sections 5(i), (iv), and (v).[173] Section 5(i) deals with the prohibition of bigamy. Section 5(ii) deals with prohibited relationships in marriage. Section 5(iii) concerns prohibition on *sapinda* relationships. Section 12 of the Hindu Marriage Act deals with voidable marriages and states that a voidable marriage may be annulled by a decree of nullity on any of the following grounds:

(a) The marriage has not been consummated owing to the impotence of the respondent.
(b) The marriage is in contravention of the condition specified in section 5(ii).[174]
(c) The consent of the petitioner or a guardian was obtained by force or by fraud.
(d) The respondent was at the time of the marriage pregnant by some person other than the petitioner.[175]

The Act prescribes that no petition for annulling a marriage shall be entertained if the petition is presented: (1) more than one year after any coercion had ceased to operate or fraud been discovered; or (2) if the parties with full consent have lived together as husband or wife after any coercion had ceased to operate or fraud been discovered.[176] The Act prescribes the same jurisdictional rules for petitions dealing with divorce, annulments and judicial separation, etc. Similar provisions on the annulment of marriage are incorporated into the Special Marriage Act[177] and Foreign Marriage Act.[178]

[173] Hindu Marriage Act 1955 (n 4) s 11, Nullity of marriage and divorce – Void marriages. Any marriage solemnised after the commencement of this Act shall be null and void and may, on a petition presented by either party thereto, against the other party be so declared by a decree of nullity if it contravenes any one of the conditions specified in clauses (i), (iv) and (v), s 5.

[174] Hindu Marriage Act 1955 (n 4) s 5 lays down the conditions of a valid marriage.

[175] ibid, s 12(1).

[176] ibid, s 12(2).

[177] Special Marriage Act 1954 (n 7) ss 24, 25, 31.

[178] Foreign Marriage Act 1969 (India) s 18.

As far as judicial statements are concerned, there are no cases that have dealt with the recognition of a foreign annulment decree. *Neerja Saraph v Jayant Saraph* is a glaring example of the misuse of foreign matrimonial processes. Neeraja was married to the respondent, a doctor in computer hardware, on 6 August 1989. Less than a month after their marriage, the husband returned to the US, leaving Neeraja in India.[179] In December 1989, she received a petition brought before the US court for the annulment of their marriage. She was forced to file a suit for damages before the Indian courts, and the suit was decreed *ex parte* for Rs 22 lakhs (Rs 2,200,000).[180] The respondent appealed and the High Court ordered a stay of execution. The Supreme Court highlighted the necessity for appropriate steps to be taken to safeguard the interests of women. The Court observed:

> [A]lthough it is a problem of private international law and is not easy to resolve, but with the change in social structure and rise of marriages with NRIs [non-resident Indians] the Union of India may consider enacting legislation safeguarding interests of women which may be examined by incorporating such provisions as–
>
> (1) No marriage between an NRI and an Indian woman that has taken place in India may be annulled by a foreign court;
> (2) Adequate alimony to the wife in the husband's property both in India and abroad.
> (3) The decree granted by Indian courts may be made executable in foreign courts both on the principle of comity and by entering into reciprocal agreements like Section 44-A of the Civil Procedure Code, making a foreign decree executable as it would have been a decree passed by that court.[181]

In *Mrs. M. v Mr. A*[182] the appellant sought a decree of nullity of her marriage which had been solemnised in Texas. Alternatively, she prayed for a decree of divorce on the ground of cruelty. The petition had been filed before the City Civil Court in Bombay under the Special Marriage Act 1954, which applied to the parties by virtue of section 18 of the Foreign Marriage Act 1969.[183] Section 18(3) of the 1954 Act reads:

> Nothing contained in this Section shall authorise any court–
>
> (a) to make any decree of dissolution of marriage, except where–
>   (i) the parties to the marriage are domiciled in India at the time of the presentation of the petition; or
>   (ii) the petitioner, being the wife, was domiciled in India immediately before the marriage and has been residing in India for not less than three years immediately preceding the presentation of the petition.[184]

The trial judge dismissed the petition on the ground that the court was not vested with the requisite jurisdiction.[185] The appellant contended that the trial judge was in error in holding that the law required that the petitioner should have been residing in India continuously for three years immediately preceding the presentation of the petition, whereas the section only referred to a period of not less than three years immediately preceding the presentation of the petition and did not refer to continuous residence.[186] Accepting the appellant's contention and permitting the appeal, the High Court held that the Foreign Marriage Act confers jurisdiction if a party is

[179] ibid [3].
[180] ibid.
[181] ibid [4].
[182] *Mrs. M. v Mr. A.* [1993] DMC 384.
[183] ibid [2].
[184] ibid [4]
[185] ibid [2].
[186] ibid.

resident for a reasonably long time – the minimum being three years. It would be entirely unreasonable to hold, particularly when interpreting a matrimonial statute, that a break in the period of residence would be fatal to a petition since, in that event, the section would have used the word 'continuous' or 'unbroken'.[187] In the absence of specific legislation, it is expected that Indian courts will apply *Y Narasimha Rao* by analogy on the annulment of marriage.

The principles of Indian private international law on the nullity of marriage generally resonate with English law and the EU practice. The UK Domicile and Matrimonial Proceedings Act 1973 provides for similar grounds of jurisdiction in divorce and nullity of marriage.[188] Rules for the recognition of foreign annulments may be found in the Family Law Act 1986 and are the same as the divorce rules discussed earlier in this chapter.[189] A similar approach is seen in the Brussels II Regulation on Jurisdiction and the Recognition of Judgment in Matrimonial Matters.[190] However, with regard to applicable law, the Rome III Regulation applicable to divorce and legal separation excludes the annulment of marriage from its scope, indicating the application of traditional private international law principles within the EU.[191]

B. Extrajudicial Divorces and Recognition in Foreign Jurisdictions

Divorce under Islamic law operates in the following ways: (1) by the pronouncement of *talaq* by the husband; (2) by mutual agreement between the parties through *khula* or *mubarat*; or (3) by judicial separation requested by either party. The controversial aspect of Islamic divorce pertains to the *talaq* as it provides a unilateral power on the husband.[192]

Case law across jurisdictions reveals divergent practices with regard to the recognition of extrajudicial divorces.[193]

US practice treats *talaq* divorces that have taken place in other countries as valid on the basis of principles of comity and substantial connection.[194] In *Seth v Seth*,[195] a court in Texas refused to uphold a divorce performed by *talaq* in Kuwait by relying on a lack of 'most significant relationship'. Though the parties were citizens of India, the court held that Texas law applied based on their ten years of residence there. Since Texas law does not allow *talaq*, the divorce could not be recognised. In *Aleem v Aleem*,[196] husband and wife, both of Pakistani descent, were married in Pakistan. The couple moved to the US and had been living in Maryland for over 20 years. The husband went to the Pakistani embassy in Washington DC and performed *talaq* in accordance with the Pakistani law. The court held that a *talaq* divorce obtained according to Pakistani law could not be enforced by comity because it was contrary to Maryland public policy.[197]

[187] ibid.

[188] Domicile and Matrimonial Proceedings Act 1973 (n 13) s 5(3).

[189] ibid. Family Law Act 1986 (n 116) ss 44(2), 45, 46.

[190] Brussels II *bis* Regulation (n 18) Art 1 states that this Regulation shall apply, to whatever is the nature of the court or tribunal, in civil matters relating to divorce, legal separation, or marriage annulment.

[191] Rome III Regulation (n 50) Art 2.

[192] SM Fallon 'Justice for All: American Muslims, Sharia Law, and Maintaining Comity with American Jurisprudence' (2013) 36 *Boston College International and Comparative Law Review* 153, 160.

[193] J Macfarlane, '*Islamic Divorce in North America: A Shari'a Path in a Secular* Society (Oxford University Press 2012); see generally P Shah, 'Distorting Minority laws, Religious and European Minority legal Systems' in P Shah and MC Foblets (eds), *Family, Religion and Law: Cultural Encounters in Europe* (Routledge, 2015) 25.

[194] Editorial Board, Minnesota Law Review 'United States Recognition of Foreign, Non judicial Divorces' (1969) 53 *Minnesota Law Review* 612–640, 616–617.

[195] *Seth v Seth* 694 SW 2d 459 (Tex. App. 1985).

[196] *Aleem v Aleem* 175 Md. App. 663 (Md. Ct. Spec. App. 2007).

[197] ibid.

Multiple factors influenced the judgment. Based on the substantial connection, Maryland law qualified as the applicable law.[198] In addition, even though the *talaq* had been pronounced in the Pakistani Embassy, it could still constitute pronouncing *talaq* within US territory thus being contrary to US public policy.[199] Further, Maryland law dictates the equal division of property. Similarly, in *Saida Banu Tarikonda v Bade Saheb Pinjarra*,[200] the Oakland court refused to recognise a triple *talaq* pronounced in India based on the violation of the public policy of due process.

Under English law, the rules on extrajudicial recognition are part of codified statutes rather than judicial decisions. Under the Family Law Act 1986, a distinction is made between divorce obtained through 'proceedings' and otherwise than by means of proceedings.[201] A procedural *talaq* is recognised in the UK if the divorce or legal separation is effective in the country where it is obtained and parties to the divorce have a connection with the place of divorce at the relevant date of divorce in the form of habitual residence or domicile there.[202] An extrajudicial divorce is recognised:

(1) if it is effective in the country where divorce is pronounced; or
(2) if the parties to the divorce were domiciled in that country or, if only one of the parties was domiciled in that country, the other parties' domicile recognises a bare *talaq*.[203]

There will be no recognition if one of the parties has been habitually resident in the UK throughout the period of one year immediately preceding the pronouncement. The Act lays down that a foreign embassy or consulate cannot be regarded as a part of a country for the purposes of section 45 of the Family Law Act 1986.[204]

A divorce granted in Bangladesh and Pakistan following the formalities under the Muslim Family Laws 1961 Ordinance would fall under the category of a procedural *talaq*.[205] However, since India has not enacted legislation and no standard procedure for *talaq* has been laid down, Muslim divorce pronounced in India would only qualify as a bare *talaq*.

With growing Muslim populations, jurisdictions will have to face increased Islamic legal issues before them. Adequate rules must be put in place so that certainty is achieved in legal relations.

VI. Conclusion

This chapter has discussed the legal framework governing jurisdiction, applicable law, and the recognition of foreign divorces in India. The analysis illustrated the existence of concurrent

[198] G Robinson, 'United States: Maryland High Court Holds Islamic 'Talaq" Divorce Unconstitutional' (2008) *Global Legal Monitor*, www.loc.gov/law/foreign-news/article/united-states-maryland-high-court-holds-islamic-talaq-divorce-unconstitutional/; see also *Ashfaq v Ashfaq* – 467 SW3d 539 (Tex. App. 2015).

[199] ibid.

[200] *Saida Banu Tarikonda v Bade Saheb Pinjarra* case No 287403 Oakland Circuit Court Family Division LC No. 2008-746484-DMhttps://cases.justia.com/michigan/court-of-appeals-unpublished/20090407_C287403_53_287403.OPN.PDF?ts=1396125828.

[201] Family Law Act 1986, (UK) (n 116); See also P Shah, 'In Pursuit of the Pagans: Muslim Law in the English Context' (2013) 45(1) *Journal of Legal Pluralism & Unofficial Law* 58–75.

[202] Family Law Act 1986 (UK) 1986 (n 116) s 46(1); see *Chaudhary v Chaudhary* [1985] FLR 476; *Qazi v Qazi* [1979] 3 WLR 833.

[203] ibid, s 46(2).

[204] This modification was undertaken after the case of *Radwan v Radwan* [1973] Fam.35.

[205] S Hossain, 'Cross Border Divorce Regime in Bangladesh' in SR Garimella and S Jolly (eds), *Private International Law: South Asian State Practice*, (Springer, 2017) 89, 110; The Muslim Family Laws Ordinance Pakistan (V111 of 1961); The Muslim Family Laws Ordinance Bangladesh (V111 of 1961) Bangladesh was part of the Pakistan in 1961 before its independence and inherited the same law.

personal laws on matrimonial matters applicable to many religious communities. The religion-based statutes depict a flexible and broader base of divorce jurisdiction and an absence of a precise position on applicable law. The Judiciary has played a dynamic role in evolving an ingenious jurisprudence on the recognition of foreign divorce decree. The current legal position dictates that the jurisdiction assumed by the foreign court as well as the grounds on which the divorce has been granted must be in accordance with the law under which the parties were married. This scenario is leading to a situation of limping marriages. The Law Commission of India, in its 65th Report, has recommended that the country accede to the 1970 Hague Convention on the Recognition of Divorces and Legal Separations or enact legislation dealing with the recognition of foreign divorce decrees. In its 219th Report, the Law Commission made further recommendations, including the registration of marriages and the inclusion of the ground of irretrievable breakdown of marriage to avoid forum shopping and limping marriages. The recommendations of the Law Commission have not been implemented.

This chapter also reflected on the position of Indian law vis-à-vis trends in other jurisdictions concerning the non-recognition of ancillary financial orders and adopting the same rules to nullity of marriage as apply to divorce. Here Indian practice resonates with the global trend.

The chapter drew attention to the problems encountered by foreign courts in recognising dower and *talaq*. The scenario is beset with uncertainty, especially because of the absence of judicial or quasi-judicial proceedings governing the process of *talaq* in India. This situation points to the need for diplomatic deliberations and judicial cooperation for evolving more inclusive conventions at the global level in the interests of promoting justice.

8

Private International Law Practice and Children: Issues of Custody and Abduction

I. Introduction

Anand and Nandini, citizens of India, married in Delhi according to Hindu rites and customs. Their marriage was registered under the Hindu Marriage Act. After marriage, the parties shifted to the US and obtained citizenship there. The couple gave birth to a child named Namrata. After marriage, disputes and differences arose between the spouses. Nandini contended that the disputes were often violent and she was physically, mentally, and psychologically abused. Nandini visited her parents in India. She took Namrata with her to India. During her stay in India, Nandini decided not to return to the US. Anand commenced an action before the New York court for custody of the child. The court awarded sole custody of Namrata to Anand. Armed with the custody order, Anand came to India and filed a *habeas corpus* petition before the Delhi High Court. Anand argued that Namrata, having been born in the US, was a US citizen and hence he was seeking the child's return to her habitual residence and the recognition of the foreign custody order. In defence, Nandini contended that Namrata's removal to India had been due to the persistent domestic violence committed by Anand. The fact that the US is a party to the 1980 Hague Child Abduction Convention while India is not, gives rise to uncertainty as to what will happen in the foregoing scenario which, while not uncommon, poses challenges on how best to safeguard the interests of a child in Namrata's position.

This chapter will therefore examine international initiatives to harmonise the conflicts of laws issues underlying the removal of a child from one jurisdiction to another. This chapter is divided into five parts, including this Introduction. Section II introduces basic concepts of the jurisprudence relating to the well-being of the child and contextualises intercountry child abduction by tracing the main elements of the 1980 Hague Abduction Convention. Section III discusses Indian judicial narratives dealing with intercountry child abduction. The focus here will be on custody laws, legislative initiatives, and judicial statements on child abduction and the recognition of foreign custody orders. Section IV critically analyses the provisions of the Bill initiated by the Ministry of Women and Child Development (MWCD) and the Law Commission of India while evaluating India's reasons for not acceding to the 1980 Hague Convention. Section V addresses the recognition of foreign custody orders and compares the practices developed in the US, EU and other jurisdictions.

II. Jurisprudence on the Well-Being of the Child: An Interplay of Public and Private International Law

A. Fundamental Concept: The Best Interests of the Child

International law, in the form of conventions and customary law, has seen a greater appreciation of the importance of safeguarding children's rights. It has laid down a comprehensive framework for ensuring that the rights of children, as a vulnerable sector of society dependent on adults to enforce their rights, are respected and protected.[1] The UN Convention on the Rights of the Child (CRC) attempted a complete statement of children's rights under international law.[2] With the coming into force of the CRC, the study of children's rights expanded to areas beyond the traditional boundaries of international law, including the private and family spheres.[3] The CRC and the efforts of human rights organisations were strengthened by the private international law legal instruments promulgated by the HCCH, focusing on the well-being of the child.[4] The best interests or welfare of the child serves as the determinative consideration in public and private international law underlying the implementation of the international framework for the safeguarding of children's rights.[5] However, none of the legal instruments have identified the key elements that constitute the best interests of the child. As a result, a lack of clarity shrouds the principle's interpretation in specific cases.[6]

B. Private International Law Responses to Child Abduction

The increase in the cross-border abduction or wrongful removal of a child by a parent finds its root in the growth in the number of transnational marriages. It has become a problem that plagues many countries. As an international collaborative response, the 1980 Hague Convention on the Civil Aspects of International Child Abduction was adopted by the HCCH on 24 October 1980.[7] As of March 2021, 103 states have ratified or acceded to the 1980 Convention.[8] India has not acceded to the 1980 Convention.

[1] JJ Garman, 'International Law and Children's Human Rights: International, Constitutional, and Political conflicts Blocking Passage of the Convention on the Rights of the Child' (2007) 41(2) *Valpaisio University Law Review*, 659–696; See also A Skelton, 'International Children's Rights Law: Complaints and Remedies' in U Kilkelly and T Liefaard (eds), *International Human Rights of Children* (Springer, 2019); Geneva Declaration of the Rights of the Child (adopted 26 September 1924, League of Nations OJ Spec. Supp. 21) Art 1; International Covenant on Civil and Political Rights (adopted 16 December 1966, entered into force 23 March 1976) 999 UNTS 171 (ICCPR); Convention on the Rights of the Child (adopted 20 November 1989, entered into force 2 September 1990) 1577 UNTS 3 (CRC).

[2] CRC (n 1).

[3] ibid, Art 18.

[4] Convention on the Law Applicable to Maintenance Obligations Towards Children (Adopted 25 October 1956 entered into force January 1962); Convention on the Civil Aspects of International Child Abduction (adopted 25 October 1980 entered into force 1 December 1983) 1343 UNTS 89; The Hague Convention on the Protection of Children and Cooperation in Respect of Intercountry Adoption (adopted 29 May 1993, entered into force 1 May 1993) 33 UNTS.

[5] P Alston, 'The Best Interests Principle: Towards a Reconciliation of Culture and Human Rights' (1994) 8(1) *International Journal of Law, Policy and Family* 1–25, 1.

[6] S Parker, 'The Best Interests of the Child – Principles and Problems' (1994) 8(1) *International Journal of Law, Policy and Family* 26–41, 27; JA Drobac, 'For the Sake of the Children: Court Consideration of Religion in Child Custody Cases' (1998) 50(5) *Stanford Law Review* 1609–1690.

[7] Abduction Convention (n 4); EP Vera, 'Explanatory Report by Elisa Perez-Vera' (*HCCH* 1981) https://assets.hcch.net/docs/a5fb103c-2ceb-4d17-87e3-a7528a0d368c.pdf.

[8] The International Child Abduction Database, www.incadat.com/index.cfm?act=text.text&.

i. Hague Abduction Convention 1980

The 1980 Convention aims to ensure the prompt return of the wrongfully removed child.[9] Its stated objectives are:

(a) to secure the prompt return of children who have been wrongfully removed or retained in a contracting state; and
(b) to ensure that rights of custody and access under the law of one contracting state are respected in other contracting states.[10]

Notwithstanding the reference to 'abduction' in its title, the substantive provisions of the 1980 Convention do not refer to abduction and deal with situations where the custodial rights of a parent have been violated. The instrument provides a mechanism for obtaining the return of a child who has been taken to another country in violation of such custodial rights.[11] The 1980 Convention provides a procedural mechanism for restoring the status quo by requiring the child to be returned to his or her habitual residence immediately preceding wrongful removal to or retention in another country.[12] The removal or retention of a child is to be considered wrongful where it is in breach of the rights of custody of the left-behind parent in the habitual residence of the child.[13] The emphasis on prompt return aims to minimise the adverse psychological effects of abduction by quickly returning the child to his or her habitual residence and allowing the jurisdiction with which the child has the closest connection (that is, the competent authority in the habitual residence) to determine custody and related matters consequent upon the breakdown of a marriage.[14] Therefore, the 1980 Convention is a return mechanism that does not determine custody and related issues, but which will prevent an abducting parent from seeking a custody order in a different contracting state from the child's habitual residence.[15]

Two conditions need to be satisfied before the 1980 Convention applies: (a) the child must be under 16 years of age; and (2) the child must have been habitually resident in a Contracting State immediately before any breach of custody or access rights.[16] The breach of custody rights and the determination of habitual residence therefore become the decisive points in assessing the legality of a child's removal from one jurisdiction to another.[17] In the absence of a definition of habitual residence under the 1980 Convention, jurisprudence has evolved fact-intensive standards to be followed in the determination of habitual residence.[18] Contracting States are required to establish

[9] L Siberman, 'Interpreting the Hague Abduction Convention: In Search of a Global Jurisprudence' (2005) 38(4) *UC Davis Law Review*, 1049–1086, 1063–1064; A Dyer, 'The Hague Convention on the Civil Aspects of International Child Abduction-towards Global Cooperation: It's Successes and Failures' (1993) 93(1) *International Journal of Child Rights* 273–292.

[10] Abduction Convention (n 4) Art 1; See also PR Beaumont and PE McEleavy, *The Hague Convention on International Child Abduction* (Oxford University Press, 1999).

[11] L Silberman, 'Hague International Child Abduction Convention: A Progress Report' (1994) 57(3) *Law and Contemporary Problems* 210–269, 211.

[12] RJ Frank, 'Note, American and International Responses to International Child Abductions' (1984) 16 *New York University Journal of International Law and Policy* 415–474, 415.

[13] Abduction Convention (n 4) Art 3.

[14] EA Schnitzer-Reese, 'International Child Abduction to Non-Hague Convention Countries: The Need for an International Family Court' (2004) 2(1) *Northwest Journal of International Human Rights* 1–19, 5.

[15] L Nakdai, 'It's 10 PM, Do You Know Where Your Children are?: The Hague Convention on the Civil Aspects of International Child Abduction' (2002) 40(2) *Family Court Review* 251–264, 253.

[16] Abduction Convention (n 4) Art 4.

[17] J Atkinson, 'The Meaning of "Habitual Residence" under the Hague Convention on the Civil Aspects of International Child Abduction and The Hague Convention on the Protection of Children' (2011) 63(4) *Oklahoma University Law Review*, 647–662, 634.

[18] T Vivatyaraphol, 'Back to Basics: Determining a Child's Habitual Residence in International Child Abduction Cases Under the Hague Convention' (2009) 77(6) *Fordham Law Review* 3332–3369.

a Central Authority.[19] Article 8 provides that a person may apply to the Central Authority of the child's habitual residence or to the Central Authority of any other Contracting State for assistance in securing the return of a wrongfully removed child.[20] Once the wrongful removal is proved, a few grounds exist to prevent the return of the child to his or her habitual residence. These include:

(1) The person or institution having the care of the child was not exercising custody rights at the time of removal or retention.[21]
(2) The left behind parent consented or acquiesced to the removal or retention.[22]
(3) The petition for the return of the child was filed a year after the wrongful removal with the result that the child has become settled within his or her new environment.[23]

The defences under the 1980 Convention are fact-based. Evidence must be furnished of the child's connections and proof of settlement in the new country. Only limited defences are envisaged based on which a child's return may be denied.

a. Grave Risk to the Child

Under Article 13 of the 1980 Convention, courts will not order the return of the child, when it can be established that return would expose the child to a 'grave risk' of physical or psychological harm or otherwise place the child in an intolerable situation.[24] However, the term 'grave risk' has not been defined. Jurisprudence shows that there is a wide variation in the approach taken by courts in dealing with allegations of grave risk.[25] Overall, courts have given a restrictive interpretation to Article 13 for the fear that to do otherwise would defeat or dilute the convention's purpose of ensuring the prompt return of a child to his or her country of habitual residence.[26]

b. Objection to Return

Courts will not order the return of a child who is of a sufficient age and maturity to understand his or her circumstances and objects to being returned to his or her habitual residence.[27] This is a fact-based analysis. It is not based on the preference of the child to be with either parent. The defence will only be applicable in cases where the child explicitly objects to being returned. Such a defence was raised in *Louise Ann Fairley v Sajjad Ahmed Rana*[28] although Pakistan had not acceded to the 1980 Convention at the time of the petition. The respondent, (a Pakistan citizen) married the petitioner (a UK citizen) in the UK. A child named Misbah Irum Rana was born to the couple. The father removed the child to Pakistan in violation of a court order. The mother petitioned the Lahore High Court to declare the father's exercise of custody over the child in Pakistan to be illegal and improper given the foreign court order. The Lahore High Court allowed the petition and held that the child should be handed over to her mother's custody. The respondent appealed to the

[19] Abduction Convention (n 4) Art 6.
[20] ibid, Art 8.
[21] ibid, Art 13(a).
[22] ibid.
[23] ibid, Art 12.
[24] ibid, Art 13(1)(b).
[25] N Bala and J Chamerland, 'Family Violence and Proving "Grave Risk" for Cases under the Hague Convention Article 13(b)' (2017) Queen's University Legal Research Paper 091/2017, 1–19, 4–5. https://papers.ssrn.com/sol3/papers.cfm?abstract_id=2987207.
[26] K Yoko, 'A Haven for International Child Abduction: Will the Hague Convention Shape Japanese Family Law?' (2015) 46(1) *California Western International Law Journal* 40–68, 60.
[27] Abduction Convention (n 4) Art 13.
[28] *Sajjad Ahmed Rana v Louise Ann Fairely* PLD [2007] Lahore 300.

Supreme Court of Pakistan. In the proceedings, the child objected to being returned to his mother. After prolonged hearings, the parties reached a compromise, which disposed of the petition.[29]

ii. Violation of Principles of Human Rights and Fundamental Freedoms

The return of the child may be refused under Article 20 of the 1980 Convention, if it would not be permitted by the principles of the requested state relating to the protection of human rights and fundamental freedoms.[30] Similar to the factual assessment associated with other defenses, Article 20 raises questions of whose human rights are affected and what constitutes fundamental freedoms. Courts have taken differing positions, with some insisting on the child's human rights and others insisting on parental rights.[31] In both cases, a limited application was preferred to prevent the gross violation of human rights.

Among private international law instruments, the 1980 Convention has been one of the most successful with more than 100 Contracting States. It has resulted in the return of hundreds of children to their habitual residence. As noted, the 1980 Convention does not deal with issues of jurisdiction, recognition, or custody. The recognition and enforcement of custody orders are instead covered by the 1996 Hague Convention on Jurisdiction, Applicable Law, Recognition, Enforcement, and Cooperation in Respect of Parental Responsibility and Measures for the Protection of Children.

iii. 1996 Hague Convention on Parental Responsibility and Protection of Children

The convention was adopted by the HCCH in 1996.[32] It provides uniform rules on jurisdiction and recognition in relation to child protection issues not contained in the 1980 Convention. First, the 1996 Convention ascribes jurisdiction and applicable law to the states in which the child is habitually resident.[33] However, in exceptional situations, the law of another Contracting State with which the situation has a substantial connection may apply.[34] Second, the 1996 Convention ensures the return of a child to his or her designated custodial parent by enforcing custody and access orders.[35] Thus, it complements the 1980 Convention by providing an alternate way to secure a child's return when both states are parties to both conventions and a return remedy in itself for states that are not parties to the 1980 Convention.[36] The 1996 Convention also fills in the gap in relation to rights of access by recognising such rights.[37] It has been generally observed

[29] S Ali, 'Intercountry Child Abductions, – Pakistan Legal Response' in SR Garimela and S Jolly (eds), *Private International Law: South Asian States' Practice* (Springer, 2017) 221–241.

[30] Abduction Convention (n 4) Art 20; K Trimmings and PR Beaumont, 'Article 20 of the 1980 Hague Abduction Convention' (2014) 9(1) *Journal of Comparative Law* 66–88.

[31] MH Weiner, 'Using Article 20' (2004) 38(3) *Family Law Quarterly* 583–622.

[32] Convention on Jurisdiction, Applicable Law, Recognition, Enforcement and Co-operation in Respect of Parental Responsibility and Measures for the Protection of Children (adopted 19 October 1996, entered into force 1 January 2002) 35 I.LM. 1391, 1396 [Protection Convention].

[33] ibid, Arts 5 and 15 (this provision abandoned the previous reliance on nationality); N Lowe, 'The 1996 Hague Convention on the Protection of Children – A Fresh Appraisal' (2002) 14(2) *Child and Family Law Quarterly* 191–206.

[34] ibid, Art 15.

[35] ibid, Art 23; GF De Hart, 'The Relationship between the 1980 Child Abduction Convention and the 1996 Protection Convention' (2000) 33(1) *New York University Journal of International Law and Politics* 83, 85.

[36] ibid, Art 50.

[37] M Groff, 'The Hague Conventions: Giving Effect to Human Rights through Instruments of Private International Law,' in J Handmaker and K Arts (eds), *Mobilising International Law for Global Justice* (Cambridge University Press, 2018) 89–118.

that, when courts have refused a return order under the 1980 Convention, they have automatically assumed jurisdiction to determine custody rights.[38] Removing this misconception, the 1996 Convention stresses that, if the child has been wrongfully removed from his or her habitual residence, jurisdiction cannot be exercised until the conditions under Article 7 of the 1996 Convention have been met.[39] The 1996 Convention provides authorities with the power to take measures to protect the person or property of the child.[40] It also ensures that measures taken are recognised in other states, stipulating only limited grounds for the refusal of recognition.[41] Thus, the 1996 Convention supplements the 1980 Convention. The two instruments together establish a system of international cooperation. India has not acceded to either convention. The next part of this chapter will deal with the legal framework in India for handling cross-border child abductions.

III. Indian Legal Framework Relating to Intercountry Child Abduction

A. Legislative Framework

The term 'custody' is not defined in any Indian statute. The law governing custody is instead addressed as part of the law on guardianship. The main statute dealing with guardianship is the Guardian and Wards Act 1890 (GWA).[42] Besides the GWA, provisions on custody matters are scattered among statutes dealing with personal matters, including the Hindu Minority and Guardianship Act 1956, the Hindu Marriage Act 1955, the Parsi Marriage and Divorce Act 1936, the Indian Divorce Act 1869 and the Special Marriage Act 1954.[43] The GWA is secular legislation which applies to all persons irrespective of religion. The GWA specifies the procedures for the appointment of guardians, their powers, and responsibilities.[44] A guardian can be appointed by the court (in the case of a parent's death or where parents have abandoned their child) or by will where parents wish someone to act as guardian of their children after their death.[45] The GWA defines a guardian as a person having the care of a minor (that is, a person under 18 years of age) and his or her property.[46] The GWA dictates that the welfare of a minor regulates the appointment of a guardian.[47] Section 17(2) details the factors to be taken into account in determining whether it would be appropriate to appoint a particular person as the guardian of a minor. Courts can take into consideration the minor's age, sex, and religion; the character and capacity

[38] ibid.

[39] Protection Convention (n 32) Art 7. The conditions include acquiescence of the person having custody, the child residing in another state for more than one year after knowing of the wrongful removal, and the child settling into his or her new environment.

[40] ibid, Arts 12, 13.

[41] ibid, Art 23

[42] Guardian and Wards Act (India) 1890 (Act No 8 of 1890).

[43] Law Commission of India, *Need to accede to the Hague Convention on the Civil Aspects of International Child Abduction (1980)* (Report No 218, 2009) [2.10]; S Jolly, 'International Parental Child Abduction: An Explorative Analysis of Legal Standards and Judicial Interpretation in India' (2017) 31(1) *International Journal of Law Policy and the Family* 20–40, 25.

[44] Guardian and Wards Act (n 42) s 17(2).

[45] ibid, s 7.

[46] ibid, s 4(2).

[47] ibid, s 7.

of the proposed guardian; the guardian's relationship with the minor; and the wishes of deceased parents.[48] The GWA specifies that the District Court where the minor ordinarily resides is to have jurisdiction on matters concerning the guardianship of a minor.[49] Reliance can also be placed on section 26 of the Hindu Marriage Act 1955, which requires a court to decide applications for the custody, maintenance, and education of minors as expeditiously as possible.[50] Similar provisions are found in the Parsi Marriage and Divorce Act 1936[51] and the Divorce Act 1869[52] which authorise courts to issue interim orders for the custody, maintenance and education of minors in proceeding under these Acts.

Statutory provisions favour the father as the natural guardian of a minor.[53] The Hindu Minority and Guardianship Act 1956 confers primary guardianship on the father in the case of a boy or unmarried girl.[54] The Act also lays down that custody of a minor below the age of five should 'ordinarily' be with the mother.[55] In *Gita Hariharan v Reserve Bank of India*,[56] the court construed section 6 of the Act (providing that in the case of a boy or an unmarried girl, the father and (after him) the mother should be the guardian) as meaning not merely referring to what happens after the father's lifetime, but also to situations where the father has gone absent.[57] As early as 1980, the Law Commission of India submitted a report to the Government of India recommending that section 6 of the GWA be amended 'to allow the mother the custody of a minor till it completes the age of 12 years'.[58] Similarly, under Islamic law, the father is the natural guardian of a minor, but custody is vested in the mother until the son reaches the age of seven and the daughter reaches puberty.[59] The paramount consideration in the custody and guardianship of children is the welfare of the minor.[60] A catena of cases has elucidated the factors determining the welfare of the child and emphasised that it is not the welfare or the interests of the parents or the statutory preference for fathers' rights that should require adjudication but the welfare of the minor.[61]

In intercountry child abduction cases, the *Hindu Minority and Guardianship Act* 1956, which has extra-territorial operation,[62] is often invoked by parents seeking guardianship rights over their child. Distressed parents also resort to the constitutional remedy of *habeas corpus* under Articles 226[63] and 32[64] of the Indian Constitution.[65] Judicial decisions may be classified into two categories based on a timeline, ie, those before the decision in *Surya Vadanan* and those after.

[48] ibid, s 17(2).
[49] ibid, s 9.
[50] Hindu Marriage Act 1955, India (Act No 25 of 1955) s 26. See also Law Commission of India Report (n 43) [2.11].
[51] Parsi Marriage and Divorce Act 1936, India (Act No 3 1936) s 49.
[52] Indian Divorce Act 1869 (Act No 4 of 1869) s 41.
[53] SA Desai and Sir D F Mulla, *Mulla Hindu Law* 21st edn (Lexis Nexis, 2013); MP Jain, *Outlines Of Indian Legal And Constitutional History* 7th edn (Lexis Nexis, 2014).
[54] The Hindu Minority and Guardianship Act 1956 (Act No 32 of 1956) s 6.
[55] ibid, s 6(a); See also *Roxann Sharma v Arun Sharma* [2015] 8 SCC 318.
[56] *Gita Hariharan v Reserve Bank of India* [1999] 2 SCC 228.
[57] ibid.
[58] Law Commission of India, *The Guardians and Wards Act, 1890 and Certain Provisions of the Hindu Minority and Guardianship Act, 1956 (1980)* (Report No 83, 1980).
[59] Law Commission of India, *Reforms in Guardianship and Custody Laws in India (2015)* (Report No 257, 2015) [2.2.13].
[60] Hindu Minority and Guardianship Act (n 55); See also *Sheoli Hati v Somnath Das* [2019] 7 SCC 490.
[61] *Gaytri Bajaj v Jiten Bhalla* [2012] 12 SCC 471; *Rosy Jacob v Jacob A. Chakramakkal* [1973] 1 SCC 840.
[62] Desai and Mulla (n 53) 26.
[63] The Constitution of India 1950, Art 226.
[64] ibid, Art 32.
[65] Law Commission of India Report 218 (43) [2.13].

B. Judicial Position before *Surya Vadanan*

Surinder Kaur Sandhu v Harbax Singh Sandhu[66] was one of the first cases where the issue of intercountry child abduction came up before a judicial forum in India. In this case, the parties were married in India and moved to England, where a child was born to them. Marital discord resulted in the husband criminally assaulting the wife, leading to his conviction and imprisonment. The husband, while on probation, removed the child from England to India.[67] The wife, in possession of a wardship order from the English court, arrived in India and petitioned the judicial magistrate for custody. The husband successfully argued that the Hindu Minority and Guardianship Act considered the father as natural guardian.[68] The wife sought special leave to appeal from the Supreme Court. Taking account of the child's best interests, the Supreme Court awarded custody to the mother. The Court held that the welfare and best interests of the child were the fundamental considerations in international parental child abduction cases.[69] The Court considered that 'the modern theory of conflict of laws prefers the jurisdiction of the State which has the most intimate contact with the issues arising in the case'.[70]

In *Jacqueline Kapoor v Surinder Pal Kapoor*[71] Jacqueline Kapoor (petitioner) was a German national and Surinder Pal Kapoor (respondent) was an Indian national. The parties married in India. Thereafter both left for Germany and became domiciled there in Dusseldorf. A child Navdeep Kapoor was born to them in Dusseldorf.[72] Their marriage was dissolved by an order dated 5 March 1993 of the Dusseldorf Family Court. The order gave custody to the mother and access rights to the father. The respondent father removed the child to India without his wife's consent.[73] The Indian court accepted the principle of intimate contact laid down in *Surinder Kaur Sandhu v Harbax Singh Sandhu*[74] as the basis of jurisdiction. It held that all relevant matters, including the birth of the child in Germany, her living there for about eight years, her knowledge of German, and her education at school and up-bringing by the mother and father, established an intimate connection between the child and the German legal system.

The law on international child abduction was substantially modified by the Supreme Court decision in *Dhanwanti Joshi v Madhav Unde*.[75] It was one of the first cases where the Supreme Court had to deal with a wrongful removal by a child's mother. In this case, the respondent Mr Madhav married the appellant (then in the US) in Omaha. The appellant Dhanwanti lived with the respondents in the US for ten months after her marriage. A male child was born to them in the US. Due to compelling circumstances, the mother (appellant) and the child left the respondent when the child was 35 days old.[76] Thereafter, the husband had no occasion to live with his wife and the child. The Supreme Court had to decide the custody of the child when he was more than 12 years old. It held that, even though the father may have obtained custody from the US court, the best interests of the child pointed to the child continuing to live with his mother who had brought up the child single-handedly since the child's removal to India.[77]

[66] *Surinder Kaur Sandhu v Harbax Singh Sandhu* [1984] 3 SCC 698.
[67] ibid [3].
[68] ibid [7].
[69] ibid [8].
[70] ibid [10].
[71] *Jacqueline Kapoor v Surinder Pal Kapoor* [1994] SCC OnLine P&H 499.
[72] ibid [1], [2].
[73] ibid [2].
[74] ibid [9].
[75] *Dhanwanti Joshi v Madhav Unde* [1998] 1 SCC 112.
[76] ibid [3].
[77] ibid [31].

This was, however, made subject to the father having visitation rights. The Supreme Court in cases declined to exercise a summary jurisdiction and refused to return the child.[78] The Court further held that:

> so far as non-Convention countries are concerned, or where the removal related to a period before adopting the Convention, the law is that the court to which the child is removed will consider the question on merits bearing the welfare of the child as of paramount importance and consider the order of the foreign court as only a factor to be taken into consideration as stated in *McKee v. McKee*[79] unless the court thinks it fit to exercise in summary jurisdiction, in the interests of the child and its prompt return for its welfare.[80]

The case of *V Ravi Chandran v Union of India*[81] further clarified the criteria to be adopted by courts in cases of child abduction. The court observed that comity and the best interests of the child were the two primary legal considerations in international child abduction.[82] Comity did not require the mindless enforcement of a foreign judgment but merely that due consideration be given to it. For this purpose, the court could order a summary or elaborate inquiry. In a summary inquiry, the court would return custody to the country from which a child has been removed unless such return could be shown to be harmful to the child. In an elaborate inquiry, the court can delve into the merits of where a child's permanent welfare lies and refuse to enforce the order of a foreign court as appropriate. It can treat the removal of a child from another country as only one of a number of relevant factors to be taken into account.[83] The question of whether to conduct a summary or elaborate procedure would be determined by considerations of the child's welfare. The summary jurisdiction to return the child would be invoked, for example, if a child had been removed from his or her native land and removed to another country where his or her native language is not spoken or the child has been detached from the social customs and contacts to which he or she has been accustomed. This is because such circumstances could be psychologically detrimental to the child's well-being.[84]

C. Legal Position after *Surya Vadanan*

In *Surya Vadanan v State of Tamil Nadu*,[85] the custody of two minor girls, both UK citizens, was in question. The appellant (Surya) and respondent (Mayura) were married in Chennai. While both were of Indian origin, Surya was a resident and citizen of the UK at the time of marriage and afterwards, Mayura acquired UK citizenship. Two girls were born to them in the UK and therefore were UK citizens. The couple's marital problems forced Mayura to return to India with the children.[86] On reaching India, Mayura petitioned under section 13(1)(i-a) of the Hindu Marriage Act for a divorce from Surya in the Coimbatore Family Court. Mayura also filed an application for custody of her daughters, but no orders were made on that application.[87] In response, Surya

[78] *Mrs. Elizabeth Dinshaw v Arvand M. Dinshaw and Anr* [1987] 1 SCC 42; *Mrs. Kuldeep Sidhu v Chanan Singh and other* AIR [1989] P&H 103; *Mrs. Jacqueline Kapoor* (n 71) (In all these cases, the abduction was carried out by fathers).
[79] *McKee v McKee* [1951] AC 352.
[80] *Dhanwanti Joshi* (n 75) [29].
[81] *V Ravi Chandran v Union of India* [2010] 1 SCC 174.
[82] ibid [35].
[83] ibid [27].
[84] ibid.
[85] *Surya Vadanan v State of Tamil Nadu* [2015] 5 SCC 450.
[86] ibid [6].
[87] ibid [9].

petitioned the English High Court to make the children wards of the Court. On 13 November 2012 the English High Court made the children wards of the Court and ordered Mayura to return the children to the UK.[88] Surya petitioned the Madras High Court for *habeas corpus*, but the petition was dismissed. Surya applied for special leave to appeal to the Supreme Court. Ordering the return of the two children to the UK for a determination of custody by the UK Court,[89] the Supreme Court summarised the legal principles applied by the Indian judiciary in intercountry child abductions until then:[90]

(1) The comity of nations does not require a court blindly to follow an order made by a foreign court but requires that the foreign order be given serious consideration.
(2) The welfare of the child is the paramount consideration.
(3) When considering the return of a child, the domestic court may conduct a summary or elaborate inquiry.
(4) The modern theory of conflict of laws recognises and prefers the jurisdiction of the state which has the most intimate contact with the issues arising in a case.[91]

The Supreme Court then commented on the principles summarised. The Court stated that the High Court had erroneously treated comity and the best interests of the child as 'contrasting principles of law'. They are not 'contrasting' in the sense of one being the opposite of the other, but are contrasting in the sense of being different principles that need to be applied to the facts of a given case.[92] The Court opined that the 'most intimate contact' and the 'closest concern' doctrines were very much alive and cannot be ignored only because their application might be uncomfortable in certain situations.[93] The Court did not elaborate on situations where the application of these doctrines would be uncomfortable. It was not appropriate that a domestic court having much less intimate contact with a child and having much less immediate concern with a child and his or her parents (in contrast to a foreign court) should take upon itself the onerous task of determining the best interests and welfare of the child.[94] The Court expressed the view that the principle of 'comity of courts' should not be jettisoned except for extraordinary and compelling reasons.[95] When deciding whether a summary or elaborate inquiry is to be conducted, the domestic court should take into account the following:

(1) The nature and effect of an interim or interlocutory order made by a foreign court.
(2) The existence of special reasons for or against repatriating a child to the foreign court's jurisdiction.
(3) The harm that might be caused, in particular, whether repatriation may cause moral, physical, social, cultural or psychological harm to the child; whether repatriation may cause harm to the parent with whom the child is in India; and whether there may be a threat to the latter's physical safety.[96]

The Court felt that, if the jurisdiction of the foreign court was not in doubt, the 'first strike' principle would be applicable. That is to say that due respect and weight must be given to a substantive

[88] ibid [13].
[89] ibid [69.1].
[90] ibid [46]–[56].
[91] ibid [24.1].
[92] ibid [48].
[93] ibid [49].
[94] ibid [49].
[95] ibid [54].
[96] ibid [56].

order prior in point of time to a substantive order passed by another court (whether foreign or domestic).[97] The first strike principle may provide certainty in terms of the recognition and enforcement of foreign judgments. However, unfortunately, it has the effect of favouring the party who can approach a favourable court first. In child abduction, the question should not be about who has approached which court first, but the welfare of the child.[98] The Court noted that nothing prevented Mayura from contesting the correctness of the interim and interlocutory orders and having them vacated or modified or even set aside.[99] The Court concluded that it could see no reason for refusing to repatriate the children and so ordered. A final order was in fact made by the English Court granting Mayura final custody rights. The case is a clear indication that repatriating a child to his or her habitual residence does not prejudice the rights of a parent who wrongfully removed the child.

The case supports the position of those who arguing for India's accession to the 1980 Convention. The Court favoured comity and contextualised the welfare of the child principle in ordering the return of the child. However, the judgment stressed that the foreign court order was only interlocutory and there was every possibility that Mayura could obtain final custody of the child (as she eventually did).[100] Thus, the judgment leaves open the question of whether the Indian courts would still have relied on comity and ordered the return of the child if the foreign court order had been final in Surya's favour.[101] *Surya Vadanan* has generally been followed in subsequent cases.[102]

The Law Commission of India has flagged that courts in India have not adhered to a consistent trend while adjudicating on abduction cases.[103] The cases reveal that a number of concepts are typically employed in child abduction cases.

D. Concepts Employed in Child Abduction Cases

i. *Welfare of the Child*

Indian judicial statements on child abduction have been fundamentally guided by the principle of the child's 'welfare'.[104] However, in the absence of legislative guidance regarding what factors should be used to assess the best interests of a minor, indeterminacy prevails and courts have given varied interpretations based on their personal ideas about what was best for the children in the cases before them, including idealised notions of parenthood coloured by varying degrees of gender bias and cultural preconceptions.[105] The emphasis of the Indian courts on the welfare of the child principle is problematic because Article 16 of the 1980 Convention prohibits judicial or administrative authorities of a Contracting State to which a child has been removed or retained

[97] ibid [52].

[98] ibid [39.1].

[99] ibid [62].

[100] M Sharma, 'Inter-Country Child Abduction: Indian Legal Response' in SR Garimella and S Jolly (eds), *Private International Law: South Asian States' Practice* (Springer, 2017) 199–220.

[101] ibid.

[102] *Tippa Srihari v State of Andhra Pradesh* [2018] SCC OnLine Hyd 123; *Chandan Mishra v Union of India* [2017] SCC OnLine Del 827.

[103] AC Lakshmanan, 'International Child Abduction – Parental Removal' (2008) 48 *Indian Journal of International Law* 427–434.

[104] L Jambholkar, 'Conflict of Laws' in SK Verma and K Kusum (eds), *Fifty Years of the Supreme Court of India: Its Grasp and Reach* (Oxford University Press, 2000) 650–681, 667.

[105] A Parashar, 'Welfare of Child in Family Laws – India and Australia' (2003) 1(1) *NALSAR Law Review* 49–72, 56.

from deciding on the merits of custody until it has been determined that the child is not to be returned or an application for return has not been lodged within a reasonable time.[106] Not being a party to the 1980 Convention, India is not bound to adhere to its principles. However, the emphasis on the welfare of the child principle as articulated in specific cases introduces uncertainty in child abduction cases.

ii. *Intimate Contact and Habitual Residence*

In contrast to reliance on habitual residence as the basis of jurisdiction under the 1980 Convention, courts in India have steadfastly invoked the doctrine of 'intimate contact' as the basis of jurisdiction in child abduction cases.[107] Decisions suggest that the intimate contact analysis is contextualised on the basis of the law of the place, which promotes the well-being of the spouses and children.[108] Habitual residence is considered only as a factors in the determination of intimate contact. Thus, reliance on intimate contact allows judicial forums to reject habitual residence as a suitable basis of jurisdiction in a given case.

a. Comity

Along with the focus on the welfare of the child principle, courts in India have also relied on 'comity' as a fundamental legal principle in child abduction cases and ordered the return of the child to his or her habitual residence. However, even in those cases where the judiciary has relied on the comity principle, it has always contextualised the issue based on the welfare of the child and stated that the 'comity of courts' does not require automatic enforcement of foreign judgments, but due consideration of the latter depending on the facts and circumstances in separate cases.[109] Such an interpretation brings uncertainty to the entire procedure. Even if equipped with a valid foreign custody order in one's favour, an aggrieved party cannot be guaranteed that such order will be recognised in India.

E. Indian Opposition to the 1980 Convention

India contemplated that acceding to the 1980 Convention would be an obstruction in protecting Indian women and children from inhospitable living conditions.[110] Numerous jurisdictions regard child abduction by a parent as an offence.[111] Section 361 of the Indian Penal Code (IPC), dealing with kidnapping, does not cover the situation where a parent abducts his or her child.[112] The general position of the Indian Government is that the rule of treating abduction as a crime can put Indian women in danger if they have taken the child out of India.[113]

[106] Abduction Convention (n 4) Art 16.
[107] P Anand, 'India' in J Stewart (ed), *Family Law: Jurisdictional Comparisons* (Sweet and Maxwell, 2011) 181–200, 195.
[108] ibid.
[109] FE Noronha, '*Private international law in India: Adequacy of Principles in Comparison with Common law and Civil Law Systems*' (Universal Law Publishing, 2010) 118–119.
[110] Press Trust of India, 'Law Min Opposed to Ratifying Child Abduction Treaty' *Hindustan Times* (Delhi, 5 September 2010) www.hindustantimes.com/delhi/law-min-opposed-to-ratifying-child-abduction-treaty/story-0vCTaReaNu928QibETdc7K.html; See also S Jolly and AV Sharma, 'Domestic Violence and Inter-country Child Abduction: An Indian Judicial and Legislative Exploration' (2021) 17(1) *Journal of Private International Law* 114–146.
[111] Silberman (n 11) 212.
[112] The Indian Penal Code 1860 (Act No 45 of 1860) s 361.
[113] L Jambholkar, 'Domestic Violence and the Hague Abduction Convention: The Indian Perspective' (2017) 57(1-2) *Indian Journal of International Law* 179.

F. Legislative Initiatives on Intercountry Child Abduction: Civil Aspects of the International Child Abduction Bill 2016 and the Protection of Children (Inter-Country Removal and Retention) Bill 2016

The mounting number of child abduction cases has resulted in a slew of legislative activity concerning intercountry abduction. The first initiatives began in 2007 through the Indian Civil Aspects of International Child Abduction Bill 2007.[114] However, the text of the Bill was not made public. An Indian Law Commission Report in 2009 pointed to the absence of progressive development on the subject and the absence of a uniform approach by the Indian judiciary. It strongly recommended that India accede to the 1980 Convention. The issue of child abduction came before the Punjab and Haryana High Court in the case of an outbound child abduction from India.[115] The Court acknowledged that the welfare of the child had been compromised due to India not being a party to the 1980 Convention. The Court commented that until India acceded to the 1980 Convention and enacted legislation to give effect to it by creating a Central Authority, inconsistency in judicial decisions would remain.[116] The Court referred the matter to the MWCD and the Law Commission 'to examine multiple issues involved in inter-country, inter-parental child removal and thereafter to consider whether recommendations should be made for enacting a suitable law for signing the Abduction Convention on child abduction'.[117]

In pursuance of the reference, the MWCD drafted the Civil Aspects of International Child Abduction Bill 2016 (the 2016 Child Abduction Bill).[118] The Law Commission in turn submitted its 263rd Report with a draft Bill entitled 'The Protection of Children (Inter-Country Removal and Retention) Bill 2016' (the 2016 Protection of Children Bill).[119] The Bills drafted by the MWCD and Law Commission were modelled on the 1980 Convention. Both stress that the best interests of the child should be the paramount consideration in child abduction disputes. The main objectives of the 2016 Child Abduction Bill are to secure the prompt return of children wrongfully removed to or retained in any Contracting State to the 1980 Convention and to ensure that rights of custody and access are respected.[120] In contrast, the 2016 Protection of Children Bill deals with the detailed functions of the Central Authority to provide assistance to help locate such children, encourage amicable solutions, and help the process of requests for the return of children.[121]

The 1980 Convention limits its application to abduction cases where the child is below 16 years of age.[122] The 2016 Protection of Children Bill explicitly states that it only applies to children who are below 16 years of age and have either been wrongfully removed to or retained in India, irrespective of nationality, religion, or status.[123] However, the 2016 Child Abduction Bill does not prescribe an age bar for abducted children. What constitutes wrongful retention

[114] A Malhotra and R Malhotra, 'India' in EE Sutherland (ed), *The Future of Child and Family Law: International Predictions* (Cambridge University Press, 2012) 144–177.

[115] *Seema Kapoor v Deepak Kapoor* [2016] SCC OnLine P&H 1225.

[116] ibid [49].

[117] ibid [11].

[118] The Civil Aspects of International Child Abduction Bill (India) 2016, https://wcd.nic.in/sites/default/files/Draft_Implemnting_Legislation_Hague_Convention_0.pdf.

[119] The Protection of Children (Inter-Country Removal and Retention) Bill (India) 2016 https://wcd.nic.in/sites/default/files/%2C%20Annexure%20III_0.pdf.

[120] Child Abduction Bill (n 118).

[121] Protection of Children Bill (n 119).

[122] Hague Abduction Convention (4) Art 4.

[123] Protection of Children Bill (n 119) s 1.

or removal remains the same under both Bills and follows the 1980 Convention.[124] The Bills go further than the 1980 Convention in providing a definition of 'habitual residence':

> '[H]abitual residence' of a child is defined as the place where the child resided with both parents; or, with one parent when they are living separately under a separation agreement or with the implied consent of the other parent or under a court order; or with a person other than a parent on a permanent basis for a significant period of time, whichever last occurred.[125]

The cultural practice prevalent in India of leaving children with grandparents has also been accounted for in the Bills. However, the invocation of the latter provisions depends on whether the child stays with someone, other than a parent, on a permanent basis for a significant period of time.[126] What constitutes a significant amount of time will depend on specific factual scenarios.

i. Institutional Mechanism

Following the 1980 Convention, both Bills provide for the constitution of a Central Authority.[127] Under the 2016 Child Abduction Bill, the Central Authority would be a person not below the rank of Joint Secretary appointed by the Central Government.[128] In the 2016 Protection of Children Bill, the Central Authority would not be a single member body, but a body with a chairperson and two others.[129] The functions of the Central Authority would include: discovering the whereabouts of a child that has been wrongfully removed or retained, taking measures to prevent further harm to the child, and securing his or her voluntary return, eliciting information about the wrongfully removed child with the appropriate authorities of a Contracting State.[130]

ii. Procedure for Application to Central Authority and Judicial Proceedings

Section 7 of the 2016 Child Abduction Bill and section 8 of the 2016 Protection of Children Bill lay down procedures for seeking assistance from the Central Authority to secure the return of a child who has been wrongfully removed or retained in India.[131] Both Bills put forward grounds whereby the Central Authority can refuse assistance. The grounds in the 2016 Child Abduction Bill include situations where it is manifest that the requirements of the 1980 Convention are not fulfilled or an application is not well founded.[132] The 2016 Protection of Children Bill does away with the term 'well founded' leaving the only grounds for refusal as the non-fulfilment of the requirements of the 1980 Convention or an incomplete application.[133] This will ensure that no application will be rejected at the preliminary stages for lack of foundation. In case of refusal, the appropriate authority or person or any other body will be informed by the Central Authority of the reasons for the same. Both Bills state that the Central Authority should not reject an application solely on the ground of lack of documents or information.[134] The Central Authority may

[124] Protection of Children Bill, s 3(1); Abduction Bill, s 3(1).
[125] Protection of Children Bill, s 2(f); Child Abduction Bill, s 2(f).
[126] Protection of Children Bill, s 2(f); Child Abduction Bill, s 2(f).
[127] Protection of Children Bill, s 4; Child Abduction Bill, s 4.
[128] Child Abduction Bill, s 4(1).
[129] Protection of Children Bill, s 4(2).
[130] Child Abduction Bill 2016, s 5(b)(c)(d)(e); Protection of Children Bill, s 6(b)(c)(d)(e).
[131] Child Abduction Bill, s 7; Protection of Children Bill, s 8.
[132] Protection of Children Bill, s 11; Child Abduction Bill, s 10.
[133] Protection of Children Bill, s 10.
[134] Protection of Children Bill 2016, s 12; Child Abduction Bill, s 11.

instead ask an applicant to provide the required documents or information. No specific time frame has been provided. The Bills have also incorporated provisions for appeal against the refusal of the Central Authority to accept an application.[135]

iii. Exceptions to Return

The 2016 Child Abduction Bill states that the court shall order the child's return to the Contracting State in which the child had his or her habitual residence provided the return application has been filed within one year from the date of removal.[136] The 2016 Protection of the Children Bill replaces the word 'shall' with 'may', making the court's decision discretionary rather than mandatory.[137] The Bills further provide that the court may pass an order for return, even it has been more than a year since the date of removal if the court is convinced that the child has not settled in his or her new environment.[138]

The grounds of exemptions provided under the Bills for returning the child to his or her habitual residence follow those of the 1980 Convention.[139] The 2016 Child Abduction Bill provides that the child need not be returned if there is a grave risk that return would expose him or her to physical or psychological harm or place the child in an intolerable situation.[140] In the 2016 Protection of Children Bill, the word 'intolerable' has been replaced with 'non-conducive'.[141] The inclusion of the term 'non-conducive' ensures that a child will not be returned to a hostile environment even though it may be tolerable. Neither Bill provides clear guidelines for this provision and India has no statute or guiding principles on ascertaining whether there is a 'grave risk and intolerable situation'. The 2016 Protection of Children Bill has additional safeguards. It provides that the child need not be returned if the person involved in the removal was fleeing from an incident of domestic violence as defined by section 3 of the Protection of Women from Domestic Violence Act 2005.[142] This is significant given that one of the major reasons for India's opposition to the 1980 Convention is the absence of specific reference to domestic violence as a ground for refusal of the return of a child.

iv. Application in Respect of Child Removed from India

The Bills have provisions for ensuring the return of a child who has been wrongfully removed from India.[143] Unlike the 1980 Convention, section 28 of the 2016 Protection of Children Bill prescribes the punishment for the wrongful removal or retention of a child.[144] The punishment is imprisonment for a term of up to one year or a fine of up to Rs 10,000 or both.

In spite of the public debate following the drafting of the Bills, the Indian Government has taken the position that it is not in India's interest to sign the 1980 Convention. The MWCD constituted a Committee chaired by Justice Rajesh Bindal of the Punjab and Haryana High Court

[135] Protection of Children Bill 2016, s 13; Child Abduction Bill, s 12.
[136] Child Abduction Bill, s 15.
[137] Protection of Children Bill, s 16.
[138] Protection of Children Bill, s 16; Child Abduction Bill, s 15.
[139] Protection of Children Bill, s 17; Child Abduction Bill, s 16.
[140] Child Abduction Bill 2016, s 16(1)(b).
[141] Protection of Children Bill, s 17(1)(b).
[142] Protection of Women from Domestic Violence Act 2005 (Act No 3 of 2005) s 3.
[143] Child Abduction Bill (n 118) s 23(1). Protection of Children Bill (n 119) s 24.
[144] Protection of Children Bill, s 28.

to draft new model legislation and advise whether India should accede to the 1980 Convention.[145] Justice Rajesh Bindal's Committee submitted its report in April 2018. The report highlighted that domestic violence and intercountry child abduction were related concepts and could not be seen in isolation.[146] It did not recommend that India sign the 1980 Convention.[147] However, the Committee recommended the creation of an Intercountry Parental Child Removal Disputes Resolution Authority.[148] The Committee gave details on global practices and the Indian situation vis-à-vis child abduction and drafted the Protection of Children (Inter-Country Removal and Retention) Bill 2018.[149] In July 2018, the MWCD formed a Committee under the National Commission for Protection of Child Rights and set up a mediation cell to solve issues of child abduction.[150] The Committee is supposed to work in tandem with the Integrated Nodal Agency, which was established by the MWCD to discuss all issues pertaining to the marital disputes of Indian citizens residing outside India.[151] At present, no legislation is pending and the courts are using the precedents discussed above to resolve child abduction disputes.

G. Comparison with Global Standards

The 1980 Convention has been one of the most successful among private international law legal initiatives and has helped to facilitate the safe and prompt return of wrongfully abducted children.[152] Major jurisdictions have put in place legal mechanisms to implement the 1980 Convention in their domestic law. The International Child Abduction Remedies Act (ICARA) was passed in 1988 to implement the 1980 Convention in the US.[153] According to ICARA, state and federal courts have original concurrent jurisdiction to hear cases arising under the 1980 Convention.[154] ICARA states that the remedies established by the 1980 Convention and ICARA are to be in addition to remedies available under other laws or international agreements.[155] ICARA provides for the designation of a Federal agency to serve as the Central Authority for the US under the 1980 Convention.[156] ICARA also sets the structure for hearing return cases, the burdens of proof applicable to return cases and to defences, relaxed rules for admissibility of documents, and guidelines for the award of fees and costs.[157]

[145] Ministry of Women and Child Development, 'Concept Note on Legislation to Address issue related to Civil Aspects of International Child Removal' (2017) https://wcd.nic.in/sites/default/files/MEENAXEE%20RAJ%20HAGUE_0.pdf; Chandigarh Judicial Academy, 'Events of the Month and Forthcoming Events' e-Newsletter (February 2017) http://cja.gov.in/E%20newsletter/e-Newsletter%20February%202017.pdf.

[146] Report of Justice Rajesh Bindal Committee to Examine Vol. I and The Civil Aspects of International Child Abduction Bill, 2016 and The Protection of Children (Inter-Country Removal and Retention) Bill 2016 (*Chandigarh Judicial Academy*, 21 April 2018) 78 http://cja.gov.in/Articles/Volume%20I%20HMJ%20Rajesh%20Bindal.pdf.

[147] S Nair, 'Inter-Country Child Abduction: Government Panel against Hague Treaty' *Indian Express* (9 May 2018) https://indianexpress.com/article/india/inter-country-child-abduction-govt-panel-against-hague-treaty-5169074/.

[148] Justice R B Committee Report (n 146) 192.

[149] ibid 205.

[150] Press Information Bureau, 'National Commission for Protection of Child Rights (NCPCR) to Constitute 'Mediation Cell' for cases of Child Custody Dispute in NRI Marital Discord' (*Press Information Bureau*, 1 August 2019) https://pib.gov.in/newsite/PrintRelease.aspx?relid=181332.

[151] ibid.

[152] Silberman (n 9) 1052–1053.

[153] International Child Abduction Remedies Act (1988) 22 USC 9001.

[154] ibid, s 9003.

[155] ibid, s 9003(g).

[156] ibid, s 9006.

[157] ibid, ss 9001–9011.

i. Implementation in the EU

a. Custody Convention

The Convention on the Recognition and Enforcement of Custody of Children and on Restoration of Custody of Children (Custody Convention)[158] was signed by the Member States of the Council of Europe in the same year as the 1980 Convention and is modelled on and complements the latter. It attempts to protect custody and access rights in international situations and facilitates the prompt restoration of the custody of a child improperly removed.[159] A party can choose to apply either under the 1980 Convention or the Custody Convention.[160] The functions of Central Authorities are elaborated as it was felt that the practical difficulties in tracing children were more complicated than the issue of divergent jurisdictional rules or applicable law.[161] It is important to mention that the Custody Convention does not lay down rules on jurisdiction and broadly provides that a decision relating to custody shall be recognised and made enforceable in every Contracting State unless the state addressed chooses to avail itself of one of the specified grounds for refusal of recognition and enforcement.[162] This is a modification in comparison to the 1980 Convention which does not provide for the recognition of custody orders. This provision is further strengthened by Article 9(3) which states that under no circumstance can a foreign decision be reviewed as to its substance.[163]

Unlike the 1980 Convention, the Custody Convention allows countries to opt for an automatic return and the restoration of a custody order with few exceptions or a rigorous process for a return order with more stringent exceptions. An automatic return order with few exceptions is provided under Article 8 which states that, if an application is made within six months of the improper removal of a child, the restoration of custody is to be immediate upon establishing the wrongful removal of the child, the child's connection based on nationality and habitual residence, and the parents' connection based on the nationality of the state in which the decision on custody was made.[164] The countries which consider that the state addressed must always retain an ultimate discretion to refuse the restoration of a child's custody, preserve their position by invoking Articles 9 and 10 and by relying on the reservation under Article 17. In these situations, return would be subject to rules of public policy, an assessment as to whether a change of circumstances has resulted in the original decision no longer being in accordance with the welfare of child,[165] and whether the child had any real connection with the state where the proceedings have been instituted.[166] Rhona Schuz notes that this Convention 'has little to commend itself to a left-behind parent who can choose between using the Custody Convention or the Abduction Convention'.[167] Further the abducting parent needs to be in violation of a custody order or decision for this instrument to be applied. This condition is not present in the 1980 Convention.[168]

[158] European Convention on Recognition and Enforcement of Decisions concerning Custody of Children and on Restoration of Custody of Children [1980] European Treaty Series No 105.

[159] Council of Europe, 'Details of Treaty No. 105' (*Council of Europe*) www.coe.int/en/web/conventions/full-list/-/conventions/treaty/105.

[160] R Schuz, *The Hague Child Abduction Convention: A Critical Analysis* 1st edn (Hart Publishing, 2013) 19.

[161] RL Jones, 'Council of Europe Convention on Recognition and Enforcement of Decisions Relating to the Custody of Children' (1981) 30(2) *The International and Comparative Law Quarterly* 467–475, 469; Custody Convention (n 158) Art 5.

[162] ibid, Art 7.

[163] ibid, Art 9(3).

[164] ibid, Art 8.

[165] ibid, Art 10 (1)(b).

[166] ibid, Art 10(1)(c).

[167] Schuz (n 160) 18.

[168] ibid 7.

b. Brussels II *bis* Regulation

The Brussels II *bis* Regulation (Brussels II Regulation) adopted in 2003 provides additional rules applicable to child return cases for courts within the EU.[169] Similar to the 1980 Convention, the court of habitual residence of the child retains jurisdiction to decide questions of custody notwithstanding an abduction.[170] In the absence of a formal definition of habitual residence, courts have interpreted the term in light of the best interest of the child.[171] The Brussels II Regulation is built on the prompt return of the child. It states that in cases of wrongful removal or retention of a child, the return of the child should be obtained without delay.[172] A failure to make such effort constitutes a violation of Article 8 of the European Convention on Human Rights (ECHR).[173] If the court of a Member State of origin decides that the child should be returned, the requirement of an *exequatur* is abolished for the enforcement of such decision and it is directly enforceable in a requested Member State. The courts of the Member State to which the child has been wrongfully removed or retained may oppose his or her return in specific cases. However, such a decision can be replaced by a subsequent decision by the court of the Member State of the habitual residence of the child prior to the wrongful removal or retention.[174] Should that judgment entail the child's return, the return should take place without any special procedure being required for recognition and enforcement of that judgment in the Member State to or in which the child has been removed or retained.[175]

The Brussels II Regulation differs from the 1980 Convention with regard to the inquiry into the child's view as to return. The 1980 Convention does not place an obligation on (and leaves it to the discretion of) the trial court to inquire whether the child objects to return.[176] However, the Brussels II Regulation reverses the burden of proof regarding the child's objections by requiring that the child be given the opportunity to be heard during the proceedings unless this appears inappropriate having regard to his or her age or degree of maturity.[177] The Brussels II Regulation does not lay down criteria for determining the age or degree of maturity required or the procedure for hearing the child. As a result, the decision to return a child depends upon the child being given an opportunity to be heard.[178] It also provides that the court cannot refuse to return the child unless the person who requested the return has been given an opportunity to be heard.[179] Notably, the Brussels II Regulation circumscribes application of the 1980 Convention by providing that a court cannot refuse to return a child based on Article 13b of the 1980 Convention if it is established that adequate arrangements have been made to secure the protection of the child after his or her return.[180]

[169] Council Regulation (EC) No 2201/2003 of 27 November 2003 Concerning Jurisdiction and the Recognition and Enforcement of Judgments in Matrimonial Matters and the Matters of Parental Responsibility, Repealing Regulation (EC) No 1347/2000 [2003] OJ L338/1.

[170] ibid, Art 10; Art 13 provides that where a child's habitual residence cannot be established, the courts of the Member State where the child is present shall have jurisdiction.

[171] R Lamont, 'Habitual Residence and Brussels II bis: Developing Concepts for European Private International Family Law' (2007) 3(2) *Journal of Private International Law* 261–281, 264.

[172] Brussels II Regulation (n 169) Art 11.

[173] *Iglesias Gi and AUI v Spain* [2003] 40 EHRR 36 [62].

[174] Brussels II Regulation (n 169) Art 11(8).

[175] ibid, Art 21.

[176] Abduction Convention (4) Art 13 (b)

[177] Brussels II Regulation (n 169) Art 11(2).

[178] JD Garbolino, 'The Impact of the Brussels II Regulation on Hague Convention Proceedings in the European Union' (*Federal Judicial Center*, March 2016) www.fjc.gov/sites/default/files/2016/Impact%20of%20Brussels%20II_0.pdf.

[179] Brussels II Regulation (n 169) Art 11(5).

[180] ibid, Art 11(4).

While the Brussels II Regulation is a coordinated document, the EU Commission considered a comprehensive modification and recast the instrument completely. The recast regulation known as Regulation (EU) 2019/1111 of 25 June 2019 deals with jurisdiction, the recognition and enforcement of decisions in matrimonial matters, matters of parental responsibility and international child abduction. Brussels II *bis* Recast was adopted by the European Council on 25 June 2019 and will apply in all EU Member States, save Denmark, from 1 August 2022.[181] The Recast Regulation modified the previous law by focusing on the voice of the abducted child.[182] Article 21 of Brussels II *bis* Recast requires that member states provide a child who is capable of forming his or her own mind with a genuine and effective opportunity to express a view, either directly or through a representative. This obligation extends to all proceedings concerned with matters of parental responsibility.[183] Article 26 stipulates that the requirements in Article 21 also apply in 1980 Convention proceedings concerned with the summary return of the child.[184] The Recast strengthens the expeditious return process which was already part of the old regulation. It stipulates that a court of first instance shall give its decision no later than six weeks after it is seised of a matter.[185] The need for expeditious proceedings is also stressed in the recitals. Recital 41 stipulates that in order to quicken the 1980 Convention process, Member States should limit the jurisdiction to hear proceedings to as few courts as possible.[186] Further, Recital 42 requires Member States to consider limiting the number of appeals to one. These measures are expected to encourage and ensure the prompt return of the child.[187]

ii. The 1980 Convention and Non–convention Countries

India's major objection to the 1980 Convention is the absence of specific provisions to protect the interests of women. India is not the only jurisdiction that has raised gender concerns regarding implementation of the 1980 Convention. Gender concerns have been elevated to the central stage of discourse in child abduction.[188] It has been pointed out that emphasis on the prompt return of the child and the restrictive interpretation of exceptions to return mechanisms have seriously affected the growing number of child abduction cases perpetrated by women owing to domestic violence.[189] Growing gender concerns have been clear from statistical data related to the 1980 Convention.[190]

[181] Council Regulation (EU) 2019/1111 of 25 June 2019 on Jurisdiction, The Recognition and Enforcement of Decisions in Matrimonial Matters and the Matters of Parental Responsibility, and on International Child Abduction [2019] OJ L178/1.

[182] The recast defines the child as any person below 18 years. See Art 2(6). This is different from the Hague Abduction Convention, European Custody Convention and Brussels II *bis* Regulation which provides for 16 years of age.

[183] Brussels II Recast (n 181) Art 21.

[184] ibid, Art 26.

[185] ibid, Art 24.

[186] ibid, recital 41.

[187] ibid, recital 42.

[188] In 2011 the Special Commission of the HCCH identified domestic violence as one of its themes. The Commission recommended the establishment of a group of experts to develop principles on the management of domestic violence allegations in return proceedings. See Hague Conference on Private International Law, *Report of Part I of the Sixth Meeting of the Special Commission on the Practical Operation of the 1980 Hague Child Abduction Convention and the 1996 Hague Child Protection Convention*, 4–6 Judges Newsletter on Child Protection, Vol. XVIII (2012), available at https://assets.hcch.net/docs/26ef0df8-c8cc-445f-8971-9a33a37ce216.pdf; Special Commission on the Practical Operation of the 1980 and 1996 Hague Conventions (25–31 January 2012), *Conclusions and Recommendations* (Part II), Nos 80–82, 1–3, https://assets.hcch.net/upload/wop/abduct2012concl_e.pdf.

[189] J Johnston, IS Edwards, M Blomquist and L Girdner, 'Prevention of Family Abduction through early Identification of Risk Factors' (Office of Juvenile Justice and Delinquency Prevention, U.S. Department of Justice, Washington, DC 2001) 1–11.

[190] N Lowe and V Stephens, Part I 'A Statistical Analysis of Applications Made in 2008 under the Hague Convention of 25 October 1980 on the Civil Aspects of International Child Abduction' (*HCCH Permanent Bureau and the International Centre for Missing and Exploited Children*, February 2018) 1 https://assets.hcch.net/docs/d0b285f1-5f59-41a6-ad83-8b5cf7a784ce.pdf.

In the absence of explicit provisions in the 1980 Convention to address domestic violence concerns, many jurisdictions have resorted to domestic legal mechanisms to protect the interest of women involved in child abduction. For instance, Japan which acceded to the 1980 Convention, by its domestic law[191] exempts the return of the child to its habitual residence if 'there is a risk that the respondent would be subject to violence, etc. by the petitioner in such a manner as to cause psychological harm to the child'.[192] Similarly, Switzerland has provided a system for raising domestic violence as a defence through the definition of 'intolerable situation' in Article 13(b) of the 1980 Convention.[193]

Recent decisions of the European Court of Justice reveal the heavy scrutiny paid by the Court to the interlinkage between domestic violence and child abduction.[194] Thus, international development reveals that, India's objections are based on a well-founded rationale.[195] In this situation, one option for India is to pursue international diplomacy and negotiations to highlight the issue of domestic violence in child abduction. Such an effort is significant because the HCCH has recognised domestic violence as a recurrent theme in child abduction, and the *Guide to Good Practice* adopted by the HCCH has stressed the need to address and develop a practice to deal with domestic violence and child abduction.[196] Alternatively, India can incorporate safety mechanisms to protect women under its domestic legislation as done by many other jurisdictions before acceding to the 1980 Convention.

iii. *Muslim Countries and 1980 Convention*

At this juncture, it is also important to discuss the fact that the 1980 Convention was adopted as a response to the increased number of marriages between different ethnic and religious communities and to protect the rights of children abducted by parents to a foreign country.[197] Though it has been ratified by 103 countries, most Muslim countries have not acceded to the 1980 Convention. Morocco, Iraq and Pakistan only became parties to the 1980 Convention in 2010, 2014 and 2017, respectively.[198] Concerning Asian and South Asian countries, even though all Asian nations are parties to the CRC, only South Korea, Singapore, the Philippines, Japan, Pakistan, Thailand, and Sri Lanka have acceded to the 1980 Convention.[199]

The religious specificities followed in Muslim countries regarding marriage, divorce, and custody matters and a presumed incompatibility with Islamic law (*sharia*), specifically its child custody rules, stand in the way of Muslim countries becoming party to the 1980 Convention.[200]

[191] Law on the implementation of the Convention on the Civil Aspects of International Child Abduction 2013 (Act No 48 of 2013).

[192] ibid, Art 28(2)(ii). See also S Yamaguchi and T Lindhorst, 'Domestic Violence and the Implementation of the Hague Convention on the Civil Aspects of International Child Abduction: Japan and US Policy' (2016) 17(4) *Journal of International Womens Studies* 16.

[193] B Bernadet, 'Regulation 2201/2003 (Brussels II *bis*) on Recognition and Enforcement of Judgments in Matters of Parental Responsibility' (2012) 46(1) *Zbornik Radova* 239–260.

[194] *OCI and Others v Romania* App no 49450/17 (ECrtHR, 21 Maxy 2019).

[195] K Singh, 'Child custody Cases in the Context of International Migration' in P Rajni and U Patricia (eds), *Marriage, Migration and Gender* (Sage Publications, 2008) 344.

[196] Guide to Good Practice under the Convention of 25 October 1980 on the Civil Aspects of International Child Abduction Part VI, Art 13(1)(b), The Hague Conference on Private International Law – HCCH, 2020, Glossary, 9, https://assets.hcch.net/docs/225b44d3-5c6b-4a14-8f5b-57cb370c497f.pdf. See also HCCH Permanent Bureau, 'Draft Guide to Good Practice on Article 13(1)(b) of the Hague Convention of 25 October 1980 on the Civil Aspects of International Child Abduction' (2017), 1 https://assets.hcch.net/docs/0a0532b7-d580-4e53-8c25-7edab2a94284.pdf.

[197] MR Walsh and SW Savard, 'International Child Abduction and the Hague Convention' (2006) 6 *Barry Law Review* 29–60, 29–30.

[198] International Child Abduction Database (n 8).

[199] ibid.

[200] AM Emon and U Khaliq, 'Private International Law, Islamic Law, and Cross-Border Child Abduction A Historico-Legal Analysis' (*Anver M. Emon*, 2016) 37–42.

Under Islamic law, the father has priority as far as custody and guardianship are concerned. Further, the best interest or welfare of the child frequently correspond with upbringing under the principles of *sharia*.[201] This religious-based inquiry has pointed ramifications in child abduction and custody cases and leads courts to conclude that it falls within the child's best interests to be raised in a Muslim community, which can protect the religious upbringing of the children.[202] With its emphasis on prompt return, the 1980 Convention does not provide a mechanism for Muslim countries to uphold their custody laws and religious practice.[203]

However, some cases decided in Muslim countries show that the latter have adopted the welfare of the child principle even to the point of overriding historical doctrines of *sharia*. For instance, in *Amina Tarar*,[204] involving a custody petition filed by the mother of a female child against the father who removed the child to Pakistan, the Lahore High Court ordered the handing over of the child to the mother's custody. Similarly, *Roshni Desai v Jahanzeb Niazi*[205] handed custody of the minor, born of a common law marriage, to the mother. However, these limited cases cannot be considered to be determinative of future legal outcomes in all jurisdictions.[206] As a solution, some scholars have suggested greater use of Article 20 of the 1980 Convention, which incorporates fundamental freedoms and human rights as an exception to return if countries with non-western religious and cultural norms join the 1980 Convention.[207] Muslim countries have also raised objection to the employment of the term 'abduction' contending that a parent cannot abduct his or her child.[208] The HCCH's Malta Process was convened to discuss the obstacles to accession by Muslim countries and to explore possible alternatives. But the Malta Process has not yielded results and differences of opinion remain with regard to law and jurisdiction in child abduction cases.[209] Thus, the implementation history of the 1980 Abduction suggests that, although it is one of the most successful private international law instruments, given the changed profile of abductions and concerns of Muslim jurisdictions, changes needs to be brought in if the 1980 Convention is to grow in its ambit and scope.[210] It should also be stressed that although the 1980 Convention has facilitated the process of the prompt and safe return of the wrongfully removed children to their habitual residence, it does not determine custody rights. Thus, one of the complex issues faced by the countries dealing with child abduction cases is the question of the recognition of foreign custody orders, especially if the foreign state is a non-signatory to the 1980 Convention. A look at the recognition and enforcement of a foreign custody order, especially among non-convention countries, is required since in many cases of child abduction a formal custody order is breached and a resort to classical principles of private international law is needed.

[201] DM Andrews, 'Note, Non-Muslim Mothers v. Egyptian Muslim Fathers: The Conflict Between Religion and Law in International Child Custody Disputes and Abductions' (2000) 23 *Suffolk Transnational Law Review* 595–632, 608.

[202] Andrews ibid. See also DSL Ong, 'Parental Child Abduction in Singapore: The Experience of a Non-Convention Country' (2007) 21(2) *International Journal of Law Policy and Family* 220–241, 232.

[203] CS Bruch, 'Religious Law, Secular Practices, and Children's Human Rights in Child Abduction Cases under the Hague Child Abduction Convention' (2000–2001) 33(1) *New York University Journal of International Law Policy* 49–58.

[204] *Imran Ali v Mst. Iffat Siddiqui and two others* PLD 2008 Karachi 198.

[205] *Roshni Desai v Jahanzeb Niazi* [2011] PLD 423 Lahore High Court.

[206] Emon and Khaliq (n 200).

[207] Beaumont and McEleavy (n 10).

[208] AG Hamid, N AHak, N M Zina and H M Jan, 'The Applicability of the 1980 Hague Abduction Convention in Muslim Countries: Particular Reference to the Malaysian Position' (2018) 32(2) *Arab Law Quarterly* 99–128, 110 https://brill.com/view/journals/alq/32/2/article-p99_99.xml?language=en#d1768962e1189.

[209] W Duncan, 'Purpose of the Malta Process' (*The Judges' Newsletter*, 2010) 12 https://assets.hcch.net/docs/8a903d75-7364-47bf-85e0-dc777d602277.pdf.

[210] CS Bruch, 'The Hague Child Abduction Convention: Past Accomplishments, Future Challenges' (1999) 1(1–2) *European Journal of Law Reform* 97–118, 114.

IV. Recognition of Foreign Custody Orders

A. Indian Legal and Judicial Position

It has been noted in chapter two that based on the comity of courts principle, section 13 of the Code of Civil Procedure provides that a judgment of a foreign court is conclusive in India under normal circumstances, in a lis between the same parties. Similarly, section 41 of the Indian Evidence Act provides that a competent court's final judgment in the exercise of matrimonial jurisdiction is conclusive proof that the legal character which it confers or takes away accrued or ceased at the time declared in the judgment for that purpose.[211] However, there are certain exceptions to this general principle, where a foreign judgment is not taken to be conclusive and may not be recognised by Indian law. Such exceptions are laid down in the six clauses (a) to (f) of Section 13.[212] Those grounds include a foreign judgment delivered by an incompetent court; a foreign judgment not on merits; a foreign judgment against international or Indian law; a foreign judgment opposed to natural justice; a foreign judgment obtained by fraud; and a foreign judgment founded on a breach of Indian law.[213] Despite statutory certainty, while dealing with issues of a foreign judgment regarding child custody, the Supreme Court of India has often overlooked the statutory principle and accorded primacy to the principle of welfare of the child.[214] In *PK Srikumar v Harshitha Gopinathan*,[215] the plaintiff husband married the defendant wife. At the time of marriage, the plaintiff was a US permanent resident. After marriage, both parties were employed and settled in the US. A child, Srihari Srikumar, was born in the US. After the minor was taken from the US by the wife, the husband initiated proceedings before the Superior Court of California, seeking custody of the child and obtained an *ex parte* order for interim custody. The Indian court observed that, having regard to the facts and circumstances of the case and in view of the fact that the child has been brought up by the mother from 2011, the wife would be the proper person to have permanent custody of the child. Therefore, the judgment passed by the foreign court was not conclusive and binding on the defendant and was not enforceable against her within the jurisdiction of Indian courts.[216]

No specific legal criteria for the recognition and enforcement of foreign custody decrees exist in India. Such criteria are important because courts subordinate to the Supreme Court can abide by them.[217] In their steadfast reliance on the welfare of the child principle, courts have often discounted the statutory provisions of the Civil Procedure Code with respect to the recognition of foreign judgments. Further, unlike foreign divorce decrees where the Supreme Court has elaborated clear principles, the field of foreign custody orders operates without clear-cut judicial decisions and is decided based on the specific facts of each case leading to a situation of uncertainty. This situation is in stark contrast to the clear and detailed provisions on recognition of foreign custody orders in other jurisdictions such as the US and EU.

B. Comparison of South Asian Positions on Foreign Custody Orders

The preceding section revealed the lack of legal clarity in India concerning the recognition of foreign custody orders in child abduction cases. An examination of the recognition of foreign

[211] The Indian Evidence Act 1872 (Act No 1 of 1872) s 14.
[212] ibid, s 13 (a)–(f).
[213] ibid.
[214] Noronha (n 109) 122.
[215] *P K Srikumar v Harshitha Gopinathan* [2015] SCC OnLine Mad 10343.
[216] ibid [63].
[217] *Shilpi Gupta v Union of India & Ors.* [2016] SCC Online Del 2561.

custody orders in other South Asian jurisdictions suggests a similar predicament and ambiguity. For instance, even though Pakistan became a party to the 1980 Convention in 2017,[218] it has not enacted legislation to implement the same. Similar to the Indian colonial legislation, Pakistan's Guardian and Wards Act regulates issues of guardianship, while the Civil Procedure Code 1972 deals with the enforcement of foreign judgments. The preferred method of enforcing foreign custody orders is by filing a writ of *habeas corpus*.[219]

Sri Lanka acceded to the 1980 Convention in 2011[220] and enacted domestic legislation entitled Civil Aspects of International Child Abduction Act No 10 of 2001 to implement the 1980 Convention.[221] Under the Act, as between parties to the 1980 Convention, foreign court orders will automatically be recognised and the child's return ordered. However, for non-Convention countries, the situation is different.[222] Sri Lanka has not entered into any conventions or agreements dealing with the reciprocal enforcement of foreign custody orders. The Reciprocal Enforcement of Judgments Ordinance No 41 of 1921[223] provides for the enforcement of the foreign judgment, but it is limited to money judgments obtained in the UK and Commonwealth countries.[224] Applications for enforcement must be made to the registering court at any time within twelve months of the date of the foreign judgment or such longer period as may be allowed by the court.[225] There is no automatic recognition or enforcement of the custody orders of foreign courts. When there is a foreign custody order in place, and the parent who has been granted the custody order wants to have the order enforced in Sri Lanka, the parent would have to institute proceedings in the District Court of Sri Lanka where he or she resides, seeking an order that he or she is entitled to legal and physical custody of the child. If the parents reside abroad, they will have to come and stay in Sri Lanka and fulfil the required number of days to qualify as a resident. The other parent would be named as respondent and have a right to be heard in the proceedings. If an order of custody is granted in favour of the applicant, he or she can remain in Sri Lanka with the child based on the rights conferred on her or him by the custody order or move back to their place of habitual residence.[226] It should also be mentioned that, the Roman-Dutch law of Sri Lanka favours the custodial right of the father during the subsistence of the marriage subject to the welfare of the child.[227]

Thus, South Asian jurisprudence is characterised by an absence of specific legal provisions concerning foreign custody orders. Each case is decided on its merits and therefore an inherent defect exists when recognition and enforcement of foreign court judgments are to sought. The uncertain position is in stark contrast to the explicit statutory provisions operating in the US and EU.

[218] Hague Conference on Private International Law, 'Pakistan Joins the 1980 Hague Child Abduction Convention' (*Hague Conference on Private International Law*, 22 December 2016) www.hcch.net/en/news-archive/details/?varevent=532.

[219] Ali (n 28) 240.

[220] Hague Conference on Private International Law, 'HCCH Details-Sri Lanka' (*Hague Conference on Private International Law*) www.hcch.net/en/states/hcch-members/details1/?sid=70.

[221] Civil Aspects of International Child Abduction Act 2001 (Act No 10 of 2001). See also R Wijeyeskera, 'Inter-country Child Abduction – Sri Lankan Legal Response' in SR Garimella and S Jolly (eds), *Private International Law: South Asian States' Practice* (Springer, 2016) 243–261.

[222] S De Soysa, 'Custody Disputes between Parents and Third Parties- An Evaluation of the Sri Lankan Law' (1985) *University of Colombo Review* 123; In cases involving minor children, Sri Lankan courts consider the best interests of child principle. See also *Weragoda v Weragoda* [1961] 59 CLW 59; *Endoris v Kiripetha* [1968] 73 NLR 20; *Premawathie v Kudalugoda Aratchiew* [1970] 75 NLR 398.

[223] The Reciprocal Enforcement of Judgments Ordinance 1921 (Act No 41 of 1921).

[224] The foreign judgment can be challenged on the ground that the foreign court lacked jurisdiction, the original judgment was obtained by fraud; that the foreign judgment was obtained in contravention of public policy and natural justice.

[225] The Reciprocal Enforcement of Judgments Ordinance 1921 (n 248) s 3(1).

[226] R Dantanarayana and J Wilson, 'Child Custody and 'Enforcement' of Foreign Child Custody Orders in Sri Lanka' (2017) 10(1) *Family Law Update* 11–14 www.esthersusin.com/.cm4all/mediadb/Family-Law-Newsletter-December-2017.pdf.

[227] ibid.

C. Recognition of Foreign Custody Order in the US

Historically, US courts have been reluctant to decide on the applicability of the full faith and credit clause in custody matters and courts have manifested differing positions.[228] The 1980 Convention has been implemented in the US through ICARA. The latter includes a full faith and credit clause that requires states to recognise the judgments of other courts ordering the return of a child pursuant to the 1980 Convention.[229] However, in the US, the 1980 Convention is not an exclusive remedy. The parties involved in child abduction may use other domestic laws to seek the return of or access to a child in the US.

As far as the non-signatories are concerned, the US does not follow a uniform approach in dealing with international child abduction cases. Such situations require reference to the classical doctrine of comity, subject to considerations of due process.

The Uniform Child Custody Jurisdiction Act (UCCJA) adopted in 1968 was intended to settle the question of the applicability of the full faith credit clause in custody disputes.[230] The UCCJA purported to reduce jurisdictional competition and provided that custody litigation should take place in a state based on factors such as whether the parties' home was in the state, emergency, significant connection, and appropriate forum.[231] The UCCJA also aimed to deter the wrongful removal of children, facilitate enforcement of out-of-state custody decrees and unify the law of states.[232] Significantly, the UCCJA provided that a custody decree rendered under proper jurisdictional requirements would be binding on all the parties and be recognised and enforced in other states in inter-state custody disputes.[233]

Section 23 of the UCCJA extends this provision to transnational custody disputes and provided that:

> the provisions of this Act relating to the recognition and enforcement of custody decrees of other States apply to custody decrees and decrees involving legal institutions similar in nature to custody institutions rendered by appropriate authorities of other nations if reasonable notice and opportunity to be heard were given to all.[234]

Although the UCCJA generated considerable optimism, it did not produce a discernible change and the need was felt for other federal legislation.

In 1997, the UCCJA was replaced by the Uniform Child Custody Jurisdiction and Enforcement Act (UCCJEA).[235] The UCCJEA is not a substantive statute dealing with custody issues and only determines which state courts have jurisdiction. The jursidictional rules broadly follow the earlier UCCJA. However, the court which has jurisdiction under UCCJEA may decline to exercise its jurisdiction if it determines that it is an inconvenient forum and

[228] M Blair, 'International Application of the UCCJEA: Scruntinizing the Escape Clause' (2004) 38/3 *Family Law Quarterly*, 547–581, 551.

[229] International Child Abduction Remedies Act (n 153) s 9003(g).

[230] Uniform Child Custody Jurisdiction Act (US) 1968, Prefatory Note.

[231] ibid, s 3; BM Bodenheimer, 'The Uniform Child Custody Jurisdiction Act' (1969) 3(4) *Family Law Quarterly* 304–316.

[232] ibid; EM Trapnell, Uniform Child Custody Jurisdiction Act (1978) 12(4) *University of Richmond Law Review* 745–748, 745.

[233] PM Hoff, 'The Uniform Child-Custody Jurisdiction and Enforcement Act' (*National Criminal Justice Reference Service*, December 2001) 5 www.ncjrs.gov/pdffiles1/ojjdp/189181.pdf; ME Moraza Choisne, 'Juridical Solutions in the U.S.A. for Parental Kidnapping in Child Custody Cases' (1990) 24(2) *Revista Juridica de la Universidad Interamericana de Puerto Rico* 309–353, 316.

[234] Uniform Child Custody Jurisdiction Act 1968 (n 230) s 23. See also MI Bodzin, 'International Parental Child Abduction: The Need for Recognition and Enforcement of Foreign Custody Decrees' (1988–1989) 3(2) *Emory Journal of International Dispute Resolution*, 205–219, 207.

[235] Uniform Child Custody Jurisdiction and Enforcement Act (US) 1997.

that a court of another state is a more appropriate forum. The UCCJEA incorporates domestic violence as well as the financial positions of parties as a factor in determining the appropriate forum.[236] This is not only a great improvement but will assist battered women. The UCCJEA specifically provides for the enforcement of 1980 Convention return orders and authorises public officials to locate and secure the return of children in 1980 Convention cases.[237] The UCCJEA contains provisions that clarify when foreign custody determinations are entitled to enforcement and when courts in the US must defer custody matters to the jurisdiction of a foreign court.[238]

Section 105 of the UCCJEA addresses the international application of the Act. It provides that US courts are to treat a foreign state as a state of the US and requires that child custody determinations made by foreign states in conformity with the UCCJEA must be recognised and enforced as mandated in Article 3.[239] However, the section contains an escape clause, providing that the UCCJEA need not be applied if the 'child custody law of the foreign country violates fundamental principles of human rights'.[240] In the absence of a definition of what constitutes a violation of fundamental principles of human rights, courts have adopted differing interpretations. In *Anwar Malik v Joohi Malik*,[241] the Maryland intermediate appellate court held that a custody order of a Pakistani court would be valid unless:

(1) the 'best interests of the child' standard had not been applied; or
(2) the order had been obtained by applying a law contrary to Maryland public policy.

In *Noordin v Abdulla (In re Custody of R)*,[242] the Washington court held that it could deny recognition and enforcement of a foreign custody decree even if the foreign court was competent. A foreign decree would not be recognised if the foreign proceedings had been conducted in a manner contrary to Washington state law and public policy and if the best interests of child had not been considered.

D. Recognition of Foreign Custody Orders in the EU

The Brussels II *bis* Regulation covers the recognition and enforcement of foreign custody orders in the European Union.[243] Article 21 states that 'a judgment given in a Member State shall be recognised in the other Member States without any special procedure being required'.[244] Importantly, under Article 2(4), the term 'judgment' refers to a decree, order or a decision of a court of any Member State.[245] No reference is made as to whether an order should be interim or final. Article 23 provides for restricted grounds for non-recognition of judgments relating to parental responsibility. These include the following:

(a) Recognition would be contrary to the public policy of the Member State where recognition is sought. The principle of the best interests of the child would be applied instead.

[236] ibid, s 207.
[237] ibid, s 302. See also Hoff (n 233) 4.
[238] ibid, s 303.
[239] ibid, s 105.
[240] ibid, s 105(c). See also Blair (n 228) 556.
[241] *Malik v Malik* 638 A.2d 1184 (Md. Ct. Spec. App. 1994).
[242] *Noordin v Abdulla (In re Custody of R)* 947 P.2d 745 (1997).
[243] Brussels II *bis* Regulation (n 169).
[244] ibid, Art 21. See Also PE McEleavy, 'Brussels II *bis*: Matrimonial Matters, Parental Responsibility, Child Abduction and Mutual Recognition' (2004) 53(2) *International Comparative Law and Quarterly* 503–512, 511.
[245] ibid, Art 2(4).

(b) The judgment was given without the child being heard, except in cases of urgency.
(c) The judgment was given in default of appearance without proper notice of the relevant documents having been given, unless the respondent unequivocally accepted the judgment.
(d) No opportunity of being heard was given to the respondent.
(e) The judgment is irreconcilable with a later judgment relating to parental responsibility given in the Member State in which recognition is sought.[246]

The Recast Regulation reiterates similar rules on recognition of custody orders to those which formed part of the Brussels II *bis* Regulation.[247] The assessment suggests that, in comparison to the Indian position, the US and the EU have enacted specific statutory position to facilitate the issue of the recognition of foreign custody orders.

V. Conclusion

This chapter analysed the complexities of intercountry parental child abduction and the international community's response through the 1980 Convention. The latter attempted to ensure the prompt return of a wrongfully removed child to his or her habitual residence. However, there are growing concerns regarding the correlation between incidents of child abduction and the presence of domestic violence. The 1980 Convention does not give due consideration and sufficient weight to such circumstances in the context of a 'grave risk' argument. This chapter explored the statutory and Indian judicial responses and highlighted the legal concepts developed by the Indian courts. In the absence of a legislative framework dealing with intercountry child abduction, the courts have applied domestic law to address wrongful child removal disputes as custody disputes based on the criteria of the best interests of the child or the welfare of the child, in contrast to the return-based approach of the 1980 Convention. India has steadfastly opposed accession to the 1980 Convention, claiming that signing it would seriously jeopardise the interests of women fleeing from domestic violence. There has been extensive legal activity on the subject, beginning with the Law Commission Report in 2009 recommending accession to the 1980 Convention. This was followed in 2016 by a reference of the High Court of Panjab and Haryana to the Law Commission of India and the MWCD to look into intercountry child abduction. As a response, Bills were drafted by the Law Commission and the MWCD as precursors to the country's accession to the 1980 Convention. These have been hotly debated by the public. However, despite these legal developments, the government decided against accession, leaving the judiciary to evolve practices based on the welfare of the child.

The situation presents further complications as the country also lacks an adequate mechanism for recognising foreign custody orders, which are often violated in child abduction cases. However, it needs to be mentioned that the domestic violence concerns advanced by India in opposing the 1980 Convention are not unique to India, as many jurisdictions facing similar scenarios have responded by incorporating domestic mechanisms specifying several conditions that would allow refusing the return of the child. Besides, many Islamic countries also oppose the 1980 Convention based on its conflict with principles of their custody laws and *sharia*. The discussion shows that, despite the 1980 Convention being one of the most successful private international law instruments, considering the changed profile of abductions and the concerns of jurisdictions, changes need to be introduced to grow the instrument's ambit and scope.

[246] ibid, Art 23.

[247] Brussels II Recast (n 181) Arts 30 and 39; Compared to the provisions of Brussels II *bis* Regulation under Art 23 which talks of the general obligation of considering the views of the child, Art 39 of the Recast provides for refusal of recognition of decisions in matters of parental responsibility only in cases where the child who is capable of forming his or her own views was not provided that opportunity.

9

Cross-Border Surrogacy and Private International Law

I. Introduction

Surrogacy is a method of reproduction where a woman carries the child of another pursuant to a contract. The understanding is that, at birth, the child will be handed over to the other party and the surrogate mother will relinquish all rights to the child.[1] Surrogacy can be categorised into traditional and gestational surrogacy based on the method used. In traditional surrogacy, the child is genetically related to the surrogate mother.[2] In gestational surrogacy, the surrogate mother is not genetically linked to the child and only acts as a gestational carrier.[3] Based on the financial considerations involved, surrogacy may be further divided into altruistic and commercial surrogacy. In altruistic surrogacy, the surrogate mother does not receive financial compensation and is motivated by emotional and humanitarian considerations.[4] Commercial surrogacy involves monetary consideration.[5]

Surrogacy may be an appealing option for infertile couples that would not otherwise be able to fulfil their dream of parenthood and for surrogate mothers who would obtain financial remuneration. However, it raises critical ethical and legal issues.[6] Data from across the world reveals the rampant exploitation of marginalised and vulnerable women. The financial vulnerability of women in many developing nations forces them to act as surrogates to the detriment of their emotional and physical health.[7] In such a situation, it is doubtful whether a woman's 'consent' to act as a surrogacy can be said to have been freely given, rather than to have been forced by their economic circumstances.[8] On an ethical level, there is the fear that surrogacy will lead to the

[1] C Carr, *Unlocking Medical Law and Ethics* 2nd edn (Routledge, 2015) 263; K Trimmings and P Beaumont, 'General Report on Surrogacy' in K Trimmings and P Beaumont (eds), *International Surrogacy Arrangements: Regulation at the International Level* (Hart Publishing, 2013) 444.

[2] K Brugger, 'International Law in the Gestational Surrogacy Debate' (2012) 35(3) *Fordham International Law Journal* 665–697; A Hofheimer, 'Gestational Surrogacy: Unsettling State Parentage Law and Surrogacy Policy' (1991–92) 19(3) New *York University Review of Law & Social Change* 571–616, 573; K Yamamoto and SAD Moore, 'A Trust Analysis of a Carriers Right to Abortion (2001) 70 *Fordham Law Review* 93, 95.

[3] Hofheimer (n 2) 574.

[4] ibid. See also V Rozée and S Unisa, *Assisted Reproductive Technologies in the Global South and North* 1st edn (Routledge, 2016) 16.

[5] Hofheimer (n 2) 574.

[6] B Steinbock, *Legal and Ethical Issues in Human Reproduction* (Ashgate, 2002) 66; P Gerber and K O'Byrne, *Surrogacy, Law and Human Rights* 1st edn (Routledge, 2016); AP Kumar, D Inder and N Sharma, 'Surrogacy and Women's Right to Health in India: Issues and Perspectives' (2013) 57(2) *Indian Journal of Public Health* 65–70; P Saxena, A Mishra and S Malik, 'Surrogacy: Ethical and Legal Issues' (2012) 37(4) *Indian Journal of Community Medicine* 211, 213.

[7] CP Kindregan Jr. and D White, 'International Fertility Tourism: The Potential for Stateless Children in Cross-Border Commercial Surrogacy Arrangements' (2013) 36(3) *Suffolk Transnational law Review* 527–626, 605.

[8] A Bailey, 'Reconceiving Surrogacy: Toward a Reproductive Justice Account of Indian Surrogacy' (2011) 26(4) *Hypatia* 715–741.

commodification and de-personalisation of reproduction since there will be a divide between a child's birth and legal parents.[9] Along with legal and ethical concerns, the conflicting approaches of jurisdictions to surrogacy gives rise to a host of private international law issues in relation to legal parentage and nationality.[10] So much was acknowledged by the General Council of the Hague Conference on Private International Law in 2010, when it enumerated the complex issues of private international law arising from the growth of cross-border surrogacy arrangements.[11] The Special Commission on the Practical Operation of the Hague Convention on Protection of Children and Cooperation in Respect of Intercountry Adoption in June 2010 inter alia noted that the rapid increase in the number of international surrogacy arrangements and expressed concern over the uncertainty surrounding the status of children born as a result of these arrangements.[12]

This chapter evaluates Indian legislative and judicial responses to cross-border surrogacy. It is divided into six parts, including this Introduction. Section II explains private international law concerns in cross-border surrogacy. Section III evaluates the legal response to surrogacy in India. Special emphasis is given to the evolution of the Surrogacy Bills with a focus on the 2019 Bill. Section IV appraises the judicial narrative on surrogacy and compares it with the legal position in Nepal. Section V examines the HCCH's efforts in highlighting legal challenges and harmonising conflict of law approaches to cross-border surrogacy.

II. Private International Law Issues in Cross Border Surrogacy

A. Legal Parentage

Domestic laws determine rules on legal parentage. Jurisdictions assign legal parentage based on the operation of law, on the fact of birth, or by agreement between the putative parents.[13] Generally, if the mother who gives birth is married, the legal presumption is that the husband is the child's legal father.[14] For instance, section 112 of the Indian Evidence Act 1872 states:

> [T]he fact that any person was born during the continuance of a valid marriage between his mother and any man, or within two hundred and eighty days after its dissolution, the mother remaining unmarried, shall be conclusive proof that he is the legitimate son of that man, unless it can be shown that the parties to the marriage had no access to each other at any time when he could have been begotten.[15]

[9] LB Andrews, *Between Strangers: Surrogate Mothers, Expectant Fathers, & Brave New Babies* (Harper & Row 1989) 101; D DeMarco, *Biotechnology and the Assault on Parenthood* (Ignatius Press, 1991) 75; S Allan, 'The Surrogate in Commercial Surrogacy: Legal and Ethical Considerations' in Paula G and K O'Byrne (eds) *Surrogacy, Law and Human Rights* (Routledge, 2016) 113–143.

[10] CF Glynn, 'Review Article: Human Rights and Private International Law: Regulating International Surrogacy' (2014) 10(1) *Journal of Private International law* 157–170, 159.

[11] Permanent Bureau, 'A Preliminary Report on the Issues Arising from International Surrogacy Arrangements' (*Hague Conference on Private International Law*, March 2012) https://assets.hcch.net/docs/d4ff8ecd-f747-46da-86c3-61074e9b17fe.pdf; Permanent Bureau, 'Private International Law Issues Surrounding the Status of Children, Including Issues Arising from International Surrogacy Arrangements, (*Hague Conference on Private International Law*, March 2011) www.hcch.net/upload/wop/genaff20llpdlle.pdf; Council on General Affairs and Policy of the Conference, 'Conclusion and Recommendations adopted by the Council on General Affairs and Policy of the Conference' (*Hague Conference on Private International Law*, 7–9 April 2010) https://assets.hcch.net/upload/wop/genaff2010concl_e.pdf.

[12] Permanent Bureau, 'Conclusions and Recommendations and Report of the Special Commission on The Practical Operation of The 1993 Hague Inter-country Adoption Convention' (*Hague Conference on Private International Law*, 17–25 June 2010) https://assets.hcch.net/upload/wop/adop2010_rpt_en.pdf.

[13] Kindregan and White (n 7) 604–619.

[14] ibid.

[15] The Indian Evidence Act 1872 (Act No 1 of 1872) s 112.

Thus, the presumption of paternity in the case of a child born through surrogacy holds in favour of the surrogate mother and her husband and not to the would-be parents. However, where surrogacy is permitted, the paternity of the child will lie with the intended parents. Since the determination of legal parentage is based on domestic parameters and varies from one state to another, cross-border surrogacy gives rise to legal complications as is apparent from judicial statements.

B. Nationality

The right to nationality is a recognised human right under various international conventions[16] and domestic jurisdictions have enacted constitutional and legislative provisions dealing with nationality. Nationality rules follow the principle of birth or descent.[17] Differing reliance on birth or descent and contradictory approaches to surrogacy lead to complications in determining the nationality of children born through cross-border surrogacy. For instance, the Ukraine, which permits commercial surrogacy,[18] assigns the would-be parents' nationality to a child born through surrogacy. However, if the intending parents are from Japan, which does not permit surrogacy, the child will not be granted Japanese nationality. The legal complications involved and the consequent risk of statelessness arising from cross-border surrogacy have been stressed in judicial statements in the *Baby Manji*[19] and *Jan Balaz*[20] cases.

III. Legal Status of Commercial Surrogacy in India

A. Constitutional and Statutory Provisions

A key constitutional question about surrogacy is whether it is part of a right to reproductive liberty. The provisions germane to the discussion are Articles 21 and 23 of the Indian Constitution. Article 21 guarantees the right to life and liberty to citizens and non-citizens.[21] Judicial dicta have consistently expanded the scope and applicability of Article 21.[22] In *Suchita Srivastava v Chandigarh Administration*,[23] in the context of abortion, the court observed:

> There is no doubt that a woman's right to make reproductive choices is also a dimension of 'personal liberty' as understood under Article 21 of India's Constitution. It is essential to recognise that reproductive choices can be exercised to procreate as well as to abstain from procreating. The crucial consideration is that a woman's right to privacy, dignity, and bodily integrity should be respected.

[16] Universal Declaration of Human Rights (adopted 10 December 1948 UNGA Res 217 A(III) (UDHR) Art 15; Convention on the Rights of the Child (adopted 20 November 1989, entered into force 2 September 1990) 1577 UNTS 3 (CRC) Art 7.

[17] Citizenship Act 1955 (Act No 57 of 1955) ss 3, 4.

[18] SN Kirshner, 'Selling a Miracle: Surrogacy through International Borders: Exploration of Ukrainian Surrogacy' (2015) 14(1) *Journal of International Business and Law* 77–98, 85.

[19] *Baby Manji Yamada v Union of India* [2008] 13 SCC 518.

[20] *Jan Balaz v Anand Municipality* AIR [2010] Guj 21.

[21] The Constitution of India 1950, Art 21.

[22] *Suchita Srivastava & Anr. v Chandigarh Administration* [2009] 14 SCR 989; *Laxmi Mandal v Deen Dayal Harinagar Hospital & Ors* [2010] 8853/2008; *Jaitun v Janpura Maternity Home & Ors* [2010] 10700/2009 (High Court of Delhi, 4 June 2010); *Sandesh Bansal v Union of India and others Writ Petition* No 9061/2008).

[23] *Suchita Srivastava* (n 22) [11].

In *KS Puttaswamy v Union of India*,[24] the constitutional right of women to make reproductive choices as part of their personal liberty under Article 21 was recognised. However, the position of surrogacy in the context of reproductive liberty has not been clarified by the court.[25] Questions have also been raised about the validity of surrogacy agreements in the context of Article 23, which prohibits forced labour and trafficking in human beings.[26] Surrogacy is a contractual arrangement to transfer a baby in the future. It could be interpreted as the sale of a baby for consideration, thus qualifying as trafficking.

The enforceability of surrogacy agreements under the Contract Act is a complex one. The conditions for a valid contract are offer, acceptance, free consent, a lawful object, a lawful consideration, and the absence of a vitiating factor (such as illegality).[27] In the context of surrogacy, where most surrogate mothers belong to the economically disadvantaged sectors of society, the question of free consent assumes complexity.[28] Although a surrogacy contract is essentially concluded between two individuals, it involves larger public concerns such as ensuring the best interests of the child and preventing the exploitation of women. Hence, whether surrogacy contracts are forbidden by law or opposed to public policy needs to be answered separately. Judicial decisions have not elaborated on the public policy or the enforceability of surrogacy agreements. In the wake of the booming number of surrogacy transactions, (now valued in the billions[29]), numerous reported instances of the exploitation of surrogates, and a lack of clarity regarding the rights of parties,[30] the Indian Council of Medical Research (ICMR) felt that it was imperative to put in place guidelines regulating the practice of Assisted Reproductive Technology (ART) in India, especially in the absence of any legislation.[31]

B. ICMR Guidelines

The ICMR Guidelines of 2005 define surrogacy as an agreement between a woman and expecting parents whereby the woman consents to carry a pregnancy, which is genetically unrelated to her or her husband, with an ultimate understanding that the child will be handed over to the party commissioning the pregnancy.[32] It restricts surrogacy to those who cannot physically or medically carry a baby to term.[33] The Guidelines prescribe financial agreements for surrogacy and dictate that the same shall cover all associated costs of pregnancy.[34] Under the Guidelines, the upper age limit for surrogates is 45 years of age[35] and a woman cannot be a surrogate more than three times in her life.[36] The surrogate mother cannot be genetically related to the child

[24] *KS Puttaswamy v Union of India* [2019] 1 SCC 1.

[25] A Ghosh and N Khaitan, 'A Womb of One's Own: Privacy and Reproductive Rights' (2017) 52 *Engage Economic and Political Weekly* 42–43 www.epw.in/engage/article/womb-ones-own-privacy-and-reproductive-rights.

[26] The Constitution of India 1950 (n 21) Art 23; See also G Palattiyil, E Blyth, D Sidhva and G Balakrishnan, 'Globalization and Cross-Border Reproductive Services: Ethical Implications of Surrogacy in India for Social Work' (2010) 53(5) *International Social Work* 686–700.

[27] Indian Contract Act 1872, s 10.

[28] ibid, ss 13, 14,16, 19, 23.

[29] S Jolly, 'Cross Border Surrogacy: Indian State Practice' in SR Garimella and S Jolly (eds), *Private International Law: South Asian States' Practice* (Springer, 2017) 175–197, 178–179; see also I Jargilo, 'Regulating the Trade of Commercial Surrogacy in India' (2016) 15(2) *Journal of International Business and Law* 337–360.

[30] Jolly (n 29) 179.

[31] National Guidelines for Accreditation, Supervision, and Regulation of ART Clinics in India 2005.

[32] ibid, 13 R 1.2.33.

[33] ibid, R 3.10.2.

[34] ibid, R 3.10.3.

[35] ibid, R 3.10.5.

[36] ibid, R 3.10.8.

and must relinquish in writing all parental rights over the child. The child born out of surrogacy is presumed to be the legitimate child of the commissioning couple, born within the wedlock, with the consent of both spouses, and with all the attendant rights of parentage, support, and inheritance.[37] It is essential to point out that these Guidelines have no legal force. Nonetheless, they have been referred to by the Indian Judiciary as a guide in a few cases involving ART.

C. Evolution of Surrogacy Regulation Bills

The Law Commission, which conducted a detailed study of the legal issues arising out of surrogacy, opined in its 228th Report[38] that surrogacy agreements would continue to be governed by the contract between the parties. The contract is supposed to contain all the terms of the relationship, including the surrogate mother's consent to bear the child, the reimbursement of all her expenses for carrying the child, and her willingness to hand over a child commissioning parents, etc. The Report provided an elaborate framework for legislation that comprehensively deals with the difficult issues of surrogacy. As a result, the Assisted Reproductive Technology (Regulation) Bill and Rules 2008 was introduced. It was subject to much modification and was followed by the Assisted Reproductive Technology (Regulation) Bill and Rules 2010, which imposed severe restrictions on foreign nationals seeking to engage Indian surrogates. Arrangements with foreign nationals would only be allowed where their countries recognised surrogacy and the child born through such surrogacy arrangement would be granted the citizenship of the commissioning couple.[39] Owing to the lapse of the earlier ART Bill 2010, the Ministry of Home Affairs circulated the Assisted Reproductive Technology (Regulation) Bill 2014.[40] The Bill proposed that surrogacy should only be available to infertile married heterosexual couples. This would effectively debar single individuals and homosexual couples.[41] The Bill also proposed to disallow surrogacy for foreign nationals, but to permit it for Overseas Citizens of India (OCIs,) persons of Indian Origin (POIs), non-resident Indians (NRIs), and foreign nationals who have been married to Indian citizens for at least two years and have obtained a medical visa for surrogacy in India.[42] Regarding the rules on nationality and citizenship, the Bill stated that children born through surrogacy in India to OCIs, POIs, and foreigners married to an Indian should not be given Indian citizenship under the Citizenship Act 1955.[43] The ART Bill 2014 further provided that a child born through ART shall be presumed to be the legitimate child of the commissioning couple and have the same rights as a biological child of such couple.[44] The birth certificate would thus be issued in the name of commissioning parents. As far as regulatory authorities are concerned, the Bill suggested the establishment of a National Advisory Board, a State Advisory Board, and a National Registry for the accreditation, regulation, and supervision of clinics to prevent misuse of ART and promote ethical and safe ART practices.[45] Most importantly, the Bill espoused the

[37] ibid, R 3.5.4. See also J Rimm, 'Booming Baby Business: Regulating Commercial Surrogacy in India' (2009) 30(4) *University of Pennsylvania Journal of International Law* 1429–1462, 1440.

[38] Law Commission of India, *Need for Legislation to Regulate Assisted Reproductive Technology Clinics as Well as Rights and Obligations of Parties to a Surrogacy* (Report No 228, 2009).

[39] The Assisted Reproductive Technologies (Regulations) Bill 2010, s 35.

[40] Ministry of Health and Family Welfare Government of India, 'The Assisted Reproductive Technology (Regulation) Bill, 2014' (2015, No V.25011/444/2011 – HR (Vol II) (Part)).

[41] ibid, s 2(p).

[42] ibid, s 60(11)(a).

[43] ibid, s 61(7); See also Jolly (n 29) 191.

[44] ibid, s 61(1).

[45] ibid, ss 3, 18, 22.

legalisation of commercial surrogacy by recognising financial transactions for surrogacy, ie, arrangements between the commissioning parents and surrogate mother.[46]

The Surrogacy Regulation Bill 2016 altered the positions adopted in the earlier Bills by only allowing altruistic surrogacy for Indian citizens[47] and prohibiting commercial surrogacy.[48] The Surrogacy Bill 2016 prescribed altruistic surrogacy only for heterosexual couples who have been married for at least five years and who have been proven to be infertile.[49] The Bill specifically laid down that a surrogate mother should be a close relative of the intending couple and a married woman between the ages of 25 and 35 years with a child of her own. This seriously restricted the usage of surrogacy.[50] However, the Bill did not define who constituted a close relative. Any child born out of surrogacy would be deemed to be a biological child of the intending couple and entitled to all rights and privileges of a natural child under any law.[51]

D. Surrogacy (Regulation) Bill 2019

The Surrogacy (Regulation) Bill 2019 was introduced after the 2016 version lapsed following dissolution of the Lok Sabha.[52] The 2019 Bill, for the most part, is identical to the 2016 Bill. This means that commercial surrogacy will be impermissible and only Indian citizens who have been married for at least five years, with one or both being infertile, can apply for an eligibility certificate, assuming that a close relative will be willing to help them out by acting as a surrogate.[53] Just as the 2016 Bill, the 2019 Bill does not allow homosexuals couples to apply for surrogacy. The Bill only recognises a legally married man and woman as a couple. The Indian Judiciary having accepted same-sex marriages,[54] the intentions of the drafters of the Bill are difficult to understand as the Bill's terms fail to accommodate the legitimate concerns of a large sector of society which is the most likely to avail itself of the benefits of ART.[55]

i. Procedure and Eligibility Criteria for Surrogacy

A certificate of eligibility is essential for availing the service of surrogacy. The certificate will be issued upon fulfilment of the following conditions:

(1) Production of a certificate from a District Medical Board of the proven infertility of one or both spouses.
(2) Acquisition of an order of parentage and custody of the surrogate child from the Magistrate's Court.
(3) Proof of insurance coverage for 16 months covering postpartum delivery complications for the surrogate.[56]

[46] ibid, s 60(3), 60(31).

[47] The Surrogacy (Regulation) Bill 2016, Lok Sabha (2018) [Bill No 257 of 2016] s 2(b) 'altruistic surrogacy' means the surrogacy in which no charges, expenses, fees, remuneration or monetary incentive of whatever nature, except the medical expenses incurred on surrogate mother and the insurance coverage for the surrogate mother, is given to the surrogate mother or her dependants or her representative.

[48] ibid, ss 3, 35, 37.

[49] ibid, s 4(ii)(a).

[50] ibid, s 4(iii)(b).

[51] ibid, s 7.

[52] Parliament of India, (17th Series, Vol III, First Session, 2019/1941 (Saka) No 21, Monday, 15 July 2019/Ashadha 24, 1941 (Saka) 78.

[53] The Surrogacy (Regulation) Bill 2019 (Bill No 156-C of 2019).

[54] *Navtej Singh Johar & Ors. v Union of India* [2018] 10 SCC 1.

[55] ibid; BBC, 'India has 2.5m Gays, Government tells Supreme Court' (*BBC*, 14 March 2012) www.bbc.com/news/world-asia-india-17363200.

[56] The Surrogacy (Regulation) Bill 2019 (n 53) s 4(iii)(a).

The 2019 Bill lays down the following eligibility criteria for intending couples:

(1) They must be Indian citizens who have been married for at least five years.
(2) The wife must be between 23 and 50 years old and the husband between 26 and 55 years old.
(3) They should not have any surviving child (biological, adopted, or surrogate), excluding a child who is mentally or physically challenged or suffers from a life-threatening disorder or fatal illness.
(4) They must meet any other conditions specified by regulations.[57]

The 2019 Bill prescribes a number of qualifications for the surrogate mother. She must be between 25 and 35 years old, a close relative of the intending couple, and a married woman with a child of her own. She must not have acted as a surrogate previously. She must possess a certificate of medical and psychological fitness for surrogacy.[58] She cannot provide her gametes for surrogacy.

ii. Legal Parentage

The 2019 Bill deals with the parentage by prescribing that no surrogacy procedure shall take place unless the intending couple has a certificate of eligibility issued by the appropriate authority. This will only be issued if a magistrate has made an order, in favour of the intending parents, concerning the parentage and custody of the child to be born through surrogacy.[59] It is easy in this case to see that deciding parentage will not be a struggle given the criminalisation of non-altruistic surrogacies. Further, the Bill states that a surrogate child will be deemed to be the biological child of the intending couple.[60] An abortion of the child requires the surrogate mother's written consent and the permission of the appropriate authority. This authorisation must comply with the Medical Termination of Pregnancy Act 1971.[61] The surrogate mother can choose to withdraw from surrogacy before the embryo is implanted in her womb.[62] Since foreign nationals, NRIs, POIs, etc are not allowed to opt for surrogacy in any form, the question of citizenship does not arise. The omission of foreign nationals is controversial because according to various accounts almost a third of the total commissions for surrogacy are from foreign-based couples.[63]

iii. Institutional Mechanism

Like the 2014 and 2016 Bills, the 2019 Bill envisages the creation of a National Surrogacy Board (NSB) and State Surrogacy Boards (SSB) to advise the Central Government on policy matters, lay down codes of conduct for surrogacy clinics, and supervise the functioning of SSBs.[64] The 2019 Regulation does not deal with surrogacy contracts within the Indian Contract Act 1782. It merely requires that a written consent from a surrogate is needed to conduct the procedure.[65]

[57] ibid, s 4(iii)(c).
[58] ibid, s 4(iii)(b).
[59] ibid, s 4(iii)(a).
[60] ibid, s 7.
[61] ibid, s 3(vi).
[62] ibid, s 6(2).
[63] A Pande, 'Cross-Border Reproductive Surrogacy in India' in ES Sills (ed) *Handbook of Gestational Surrogacy: International Clinical Practice and Policy Issues* (Cambridge University Press, 2016) 143–148; See generally AL Burpee, 'Momma Drama: A Study of How Canada's National Regulation of Surrogacy Compares to Australia's Independent State Regulation of Surrogacy' (2009) 37 *Georgia Journal of International & Comparative Law* 305–338.
[64] The Surrogacy (Regulation) Bill 2019 (n 53) ss 14, 22.
[65] ibid, s 6

The Surrogacy Bill 2019 was passed by the Lok Sabha and referred to a Select Committee of Rajya Sabha.[66] The Select Committee report made recommendations and stated that consideration should be given to commercial surrogacy as it would be challenging in practice for intending parents to find a close relative who is willing to go through the commitment of acting as a surrogate.[67] It was asserted that an absolute prohibition would only lead to greater exploitation of women as the current magnitude of the surrogacy industry was such that would be unlikely to vanish. On the contrary, it was likely to find its way underground, leading to more rampant exploitation.[68] Similarly, it was also too rigid to mandate a five-year waiting period for an intending couple before being eligible to try the surrogacy route. The five years should be reduced to a lesser number.[69] The Select Committee recommended that consideration be given to the interests of widows and divorcees, as that had been overlooked. If surrogacy applications are rejected, a review or appeal procedure should be in place. The Union Cabinet on 26 February 2020 approved the Surrogacy (Regulation) Bill 2020, incorporating the recommendations of the Rajya Sabha Select Committee. The 2020 Bill allows a 'willing' woman to be a surrogate mother and proposes that the law benefit widows and divorced women in addition to infertile Indian couples.[70] However, the full text of the 2020 Bill has not been made public. The legislative effort of the government has been supplemented by judicial statements on surrogacy revealing the complex legal and social issues involved.

IV. Judicial Statements on Surrogacy: Public Policy Narratives

A. The *Baby Manji* Case

Baby Manji Yamada was born through a surrogacy agreement between a Japanese couple and an Indian surrogate mother in 2007. Dr Yuki Yamada and Dr Ikufumi Yamada were the biological parents of baby Yamada.[71] There was matrimonial discord between the biological parents and the couple separated. The child was born on 25 July 2008. As Japan bans commercial surrogacy, the Japanese authorities, informed Dr Yuki Yamada that the birth mother would be regarded as the legal mother and Dr Yki Yamada would only be able to bring the child to Japan by adopting her under Japanese and Indian laws and obtaining an Indian passport.[72] The adoption was problematic. Indian law does not allow a single father to adopt a baby girl.[73] Dr Yamada applied for an Indian passport for Manji, a document that requires an Indian birth certificate. A birth certificate can only be issued with the names of both parents. Dr Yamada could be identified as the father. However, the authorities were unsure about who should be classified as the mother.

[66] ibid.

[67] Select Committee, 'Report of the Select Committee on The Surrogacy (Regulation) Bill, 2019 Presented to the Rajya Sabha' (*PRS*, 5 February 2020) 3 www.prsindia.org/sites/default/files/bill_files/Select%20Comm%20Report-%20Surrogacy%20Bill.pdf.

[68] ibid 14.

[69] ibid 25

[70] Special Correspondent, 'Cabinet Approves Surrogacy Bill' *The Hindu* (26 February 2020) www.thehindu.com/news/national/cabinet-clears-surrogacy-regulation-bill/article30921456.ece.

[71] *Baby Manji* (n 19) [4]; See also J Reddy, 'Indian Surrogacy: Ending Cheap Labor' (2020) 18(3) *Santa Clara Journal of International Law* 92–123, 101.

[72] ibid [4]. See also S Jolly, 'Surrogacy and Family Ties: A Comparative Analysis of Indian and Japanese Legal Framework' (2010) 2 *University Institute Legal Studies Journal* 299.

[73] Central Adoption Resource Authority, 'Eligibility Criteria for Prospective Adoptive Parents' (*CARA, Ministry of Women & Child Development*) http://cara.nic.in/Parents/eg_ri.html.

On these grounds, the municipal council refused to grant a birth certificate for Manji.[74] Meanwhile, an NGO called Satya petitioned the Rajasthan High Court to prevent Manji from being taken out of India. The Rajasthan High Court required Manji to be brought to them within four weeks. In response, Dr Yamada's mother filed a writ petitioning on Manji's behalf to the Supreme Court of India.[75] After a lengthy discussion on surrogacy, the Supreme Court granted temporary custody of Manji to the petitioner.[76] The Court disposed of the petition with a direction that, if any person has any grievance, it should be ventilated before the Commission constituted under the Act.[77] After the judgment, the Jaipur passport office granted a special dispensation and issued Manji with an identity certificate. The Japanese Embassy in New Delhi granted Manji a one-year Japanese visa on humanitarian grounds and Manji's grandmother was able to take her to Japan.[78]

B. The *Jan Balaz* Case

In *Jan Balaz v Anand Municipality and ors*.[79] the Balaz couple entered into a surrogate agreement with Martha Immanuel Christi. The child was biologically related to the father Jan Balaz and the surrogacy resulted in the birth of twins.[80] Jan Balaz applied to the Anand Nagarpalika municipality for the registration of the birth of the children. The municipality issued birth certificates for the children in accordance with the Registration of Birth and Deaths Act 1969. In the birth certificates, the surrogate's name was given as the mother of the children.[81] Although German nationals, Jan Balaz and his wife were working in the UK. They had to obtain a visa from the UK consulate in India to take their children to the UK. Since the babies were born in India and are Indian citizens, the petitioner applied for an Indian passport.[82] The petitioner was shown as the father, and the surrogate's name was given as the mother.[83] The children were issued a passport on that basis. Later, Jan Balaz received a notice from the Indian Ministry of External Affairs' Regional Passport Office, requesting the surrender of the children's passports as the issue of the passport had been queried before the High Court of Gujarat.[84] Jan Balaz petitioned the High Court of Gujarat for an order that the passport office return the passports to enable the twins to fly to Germany and apply there for German citizenship. Jan Balaz contended that, as Indian citizens, the twins' right to travel could not be violated under Article 21 of the Indian Constitution.[85] The passport office argued that the surrogate could not be treated as the twins' mother for under section 3 of the Citizenship Act 1955. They argued that section 6(2)(a) of the Passports Act 1967 only allowed Indian citizens to apply for a passport to visit a foreign country. The petitioners argued that surrogacy was not prohibited in India and the children were born

[74] TNN, 'Japanese Baby Finally Gets Birth Certificate' *The Times of India* (Jaipur/Vadodra, 10 August 2008) https://timesofindia.indiatimes.com/city/jaipur/Japanese-baby-finally-gets-birthcertificate/articleshow/3346424.cms.

[75] *Baby Manji* (n 19) [2]; see also S Rajan, 'Resolving Statelessness Arising out of Surrogacy in India: A Legal Analysis' (2014–2015) 14 ISIL *Year Book of International Humanitarian and Refugee Law* 14 177–198, 187.

[76] K Points, 'Commercial Surrogacy and Fertility Tourism in India: The Case of Baby Manji' (*The Kenan Institute for Ethics at Duke University*) 6 https://kenan.ethics.duke.edu/wp-content/uploads/2018/01/BabyManji_Case2015.pdf.

[77] *Baby Manji* (n 19) [18].

[78] 'Surrogate Baby Born in India Arrives in Japan' *Hindustan Times* (3 November 2008) www.hindustantimes.com/world/surrogate-baby-born-in-india-arrives-in-japan/story-clfjpEmKM0wORsHNmwG7CP.html.

[79] *Jan Balaz* (n 19).

[80] ibid [2].

[81] ibid [3].

[82] ibid [4].

[83] ibid.

[84] ibid.

[85] ibid [5].

to a surrogate who was an Indian citizen.[86] It should be noted that Germany does not recognise surrogacy and the children could not obtain direct citizenship there.

The court identified the ethical and legal issues and stressed the need for certainty as it would impact the lives of children if they were held not to have a legal parentage or identity and to be 'stateless'. The court relied on the 228th Law Commission Report and referred to the legal systems of the Ukraine, Japan, and Germany before reaching a conclusion.[87] The court pointed out that commercial surrogacy has never been considered illegal in India and the 228th Report proposed legislation to regulate ART clinics as well as the rights and obligations of parents to a surrogacy. The court also considered the flip end of things by examining how other jurisdictions handled such situations. In California, surrogacy agreements are accepted, but no statute exists to regulate them and the courts rely on the Uniform Parentage Act to deal with surrogacy agreements.[88] The court noted that the Supreme Court of Japan in interpreting the Civil Code of Japan held that a mother who physically gave birth to a child should be considered as the legal mother. This effectively denied the recognition of surrogacy altogether.[89] In Germany, where the law was stricter, artificial insemination and embryo donations were classified as criminal and not permitted by law.[90]

The court recognised the gestational mother as the real mother due to a lack of a law on the subject. The ova donor was not considered a mother at all. However, she has other rights, such as the right to privacy and cannot be forced to disclose her identity. Until legislation was enacted, the wife of the biological father could not be treated as the legal or natural mother.[91] Since both the egg donor and the gestational mothers were Indian and the children had been born an Indian national, they were also Indian nationals.[92] Even if the babies were considered illegitimate, they had been born in India and for that reason were entitled to Indian citizenship by birth under section 3(1)(c)(ii) of the Citizenship Act 1955.[93] With respect to the passports, the court held that they had been issued under section 4(2)(b) of the Passports Act. A passport only established a person's identity. But identity was not an issue in the case, as the mother was known and the children were Indian nationals.[94] The court stressed the urgent need for a detailed law on surrogacy and commented that the ICMR guidelines were insufficient.[95] The Union of India appealed against the decision.

The Supreme Court explored the possibility of adoption on humanitarian grounds by the Central Adoption Research Authority of India.[96] The Authority informed the Court that they were only concerned with issues relating to abandoned children.[97] The Supreme Court ordered the Authority to reconsider, even if that would give rise to a precedent.[98] Germany offered to issue a German visa to the children for adoption in Germany and the Balaz couple was allowed to adopt the children under German law.[99] Though the diplomatic dialogue between Germany and

[86] ibid [6].
[87] ibid [10].
[88] ibid [11].
[89] ibid [12], [14], [16].
[90] ibid [13].
[91] ibid [16].
[92] ibid [16], [17].
[93] ibid [17].
[94] ibid [18].
[95] ibid [21].
[96] Y Ergas, 'The Transnationalization of Everyday Life: Cross-Border Reproductive Surrogacy, Human Rights and the Re-Visioning of International Law' (Deconstructing and Reconstructing "Mother" Workshop, Columbia University, 12 March 2012) 20 http://claradoc.gpa.free.fr/doc/444.pdf.
[97] See T Lin, 'Born Lost: Stateless Children in International Surrogacy Arrangements' (2013) 21(2) *Cardozo Journal of International and Comparative Law* 545–588, 573–574.
[98] ibid.
[99] S Mortazavi, 'It Takes a Village to Make a Child: Creating Guidelines for International Surrogacy' (2012) 100(6) Georgetown *Law Journal* 2249–2290, 2275–2276; See also A Guha and N Chauhan, 'Regulation of Commercial Surrogacy in India: Some Suggestions' (2015) 6(2) *Indian Journal of Law and Justice* 92–99, 95.

India allowed the Balaz couple to take the children to Germany, this did not resolve the questions of legal parentage and nationality.

C. Reflections from Nepal

It is essential to understand that one nations' policy on surrogacy directly impacts other nations' positions and attitudes to surrogacy. India's laws have influenced Nepal's position on surrogacy. Nepal's encounter with surrogacy arose following the Cabinet's decision on 2 June 2014 (2071BS) allowing surrogacy services for foreign couples.[100] Nepal emerged as a hub for commercial surrogacy in Asia after surrogacy was banned in Thailand and legal complications arose in India. Advocates Pushpa Raj Pandey[101] and Prabin Pandak[102] filed two different writ petitions for declarations that the Cabinet decision was void and surrogacy was contrary to public policy and Articles 12(1), 12(2), 13(1), 20(3), 22, 27 and 29(3) of the Interim Constitution of Nepal 2063(BS). Since the two writs were filed on the same date, raising the same subject matter, the Supreme Court delivered a single judgment for both cases.

The petitioners contended that the absence of a proper law harmed the reproductive right of women guaranteed by the Constitution and forced women who were illiterate, poor and disadvantaged to work as surrogates. The Supreme Court held that the relationship of father, mother, and child could be established biologically or legally. Unregulated surrogacy could violate public policy and the public interest. The Supreme Court thus laid down 15 guidelines, including the following:

(1) As the mother's womb can never be commercialised, commercial surrogacy has to be banned entirely.
(2) If a medical board has certified that a Nepali married couple is incapable of producing children because of infertility or a weak health condition, they can seek a surrogacy.
(3) Foreign nationals, same-sex couples, or single men and women should not be eligible to seek a surrogacy.
(4) Women can be surrogates only out of altruistic feelings with full and free consent.
(5) In order to be a surrogate, a woman has to meet specific criteria as to age and her capability of producing a child from a health perspective. She should be married and have a child. She should not be permitted to be a surrogate more than once and consent from her husband or at least a leading member of her family.
(6) The surrogacy service is only to be provided by health institutions which fulfil the criteria prescribed by law.
(7) A married infertile couple wishing to engage a surrogacy service and a woman who wants to be a surrogate should first apply to a prescribed authority and they will only be allowed to make use of a surrogacy service after necessary inquiries have been undertaken by the authority.
(8) Clarity is needed in determining the legal parents of the child born from surrogacy, as well as their rights and duties. The Evidence Act of Nepal provides for a presumption of paternity in favour of the surrogate mother and spouse, rather than the intended parents.[103]

[100] R Prajuli, 'Surrogacy in Nepal: Threat to Reproductive Right' *The Himalayan Times*, 18 August 2015.

[101] *Pushpa Raj Pandey v office of Prime Minister, Ministry of Health and Population including others*, Writ No 072-WO-0119 (2073 BS).

[102] *PrabinPandak v Office of Prime Minister and others*, Writ No 072-W0-0120 (2073 BS).

[103] Evidence Act 1974, (Nepal) s 6(d) and 6(d1) – Unless proved otherwise. The following children born in a wedlock situation shall be presumed to be born from a married husband: (1) child born within 180 days of their marriage;

(9) The law has to prescribe the forum having jurisdiction to hear cases related to surrogacy.
(10) The law should stipulate a penalty by way of a fine, imprisonment or both, for the violation of surrogacy laws.[104]

As far as the petitions were concerned, although the Court affirmed the applicants' claims, it became unnecessary to issue a prerogative writ because the Cabinet had itself overruled its earlier decision to allow foreign nationals to seek surrogacy in Nepal.

Despite the judicial guidelines, Nepal's legislature failed to address concerns over surrogacy in the new Civil Code. While the Civil Code deals with artificial insemination and the related question of paternity,[105] it is silent on surrogacy. It can be observed that the public policy dimension is likely to be a hindrance to legalising surrogacy practices in Nepal. If one sees the interpretation of public policy from the perspective of private international law, the court has adopted a very broad approach in defining public policy and, by conflating it with the public interest, it has laid the possibility of invoking public policy whenever it finds anything new contrary to traditional practices, thereby narrowing the possibility of applying the rules of private international law. This has to be seen against the background of existing uncertain judicial decisions on public policy. In *Suman Panta v Immigration Department*,[106] the court impliedly recognised same-sex marriage by ignoring the potential public policy concerns. On the other hand, it interpreted the public policy widely to restrict the practice of surrogacy without trying to reconcile the situation by applying rules of private international law. If we see both issues together, the degrees of social sensitivity involved are similar, but the invocation of public policy led to different outcomes; one to recognition, the other to non-recognition. Thus there is a need to bring more clarity and direction to the operationalsation of public policy to bring judicial certainty.

V. Legal Initiatives for Harmonisation and India's Role

There is no convention regulating surrogacy at the international level. Owing to the legal inconsistencies in the practice of domestic jurisdictions, international surrogacy arrangements have thrown up a host of legal issues, including in respect of nationality and legal parentage. In 2015 the HCCH formed a Working Group to look into the legal issues and implications of cross-border surrogacy. The Working Group met in 2016, 2017, 2018 and 2019.[107] India has been a member of the Working Group and has been actively engaging in its discussion.[108] The Working Group has identified the question of parentage as one of the complex issues arising out of surrogacy. The group defined parentage as 'the relation between the parent and the child such

(2) child born within 282 days from the date of dissolution of marriage. A child born out of artificial insemination based on the consent of husband and wife shall be presumed to belong to a married husband.

[104] On file with the authors.

[105] The National Civil (Code) Act 2017 (2074)(BS) Nepal, s 109. If any child is born by using the sperm of another person, upon the consent of the married couple, such child shall be considered to belong to the husband within the marital relationship, and therefore paternity shall be determined accordingly.

[106] *Suman Panta v Immigration Department and others*, NKP [2074] decision No 9921 [SC]. Applicant a Nepali national contracted gay marriage with a US National in 2015. Supreme Court of Nepal, based on the equality clause, held that the Constitution of Nepal prevents discrimination on the ground of sexual orientation.

[107] 'The Parentage/Surrogacy Project' (*Hague Conference on Private International Law*) www.hcch.net/en/projects/legislative-projects/parentage-surrogacy.

[108] Council on General Affairs and Policy, 'Report of the Experts' Group on the Parentage/Surrogacy Project (meeting from 29 October to 1 November 2019)' (*Hague Conference on Private International Law*, March 2020) Annex https://assets.hcch.net/docs/d435cffc-65ce-4047-b603-ff63ed20591c.pdf.

as established by law'.[109] The Working Group concluded its March 2020 meeting by endorsing the formulation of a convention dealing with the recognition of foreign judicial decisions on legal parentage and a protocol on the recognition of foreign judicial decisions on legal parentage rendered as a result of an international surrogacy arrangement.[110] However, the Working Group opined against articulating a position for or against surrogacy. The Working Group has already made significant progress in developing draft provisions for a possible future protocol dealing with the recognition of foreign judicial decisions on legal parentage.

The Working Group recommended that the protocol only apply to the recognition of judgments on legal parentage and not to the rights and obligations which derive therefrom, such as maintenance, succession, or nationality.[111] It elaborated that, for the recognition of legal parentage, it should employ jurisdictional requirements based on the child's habitual residence, the respondent's habitual residence,[112] and a real and substantial connection.[113] The Working Group also expounded specific grounds of non-recognition, including grounds of public policy, the best interests of the child, the lack of due process, and inconsistent judgments or parallel proceedings.[114] The Working Group felt that a uniform applicable law at the time of child's birth would help ensure the continuity of legal parentage in cross-border cases in the absence of a foreign judgment on legal parentage.[115]

The Working Group proposed the adoption of a protocol on legal parentage established as a result of international surrogacy agreements (ISA). Most experts in the Working Group agreed that judgments rendered post-birth in the state of origin of the ISA should be recognised by operation of law in all other Contracting States. The Working Group reaffirmed the central importance of the surrogate mother's free and informed consent as a condition for recognition of the judgment on legal parentage.[116] It underlined the desire to prevent the abduction, sale, or trafficking of women and children in the context of ISAs, taking into account the Optional Protocol to the Convention on the Rights of the Child on the Sale of Children, Child Prostitution, and Child Pornography of 20 May 2000. These discussions are still at an initial stage and the Working Group is expected to submit its report to the Council on General Affairs and Policy (CGAP) by 2022 in order for CGAP to make a final decision on whether to proceed with the project.[117]

VI. Conclusion

This chapter analysed the booming cross-border surrogacy industry and the differing standards followed by jurisdictions in respect of legal parentage and nationality. This chapter evaluated the legal status of surrogacy in India. The assessment revealed that the legal position under the Constitution and the Contract Act vis-a-vis surrogacy was unclear and has not been agitated before the courts. However, the limited judicial statements in the *Baby Manji* and *Jan Balaz* cases have highlighted the painful saga of children born through surrogacy caught in legal imbroglios. For instance, in 2008 Manji Yamada born through surrogacy could not leave India for 12 months

[109] ibid.
[110] ibid [1].
[111] ibid [4].
[112] ibid noting that the state might be the respondents in certain jurisdictions.
[113] ibid [2].
[114] ibid [3].
[115] ibid [4].
[116] ibid [5].
[117] ibid.

after her birth because of a lack of clarity concerning her nationality. The scenario presents uncertainty and violates the rights of the parties involved. The chapter traced the legal initiatives undertaken by the Government of India through successive Surrogacy Regulation Bills. The assessment of these Bills showed that the Surrogacy (Regulation) Bill 2014 makes a marked shift from the pro-surrogacy position articulated by the ART Bill 2010 that allowed foreign nationals to access surrogacy with a requirement to follow medical visa rules. Surrogacy Bills in 2014, 2016, and 2019 only recognised the rights of infertile heterosexual couples to access surrogacy and ignored the rights of single parents. They also sought to prohibit foreign nationals from availing of surrogacy services. The Surrogacy Regulation Bills of 2016 and 2019 altered the positions adopted in the earlier Bills by allowing only altruistic surrogacy for Indian citizens and prohibiting commercial surrogacy outright. Starting from 2008, five Bills have been put forward. This demonstrates the government's seriousness in regulating surrogacy. However, the divergent positions articulated by the Bills and the sudden shift to discouraging of surrogacy gives rise to ambiguity for the parties involved in surrogacy. There is a strong need to have more deliberation and the Law Commission's 288th Report can serve as a useful template.

PART IV

Law of Obligations

10

The Applicable Law in Contractual Obligations*

I. Introduction

As we have seen, private international law deals with disputes arising among private individuals which contain a foreign (international) element. At the same time, the circumstances in which a dispute will include a foreign element are not uniformly defined. Its meaning has been reported to differ across national and international instruments.[1] Nonetheless, the expression generally refers to disputes which are not purely domestic by nature and therefore consist of a transnational element.[2] This may be the position when the parties or their establishments are located in different countries or when the agreement is concluded or performed overseas.[3]

The identification of the law that will govern a contractual obligation will depend on the conflict of law rules of the forum which is adjudicating a dispute,[4] which will be determined once the court has established its jurisdiction. In doing so, the court will apply its principles of private international law to identify the applicable law (also known as the governing law). In this respect, the determination of the applicable law may be referred to as the second pillar in private international law, the first being jurisdiction.

The rules on contractual obligations are generally confined to international disputes arising in connection to contracts on the sale of goods, services, immovable property, insurance, the transfer or licensing of intellectual property, agency or franchise agreements, to name a few. The rules on contractual obligations do not extend to disputes arising in connection to family matters,

*This chapter draws extensively on the following articles published by the author on the subject: S Khanderia, 'Indian Private International Law *vis-à-vis* Party Autonomy in the Choice of Law' (2018) 18(1) *Oxford University Commonwealth Law Journal* 1 [Khanderia, *Party Autonomy*]; S Khanderia, 'The Ascertainment of the Applicable Law in the Absence of Choice in India and South Africa: A Shared Future in the BRICS' [2020] *Oxford University Commonwealth Law Journal* DOI: 10.1080/14729342.2020.1773019 [Khanderia, The Ascertainment of the Applicable Law]; S Khanderia and S Peari, 'Party Autonomy and the Choice of Law under Indian and Australian Private International Law' [2020] *Commonwealth Law Bulletin* 1, DOI: 10.1080/03050718.2020.1804420 [Khanderia & Peari, *Party Autonomy in India and Australia*]; and S Khanderia, Practice does not Make Perfect: Rethinking the Doctrine of 'The Proper Law of the Contract' – A Case for the Indian Courts' (2020) 16(3) *Journal of Private International Law* 423. [Khanderia, *Practice does not Make Perfect*].

[1] See the Hague Conference on Private International Law [HCCH], 'Commentary on the Hague Principles on Choice of Law in International Contracts' (approved 15 March 2015) [1.13] www.hcch.net/en/instruments/conventions/full-text/?cid=135 [Commentary to Hague Principles].

[2] See for instance, ibid, [1.13]–[1.22] referring to Art 1(2) of the Hague Principles; and HCCH Convention on Choice of Court Agreements (concluded 30 June 2005) 44 I.L.M. 1294 Art 1(2) [HCCA] read along with T Hartley and M Dogauchi, 'Explanatory Report on the 2005 Hague Convention on Choice of Court Agreements' (HCCH Publications 2007) 33[11] www.hcch.net/upload/expl37e.pdf [HCCA, Hartley & Dogauchi Report]; and the decision of the Delhi High Court in *Gas Authority of India Ltd v SPIE CAPAG, SA & Ors* [1993] (27) DRJ.

[3] ibid.

[4] JHC Morris and GC Cheshire, 'The Proper Law of a Contract in the Conflict of Laws' (1940) 56 *Law Quarterly Review* 320, 333, 334; and M Whinchop and M Keyes, 'Putting the Private Back into Private International Law: Default Rules and the Proper Law of the Contract' (1997) 21 *Melbourne University Law Review* 515, 517.

insolvency, the governance of trusts or choice-of-court agreements, all of which are regulated by special rules. This chapter discusses the principles of Indian private international law vis-à-vis the identification of the applicable law in contractual obligations (ie matters of contract). What law will govern a dispute arising from an agreement for the sale of furniture before an Indian court between a seller (a person residing and domiciled in France) who alleges that the buyer (a person residing and domiciled in India) has failed to pay for the goods? Or what law will the Indian court apply to decide the rights and liabilities of contractual parties, if one alleges that the other was a minor or had misrepresented specific facts at the time of the conclusion of the contract? These are questions that will be addressed in this chapter.

This chapter is divided into five parts (including this Introduction). Section II will examine the principles of Indian private international law on applicable law in contractual obligations. This part is further divided into four sub-sections. Section A will provide an overview of the development of the doctrine of the proper law of the contract, which is the mechanism to identify the applicable law. Section B will discuss the means to identify the proper law of the contract in India. Besides, this section will examine the application of the proper law of the contract to contracts concluded online (e-commerce transactions). In doing so, it will discuss the choice of law implications when there are conflicting standard terms in an international commercial contract. It will accordingly analyse the legal provisions and solutions adopted by the Indian courts to resolve such predicaments, particularly in this era of heightened e-commerce transactions. Section III will analyse the scope and the extent of the applicable law governing disputes on the formal, material or essential validity of the contract; the performance of the contract; and the capacity of the parties. Section IV will reflect on Indian private international law in light of trends from other jurisdictions, such as the EU, the UK, China, Russia, Australia, Canada and Nepal. This section will also examine the possible uses of the Hague Principles on the Choice of Law in International Commercial Contracts (Hague Principles) in developing and supplementing Indian conflict of law rules on applicable law in contractual matters. Section V will provide concluding remarks.

II. Identification of the Applicable Law in Contractual Obligations in India

A. Development of the Doctrine of the Proper Law of the Contract: An Overview

In India, the rules to identify the applicable law in contractual obligations have not been codified. In such circumstances, the rules to determine the applicable law for disputes arising from a contractual obligation with a foreign element have been developed by judicial dicta. In this respect, the principles of English common law have been instrumental in shaping the principles of Indian private international law. In English common law, the mechanism to identify the applicable law is through the doctrine of the proper law of the contract which was developed in the seminal case of *Vita Food Products Incorporated v Unus Shipping Company*.[5] The Privy Council was seised of a dispute which arose from a transportation contract concluded between a Nova Scotian and an American corporation.[6] The agreement was evidenced by a bill of lading which

[5] [1939] AC 277.
[6] ibid.

exempted the master from liability from damage that could occur to the products by negligence in transporting the same.[7] The exemption clause contravened the Hague-Visby Rules which were applicable in Newfoundland – the place from where the products were shipped.[8] The parties had, however, chosen English law to govern the contract.[9] The court was, accordingly, called upon to adjudicate the validity of the parties' choice of English law. The Privy Council per Lord Wright referred to the proper law of the contract as:

> the law, which the parties intended to apply. That intention is objectively ascertained, and, if not expressed, will be presumed from the terms of the contract and the relevant surrounding circumstances.[10]

The decision of the Privy Council in *Vita Food*[11] has formed the genesis of development of the doctrine in India.

The decision of the Calcutta High Court in *Indian General Investment Trust v Raja of Khalikote* was the first reported case in which the Court discussed the doctrine of the proper law of the contract while adjudicating a dispute concerning a loan agreement between the respondent Raja for himself and on behalf of his minor son and the petitioner on the security of a certain property.[12] The Court stated that:

> the proper law of a contract means that law which a court is to apply in determining the obligations under the contract. In deciding these matters, there are no rigid or arbitrary criteria such as *lex loci contractus* or *lex loci solutionis*. The matter depends on the intention of the parties to be ascertained in each case on a consideration of the terms of a contract the situation of the parties and generally on all the surrounding facts from, which is to be gathered the intention of the parties.[13]

Subsequently, the Supreme Court in *Delhi Cloth and General Mills Co Ltd v Harnam Singh*, upon being seised of a dispute arising from a sale-agreement between two merchants residing in Lyallpur (Pakistan) and India in which the law of Lyallpur was chosen, defined the proper law of the contract as:

> the law of the country in which the contract is localised. Its localisation will be indicated by what may be called the grouping of its elements as reflected in its formation and its terms. The country in which its elements are most densely grouped will represent its natural seat the country with which the contract is, in fact, most substantially associated and in which lies its natural seat or centre of gravity.[14]

In *National Thermal Power Corporation v Singer Corporation*,[15] the Supreme Court introduced greater clarity on the interpretation of the doctrine of the proper law of the contract. Examining two international commercial agreements between National Thermal Power (an Indian company) and Singer (an English company) in which the English legal system was selected, the court stated that the proper law of the contract is:

> the legal system, by which the parties intended the contract to be governed, or where their intention is neither expressed nor to be inferred from the circumstances, the system of law with which, the transaction has the closest and most real connection.[16]

[7] ibid.
[8] ibid.
[9] ibid.
[10] ibid 290.
[11] ibid.
[12] AIR [1952] Cal 508 [8] per Sinha J.
[13] ibid.
[14] AIR [1955] SC 590 [36].
[15] [1992] 3 SCC 551.
[16] ibid [14], referring to A Dicey, J Morris and L Collins (eds), *Dicey and Morris on the Conflict of Laws*, 11th edn (Sweet and Maxwell, 1987) Rule 180: Sub-Rule (1), which defines 'the proper law of the contract'.

In doing so, the Court formally introduced the tripartite hierarchy that the proper law of a contract would be determined by assessing the express, implied or objective choice, thus, building on the foundations of *Vita Food*.[17] Besides, the Court clarified that the proper law of the contract refers to the substantive principles of the domestic law of the chosen system.[18] In an arbitration agreement, the Court stated that the proper law is 'normally the same as the proper law of the contract'.[19]

B. Identification of the Proper Law of the Contract

As has been shown above, the proper law of the contract comprises the express or the implied choice of the parties. In its absence, the system of law with which the contract has its closest and most real connection will be applied. This section will examine the interpretation given to each of these aspects in Indian private international law.

i. *Express Choice of Law*

a. Parameters of Party Autonomy

Historically, the parties' autonomy to choose a law was limited to a legal system which bore a connection to the contract.[20] In this respect, Cheshire's objective interpretation of party autonomy[21] found favour in defining the limits of the parties' express choice of law to govern their contract.[22] Anzilotti and Batifol's[23] theory of localisation which was endorsed by French law[24] formed the backbone of Cheshire's interpretation of party autonomy in the choice of law.[25] According to Cheshire, parties can select a proper law by localising the contract and grouping the individual elements of their agreement to find its centre of gravity.[26] The legal system with which the contract is 'most substantially associated' after being localised would then govern the contract.[27] For instance, if the parties desire to select English law to govern the contract, they would have to 'localise' the contract by grouping the elements of the agreement (such as the *locus contractus*, the *locus solutionis*, the currency of the transaction, the seat of arbitration (if any)

[17] (n 5).

[18] *National Thermal Power Corporation* (n 15) headnote [4].

[19] ibid [20]–[22].

[20] See *Delhi Cloth and General Mills Co Ltd v Harnam Singh*, AIR [1955] SC 590, [37]; *Rabindra N Maitra v Life Insurance Corporation of India*, AIR [1964] Cal 141, [18]–[29]; and *British India Steam Navigation Co Ltd v Shanmughavilas Cashew Industries*, [1990] 3 SCC 481 [37].

[21] GC Cheshire, *Private International Law*, 6th edn (Clarendon Press, 1961) 215; and M Wolff, 'The Choice of Law by the Parties in International Contracts' (1937) 49 *Juridical Review* 110, referring to Cheshire's objective interpretation to party autonomy.

[22] S Khanderia, 'Indian Private International Law *vis-à-vis* Party Autonomy in the Choice of Law' (2018) 18(1) *Oxford University Commonwealth Law Journal* 1, 1 [Khanderia, Party Autonomy].

[23] Anzilotti, "Il principio dell'autonomia dei contraenti nei rapporti fra l'art. 9 delle disposizioni preliminari al codice civile e l'art. 58 del codice di commercio", *Scritti di diritto internazionale privato*, Vol 3 (Padova 1960) 633 (translated version).

[24] See J Blom, 'Choice of Law Methods in the Private International Law of Contract' (1980) 18 *Canadian Yearbook of International Law* 161, 175 referring to H Batiffol, *Les conflits de lois en matière de contrats: Étude de droit international privé comparé* (Paris 1938).

[25] ibid.

[26] ibid.

[27] ibid.

and the language of the contract) in a manner that the agreement becomes 'most substantially associated' with the law of that legal system. Cheshire's objective interpretation of party autonomy was adopted by the Supreme Court in *Delhi Cloth and General Mills Co Ltd v Harnam Singh*.[28] As indicated, the Court was seised of a dispute arising from a contract for the sale of cloth between a Pakistani and an Indian merchant and the parties had chosen the law of Lyallpur to govern the agreement.[29] Although the parties had chosen the law of Lyallpur, which was connected to the contract by the plaintiff's residence there, the Court clarified that Indian private international law prohibits the parties from

> picking out whatever laws they like from any part of the globe and agreeing those laws shall govern their contract.[30]

The Court rejected the notion that the parties could choose any law as such freedom would produce 'strangely unrealistic results'.[31] Instead, the Court stressed that the selection should be restricted to the choice of 'the law of the country in which the contract is localised'.[32]

The Supreme Court in *British India Steam Navigation Co Ltd v Shanmughavilas Cashew Industries*[33] similarly adopted Cheshire's objective interpretation in ascertaining the limitations to party autonomy under the Indian private international law. The Court was seised of a dispute arising from a contract evidenced by a bill of lading between a company in India and England in which the proper law was expressly stipulated as the English legal system.[34] The Court emphasised that the parties did not have the right 'to choose a wholly unconnected law which was not otherwise the proper law of the contract'.[35] Accordingly, the Court stated that it could exercise its 'residual power to strike down for good reasons' such clauses if the choice of law was not connected to the contract.[36]

The decisions of the courts in *Delhi Cloth and General Mills*[37] and *British India Steam Navigation*[38] no longer represent the current position on the subject. The current position has been stipulated in the Supreme Court's dictum in *National Thermal Power*.[39] The Court per Thommen and Agarwal JJ referred to Dicey's subjective interpretation of party autonomy which permits the parties to choose any foreign law to govern their international contract, regardless of whether or not it has a nexus with the parties or their transaction.[40] The Court stated that:

> the expressed intention of the parties is generally decisive in determining the proper law of the contract.[41]

The Court further referred to the decision of the Privy Council in *Vita Food*.[42] It enunciated that the only limitation to the autonomy of the parties to select any foreign law to govern their

[28] *Delhi Cloth and General Mills Co Ltd* (n 20) [37].
[29] ibid.
[30] ibid [37].
[31] ibid [36].
[32] ibid, referring to Cheshire, *Private International Law*, 6th edn (OUP, 1961) 203.
[33] [1990] 3 SCC 481 [31].
[34] ibid.
[35] ibid.
[36] ibid.
[37] (n 22).
[38] (n 35).
[39] (n 17).
[40] ibid [14], referring to Dicey, Morris and Collins (n 12) Rule 180: Sub-Rule (1), which defines 'the proper law of the contract'.
[41] ibid.
[42] (n 5).

contract was that the choice should be bona fide, legal and not opposed to public policy.[43] If the parties have expressly chosen the proper law of the contract, then in the absence of 'an unmistakable indication to the contrary', such a law will also govern the arbitration agreement.[44] Subsequently, the Supreme Court in *Modi Entertainment Network and Another v WSG Cricket Pte Ltd*[45] confirmed the parties' right to select any law, including that of a neutral legal system. The parties there had concluded an international contract under which, the respondent granted a licence to the appellant (an Indian company) to telecast a cricket tournament organised by the International Cricket Conference (ICC) in Kenya on Indian television. The parties agreed that the English court would have jurisdiction over, and English law would govern, any dispute arising from the contract. Referring to the dictum in *National Thermal Power*,[46] the Court per Syed Shah Mohammed Quadri and Arijit Pasayat JJ accepted the parties' choice in favour of the neutral English law and emphasised that the selection would only be disregarded if it was not bona fide, legal or was in contravention of public policy.

The decisions of the Supreme Court in *National Thermal Power*[47] and *Modi Entertainment Network*[48] represents the current legal position in India by the constitutional mandate stipulated in Article 141.[49] Courts across the country have consistently accepted the dicta.[50]

In *Kumarina Investment Ltd v Digital Media Convergence Ltd & Anr*, the Telecom Dispute Settlement and Appellate Tribunal (TDSAT) in New Delhi referred to the provisions of the Rome I Regulation in obiter remarks and stated that the parties to an international contract could also select different laws to govern parts of the contract that are separable from one another.[51] In doing so, the court impliedly accepted the principle of *dépeçage* which permits the parties to an international contract to select different laws to govern parts of the contract that are separable from one another.

b. Choice of Soft Law or Non-state Law

The terms 'soft law' and 'non-state law' refer to 'non-binding legal instruments',[52] which have 'no legally binding force and can only be applied through voluntary acceptance'.[53] Such laws may be in the form of *inter alia* model laws, the *lex mercatoria* used by global merchants, restatements by scholars, or codifications of customs and usages promulgated by international

[43] (n 15) [14].
[44] ibid [24].
[45] [2003] 4 SCC 341.
[46] *National Thermal Power Corporation* (n 15) [14].
[47] ibid.
[48] (n 47).
[49] See Art 141 of the Constitution of India 1950 which states that '[t]he law declared by the Supreme Court shall be binding on all courts within the territory of India'.
[50] See for instance *Rhodia Ltd and Others v Neon Laboratories Ltd* AIR [2002] Bom 502; *White Industries Australia Ltd v Coal India Ltd* [2004] 2 Cal LJ 197; *Swatch Ltd. v Priya Exhibitors Pvt Ltd* (101) DRJ 99; *Shree Precoated Steels Ltd. v Macsteel International Far East Ltd. & Anr* [2008] 2 Bom CR 681; and *Max India Ltd. v General Binding Corporation* [2009] (112) DRJ 611 (DB).
[51] [2010] TDSAT 73 [27].
[52] See, HD Gabriel, 'The Advantages of Soft Law in International Commercial Law: The Role of UNIDROIT, UNCITRAL, and the Hague Conference' (2009) 34 *Brooklyn Journal of International Law* 658; and MJ Bonell, *An International Restatement of Contract Law: The UNIDROIT Principles of International Commercial Contracts* (Transnational Publishers, 2005) 200–208.
[53] MJ Bonell, 'Soft Law and Party Autonomy: The case of the UNIDROIT Principles' (2005) 51 *Loyola Law Review* 229, 229.

non-governmental organisations.[54] The UNIDROIT Principles on International Commercial Contracts (PICC),[55] the UNCITRAL Model Law on International Commercial Arbitration,[56] and the International Chamber of Commerce's (ICC) INCOTERMS[57] are examples.[58] Of their many benefits, soft or non-state laws have in recent times gained popularity, because they do away with the 'inherent difficulties' present in the harmonisation of positive or binding law, which may not be feasible given varying legal cultures among jurisdictions adopting civil and common law traditions.[59] Moreover, soft law, unlike the binding character of positive law, does not need to be ratified and can, therefore, be adopted and applied in a 'pick-and-choose' fashion.[60] Legislators and judges may selectively borrow provisions of soft law according to the needs and demands of their legal system as opposed to adopting an entire instrument.[61] Besides, the parties to an international contract may select a soft law instrument (in whole or part) to govern their agreement either because of the neutrality of such instrument or because its 'rules reflect their business relationship better than domestic or other international law'.[62]

Indian private international law permits the parties expressly to select a non-state law to govern their international arbitration agreements. Section 28 of the Arbitration and Conciliation Act 1996 (ACA) accordingly mandates a tribunal to 'decide the dispute in accordance with the rules of law designated by the parties'.[63] The legislation additionally empowers the tribunal to refer to and apply such rules when appropriate, provided that the parties have expressly authorised the application of those rules.[64] An obiter of the Delhi High Court, however, indicates that *lex mercatoria* is not considered as soft law in India.[65] This was the position in *National Highways Authority of India v Sheladia Associates, INC*, where the court was called upon to adjudicate a dispute arising from a contract to provide construction supervision services. The agreement contained an arbitration clause.[66] The court stated:

> [T]he expression '*lex mercatoria*' is not found in arbitration clauses, and some commentators have doubted whether it has any meaning. Those who do assign it a meaning differ as to whether it is a separate body of international commercial law or equivalent to freedom from strict legal constraint.[67]

The parties are, nonetheless free to select other 'general principles of law recognised by civilised nations'.[68]

The courts have in the past referred to the PICC while adjudicating domestic contracts to resolve ambiguities that were not addressed by the Indian Contract Act 1872[69] (ICA). This was

[54] Gabriel (n 52) 658, 659.

[55] UNIDROIT, 'UNIDROIT Principles on International Commercial Contracts, 2016' www.unidroit.org/english/principles/contracts/principles2016/principles2016-e.pdf [PICC].

[56] The text of the UNCITRAL Model Law on International Commercial Arbitration is available at: https://uncitral.un.org/sites/uncitral.un.org/files/media-documents/uncitral/en/19-09955_e_ebook.pdf.

[57] For detailed information on the ICC Incoterms, visit: iccwbo.org/resources-for-business/incoterms-rules/incoterms-2020/.

[58] See Gabriel (n 52) 659, 660; and AD Robilant, 'Genealogies of Soft Law' (Summer 2006) 54(3) *The American Journal of Comparative Law* 499, 500.

[59] Gabriel, ibid 660–663.

[60] ibid 664–665.

[61] ibid 664 et seq.

[62] ibid 669.

[63] Section 28(2) of the ACA.

[64] ibid, s 28(1)(b)(iii).

[65] *National Highways Authority of India v Sheladia Associates* INC [2009] 113 DRJ 835.

[66] ibid.

[67] ibid [30].

[68] ibid.

[69] The Indian Contract Act 1872 (Act 9 of 1872) [ICA]. See s 1(1) which states that the legislation applies to the whole of India – except the States of Jammu and Kashmir.

the position in *Sandvik Asia Pvt Ltd v Vardhman Promoters Pvt Ltd*[70] and *Hansalaya Properties v Dalmia Cement (Bharat) Ltd.*[71] At the same time, in the absence of a corresponding provision of a similar nature or of case-law dealing with the question, there is no clarity on whether the parties to an international contract may expressly select soft law in matters of litigation. A close look at the Supreme Court's dictum in *National Thermal Power*[72] indicates that Indian private international law does not permit parties to choose a non-state law if the dispute is being adjudicated before a court (and not through arbitration). In the present case, the Court re-defined the doctrine of the proper law as a 'legal system' which the parties may have expressly or impliedly selected and further elaborated that the expression refers to the 'substantive principles of domestic law'.[73] The remarks of the TDSAT in *Kumarina Investment*[74] in this context further substantiate this interpretation. The TDSAT was called upon to adjudicate the validity of the parties' choice of neutral law (that is, the English legal system) to govern their international agreement. The respondents, being a company incorporated in India, concluded a contract with the petitioners who were situated in Cyprus and operating in Israel. Under the contract, the respondents agreed to permit the petitioners to stream certain television channels on a website in Israel. A dispute arose when the former allegedly discontinued transmission of some channels. Upholding party autonomy in the choice of law, the TDSAT referred to European conflict-of-law principles as espoused in the Rome I Regulation, which permit the incorporation by reference of non-state laws (such as the PICC) as terms of a contract, in contrast to the selection of non-state laws as applicable law. The TDSAT held that the latter was not possible because non-state laws do not constitute any national legal system.[75]

c. Limitations to the Express Choice of Law

The choice must be '*bona fide, legal and not opposed to public policy*': As indicated above, the Supreme Court in *National Thermal Power* referred to the dictum in *Vita Food*[76] and stipulated that the only limitation to the autonomy of the parties to select any governing law for the disputes arising from their international contract was that the choice should be bona fide, legal and not opposed to public policy.[77] At the same time, the precise connotation of this expression remains unclear in English common law and under Indian private international law. Academic writings enunciate that the choice of law would not be considered to be bona fide if it is not made in good faith.[78] For this reason, the examination of a choice as bona fide

[70] (2007) 94 DRJ 762. Also see Khanderia, *Party Autonomy* (n 22) 14; and S Khanderia, 'Practice does not Make Perfect: Rethinking the Doctrine of 'The Proper Law of the Contract' – A Case for the Indian Courts' (2020) 16(3) *Journal of Private International Law* 423. [Khanderia, *Practice Does not Make Perfect*].

[71] [2008] 106 DRJ 820 (DB). Also see Khanderia, *Party Autonomy*, ibid 14; and Khanderia, *Practice does not Make Perfect*, ibid 433–434.

[72] (n 15).

[73] ibid [14], referring to Dicey, Morris and Collins (eds), *Dicey and Morris on the Conflict of Laws* (n 16) Rule 180: Sub-Rule (1), which defines 'the proper law of the contract'. FA Mann, The Proper Law in the Conflict of Laws (1987) 36 *International and Comparative Law Quarterly* 437, 437–438. [Mann, *The Proper Law in the Conflict of Laws*].

[74] (n 51) [27].

[75] ibid, referring to A Bonomi, 'Rome I Regulation on the Law Applicable to Contractual Obligations' (2010) 10 *Yearbook of Private International Law* 165, 169.

[76] (n 5).

[77] (n 15) [14].

[78] P Kincaid, 'Rationalising Contract Choice of Law Rules' (1993) 8(1) *Ottago Law Review* 93, 112.

is subjective.[79] Dicey,[80] Morris[81] and Kelly[82] articulate that the parties' choice of law will be regarded to have been made in bad faith if it contradicts the overriding mandatory norms of the legal system which has the closest connection with the contract. Such a legal system (with the closest connection) may be the forum state or any other country. The decision of the House of Lords in *The Hollandia*[83] further substantiates this interpretation. The court disregarded the parties' choice of Dutch law for not being bona fide and legal because it contradicted the overriding mandatory norms espoused in the Hague-Visby Rules.[84] The Hague-Visby Rules were applicable in the UK under the provisions of the English Carriage of Goods by Sea Act 1971.[85]

The circumstances in which the choice of law will contravene the overriding mandatory norms of a legal system are similarly nebulous. In this respect, Nygh (1999) demonstrates the close relationship and interlinkage between mandatory norms and public policy.[86] The author opines that a rule or law will assume a mandatory character when the state desires it to be applicable regardless of the choice of another legal system.[87] A provision will generally be mandatory if it endeavours to protect public interest and values and is, therefore, exceptional yet imperative by nature.[88] Mandatory rules are, consequently, a subspecies of public policy insofar as they perform certain special functions such as a marriage law which prohibits polygamy.[89] Public policy, on the other hand, seeks to protect the general, yet essential, social concepts of the forum.[90] The term 'public policy' refers to legislation of the forum state which is intended to have effect regardless of the choice of the parties.[91] Such a statute is therefor, intended to operate in the form of mandatory law of the forum.[92]

In Indian private international law, it seems that the criterion to identify if the choice of the law violates an overriding mandatory norm is the same as that to gauge the contravention of public policy. The decision of the Supreme Court in *Renusagar Power Co Ltd v General Electric Co*[93] illustrates this point. The Court clarified that in matters of international commercial arbitration,[94] the validity of the parties' choice of law must be tested against the public policy of India. The choice would be construed as being against the public policy of India if it is against 'some fundamental principle of justice ... prevalent concepts of good morals [or] deep-rooted traditions of the commonweal'.[95] Further, in *Ssangyong Engineering &*

[79] ibid, referring to JHC Morris, 'The Proper Law of a Contract: A Reply' (1950) 3 *International Law Quarterly* 197, 202–203 at ff 15 [Morris, *The Proper Law*].

[80] See *Dicey and Morris on the Conflict of Laws* (n 16) 756.

[81] JHC Morris, 'The Scope of the Carriage of Goods by Sea Act 1971' (1979) 95 *Law Quarterly Review* 59, 66 [Morris, *Scope of Carriage*]; and Morris, *The Proper Law* (n 79) 202–203.

[82] Kincaid (n 78) 112, referring to D St L Kelly, 'Reference, Choice, Restriction and Prohibition' (1977) 26 *International and Comparative Law Quarterly* 857, 870–871 at ff 20.

[83] [1982] 1 All ER 1076, 1080. Also see, *Dicey and Morris on the Conflict of Laws* (n 16) 756; and Morris, *Scope of Carriage* (n 81) 66, which state that a choice of law would be disregarded for not being '*bonafide*' if it contravened the overriding mandatory norms of the legal system with which the contract has its closest connection.

[84] ibid.

[85] ibid.

[86] PE Nygh, *Autonomy in International Contracts* (OUP, 1999) 199 et seq.

[87] ibid 199.

[88] ibid referring to Savigny, *Treatise on the Conflict of Laws,* 2nd edn (Gutherie translation 1880) 76.

[89] ibid 199–207.

[90] ibid 206–207.

[91] Nygh (n 86) 456.

[92] ibid.

[93] [1994] Supp (1) SCC 644.

[94] See s 2(f) of the Arbitration and Conciliation Act 1996 [ACA] Act No 26 of 1996, which defines the term 'international commercial arbitration'.

[95] ibid [51]–[57], referring to the dictum of Cardozo J in *Louchs v Standard Oil Co. of New York*, 224 N.Y. 99, 120 N.E. 198.

Construction Co. Ltd. v National Highways Authority of India (NHAI)[96] the Supreme Court clarified that the public policy of India would be violated in an international commercial arbitration agreement if the choice of the law violates: (1) the fundamental policy or the interests of the Republic; and (2) the most basic notions of justice and morality.[97]

In matters of litigation, there are isolated dicta which offer persuasive assistance to ascertain when the parties' express choice of law will be disregarded for being bona fide, legal, or against public policy. Existing case law does not stipulate broad guidelines for the courts to follow. Instead, judicial dicta merely indicate that the parties' choice will be construed as opposed to public policy if it is illegal and, therefore, null and void under the provisions of the ICA. For this reason, agreements in restraint to trade will be construed as opposed to public policy because they are illegal and, thus, null and void under Section 27 of the ICA.

For instance, the Bombay High Court in *Taprogge Gesellschaft MBH v IAEC India Ltd* refused to give effect to the parties' choice of German law on the ground that the agreement contained a clause which, if given effect to, would result in the violation of an imperative rule under the ICA.[98] The plaintiff was a company incorporated in Germany and engaged in the business of manufacturing cooling water filters. The defendants, an Indian company and agents of the plaintiffs, were made to sign a declaration with the latter under which they would sell or offer for sale some of the plaintiff's products. Striking down the choice of German law, the Court per Guttal J stressed that although the agreement and its performance were valid under that law, it operated as a restraint to trade and was thus unenforceable.[99] The Court further elaborated that sections 23 and 27 of the ICA espouse the public policy of India and are therefore imperative and will be given effect to, regardless of whether the parties have selected another legal system.[100] While section 23 declares as void all agreements which are against the public policy of India, section 27 prohibits agreements that restrain any person from exercising a lawful profession, trade or business. In a related vein, the TDSAT in *Kumarina Investment Ltd*, when called upon to examine the validity of the parties' choice in favour of the neutral English legal system elaborated that the contravention of the public policy of India could be ascertained against the criteria stipulated in the relevant provisions of the ICA and, in particular, sections 23, 27 and 28.[101] Such choice-of-law clauses will accordingly be considered as illegal when they operate in restraint of trade, restrict any party from enforcing its rights under the contract, or otherwise extinguish or discharge the liability of a party.[102]

d. Protection of Weaker Parties

Indian private international law does not stipulate any special rules to regulate the freedom of the parties in selecting a foreign law in international contracts which have been concluded between persons possessing unequal bargaining power. Typical illustrations of such agreements include consumer, insurance and employment contracts. Considered as vulnerable, consumers, employees and others with lesser bargaining power need to be protected from party autonomy for several

[96] [2019] SCC Online SC 677 [13], [28] and [37].
[97] ibid.
[98] AIR [1988] Bom 157.
[99] ibid [21]–[22].
[100] ibid.
[101] *Kumarina Investment Ltd* (n 51) [11], [14], [16], [17], while referring to the Supreme Court's dictum in the *National Thermal Power* (n 15).
[102] ibid.

reasons.[103] First, such parties are susceptible of being less informed as regards the content of the chosen law when compared to the stronger party in the agreement, such as a business person, employer or principal who routinely engages in concluding contracts and is thus more familiar with the contents of the law that are likely to be advantageous to it.[104] Second, weaker parties are also economically dependent on the other party and are therefore likely to succumb to a choice of law clause.[105] Third, such parties are also likely to be disadvantaged due to the lack of information and experience (in comparison to the stronger party) and, thus, capable of agreeing on the chosen law too quickly.[106] Judicial dicta indicate that a domestic contract with a weaker party will be presumed to be unfair, unreasonable and unconscionable and thus opposed to the public policy of India under section 23 of the ICA.[107] In such circumstances, the court will declare the contract as void for taking advantage of 'oppressed or depressed people'.

This was the position in *Central Inland Water Transport Corporation Ltd v Brojo Nath Ganguly*.[108] The Supreme Court refused to give effect to a contract which permitted the employer (a government-owned corporation) to dismiss the employee without cause by giving three months' notice or pay in lieu.[109] The Court stated that the contract was unconscionable and opposed to public policy.[110] Accordingly, such agreements would be construed as void, illegal and opposed to public policy.[111] They will not be given effect if they result in taking advantage of 'oppressed or depressed persons'.[112] In *Amrit Banaspati Co Ltd v State of Punjab*,[113] the Supreme Court provided indicia to assess the circumstances in which contracts with weaker parties would be conceived as a contraventions of public policy under section 23 of the ICA. The Court illustrated that an agreement with a weaker party would be presumed to contravene the public policy of India whenever the

> inequality of bargaining power is the result of the great disparity in the economic strength of the contracting parties. It will apply where the inequality is the result of circumstances, whether of the creation of the parties or not. It will apply to situations in which the weaker party is in the position in which he can obtain goods or services or means of livelihood only upon the terms imposed by the stronger party or go without them. It will also apply where a man has no choice, or rather no meaningful choice, but to give his assent to a contract or to sign on the dotted line in a prescribed or standard form or to accept a set of rules as part of the contract, however unfair, unreasonable and unconscionable a clause in the contract may be.[114]

A contract with a weaker party will, accordingly, be tested to gauge if:

(1) there is a significant disparity in the economic strength of the parties;[115]
(2) one party cannot trade in goods or services except on the terms of the other,[116] or

[103] G Rühl, 'The Protection of Weaker Parties in the Private International Law of the European Union: A Portrait of Inconsistency and Truancy' (2014) *Journal of Private International Law* 335, 339 et seq.
[104] ibid 342.
[105] ibid 343, 344.
[106] ibid 344, 345.
[107] See, *Central Inland Water Transport Corporation Ltd v Brojo Nath Ganguly* [1986] 2 SCR 278. See also, N Bhadbhade, *Pollock and Mulla on the Indian Contract and Specific Relief Acts* 14th edn (Lexis Nexis Publications, 2014) 562; and A Singh, 'Law of Contract and Specific Relief' 12th edn (Eastern Book Company, Lucknow) 285.
[108] *Central Inland Water Transport Corporation Ltd* (n 107).
[109] ibid.
[110] ibid.
[111] ibid.
[112] ibid.
[113] AIR [1992] SC 1075; and Bhadbhade (n 107) 563–564.
[114] *Amrit Banaspati* ibid 1611.
[115] ibid; and Bhadbhade (n 107) 563–564.
[116] ibid.

(3) one party has no meaningful choice except to accept the terms proposed by the other, however unreasonable.[117]

If the court finds any of the above aspects, it will declare the contract void under section 23 of the ICA. Having regards to the principles just discussed, it is likely that party autonomy in the choice of law will not be absolutely prohibited or limited in contracts which have been concluded with a weaker party under Indian private international law. Instead, a choice of law may be disregarded if the agreement contains terms which are unreasonable or unconscionable and results in the contravention of public policy.

ii. Implied Choice of Law

The implied choice of the parties operates as the second tier in identifying the proper law of the contract. The Supreme Court in *National Thermal Power* confirmed that the implied choice of the parties would play a prominent role when the parties have not expressly selected the proper law to govern their contract.[118] At the same time, there is no dictum in which the courts have identified the applicable law by referring to the implied choice of the parties. The existing judicial dicta are primarily in the form of obiter observations and merely suggest possible mechanisms that the judiciary will adopt in such circumstances. A close examination of existing dicta indicates that the courts do not adopt different criteria for the determination of the implied choice of the parties and the proper law of the contract when the parties have not made any choice at all. In this respect, the practice of the Indian courts resonates with the principles of English common law.

The judicial trend in England has been to impute an intention to the parties even when it is sufficiently clear that the parties did not think about the matter at the time of the conclusion of the contract. The decision of the House of Lords in *Amin Rasheed Shipping Co v Kuwait Insurance Co*[119] is pertinent. The standard term contract employed English terminology to govern an insurance policy issued by a company in Kuwait to a Liberian corporation in Dubai.[120] The contract contained no choice of law clause.[121] Accordingly, the court per Lord Diplock inferred or instead imputed English law as the law intended by the parties to govern their contract.[122] Lord Simonds in an obiter, however, stressed that the search for imputed intentions must be prioritised over the 'closest and most real connection' test.[123] The latter must therefore be employed only when the former 'fails that enquiry'.[124]

A plethora of judicial dicta in India illustrates that the courts in India will similarly impute an intention on the parties to ascertain whether they have made a tacit choice of law. For instance, in *State Aided Bank of Travancore v Dhrit Ram*, the Privy Council stated that, in the absence of an express choice of law, the judiciary would identify the applicable law by referring to what 'just and reasonable persons' would have done 'if they had thought about the question when they had made the contract'.[125] In doing so, the court would look at the place of the conclusion

[117] ibid.
[118] (n 15) [13].
[119] [1984] AC 50.
[120] ibid.
[121] ibid.
[122] [1984] AC 50.
[123] ibid 9.
[124] JE Jaffey, 'The English Proper Law Doctrine and the EEC Convention' (1984) 33 *International and Comparative Law Quarterly* 531, 533, referring to *Amin Rasheed Shipping Corp.* (n 119).
[125] AIR [1943] PC 6 [2].

of the contract, its performance and the nature of the business or transaction as relevant factors.[126] Further, in *Delhi Cloth and General Mills Co. Ltd. v Harnam Singh and Others*, the Supreme Court stated that the proper law of the contract, in the absence of an express choice would be identified by imputing an intention on the parties.[127] The intention would be imputed by applying the objective test to determine the country with which the contract has the closest connection.[128] In a related vein, the Calcutta High Court in *Rabindra N Maitra v Life Insurance Corporation of India* indicated that the proper law of the contract would be identified by applying the theory of localisation in the absence of an express choice of law.[129] In other words, the Court made no reference to the implied choice of the parties. Instead, it referred to Cheshire's theory of localisation.[130] It stated that in the absence of choice, the proper law of the contract would be identified by looking for the centre of gravity of the agreement.[131] The court would, accordingly, apply the law of the legal system with which 'the contract appears most properly to belong'.[132] The decision of the Supreme Court in *National Thermal Power*[133] resonates with the earlier decisions in *Delhi Cloth and General Mills*[134] and *Rabindra N Maitra*[135] which demonstrates the lack of different criterion to identify the proper law through the parties' implied choice and when the parties have not made any choice. The court per Thommen and Agarwal JJ stated that in the absence of an express choice, the implied choice would be identified by imputing an intention on the parties

> by applying an objective test to determine what the parties would have, as just and reasonable persons intended as regards the applicable law had they applied their minds to the question.[136]

The intention of the parties concerning the applicable law would be identified by looking at:

> the place where the contract was made, the form and the object of the contract, the place of performance, the place of residence or the business of the parties, reference to the courts having jurisdiction and some other links are examined by the courts to determine the system of law with which, the transaction has the closest and most real connection.[137]

iii. Absence of Choice of Law and the 'Closest and Most Real Connection Test'

The decision of the Privy Council in *Vita Food* merely indicated that in the absence of choice, the proper law of the contract would be identified by looking at 'the terms of the contract and the surrounding circumstances'.[138] However, it did not clarify the mechanism for the same. A subsequent decision of the Privy Council's decision in *Bonython v Commonwealth*

[126] ibid.
[127] (n 20) [43] referring to the decision of the English court in *Mount Albert Borough Council v Australasian Temperance, etc. Society* [1937] 4 All ER 214, 240.
[128] ibid.
[129] (n 20) [22].
[130] See text accompanying notes 20–28.
[131] ibid.
[132] *Rabindra Maitra* (n 20) [22].
[133] (n 15).
[134] (n 20).
[135] ibid.
[136] *National Thermal Power* (n 15) [16]–[17] referring to *Mount Albert Borough Council* (n 127).
[137] ibid.
[138] (n 5) 290.

of Australia[139] clarified that, in the absence of choice, the proper law would be identified by applying the closest and most real connection test.[140] The decision of the Privy Council thus forms the genesis of the development of the 'closest and most real connection' test under the English common law. The closest and most real connection test was propagated by Westlake and Cheshire.[141] The principle involves the application of Batiffol's theory of localisation as endorsed by French law,[142] which has been discussed in brief in the section discussing the historical development of party autonomy in Indian private international law. According to this principle, the court must locate the centre of gravity of a contract to determine its proper law when the parties have not expressly selected the same.[143] As indicated above, the Supreme Court in *National Thermal Power Corporation*[144] stipulated the application of the test in the absence of the parties' express or implied choice. In such circumstances, the court will identify the proper law of the contract by finding 'the system of law with which, the contract has the closest and most real connection'.[145] Therefore, the 'system of law' as opposed to a place which bears a close and most real connection to the contract would be relevant. In this respect, Lord Diplock in *Amin Rasheed Shipping Co v Kuwait Insurance Co* clarified that the 'system of law' in a contract where the documents use English terminology would be England irrespective of whether the transaction was more closely connected with Kuwait as a place.[146] The criterion which the courts have employed to interpret the closest and most real connection test has varied over time and may be divided into two categories. These are: (1) the theory of localisation; and (2) the test of the parties' imputed intentions.

a. Theory of Localisation

Historically, the theory of localisation played a crucial role while assisting the courts to ascertain the proper law of the contract, even when the parties had expressly chosen the same. Its application was initially endorsed by the Supreme Court in *Delhi Cloth and General Mills* which stated that the mechanism to identify the proper law of a contract would be by localising the contract after searching for its centre of gravity.[147] Subsequently, the Calcutta High Court in *Rabindra N Maitra*[148] stipulated a list of factors that would be relevant in finding the centre of gravity of the contract. These are:

> the domicile and even the residence of the parties; the national character of a corporation and the place where its principal place of business is situated; the place where the contract is made and the place where the contract is to be performed; the fact that [a] certain stipulation is valid under one law but void under another; the nature of the subject-matter or its situs … and in short, any other fact which serves to localise the contract.[149]

[139] [1951] AC 201.
[140] ibid 219.
[141] See GC Cheshire, *Private International Law* (Clarendon Press 1957) 249 et seq; and N Bentwich, *Westlake's Private International Law* 7th edn (Sweet & Maxwell 1925) 299 et seq.
[142] J Blom, 'Choice of Law Methods in the Private International Law of Contract' (1980) 18 *Canadian Yearbook of International Law* 161, 175.
[143] JE Jaffey (n 124) 531, 533, 534.
[144] *National Thermal Power Corporation* (n 15) [14].
[145] ibid.
[146] [1983] 2 All ER 884.
[147] *Delhi Cloth and General Mills Co Ltd* (n 20) [37].
[148] (n 20) [29].
[149] ibid.

Similarly, in *National Thermal Power*, the court considered:

> the place where the contact was made, the form and object of the contract, the place of performance, the place of business or performance of the parties, the reference to the courts having jurisdiction and such other links[150]

to be relevant while identifying the system of law with which the contract has the closest and most real connection.

b. Test of the Parties' Imputed Intentions

The test of the imputed intention of the parties has been a disguised method to identify the parties' implied choice of the applicable law. Judicial dicta and in particular the decision of the Supreme Court in *National Thermal Power* demonstrate that Indian private international law does not differentiate between the mechanism to identify the parties' implied choice and their imputed intention in the absence of a choice of the governing law.[151] The criteria which the courts have employed to discern the imputed intentions of the parties, while identifying the system of law with which the contract has its closest and most real connection, have been convoluted and far from uniform. In some decisions, the courts have demonstrated a preference for identifying the proper law by contemplating what 'just and reasonable persons' would have done 'had they thought about the matter'.[152] In other cases, the courts have invoked certain presumptions to gauge the imputed intentions of the parties.

iv. The 'Just and Reasonable Person' Test

In *Brijraj Marwari & Ors v Anant Prasad*, which was the first such opinion on the subject in the pre-Independence era, Edgley J mentioned that imputed intentions should be determined by contemplating what 'just and reasonable persons' would have done 'had they thought about the matter'.[153] In *National Thermal Power*, the Supreme Court similarly stated that it would impute an intention on the parties by looking at what 'just and reasonable persons intended as regards the applicable law had they applied their minds to the question'.[154] Accordingly, the Court indicated that the imputed intentions would be identified by looking at factors such as the *locus contractus*, the *locus solutionis*, the parties' place of residence, the form and object of the agreement, and the jurisdiction of the court.[155]

v. Presumptions

Presumptions, which are 'prima facie inferences'[156] that are 'rebuttable by the surrounding circumstances of the case',[157] are another mechanism which the courts have employed to discern

[150] (n 15) [16], [18] referring to the decision of the English court in *Mount Albert Borough Council* (n 127) 107.
[151] ibid [16]–[17] and text accompanying notes 118–137.
[152] See section II.A.ii of this chapter.
[153] AIR [1942] Cal 509 [2].
[154] (n 15) [16].
[155] ibid [17].
[156] M Schmitthoff, 'Doctrine of the Proper Law of the Contract in the English Conflict of Laws' (1940) 28 *The Georgetown Law Journal* 447, 453.
[157] ibid.

the imputed intentions of the parties. Their relevance was recognised by the Supreme Court in *Dhanrajamal Gobindram v Shamji Kalidas & Co*[158] and occasionally by some other lower courts in India.[159] In *Dhanrajamal Gobindram*, the Court stipulated the following presumptions as relevant to in ascertaining the proper law of the contract in the absence of an express choice:

(1) *lex loci contractus*: Under this presumption, the courts may assume that the parties intended to be governed by the law of the place at which the agreement was concluded, even if the meeting was transitory or fleeting and has no other connection with the contract.[160]
(2) *lex loci solutionis:* Under this presumption, the law of the place of the performance of the contract would be relevant in identifying the applicable law in the absence of choice.[161]
(3) *lex fori*: Under this presumption, the parties are treated as having intended that the law of the place of arbitration or litigation is to govern disputes arising from their contract.

The Court clarified that the *lex loci contractus* would be applicable only when it coincides with the *lex loci solutionis*. It was, therefore, 'an accepted rule' that in all other circumstances, the *locus solutionis* or the place of the performance would gain priority over the *locus contractus*.[162] At the same time, there was no clarity on how the place of performance would be identified under the Indian private international law. Would it be the place from where the goods or services are sold or rendered or the place where they are delivered? How would the *locus solutionis* be ascertained if there is more than one place of performance?

In the absence of any judicial dictum, the use of the *locus solutionis* remains a contentious issue under the Indian conflict of law rules on applicable law. There have been isolated cases where the courts have in an *obiter dicta* commented on the mechanism to identify the *locus solutionis*.[163] Nonetheless, these decisions were directly pertinent to the ascertainment of the proper law. In *Shanmugham Chettiar v Annamalai Chettiar*, the Madras High Court expressed that the *locus solutionis* should be identified within the parameters of sections 47 to 49 of the ICA which stipulate the principles concerning the place and the time of performance of a contract.[164] The Court stated that, as a general rule, the place of the performance of the contract would be the 'place where the promise ought to be performed'.[165] If the promisee fails to stipulate a 'proper place', then the promisor may ask for a reasonable place.[166] The place of the performance would therefore depend on the type of the contract and the persons who may be regarded as a promisor and promisee in each case.[167] For instance, in a dispute for the sale of goods or services, the promisor may be the buyer if the dispute arises in connection to the non-payment for the goods or the service. Conversely, in a dispute for non-delivery, the promisor would be the seller or the service provider.[168] The court in *Shanmugham Chettiar* further indicated that it may at its discretion permit the promisee to avail of the principles of common law which require that 'the debtor

[158] AIR [1961] SC 1285.
[159] *M/S Lachman Das Sat Lal* AIR [1958] Punjab 258; *CV Kunhiman v PMK Idrosekutty* AIR [1958] Ker 126 [9]; and *Compagnie de Saint Gobain v Fertiliser Corporation of India Ltd*, ILR (1970) II Delhi.
[160] *Dhanrajamal Gobindram* (n 158) [28].
[161] ibid.
[162] ibid [29]. Also see, *Compagnie de Saint Gobain* (n 159).
[163] See, *Shanmugham Chettiar v Annamalai Chettiar* AIR [1974] Mad 305 and *LN Gupta & Anr v Smt Tara Maini* ILR (1984) I Del.
[164] *Shanmugham Chettiar*, ibid [6].
[165] ibid.
[166] ibid.
[167] See Khanderia, *Practice does not Make Perfect* (n 70) 444–445.
[168] ibid.

should seek the creditor'.[169] The acceptance of the common law principle that 'the debtor should seek the creditor' has, nonetheless, been far from uniform.

For instance, in *Firm Hira Lal Girdhari Lal & Anr v Baij Nath Hardial Khatri*, the Punjab High Court stated that the common law rule was inapplicable in India.[170] The courts would examine the contract as a whole, including the course of dealings between the parties and the creditor's ordinary place of business or residence, to identify where the money was paid.[171] Conversely, in *SP Consolidated Engineering Co (P) Ltd v Union of India & Anr*,[172] *State of Punjab v AK Raha (Engineers) Ltd*,[173] and *LN Gupta & Anr v Smt Tara Maini*[174] the High Courts of Calcutta and Madras indicated acceptance of the common law principle in the interests of justice, equity and good conscience.

Subsequently, the Supreme Court in *Renusagar Power Co Ltd v General Electric Co* stated that the *lex loci solutionis* refers to 'the law of the place where the debt or liability is payable'.[175] The Court in the present case was called upon to clarify the date for the conversion of the money payable for the performance of the parties' international commercial contract. It, thus, appears that the *lex loci solutionis* will be the place of payment by the constitutional mandate under Article 141 which states that 'the law declared by the Supreme Court shall be binding on all courts within the territory of India'.

In respect of the *lex fori*, the court in *Dhanrajamal Gobindram* stipulated that 'if the courts of a particular country were chosen, it is expected, unless there be an expressed intention or evidence, that they would apply their own law to the case'.[176] This position was confirmed by the Supreme Court in *British India Steam Navigation Co Ltd.*[177] However, in *National Thermal Power*, the Supreme Court stressed the extreme caution with which, arbitration clauses should be relied on to ascertain the proper law.[178] The Court per Thommen and Agarwal JJ stated that 'the mere selection ... will not, in the absence of any other relevant connecting factor with that place, be sufficient to draw an inference'.[179] The Court remarked that having regard to 'the rest of the contract and the surrounding circumstances', other factors should additionally play a crucial role while imputing intention in favour of the application of the law of the place of the arbitration.[180]

At present, the exact relevance of the presumption in favour of the *lex fori* in the conflict of law rules of India on the applicable law remains ambiguous.[181] The Supreme Court has in

[169] (n 163) [7].
[170] AIR [1960] Punjab 450 [9].
[171] ibid.
[172] AIR [1966] Cal 259 [14].
[173] AIR [1964] Cal 418 [13].
[174] ILR [1984] I Del [7].
[175] *Renusagar Power Co Ltd* (n 93) [107], defining the term 'money of payment'.
[176] ibid [29].
[177] *British India Steam Navigation Co Ltd* (n 20). See also, *Fertiliser Corporation of India v Chemical Construction Corporation* [1973] 75 Bom LR 335 [21].
[178] *National Thermal Power Corporation* (n 15).
[179] ibid.
[180] *National Thermal Power* (n 15) [15], [45].
[181] See in this respect, JL Neels, 'Choice of Forum and Tacit Choice of Law: The Supreme Court of India and the Hague Principles on Choice of Law in International Commercial Contracts (an appeal for an inclusive comparative approach to private international law)' in UNIDROIT (ed) *Eppur si muove: The Age of Uniform Law. Essays in Honour of Michael Joachim Bonell to celebrate his 70th birthday* (2016) 358, 365 et seq. [Neels, Choice of Forum and Tacit Choice of Law]; JL Neels, 'The Role of the Hague Principles on Choice of Law in International Commercial Contracts in Indian and South African Private International Law' (2017) 22 *Uniform Law Review / Revue de droit uniforme* 443, 446; and JL Neels 'Indian perspectives on the Hague Principles' in D Girsberger, T Kadner Graziano and JL Neels (gen eds), *Choice of Law in International Commercial Contracts. Global Perspectives on the Hague Principles* (OUP, 2021) 481–483 [24.11]–[24.13].

Modi Entertainment Network and another,[182] *Shreejee Traco (I) Pvt Ltd v Paperline International Ltd*[183] and *Union of India v Hardy Exploration and Production (India) INC*[184] stated that the parties' choice of an arbitration venue or seat would create a strong prima facie presumption of the parties' intentions vis-à-vis the applicable law. In doing so, the Court did not refer to the selection of the place of arbitration or forum as merely one of the indicators in discerning the parties' choice of applicable law. As a result, it appears that the parties' choice of forum may exclusively be construed as a presumption of their choice of governing law.

vi. Identification of the Proper Law of the Contract in E-commerce Transactions

The term e-commerce refers to transactions that take place over the internet. Such transactions often contain contradictory standard terms which are obligations contained at the back of the contract. The standard terms of a contract are rarely read until litigation arises and are more susceptible to contradictions if the agreement is concluded between large entities. The predicament which occurs as a result of contradictory standard terms is known as the 'battle of forms'.[185] In international contracts which have been concluded over the internet, the parties' standard terms will often contain their choice of the applicable law, which are likely to be contradictory. For instance, A (a seller which is a company incorporated in Greece) may designate Greek law in its standard terms while concluding a contract to sell certain products to B (a buyer who resides in Delhi). However, B may have designated Indian law to govern the contract when accepting A's offer to sell the product. Suppose that A wants to sue B for the failure to pay for the goods. A initiates proceedings against B before the courts in Delhi which is the place of B's residence. What law will the Indian courts apply to decide the rights and the liabilities of the parties? Will it be Greek or Indian law? The answer will depend on whether the parties agreed on the applicable law. Whether they decided on the applicable law will in turn depend on whether the contract is valid, considering that it contains contradictory terms. Indian private international law does not clarify the mechanism to resolve the predicament in contradictory choice of law clauses. To date, the courts have not been presented with an opportunity to address the matter. In such circumstances, the courts are likely to refer to domestic principles as enunciated in the ICA to resolve such ambiguities. The general principles of Indian law of contract prescribe the last-shot method, which is stipulated in section 7 of the ICA.[186] According to this principle, the terms of the offer and acceptance must be *identical*.[187] Accordingly, the contract would not be concluded if the offer and acceptance do not constitute a mirror-image of each other.[188] Thus, if a person presents new terms to the offeror, instead of accepting the offer, this will

[182] (n 45) [16].
[183] [2003] 9 SCC 79 [7].
[184] Civil Appeal No 4628 of 2018 [2].
[185] TK Graziano, 'Solving the Riddle of Conflicting Choice of Law Clauses in Battle of Forms Situations: The Hague Solution' (2013) 14 *Yearbook of Private International Law* 71, 73.
[186] See the decisions of the Supreme Court in *Satyabrata Ghose v Mugneeram Bangur & Co*, [1954] SCR 310. Also see *Superintendence Company of India (P) Ltd v Krisha Murgai*, AIR [1980] SC 1717, 1721–22. For a detailed discussion on the battle of forms in India see, S Khanderia, 'International Approaches as Plausible Solutions to Resolve the Battle of Forms under the Indian Law of Contract' (2019) 1 8 *Global Journal of Comparative law* 13–17 [Khanderia, International Approaches as Plausible Solutions].
[187] See, *Haji Mohd Haji Jiva v E Spinner, ILR* (1900) 24 Bom 510 per Sir Jenkins CJ. Also see, Singh (n 107) 37.
[188] See ss 2(b), 2(h), 7 and 9 of the ICA.

constitute a counter-offer under the provisions of the ICA.[189] The contract is considered to have been concluded on the terms of the counter-offer if the person to whom it is made absolutely and unconditionally accepts the same.[190] According to the last-shot method, the court will apply Indian law to adjudicate the dispute.

III. Scope of the Proper Law of the Contract

This section will examine the scope of the proper law in adjudicating disputes arising from particular aspects of a contract such as its formal, material or essential validity; its performance; and the capacity to contract.

i. Formation, Interpretation, and Essential and Material Validity of the Contract

Historically, the *lex loci contractus* was applicable in adjudicating disputes arising from international commercial contracts on questions of capacity and on formal and material validity. With the advent of international trade and globalisation, the application of the law of the place of contracting may no longer be justifiable and may often be fortuitous. Today, the putative proper law is the relevant yardstick to adjudge most aspects of an international contract. It is the law that would have been applicable if the contract had come into existence. In this context, the Supreme Court in *National Thermal Power* stipulated that the proper law of the contract governs the entire gamut of the agreement such as its validity, legality, effect, and the interpretation of ant arbitration agreement.[191] The proper law of the contract will decide all questions concerning the arbitration clause.[192] Similarly, the Supreme Court in *Union of India v Hardy Exploration and Production (India) Inc.* clarified that the proper law of the contract is 'the law governing the contract which creates the substantive rights of the parties, in respect of which the dispute has arisen'.[193] Thus, all questions or disputes on whether the contractual obligations are legally binding or whether they conform to the formal requirements (for instance, if the contract has to be in writing, must be evidenced by a certain minimum number of witnesses, and if it was actually formed or concluded) will be determined by the putative proper law.

ii. Performance of the Contract

The Bombay High Court in *Taprogge Gesellschaft MBH* refused to give effect to the parties' choice of German law insofar as it operated in restraint to trade and infringed the provisions of the ICA.[194] Consequently, although the putative proper law governs most aspects including the essential validity of a contract, the agreement will be *void ab initio* under the principles of Indian private international law if its performance is illegal under the law of the Republic.

[189] ibid, s 9. See also, the Supreme Court's decision in *UP Rajkiya Nirman Nigam Ltd v Indure Pvt Ltd & Ors* [1996] 2 SCC 667.
[190] See *Col. DI Macpherson v MN Appanna & Anr* AIR [1951] SC 184 per Saiyid Fazl Ali J.
[191] (n 15) [6].
[192] ibid [23].
[193] *Hardy Exploration* (n 184) [7].
[194] See in this respect, the decisions in *Taprogge Gesellschaft MBH* (n 98). See also, *Kumarina Investment Ltd* (n 51).

In other words, performance of the contract will be tested under the putative proper law and the *lex fori* (in this case, Indian law). The proper law of the contract would, nonetheless, determine whether an arbitration clause binds the parties when one of them alleges that the contract is void, voidable, illegal or cannot be performed due to frustration.[195]

iii. Capacity to Contract

Under Indian law, minors (namely, persons below 18 years of age) and persons of unsound mind lack the capacity to enter into a contract. All agreements which are concluded with minors or persons of unsound mind are null and void under sections 10, 11 and 12 of the ICA. A minor is, nonetheless, construed as being capable, if the agreement was for the benefit of the minor.[196] Accordingly, loan agreements under which the minor is a beneficiary are valid.[197] Conversely, agreements which obligate a minor to perform a service instead of a sum of money are not construed as being for the benefit of the money and are thus invalid.[198] In a related vein, a person with an unsound mind is considered as capable 'if, at the time when he makes [a contract], he is capable of understanding it and of forming a rational judgment as to its effect upon his interests'.[199]

Indian private international law does not, however, have an exact position as regards the law that will govern the contractual capacity of a person. The High Court of Madras, while determining contractual capacity in an older judgment, favoured the application of the *lex loci contractus*. This was the position in *TNS Chockalingam Chettiar v VPS Mohammad Hussain and ors* where the Court was called upon to decide contractual capacity in a mercantile contract where one of the defendants had acted as surety for another defendant by endorsing certain bills of exchange.[200] Referring to Dicey's Rule 158, the Court per Ramesan J articulated that a mercantile contract would be null and void if any party lacks capacity under the *lex loci contractus*.[201] Subsequently, the Supreme Court in an *obiter dictum* in *Technip SA v SMS Holding (Pvt) Ltd & Ors* opined that the *lex loci domicilii* (the law of the domicile of the person) should be applicable subject to the public policy of India.[202] The Court was called upon to determine whether a company incorporated in France had acquired a company in India.[203] Nonetheless, the opinion does not have binding value being obiter. The stance of Indian private international law as regards the contractual capacity of a minor is therefore ambiguous. There is no judicial dictum to clarify the law that will govern disputes concerning the capacity of a company or other legal persons. In such circumstances, it appears that the English common law rule will be applied, that is, resort will be made to the law of the place of incorporation of the company.[204]

[195] *National Thermal Power Corporation* (n 15) [23].

[196] See ss 10 and 11 of the ICA. See also, *Mohri Bibi v Dhuromdas Ghose* [1903] 30 IA 114; *Raj Rani v Prem Adib* AIR [1949] Bom 215; and *Mathai v Joseph Mary* [2015] 5 SCC 622.

[197] See, *A.T. Raghava Chariar v O.A Srinivasa* [1916] 31 MLJ 575; and *Fernandez v Gonsalves* AIR [1925] Bom 97.

[198] See *Raj Rani* (n 196).

[199] Section 12 of the ICA.

[200] See EA Fredericks, Contractual Capacity and the Conflict of Laws in Common Law Jurisdictions (Part 2): Australasia, North America, Asia and Africa (2020) 41(1) *Obiter* 10, 30–31 referring to *TNS Chockalingam* AIR [1933] Mad 756.

[201] *TNS Chockalingam*, ibid, referring to Berriedale Keith (ed) *Dicey, on The Conflicts of Laws* 4th edn (Stevens, 1927) 599.

[202] Fredericks (n 200) 31–32 referring to *Technip SA*, [2005] 60 SCL 249 SC.

[203] ibid.

[204] See, P Rogerson, *Collier's Conflict of Laws* 4th edn (CUP, 2016) 320 at ff 150, referring to *Haugesund Kommune v Depfa ACS Bank* [2010] EWCA Civ 579, [2011] 1 All ER 190.

IV. Reflections on Indian Law: Some Insights based on Global Trends

Globally, the applicable law is identified by referring to the parties' express or implied (tacit) choice and, in its absence, by determining the legal system with which the contract has the closest connection. It is a generally accepted rule that the governing law regulates all disputes arising in relation to consent, material validity, interpretation, performance and legality.[205] Indian private international law essentially adopts a similar position to English common law. However, excessive reliance on English common law principles together with the absence of codified rules has contributed to uncertainty concerning the method that will be adopted in identifying the proper law of the contract in India. In comparison, several jurisdictions have codified the rules on the subject to enhance predictability and certainty in judicial decisions.

The conflict of law rules of the EU serves as a prominent example. The provisions of the Rome I Regulation, which replaced the Rome Convention, stipulate clearly-defined rules to assist courts to ascertain the applicable law for contractual obligations. Prior to Brexit, which came into effect on 31 January 2020, the provisions of the Rome I Regulation[206] were applicable in the UK, to determine the applicable law for contractual obligations. The UK has since enacted the Law Applicable to Contractual Obligations and Non-Contractual Obligations (Amendment etc) (EU Exit) Regulations 2019 to carry forward the provisions of Rome I and II. The conflict of law rules of the EU have influenced the codifications of several civil law jurisdictions such as Japan,[207] South Korea,[208] Turkey[209] and India's BRICS[210] partners, (that is, Russia[211] and China).[212] More recently, the Asian Principles of Private International Law (APPIL), a set of non-binding principles drawn by academics from ten East and Southeast Asian countries also reflect the experiences in the EU in this context.[213] Among these are some common law jurisdictions such as Hong Kong and Singapore where the principles of private international law have traditionally been stipulated by case law and the doctrine of *stare decisis*.[214] The APPIL, albeit recommendatory by nature, attempt to harmonise the conflict of law rules inter alia on applicable law in civil and commercial matters.[215] The APPIL endeavour to complement and supplement the private international laws in these legal systems for the benefit of the legislators and the judiciary.[216] This section draws on

[205] See for instance, Art 12 of the Rome I Regulation; Art 6 and 17 of the Act of Private International Law 2016, South Korea [South Korean PIL]; Art 1215 of the Civil Code of the Russian Federation 2015 [Civil Code of Russia]; Art 32 of the Turkish Code on Private International Law and International Civil Procedure 2007 [Turkish PIL]; and Art 9 of the Hague Principles.

[206] See Regulation (EC) No 593/2008 of the European Parliament and the Council on the Law Applicable to Contractual Obligations (Rome I Regulation). The Rome I Regulation superseded the Convention on the Law Applicable to Contractual Obligations, 19 June 1980, 80/934/EEC [Rome Convention]. The Rome I Regulation is applicable to all the Members of the EU (except Denmark).

[207] See Japanese Act on the General Rules on the Application of Laws 2007 [Japanese PIL].

[208] See the South Korean PIL.

[209] See the Turkish PIL.

[210] BRICS is an acronym for Brazil, Russia, India, China and South Africa.

[211] See Civil Code of Russia.

[212] See the Law of the People's Republic of China on the Laws Applicable to Foreign-Related Civil Relations 2010 [Chinese PIL] read along with the Rules of the Supreme People's Court on Related Issues Concerning the Application of Law in Hearing Foreign-Related Contractual Dispute Cases Related to Civil and Commercial Matters [the 2007 Interpretation].

[213] See generally, WZ Chen and G Goldstein, 'The Asian Principles of Private International Law: Objectives, Contents, Structure and Selected Topics on Choice of Law' (2017) 13(2) *Journal of Private International Law*, 411–434.

[214] ibid 412–414.

[215] ibid.

[216] ibid.

the experiences of some major jurisdictions while reflecting on the Indian conflict of law rules on choice of law. In particular, it urges codification of the principles of Indian private international law. Pending codification, it is suggested that the Supreme Court by the power conferred through Article 141 of the Constitution of India draft guidelines that would assist adjudicators and interested parties in future concerning identification of the proper law of a contract.

i. Express Choice of Law

In general, the doctrine of party autonomy in choice of law has been adopted in the private international laws of several countries,[217] including common law jurisdictions such as Australia,[218] Canada[219] and Hong Kong.[220] Likewise, Part 6 of the National Civil Code Act 2017 which codifies the principles of private international law of Nepal, acknowledges the acceptance of party autonomy in choice of law in cross-border disputes in matters of contract.[221] These legal systems all permit the choice of any foreign law, regardless of whether or not the chosen law has a connection with the parties or their transaction. Likewise, the principle has also been widely accepted among civil law countries, especially in the EU.[222] The Rome I Regulation applicable in the EU permits the parties to select any law to govern their contract.[223] However, party autonomy in the choice of law does not extend to the selection of soft law. Instead, the provisions of non-state law such as the PICC may only be incorporated by reference as terms of the parties' contract.[224] The parties may select different laws for those parts of their agreement which are separable.[225] The applicable law will govern all aspects concerning interpretation, performance, breach of obligations, consequences of nullity, prescription, and the limitation period.[226] Several other civil law jurisdictions such as Japan,[227] South Korea,[228] Mexico,[229] Venezuela[230] and India's BRICS partners (Russia[231] and China),[232] have similarly embraced the doctrine of party autonomy in the choice of law. The principle has also found favour in South Africa,[233] which has a hybrid legal system but whose conflict of law rules have been shaped by the principles of the common law.[234] The private international law of Brazil is,

[217] See in this respect, Khanderia, *Party Autonomy* (n 22) 3–6.
[218] See Nygh (n 86) 445–451.
[219] See S Pitel and N Rafferty, *Conflict of Laws* 1st edn (Irwin Law Publishers 2010) 271–274.
[220] See G Johnston, *The Conflict of Laws in Hong Kong* 2nd edn (Sweet and Maxwell, 2012) 189; and LC Wolff, 'Hong Kong's Conflict of Contract Laws: Quo Vadis?' (2010) 6(2) *Journal of Private International Law* 465, 471–472.
[221] Art 709(1) of the National Civil Code Act 2017 (Nepalese PIL).
[222] See Art 3(1) read along with Recital 11 to the Rome I Regulation.
[223] ibid.
[224] See Recital 13 to the Rome I Regulation.
[225] See Art 3(1) read along with Recital 11 to the Rome I Regulation.
[226] Art 12 of the Rome I Regulation.
[227] Art 7 of the Japanese PIL.
[228] Art 25 of the South Korean PIL.
[229] Art 7 of the Inter-American Convention on the Law Applicable to International Contracts [Mexico City Convention].
[230] ibid.
[231] Art 1210 of the Civil Code of Russia.
[232] Art 3 of the Chinese PIL; and PE McEleavy, 'Current Developments: Private International Law' (2011) 60 *International and Comparative Law Quarterly* 1065, 1085.
[233] See *Guggenheim v Rosenbaum*, [1961] (2), (4) SA 21 (W) [31A]; *Creutzburg v Commercial Bank of Namibia Ltd* [2006] 4 All SA 327, 330; and *Representative of Lloyds v Classic Sailing Adventures (Pty) Ltd* [2010] (5) SA 90 (SCA). Also see, C Forsyth, *Private International Law – The Modern Roman-Dutch Law Including the Jurisdiction of the High Courts* 5th edn (Juta Publications, 2012) 317–327; R Oppong, *Private International Law in Commonwealth Africa* 1st edn (CUP, 2013), 133, 135; Van Niekerk and C Schulze, *The South African Law of International Trade: Selected Topics* (Saga Legal Publications, 2016) 60–62; EA Fredericks and JL Neels, 'The Proper Law of a Documentary Letter of Credit: Part 1' (2003) *South African Mercantile Law Journal* 63, 63.
[234] See, Forsyth, ibid 316.

however, reported to limit the choice of a neutral legal system to international disputes that would be resolved by arbitration.[235] In matters of litigation, Brazil's conflict of law rule on the applicable law permits only an indirect selection of a legal system.[236] The choice of a governing law must therefore be achieved by localising the contract in a particular country.[237]

Further, the 2015 Hague Principles on the Choice of Law in International Commercial Contracts (Hague Principles)[238] also advocate party autonomy in the choice of law. The Hague Principles are a set of non-binding recommendations that aim to assist inter alia legislators, the judiciary, and arbitrators in interpreting,[239] developing[240] and supplementing[241] the rules of private international law on party autonomy in the choice of law.[242] The Hague Principles encourage the extension of party autonomy to the choice of *any* law. Article 3 thus recommends that, unless the private international law of the *lex fori* provides otherwise, the parties should be permitted to select rules of law which are 'generally accepted on an international, supranational, or regional level as a neutral and balanced set of rules'.

The principles of Indian private international law vis-à-vis party autonomy in the choice of law thus resonates with the global practice on the subject to a considerable extent. At the same time, it is suggested that Indian private international law seek inspiration from the Hague Principles and extend the principle of party autonomy to the choice of soft law and non-state rules in matters of litigation, as has been done in arbitration. The Hague Principles have been implanted by legislation in Paraguay and are likely to be implemented in Australia as well.[243]

That said, unlike most other civil law jurisdictions, Indian private international law fails to provide any clarity on the precise limitations to the parties' selection. What does the expression 'bona fide' denote? Is the choice of a non-state law acceptable? Are there special rules to protect the interests of weaker parties from the dangers of party autonomy?

The courts in India have consistently referred to the decision of the Privy Council in *Vita Food*,[244] to state that the parties' express choice will be disregarded if it is not bona fide, legal or when it is opposed to public policy. At the same time, the circumstances in which a choice of law may be regarded as bona fide have remained nebulous in Indian private international law. In this manner, the practice of Indian courts resonates with the other common law jurisdictions such as Australia,[245] Canada[246] and Hong Kong[247] which do not clearly explain the scope and meaning

[235] See Art 9 of the Law of Introduction to the Brazilian Civil Code 1942 read along with MM Albornoz, 'Choice of Law in International Contracts in Latin American Legal Systems' 2010 *Journal of Private International Law* 23; and N DeAraujo and FGC Saldanha 'Recent Developments and Current Trends on Brazilian Private International Law Concerning International Contracts' 2013 *Panorama of Brazilian Law* 73.

[236] See Albornoz, ibid 37.

[237] ibid.

[238] See Art 1(2) of the HCCCA; Art 1(2) of the Hague Principles.

[239] ibid. Commentary to the Hague Principles (n 1), which defines 'interpretation' as 'the process of explaining, clarifying or construing the meaning of existing rules of private international law'.

[240] ibid. The term 'development' has been defined as the 'addition of new rules, where none existed before, or effecting fundamental changes to pre-existing ones'.

[241] ibid. The term 'supplementation' has been defined as 'the refinement of an existing rule of private international law, which does not sufficiently or appropriately provide for a particular type of situation'.

[242] ibid, para 4 of the Preamble of the Hague Principles, which limits its application to international commercial contracts. For a detailed discussion the Hague Principles, see JL Neels, 'The Nature, Objective and Purposes of the Hague Principles on Choice of Law in International Contracts' (2014) 15 *Yearbook of Private International Law* 45–56.

[243] See Y Nishitani, 'Party Autonomy in Contemporary Private International Law – The Hague Principles on Choice of Law and East Asia' (2016) 59 *Japanese Yearbook of International Law* 300, 305.

[244] (n 5).

[245] See Nygh (n 86) 445–451.

[246] See Pitel and Rafferty (n 219) 271–274.

[247] See Johnston (n 220) 189; and Wolff (n 220) 468–472.

of the expression 'bona fide, legal and opposed to public policy'. Nepalese private international law, on the other hand, does not expressly indicate any limitation to party autonomy in the choice of law in its codification. At present, in Indian law, it appears that a choice of law will not be bona fide if it contravenes an overriding mandatory provision in Indian law. Interested parties have to peruse a jungle of case-law to speculate on the possible meaning that the court may attach to these limitations.

In comparison, civil law jurisdictions such as the EU clearly define the limitations of party autonomy in the choice of law. In this respect, the Rome I Regulation clearly provides that the parties' choice of law will be disregarded when it violates the overriding mandatory provisions and the contravention of the public policy of the forum operate as limitations to the parties' choice of law.[248] Further, the Rome I Regulation clearly enunciates the relevant factors that the court would have to take into account to determine whether a norm may be considered as an overriding mandatory provision.[249] A court may, therefore, refuse to give effect to the parties' choice of law if it is 'crucial … for safeguarding its public interests, such as its political, social or economic organisation'.[250]

Besides, the Rome I Regulation additionally contains certain special rules to regulate the application of the doctrine of party autonomy for agreements concluded between parties with unequal bargaining power – such as carriage, consumer, insurance and employment contracts.[251] The Rome I Regulation limits the applicability of the doctrine in various ways.[252] For instance, in carriage and insurance contracts, the Rome I Regulation 'limits the breadth of choice afforded to the parties'.[253] However, in consumer and employment contracts, the Rome I Regulation limits the parties' freedom to ensure that the choice of law does not deprive the weaker party of the protection of a mandatory law which would be applicable in the absence of choice.[254]

Likewise, the private international laws of Japan,[255] South Korea,[256] Russia,[257] China,[258] Mexico[259] and Venezuela[260] limit the parties' autonomy to choose a law provided that it does not derogate the overriding mandatory provisions or the public policy of the forum. Further, the codifications of Japan,[261] South Korea[262] and China[263] contain special rules for the protection of weaker parties such as employees, consumers or insurance-policy holders.

The legislators in India must, therefore, keep these global developments in mind while codifying the country's private international law. In the meanwhile, it is suggested that the courts must exercise extreme caution in this context, and no reference to the limitations must be made unless explicitly clarified within the decision itself.

[248] See Recital 15 read along with Arts 3(3), 9 and 21 of the Rome I Regulation.
[249] ibid, Art 9.
[250] ibid.
[251] ibid, Arts 5–8.
[252] ibid; and Rühl (n 103) 345 et seq.
[253] ibid, Arts 5(2) and 7(3); and Rühl, ibid 347.
[254] ibid, Arts 6(2) and 8(1); and Rühl, ibid 350–351.
[255] Arts 11 and 12 of the Japanese PIL.
[256] Arts 7 and 10 of the South Korean PIL.
[257] Arts 1192 and 1193 of the Civil Code of Russia.
[258] Arts 4 and 5 of the Chinese PIL.
[259] Arts 11 and 18 of the Mexico City Convention.
[260] ibid.
[261] Arts 11 and 12 of the Japanese PIL.
[262] Arts 27 and 28 of the South Korean PIL.
[263] Arts 16, 42 and 43 of the Chinese PIL.

In doing so, the lawmakers may refer to the codifications of the civil law jurisdictions and, in particular, the Rome I Regulation, which clarifies the circumstances in which the parties' choice may be construed as a contravention of the overriding mandatory norms or the public policy of the *lex fori*.[264]

As regards the selection of non-state rules, an examination of the judicial dicta per *National Thermal Power Corporation*[265] and *Kumarina Investment Ltd*[266] indicates that the parties may incorporate by reference, the provisions of such a law but not entirely select their application to govern their international contract. There is, however, no express clarification to this effect. Having regard to their many benefits as indicated above, it is suggested that the lawmakers approve of their selection in matters of litigation – as is already the case for arbitration.[267]

ii. Implied Choice of Law

The Indian private international law does not stipulate any clear criteria to identify the proper law of a contract through the implied choice of the parties. At present, the courts merely impute an intention over the parties by employing the same set of factors if the parties had not chosen any law.

Academic and scholarly writings report that, in common law, the implied choice of the parties is in practice, 'merely a judicial mode of expressing the rule that the proper law is that of the country with which, the transaction has the most real connection'.[268] This observation holds true for India. There is, therefore, no real distinction in the methods employed to identify the governing law when the parties have not expressly selected the same.[269]

In comparison, an analysis of the codifications of the civil law jurisdictions demonstrates the requirement of a stringent assessment of the contractual terms before inferring the parties' choice in favour of any particular legal system.[270] In the EU, the promulgation of the Rome I Regulation increases the level of stringency that was applicable under the Rome Convention to determine the tacit choice of the parties. Under the Rome Convention, the inferred choice of the parties had to be 'demonstrated with reasonable certainty by the terms of the contract and the surrounding circumstances of the case'.[271] In comparison, the Rome I Regulation mandates that such a choice should be 'clearly demonstrated by the terms of the contract or the circumstances of the case'.[272] Under the Rome Convention, the court was therefore more likely to infer that the parties intended to select the law of a particular legal system.[273] The current conflict of law rules in the Rome I Regulation, on the other hand, reduce the possibility of judicial discretion by leaving little scope for inferring the parties' choice of the applicable law.[274] In this respect, the

[264] See Recital 28, 34 and 37 read along with Arts 9 and 21 of the Rome I Regulation.
[265] *National Thermal Power Corporation* (n 15).
[266] *Kumarina Investment Ltd* (n 51).
[267] See s 28 of the ACA.
[268] JD Falconbridge, *Selected Essays in the Conflict of Laws*, 2nd edn (Canada Law Book Co, 1954) 351. Also see, Morris (n 81) 198; and BA Marshall, 'Reconsidering the Proper Law of the Contract' (2012) 13 *Melbourne Journal of International Law* 505, 512.
[269] See in this context Lord Collins of Mapesbury and J Harris (eds) *Dicey, Morris and Collins on the Conflict of Laws: Vol 2*, 15th edn (Sweet and Maxwell, 2012).
[270] But see Art 7 of the Japanese PIL which does not make any room for identifying the parties' intentions by referring to their tacit choice.
[271] See Art 3(1) of the Rome Convention.
[272] ibid.
[273] Nygh (n 86) 111.
[274] ibid 110.

Giuliano and Lagarde Report suggest, as indicators to decipher the tacit choice of the parties, the use of standard forms of contract which are known to be governed by a particular legal system (such as a Lloyds marine insurance policy), as well as the use of previous dealings between the parties in relation to a contract containing an express choice of law or the incorporation or reference to provisions of a particular legal system.[275]

The approach of the Rome Convention continues to find a place in the private international laws of Turkey[276] and South Korea.[277] In the absence of an express selection, the choice of law must be reasonably (and not clearly) demonstrated under the laws of these legal systems. Nonetheless, most other civil law jurisdictions have favoured the application of a stricter test to discern the implied or the tacit choice of the parties. For instance, the Civil Code of Russia mandates that the tacit choice must 'clearly ensue from the terms and conditions of the contract or the complex of circumstances of the case'.[278] In China, the conflict of law rule permits the courts to infer a choice in favour of a particular legal system exclusively when both (or all) the parties invoke the law of the same region, and neither has objected to its application.[279] In a related vein, the private international law of Mexico and Venezuela as stipulated in the Inter-American Convention on the Law Applicable to International Contracts (Mexico City Convention) mandates that the inferred choice 'must be evident from the parties' behaviour and from the clauses of the contract, considered as a whole'.[280] Similarly, the Hague Principles recommend that the tacit choice must 'appear clearly from the provisions of the contract or the circumstances'.[281] As the Commentary clarifies, the intention must be real and apparent as opposed to being imputed to the parties.[282]

The codification of the rules of private international law in India should address the anomalies that currently prevail on this aspect. The factors to discern the inferred choice must be different from that adopted when the parties have not made any choice and must confer little leeway on the courts in speculating whether or not a choice was made.[283] Thus, it is suggested that the lawmakers must mandate the adoption of a strict test to identify the implied choice of law, much as has been adopted in several civil law jurisdictions, including India's BRICS partners, China[284] and Russia.[285] The parties choice in favour of a legal system must appear clearly from the terms of the contract. This approach has also been endorsed by the Hague Principles.[286]

iii. Absence of Choice of Law

It was seen that the criteria to discern 'the system of law with which the transaction has the closest and most real connection' has been far from uniform in India. In some cases, the courts have relied on the theory of localisation, while in more recent decisions, the test of the imputed intention has found favour among the judiciary. Further, the application of the test of the imputed

[275] M Giuliano and P Lagarde (1980) *Report on the Convention on the Law Applicable to Contractual Obligations* [1980] OJ C282/1, 23 [Giuliano-Lagarde Report].
[276] See Art 24 of the Turkish PIL.
[277] See Art 25 of the South Korean PIL.
[278] See Art 1210 of the Civil Code of Russia.
[279] See Art 3 of the Chinese PIL.
[280] See Art 7 of the Mexico City Convention.
[281] See Art 4 of the Hague Principles. See also, JL Neels and EA Fredericks, 'Tacit Choice of Law in The Hague Principles on Choice of Law in International Contracts' [2011] *De Jure* 101, 104.
[282] See Commentary to the Hague Principles (n 1) [4.6].
[283] See Nygh (n 86) 111.
[284] Art 1210 of the Civil Code of Russia.
[285] Art 3 of the Chinese PIL.
[286] Art 4 of the Hague Principles.

intentions has been inconsistent. In some cases, the courts have relied on presumptions in favour of the *lex loci contractus*, *lex loci solutionis* and the *lex fori*. An examination of more recent decisions indicates that the excessive reliance on these presumptions has been done away with.[287] The *lex fori*, however, continues to play some role in identifying the proper law in the absence of choice. The approach of the Indian courts on the matter thus impedes international trade and hampers access to justice in the country by being unpredictable and uncertain. The practice of the Indian courts resonates with that of other common law systems which have similarly held fast to the 'closest and most real connection' test that was formulated by the Privy Council in *Bonython*.[288] The courts do not follow a consistent interpretation of the 'closest and most real connection' test. On some occasions, the test has been interpreted to refer to the imputed intentions of the parties and, on other occasions, to the application of the theory of localisation.[289] Regardless of these subtle differences, a set of similar indicators are relevant in the common law jurisdictions such as Australia,[290] Canada,[291] Hong Kong[292] and South Africa,[293] all of which adopt the 'closest and most real connection' test to identify the governing law in the absence of choice. Among civil law jurisdictions, the conflict of law rules on applicable law stipulated in the Mexico City Convention, which is applicable in Mexico and Venezuela, resonates with the common law's 'closest and most real connection' test. These legal systems mandate the court to invoke the law of the state with which, the contract has its 'closest ties'.[294] In contrast, Nepalese private international law does not stipulate the application of the 'closest and most real connection' test when the parties have not expressly selected the chosen law to govern their contract. Instead, the National Civil Code Act 2017 prescribes the application of the *lex loci contractus* for all contracts which have been concluded in Nepal.[295] For international contracts which have not been concluded in Nepal, the codification prescribes the application of the law of the place of performance by the *lex loci solutionis* rule, unless it cannot be ascertained. In the latter situation, the *lex loci contractus* will prevail.[296] At the same time, Nepalese private international law does not clarify whether the place of performance refers to the place where goods are sold or purchased or where services are supplied.

In comparison, the presumption of the characteristic performance plays a significant role in determining the governing law in the absence of choice in the codifications of several civil law systems. Drawing on the Swiss lead,[297] the term 'characteristic performance' has been understood to mean 'performance for which payment is due'.[298] As a general rule, the law of the country of the habitual residence of the characteristic performer would govern the contract in the absence of an express or tacit choice.[299] In some circumstances, the characteristic performer's chief administration or principal place of business would apply if the transaction has been entered into in the course of the person's trade or profession, would govern the contract in the absence of an

[287] See the decisions of the Supreme Court of India in *Modi Entertainment Network* (n 45); *Shreejee Traco* (n 183); and *Hardy Exploration* (n 184).

[288] *Bonython* (n 139).

[289] See for instance, the approach of the South African courts on the subject as enunciated in [Khanderia, The Ascertainment of the Applicable Law] (n 1) 1, 6–12.

[290] See Nygh (n 86) 453–456.

[291] See Pitel and Rafferty (n 219) 275–277.

[292] See Wolff (n 220) 472–474.

[293] See Khanderia, [The Ascertainment of the Applicable Law] (n 1)12–18.

[294] Art 9 of the Mexico City Convention.

[295] Art 709(2) of the National Civil Code Act 2017 [Nepalese PIL].

[296] ibid.

[297] Forsyth (n 233) 335.

[298] Giuliano-Lagarde Report (n 275).

[299] See Art 4 of the Rome Convention and Art 4 of the Rome I Regulation.

express or tacit choice.[300] It is suggested that the lawmakers in India should consider the application of the presumption of the characteristic performance to identify the applicable law in the absence of a choice of law, when codifying Indian private international law so that the interested parties are in a position to know beforehand the law that will govern their contract in the event that they fail to agree upon the same.

Research demonstrates that applying the law of the habitual residence, the place of chief administration, or the principal place of business of the characteristic performer is beneficial for the following reasons. First, as justified in the Giuliano and Lagarde Report by way of the preference for this test, the presumption of characteristic performance has the ability to

> define the connecting factor of the contract from the inside, and not from the outside by elements unrelated to the essence of the obligations such as the nationality of the contracting parties or the place where the contract was concluded.[301]

Second, the characteristic performer is the party who is familiar with the law of one's habitual residence and who is 'without a language barrier'.[302] Third, the characteristic performer is more likely to enter into a considerable amount of agreements in his or her professional pursuit and, hence, it should be more convenient for the same law to govern all contracts without choice of law clauses into which this party enters.[303] Fourth, it is the party who is more interested in the performance of the relevant obligations and would 'make more effort and observe more regulations than the one who pays'.[304]

In the EU, the Rome I Regulation stipulates certain fixed-style rules to decipher the characteristic performance in certain major types of contracts such as those involving the sale of goods (including those sold by auction), the supply of services, and the transfer of immovable property.[305] The mechanism employed to discern the applicable law in the absence of choice thus reduces judicial discretion. The conflict of law rules on the applicable law in the absence of choice in Japan,[306] Korea,[307] Turkey,[308] China[309] and Russia[310] similarly imbibe the presumption of characteristic performance to identify the governing law in the absence of choice. The law of the country of the habitual residence, central administration, or principal place of business of the characteristic performer would govern the contract in such circumstances. The private international laws of Korea,[311] China[312] and Russia[313] stipulate fixed-style rules to reduce the discretion

[300] ibid.

[301] Giuliano-Lagarde Report (n 275); and O Vondracek, 'Art. 4 of the Roman Convention on the Law Applicable to Civil and Commercial Obligations: A Fruitful Compromise: Analysis of the Rules of the Law of Characteristic Performance and the Property Law of Contract' (2007) 8 *Common Law Review* 32, 33.

[302] ibid.

[303] C Okoli and G Ariste, 'The Operation of the Escape Clauses in the Rome Convention and Rome I Regulation' (2012) 8 *Journal of Private International Law* 513, 516.

[304] Vondracek (n 301) 32. Also see, Forsyth (n 233) 335–336.

[305] ibid.

[306] Art 8 of the Japanese PIL.

[307] Art 25 of the South Korean PIL.

[308] Art 25 of the Turkish PIL.

[309] Art 4 of the Chinese PIL.

[310] Art 1211 of the Civil Code of Russia.

[311] Art 25 of the South Korean PIL.

[312] Art 4 of the Chinese PIL read along with the 2007 Interpretation. For a detailed discussion on the principles of Chinese private international law on the subject, see G Tu and M Xu, 'Contractual Conflicts in the People's Republic of China: The Applicable Law in the Absence of Choice' [2011] *Journal of Private International Law* 179; J Liang, 'Statutory Restrictions on Party Autonomy in China's Private International Law of Contract: How Far Does the 2010 Codification Go?' [2012] *Journal of Private International Law* 77; Q He, 'The EU Conflict of Laws Communitarization and the Modernization of Chinese Private International Law' [2012] *Rabels Zeitschrift für ausländisches und Internationales Privatrecht / The Rabel Journal of Comparative and International Private Law* 47; and Z Huo, 'An Imperfect Improvement: The New Conflict of Laws Act of the People's Republic of China' [2011] *International and Comparative Law Quarterly* 1065.

[313] Art 1211 of the Civil Code of Russia.

of the courts in interpreting or identifying the characteristic performer. In comparison, the codifications of Japan[314] and Turkey[315] have not enumerated any fixed-style rules; and the determination of the characteristic performer is left to the discretion of the courts. Further, in the EU, the predictability and certainty created by the fixed-style rules are balanced by an escape clause. The Rome I Regulation permits the court to invoke the law of another legal system if it appears from all the circumstances of the case that the contract is 'manifestly more closely connected' with that country.[316] In this manner, the escape clause, balances predictability with flexibility by allowing the application of the rules of another country when the law derived from the fixed-style rules have no real connection with the parties or the transaction. In certain circumstances, however, the court may find it arduous to identify the applicable law by invoking the fixed-style rules or the escape clause. In such scenarios, the Rome I Regulation permits the court to invoke the law of another country with which the contract is 'most closely connected'.[317] The court may weigh the relevant factors to locate the centre of gravity of the contract.[318] The common law's 'closest and most real connection' test, therefore, operates as a last resort under the provisions of the Rome I Regulation.[319] This mechanism is, however, not applicable to certain special agreements with weaker parties such as consumer, insurance or employment contracts – for which there are special rules to discern the applicable law in the absence of choice.[320]

The legislators in India should, in particular, seek inspiration from the provisions on the conflict of law rules in the EU (in particular) for the following reasons. First, the Rome I Regulation reduces the possibility of judicial discretion by incorporating certain fixed-style rules to precisely identify the characteristic performer for certain popular contracts.[321] The fixed-style rules will eliminate the ambiguities in the interpretation of the *lex loci solutionis* as it presently stands in Indian law. However, it is suggested that the reference to the characteristic performer's habitual residence, central administration or principal place of business should be avoided for it is susceptible to being fortuitous in situations when the transaction in question may not have any connection with the contract.[322] Instead, it is suggested that Indian law refer to the place from where the characteristic performer carried out the obligation in order to identify the governing law in the absence of a choice of law agreement. Second, the inclusion of the escape clause in the Rome I Regulation balances predictability with flexibility by permitting the adjudicator to acknowledge a closer connection of the contract with another country.[323] The courts in India should, however, additionally authorise the court to apply the principles of non-state law in the interest of justice and equity. The Indian courts may seek inspiration from the private international law of Mexico and Venezuela.[324] The Mexico City Convention permits

[314] Art 8 of the Japanese PIL.

[315] Art 25 of the Turkish PIL.

[316] See Art 4(3) of the Rome I Regulation.

[317] ibid, Art 4(4); and U Magnus 'Article 4 Rome I Regulation: The Applicable Law in the Absence of Choice' in Ferrari and Leible (eds), *Rome I Regulation. The Law Applicable to Contractual Obligations in Europe* (Sellier European Law Publishers, 2009) 27, 28, 49.

[318] ibid.

[319] ibid.

[320] ibid, Art 5–8.

[321] ibid, Art 4(1) and (2).

[322] See in this respect, CSA Okoli, *Place of Performance: A Comparative Analysis* (Hart, 2020) 63–72 [Okoli, *Place of Performance*]. Okoli examines the pros and cons of applying the law of the habitual residence/central administration/principal place of business of the characteristic performer in the absence of a choice under the Rome I Regulation.

[323] See Art 4(3) of the Rome I Regulation. See also, Art 1211(2) of the Civil Code of Russia; and Art 5 of the 2007 Interpretation (China), which incorporate an escape clause that resembles the clause in the Rome I Regulation.

[324] See Arts 9 and 10 of the Mexico City Convention.

the courts to 'take into account' and 'apply' 'the general principles of international commercial law recognised by international organisations' (ie soft law or non-binding legal principles such as the PICC) if the interests of 'justice and equity' so demand, while finding the law of the state with which the transaction has the closest ties.[325] Third, the Rome I Regulation is the only codification to incorporate a provision that is similar to the 'closest and most real connection' test as applicable in India and other common-law jurisdictions.[326] The instrument, therefore, accommodates unforeseen circumstances when the applicable law cannot be identified by any other means. At present, the codification of no other civil law jurisdiction has made room for a provision of a similar kind.

iv. Applicable Law in E-commerce Transactions

National laws prescribe different solutions to resolve the predicament of the battle of forms as a result of contradictory standard terms.[327] However, none of these solutions is specifically tailored to resolve the dilemma when the parties have stipulated different governing laws for their international contract in their standard terms. In other words, the solutions would apply as a general rule to resolve any predicament which arises as a result of contradictory standard terms. The last-shot method which finds a place in Indian law is also applicable in other common law countries such as India, the UK, Australia and South Africa.[328] Likewise, China, which is a civil law system, has also employed the last-shot rule to resolve the predicament in contradictory standard terms.[329] In India when there are contradictory standard terms, the terms of the counter-offer will prevail in total if the offeror has accepted them.[330] Among EU countries, the Dutch courts have adopted the first-shot rule[331] according to which the obligations stipulated in the first set of standard terms will prevail if the contract contains contradictory terms, unless they have expressly been rejected by the other party.[332] These are the first-shot method and the knock-out rule. The last-shot and first-shot rules are arbitrary, insofar as they fail to justify the basis for considering the contract to have been concluded on one party's standard terms. The judiciaries in other EU countries such as France, Germany, Austria, Lithuania, Estonia and Poland have, however, favoured the knock-out rule.[333] Under the knock-out rule, contradictory clauses are cancelled and the contract is concluded on terms, which are common in substance.[334] The contradictory terms are replaced with default rules as applicable under national law.[335] The knock-out rule, thus, attempts to balance the interests of both parties to the contract as far as practicable. The application of this rule results in the 'cancellation' of contradictory terms in a contract.

[325] See, JA Moreno Rodrigues and MM Albornoz 'Reflections on the Mexico City Convention in the Context of the Preparation of the Future Hague Instrument on International Contracts' [2011] *Journal of Private International Law* 491, 504–507; and FK Juenger, 'Contract Choice of Law in the Americas' (1997) 45 *American Journal of Comparative Law* 195, 204. Also, see generally, FK Juenger, 'The Inter-American Convention on the Law Applicable to International Contracts: Some Highlights and Comparisons' (1994) 42 *The American Journal of Comparative Law* 381.

[326] See Art 4(4) of the Rome I Regulation.

[327] For a detailed discussion on the various solutions to the battle of forms, see Khanderia, International Approaches as Plausible Solutions (n 186) 3–7.

[328] Graziano (n 185) 75–76.

[329] ibid.

[330] ibid.

[331] ibid 76–77.

[332] ibid.

[333] ibid 77–79.

[334] ibid.

[335] ibid.

In such circumstances, the court would apply conflict of law rules to identify the applicable law in the absence of choice. To illustrate, consider a scenario which is similar to the one discussed above.[336] A (a seller which is a company incorporated in Greece) designated Greek law in its standard terms when concluding a contract to sell certain products to B (a buyer who resides in Delhi). B designated Indian law to govern the contract when accepting A's offer to sell the product. A sues B for failure to pay for the goods, but initiates the proceedings before the courts in France which was the chosen forum in the parties' contract. The French court will apply the knock-out rule and 'cancel' or disregard contradictory choice of law clauses. Instead, it will invoke the provisions of the Rome I Regulation, which prescribe mechanisms for identifying applicable law in the absence of choice. Accordingly, the French court will apply Greek law to adjudicate the dispute under Article 4 of the Rome I Regulation by being the place of incorporation of the seller.

The Hague Principles propose a novel solution under Article 6(1)(b) which specifically aims to address the battle of forms arising from conflicting choice of law clauses insofar as these are regarded as independent agreements that are separable from the rest of the contract. The solution attempts to reconcile contradictions to the maximum possible extent. In this respect, it provides that:

> if the parties have used standard terms designating two different laws, and under both of these laws the same standard terms prevail, the law designated in the prevailing terms applies; if under these laws different standard terms prevail, or if under one or both of these laws no standard terms prevail, there is no choice of law.[337]

Accordingly, Article 6(1)(b) recommends an examination of the type of solution proposed at the national level in case of a contradiction between terms.[338] It encourages the adjudicating authority to analyse whether the parties (whose terms are contradictory) belong to legal systems which follow the last-shot, first-shot or the knock-out rule.[339] If all the parties belong to jurisdictions which adopt the last-shot rule, Article 6 of the Hague Principles recommends that the adjudicator invoke that method.[340] The same principle would apply when all parties belong to countries adopting the first-shot or the knock-out rule.[341] In doing so, it endeavours to reconcile the solution as far as possible by preventing the arbitrary or unjustifiable application of the resolution adopted by the legal system where only one party belongs.[342] Article 6, however, proposes the application of the knock-out rule if the parties belong to jurisdictions which imbibe different solutions to redress the battle of forms.[343] Applying this principle, the court or arbitrator would then cancel or knock-out the contradictory choice of law clauses and identify the governing law by invoking the conflict of law rule on the absence of choice of the *lex fori*.[344]

Unlike the current approach adopted in the domestic realm in India, namely, the last-shot method as a general rule, the solution under the Hague Principles is not arbitrary. It favours the formation of the contract as far as possible. As indicated above, the Hague Principles recommends a reconciliation of the conflicting terms based on the approaches adopted at the domestic level.

[336] See the text accompanying notes 185–186.
[337] Art 6(1)(b) of the Hague Principles.
[338] See Graziano (n 185) 92; and Commentary to Art 6(1)(b) the Hague Principles (n 1).
[339] See Graziano, ibid 89–90; and Commentary to Art 6(1)(b) of the Hague Principles, ibid, scenarios 2a and b.
[340] See Graziano, ibid; and Commentary Art 6(1)(b) of the Hague Principles, ibid, scenarios 2a and b.
[341] See Graziano, ibid; and Commentary Art 6(1)(b) of the Hague Principles, ibid, scenarios 2a, 2b and 4.
[342] See Khanderia, International Approaches as Plausible Solutions (n 186) 26.
[343] See Graziano (n 185) 97–99; and Commentary Art 6(1)(b) of the Hague Principles (n 1) scenario 7.
[344] See Graziano, ibid 91.

Where this is not possible, incorporating the solution proposed by the Hague Principles in India would mandate adjudicators to invoke the knock-out rule and identify the proper law as if the parties had not made any choice in the first place. Adopting the Hague Principles in Indian private international law would, however, necessitate a complete reform of the Republic's conflict of law rules on applicable law according to the suggestions advanced above.

V. Conclusion

In this chapter, we discussed the principles of Indian private international law to identify the applicable law in matters of contract. It was seen that the English common law has been instrumental in shaping the principles of Indian law on the subject. The applicable law is determined through the doctrine of the proper law of the contract. In the absence of codification, the Supreme Courts dicta in *National Thermal Power*[345] has provided some guidelines concerning the identification of the proper law of the contract. In India, the applicable law will chiefly depend on the express choice of the parties. In matters of international commercial arbitration, the parties right to choose a governing law extends to the choice of soft law or non-state law. However, whether the parties can select a soft-law or a non-state law to govern their international contract in matters of litigation remains unknown.

It was seen that the parties' choice of law would prevail unless it is not bona fide, legal or is opposed to the public policy of India. However, the courts have not, as a matter of fact, disregarded the parties' choice because it was not bona fide or legal. The parameters within which those limitations will operate in practice, remain unknown. At present, it appears that the choice will not be bona fide if it contradicts an overriding mandatory provision in Indian law. It was also seen that a choice is likely to be considered to contradict an overriding mandatory provision in India if it violates the public policy of the Republic. In other words, the expressions 'overriding mandatory provision' and 'public policy' have been used interchangeably in India.

In the absence of an express choice, the proper law will depend on the implied choice of the parties. However, a close examination of existing dicta indicates that the identification of the proper law through the implied choice of the parties is illusory. This is because the courts will in fact impute an intention on the parties while searching for the proper law. In doing so, the court will refer to the same indicia as it would if the parties had not made any choice. The 'closest and most real connection test' which is the mechanism to identify the applicable law in the absence of choice is equally nebulous. The criterion which the courts have employed to interpret the test has varied over time. Occasionally, the courts have employed the theory of localisation to search for the centre of gravity of the contract. Accordingly, the applicable law will depend on the individual factors of the agreement which have the closest connection with the contract.

In some cases, the courts have demonstrated a preference for the test of the imputed intentions of the parties to discern applicable law. It was seen that the court may refer to the intentions of 'just and reasonable persons' or it may invoke the presumptions of the *lex loci contractus*, *lex loci solutionis* or *lex fori* to discern their imputed intentions. The *lex loci solutionis* will apply if it coincides with the *lex loci solutionis*. When it differs, the latter will prevail. However, the courts have not sufficiently clarified the mechanism to identify the place of performance if the *lex loci solutionis* is presumed to be what the parties intended. The *lex fori* will apply to the extent that there are factors to substantiate that the parties intended its application.

[345] (n 15).

The chapter demonstrated how the lack of codification has contributed to considerable unpredictability and uncertainty in Indian law. In this respect, it suggested that Indian private international law should be codified. In the meanwhile, the Supreme Court should stipulate clear guidelines to identify the applicable law in international disputes in matters of contract. It was suggested that the lawmakers in India focus on the focus on the following aspects when codifying the law:

(1) Lawmakers should seek inspiration from the Hague Principles and extend the principle of party autonomy in the choice of law to the choice of soft law and non-state law.[346]
(2) The limitations to the parties' choice should be clearly defined. The courts should refrain from referring to the expression bona fide unless the term is defined or clarified in the decision. In this respect, the lawmakers should refer to the private international laws of civil law jurisdictions, in particular the EU, and permit the courts to disregard the parties' choice of law when it contradicts overriding mandatory norms or public policy. The law must provide clear indicia to identify the violation of an overriding mandatory norm or the public policy of India.
(3) The law should clearly address how the rights of weaker parties will be protected from the dangers of party autonomy. Lawmakers should refer to the provisions of the Rome I Regulation which contain special rules to regulate the application of party autonomy to agreements between parties with unequal bargaining power, such as may be typical in carriage, consumer, insurance and employment contracts.[347]
(4) The law should clearly demarcate mechanisms to identify proper law through the implied choice of the parties, when the parties have not made any express choice. Lawmakers should seek inspiration from the Rome I Regulation and the Hague Principles which advocate that the parties to a contract should be considered to have made an implied choice only if the terms of the contract and the circumstances of the case *clearly demonstrate* a choice in favour of that law.[348]
(5) The law should replace the vague and convoluted 'closest and most real connection test' with the characteristic performance test which has found a place in the conflict of laws of several civil law jurisdictions and, in particular, the Rome I Regulation. The law should stipulate certain fixed-style rules to identify the characteristic performer in certain common contracts. The law of the place from where the characteristic performer performed the contract as opposed to habitual residence, place of chief administration, or principal place of business should be applied. These last three connecting factors may not coincide with the place of characteristic performance and are likely to be fortuitous.[349]
(6) Predictability should be balanced by an escape clause which permits the law of another country to apply if the contract is manifestly more closely connected with such country.[350] The law should additionally allow courts to consider and apply general principles of international commercial law (such as the PICC) in the interest of justice and equity. This approach finds favour in the Mexico City Convention.[351]
(7) The law should prescribe mechanisms to address the battle of forms and contradictory choice of law clauses in standard form contracts.[352] The arbitrary last-shot rule, which is currently the general conflict of law rule in India, should be replaced with the solution prescribed in the Hague Principles.

[346] See Art 3 of the Hague Principles.
[347] Arts 5–8 of the Rome I Regulation.
[348] ibid, Art 3; and Art 4 of the Hague Principles.
[349] See Okoli, *Place of Performance* (n 303) 63 et seq.
[350] See paras 1 and 2 of Art 4(3) of the Rome I Regulation.
[351] See Arts 9 and 10 of the Mexico City Convention.
[352] See Art 6(1)(b) of the Hague Principles.

11

The Applicable Law in Non-Contractual Obligations

I. Introduction

The term 'non-contractual obligations' has not been uniformly defined until late. In the conflict of laws, such obligations generally refer to cross-border disputes in connection with tortious claims for damage caused due to inter alia negligence, misrepresentation, nuisance or defamation. The identification of the applicable law in matters of tort is considered as 'one of the most vexed questions in the conflict of laws'.[1] This is because unlike the identification of the applicable law in matters of contract, the question in tortious issues is likely to include 'far more diverse range of interests and duties'.[2] Moreover, the parties are likely to be strangers who did not predict the occurrence of harmful behaviour.[3] Consider for example a scenario where A (a person in Delhi) has suffered an injury caused from a faulty hairdryer that was manufactured by B (a company which has its principal place of business in Paris). The question of whether A can claim damages for the harm will essentially depend on the applicable law, taking into account that the dispute contains a foreign element, namely, that the product was manufactured overseas. In a related vein, what happens when A (resident in Mumbai) has been injured in a motor vehicle accident in New South Wales while on holiday due to the rash and negligent driving of a taxi driver? Can the employer be vicariously liable for the employee's action? All of these questions require the identification of the applicable law (insofar as the tort is international) to determine the rights and liabilities of the alleged tortfeasor and the victim. In some cases, the tort or delict may arise from a contractual obligation, for instance, from an employment contract. What are the remedies of a person who has waived his or her right to compensation under the agreement, if he or she is injured abroad in the course of employment by the negligent act of a co-worker?[4] Such issues would necessitate a classification to understand the nature of the dispute, namely, whether it arises from a contractual or a non-contractual obligation.

This chapter examines the principles of Indian private international law in identifying the applicable law in non-contractual matters. It is divided into four parts. Section II (section I being this Introduction) analyses the mechanism to determine the applicable law in such matters.

[1] A Mills, *Party Autonomy in Private International Law* (Cambridge University Press, 2018) 395 [Mills, *Party Autonomy*]; referring to SC Symeonides, 'Rome II and Torts Conflicts: A Missed Opportunity' (2008) 56(1) *American Journal of Comparative Law*, 173, 188.

[2] A Briggs, *The Conflict of Laws* 4th edn (OUP, 2019) 247.

[3] ibid.

[4] See *Sayers v International Drilling Co NV* [1971] 1 WLR 1176.

Sub-section A of section II discusses the strict application of the common law's 'double actionability' rule to cross-border disputes involving tortious claims. Sub-section B highlights the nuances of extending the rule to complex tortious claims in matters such as product liability, defamation, unfair competition, unjust enrichment or intellectual property. Section III reflects on the position of Indian private international law vis-à-vis global trends on the subject and suggests possible ways to develop the law. Section III.A, accordingly, considers the legal position in other common law jurisdictions such as the UK, Australia and Canada. The conflict of law rules in civil law systems such as those of the EU, Russia, China, South Korea and Turkey will also be examined. Some suggestions to develop Indian private international law will be suggested in section III.B. Section IV provides concluding remarks.

II. Identification of Applicable Law in Non-Contractual Obligations in India

A. Double Actionability Rule

i. Historical Origins of the Rule: An Overview

The principles of private international law on the subject have not been codified in India. In such circumstances, the means of identifying the applicable law for non-contractual obligations rests on the doctrine of *stare decisis* and has been developed by case law. The principles of English common law have played an instrumental role in shaping Indian conflict of law rules on applicable law in non-contractual obligations. The doctrine of double actionability, which was developed in the seminal case of *Phillips v Eyre*,[5] was the relevant rule in identifying the applicable law in non-contractual obligations under the English common law.

In *Phillips*, the Queen's Bench was seized of a dispute against the Governor of Jamaica for an assault committed against an Englishman.[6] The act of the Governor was, nonetheless, indemnified under Jamaican law.[7] Accordingly, the court had to determine whether the Governor could be held liable under English law. The court invoked the doctrine of double actionability.[8] It stated that an act which was committed overseas would be considered as a tort if the act was actionable: (1) as a tort under English law (*lex fori*); and (2) as a wrong under the law where the act was committed (*lex loci delicti commissi*).[9]

It was irrelevant whether the act constituted a tort under the law of the *lex loci delicti*.[10] It would suffice if the plaintiff could demonstrate that the defendant's behaviour was a civil wrong in some way under the legal principles of that country.[11]

However, the plaintiff's claim would succeed if it demonstrated that the defendant was also liable under the English law of tort. In this manner, the doctrine mandated the 'concurrent

[5] [1870] LR 6 QB 1.
[6] ibid.
[7] ibid.
[8] ibid 28, 29.
[9] ibid.
[10] See, JHC Morris, 'The Proper Law of Tort' [1951] *Harvard Law Review* 881, 888; and JG Collier, *The Conflict Of Laws* 3rd edn (CUP, 2001) 222–223.
[11] ibid.

application' of two laws to determine the defendant's liability in any cross-border action based on tort.[12] Torts committed in England would, however, be governed by domestic law.[13]

Subsequently, in *Boys v Chaplin*,[14] the House of Lords developed a 'flexible exception' rule that resembled JHC Morris' theory of 'the proper law of the tort',[15] to avoid the mechanical application of the doctrine of double actionability. According to this exception, the court will apply the legal principles of a system of law which has the most significant relationship with the parties and the issue, instead of applying double actionability, if there are 'clear and satisfying grounds'.[16] The court was seised of a dispute between two English soldiers who were involved in a car accident in Malta.[17] The defendant was liable under English and Maltese law. Nonetheless, the quantum of damages differed, as Maltese law did not permit the plaintiff to claim compensation for pain and suffering.[18] The court applied English law because it had a significantly closer connection with the dispute. In *Red Sea Insurance Company Limited v Bouygues SA and Others*, the House of Lords subsequently clarified that the flexible exception rule permitted the court to displace the *lex fori* or the *lex loci delicti*.[19] The law of the legal system derived under the flexible exception would then govern only particular issues of the claim (for instance, the part concerning damages).[20]

In the UK, the double actionability rule has been replaced with the enactment of the Private International Law (Miscellaneous Provisions) Act 1995 (1995 Act) which defines the method of identify the applicable law in all non-contractual obligations except defamation. Disputes on defamation with a foreign element would, accordingly, still be regulated by the doctrine of double actionability. The 1995 Act did away with the obligation of the claimant to prove the liability of the tortfeasor concurrently under the laws of two legal systems, the *lex fori* and the *lex loci delicti*. Instead, it mandated the sole application of the *lex loci delicti*. In certain circumstances, a 'flexible exception' could displace the *lex loci delicti* rule with the law of another country if 'one or more of the issues had a substantially more significant relationship' with the legal system of that other country.[21] When deciding whether to apply the exception, the court would consider factors such as any common domicile and residence of the parties,[22] the place where the harmful effect of the tort was felt,[23] or whether the tort arose from a pre-existing contractual relationship between the parties.[24] Given this latter factor, some scope for the operation of party autonomy in the choice of law governing a tortious act was indirectly permitted by the 1995 Act.[25] But the court would disregard the applicable law indicated by the 1995 Act, if that law violated the public policy of England.[26]

[12] See A Mills, 'The Application of Multiple Laws under the Rome II Regulation' in J Ahern and W Binchy (eds), *The Rome II Regulation on the Law Applicable to Non-Contractual Obligations: A New Litigation Regime* (Martinus Nijhoff Publishers, 2009) 140.

[13] See *Szalatnay-Stacho v Fink* [1947] KB 1 CA; Mills, *Party Autonomy* (n 1) 397.

[14] [1971] AC 356.

[15] Morris, (n 10) 888.

[16] *Boys* (n 14) 391H.

[17] ibid.

[18] ibid.

[19] [1995] 1 HKLR 224, 229.

[20] ibid. See also Briggs, *Conflict of Laws* (n 2) 263.

[21] ibid, s 12.

[22] Collier (n 10) 232; and P Stone, 'Product Liability under the Rome II Regulation' in J Ahern and W Binchy (eds), *The Rome II Regulation on the Law Applicable to Non-Contractual Obligations: A New Litigation Regime* (Martinus Nijhoff Publishers, 2009) 175.

[23] ibid.

[24] See *Johnson v Coventry Churchill International*, [1992] 3 All ER 14; *Morin v Bonhams & Brooks*, [2003] EWCA Civ 1802; *Trafigura Beheer v Kookmin Bank*, [2006] 2 Lloyd's Rep. 455; Stone (n 32) 174; Mills, *Party Autonomy* (n 1) 402.

[25] See Mills, *Party Autonomy*, (n 1) 397, 398.

[26] Section 14(3)(a) of the 1995 Act; and Collier (n 10) 235.

The 1995 Act was in due course superseded by the Rome II Regulation,[27] which applied in the UK until Brexit. The UK has since enacted the Law Applicable to Contractual Obligations and Non-Contractual Obligations (Amendment etc) (EU Exit) Regulations 2019 to carry forward the application of Rome I and II post-Brexit. However, matters of defamation are outside the scope of the Rome II Regulation. Therefore, double actionability continues to be applied in matters of defamation.[28]

ii. Application of the Double Actionability Rule in India

Indian courts will likely apply a test of double actionability in all disputes involving tortious breaches. This last statement, however, is not certain in the absence of explicit endorsement by the Supreme Court.[29] To date, there have only been two reported cases on the law applicable to tortious claims with foreign elements.[30] Both disputes were in respect of the tort of negligence. Otherwise, existing dicta are merely of persuasive, as opposed to authoritative, value.

The doctrine of double actionability was considered by the Rajasthan High Court in *Kotah Transport Ltd v Jhalawar Transport Services Ltd*.[31] The case involved an action against a driver for reckless driving leading to the collision of two buses and injury to the plaintiff.[32] The accident took place in India, but the Court referred to English common law 'in the interest of justice, equity and good conscience' and considered what would happen if the tort had occurred in a different country.[33] In such a situation, the Court suggested that the principle of double actionability would apply:[34]

> [W]hether an act done in a foreign country is or is not a tort (in India) depends upon the combined effect of the law of the country where the act is done (*lex loci delicti commissi*) and of the law of the forum (*lex fori*).[35]

In *Sona Devi v Anil Kumar*, the Punjab and Haryana High Court likewise invoked the doctrine of double actionability.[36] The case concerned the accidental drowning of pilgrims due to reckless driving by a tour operator. The pilgrims were on the way to religious sites in northern India via Nepal. The issue was whether the defendant's wrong was actionable in India.[37] Kannan J noted that India had no equivalent to the 1995 Act prescribing the application of the law of the place of the commission of the tort (*lex loci delicti*) to a tort with a foreign element.[38]

The Court observed that 'in England, the statutory provisions govern and displace common law'.[39] In contrast, in the absence of statutory provisions, 'India will continue to be

[27] Regulation (EC) No 864/2007 of the European Parliament and of the Council of 11 July 2007 on the Law Applicable to Non-Contractual Obligations [2007] OJ L199/40 [Rome II Regulation].

[28] See Briggs, *Conflict of Laws* (n 2) 275–276.

[29] See in this respect Art 141 of the Constitution of India 1950, which provides that 'the law declared by the Supreme Court shall be binding on all courts within the territory of India'.

[30] See *Kotah Transport Ltd v Jhalawar Transport Services Ltd* AIR [1960] Raj 224; and *Sona Devi v Anil Kumar* [2011] 3 TAC 552.

[31] ibid.

[32] ibid.

[33] ibid [31]–[32].

[34] ibid.

[35] ibid [31]–[32] referring to A Dicey, J Morris and L Collins (eds), *Dicey and Morris on the Conflict of Laws*, 11th edn (Sweet and Maxwell, 1987) Rules 180–181.

[36] *Sona Devi* (n 30).

[37] ibid.

[38] Section 11 of the 1995 Act.

[39] *Sona Devi* (n 30) [6].

governed by the principles of common law themselves'.[40] The claimants would therefore have to prove that the tour operator's act was actionable: (1) as a tort under Indian law; and (2) as a wrong 'though not necessarily as a tort'[41] under the law of the place where the act was done. The Court did not mention the concurrent application of two laws (as under English common law).[42] Instead, the Court held that, if both conditions were satisfied, Indian common law would mandate the exclusive application of domestic (that is, Indian) law.[43] Thus, the Court appears to have misunderstood how the double actionability rule was applied by the Queen's Bench in *Phillips v Eyre*.[44] The Court also cited the respective decisions of the English and American courts in *Harding v Wealands*[45] and *Babcock v Jackson*.[46] It confirmed the existence of an exception to the doctrine of 'double actionability' in India.[47]

In *Harding*, the House of Lords decided applied the *lex fori* as a flexible exception to the double actionability rule when adjudicating upon a dispute arising from an accident between two persons who went on holiday from England to New South Wales.[48] The court did so on the basis that England bore a significant connection with the parties and their claim.[49] Similarly, in *Babcock*, the New York Court of Appeals applied the *lex fori* as the law applicable to a motor vehicle accident involving a couple from New York on holiday in Ontario.[50] The court justified the application of New York law, which was the *lex fori*, by reference to the close relationship between the parties and New York.[51] It rejected the application of Ontario law, the *locus delicti*, since Ontario had no other connection with the parties apart from fortuitously being the place where their accident occurred.[52] The court invoked the 'centre of gravity' principle which hinges on the 'grouping the elements' to determine applicable law.[53]

Kannan J thus drew an analogy between the facts in *Sona Devi*[54] and those of *Harding*[55] and *Babcock*.[56] He elaborated:

> The 'double actionability' rule has been said to be flexible. If all, or virtually all of the significant factors so indicate, a particular issue or even the entire question of liability may be governed instead by the law of the country which has the most significant relationship with the occurrence in question and with the parties. Thus, a claimant may recover even though the law of the place of the tort would have disallowed some or all of his claim. Likewise, he may recover in respect of a tort actionable under the law of the place where it occurred even though the conduct would not have been actionable as a tort if it has occurred in England. For this exception to apply, the connection between the case and the country whose law is to be denied application must be so weak that the law has no interest in being applied to the particular dispute, and no other law should be applied instead.[57]

[40] ibid.
[41] ibid.
[42] See *Phillips* (n 5).
[43] *Sona Devi* (n 30) [6].
[44] See *Phillips* (n 5).
[45] [2006] UK HL 32.
[46] [1963] 2 LlR 286.
[47] *Sona Devi* (n 30) [6].
[48] (n 45).
[49] ibid.
[50] (n 46). Also see generally TJB, 'The Impact of Babcock v. Jackson on Conflict of Laws' (1966) 52(2) *Virginia Law* 302, 303 et seq; RH Chappell Jr, '*Lex Loci Delicti* and *Babcock v. Jackson*' (1966) 7 *William and Mary Law Review* 249, 250 et seq; and ME Solimine, 'The Impact of *Babcock v. Jackson*: An Empirical Note' (1993) 56 *Albany Law Review* 773, 774.
[51] ibid.
[52] ibid
[53] ibid.
[54] (n 31).
[55] (n 45).
[56] (n 46).
[57] (n 31) [8].

Whether the application of the flexible exception indirectly extends the doctrine of party autonomy in choice of law to non-contractual matters remains unknown. As indicated above, in England, the exception enables the courts to apply the law of another country if a dispute arose from a pre-existing contractual relationship between the parties.

It has not been necessary in tortious matters to limit the application of the governing law if the same contravenes an overriding Indian mandatory norms or public policy. This may be due to India's strict adherence to the double actionability rule. The application of the *lex fori* under the rule serves as a:

> filter whereby the courts can screen out unfamiliar or controversial torts without the need to rely on spurious characterisations or arguments of public policy.[58]

B. Application of Double Actionability as a Uniform Principle?

In recent times, the growth of international trade and commerce has given rise to more complex tortious claims, such as those arising from environmental damage, the infringement of intellectual property, the use of defective or inherently dangerous products (product liability), unfair competition, and unjust enrichment. Such eventualities have prompted several legal systems to develop special rules for the determination of particular types of tortious claims. Indian private international law will likely resort to the double actionability rule to determine the applicable law for all tortious disputes before an Indian court. This section will analyse particular tortious claims and sketch out how double actionability might apply to such matters.

i. Product Liability

There has been no case where the Indian courts have had the opportunity to identify, or even comment on, the law that will govern a cross-border dispute in connection with product liability. Product liability is a private law measure which aims to determine the civil liability of the manufacturer due to injury caused to a person or property through the use of a defective or inherently dangerous product.[59]

Rules on product liability have recently been at the forefront of the news, especially in connection with innovations such as the introduction of autonomous vehicles incorporating artificial intelligence (AI)[60] in place of human effort. The inclusion of a Global Positioning System (GPS), Light Detection and Ranging (Lidar), cameras, ultrasonic sensors, parking sensors and automatic brakes are common features of such vehicles.[61] Like most other products, when something goes wrong, autonomous vehicles may endanger the life or safety of a user (the driver) or third parties (pedestrians) as a result of a defective component or faulty design.

[58] KF Tsang, 'Double Actionability: An Outdated Rule in Modern Times' (2017) 86 *University of Missouri-Kansas City Law Review*, 73, 81 referring to A Dickinson, 'Further Thoughts on Foreign Torts – *Boys v. Chaplin* Explained? (*Red Sea v. Bouygues*)' [1994] *Lloyd's Maritime and Comparative Law Quarterly* 463, 463.

[59] See M Tulibacka, *Product Liability Law in Transition: A Central European Perspective* (Ashgate Publishers, 2009) 4.

[60] S Pradhan and R Patnaik, 'Internet and Society: Latest Developments in Cyberspace' (2018) 6(2) *Nirma University Law Journal* 21, 30; M Xu et al., 'The Fourth Industrial Revolution: Opportunities and Challenges' (2018) 9(2) *International Journal of Financial Research* 90, 93; and K Schwab, 'The Fourth Industrial Revolution' (2016) *World Economic Forum* 7, available at: https://luminariaz.files.wordpress.com/2017/11/the-fourth-industrial-revolution-2016-21.pdf.

[61] See, SH Williams, 'Technological Opacity, Predictability, and Self-Driving Cars' (2016) 38 *Cardozo Law Review* 121, 137–145; and J De Bruyne and C Vanleenhove, 'The Rise of Self-Driving Cars: Is the Private International Law Framework for Non-Contractual Obligations Posing a Bump in the Road?' (2018) 5(1) *IALS Student Law Review* 14, 15–16.

Consider the following example: A (a permanent resident of Delhi) is riding in a self-driving car manufactured by B (a company with a statutory seat in Germany and its principal place of business in Bangalore) while A is on holiday in Greece. The car collides with a truck. The truck is being driven by C (a permanent resident of Greece). The accident critically injures A. C is unharmed, but C's truck has been damaged. A sues B in Bangalore. C sues A for the damage caused to C's truck. What law will govern: (1) A's action against sues B; and (2) C's action against A? The accident was not caused by anyone's negligence. It was instead caused by a defective component in the car. Can B be held liable to A for the defect in the car and (if so) to what extent? Will A be expected to compensate C for the damage to C's truck even though the accident was not caused by A's fault? In cross-border disputes, the ascertainment of such liability is likely to become more complicated, because it may require the identification of several applicable laws in order to determine the parties' respective rights and liabilities.

In India, it appears that the courts will apply 'double actionability' to cross-border claims involving issues of product liability. According to that doctrine, the plaintiff would be under an onus to prove: (1) that the alleged wrong is actionable under the law of the country where it was committed or occurred (*lex loci delicti*); and (2) that the act is simultaneously actionable as a tort under Indian law. In cases of product liability, the interpretation of the place of the commission of the wrong may be difficult. Does the *locus delicti* refer to the place: (1) where the defective or damaged product was manufactured; or (2) where the accident arose and injured a person?

Consider a second scenario. A (an Austrian tourist travelling to Delhi) is injured by a shock from an electronic trimmer manufactured by B (a company incorporated in China). How would the place of commission or occurrence of the tort be identified, assuming that the court in India has jurisdiction as the place where the cause of action arose? Would the *locus delicti* be: (1) China where the electronic trimmer was manufactured; or (2) India where its use injured the tourist? If the place of the commission of the tort is construed to mean the place of manufacturing (China), the plaintiff would be under an onus to prove the defendant's liability under Chinese and Indian substantive law.

Under the Indian law of tort, the application of the seminal case of *Donoghue v Stevenson*[62] would normally impose a duty of care towards consumers on the manufacturer of a product. The manufacturer is responsible for damage caused by the sale of a defective product. *Donoghue*, which has been instrumental in shaping the English common law of tort and the doctrine of negligence, concerned damage caused to the person, Donoghue suffered shock and gastroenteritis by drinking from a ginger beer bottle which contained a decomposed snail. The House of Lords per Lord Atkin held the manufacturer to be liable for negligence for the sale of a defective product. It justified its decision by stating that:

> a manufacturer of products, which he sells in such a form as to show them to reach the ultimate consumer in the form in which they left him with no reasonable possibility of intermediate examination and with the knowledge that the absence of reasonable care in the preparation or putting up of the products will result in an injury to the consumer's life or property, owes a duty to the consumer to take reasonable care.[63]

However, the substantive principles of Indian law do not hold a manufacturer liable for accidents caused by a motor vehicle (including an autonomous vehicle). The principles in *Donoghue*[64] have not been extended to such claims. Instead, claims for accidents from the use of a motor vehicle are

[62] [1932] AC 562. See also, WVH Rogers, *Winfield & Jolowicz on Tort* 18th edn (Sweet & Maxwell, 2010) 498–501.
[63] ibid 599.
[64] ibid.

subject to a principle of strict liability which holds the user of a vehicle liable for all the damage resulting from its use. The Indian law of tort which regulates such matters is stipulated by the Motor Vehicles Act 1988[65] (MVA). The legislation defines a 'motor vehicle' as:

> *any* mechanically propelled vehicle adapted for use upon roads whether the power of propulsion is transmitted thereto from an external or internal source and includes a chassis to which a body has not been attached and a trailer, but does not include a vehicle running upon fixed rails or a vehicle of a special type adapted for use only in a factory or in any other enclosed premises or a vehicle having less than four wheels …[66]

In contrast to the general duty of care in *Donoghue*,[67] the MVA adopts the principle of strict liability developed in *Rylands v Fletcher*.[68] That means that:

> the person who, for his own purpose brings on his land, and collects and keeps there anything likely to [make] mischief if it escapes, must keep it in at his peril; and if he does not do so, is *prima facie* answerable for *all* the damage, which is the natural consequence of its escape.[69]

The Supreme Court in *Kaushnuma Begum and Ors v The New India Assurance Co. Ltd*[70] extended the principle of strict liability to accidents involving the use of a motor vehicle. The Court was called upon to determine the liability of the defendant who had allegedly killed a pedestrian when the wheel of the jeep that the former was driving, burst.[71] The Court held the defendant liable for the death of the plaintiff.[72] It justified its position by stating that:

> in view of the fast and constantly increasing volume of traffic, the motor vehicles upon the road may be regarded to some extent as coming within the principle of liability defined in *Rylands v Fletcher*. From the point of view of the pedestrian, the roads of this country have been rendered by the use of the motor vehicles highly dangerous … Where a pedestrian without negligence on his part is injured or killed by a motorist whether negligently or not, he or his legal representatives as the case may be should be entitled to recover damages if the principle of social justice should have any meaning at all. In order to meet to some extent, the responsibility of the society to the deaths and injuries caused in road accidents, there has been a continuous agitation throughout the world to make the liability for damages arising out of motor vehicles accidents as a liability without fault.[73]

It would, consequently, be irrelevant whether the accident was caused by the fault or negligence of the defendant. The Court clarified that the only defence available to the defendant who is strictly liable for the accident caused by the use of the motor vehicle would be to demonstrate that it was caused by: (1) the fault of the plaintiff; or (2) an act of God.[74] The extension of the doctrine of 'double actionability' to identify the applicable law in product liability cases involving a motor vehicle such as a self-driving car may therefore result in the failure of a claim as a result of the claimant's inability to prove that the relevant act is actionable under the *lex fori* and the *lex loci delicti*.

[65] Act No 59 of 1988.
[66] ibid, s 2(28).
[67] (n 69).
[68] (1868) LR 3 HL 330, 339, 340. See also, A Sapre, *Ratanlal & Dhirajlal: The Law of Torts* 28th edn (Lexis Nexis, 2018) 498 et seq.
[69] ibid.
[70] AIR [2001] SC 485.
[71] ibid.
[72] ibid.
[73] ibid [18], referring to *Gujarat State Road Transport Corporation, Ahmedabad v Ramanbhai Prabhatbhai & Anr* [1987] (3) SCC 234.
[74] ibid.

The application of the law of the place of the commission of an accident (that is, the *lex loci delicti* rule) may not hold the driver liable at all for an accident which has not occurred by his or her fault. Instead, in a product liability case, where the accident has been caused by the failure of a component (for instance, because the automatic brakes failed), the *lex loci delicti* may hold the manufacturer liable for the defect which has caused the injury. In comparison, under Indian law, the defendant (driver of the vehicle) would, however, be strictly liable for the 'non-natural use of land',[75] regardless of whether a defect in the vehicle caused the accident. To illustrate, suppose an Austrian tourist is driving a self-driving car manufactured in Ohio while on holiday in India. The vehicle fails to locate a divider on the road and fatally injures the driver, resulting in the driver's death. The family of the driver sues the car company in India for the tort of negligence in producing a defective component. The Indian court would have jurisdiction by being the place where the cause of action arose. Under the doctrine of double actionability, the plaintiffs would have to prove the liability of the car manufacturer under the substantive law of Ohio and India. While the car manufacturer may be liable for the tort of negligence under Ohio law, the substantive law of tort in India would on the contrary hold the driver strictly responsible for the non-natural use of land. The claim would therefore fail because the plaintiffs would be unable to prove the liability of the car manufacturer under the *lex loci delicti* and the *lex fori*. The driver of the care may have committed no wrong under the *lex loci delicti*. Conversely, the *lex fori* (Indian law) would hold the driver (and not the manufacturer of the car) responsible under the law of tort.

ii. Defamation

In cross-border tortious claims in defamation, the place of publication may differ from the country where the material is printed or issued or the place where a reputation has been damaged. Identifying the applicable law may not be straightforward. Under the double actionability rule, the victim would have to prove that the defamatory behaviour was actionable under the law of the country where it originated and in India.[76] Consider the following scenario: A (a permanent resident of Delhi) sues B (a permanent resident of Sydney) for libellous material published in Sydney. The place of the occurrence of the tort may be: (1) Sydney (the place where the material was published); (2) India (where A's reputation has been damaged); or (3) both. Under present principles of Indian private international law, A would have to prove that the act is actionable under the laws of India and New South Wales.

iii. Unjust Enrichment

Unjust enrichment occurs when one person is enriched at the expense of another.[77] A claim for unjust enrichment may arise when a person has received money: (1) by mistake; (2) by taking advantage of another's position; or (3) for a purpose that has failed.[78] In such circumstances, the person enriched is under an obligation 'by the ties of natural justice and equity, to refund

[75] ibid.

[76] For a detailed discussion on the law of tort on defamation in India, see Sapre (n 68) 269–328.

[77] See A Singh, *Law of Contract and Specific Relief* 12th edn (Eastern Book Company, 2017) 558 referring to the decision of the English court in *Moses v Macferlan* [1760] 2 Burr 1005, 1012.

[78] ibid.

the money'.[79] In other words, the principal remedy for unjust enrichment would be restitution or disgorgement of the benefit obtained.[80] A claim for unjust enrichment may involve a foreign element where, for instance, a person in India has been enriched in India at the expense of a person overseas. Such claims would be subject to double actionability where the plaintiff would have to prove the defendant's liability to make restitution under Indian law and the relevant foreign law. In India, the Supreme Court has in *Ms Nagpur Golden Transport Co v Ms Nath Traders & Ors*[81] and *Indian Council for Enviro-Legal Action v Union of India*[82] observed that unjust enrichment is neither founded on consent nor wrongdoing. The cause of action not based on contract or tort, but is a cause of action in its own right.[83] Occasionally, however, the Supreme Court has referred to claims of unjust enrichment as based on 'implied contracts'. Consequently, a cross-border claim based on unjust enrichment may fail as a result of the application of double actionability by not being a tort under the *lex fori* (Indian law).

iv. Environmental Torts

An environmental tort would give rise to a cross-border claim when nuisance or pollutants cross boundaries.[84] This may be the position when contaminants in a river from an industry in one country (for example, Bangladesh) adversely affect the health and safety of citizens in another nation (for example, India) who have access to drinking water drawn from the contaminated river. There is no clarity on whether the doctrine of double actionability extends to cross-border claims on environmental pollution under Indian private international law. In this connection, the Supreme Court's dictum in *Union Carbide and Others v Union of India and Others*[85] deserves mention. The decision is considered seminal under Indian law, as the first case in which the Court was called upon to rule on an international tort. The dispute arose from the leakage of lethal gas from a plant in Bhopal that was owned and controlled by an American parent corporation. The leakage resulted in the death of hundreds of Indians.[86] The Court applied Indian law to the dispute.[87] However, it did not comment on how it determined the applicable law. It appears that the Court applied the exception to double actionability. Thus, Indian law may have been applied because India had the most significant connection to the claim. In all other disputes where the Court applies double actionability to identify the applicable laws, it will first ascertain whether the tort was actionable in the foreign country where the cause of action giving rise to the tort occurred and secondly whether the claim is valid under the Indian law of tort.

Under the Indian law of tort, a claim for environmental damage would generally be actionable in negligence if the defendant breached a duty of care towards the victims. The injured party may claim damages caused by the wrongdoer's negligence. In certain circumstances, the tortfeasor may be subject to absolute liability, if the environmental damage has been caused by a hazardous

[79] ibid.

[80] [2011] 12 SCC 745.

[81] AIR [2012] SC 357, referring to Lord Wright in *Fibrosa Spolka Akcyjna v Fairbairn Lawson Combe Barbour Ltd* [1942] 2 ALL ER 122 (HL).

[82] (2011) 8 SCC 161 152–154, 159 and 161.

[83] ibid.

[84] See S Pitel et al '*Private International Law in Common Law Canada: Cases, Texts and Materials*' 4th edn (Emond Publishing, 2016) 684 (Pitel, *Private International Law in Common Law Canada*).

[85] [1991] 4 SCC 584. For a detailed discussion, see U Baxi, *Inconvenient Forum and Convenient Catastrophe: The Bhopal Case*, Bombay 1986.

[86] ibid.

[87] ibid.

or inherently dangerous activity.[88] In such circumstances, the negligence of the tortfeasor would be irrelevant.[89] Cross-border environmental damage will therefore be actionable in India if, in addition to being tortious under Indian law, the damage was caused by conduct considered wrongful under the law of the foreign country where the act originated.

v. Unfair and Restrictive Trade Practices

An unfair or restrictive trade practice may have a cross-border effect when it adversely constrains competition in another country. For instance, the act of a foreign manufacturer who agrees with a supplier in another country to put a ceiling on the sale of a product to increase its price would be construed as restrictive under the legal principles of some countries such as India.[90] Likewise, a practice may be unfair when a foreign manufacturer of athletic clothing falsely represents that the use of a certain type of sweatpants will facilitate weight loss. A person who has suffered harm or injury as a result of the unfair or restrictive trade practice of a foreign entity and who is suing before a court in India would therefore have to prove that the act was: (1) actionable as a wrong under the law of the foreign country where it originated; and (2) actionable under the domestic provisions of Indian law of tort. In India, such activities are generally considered as anti-competitive and so are prohibited under the Competition Act 2002[91] (CA). Such activities are additionally actionable as torts under Indian law. A restrictive trade practice will become a tort. It will be regulated by the provisions of the Consumer Protection Act 1986[92] (CPA) when it 'tends to bring about manipulation in price or its conditions of delivery or to affect the flow of supplies in the market relating to goods or services … to impose on the consumers, unjustified costs or restrictions'.[93] Likewise, an unfair trade practice would become a tort if 'promotes the sale, use or supply of any goods or … service' by adopting an unfair or deceptive practice.[94] Accordingly, cross-border claims which satisfy the prerequisites of the CPA may be actionable under the double actionability rule.

vi. Intellectual Property

The application of the doctrine of double actionability to the infringement of intellectual property rights would invariably result in the application of Indian law which will be the *lex loci delicti* and the *lex fori*. Consider the following illustrations. A (a company incorporated in Delhi) allegedly infringes a registered trademark in the name of 'Sav-n-More' which is owned by B (a company incorporated in Singapore) and used by B to sell clothes online across the globe, including India. A starts a website under the name of 'Sav-n-More Ltd' to sell clothes in India. Accordingly, B sues A in the courts of Delhi for infringement of the trademark. In this illustration, the *lex loci delicti* and *lex fori* are both Indian law. Similarly, consider the infringement of a geographical indication such as 'Champagne' (a form of wine made from grapes grown in the area by the same name in France) which refers to a sign or symbol to identify

[88] See the decision of the Supreme Court in *MC Mehta v. Union of India*, [1987] 1 SCC 395. Also see Sapre (n 68) 509–511.
[89] ibid.
[90] See s 27 of the ICA.
[91] Act No 12 of 2003.
[92] Act No 68 of 1986.
[93] ibid, s 2(nnn).
[94] ibid, s 2(r).

goods originating from a specific region that gives the product a distinct quality, reputation or characteristic. Assume that A (a manufacture in India) has infringed a geographical indication by manufacturing wine by the name of 'Champagne'. The infringement occurred in India. The *lex loci delicti* and the *lex fori* would result in the application of Indian law.

III. Reflections on Indian Law: Some Insights Based on Global Trends

A. General Remarks

As we have seen, Indian private international law continues to hold fast to the doctrine of 'double actionability'. In contrast, global trends demonstrate that the development of conflict of law rules on applicable law for non-contractual obligations has been revolutionised. The doctrine of double actionability has been discarded in most jurisdictions, including 'mature common law systems'[95] such as Canada,[96] Australia[97] and New Zealand[98] for being 'notoriously difficult to understand and apply'.[99] India's BRICS partners, Russia and China, have also abandoned the double actionability rule which was historically employed to determine applicable law in disputes[100] for operating in favour of the defendant to the disadvantage of the plaintiff, leading to 'absurd and anomalous results'.[101] The principles of Australian and Canadian private international law prescribe the strict application of the *lex loci delicti* (the law of the place of the occurrence of the tort) which found a place in the UK's 1995 Act.[102] The 1995 Act's flexible exception rule does not find any place under the laws of these legal systems.[103] There is no reported case in which the courts have clarified whether the *lex loci delicti* rule would be disregarded if it contravenes an overriding mandatory norm or the public policy (*ordrè public*) of Australia or Canada.

In Australia, the courts confirmed the strict application of the *lex loci delicti* in the leading cases of *John Pfeiffer Pty Ltd v Rogerson*[104] and *Regie Nationale des Usines Renault SA v Zhang*.[105] In both cases, the High Court of Australia rejected the common law's flexible exception for its ability to undermine certainty and predictability.[106] The dicta underscored the importance of

[95] See A Briggs, *Private International Law in Myanmar* (OUP, 2015) 108. [Briggs, *PIL in Myanmar*].
[96] See Pitel (n 84) 651.
[97] See Davies et al, *Nygh's Conflict of Laws in Australia* 9th edn (LexisNexis Butterworths, 2020) 424 [*Nygh's Conflict of Laws*].
[98] See s 10 of the Private International Law (Choice of Law in Tort) Act 2017 [New Zealand PIL Act].
[99] See *Nygh's Conflict of Laws* (n 97) 424. See also R Mortenson et al, *Private International Law in Australia* 3rd edn (Lexis Nexis, 2011) 443–445 for other mechanism that were historically employed in Australia to identify the applicable law.
[100] See SC Symeonides, *Codifying Choice of Law Around the World: An International Comparative Analysis* (OUP, 2014) 83.
[101] See Z Huo 'An imperfect improvement: the new conflict of laws act of the People's Republic of China' [2011] *International and Comparative Law Quarterly* 1065, 1089.
[102] See the decision of the Australian courts in *John Pfeiffer Pty Ltd v Rogerson* [2000] 203 CLR 503; and *Regie Nationale des Usines Renault SA v Zhang* [2002] 210 CLR 491; and the decisions of the Canadian courts in *Tolofson v Jenson* [1994] 3 SCR 1022; and *Wong v Lee* [2002] OJ No 885.
[103] ibid.
[104] [2000] 203 CLR 503.
[105] [2002] 210 CLR 491.
[106] Also see Australian Law Reform Commission Report [ALRC], 'Choice of Law' Report No 58, Ch 6, available at: www8.austlii.edu.au/cgi-bin/download.cgi/cgi-bin/download.cgi/download/au/other/lawreform/ALRC/1992/58.pdf which recommended the application of the a flexible exception to displace the *lex loci delicti* if law of another country was the proper law of the tort and had a significant relationship with its occurrence and the parties.

exclusively applying the law of the place of the tort for being uniform, respecting territorial sovereignty and for respecting the parties' reasonable expectation. In *Distillers Co (Biochemicals) Ltd v Thompson*[107] the court clarified the mechanism to identify the place of the commission (or the occurrence) of the tort. Accordingly, it stated the

> right approach is, when the tort is complete, to look back over a series of events constituting it and ask, where in substance did the cause of action occur?[108]

In the absence of any statutory provisions, there is no special mechanism to identify the applicable law in complex disputes such as product liability and defamation. Over time, the courts have, however, interpreted the *lex loci delicti* rule while adjudicating such complex disputes. In product liability cases, the mechanism to identify the *lex loci delicti* depends on the type of claim. The law of the country where the product was manufactured would govern any dispute which arises from the damage which has been caused by a defect in the good.[109] Conversely, the law of the country where the product was marketed or sold would govern disputes which arise from the damage that has been caused from the product where the manufacturer has failed to warn the user of the inherent risks associated therein.[110] The place of manufacture would be irrelevant in the latter type of disputes. In cross-border disputes arising in connection with defamation, the *lex loci delicti* refers to the laws of all the countries connected to the claim where the material was received.[111] For instance, in a lawsuit concerning the publication of libelous material, which has been distributed in India, Australia and New Zealand, the Australian court would individually invoke the defamation laws of all three countries.[112] In common law Canada, the application of the *lex loci delicti* has been justified on the ground that people ordinarily presume 'to be governed by the law of the place where they happen to be and expect that the concomitant legal benefits and responsibilities will be defined accordingly'.[113]

The strict application of the *lex loci delicti* rule was confirmed by the Supreme Court in *Tolofson v Jenson*[114] and *Wong v Lee*.[115] Although leading scholars have argued in favour of the flexible exception rule to prevent injustice when both the parties are residents or nationals of the forum,[116] these opinions have not found favour among the courts.[117] The Canadian judiciary has frowned upon its application given its ability to hamper certainty and create or prolong litigation with the task of tracing the relevant contacts and weighing them qualitatively against one another.[118] In *Wong*, the Court accordingly stated the *lex loci delicti* would apply 'notwithstanding a high degree of connection between [the] litigants and the place of the forum'.[119] In due course, the Canadian courts have interpreted the *lex loci delicti* rule while identifying the applicable law for certain particular types of torts. In the absence of any statutory provisions, this mechanism

[107] [1971] AC 458.
[108] ibid 469.
[109] See *Distillers Co (Biochemicals) Ltd* (n 107); *John Pfeiffer* (n 102); and *Pulido v RS Distributions Pty Ltd* [2003] 177 FLR 401. See also, Mortenson et al (n 99) 448; and *Nygh's Conflict of Laws* (n 97) 428.
[110] See *Distillers Co (Biochemicals) Ltd* ibid; *John Pfeiffer* ibid; and *Pulido* ibid. See also, Mortenson ibid, 448; and *Nygh's Conflict of Laws* ibid 428.
[111] *Nygh's Conflict of Laws* ibid 452–453.
[112] ibid.
[113] Pitel (n 84) 650.
[114] [1994] 3 SCR 1022. Also see Pitel ibid 651.
[115] [2002] OJ No 885.
[116] See Pitel (n 84) 658–659, 673–675.
[117] ibid, referring to *Wong* (n 102).
[118] ibid 659.
[119] ibid 676–675 referring to *Wong* (n 102).

(to interpret the *lex loci delicti*) has not been clearly defined and remains open to interpretation. Nonetheless, a close examination of the interpretation of the *lex loci delicti* in complex cases on tortious liability indicates that the place of the commission or occurrence of the tort is understood to mean the place of the damage in such disputes. In product liability cases, the place of the occurrence of the tort refers to the place of direct (and not consequential) injury, provided that: (1) the goods have entered through the usual channels of trade; and (2) the manufacturer could have reasonably foreseen its consumption in the country of harm.[120] Likewise, in defamation cases, the place of tort has been interpreted as the place where the victim has suffered an injury to his or her reputation.[121] The place of publication would be irrelevant if the reputation has been injured in another country by being the victim's place of residence or business.[122] In case of unfair competition or restraint of competition, the place of tort will be construed as the place(s) where the effect has been felt.[123] The governing law in claims arising from unjust enrichment will be the country which is most closely connected with the causal act.[124] Thus, for instance, the applicable law in a claim to restore the benefits of unjust enrichment arising in connection to a person's ownership of immovable property will be that of the country where the land is situated.[125] In cross-border disputes concerning the infringement of intellectual property in Canada, the *lex loci delicti* will be the local law (of the province) provided that the legislation affords protection to that right.[126] For instance, the governing law in a claim concerning piracy occurring in Canada of copyrighted material, in the form of a software which has been registered in Australia, would be that of Canada under the *lex loci delicti* rule. The governing law would not be Australian law, even though Australia is the place where the right is protected by registration.[127]

In comparison, the private international law of New Zealand resonates with the provisions of the 1995 Act insofar as it prescribes the application of the *lex loci delicti* coupled with the flexible exception rule.[128] There is, however, no reported case on the development of special rules in particular torts in New Zealand.

Russian and Chinese private international law has similarly displaced the convoluted double actionability rule in favour of certain clear, predictable rules to identify the applicable law in cross-border disputes on non-contractual matters. As such, the mechanism to identify the applicable law depends on whether the claim is of a general or special nature in these legal systems.[129] Under the laws of both these countries, the law expressly chosen by the parties will govern the dispute under the doctrine of party autonomy, provided that the choice is made *ex-post* (that is, after the injury has occurred).[130] The restrictions to party autonomy 'aim to prevent the socially stronger party from imposing its unilateral choice on the weaker party'.[131] Russian private international

[120] *Morgan v Pyle National (Canada) Ltd* [1973] 43 DLR (3d) 239 (SCC); and J Walker, *Halsbury's Laws of Canada: Conflict of Laws* (Lexis Nexis, 2016) 556, 563.

[121] See Walker, ibid 566–567 referring to *Gorton v Australian Broadcasting Commission* [1974] 22 FLR 181; and *Maple v David Syme & Co* [1975] 1 NSWLR 97 (Sup. Ct. NSW) ff 4.

[122] ibid.

[123] See Walker ibid 569.

[124] ibid 569–570.

[125] ibid 570.

[126] ibid 567.

[127] ibid 567, ff 1.

[128] see ss 7 and 8 of the New Zealand PIL Act.

[129] See Arts 1219–1223 of the Civil Code of the Russian Federation 2015 [Civil Code of Russia] and Arts 44–47 of the Law of the People's Republic of China on the Laws Applicable to Foreign-Related Civil Relations, 2010 [Chinese PIL].

[130] Art 1219(3) of the Civil Code of Russia; and Art 44(3) of Chinese PIL.

[131] See Z Huo 'An imperfect improvement: the new conflict of laws act of the People's Republic of China' [2011] *International and Comparative Law Quarterly* 1065, 1089.

law, however, further limits party autonomy to the choice of the law of the forum (*lex fori*).[132] In the absence of an express choice, the habitual residence of the parties obtains the pride of place, provided that it is common.[133] In the absence of such commonality, the *lex loci delicti* will be applicable as a general rule in these countries to determine the rights and obligations between the parties.[134] However, neither Russian nor Chinese private international law provide any guidance to resolve the ambiguities that may arise if the event giving rise to the tort and damage happens to occur in different countries.

In Russia, there are special rules to identify the applicable law for claims arising in connection to product liability, unfair competition and unjust enrichment. In cases of product liability, the victim may choose to be governed by the law of the place where: (1) she or he has a residence or principal place of business; (2) the manufacturer has its residence or principal place of business; or (3) the place where the goods were acquired.[135] Disputes concerning unfair competition and unjust enrichment will be governed respectively by the law of the country whose market has been affected and the place where the causal act took place.[136]

In China, there are special rules to identify the applicable law for claims arising in connection to product liability, defamation, the infringement of intellectual property, unjust enrichment and *negotiorum gestio* (claiming payment for the voluntary management of the affairs of another). The applicable law in cross-border product liability cases is that of the habitual residence of the victim. This rule may be departed in two circumstances: (1) when the victim instead prefers the application of the law of the principal place of business of the manufacturer or the place of damage; or (2) the tortfeasor (ie manufacturer) has not engaged in any business in the country of the victim's habitual residence.[137] In a related vein, cross-border disputes on defamation occurring on the internet are governed by the habitual residence of the victim.[138] At the same time, disputes concerning the infringement of intellectual property will be regulated by the law of the place where the right is protected (*lex loci protectionis*).[139] In the case of unjust enrichment and *negotiorum gestio*, the law of the common habitual residence of the parties is applicable; failing which, the law where the causal fact took place would govern the dispute.[140]

The codifications of Russia[141] and China[142] authorise a court to refuse to apply the governing law if it contravenes an overriding mandatory provision or the public policy (*ordrè public*) of the forum.

The doctrine of double actionability does not find a place in the principles of private international law of India's neighbour, Nepal. Part 6 of the National Civil Code Act 2017 which codifies the principles of private international law of this country prescribes the application of the *lex loci delicti* as a general rule to govern all tortious claims which involve a foreign element.[143] Therefore, it appears that party autonomy in the choice of law is not recognised under Nepalese private international law of tort. In certain circumstances, the law of the place of the occurrence of the consequences would, however, override the application of

[132] Art 1219(3) of the Civil Code of Russia.

[133] ibid; Art 44(2) of the Chinese PIL.

[134] Art 1219(1) of the Civil Code of Russia; Art 44(1) of the Chinese PIL.

[135] Art 1221 of the Civil Code of Russia.

[136] ibid, Arts 1222 and 1223.

[137] Art 45 of the Chinese PIL.

[138] ibid, Art 46

[139] ibid, Art 50.

[140] ibid, Art 47.

[141] Arts 1192 and 1193 of the Civil Code of Russia.

[142] Arts 4 and 5 of the Chinese PIL.

[143] Art 712(1) of the National Civil Code Act 2017 (Nepalese PIL).

the *lex loci delicti* rule, unless the former cannot be identified.[144] In such circumstances, the *lex loci delicti* would continue to govern the tortious claim.[145] In cross-border disputes on unjust enrichment, the National Civil Code Act 2017 stipulates the application of the law of the country where the act was done, as a special rule.[146] There apart, the codification does not prescribe any other special rules for other forms of non-contractual obligations such as product liability, unfair competition or the infringement of intellectual property, to name a few.

The doctrine of double actionability has not been reported to have been relevant in identifying the applicable law in the EU, South Korea or Turkey.

In the EU, the law on the subject is regulated by the provisions of the Rome II Regulation. The identification of the governing law primarily depends on the express and implied (or tacit) choice of the parties.[147] The parties are free to choose the governing law *ex-ante* and *ex-post* – i.e. before and after the injury occurred.[148] The choice of a soft law or a non-state law such as the Principles of European Tort Law (PETL)[149] is, however, not permitted under the Rome II Regulation,[150] except if the parties have incorporated the terms of such non-binding legal provisions by reference into their contract.[151] In this manner, the application of the doctrine of party autonomy under the Rome II is similar to that under the Rome I Regulation.[152] In the absence of an express selection, the tacit choice of the law by the parties will govern the disputes provided that their intentions of being regulated by that legal system can be 'demonstrated with reasonable certainty by the facts of the case'.[153]

In the absence of an express or tacit choice, the identification of the applicable law depends on whether the claim is of a general or complex nature. The general rule is prescribed in Article 4, which stipulates the application of the law of the habitual residence of the parties will apply provided that it is common.[154] The habitual residence, thus, obtains the pride of place.[155] In the absence of such commonality, the law of the place where the actual damage occurs would govern the dispute under the *lex loci damni* rule.[156] The place where the event giving rise to the tort or the consequential injury occurs is, therefore, irrelevant.[157] To illustrate, the law that would govern a dispute arising between two Australians as a result of a personal injury in a motor vehicle accident in Rome due to the negligence of the driver would be that of Australia, due to the

[144] ibid, Art 712(2).

[145] ibid.

[146] ibid, Art 713. For the definition of 'unjust enrichment' under Nepalese law, see Art 664.

[147] TK Graziano, 'Freedom to Choose the Applicable Law in Tort – Articles 14 and 4(3) of the Rome II Regulation' in J Ahern and W Binchy (eds), *The Rome II Regulation on the Law Applicable to Non-Contractual Obligations: A New Litigation Regime* (Martinus Nijhoff Publishers, 2009) 113 et seq.

[148] ibid 116–117.

[149] See F Busnelli et al, *Principles of European Tort Law: Text and Commentary* (2005) available at https://link.springer.com/book/10.1007/3-211-27751-X.

[150] Graziano (n 147) 119.

[151] ibid.

[152] See Recital 13 to the Rome I Regulation.

[153] Graziano (n 147) 119–120.

[154] See Art 4(2) of the Rome II Regulation. See also, J von Hein, 'Article 4 and Traffic Accidents' in J Ahern and W Binchy (eds), *The Rome II Regulation on the Law Applicable to Non-Contractual Obligations: A New Litigation Regime* (Martinus Nijhoff Publishers, 2009) 160–165 [von Hein, *Article 4 and Traffic Accidents*]; and J von Hein, 'Article 4 in Rome Regulations: Commentary on the European Rules of the Conflict of Laws' (Calliess eds) 509–517 [von Hein, *Article 4 Rome II*].

[155] Art 4(2) of the Rome II Regulation; von Hein, *Article 4 and Traffic Accidents*, ibid 160–165; and von Hein, *Article 4 Rome II*, ibid 509–517.

[156] Recitals 6 and 18 and Art 4(1) of the Rome II Regulation; von Hein, *Article 4 and Traffic Accidents*, ibid 158–160; and von Hein, *Article 4 Rome II*, ibid 497–509.

[157] ibid.

common residence of the persons involved. If, however, the dispute arose between an Australian and a French driver, the law that will govern would be that of Italy as the place where the damage occurred. It would, therefore, be irrelevant that the person injured eventually died in Australia due to the injury.

As a last resort, the Rome II Regulation permits, through an 'escape clause', the application of the law of another legal system provided that the tort in question is 'manifestly more closely connected' with that country.[158] The instrument does not stipulate a set of indicative factors to illustrate the circumstances in which the escape clause may be invoked. The commentaries, however, clarify that its application would be permitted only when another country is significantly more closely connected to the dispute.[159] In doing so, the EU's conflict of law rules retains the flexibility in identifying the applicable law in non-contractual matters – as was the case in contractual issues. Unlike the exception developed by the English court in *Boys v Chaplin*,[160] the Rome II Regulation does not permit the law derived under the escape clause to apply exclusively to a particular issue of the claim.[161] In other words, the law derived under the escape clause will govern the (entire) dispute and not merely an issue.

Articles 5–12 of the Rome II Regulation operate as *lex specialis* rules to identify the applicable law for complex cases for which the general rule may be inappropriate. The special rules govern disputes arising from product liability,[162] unfair competition,[163] environmental damage,[164] the infringement of intellectual property,[165] industrial action,[166] unjust enrichment,[167] *negotiorum gestio*[168] (claiming payment for the voluntary management of the affairs of another) and *culpa in contrahendo* (the parties' standard of conduct in pre-contractual dealings).[169] The rules are formulated to balance the interests of the parties and, thus, prevent injustice. For instance, Article 5 of the Rome II Regulation stipulates the conflict of law rule on the applicable law for disputes arising from the use of a defective product. In this respect, the term 'product' has been interpreted according to Article 2 of the Product Liability Directive as all movables, including those incorporated into another immovable.[170] The express and inferred choice of the parties remains as a defining factor to discern the applicable law for disputes on product liability. In the absence of such choice, the law of the habitual residence of the parties is similarly applicable (as for general disputes involving tortious claims) to the extent that it is common to the victim and the tortfeasor.[171]

[158] See Art 4(3) of the Rome II Regulation; Stone (n 22) 196; R Fentiman, 'The Significance of Close Connection' in J Ahern and W Binchy (eds), *The Rome II Regulation on the Law Applicable to Non-Contractual Obligations: A New Litigation Regime* (Martinus Nijhoff Publishers, 2009) 85 et seq.; and C Schmid and T Pinkel, 'Article 5 Rome II' in Calliess (ed) *Rome Regulations: Commentary on the European Rules of the Conflict of Laws* (Wolters Kluwer 2015) 562–566.

[159] See, Stone, ibid 196. Also see Fentiman, ibid 85; and Schmid and Pinkel, ibid 562–566.

[160] [1971] AC 356.

[161] Briggs, *Conflict of Laws* (n 2) 263.

[162] Art 5 of the Rome II Regulation.

[163] ibid, Art 6. But see Art 6(4) which states that party autonomy does not extend to disputes arising in relation to unfair competition.

[164] ibid, Art 7.

[165] ibid, Art. 8. But see Art 8(3) which states that party autonomy does not extend to disputes arising in relation to the infringement of intellectual property.

[166] ibid, Art 9.

[167] ibid, Art 10.

[168] ibid, Art 11.

[169] ibid, Art 12.

[170] Schmid and Pinkel (n 158) 544–545.

[171] Art 4(2) of the Rome II Regulation. Also see von Hein, *Article 4 Rome II* (n 154) 509–517.

In the absence of commonality, the Rome II Regulation imbibes a 'seven-step cascade system of connecting factors' to identify the applicable law.[172] In such circumstances, the law of the place where: (1) the person suffering the damage has its habitual residence; (2) the product was acquired; or (3) the damage occurred (*lex loci damni*) would govern the dispute provided that the product in question was marketed in either of these jurisdictions.[173] The law of the habitual residence of the tortfeasor (namely, the manufacturer) would, however, be applicable if the defective product in question was not reasonably foreseen to be marketed in those countries.[174] Nonetheless, the law of another country may be invoked in the form of an 'escape clause' provided that such legal system is 'manifestly more closely connected' with the dispute.[175] To illustrate, the law that would govern a dispute before a French court adjudicating the liability of the manufacturer of a self-driving car produced in Ohio, which resulted in an injury to its user (habitually resident in France) while driving to work in Paris, would primarily depend on the choice of the parties. In the absence of an express or implied choice, the law that would govern the dispute would be French law by being the habitual residence of the victim if the car had been marketed in that jurisdiction. If the car had not been marketed in France, then the law of the place where the car was acquired, for instance, Scotland would apply if it had been marketed there. The law of the habitual residence of the manufacturer (Ohio) would, however, apply if the marketing in France or Scotland had not been foreseeable. In the present scenario, however, the court may at its discretion invoke the escape clause and apply the French law since it is manifestly more closely connected with the tort by being the place where the victim habitually resides and the place of injury.

Tortious claims for damages arising from an act of unfair competition and restriction of competition are governed by the law of the country 'where competitive relations or the collective interests of consumers are, or are likely to be, affected', except when it adversely affects the interests of a specific competitor.[176] In such circumstances, the general rule prescribed in Article 4 would be applicable.[177] The doctrine of party autonomy is, however, not extended to claims for unfair competition.[178] Similarly, disputes for environmental damage would be governed by the law of the country where the event giving rise to the damage occurred.[179] Disputes arising from the infringement of intellectual property shall be governed by the law of the place where the right is granted under the *lex loci protectionis* rule.[180] At the same time, non-contractual obligations concerning the liability of a worker or an employer for damages in the course of an industrial action would be governed by the law of the place where the action has or will be taken.[181] The governing law may be displaced if it contravenes an overriding mandatory norm or the public policy of the forum-state.[182]

[172] Schmid and Pinkel (n 158) 546.

[173] Art 5(1) of the Rome II Regulation; and Schmid and Pinkel, ibid 546 et seq.

[174] ibid, Art 5(2); and Schmid and Pinkel, ibid 555–556.

[175] See Stone (n 22) 196. Also see Fentiman (n 158) 85; and Schmid and Pinkel, ibid 562–566.

[176] Art 6(1) and (2) of the Rome II Regulation; and S Augenhofer, *Unfair Competition and Acts Restricting Free Competition: Commentary on the European Rules of the Conflict of Laws* (Calliess eds) 570–602.

[177] ibid, Art 6(2).

[178] ibid, Art 6(4).

[179] ibid, Art 7. Also see, J von Hein, *Environmental Damage: Commentary on the European Rules of the Conflict of Laws* (Calliess eds) 603–624.

[180] See Art 8 of the Rome II Regulation. See also, K de la Durantaye, *Infringement of Intellectual Property: Commentary on the European Rules of the Conflict of Laws* (Calliess eds) 526–642.

[181] ibid, Art 9. Also, Rödl, *Industrial Action: Commentary on the European Rules of the Conflict of Laws* (Calliess eds) 643–657.

[182] ibid, Arts 16 and 26. See also, Briggs, *Conflict of Laws* (n 2) 256 which clarifies that the Rome II Regulation does not follow the trend found in the Rome I Regulation that defines the circumstances in which the applicable law will be considered to override a mandatory provision of the forum-state in the EU.

In certain circumstances, the provisions of the Rome II Regulation may be replaced by the 1971 Hague Traffic Accidents Convention (1971 Hague Convention])[183] or the 1973 Hague Convention on the Law Applicable to Products Liability (1973 Hague Convention).[184] This is because 12 EU states have ratified the 1971 Convention. On the other hand, six EU states have ratified the 1973 Hague Convention. Austria, Czechoslovakia, Belgium, France, Luxemburg, Lithuania, Latvia, the Netherlands, Poland, the Czech Republic, Slovakia, Slovenia and Spain have ratified the 1971 Hague Convention. Finland, France, Luxemburg, the Netherlands, Norway and Spain, have ratified the 1973 Hague Convention. The precise relationship between the 1971 and the 1973 Hague Conventions and the Rome II Regulation has been subjected to much debate.[185] Although some academic writings opine that the conflict of law rules of the Rome II Regulation would undoubtedly take precedence among its signatories,[186] others confirm that this would depend on the Member State before which the claim has been raised.[187]

As the name suggests, the scope of the 1971 Hague Convention is limited to the determination of the governing law for transnational disputes arising from traffic accidents. In comparison, the 1973 Hague Convention specifically addresses the conflict of law issues on the applicable law for cross-border disputes arising as a result of damage caused by the use of a defective product. For example, consider a French court which has been called upon to decide the rights and liabilities of the parties arising out of an accident. The accident resulted in an injury to an Australian tourist in France. The accident was due to the negligent driving of a French driver. The French court would refer to the 1971 Hague Convention to determine the applicable law. In contrast, the conflict of law rules on applicable law stipulated in the 1973 Hague Convention would be invoked if the damage had been caused by the failure of a component of the product, including the car itself.

The private international laws of South Korea[188] and Turkey[189] recognise party autonomy in choice of law as a general conflict of law rule.[190] However, the parties may choose any law to govern their dispute arising out of a non-contractual obligation after (*ex post*) and not before (*ex ante*) the injury occurred.

In the absence of an express choice, South Korean private international law prescribes the application of the law of the place where the tort occurred (*lex loci delicti*) as a general rule.[191] However, if the victim and the tortfeasor have a common habitual residence, then the law of that country will apply.[192] The general rule is displaced in disputes arising from the infringement of intellectual property and unjust enrichment. Such disputes will respectively be governed by the

[183] The text of the 1971 Hague Convention on Traffic Accidents is available at: www.hcch.net/en/instruments/conventions/full-text/?cid=81. For a list of signatories to the 1971 Convention, visit: www.hcch.net/en/instruments/conventions/status-table/?cid=81.

[184] The text of the 1973 Hague Convention on the Law Applicable to Products Liability is available at: www.hcch.net/en/instruments/conventions/full-text/?cid=84.

[185] For a detailed discussion on the relationship between the Rome II Regulation and the 1971 Hague Convention, see, von Hein, *Article 4 and Traffic Accidents* (n 161) 157; CI Nagy, 'The Rome II Regulation and Traffic Accidents: Uniform Conflict Rules with Some Room for Forum Shopping – How so?' (2010) 6(1) *Journal of Private International Law* 93, 108, available at SSRN: https://ssrn.com/abstract=1737713; AE Menendez, 'Road Traffic Accidents: From the Hague Convention of 4 May 1971 to Regulation (EC) No. 864/2007 (Rome II)' (2007) 7 *Anuarioespanol Derecho International Private* 505; and M Krvavac, 'The Hague Convention on the Law Applicable to Traffic Accidents and Rome II Regulation' (2018) 79 *Collection of Papers Faculty of Law, NIS* 141.

[186] von Hein, *Article 4 and Traffic Accidents* (n 154) 157.

[187] Nagy (n 185) 108; and Bruyne and Vanleenhove (n 61) 24.

[188] Art 33 of the Act of Private International Law 2016 [South Korean PIL].

[189] Art 34(5) of the Turkish Code on Private International Law and International Civil Procedure 2007 [Turkish PIL].

[190] Art 33 of the South Korean PIL.

[191] ibid, Art 32(1).

[192] ibid, Art 32(2).

lex loci protectionis rule (the law of the place where the intellectual property was granted)[193] and the law of the country where the act took place.[194] South Korean private international law permits the courts to refuse to apply the governing law if it contravenes an overriding mandatory norm.[195] Whether the contravention of the public policy of South Korea will similarly displace the governing law, remains ambiguous.

Turkish private international law prescribes the application of the *lex loci delicti* as a general rule in the absence of a choice, unless the damage occurred in a different country.[196] In the latter circumstance, the *lex loci damni* would govern the claim.[197] As a last resort, Turkish private international law balances predictability with flexibility by making provision for an 'escape clause'.[198] In such circumstances, the *lex loci damni* may be displaced by the law of another country if the relationship arising from the tort is 'more closely connected with that country'.[199] The general rule is displaced in certain complex cases. Accordingly, damages arising from the infringement of intellectual property would be governed by the law of the country where the right is protected (*lex loci protectionis*).[200] Likewise, cross-border disputes in defamation would be governed by the law of the habitual residence of the victim, the habitual residence/place of business of the tortfeasor or the *lex loci damni*, depending on the choice of the victim.[201] These apart, non-contractual liability for damage arising from the use of a product may be regulated by the law of the habitual residence of the victim or the place of business of the manufacturer, depending on the choice of the victim.[202] The applicable law for cross-border disputes on claims concerning unfair competition and restraint of competition would be that of the country whose market is directly affected.[203] Lastly, claims arising from unjust enrichment are governed by the law applicable to the existing transaction or the place where the unjust enrichment occurred.[204]

In contrast, India has been unmoved by global developments insofar as it continues to embrace the doctrine of double actionability to identify the applicable law from cross-border disputes on tort. In the present era, the principle finds a place under the private international laws of some common law systems such as Hong Kong[205] and Singapore.[206] Besides, the principle continues to find a place in the codification of the Japanese private international law.[207] The rule has been severely criticised because it 'appears to co-mingle the law dealing with what we would call today jurisdiction and the choice of law'.[208] The first criterion which tests whether the act is actionable as a tort under the *lex fori* concerns the determination of jurisdiction of the court in an international matter.[209] It is only the second criterion which tests

[193] ibid, Art 24.
[194] ibid, Art 31.
[195] ibid, Art 7.
[196] Art 34(2) of the Turkish PIL.
[197] ibid.
[198] ibid, Art 34(3).
[199] ibid.
[200] ibid, Art 4(3).
[201] ibid, Art 35.
[202] ibid, Art 36.
[203] ibid, Arts 38 and 39.
[204] ibid, Art 39.
[205] See, Art 8 of the Basic Law of the Hong Kong Administrative Region of the People's Republic of China.
[206] See, *Goh Chok Tong v Tang Liang Hong* [1997] I SLR (R) 811; and *Rickshaw Investments Ltd v Nicolai Baron von Uexkull* [2007] 1 SLR 377.
[207] See Art 22(2) of the Japanese Act on the General Rules on the Application of Laws 2007 [Japanese PIL]. Also see K Takahashi, 'A Major Reform of Japanese Private International Law' [2006] *Journal of Private International Law* 311, 333; and SC Symeonides, *Codifying Choice of Law Around the World: An International Comparative Analysis* (OUP, 2014) 84.
[208] See Pitel (n 84) 651.
[209] ibid.

whether the claim is actionable as a wrong under the *lex loci delicti* that appears to be the application of a choice of law rule.[210] Thus, the claimant must 'win twice to win once' for its claim to be successful.[211] In this manner, the rule is chauvinistic by mandating the application of the *lex fori* and prevents access to justice. Moreover, Indian law does not clarify whether the application of the double actionability rule will result in: (1) the concurrent application of the *lex fori* and the *lex loci delicti* (the original position prescribed in *Phillips v Eyre);*[212] or (2) the claim being exclusively governed by the *lex fori* after the claimant demonstrates its actionability under the two laws? As was shown above, in *Sona Devi* the Court indicated the exclusive application of the *lex fori* after the claimant has demonstrated actionability under the two laws.[213] Regardless of its interpretation, legal scholars have criticised the application of the double actionability rule for its susceptibility to presenting a 'false conflict'.[214] A false conflict occurs when the laws of the *lex fori* and the *lex loci delicti* differ, but only one of them is more suited to governing a dispute.[215]

Consider the following illustrations. A (an Austrian tourist travelling to Delhi) is injured in a traffic accident caused by the reckless driving of B (a permanent resident of Delhi). A sues B in a court in Delhi. In this situation, one legal system (the Indian legal system) would plainly be more suitable than the other (the Austrian legal system) in terms of determining the parties' rights and liabilities in respect of each other. Suppose now that A (an American tourist travelling to Delhi) is injured by a shock from an electronic shaver manufactured by B (a company incorporated in China). In this situation, one legal system would be plainly more suited for determining the rights and liabilities of the parties. That would be the Chinese legal system as the defective product was manufactured in its territory and the injured tourist was not Indian. The application of Indian law may accordingly not be justified unless the damage occurred in its territory. The application of the doctrine of double actionability thus presents 'a needless complication'.[216]

B. Moving Past the Obsolete Double Actionability Rule

In light of the foregoing examination of global trends, it is suggested that India abandon the obsolete double actionability rule in favour of clear predictable rules which promote and do not impede access to justice in the Republic. Lawmakers should separate the mechanism for identifying applicable law in disputes on general tortious claims such as nuisance, negligence, or assault and the mechanism for dealing with applicable law in more complex matters such as product liability, environmental damage and unfair competition. Although the promulgation of a statute to this effect is recommended, the Supreme Court of India should in the meanwhile invoke the power conferred upon it by Article 141 of the Constitution[217] to draft guidelines on the subject.

[210] ibid.

[211] Briggs, *Conflict of Laws* (n 2) 274.

[212] (n 5).

[213] *Sona Devi* (n 30) [6].

[214] See B Currie, 'The Constitution and the Choice of Law: Governmental Interests and the Judicial Function' (1958) 26 *University of Chicago Law Review* 9, 10; and JHC Morris, *The Conflict of Laws* 3rd edn (Stevens & Sons, 1984) 527, 529–530; and Tsang (n 58) 88.

[215] ibid.

[216] Tsang (n 58) 90 referring to the remarks of the Australian court in *Breavington v Godleman* 169 CLR 41, 77 (Austl. 1988); and the Supreme Court of Canada in *Tolofson* (n 62) ff 92 which discarded the principle.

[217] See Art 141 of the Constitution of India 1950 which states that '[t]he law declared by the Supreme Court shall be binding on all courts within the territory of India'.

i. Express Choice of Law

It is suggested that Indian private international law recognises the parties' choice of law as a chief factor for identifying the governing law in all cross-border disputes involving non-contractual matters. As has been shown above, the principle has found favour in the laws of a number of civil law jurisdictions. However, in contrast to the Rome II Regulation,[218] the laws of Russia,[219] China,[220] South Korea[221] and Turkey[222] merely permit parties to choose the governing law *ex-post* (after the dispute has arisen). These legal systems have limited party autonomy to protect the interest of the victim, especially if the tortfeasor is a big corporation.

The approach found under the Rome II Regulation, which permits parties to choose governing law *ex ante* and *ex post*,[223] is more favourable for adoption in Indian private international law. The exploitation of weaker and more vulnerable parties, such as consumers or insured persons, may be prevented by limiting an *ex ante* choice of law when it contravenes the overriding mandatory provisions or public policy of India.

As we have seen in chapter 10 on 'The Applicable Law in Contractual Obligations', party autonomy in the choice of law in matters of a contract is permitted in India to the extent that it does not violate the public policy of the forum. In this respect, contracts with weaker parties will be construed to be unconscionable and opposed to the public policy of India under Section 23 of the ICA if:

(1) there is a great disparity in the economic strengths of the parties;[224]
(2) one party cannot trade in goods or services except on the terms of the other,[225] or
(3) one party has no meaningful choice except to accept the terms proposed by the other however unreasonable.[226]

It is suggested that Indian private international law further extend the principle of party autonomy to the choice of soft law and non-state law. Parties may prefer the choice of non-binding legal principles such as soft law and non-state law because 'such instruments can reflect their business relationship better than domestic or international law'.[227] At the same time, unlike in the field of contract, there is a dearth of non-binding legal instruments in matters of tort. The PETL seems to be the only feasible option as of now.

ii. Implied Choice of Law

In the absence of an express choice, the courts in India should ascertain if the parties have impliedly or tacitly chosen a law. It is suggested that India adopt an approach which is similar to that under the Rome II Regulation and recognise the parties' implied choice of law as identifying the applicable law in cross-border tortious disputes. In doing so, however, lawmakers

[218] See Art 14 of the Rome II Regulation.
[219] See Art 1219(3) of the Civil Code of Russia.
[220] See Art 44(3) of the Chinese PIL.
[221] See Art 33 of the South Korean PIL.
[222] See Art 34(5) of the Turkish PIL.
[223] See Art 14 of the Rome II Regulation.
[224] *Amrit Banaspati Co Ltd v State of Punjab* AIR [1992] SC 1075.
[225] ibid.
[226] ibid.
[227] HD Gabriel, 'The Advantages of Soft Law in International Commercial Law: The Role of UNIDROIT, UNCITRAL, and the Hague Conference' (2009) 34 *Brooklyn Journal of International Law* 658, 669.

should prefer a strict test (as in the Rome I Regulation[228]), as opposed to a more lenient yardstick (as in the Rome II Regulation). The latter would only permit the court to identify the intentions of the parties if it is 'demonstrated with reasonable certainty by the facts of the case'.[229] In comparison, the Rome I Regulation mandates that in matters of contract the implied choice should be '*clearly* demonstrated by the … the circumstances of the case'.[230] The incorporation of a stringent standard will reduce the possibility of discretion the judges by leaving little scope for inferring a choice of applicable law.[231]

iii. Absence of a Choice of Law

In the absence of choice, the identification of the applicable law should depend on whether the claim is of a general or special nature.

a. General Rule

The general rule should extend to all tortious claims of a common nature such as negligence, nuisance and assault. Although several countries have prescribed a special rule to identify the applicable law for cross-border disputes arising from tortious claims in defamation, it is suggested that the general rule should be extended to matters of defamation in India. In general, it is suggested that lawmakers in India adopt an approach which is similar to that under the Rome II Regulation when stipulating the mechanism to identify the applicable law in non-contractual matters. Accordingly, the common habitual residence rule should have pride of place under the reformed Indian private international law for its ability to strike 'a fair balance between the interest of the person claimed to be liable to foresee the applicable law and the interests of the person sustaining the damage'.[232] Besides the EU,[233] several legal systems such as those of Russia,[234] China[235] and South Korea[236] have stipulated the common habitual residence rule as the chief means of identifying the applicable law in disputes involving general tortious claims. In the absence of commonality, the application of the *lex loci damni* or the law of the place where the damage occurred is suggested for several reasons. First, the application of the *lex loci damni* will preserve the legal values entrenched in the domestic principles of tort law, namely, the deterrence of tortious acts, the control of delictual behaviour, and the provision of compensation for wrongs suffered.[237] The rule thus complements the chief aim of the law of tort, which is to compensate the victim for another's wrongful behaviour.[238] The place of direct (as opposed to indirect or consequential) damage should be considered for reasons of predictability. Second, the rule does away with inherent difficulties in locating the place of the commission or the occurrence of the tort, by mandating the application of the law of the place where damage was sustained.[239]

[228] See Art 3 of the Rome I Regulation.
[229] ibid, Art 14.
[230] ibid, Art 3(1).
[231] See PE Nygh, *Autonomy in International Contracts* (OUP, 1999) 110.
[232] See von Hein, *Article 4 Rome II* (n 150) 497 referring to the Rome II Regulation.
[233] See Art 4 of the Rome II Regulation.
[234] See Art 1219(2) of the Civil Code of Russia.
[235] See Art 44(2) of the Chinese PIL.
[236] See Art 32(1) of the South Korean PIL.
[237] P Jurčys, 'Applicable Law to Intellectual Property Infringements in Japan: Alternative *Lex Loci Protectionis* Principle' (2010) 24(2) *International Review of Law, Computers & Technology* 193, 195–196.
[238] ibid 195.
[239] ibid 497, which discusses the dissatisfaction with the *lex loci delicti*.

Third, the application of the *lex loci damni* has several economic benefits because it distributes the cost of obtaining legal information among the parties.[240] Last, it enables the tortfeasor to predict the likely consequences of his or her act, insofar as the place where the act is likely to injure another person will normally be foreseeable.[241] By contrast, the *lex loci delicti rule* which finds favour in the laws of Canada,[242] Australia,[243] Russia,[244] China[245] or South Korea[246] is undesirable. This is because the latter rule significantly increases the victim's cost of obtaining legal information by 'frustrating the victim's legitimate desire to structure the insurance of his protected interests according to the standards of his legal environment'.[247]

b. Particular Torts

In complex cases, the direct application of the law of the country where the damage occurred may not be practicable having regard to the special circumstances under which injuries from such torts occur. Categories of particular torts for which a special conflict of law rule must be considered are examined below.

iv. Product Liability

The Rome II Regulation's seven-step cascading system is the most suitable for identifying the applicable law in cross-border disputes on product liability. The conflict of law rule in the Rome II Regulation offers a predictable solution where every dispute arising out of a product liability claim is subjected to a foreseeable set of principles that are known to the parties in advance. Moreover, the Rome II Regulation balances certainty concerning the identification of the applicable law with flexibility in the form of the escape clause, which permits the court to invoke the law of another country provided it is manifestly more closely connected with the tort. In comparison, the private international laws of other civil law jurisdictions such as Turkey,[248] Russia[249] and China[250] are susceptible of being unpredictable insofar as they confer a choice to the victim to select a law from the available options indicated therein according to his or her convenience. The conflict of law rule in common law jurisdictions such as Australia and Canada, which adopt the *lex loci delicti* is similarly unpredictable and is not feasible for not being flexible.

Accordingly, India's convoluted double actionability rule should be replaced with the common habitual residence rule as the primary mechanism to identify the applicable law in cross-border disputes on product liability. In the absence of commonality, the applicable law should be that of: (1) the habitual residence of the victim; (2) the place of acquisition of the product; or in its absence; (3) the place of damage, provided that the goods were marketed in these countries. The law of the manufacturer should be applicable only when the product has not been marketed in any of these jurisdictions. As a last resort, the escape clause should permit

[240] ibid.
[241] ibid 497–498.
[242] See *Tolofson* (n 102); and *Wong* (n 102).
[243] See *John Pfeiffer* (n 102); *and Distillers* (n 107).
[244] Art 1219(2) of the Civil Code of Russia.
[245] See Art 44(2) of the Chinese PIL.
[246] See Art 32(1) of the South Korean PIL.
[247] von Hein, *Article 4 Rome II* (n 154) 502.
[248] See Art 36 of Turkish PIL.
[249] See Art 1221 of the Civil Code of Russia.
[250] See Art 45 of the Chinese PIL.

the application of the law of another country, which has a significantly close connection with the damage, for instance when the tort arises from a contractual relationship between the parties.

v. Unfair Competition and Restrictive Trade Practices

It is suggested that the law of the country which has been adversely affected by an unfair or restrictive trade practice should govern the dispute arising in connection such claim. This conflict of law rule has presently been accepted in the private international laws of the EU,[251] Turkey,[252] Russia[253] and Canada.[254] The means for identifying the governing law for general tortious claims should, nonetheless, continue to apply if the unfair or restrictive trade practice merely affects the interests of a specific competitor (and not several competitors).[255] This approach finds a place in the Rome II Regulation.[256] Such disputes should, therefore, be adjudicated according to the law of the common habitual residence of the parties.[257] The law of the country where the damage occurs should be applicable only in the absence of such commonality.[258]

vi. Unjust Enrichment

Disputes where one person has suffered damage by being unjustly enriched by another are not presently recognised as tortious under the domestic law in India. Consequently, disputes involving a claim for unjust enrichment before a court in India will fail the test of double actionability. It is suggested that claims arising in such matters should be recognised under Indian private international law and subjected to the law of the country where the causal act occurred. For instance, the governing law in a dispute relating to unfinished work by a contractor in Paris who was hired and was paid in advance by a person in New Delhi to paint the latter's home will be that of India, the place where the act (of painting) occurred. This approach has been accepted in the private international laws of the EU,[259] South Korea,[260] Japan,[261] Russia,[262] China,[263] Canada[264] and Nepal.[265]

vii. Environmental Torts

At present, only the Rome II Regulation prescribes a mechanism for identifying the applicable law for cross-border torts arising from environmental damage.[266] In India, although the injury arising from environmental damage is recognised as a tort under domestic law, the application

[251] See Art 6 of the Rome II Regulation.
[252] See Art 38–39 of the Turkish PIL.
[253] See Art 1222 of the Civil Code of Russia.
[254] Walker (n 120) 569–570.
[255] See Art 6(2) of the Rome II Regulation.
[256] ibid.
[257] ibid.
[258] ibid.
[259] ibid, Art 10.
[260] Art 31 of the South Korean PIL.
[261] Art 14 of the Japanese PIL. See also, Takahashi (n 207) 334–336.
[262] Art 1223 of the Civil Code Russian Federation.
[263] Art 47 of the Chinese PIL.
[264] See Walker (n 120) 569–570.
[265] See Art 713 of Nepalese PIL.
[266] See Art 7 of the Rome II Regulation.

of double actionability is likely to subject a tortfeasor to different liabilities with the concurrent application of foreign and national law. For instance, a dispute before a court in India arising from lung injury to persons in Darjeeling due to the escape of poisonous fumes from China would be subjected to the principles of absolute liability under the Indian law of tort, but may require proof of negligence under Chinese law. To avoid such complexities, it is therefore suggested that the present rule be replaced with the application of the law of the country where the damage occurs. Accordingly, the rights of persons in India experiencing an injury as a result of an environmental wrong originating in a foreign country should be decided under the Indian law of tort.

viii. Intellectual Property

It is suggested that the law of the place of the protection of the intellectual property (*lex loci protectionis*) should govern all cross-border claims. This approach finds a place in the private international laws of the EU,[267] China,[268] South Korea[269] and Turkey.[270] The application of double actionability is inappropriate because it obligates the claimant to prove the actionability of the act under the law of the place of the occurrence (*lex loci delicti*) and the *lex fori*. However, in disputes concerning the infringement of intellectual property, the *lex loci delicti* and the *lex fori* will coincide and in an Indian case both refer to Indian law.

IV. Conclusion

In this chapter, we have seen the methods employed by Indian private international law to identify the applicable law in cross-border disputes in non-contractual matters. The lack of experience of Indian courts in adjudicating such disputes was demonstrated. To date, there have only been two cases in which the courts have discussed the mechanism that will be employed in such matters.[271] It was seen that, in the absence of black letter law on the subject, the courts have held firmly to the traditional yet obsolete principles of English common law which stipulate the double actionability rule.[272] Although the UK abandoned the rule with the promulgation of the 1995 Act, in India the courts have explicitly stated that they continue to adhere to the common law principles and not English statutes.[273]

The application of double actionability rule presents several problems. In particular, it seriously debilitates access to justice by requiring the claimant to prove that the act for which it is claiming damages is actionable under the laws of two legal systems. Thus, the claimant must prove that the act was prohibited as: (1) a wrong (not necessarily a tort) under the law of the country where it occurred (*lex loci delicti*); and (2) a tort under Indian law (*lex fori*). In India, the application of double actionability is confusing, to say the least, and unpredictable. The original intention underlying the doctrine was for the laws of the two countries to be applied concurrently once the claimant establishes actionability under the two legal systems. In Indian private

[267] ibid, Art 8.
[268] See Art 50 of the Chinese PIL.
[269] See Art 24 of the South Korean PIL.
[270] See Art 4(3) of the Turkish PIL.
[271] See *Kotah Transport* (n 30); and *Sona Devi* (n 30).
[272] See *Phillips* (n 5).
[273] See *Sona Devi* (n 30) [6].

international law, however, the court has said that the *lex fori* (that is, Indian law) alone will be applied once the claimant has shown actionability under the two legal systems. The exclusive application of the *lex fori* is parochial and chauvinistic.

On the other hand, an inflexible application of the *lex locus delicti* does not come without problems. For instance, consider tortious claims for environmental damage. Is the tort considered to have occurred at the place where the act resulting in the injuries in the form of pollutants originated or is the place where the effects were actually felt from exposure to those pollutants? Similarly, with defamation, is the *locus delicti* the place where libellous material was published or spoken or is it the place where the effects of the material were actually felt by an aggrieved party? The predicament of locating the *locus delicti* persists in most tortious claims.

This chapter demonstrated that Indian law is far behind global trends. The laws of most countries (including common law systems such as Australia, Canada and New Zealand) have discarded the double actionability rule.[274] The laws of other countries (such as in the EU, South Korea and Turkey) have never accepted the convoluted double actionability rule. This chapter consequently urged legislative reform in India. It suggested that the Supreme Court invoke its constitutional powers under Article 141 to set out guidelines that define the mechanisms that the courts will employ to identify applicable law. In this connection, the chapter highlighted the potential inspiration that India may draw from the Rome II Regulation.

This chapter suggested that new principles of Indian private international law on applicable law in non-contractual matters must incorporate party autonomy in the choice of law as a cornerstone. Concerns regarding the exploitation of weaker parties may be addressed by limiting the validity of choice of law to situations in which it does not violate public policy.[275] The adjudicating authority must be able to disregard a choice of law as unconscionable if inter alia the parties agreed on the law merely because the weaker party had no alternative but to accept what the party in a stronger bargaining position put forward.[276] In the absence of an express choice of law, the parties' implied or tacit choice should be ascertained, provided that it can be clearly inferred from the facts of the case.

The chapter further argued that, in the absence of an express or a tacit choice of law, applicable law should be determined by reference to whether a claim is general or special in nature. For general claims, the common habitual residence rule should hold pride of place under any reformed Indian private international law. This will balance the interests of both parties, If the parties do not have a common habitual residence, the law of the place where the direct damage (*lex loci damni*) should govern their dispute. It was also suggested that predictability must be balanced with a flexible escape clause which will permits the court to apply the law of another country if it is manifestly more closely connected with a dispute.

Lastly, the chapter proposed choice of law rules to govern special claims in complex areas, such as product liability, unfair competition, environmental damage and the infringement of intellectual property.

[274] See the text accompanying notes 95–128.
[275] See in this respect s 23 of the ICA.
[276] See in this respect *Amrit Banaspati* (n 220).

PART V

Recognition and Enforcement

12

The Recognition and Enforcement of Foreign Judgments

I. Introduction

Under the traditional concept of sovereignty, every country has exclusive jurisdiction over its territory and its population.[1] For this reason, courts in a state other than where a judgment was pronounced were not historically permitted to give extraterritorial effect to such decisions.[2] In modern times, however, burgeoning agreements among persons, both natural and artificial, have resulted in escalating international trade and commerce and rendered these conventional principles of international law as redundant. A decision arising out of litigation or arbitration may have an impact outside its national borders when the party against whom it is pronounced (also known as the judgment-debtor or award-debtor) has assets in another jurisdiction.[3] In such circumstances, the failure to provide a remedy to the plaintiff would render the decision as merely *brutum fulmen*.[4] The notion of sovereignty does not traditionally prevent a court from refusing to give effect to the decision of a foreign court. However, states have increasingly accommodated the changes caused by the free movement of people and acknowledged the outcome of these judgments by recognising or enforcing them.[5] As Edwards articulates, 'enlightened social values and the facilitation of international relations [call for the recognition and enforcement of foreign judgments]'.[6] A place must, therefore, be found to do justice and 'foster the free flow of commerce and community interrelationships in a shrinking world'.[7] The recognition and enforcement of foreign decisions are therefore conceived as the third pillar of private international law.

This chapter discusses the principles of Indian private international law on the recognition and enforcement of foreign judgments. It is divided into six parts. Section II (section I being this Introduction) provides an overview of the statutory framework on the subject as found in the Code of Civil Procedure 1908 (CPC).[8] It sheds light on the significance of the doctrine of obligation in determining the eligibility of foreign judgments for recognition in India. Section III examines the grounds on which a foreign judgment will be eligible for recognition and

[1] R Michaels 'Recognition and Enforcement of Foreign Judgments in Max Planck Encyclopaedia of Public International Law' available at https://scholarship.law.duke.edu/cgi/viewcontent.cgi?article=2699&context=faculty_scholarship.

[2] ibid.

[3] AB Edwards (Updated by E Kahn), 'Conflict of Laws', in WA Joubert (ed), *The Law of South Africa Vol 2 Part 2* 2nd edn (LexisNexis/Butterworths, 2003) 384, fn 10; and C Forsyth, *Private International Law* 5th edn, (Juta, 2012) 417.

[4] Forsyth, ibid 417.

[5] See Pitel et al, *Private International Law in Common Law Canada: Cases, Texts and Materials* 4th edn (Emond Publishing, 2016) 393 [Pitel, *Private International Law in Common Law Canada*].

[6] See Forsyth, (n 3) 417.

[7] ibid.

[8] Act No 5 of 1908.

enforcement in India. In particular, it discusses the notion of 'international competency' which is the chief indicator to determine the validity of foreign judgments under Indian law. Section IV examines the grounds on which a court may refuse to recognise or enforce a foreign judgment in India. Section V reflects on the principles of Indian private international law based on global trends. It considers the practices of other jurisdictions such as the EU, Australia, New Zealand, Canada, South Africa and Nepal. Further, this section examines whether India should accede to the 2005 Hague Convention on Choice of Agreements (HCCCA)[9] and the 2019 Hague Judgments Convention on the Recognition and Enforcement of Foreign Judgments in Civil and Commercial Matters (the Judgments Convention),[10] which stipulate rules on the recognition and enforcement of foreign judgments. Section VI provides concluding remarks.

II. The Recognition and Enforcement of Foreign Judgments

A. The Statutory Framework

In India, the recognition and enforcement of foreign judgments (including those sounding in money)[11] are regulated by sections 13, 14 and 44-A of the CPC, which extend to the entire country, except the Union Territories of Jammu and Kashmir, the State of Nagaland and other tribal areas.[12] The CPC defines the term 'judgment' as a 'statement given by the judge of the grounds of a decree or order'.[13] Accordingly, a decision pronounced by a court in a jurisdiction

[9] See M Dogauchi and T Hartley, The Permanent Bureau: Hague Conference on Private International Law – Preliminary Document No. 26, Preliminary Draft Convention on Exclusive Choice of Court Agreements, Explanatory Report (December 2004) www.hcch.net/en/publications-and-studies/details4/?pid=3512 [Dogauchi/ Hartley Report].

[10] The text of the 2019 Judgments Convention is available at: https://assets.hcch.net/docs/23b6dac3-7900-49f3-9a94-aa0ffbe0d0dd.pdf. For a detailed discussion on the events leading up to the draft Judgments Convention, see PH Pfund, 'The Project of the Hague Conference on Private International Law to Prepare a Convention on Jurisdiction and the Recognition/Enforcement of Judgments in Civil and Commercial Matters' (1998) 24(1) *Brooklyn Journal of International Law* 7; B Smith, 'The Proposed Hague Convention on Jurisdiction, Recognition and Enforcement of Judgments' (1999) 12(2) *Revue Québécoise de Droit International* 73; C Kessedjian, 'The Permanent Bureau, Hague Conference on Private International Law: Preliminary Document No 7 – International Jurisdiction and Foreign Judgments in Civil and Commercial Matters' (1997), www.assets.hcch.net/docs/76852ce3-a967-42e4-94f5-24be4289d1e5.pdf; P Nygh and F Pocar, Hague Conference on Private International Law: Preliminary Document No. 11 – Preliminary Draft Convention on Jurisdiction and Foreign Judgments in Civil and Commercial Matters (2000), www.hcch.net/en/publications-and-studies/details4/?pid=3494&dtid=35 (Nygh/Pocar Report); The Permanent Bureau, Hague Conference on Private International Law: Preliminary Document No. 16 – Some Reflections on the Present State of Negotiations on the Judgments Project in the Context of the Future Work Programme of the Conference (2002), www.hcch.net/en/publications-and-studies/details4/?pid=3500; Permanent Bureau & Co-Reporters, Hague Conference on Private International Law: Summary of the Outcome of the Discussion in Commission II of the First Part of the Diplomatic Conference (6-20 June 2001), www.hcch.net/en/publications-and-studies/details4/?pid=3499&dtid=35; ATV Mehren, 'Drafting a Convention on International Jurisdiction and the Effects of Foreign Judgments Acceptable Worldwide: Can the Hague Convention Project Succeed' (2001) 49 *American Journal of Comparative Law* 191; GF Calliess, 'Value-added Norms, Local Litigation and Global Enforcement: Why the Brussels Philosophy Failed in the Hague' (2004) 5 *German Law Journal* 1490; K Woestehoff, 'The Drafting Process for a Hague Convention on Jurisdiction and Judgments with Special Consideration of Intellectual Property and E-Commerce' (2005) *LLM Theses and Essays*, Paper No 54, 13, www.digitalcommons.law.uga.edu/stu_llm/54; RA Brand, 'Community Competence for Matters of Judicial Cooperation at the Hague Conference on Private International Law: A View from the United States' (2002) 21 *Journal of Law and Commerce* 191; and S Khanderia, 'The Hague Judgments Project: Assessing its Plausible Benefits for the Development of the Indian Private International Law' [2019] *Commonwealth Law Bulletin* 452, 452–457 [Khanderia, *The Hague Judgments Project*].

[11] A money-judgment is a decision which imposes the judgment-debtor with the duty to pay in the form of damages. A non-money judgment, on the other hand, does not involve any such duty to pay and, instead, merely mandates the judgment-debtor to perform a certain action as stipulated in the decision of the foreign court.

[12] See s 1(2) of the CPC.

[13] ibid, s 2(9) read along with ss 2(2) and (14) of the CPC.

outside India is a foreign judgment.[14] At the same time, the statute does not define the terms 'recognition' and 'enforcement'. However, the 'recognition' of a judgment is commonly understood to mean the act of one court (popularly referred to as the requested or recognising court) of accepting or acknowledging the legal effect of a foreign judgment as was intended by the forum pronouncing the decision (also known as the court of origin).[15] 'Enforcement', on the other hand, is the requested court's act of compelling the judgment-debtor to comply with the decision of the foreign forum.[16] In other words, while enforcement requires the requested court to order the judgment-debtor to perform or refrain from performing the act as mandated under the decision of the foreign forum, recognition merely involves the acknowledgement of the effect the decision of the court of origin in the recognising state.[17] For this reason, while a judgment may be recognised without enforcement, there can be no enforcement without recognition.[18]

B. The Relevance of the 'Doctrine of Obligation'

Predicated on English common law,[19] the doctrine of obligation 'retains the pride of place as the preferred theory,'[20] when determining the eligibility of foreign judgments sounding in money for recognition or enforcement in countries such as India. As such, the doctrine of obligation must be distinguished from the principles of reciprocity or comity, which are some other justifications that exist to recognise and enforce a foreign judgment. The principle of reciprocity involves the willingness and cooperation among nations to conclude mutually accepted agreements whereby states agree to give effect to each other's judgments.[21] Globally, the doctrine of reciprocity has, however, lost its relevance by fostering 'an unwelcome situation'[22] and being detrimental to litigants when states have not been able to agree to the enforcement of each other's judgments.[23] In contrast, the doctrine of comity, which received its theoretical basis in the American decision of *Hilton v Guyot*,[24] concerns the 'voluntary deference'[25] that states pay to the laws of one another regardless of any such mutual agreement. Comity is, thus, an act of:

> recognition by one nation of the legislative, executive and judicial acts of another nation ... having due regard to the international duty and convenience, and to the rights of its citizens or of other persons who are under the protection of its laws.[26]

[14] ibid, s 2(5) and (6).

[15] H Silberberg, 'The Recognition and Enforcement of Foreign Judgments in South Africa' [1977] *Institute of Foreign and Comparative Law, UNISA, Pretoria* 6; and Hague Conference on Private International Law, Judgments Convention: Revised Preliminary Explanatory Report (Note 10 of May 2018) 22–23 www.hcch.net/en/projects/legislative-projects/judgments/special-commission (Explanatory Report to the Judgments Convention).

[16] ibid.

[17] Forsyth (n 3) 418.

[18] ibid.

[19] For a detailed discussion on the principles of the English common law on the recognition and enforcement of foreign judgments, see Collins (ed), *Dicey, Morris and Collins on the Conflict of Laws: Vol 1* 15th edn (Sweet and Maxwell, 2012), 663–673 and 689–711.

[20] See C Roodt, 'Recognition and Enforcement of Foreign Judgments: Still a Hobson's Choice among Competing Theories?' (2005) 38(1) *The Comparative and International Law Journal of Southern Africa* 15, 17, referring to the application of the doctrine in common law systems.

[21] Roodt (n 20) 18.

[22] Michaels (n 1). Also, see generally, W Southard 'The Reciprocity Rule and the Enforcement of Foreign Judgments' (1977) 16 *Columbia Journal of Transnational Law* 327.

[23] ibid.

[24] 159 US 113.

[25] Roodt (n 20) 15, 18.

[26] *Hilton* (n 24) 163–164.

The recognition and enforcement of a foreign judgment based on comity therefore constitutes an act of courtesy as opposed to being 'a matter of absolute obligation'.[27] It is the decision to treat the foreign judgments of another court with respect 'in the hope that foreign courts would enforce one's own judgments'.[28] In comparison, the traditional common law rules on which Indian private international law is based have 'grown out of the rejection of the principle of comity or reciprocity'[29] and instead prefers the application of the doctrine of obligation.

The doctrine of obligation is perceived as a facet of the theory of vested rights.[30] Accordingly, foreign judgments cannot have any extraterritorial effect in India unless the judgment-debtor owes an obligation to the judgment-creditor under the law of the state of origin (ie the country in whose territory the decision was pronounced).[31] Accordingly, the judgment-creditor may enforce a decision of a foreign court against the judgment-debtor if the latter owed an obligation to the former, by initiating a new legal proceeding based on an action of debt before the recognising (also known as the requested) forum.[32] In other words, the decision of the foreign court will constitute a new cause of action in proceedings for recognition and enforcement in the requested forum.[33] Such a suit must be initiated within three years from the date on which the foreign judgment was pronounced.[34] For this reason, foreign judgments sounding in money do not have any automatic effect in India. Instead, such judgments merely constitute 'evidence for the creation of an obligation'.[35]

The doctrine of reciprocity has limited application under section 44A of the CPC. The judgments of superior courts[36] from foreign countries which have been designated as 'reciprocal' will be recognised and enforced automatically without the need to institute a fresh legal proceeding. The UK,[37] Burma, the former British Colony of Aden, Fiji, Singapore, the Federation of Malaya, Hong Kong, Trinidad and Tobago, New Zealand, Bangladesh, Papua New Guinea and the United Arab Emirates have accordingly been designated as reciprocating territories in the Official Gazette of the Central Government.[38] Proceedings in India for the enforcement of a foreign judgment must be initiated within twelve years from the date when the foreign judgment was pronounced.[39] Accordingly, the rules to determine the eligibility of foreign judgments

[27] HL Ho, 'Policies underlying the Enforcement of Foreign Commercial Judgments' (1997) 46 *International and Comparative Law Quarterly* 443, 451.

[28] Michaels (n 1).

[29] See S Khanderia, 'Embarking on New Frontiers in the South African Law on Recognition and Enforcement of Foreign Judgments – Is Comity Really "Unreliable" Festschrift for Prof Christopher Forsyth', *Eleven International Publishing* (on record with author) [Khanderia, *Embarking on New Frontiers*] referring to A Briggs, 'Recognition of Foreign Judgments: A Matter of Obligation' (2013) 129 *Law and Quarterly Review* 87 [Briggs, *A matter of Obligation*].

[30] S Harder, 'The Effects of Recognised Judgments in Civil and Commercial Matters' (2013) 62(2) *International and Comparative Law Quarterly* 441, 449; and RD Carswell, 'The Doctrine of Vested Rights in Private International Law' (1959) 8 *International and Comparative Law Quarterly* 268, 279–280.

[31] Briggs, *A matter of Obligation* (n 29) 87.

[32] Roodt (n 20) 17.

[33] See Khanderia, *The Hague Judgments Project* (n 10) 466–467. Also see Harder (n 30) 449; and Carswell (n 30) 279–280.

[34] See CK Takwani, *Civil Procedure with Limitation Act 1963* 8th edn (Eastern Book Company, 2017) 137.

[35] See Khanderia, *The Hague Judgments Project* (n 10) 466.

[36] See the decision of the Bombay High Court in *Kevin George Vaz v Cotton Textiles Exports Promotion Council* (2006) 5 Bom CR 555, which clarifies that a judgment of the Labour Tribunal of Hong Kong, which has not been designated as a superior court would not be subject to the special procedure as enunciated in s 44A of the Code of Civil Procedure 1908.

[37] See in this context the Foreign Judgments (Reciprocal Enforcement) Act 1933.

[38] See, the website of the High Court of Punjab, Haryana and Chandigarh, www.highcourtchd.gov.in/sub_pages/left_menu/Rules_orders/high_court_rules/vol-I-pdf/chap12pArts.V1.pdf, for a list of the courts of these territories that have been designated as 'superior' for s 44A.

[39] See Art 136 of the Schedule of the Limitation Act 1963, Act No 36 of 1963.

sounding in money for recognition or enforcement in countries such as India 'focus less on the public relations of comity or duty between States and more on the private law relations between the parties'.[40] The determination of the extraterritorial impact of foreign judgments in a common law system is thus rooted on the recognising forum's national law as opposed to any pre-existing international obligations such as reciprocity or comity.[41]

III. Determining Eligibility of a Foreign Judgment

A. International Competency of a Foreign Court: An Overview

The eligibility of every foreign judgment in a civil and commercial matter for recognition and enforcement in India chiefly depends on the determination of the 'international jurisdiction' or 'international competency' of the court of origin. The prerequisite of a foreign forum's international competency is thus equally relevant for a foreign judgment which has been pronounced by a superior court in a reciprocating country. Judicial dicta have stressed the significance of the international competency of the court of origin in assessing eligibility. The court per Mitter J in the seminal case of *Chormal Balchand Firm v Kasturi Chand Seraogi and Anr* accordingly enunciated that the competency of the foreign court 'over the subject-matter and the person brought before them' is of utmost importance when determining the jurisdiction of the foreign court in the 'international sense'.[42] In a related vein, the Supreme Court in *Sankaran Govindan v Lakshmi Bharathi* held that 'unless a court has jurisdiction in the international sense, a judgment delivered by that court would not be recognised or enforced in India',[43] insofar as it violates the provisions of the CPC.[44] The terms 'international jurisdiction' or 'international competency' have, however, not been formally defined anywhere, neither at English common law nor in Indian private international law. In practice, it has been understood to mean the entitlement of a foreign court to summon a defendant and subject the latter to its jurisdiction. In the context of the recognition and enforcement of foreign judgments sounding in money, it connotes the 'cumulative effect' of the foreign judgment in two legal systems, namely, that of the state of origin and the recognising state.[45] At the same time, the determination of international competency does not involve the application of any other law except the recognising court's own domestic law.[46] In other words, the eligibility of the court of origin vis-à-vis its international competency is tested against the principles of private international law of the recognising state, in this case India.

[40] Michaels (n 1) [8].

[41] Briggs, *A matter of Obligation* (n 29) 87; and D Kenny, 'Re Flightlease: The 'Real and Substantial Connection' Test for Recognition and Enforcement of Foreign Judgments Fails to Take Flight I Ireland' (2014) 63 *International and Comparative Law Quarterly* 197, 200.

[42] *Chormal Balchand Firm v Kasturi Chand Seraoji and Anr* ILR [1936] 63 Cal 1033 [8], referring to the decision of the English court in *Pemberton v Hughes*, [1899] 1 Ch 781 (CA), 790 per Lindley MR.

[43] [1975] 3 SCC 351, 361, referring to the decisions of the English court in *Boswell v Cloaks* [1884] 27 Ch D 424; *Abouloff v Oppenheimer* [1882–83] LR 10 QBD 259; and *Vadala v Lawes* [1890] 25 QBD 310. See also, *R Gajambal & Ors v Rukn Ul Mulk Syed Abdul Wajid* AIR [1963] SC 1.

[44] See s 13(a) of the CPC.

[45] E Spiro, 'The Incidence of Jurisdiction in the Recognition and Enforcement of Foreign Judgments' [1978] *Acta Juridica* 59, 7.

[46] see *Chormal Balchand* (n 42) [8], referring to the decision of the English court in *Pemberton v Hughes* [1899] 1 Ch 781 (CA), 790 per Lindley MR. Also see Spiro (n 45) 72.

B. The Grounds on which a Foreign Court is Considered as 'Internationally Competent'

The grounds on which a foreign court will be considered to be internationally competent under Indian law have not been clarified by statute. Instead, section 14 of the CPC merely indicates that every foreign judgment will be presumed to have been pronounced by a court of competent jurisdiction. In *Chormal Balchand*,[47] the Calcutta High Court stipulated six grounds on which a foreign court will be considered as internationally competent under Indian law for the recognition and enforcement of foreign monetary and non-monetary judgments[48] *in personam*. There are no reported dicta which prescribe the factors to assess the eligibility of foreign judgments for actions *in rem*. A foreign court is considered to possess international jurisdiction under Indian private international law if the judgment-debtor:

(1) was a subject (national) of the foreign country (namely the state of origin) at the time of the commencement of the proceedings;[49]
(2) was a resident in the territory of the foreign state at the time of the commencement of the proceedings;[50]
(3) had chosen the jurisdiction of that (foreign) court in its character as a plaintiff in the original case;[51]
(4) had voluntarily appeared before that court;[52]
(5) had submitted to the jurisdiction of that court in any manner;[53] or
(6) owned immovable property, in respect of which the cause of action arose, located in the territory of that (foreign) forum and the judgment-debtor was present in the territory of the state of origin at the time when the cause of action arose.[54]

The acceptance of the sixth ground (relating to the situs of immovable property), has, however, remained ambiguous. In *Andhra Bank Ltd v R Srinivasan & Ors*,[55] the Supreme Court referred to a dictum in *Emanuel v Symon*[56] per Buckley LJ. It clarified that a foreign court will be considered to possess international jurisdiction under Indian law in five circumstances.[57] In doing so, it did not acknowledge the *situs* of immovable property as a relevant factor to establish the eligibility of a foreign judgment sounding in money.[58] Thus, while the *situs* of the immovable property constitutes a ground for internal jurisdiction for the purpose of recognition and enforcement of domestic judgments,[59] the same is not applicable while determining the 'international

[47] *Chormal Balchand* (n 42) [9]–[10].

[48] See in this respect SR Garimella, 'India' in A Reyes (ed), *Recognition and Enforcement of Judgments in Civil and Commercial Matters* (Hart Publishing, 2019) 303; and A Chong, 'Moving towards harmonisation in the recognition and enforcement of foreign judgment rules in Asia' (2020) 16(1) *Journal of Private International Law* 31, 57, DOI: 10.1080/17441048.2020.1744256 which states that the principles of Indian private international law on the recognition and enforcement of a foreign judgment do not distinguish between a monetary and a non-monetary judgment.

[49] ibid.

[50] ibid.

[51] ibid.

[52] ibid.

[53] ibid.

[54] ibid. But see *Andhra Bank Ltd v R Srinivasan & Ors* [1962] 3 SCR 391 [11], in which, the Supreme Court did not acknowledge this factor as ground to determine the international jurisdiction of a foreign forum.

[55] *Andhra Bank* ibid.

[56] [1908] 1 KB 302.

[57] *Andhra Bank* (n 54) [11].

[58] ibid.

[59] see ss 16–18 of the CPC.

jurisdiction' of a foreign forum. There is no reported dictum where the Indian judiciary has recognised or enforced foreign judgments from foreign forums that have based their jurisdiction exclusively on the *situs* of immovable property.

The eligibility of foreign judgments sounding in money thus generally rests on the allegiance or obedience of the judgment-debtor towards the state of origin. As the Supreme Court in *Andhra Bank Ltd v R Srinivasan & Ors* indicated:

> [J]urisdiction depends on the physical power, and since the right to exercise that power ... is exercisable only against persons who are within the territory of the sovereign whom the court represents, the rule of common law has always been that jurisdiction is confined to persons who are within the reach of the process of the court at the time of the service of the writ.[60]

The significance of the allegiance of the judgment-debtor towards the court of origin plausibly justifies the requirement of 'presence' in that territory in disputes on rights *in rem* immovable property – provided this ground is a valid base to establish the international jurisdiction of the foreign forum under Indian private international law.

Against this backdrop, the grounds on which foreign judgments sounding in money would be construed as eligible for recognition and enforcement under Indian private international law can be divided into three broad categories, namely: (1) nationality; (2) residence; and (3) submission. A fleeting, temporary or transitory presence of the defendant in the state of origin at the time of initiation of proceedings, (which constitutes a valid base under English common law),[61] is not of any significance under the Indian law on the subject.

i. The Nationality of the Judgment-Debtor

Indian law adopts the principles of English common law as stipulated in *Emanuel*,[62] whereby the nationality of the defendant as opposed to his or her presence is relevant to establish the international competence of a foreign court.[63]

The decision of the courts in *Chormal Balchand*[64] and *Andhra Bank Ltd*[65] indicates that the terms 'subject' and 'national' have been employed interchangeably in the context of recognition and enforcement of foreign judgments. The dicta did not, however, clarify the scope and the meaning of these expressions. In its subsequent decision in *State Trading Corporation v CIT*, the Supreme Court clarified that the term 'subject' refers to the relation of a person with the state.[66] A subject is thus also referred to as an 'inhabitant' or a 'citizen' in Indian law, depending on the form of government in the place where the subject lives.[67] At the same time, the parameters to identify the 'nationality' and the 'citizenship' of a person as a 'subject' of a state are not identical,[68] but are nonetheless related. While 'nationality' concerns the judgment-debtor's identity in international law, 'citizenship' indicates his or her relation 'to the State in its national or municipal aspect'.[69] Therefore, 'citizenship, as distinct from nationality, is a creature solely of domestic law'.[70]

[60] *Andhra Bank* (n 54) [6].
[61] See *Dicey, Morris and Collins on the Conflict of Laws* (n 19) 690–696.
[62] (n 56).
[63] See the decision of the Supreme Court in *Andhra Bank* (n 54) [11]. See also, Chong (n 48) 42.
[64] *Chormal Balchand* (n 42) [8].
[65] *Andhra Bank* (n 54) [11].
[66] AIR [1963] SC 1811 [71]–[72].
[67] ibid [72].
[68] ibid [73].
[69] ibid.
[70] ibid [53].

It refers 'to [the] rights which a State sees fit to confer upon certain individuals who are also its nationals'.[71] In other words, citizenship denotes a person's 'highest political status' in a state and confers on him or her political and civil rights.[72] On the contrary, nationality does not confer any such civil or political rights. A person is considered to be a national of a country when 'he owes allegiance to a particular sovereign authority'.[73] For this reason, a person may be a national of a state but not a citizen because of his or her allegiance towards that country.[74] A national will not necessarily be permitted to participate in its civil and political activities.[75] Such a limitation may stem from the person's exclusion from the metropolitan territory as defined under the law of that nation.[76] A national may be a citizen if the state allows him or her to participate in the civil and political rights of the state.[77] As regards companies, nationality is determined by their place of incorporation and the country from where they derive their legal personality.[78] By this principle, a company incorporated in the state of origin will be considered as a national of that territory, regardless of whether its shareholders hold a different nationality.[79]

ii. The Residence of the Judgment-Debtor

The 'residence' of the judgment-debtor at the time of the commencement of the proceedings, as opposed to the 'domicile' of the judgment-debtor, is relevant in establishing the competency of the foreign forum for the purpose of the recognition and enforcement of its judgment.[80] In this respect, the Supreme Court in *Union of India v Dudh Nath Prasad* has clarified that the terms 'residence' and 'domicile' may be employed interchangeably, because they both refer to 'permanent home'.[81] Nonetheless, they 'etymologically' have different connotations in private international law.[82]

In *Yogesh Bharadwaj v State of UP*, the Supreme Court enunciated that 'residence' refers to a physical fact, which connotes a person's 'bodily presence as an inhabitant'.[83] The residence of a person is accordingly established by any period of presence in a country, provided that it is not transitory, fleeting or casual.[84] In comparison, domicile, unlike residence, involves more than a physical presence and refers to a person's intention to reside permanently in a country, 'not for a mere special or temporary purpose'.[85] In other words, the domicile is of the whole country.[86] Therefore, 'no one can be without a domicile and no one can have two domiciles'.[87]

Although the intention of a person is not relevant in establishing his or her residence in a foreign forum, it must be voluntary and lawful.[88] Therefore, a person cannot be considered as

[71] ibid [53].
[72] ibid [73].
[73] ibid [73]. Also see *Hari Narayanan v Meenakshi Narayanan* [2007] SCC OnLine Mad 1525.
[74] ibid.
[75] ibid.
[76] ibid.
[77] ibid.
[78] ibid [48]–[52]; *McLeod & Co. Ltd v State of Orissa and Ors* [1984] 1 SCC 434 [7]; and *TDM Infrastructure (P) Ltd. v UE Development India Pvt. Ltd* [2008] 14 SCC 271 [35].
[79] ibid.
[80] See *Chormal Balchand* (n 42) [8].
[81] [2000] 2 SCC 20 [26].
[82] ibid.
[83] [1990] 3 SCC 355 [11].
[84] ibid [17], [20] and [21].
[85] ibid [11].
[86] ibid [9], [12] and [14].
[87] ibid [9], [12] and [14].
[88] ibid [20].

a resident if he or she is staying in a jurisdiction in violation of immigration laws or as a result of 'enforced presence by reason of kidnapping or imprisonment'.[89] Further, it is the habitual as opposed to the ordinary residence of a judgment-debtor in the state of origin that is relevant.[90] A person may be an ordinary resident in a country if his or her inhabitation there 'is not casual or uncertain, but is in the ordinary course of his life'.[91] In comparison, habitual residence is of a longer duration even though there is no minimum requirement in terms of such period.[92]

There are, however, no clear indicia to determine the residence of artificial persons in Indian private international law. The Supreme Court in *McLeod & Co. Ltd* stated that, unlike nationality and domicile, residence of a company cannot be 'easily established'.[93] There are no uniform criteria and the mechanisms employed vary depending on the issues in a dispute.[94] However, the court indicated that a company, like an individual, might have more than one residence at a given time.[95] In the absence of any fixed yardstick to assess a company's residence in the context of the recognition and enforcement of foreign judgments, the courts will likely refer to the principles of English common law that have been stipulated by the Court of Appeal in *Adams v Cape Industries plc*.[96] In *Adams*, the court stated that it would examine the relationship between such person and the corporation; and whether he had the power to bind the latter contractually to determine the residence of the corporation.[97] Thus, it would assess factors such as the manner of acquisition of the business premises, the degree of control by the corporation, the display of the corporation's name, the payment of the representative and the reimbursement of the expenses.[98]

iii. The Submission of the Judgment-Debtor

The failure of a judgment-debtor to submit to the jurisdiction of the court of origin, in circumstances where he or she is not a subject or resident of the state in which the court is located, would render the foreign judgment unenforceable in India. Nonetheless, the foreign judgment (which initially lacks extraterritorial effect in India because the judgment-debtor has not submitted to the jurisdiction of the court of origin) may become enforceable upon the occurrence of certain subsequent events. An example is when the court of origin has ceased to be 'international' (for instance, by accession).[99] In such a circumstance, the relation of the judgment-debtor is altered *qua* the state of origin and she or he is no longer a foreigner under Indian law.[100] In all other cases, the requirement of the judgment-debtor to submit to the jurisdiction of the court of origin either expressly or implicitly is indispensable. The competency of the court of origin continues to be unimpaired even with the death of the judgment-debtor – in which case the successor(s) may be brought on record – without the need for re-submission.[101]

[89] ibid.
[90] See *Sankaran Govindan v Lakshmi Bharathi and Ors* [1974] AIR 1764 [20] and [35].
[91] ibid [18].
[92] ibid.
[93] *McLeod* (n 78) [8].
[94] ibid.
[95] ibid.
[96] [1990] Ch 433. P North and JJ Fawcett, *Cheshire and North's Private International Law* 13th edn (OUP, 2006), 409–411, referring to the English common law on the subject.
[97] ibid.
[98] ibid.
[99] *Bhagwan Shankar Surdi v Rajaram Bapu Vithal Nanajkar* ILR [1952] Bom 65 (FB):(1951) [53]. See also, Khanderia, *The Hague Judgments Project* (n 10) 468.
[100] *Bhagwan Shankar*, ibid [53].
[101] *Andhra Bank* (n 54).

Express submission to the jurisdiction of a foreign court may occur when the plaintiff has initiated proceedings against the defendant in the court of origin, as this would indicate acceptance of the jurisdiction of that court.[102] The plaintiff may not necessarily have many choices as to whether or not it would like to sue the defendant in the court of origin, having regard to the conflict of law rules of jurisdiction of that forum. These factors, however limited they may be, do not diminish the fact that the plaintiff had consented to submit to the jurisdiction of the court of origin.

The place where the cause of action arose (for example, the place of performance of a contract or the place of occurrence of a tort) has not *explicitly* been identified in judicial dicta as a valid basis for a foreign court to assume international jurisdiction. Nonetheless, such foreign judgments will be recognised or enforced in India if the defendant had submitted to the jurisdiction of the foreign-forum.

To illustrate, suppose A (a resident and domiciliary of state Y (India)) is hit by another car which is being driven by B (a resident and domiciliary of state Z (New South Wales)), while on holiday in a state X (Ontario). A suffers injuries and initiates proceedings against B in Ontario, the place where the accident arose. However, the court declares the decision in favour of B (and, thus, against A). The court in Ontario awards damages to B. The judgment must be recognised and enforced in India (the place of A's residence). The act of initiation of the proceedings demonstrates the plaintiff's (A's) submission to the jurisdiction of the Ontario court, although A did not have much choice in doing so, having regard to the rules of direct jurisdiction in Ontario.

Consider another situation. Plaintiff A (a resident of state X (India)) is considered to have submitted to the jurisdiction of a court in state Z (Germany) if it initiates proceedings against defendant B (a resident of state Y (New York)) based on the fact that the contract between A and B had been performed in Munich, the place of delivery of the goods. The decision of the German court is pronounced against A, who is ordered to pay damages of €500. A now assumes the character of the judgment-debtor in the recognising court. Here, the court of origin (German court) assumed jurisdiction and pronounced a judgment sounding in money which is capable of being recognised and enforced in India, not because of the residence or nationality of the defendant but by the submission of the plaintiff.

Similarly, the parties' decision to confer jurisdiction to a foreign court through a choice of court agreement is an act of express submission.[103] It forms a valid base of international competency.[104] As we have seen in chapter 5 on 'Jurisdiction', in *Modi Entertainment Network and Another v WSG Cricket PTE Ltd*,[105] the Supreme Court has upheld the validity of a choice of court agreement in favour of a foreign forum. The Court did not address the question of recognition and enforcement of judgments resulting from choice of court agreements. However, it is presumed that the court of origin, which has assumed jurisdiction on such a ground will be 'internationally competent' under Indian law. In comparison, implied or tacit submission occurs by the conduct of the parties.[106] Thus, the voluntary and unconditional appearance of the judgment-debtor to argue a case on the merits is an act of implied submission.[107] The judgment-debtor cannot subsequently deny an act of submission before the foreign forum, unless its appearance was merely to contest the jurisdiction of the court of origin or request for a stay or dismissal of the proceedings.

[102] See *Chormal Balchand* (n 42) 1043 [9]–[10]; and *Andhra Bank* (n 54) [9]–[11].
[103] See Khanderia, *The Hague Judgments Project* (n 10) 462–464.
[104] ibid.
[105] [2003] 4 SCC 341.
[106] *Y Narasimha Rao & Ors v Y Venkata Lakshmi & Anr* [1991] 3 SCC 451, 461 [16].
[107] *Chormal Balchand* (n 42) [9], [10] and [12]; *Andhra Bank* (n 54) [9], [11].

IV. The Disqualification of a Foreign Judgment from Recognition or Enforcement

Section 13 of the CPC stipulates six grounds on which a foreign judgment will be considered as inconclusive under Indian law and will, therefore, be denied recognition or enforcement. Besides being ineligible for not being pronounced by a court of 'international competence', Section 13 permits an Indian court to deny recognition or enforcement of a foreign judgment (including those given under section 44-A of the CPC) on the following grounds:

(1) where the foreign judgment has not been given on the merits of the case;
(2) where the foreign judgment appears on the face of the proceedings to be founded on an incorrect view of international law or a refusal to recognise the law of India in cases in which such law is applicable;
(3) where the proceedings in which the foreign judgment was obtained are opposed to natural justice;
(4) where the foreign judgment has been obtained by fraud;
(5) where it sustains a claim founded on a breach of any law in force in the States.

The scope of each of these factors will be discussed below.

i. When the Foreign Judgment has not been Given on the Merits[108]

The Supreme Court in *International Woollen Mills v Standard Wool (UK) Ltd* clarified that a foreign judgment would not be regarded as having been given on the merits of the case if the decision has not been based on evidence and is instead the result of summary proceedings due to the failure of the defendant's appearance before the forum.[109] Such decisions will be considered as inconclusive and not final and binding under Indian law.[110] Thus, in judgments pronounced *ex parte*, the court in India ought to be satisfied that the foreign forum had applied its mind to the evidence submitted by the plaintiff in the absence of the defendant.[111] At the same time, the mere fact that the judgment is *ex parte* would not in itself render it inconclusive, if it is apparent from the decision that the court of origin had considered the oral and documentary evidence produced by the plaintiff and had applied its mind to the matter.[112] Indian private international law does not, however, permit *suo moto* investigation into the merits of foreign judgments.[113] In other words, the Indian court would not review the merits unless the judgment-debtor alleges that the decision was made in default or has not been based on evidence.[114] If the judgment-debtor succeeds in proving that the foreign court did not pronounce its decision on the merits of the case, then the judgment will be unenforceable in India.

[108] s 13(b) of the CPC.
[109] [2001] 5 SCC 265. See also, *Marine Geotechnics LLC v Coastal Marine Construction & Engineering Ltd* [2014] 2 Bom CR 769 [20]; *Chintamoni Padhan v Paika Samal* AIR [1956] Ori 136; *Dhirajlal v Navinbhai Dave* [2011] (4) Mh.L.J; *Golian Consultants Ltd v Jagdarshan Singh* [2014] SCC Online P&H 16406; *BNP Paribas v Atit Omprakash Agarwal* [2017] SCC Online Bom 9063 [10].
[110] ibid.
[111] See Chong (n 48) 41.
[112] ibid.
[113] See *Marine Geotechnics* (n 109).
[114] *International Woollen Mills* (n 109).

ii. When the Proceedings in which the Judgment was Obtained are Opposed to Natural Justice[115]

A foreign judgment which has otherwise been decided on the merits can be rendered inconclusive if it involves procedural abnormalities.[116] In such circumstances, it may be vitiated on the ground that it has violated fundamental principles of natural justice. This may be the position when the decision of the foreign court has been passed without apprising the judgment-debtor of the appropriate procedure[117] or is one which, albeit based on evidence, has failed to provide the defendant with a fair chance to be heard and put forward a defence.[118]

iii. When the Judgment has been Obtained by Fraud[119]

A foreign judgment will be considered as inconclusive under Indian law if it has been obtained by practising fraud on the court of origin.[120] In other words, the deception must be extrinsic as opposed to intrinsic (that is, the fraud must have affected the way in which the case was heard) to create a valid defence. An example of extrinsic fraud would be the suppression of material facts and evidence from the court of origin.[121] The fraud should be of such a nature that it could only have been discovered after the judgment was pronounced.[122] In such circumstances, the foreign judgment would not create *res judicata* or be enforceable and the case would therefore have to be tried again on the merits.[123] A deceitful act, which was within the knowledge of the judgment-debtor before the pronouncement of the decision would not impair its enforceability.[124]

iv. When the Judgment is Pronounced in Violation of a Law in Force in India[125]

The CPC prohibits the recognition of a foreign judgment when it appears on the face of the proceedings to have been founded on an incorrect view of international law.[126] Likewise, a foreign judgment will be denied effect in India if it operates as a refusal to recognise the law of India in cases in which such law is applicable[127] or if it sustains a claim founded on a breach of any law

[115] Section 13(d) of the CPC.

[116] ibid, read along with Art 14 of the Constitution of India 1950; and *Maneka Gandhi v Union of India* [1978] 1 SCC 248, as per which, the right to be heard is constitutionally mandated. Also see generally MP Singh, *VN Shukla's Constitution of India* 12th edn (Eastern Book Co, 2013) 67–86.

[117] *Y Narasimha Rao* (n 107) 461 [18].

[118] ibid.

[119] Section 13(d) of the CPC.

[120] *Masterbaker Marketing Ltd v Noshir Mohsin Chinwall* [2015] SCC Online Bom 559 [19]; and *Abraaj Investment Management Ltd v Neville Tuli* AIR [2015] 6 Bom R 555 [59]. Also see Khanderia, *The Hague Judgments Project* (n 10) 471–472.

[121] *Abraaj Investment* ibid [59].

[122] ibid.

[123] See *Sankaran Govindan* (n 90) 361, referring to the decisions of the English court in *Boswell v Cloaks* [1884] 27 Ch D 424; *Abouloff* (n 43); and *Vadala* (n 43); and Khanderia, *The Hague Judgments Project* (n 10) 471–472.

[124] See *Sankaran Govindan* ibid 361.

[125] Section 13(c) and (f) of the CPC.

[126] ibid, s 13(c).

[127] ibid.

in force in India.[128] There is no dictum where the courts have had the opportunity to elaborate how an incorrect understanding of international law may prevent foreign judgments in civil and commercial matters from being recognised and enforced in India.

A decision of a foreign court on a matrimonial matter will be unenforceable if it has granted a divorce on a ground which is not recognised under Indian law. The Supreme Court in *Y Narasimha Rao & Ors v Y Venkata Lakshmi & Anr* stressed that:

> the jurisdiction assumed by the foreign court as well as the grounds on which the relief is granted must be in accordance with the matrimonial law under which the parties are married.[129]

Thus, if the parties were married under Indian law, the dissolution of their marriage must be based on grounds that are recognised under Indian law.[130] The Court, consequently, refused to recognise dissolution of a marriage which was granted by a court in Missouri based on the irretrievable breakdown of marriage, a ground which then did not find a place in the Hindu Marriage Act 1955.[131]

Similarly, the decision of a foreign court in a contract for the breach of performance must conform to the provisions of Indian law if the agreement was to be performed in the Republic. Although there is no *direct* dictum to this effect, such judgments would ostensibly be regarded as inconclusive (and thus unenforceable) if they award damages for a breach of a contract which has to be performed in India but is illegal under the Republic's law.[132] The decision of the Bombay High Court in *Taprogge Gesellschaft MBH v IAEC India Ltd*[133] sheds some light on this aspect and could be persuasive in interpreting Section 13(f). As discussed in chapter 10 on applicable law in contractual obligations, the Court refused to give effect to the parties' choice of German law insofar as the agreement operated in restraint of trade and was contradictory to sections 23, 27 and 28 of the ICA.[134] The Court held that these provisions have extraterritorial application regardless of the choice of any other law.[135] Likewise, in *Securities and Exchange Board of India v Pan Asia Advisors Ltd and Anr*,[136] the Supreme Court approved the decision of the Securities and Exchange Board of India under the Securities and Exchange Board of India Act 1992.[137] The Board prohibited non-resident Indian companies from issuing securities outside the Republic insofar as the same amounted to fraudulent activity and violated the interests and welfare of investors in India.[138] A decision by a foreign court which fails to secure such rights is not recognisable and enforceable in India.[139]

In this manner, Indian private international law indirectly recognises the contravention of public policy of the Republic as a valid ground to disqualify a foreign judgment from recognition and enforcement in the country, even though public policy has not been explicitly indicated in CPC section 13.

[128] ibid, s 13(f).
[129] *Y Narasimha Rao* (n 106) [13].
[130] ibid.
[131] ibid.
[132] Khanderia, *The Hague Judgments Project* (n 10) 472.
[133] AIR [1988] Bom 157.
[134] ibid; and Khanderia, *The Hague Judgments Project* (n 10) 472–473.
[135] ibid.
[136] [2015] 14 SCC 71. Also see Khanderia, *The Hague Judgments Project* (n 10) 473.
[137] Act No 15 of 1992.
[138] ibid.
[139] Khanderia, *The Hague Judgments Project* (n 10) 473.

V. Reflections on Indian Law: Some Insights Based on Global Trends

A. General Remarks

i. Bases of Jurisdiction

The principles of Indian private international law on the subject generally resonate with practice across other common law systems such as Australia,[140] New Zealand,[141] South Africa,[142] and Nepal,[143] which similarly employ the concept of 'international jurisdiction' as the cornerstone to determine eligibility of a foreign judgment for recognition and enforcement. The doctrine of obligation underlines this area of the law and a foreign judgment will have no effect in any of these jurisdictions unless the judgment-debtor conducted himself before the foreign court in a certain manner,[144] which will be assessed according to the *lex fori*. At the same time, the private international laws of South Africa[145] and New Zealand[146] (but not Australia)[147] demonstrate some indication as regards the acceptance of the principle of comity as a factor to determine the international jurisdiction of the foreign court. As indicated above, comity is a voluntary and discretionary principle that a state employs with an expectation that the state of origin will reciprocate by similarly giving effect to its court decisions.[148] Although comity does not constitute the chief basis for the recognition and enforcement of foreign judgments, it is a crucial factor in these countries in the determination of the international jurisdiction of a foreign court.[149] There are subtle differences in the practice of Indian courts vis-à-vis other common law jurisdictions such as South Africa,[150] Australia[151] and New Zealand,[152] where the grounds of international competency have been predicated on English common law and have similarly been clarified by

[140] See Davies, Bell and Brereton (eds), *Nygh's Conflict of Laws in Australia* 8th edn (Lexis Nexis, 2010) 895–896 [*Nygh's Conflict of Laws*].

[141] M Hook and J Wass, *The Conflict of Laws in New Zealand* (Lexis Nexis 2020) 368–380.

[142] Forsyth (n 3) 417 et seq; and Khanderia, *The Hague Judgments Project* (n 10) 416 et seq.

[143] See s 37(a) of the Mutual Legal Assistance Act 2014, Act No 7 of 2070 (2014).

[144] see Chong (n 48) 42.

[145] PN Okoli, 'Promoting Foreign Judgments: Lessons in Legal Convergence from South Africa and Nigeria' (Wolters Kluwer, 2019) 108–111, referring to the decisions of the South African court in *Laconian Maritime Enterprises Ltd. v Agromar Lineas* [1986] (3) 509 (D & LCD) 513; *Jones v Krok* [1995] (1) SA 677 (A); and *Richman v Ben Tovim* [2006] (2) SA 591 (C). Also see, A Morgan and A Kennedy, 'When Considering whether to Recognise and Enforce a Foreign Money Judgment, Why Should the Domestic Court Accord the Foreign Court International Jurisdiction on the Basis that the Judgment Debtor was Domiciled There? An Analysis of the Approach Taken by Courts in the Republic of South Africa' (2020) *Journal of Private International Law* 16(3) 549, 562–569, referring to the decision of the Constitutional Court in *Government of the Republic of Zimbabwe v Fick* Case, CCT 101/12 [2013] (5) SA 325. But see Forsyth (n 3) 437, which criticises the application of comity for being 'devoid of precise meaning' and, thus, susceptible to be employed as 'a veil for judicial discretion'.

[146] Hook and Wass (n 141) 352.

[147] See *Nygh's Conflict of Laws* (n 140) 904 which reports that attempts to persuade the Australian courts to recognise and enforce foreign judgments on the basis of reciprocity or comity have failed.

[148] See text accompanying notes 24–28. See also, Okoli (n 145) 84–86; and Morgan and Kennedy (n 145) 566–569.

[149] See Okoli ibid 108–111; Morgan and Kennedy, ibid 562–569; and Hook and Wass (n 141) 352.

[150] For a discussion of South African law, see Forsyth (n 3) 417 et seq; Van Niekerk and C Schulze, *The South African Law of International Trade: Selected Topics* (SAGA Legal Publications, 2011) 319–321; and S Khanderia, 'The Hague Conference on Private International Law's Proposed Draft Text on the Recognition and Enforcement of Foreign Judgments: Should South Africa Endorse it?' (2019) 63(3) *Journal of African Law* 413, 416 et seq [Khanderia, *Recognition and Enforcement of Foreign Judgments in South Africa*].

[151] For a discussion of Australian law, see *Nygh's Conflict of Laws* (n 140) 895–904.

[152] For a discussion on New Zealand law, see Hook and Wass (n 141) 368–380.

judicial dicta.[153] The private international laws of these jurisdictions consider a foreign forum as internationally competent if it based its jurisdiction on: (1) the residence or submission of the judgment-debtor in the territory of the court of origin at the time of commencement of the proceedings; or (2) the submission of the judgment-debtor before that forum.[154] However, the laws of South Africa and New Zealand additionally acknowledge the presence of the judgment-debtor in the territory of the court of origin at the time of commencement of the proceedings as a valid basis for the international jurisdiction of a foreign forum.[155]

As we have seen above, the presence of the judgment-debtor does not confer international competency on a foreign forum under Indian law. The Asian Principles for the Recognition and Enforcement of Foreign Judgments (Asian Principles), which are a form of soft-law and aim to promote harmonisation of rules in Asia, however, advocate the recognition and enforcement of foreign monetary judgments based on inter alia the presence of the judgment-debtor in the state of origin.[156] In comparison, Indian law continues to hold firmly to the traditional principles of English common law where nationality, as opposed to presence will constitute a valid basis of international jurisdiction.[157] In this respect, the principles of Indian private international law are more advanced when compared to the laws of South Africa or New Zealand, insofar as Indian principles effectively prevents the arbitrariness which would occur if its courts were permitted to recognise and enforce foreign judgments based on the mere presence of a judgment-debtor. The acceptance of 'mere presence' as a ground to confer international jurisdiction has been subjected to severe criticism in South Africa[158] and New Zealand[159] as being arbitrary. The ground permits a foreign forum to assume jurisdiction based on the transitory or fleeting presence of the judgment-debtor. It is, therefore, susceptible to render a judgment unenforceable and ineffective if the defendant escaped the jurisdiction without any assets to freeze or confiscate.[160]

As we have seen in chapter 5 on 'Jurisdiction', the presence of the defendant does not constitute a valid basis for an Indian court to assume jurisdiction in an international civil or commercial matter. It is, therefore, only fair that mere presence is not recognised as a ground that confers international jurisdiction on a foreign forum under Indian law. In contrast, Canada, which is also a common law country, has embraced the doctrine of comity as a 'touchstone', which forms an 'informing principle of private international law'.[161] Canadian private international law thus

[153] Note that Nepalese private international law on the subject, which is stipulated in s 37(a) of the Mutual Legal Assistance Act, merely indicates the competence of the foreign court as an indispensable factor to give effect to a foreign judgment – but does not make any mention on the factors which would be considered to ascertain the international jurisdiction of that court.

[154] For a discussion of South African law, see Forsyth (n 3) 417 et seq; Van Niekerk and Schulze (n 150) 319–321; and Khanderia, *Recognition and Enforcement of Foreign Judgments in South Africa* (n 150) 416 et seq. For a discussion of Australian law, see *Nygh's Conflict of Laws* (n 140) 895–904. For a discussion on New Zealand law, see Hook and Wass (n 141) 368–380.

[155] See Khanderia, *Recognition and Enforcement of Foreign Judgments in South Africa* (n 150) 418–419; and Hook and Wass, ibid 369–372.

[156] See Article 2(a) of the Asian Principles for the Recognition and Enforcement of Foreign Judgments 2020, Asian Business Law Institute, available at https://info.sal.org.sg/abli/ebooks/recognition-enforcement-foreign-judgments/ [Asian Principles].

[157] See text accompanying notes 63–79.

[158] Forsyth (n 3) 430; R Oppong 'Mere Presence and International Competence in Private International Law' (2007) 3 *Journal of Private International Law* 321; C Schulze 'International Jurisdiction in Claims Sounding in Money: Is *Richman v Ben-Tovim* the Last Word?' (2008) 20 *South African Mercantile Law Journal* 61; and GMN Xaba 'Presence as a Basis for the Recognition and Enforcement of Foreign Judgments sounding in Money: The "Real and Substantial Connection" Test Considered' (2015) 36(1) *Obiter* 121.

[159] Hook and Wass (n 143) 32–33.

[160] Forsyth (n 3) 430; and Khanderia, *Recognition and Enforcement of Foreign Judgments in South Africa* (n 150) 418–419.

[161] J Blom 'The Enforcement of Foreign Judgments: Morguard Goes Forth into the World' (1997) 28 *Canadian Business Law Journal* 373, 374 [Blom, *Morguard Goes Forth into the World*].

does away with the principle of international jurisdiction, which mandates the assessment of the jurisdiction of the foreign forum according to principles of domestic law. Canadian courts have replaced the 'rigid and outmoded nineteenth-century principles with a flexible test of real and substantial connection'.[162] Although the application of the test is limited to the recognition and enforcement of inter-provincial judgments,[163] it has since evolved into a crucial constitutional standard which is extended to foreign judgments as well.[164] Under Canadian private international law, a foreign decision will be eligible for recognition and enforcement in Canada if the court of origin had a 'significant connection' with the cause of action, or 'when the defendant has "participated in something of significance or was actively involved in that foreign jurisdiction"'.[165] The Supreme Court of Canada has accordingly stipulated a flexible list of presumptive connecting factors to interpret the 'real and substantial connection' test.[166] Consequently, apart from the traditional jurisdictional bases of residence and submission (express and implied), foreign judgments which are pronounced by a court where the cause of action occurred will also be eligible for extraterritorial effect in Canada.[167]

In a related vein, comity and reciprocity similarly form the backbone of the law on the recognition and enforcement of foreign judgments in the EU, which is largely a civil law jurisdiction.[168] The law on the subject on the continent has been harmonised at the supranational level with the promulgation of the Brussels I *bis* Regulation[169] and the Lugano Convention.[170] In general, the application of the provisions of these instruments is limited to the recognition and enforcement of judgments from other Member States. The provisions are, therefore, not applicable when a court in the EU is requested to recognise or enforce a decision from a third party, in which case the internal law of the requested state will apply. Unlike the practice of most common law jurisdictions (including India), the Brussels I *bis* Regulation and the Lugano Convention clearly define the grounds on which a court may give effect to a foreign judgment from another Member State. In particular, the instruments abolish the requirement of *exequatur*[171] and thus facilitate the free movement of judgments by making a provision for the automatic recognition and enforcement of judgments in civil and commercial matters.[172] A court in the EU would give effect to a judgment from another Member State if its jurisdiction was based on the domicile[173] or the

[162] Kenny (n 41) 197–198. See also, A Briggs, 'Crossing the River by Feeling the Stones: Rethinking the Law on Foreign Judgments' (2004) 8 *Singapore Yearbook of Private International Law* 1, 1 [Briggs, *Crossing the River*]; and S Pitel, 'Enforcement of Foreign Judgments: Where Morguard Stands after Beals' (2004) 40 *Canadian Business Law Journal* 189, 202 [Pitel, *Where Morguard Stands after Beals*].

[163] See the decision of the Supreme Court of Canada in *Morguard Investments Ltd. v De Savoye* [1990] 3 SCR 1077 [1098].

[164] Blom, *Morguard Goes Forth into the World* (n 161) 377.

[165] [2003] SCC 72 [23]; J Goodman and J Talpis '*Beals v Saldana* and the Enforcement of Foreign Judgments in Canada' (2004) 40 *Canadian Business Law Journal* 227, 228–229; and Pitel, *Where Morguard Stands after Beals* (n 162) 194.

[166] See *Club Resorts v Van Breda*, [2012] SCC 17 [19].

[167] ibid.

[168] See H Alavi 'A Step Forward in the Harmonisation of European Jurisdiction: Regulation Brussels I Recast' (2015) 8(2) *Baltic Journal of Law and Politics* 159, 163; and Chong (n 48) 53–54 which states that reciprocity is a pre-requisite to the recognition and enforcement of foreign judgments in all civil law jurisdictions.

[169] Brussels Convention on Jurisdiction and Enforcement of Judgments in Civil and Commercial Matters, 27 September 1968 (the Brussels Convention), which is now replaced by Regulation (EU) No 1215/2012 of The European Parliament and of the Council of 12 December 2012 on Jurisdiction and the Recognition and Enforcement of Judgments in Civil and Commercial Matters (the Brussels I *bis* Regulation).

[170] In the European Economic Area, the Brussels Recast is supplemented by the Convention on Jurisdiction and the Recognition and Enforcement of Judgments in Civil and Commercial Matters (2007) www.ec.europa.eu/world/agreements/downloadFile.do?fullText=yes&treatyTransId=13041 (Lugano Convention).

[171] See in this respect, LJE Timmer, 'Abolition of *Exequatur* under the Brussels I Regulation: Ill Conceived and Premature' (2013) 9 *Journal of Private International Law* 129.

[172] See Art 36 of the Brussels I *bis* Regulation; and Art 33 of the Lugano Convention.

[173] See Arts 4, 62 and 63; and Arts 2, 59 and 60 of the Lugano Convention.

express or implied submission of the judgment-debtor.[174] The presence, residence or the nationality of the judgment-debtor is therefore an irrelevant factor in establishing the validity of the foreign judgment. Likewise, a court is obligated to recognise or enforce the judgment of a court in another Member State if the cause of action arose in the latter's territory, either because the performance of the contract or the occurrence of the delict took place in its territory.[175] Besides, these instruments stipulate some exclusive bases of jurisdiction and judgments pronounced in violation of these grounds will therefore be denied recognition or enforcement. Accordingly, the jurisdiction of a foreign court in a dispute arising in connection to a right in immovable property must be based on its *situs*,[176] while that concerning a dispute on the validity or registration of intellectual property or an analogous right must be predicated on its *locus protectionis* (place of protection).[177] In a related vein, the jurisdiction of the foreign court for disputes concerning the validity of the constitution or dissolution of a company must be based on its seat.[178] In contrast, the court's jurisdiction in a dispute concerning the validity of an entry in a public registry must be based on the place where the register is kept.[179]

ii. Grounds for Denial

In general, the principles of Indian private international law resonate with the trends in other jurisdictions such as Australia,[180] New Zealand,[181] Canada[182] South Africa[183] and Nepal[184] which similarly prohibit the recognition or enforcement of a foreign judgment if it was obtained by fraud, contrary to public policy, was opposed to natural justice. Likewise, the Brussels I *bis* Regulation and the Lugano Convention similarly prohibit the recognition or enforcement of a foreign judgment from another Member State if it contravenes the public policy of the recognising state.[185] Although fraud has not explicitly been stipulated as a ground to deny the recognition or enforcement of a foreign judgment, it is 'subsumed under the public policy exception'.[186] Besides, EU law prohibits a foreign judgment from another Member State from being recognised or enforced if it:

(1) is a result of default proceedings or the failure to notify the defendant on a timely basis of the commencement of proceedings before the rendering court;[187] or,
(2) is inconsistent with an earlier judgment between the same parties in the same cause of action before: (a) the recognising court; or (b) another court.[188]

Although the rules in common law jurisdictions, including India, do not expressly stipulate that recognition or enforcement of a foreign judgment would be denied if it results in inconsistent judgments, 'it

[174] See Arts 25 and 26 of the Brussels I *bis* Regulation; and Arts 23 and 24 of the Lugano Convention.
[175] See Art 5 of the Brussels I *bis* Regulation; and Art 7 of the Lugano Convention.
[176] See Art 24(1) of the Brussels I *bis* Regulation; and Art 22(1) of the Lugano Convention.
[177] See Art 24(4) of the Brussels I *bis* Regulation; and Art 22(4) of the Lugano Convention.
[178] See Art 24(2) of the Brussels I *bis* Regulation; and Art 22(2) of the Lugano Convention.
[179] See Art 24(3) of the Brussels I *bis* Regulation; and Art 22(3) of the Lugano Convention.
[180] See *Nygh's Conflict of Laws* (n 140) 921–935.
[181] See Hook and Wass (n 141) 394 referring to s 6(1) and (2) of the Reciprocal Enforcement of Judgments Act 1934.
[182] See J Walker, *Halsbury's Laws of Canada: Conflict of Laws* (Lexis Nexis, 2011) 477–485.
[183] See Forsyth (n 3) 417; and Van Niekerk and Schulze (n 150) 319–321; and Khanderia, *Recognition and Enforcement of Foreign Judgments in South Africa* (n 150) 420 et seq.
[184] Section 37(3) of the Mutual Legal Assistance Act 2014.
[185] See Art 45 of the Brussels I *bis* Regulation; and Art 34 of the Lugano Convention.
[186] see Chong (n 48) 49.
[187] ibid.
[188] ibid.

is a generally accepted practice that a local judgment will prevail over a conflicting foreign judgment dealing with the same issue between the same parties' if the former precedes the latter.[189]

The principles of private international law of common law countries do not, however, clarify the position if a subsequent local judgment, which concerns a matter between the same parties and the same cause of action, will similarly gain priority over an existing foreign judgment.[190] Scholarly writings opine that, in such circumstances, it is likely that common law countries would follow the position under English law and prioritise the recognition and enforcement of an earlier foreign judgment.[191] In this respect, the principles of private international law of Nepal on the subject deserve mention insofar as they provide considerable clarity over the matter, unlike most other common law jurisdictions discussed above. Section 37 of the Mutual Legal Assistance Act 2014 clarifies that a local judgment in a dispute between the same parties and the same subject matter will have precedence over a foreign decision if it was filed or pronounced before the latter.[192] In such circumstances, the foreign judgment will not be recognised or enforced.[193] Similarly, a foreign judgment which has already been recognised and enforced or is in the process of being recognised or enforced, will gain precedence over any other judgment and will prevent any other judgment, including a local one, from being recognised or enforced in Nepal.[194]

Unlike the principles of Indian private international law, the rules in other jurisdictions promote fairness and respect for the courts in other countries by prohibiting a foreign judgment from being contested on the merits of the case.[195] Therefore, a foreign judgment would be recognised even if it is void.[196] Judgment debtors aggrieved by the decision of the court of origin may therefore only initiate appellate proceedings to challenge the findings of the court of origin.[197] Besides, these legal systems additionally permit its court to refuse to give effect to a foreign judgment if it is penal by nature.[198] This ground does not explicitly find a place in Indian law. In this respect, the Asian Principles, however, advocate the recognition and enforcement of foreign money judgments which are penal in nature.[199]

B. Should India Accede to the Hague Conventions on the Recognition and Enforcement of Judgments?

At the international level, the HCCCA and the Judgments Convention, which have been negotiated under the auspices of the HCCH, endeavour to harmonise the law on the recognition and enforcement of foreign judgments in civil and commercial matters.[200] However, India is not a

[189] Chong (n 48) 52.

[190] ibid.

[191] ibid 52–53.

[192] Section 37(3)(b)-(c) of the Mutual Legal Assistance Act 2014.

[193] ibid.

[194] ibid, s 37(3)(d).

[195] For the principles of the Australian law, see *Nygh's Conflict of Laws* (n 140) 907–910; For the principles of the South African law, see *Joffe v Salmon* [1904] TS [317], [319]; *Gabelsberger v Babl* [1994] (2) SA 677; Forsyth (n 3) 468–469; Oppong (n 158) 332–333; and Khanderia, *Recognition and Enforcement of Foreign Judgments in South Africa* (n 150) 420.

[196] See Khanderia, *The Hague Judgments Project* (n 10) 471 ff, 142.

[197] ibid.

[198] ibid.

[199] See Principle 6 of the Asian Principles.

[200] For a detailed discussion on the meaning of civil and commercial matters, see HCCH, 'Note on Article 1(1) of the 2016 Preliminary Draft Convention and the Term "Civil or Commercial Matters"', Preliminary Document No 4 of December 2016 for the attention of the Special Commission of February 2017 on the Recognition and Enforcement of Foreign Judgments.

signatory to either convention. Unlike the vague and convoluted principles on the subject that exist under Indian law, the HCCCA and the Judgments Convention strive to enhance predictability by enabling interested parties to know in advance the grounds on which a foreign decision in a civil or a commercial matter which has been pronounced in the court of a Contracting State, may be recognised or enforced in the territory of another Contracting State.[201] The HCCCA has to date been ratified by the EU, Denmark, Montenegro, Mexico, Singapore and the UK.[202] Besides, China, the Republic of North Macedonia, the US, Australia and Israel will shortly enact the HCCCA into law.[203] On the other hand, the Judgments Convention has so far been signed by Ukraine, Uruguay and Israel.[204] The Judgments Convention will come into force on the first day of the month following ratification by two states.[205]

The HCCCA, which governs the operation of exclusive choice of court agreements among its Contracting States[206] reinforces access to justice and facilitates the free movement of judgments arising from such contracts.[207] Article 8 of the HCCCA mandates the recognising court in a Contracting State to 'be bound by the findings of fact on which the state of origin based its jurisdiction'.[208] A court in a Contracting State is generally prohibited from refusing to give effect to a foreign judgment from the court of another Contracting State, when the latter court has been designated by the parties' choice of court agreement as the forum to resolve the parties' disputes. Exceptions are stipulated in Article 9. The grounds in Article 9 largely resonate with those found under Indian private international law. The HCCCA accordingly permits the requested court to refuse recognition or enforcement of a foreign judgment if the latter was obtained in violation of the principles of natural justice[209] or by fraud;[210] if the judgment contravenes the public policy of the requested state;[211] or if the judgment is inconsistent with an existing judgment in a dispute between the same parties on the same subject-matter.[212] Nonetheless, the HCCCA provides significant clarification of the position that should be adopted by a requested court in a Contracting State when deciding whether to recognise or enforce a judgment of a Contracting State which has assumed jurisdiction in violation of a choice of court agreement. The HCCCA accordingly permits the requested court to refuse to recognise or enforce a foreign judgment if the court of origin had assumed jurisdiction when the choice of court agreement was null and void[213] or was concluded among parties who lacked the capacity to enter into the agreement.[214]

[201] But see Art 2(1) and (2) of the HCCCA and the Judgments Convention for a list of matters which are excluded from the scope of these Conventions.

[202] visit www.hcch.net/en/instruments/conventions/status-table/?cid=98 for the list of signatories.

[203] ibid; and Chong (n 48) 61.

[204] See www.hcch.net/en/instruments/conventions/status-table/?cid=137.

[205] Art 29 of the Judgments Convention.

[206] Art 2(1)(a) read along with Art 3 of the HCCCA. Also see Art 19 of the HCCCA, which permits the Contracting States to limit the scope of the HCCA to the choice of courts that have some connection with the parties or their transaction. But see, Art 25 of the HCCCA for the meaning of 'State' in case of a non-unified legal system.

[207] Khanderia, *The Hague Judgments Project* (n 10) 458. But see Art 22 of the HCCCA, which additionally permits the Contracting States to reciprocally declare that its courts would furthermore recognise and enforce judgments that pertain to non-exclusive choice of court agreements from other Contracting State.

[208] ibid, Art 8(2) read along with Art 13. See also, T Hartley and M Dogauchi, 'Explanatory Report on the 2005 Hague Convention on Choice of Court Agreements' (HCCH Publications, 2007) 65 www.hcch.net/upload/expl37e.pdf [HCCCA, Hartley-Dogauchi Explanatory Report], which clarifies that the applicability of the concerned provision is limited to circumstances when the forum of the Contracting State 'bases its jurisdiction' under the Convention – ie as a result of the choice of court agreement. cf Art 8(3) of the HCCCA.

[209] ibid, Art 9(c).

[210] ibid, Art 9(d).

[211] ibid, Art 9(e).

[212] ibid, Art 9(f), (g).

[213] ibid, Art 9(a).

[214] ibid, Art 9(b); and HCCCA, Hartley-Dogauchi Explanatory Report (n 208) 31.

As we have seen above, under Indian law, although submission to a foreign court as a result of the parties' choice of court agreement constitutes a valid base of 'international competency', there is no clarity on whether the assumption of jurisdiction in violation of such an agreement would affect the recognition and enforcement of the decision in India. Consider a scenario when two parties, A and B, have concluded a forum selection agreement to resolve disputes that may arise in connection to their international contract on the sale of goods, say, 100 pairs of cotton socks in favour of the courts in Pretoria, South Africa. Further, assume that the courts in Brazil assume jurisdiction on the ground that the contract was to be performed within its jurisdiction. The decision is pronounced against B who has assets in India and is required to pay damages of Rs10,000 to A. Will the judgment of the Brazilian court be eligible for recognition and enforcement in India even though the court assumed jurisdiction in violation of the choice of court agreement but on the basis of another valid ground?

The Judgments Convention extends its scope to decisions which do not arise from a choice of court agreement regulated by the HCCCA.[215] As such, the Judgments Convention mandates requested courts to do away with any special procedures involved in the recognition and enforcement of foreign judgments and prohibits the review of the merits of the original decisions. In doing so, it simplifies processes and reduces the related costs involved in giving extraterritorial effect to court decisions.[216] In particular, Article 5 stipulates 13 'indirect' and permissible grounds of jurisdictional bases or filters to determine the eligibility of foreign judgments by courts of origin in Contracting States in civil and commercial matters.[217] This is to be contrasted with 'direct' jurisdiction, which concerns the rules on which a rendering court may assume jurisdiction over a matter. Indirect jurisdiction relates to the 'indirect' control that a recognising court is permitted to exercise over the court of origin through the recognition and enforcement of the latter's judgments.[218] Therefore, grounds of 'indirect' jurisdiction exhibit a power, which the recognising court exercises over the court of origin, through the process of recognition, by determining whether the jurisdiction was exercised properly or not.[219] In comparison, 'direct' jurisdiction is described as a privilege insofar as it provides the court of origin with the freedom to exert jurisdiction, without conferring the recognising court with the right to prevent the former from exercising the same.[220] The requested court in a Contracting State is therefore under an obligation to recognise or enforce a foreign judgment from another Contracting State, if the latter's courts have based jurisdiction on any one of the 13 grounds indicated in the Judgments Convention.[221] In general, the Judgments Convention prescribes grounds which are similar to those found under Indian law, to establish the international jurisdiction of the foreign forum. A court in a Contracting State is thus obligated

[215] See HCCA, 'Convention of 2 July 2019 on the Recognition and Enforcement of Foreign Judgments in Civil or Commercial Matters: Explanatory Report' (2020) Pre-Publication Version, 6 [20], available at: http://assets.hcch.net/docs/a1b0b0fc-95b1-4544-935b-b842534a120f.pdf [Explanatory Report to the Judgments Convention].

[216] Hague Conference on Private International Law 'Overview of the Judgments Project': www.hcch.net/en/projects/legislative-projects/judgments 3 and 17; and ATV Mehren, 'Enforcing Judgments Abroad: Reflections on the Design of Recognition Conventions' (1998) 24 *Brooklyn Journal of International Law* 17, 23.

[217] See Explanatory Report to the Judgments Convention (n 215) 26 [114].

[218] See R Michaels, 'Some Fundamental Jurisdictional Conceptions as Applied in Judgments Conventions' Research Paper No 123, (August 2006) *Duke Law School Legal Studies, Research Papers Series* 1, 8 (Michaels, *Some Fundamental Jurisdictional Conceptions*).

[219] ibid.

[220] ibid.

[221] See Art 5 of the Judgments Convention.

to recognise or enforce a foreign judgment from another signatory if it based its jurisdiction on inter alia:

(1) being the place of the habitual residence of the judgment-debtor;[222]
(2) the submission (express or implied) of the judgment-debtor;[223]
(3) being the place where the cause of action arose, either because as the place of the performance of a contract[224] or (in the case of a non-contractual obligation) as the place where an act or omission that directly caused harm occurred.[225]

However, unlike the principles of Indian private international law which are ambiguous to this effect,[226] the Judgments Convention unequivocally recognises the jurisdiction of a foreign court which is based on the *situs* of the immovable property as a valid ground. In this respect, the Judgments Convention provides that, in disputes arising from a short-term lease, a tenancy or a contractual obligation which is *secured by* a right *in rem* over immovable property, the jurisdiction of the foreign forum may be based on the *situs* of the immovable property[227] or any of the other 12 indirect grounds. In other words, such disputes are subject to the rules on indirect jurisdiction.

However, foreign judgments arising from disputes which solely concern rights *in rem* over immovable property or long-term tenancies which exceed six months are subject to the rule of exclusive jurisdiction stipulated in Article 6. As opposed to the 'indirect' bases which are permissible, Article 6 mandates the recognising court to give effect to the foreign judgment (from a court of another Contracting State) 'if and only if' the latter assumed jurisdiction on that ground.[228] In other words, jurisdiction assumed on any other ground would render the judgment invalid for recognition and enforcement in another Contracting State. In such matters, the requested court is thus permitted to recognise and enforce such judgments 'if and only if' the *forum rei sitae* (the court in which the immovable property is situated) has decided them.[229] To illustrate, suppose A, habitually resident in state X (New South Wales) enters into an agreement with B in state Z (France) to purchase immovable property situated in state Y (Greece), which is secured by a mortgage guaranteed by a bank in state Z (New York).[230] A defaults in the mortgage. The courts of state X (Australia) or Y (Greece) may assume 'indirect' jurisdiction by being the place of habitual residence of the judgment debtor and the *situs* of the property in a dispute concerning a contractual obligation secured by a right *in rem* over immovable property. However, a proceeding against A, who is habitually resident in state Y (Greece) in a dispute arising from his failure to register the sale deed for immovable property in state Z (New York) may exclusively be initiated in state Z (New York), by being the *situs* of the property.

[222] ibid, Art 5(a). For disputes arising out of activities carried out by natural persons, see Art 5(b), which regards the principal place of business of the judgment-debtor at the time of the initiation of the proceedings in the court of origin. Alternatively, Art 5(d) provides that, the fact that the defendant had a branch, agency or other establishment without a separate legal entity in the state of origin may also be considered provided that the judgment arose out of the activities of these establishments.

[223] ibid, Art 5(c), (e), (f), (k), (l) and (m).

[224] ibid, Art 5(g).

[225] ibid, Art 5(j).

[226] See the text accompanying notes 54–61.

[227] ibid, Art 5(h) and (i).

[228] ibid, Art 6 read along with Explanatory Report to the Judgments Convention (n 215) 53–55.

[229] ibid.

[230] For a similar illustration, see Permanent Bureau: Hague Conference on Private International Law – Explanatory Note Providing Background on the Proposed Draft Text and Identifying Outstanding Issues (April 2016), 38 [168], available at www.assets.hcch.net/docs/e402cc72-19ed-4095-b004-ac47742dbc41.pdf.

The Judgments Convention prescribes grounds which are similar to those under the HCCCA to permit a requested court in a Contracting State to refuse to recognise or enforce a foreign judgment from another signatory state. A foreign judgment in a civil or a commercial matter will therefore be denied recognition or enforcement if it was a result of proceedings which violated the fundamental principles of natural justice;[231] it was obtained by fraud;[232] it contravened the public policy of the forum;[233] or if the court of origin had assumed jurisdiction in contravention to a choice of court agreement.[234] At the same time, the Judgments Convention additionally addresses the predicaments that may arise during the recognition and enforcement of conflicting judgments from parallel proceedings, a factor which is not addressed under the HCCCA.[235] The Judgments Convention accordingly permits the recognising court to refuse (or to postpone) recognition or enforcement of a foreign judgment, if proceedings between the same parties in the same cause of action are pending before it, provided that it was seised before the court of origin.[236]

It is suggested that India ratifies both Hague Conventions to promote predictability and access to justice in the Republic. At present, Indian law on the subject lacks transparency or consistency. As a result of the lack of codification, interested parties must peruse a jungle of case law to decipher the factors which confer a foreign court with the requisite 'international jurisdiction' or 'competency' when the judgment of that forum would have to be recognised or enforced in India. In particular, India's accession to the HCCCA would foster the Republic's goals of promoting party autonomy in the choice of the court and would accordingly introduce certainty that the courts in the Republic will not recognise or enforce a foreign judgment in a forum that has assumed jurisdiction in contravention of a choice of court agreement. These apart, the introduction of the HCCCA and the Judgments Convention into Indian law will promote predictability as regards the country's stance on the 'public policy' and 'inconsistent judgments' exceptions, both of which are presently impliedly accepted in the Republic.

VI. Conclusion

In this chapter, we have examined the principles of Indian private international law on the recognition and enforcement of monetary and non-monetary foreign judgments. The law on the subject is stipulated in sections 13, 14 and 44-A of the CPC. In particular, we saw that the doctrine of obligation forms the backbone of the law on the subject. The principle is based on the premise that the judgment debtor owes an obligation to the judgment creditor under the law of the state which passed the decision. For this reason, a foreign judgment cannot have an automatic effect in India. Instead, the foreign judgment merely constitutes a cause of action which must be recognised or enforced by initiating a fresh legal proceeding in India. The principle of reciprocity thus has a limited effect in the Republic to the extent that Indian law permits foreign judgments from the superior courts of certain countries which have been notified as such by the Central Government to have an automatic effect in the country. At the same time, it was seen that all foreign judgments, regardless of whether or not from a reciprocating country, must conform

[231] Art 7(a) of the Judgments Convention.
[232] ibid, Art 7(b).
[233] ibid, Art 7(c).
[234] ibid, Art 7(d).
[235] ibid, Art 7(2).
[236] ibid read along with the Explanatory Report to the Judgments Convention (n 215) 62–63 [273]–[276].

to the requirement of being pronounced by a court which possesses international jurisdiction and is thus considered as 'internationally competent' under Indian law. The principles on which a foreign court is considered as internationally competent have not been clarified by statute. In such circumstances, judicial dicta have enunciated that the nationality or the habitual residence of the judgment debtor will constitute valid grounds conferring international jurisdiction on a foreign forum. Likewise, the express or implied submission of the judgment debtor will also confer international competency on the foreign court. This chapter shed light on 'cause of action' impliedly being recognised under Indian law.

Further, this chapter demonstrated that Indian law does not adopt a clear position on the *situs* of the immovable property as a valid basis, insofar as some decisions have not recognised this factor to be relevant in establishing the competency of the foreign forum. Any foreign decision in a civil or a commercial matter which is pronounced by a court of international competency may, nonetheless, be denied effect in India if the judgment debtor proves that the proceedings violated the fundamental principles of natural justice, the decision was obtained by fraud, or the judgment contravenes the principles of international or domestic law. Further, it was seen that public policy and inconsistent judgments have impliedly been recognised as grounds that permit an Indian court to deny giving effect to a foreign judgment.

Lastly, the chapter reflected on the position of Indian law vis-à-vis trends in other jurisdictions. In doing so, the chapter took a bird's eye view in comparing Indian law with the laws of Australia, New Zealand, Canada, South Africa, Nepal and the EU. The chapter additionally embarked on India's position at the HCCH and deliberated whether the Republic should accede to the HCCCA and the Judgments Convention, two instruments which attempt to harmonise and unify the law on recognition and enforcement of foreign judgments. It was seen that, although the principles of Indian private international law generally adhere to the provisions of the HCCCA and the Judgments Convention, the Republic will nonetheless benefit by acceding to these two instruments, thereby promoting predictability and access to justice in India.

13

The Recognition and Enforcement of Foreign Arbitral Awards

I. Introduction

Arbitration, which is an alternative dispute resolution mechanism, has in recent times increasingly been preferred to litigation by parties for the adjudication of their disputes. This is because arbitration has the benefits of being flexible and neutral. Unlike proceedings before a court, arbitration is not cumbersome.[1] The parties may, accordingly, decide to adjudicate their disputes by arbitration at a venue of their choice, depending on their convenience. They can also choose the procedural rules that will govern the arbitration process.[2] Moreover, the law regulating arbitration has evolved at a fast pace, when compared to litigation, with considerable efforts to harmonise the legal principles on the subject.[3] The international instruments in the form of the 1985 UNCITRAL Model Law on International Commercial Arbitration (UNCITRAL Model Law)[4] have been universally accepted, thus rendering the law on the subject predictable and certain.

In the context of recognition and enforcement, the successful efforts to harmonise the legal principles with the enactment of the 1927 Geneva Convention on the Execution of Foreign Arbitral Awards (1927 Geneva Convention);[5] and UNCITRAL's 1958 Convention on the Recognition and Enforcement of Foreign Arbitral Awards (popularly known as the New York Convention)[6] have accelerated the free movement of arbitral award and have thereby promoted access to justice. Most importantly, unlike in the case of litigation, the parties do not have to familiarise themselves with the vastly differing rules of another jurisdiction or peruse a jungle of case law to ascertain the legal position in a country. As we have seen in the preceding chapter on the recognition and enforcement of foreign judgments, the law on the subject obligates the parties to familiarise themselves with the law of the country where the decision is to be recognised or enforced if it is

[1] See G Cuniberti, 'Beyond Contract – The Case of Default Arbitration in International Commercial Disputes' (2009) 32(2) *Fordham International Law Journal* 417, 423–427.

[2] ibid 430.

[3] For a detailed discussion on the history of international treaties on arbitration, see A Nussbaum, 'Treaties on Commercial Arbitration – A Test of International Private-Law Legislation' (1942) 56 *Harvard Law Review* 219; and P Tercier, 'The 1927 Geneva Convention and the ICC Reform Proposals' (2008) 2 *Dispute Resolution International* 19.

[4] The text of the UNCITRAL Model Law is available at: www.uncitral.org/pdf/english/texts/arbitration/ml-arb/07-86998_Ebook.pdf. For a detailed discussion on the UNCITRAL Model Law, see JMH Hunter, 'The UNCITRAL Model Law' (1985) 13 *International Business Law* 399; and R Sorieul, 'The Influence of the New York Convention on the UNCITRAL Model Law on International Commercial Arbitration' (2008) 2(1) *Dispute Resolution International* 27–42.

[5] The official text of the 1927 Geneva Convention may be accessed in the League of Nations, '*Treaty Series*' vol 92, 301, available at: https://treaties.un.org/doc/Publication/UNTS/LON/Volume%2092/v92.pdf.

[6] The official text of the New York Convention is available at the United Nations, *Treaty Series*, Vol 330, 3, https://treaties.un.org/pages/ViewDetails.aspx?src=TREATY&mtdsg_no=XXII-1&chapter=22&clang=_en.

pronounced in their favour so that the judgment does not become *brutum fulmen*. In comparison, the unification of the law of arbitration has effectively addressed the roadblocks that have prevailed in proceedings before a court. For this reason, scholars recommend the application of arbitration as a default mechanism to resolve international commercial disputes.[7]

In India, unlike the law on the recognition and enforcement of foreign judgments, the principles that regulate the recognition and enforcement of foreign awards have been predicated on well-defined grounds and are thus predictable and certain. One of the primary reasons for these developments in Indian private international law on the subject may be attributed to the Republic's pro-activeness in acceding to international conventions on the subject.

This chapter discusses the law on the recognition and enforcement of foreign arbitral awards in India. It is divided into six parts. Section II (section I being this Introduction) provides a general overview of the law on the recognition and enforcement of foreign arbitral awards in India. It discusses the statutory framework of the law on the subject in section II.A. Section II.B subsequently discusses the scope and meaning of foreign arbitral awards as interpreted under the provisions of the Arbitration and Conciliation Act 1996 (ACA). Section II.C assesses the law on foreign arbitral awards under the New York Convention or the 1927 Geneva Convention, by reference to Indian case law. Section III discusses the execution of foreign arbitral awards in India. In doing so, it highlights the statutory requirements in the ACA which prohibit the Indian court to annul a foreign award which has been given under foreign law in section III.A. Section III.B discusses the procedural requirements to recognise or enforce a foreign arbitral award which has been issued under the New York Convention or the 1927 Geneva Convention. Section IV discusses the grounds on which an Indian court may refuse to recognise or enforce a foreign arbitral award under the New York Convention or the 1927 Geneva Convention. Section V provides concluding remarks. It has not been deemed necessary to reflect on the position of Indian law on the subject, given the country's ratification of the 1927 Geneva Convention and the New York Convention, which have been universally accepted and have resulted in the harmonisation of Indian law on the subject with global trends.[8]

II. The Law on the Recognition and Enforcement of Foreign Arbitral Awards

A. The Statutory Framework

In general, in India, the law on arbitration is stipulated in the Arbitration and Conciliation Act 1996[9] (ACA), which draws on the provisions of the UNCITRAL Model Law. The legislation consolidates the legal provisions on the subject by repealing the Arbitration (Protocol and Convention) Act 1937 (which gave effect to the provisions of the 1927 Geneva Convention) and the Foreign Awards (Recognition and Enforcement) Act 1961 (1961 Act) (which gave effect to the provisions of the New York Convention). The ACA was thus enacted to foster India's ability to meet international standards and best practices concerning the recognition and enforcement of

[7] See in this respect, Cuniberti (n 1) 417 et seq.

[8] For a list of signatories to the 1927 Geneva Convention, visit: http://treaties.un.org/pages/LONViewDetails.aspx?src=LON&id=550&chapter=30&clang=_en. For a list of Contracting States of the New York Convention, visit: http://treaties.un.org/pages/ViewDetails.aspx?src=TREATY&mtdsg_no=XXII-1&chapter=22&clang=_en.

[9] Act No 26 of 1996.

domestic and foreign arbitral awards.[10] The mechanism to regulate the recognition and enforcement of foreign arbitral awards is stipulated in Part II of the ACA which implements India's obligations under the 1927 Geneva Convention and the New York Convention.

The expressions 'recognition' and 'enforcement' have not been defined in the 1927 Geneva Convention, the New York Convention or the ACA. The Official Commentary to the New York Convention, however, interprets the term 'recognition' as the 'legal force and effect of an award'.[11] On the other hand, 'enforcement' is 'the forced execution of an award previously recognized by the same State'.[12] Although some jurisdictions may require a foreign award creditor to seek recognition and enforcement of an award,[13] Indian private international law permits an application for the recognition of the foreign arbitral award to be requested independently, to 'shield against re-agitation of issues with which the award deals'.[14]

Section 44 to 52 of ACA stipulate the requirements for the recognition and enforcement of foreign arbitral awards, which have been rendered under the New York Convention. Likewise, sections 53 to 60 of the ACA govern the recognition and enforcement of foreign arbitral awards which have been given under the 1927 Geneva Convention. Foreign arbitral awards which have not been given under either of these international instruments are not regulated under the provisions of the ACA.

B. The Scope and Meaning of a 'Foreign Arbitral Award'

A 'foreign arbitral award' that is given under the New York Convention is defined under section 44 of the ACA. It is one which has been made in a 'reciprocating' territory to settle disputes 'on differences between persons arising out of legal relationships' in an international commercial[15] matter by arbitration[16] pursuant to an agreement which is evidenced in writing.[17] The parties' intention to settle their disputes by arbitration must therefore be clearly established by their conduct since its effect is to exclude the authority of national courts to adjudicate upon disputes.[18] Indian law will consider an arbitration agreement to have been concluded, even when it has not been signed or when there is no exchange of documents. An example is when the parties have accepted other aspects of the contract which contains the arbitration clause.[19]

[10] For the development of international commercial arbitration in India, see TS Work, 'India Satisfies Its Jones for Arbitration: New Arbitration Law in India' (1997) 10 *Transnational Law* 217; and FS Nariman, 'India and International Arbitration' (2009) 41 *George Washington International Law Review* 367.

[11] See UNCITRAL Secretariat, 'Guide on the Convention on the Recognition and Enforcement of Foreign Arbitral Awards' (New York 1958), Commentary to Article 1(1), 9 [7]–[8] [Commentary to the New York Convention], available at: www.uncitral.org/pdf/english/texts/arbitration/NY-conv/2016_Guide_on_the_Convention.pdf.

[12] ibid.

[13] ibid, 9 [9]–[10].

[14] ibid, 10, [11], referring to the decision of the Supreme Court of India in *Brace Transport Corporation of Monrovia, Bermuda v Orient Middle East Lines Ltd. & Ors* 12 October 1993, Civil Appeals Nos 5438–39 of 1993.

[15] See Art I(3) of the New York Convention.

[16] Section 44 of the ACA read along with Art I of the New York Convention. See also, generally, J Gill, 'The Definition of Award under the New York Convention' (2008) 2 *Dispute Resolution International* 114.

[17] Section 44(a) of the ACA read along with s 7 of the ACA, which describes the circumstances in which, an arbitration agreement will be construed to be in writing. See also, generally, L Boo, 'The Writing Requirement in Contemporary Practice: Is There Really a Need for Change' (2008) 2 *Dispute Resolution International* 75.

[18] See the decision of the Supreme Court in *Cheran Properties Ltd. v Kasturi & Sons Ltd. & Ors* Civil Appeal Nos 10025–10026 of 2017, 22, fn 10, referring to C Partasides and N Blackaby, *Redfern and Hunter on International Arbitration* 5th edn (OUP, 2009) 89–90; and Commentary to Art II(1) of the New York Convention (n 11) 44, [17], referring to *Smita Conductors Ltd. v Euro Alloys Ltd* AIR [2001] SCW 3517.

[19] ibid.

The New York Convention does not mandate reciprocity as a fundamental criterion. Accordingly, a Contracting State is not obligated to limit the recognition or enforcement of foreign arbitral awards to those made in another signatory.[20] A state may, instead, decide to recognise and enforce a foreign arbitral award from any country (regardless of whether it is a signatory). The New York Convention, nonetheless, permits Contracting States to make a reservation and only recognise and enforce arbitral awards made in another signatory.[21] India has opted in favour of the application of the principle of reciprocity. Foreign arbitral awards which have been given in a reciprocating territory notified as such in the Official Gazette of the Central Government will be recognised or enforced in the Republic.[22] At present, India has notified the following signatories as reciprocating:[23] Australia, Austria, Belgium, Botswana, Bulgaria, Central African Republic, Chile, Cuba, Czech, Slovak (the former Czechoslovak Socialist Republic), Denmark, Ecuador, the Arab Republic of Egypt, Finland, France, Germany, Ghana, Greece, Hong Kong, Hungary, Italy, Republic of Ireland, Japan, Republic of Korea, Kuwait, Malagasy Republic, Malaysia, Mexico, Morocco, the Netherlands, Nigeria, Norway, the Philippines, Poland, Romania, Russia, San Marino, Singapore, Spain, Sweden, Switzerland, the Syrian Arab Republic, the United Republic of Tanzania, Thailand, Trinidad and Tobago, Tunisia, the UK, and the US.[24] However, the break-up of a territory which has been notified as 'reciprocating' would not affect the enforceability of awards rendered in that country after its political separation.[25] In other words, a state (which has been politically separated) will therefore continue to be recognised as a reciprocating territory under Indian law.[26]

Although the provisions of the ACA do not define the term 'commercial', regard may be had to its interpretation in the UNCITRAL Model Law on which the provisions of the legislation are predicated.[27] In general, the courts in India construe a broad as opposed to a restricted meaning to the term 'commercial'.[28] An agreement would be 'commercial' whether or not it arises from a contract[29] and would include transactions for the sale of goods and services,[30] factoring and leasing, to name a few. The ACA provides that a commercial arbitration agreement would be considered as 'international' when any of the parties is a foreign national or habitually resident outside India. Where party to the arbitration agreement is a body corporate whose central management and control are outside India, the agreement will also be treated as international.[31] Although the statute denotes that the place of performance is irrelevant when determining

[20] See Art I(3) of the New York Convention. See also, generally, WW Park, 'Non-Signatories and the New York Convention' (2008) 2 *Dispute Resolution International* 84.

[21] ibid.

[22] Section 44(b) of the ACA.

[23] See the website of the ICC, available at: http://library.iccwbo.org/content/dr/COUNTRY_ANSWERS/CA_SUPP_0029_31.htm?l1=Country+Answers&l2=India.

[24] ibid.

[25] See the decision of the Supreme Court in *Transocean Shipping Agency Pvt Ltd v Black Sea Shipping & Ors* [1998] (2) SCC 281, 284.

[26] ibid.

[27] See Art I of the UNCITRAL Model Law.

[28] See Commentary to Art 1(3) of the New York Convention (n 11) 33, 34 [85]–[86]; referring to the decision of the High Court of Gujarat in *Union of India & Ors v Lief Hoegh & Co. & Ors* 4 May 1982; and M Pryles, 'Reservations Available to Member States: The Reciprocal and Commercial Reservations', in E Gaillard and D Di Pietro (eds), *Enforcement of Arbitration Agreements and International Arbitral Awards: The New York Convention in Practice* (Cameron May, 2008) 161, 178–79.

[29] Section 44 of the ACA read along with ss 2(f) and 7 of the ACA; *Gas Authority of India Ltd v SPIE CAPAG, SA & Ors* [1993] (27) DRJ; and *Enercon (India) Limited & Ors. v Enercon GmbH & Anr* Civil Appeal No 2806 of 2014 [79].

[30] See in this regard, the decision of the Supreme Court in *R.M. Investment and Trading Co. (P) Ltd v Boeing Co.*, [1994] SCC (4) 541.

[31] Section 2(f) of the ACA.

whether an arbitration agreement is 'international', the dictum of the Delhi High Court in *Gas Authority of India Ltd v SPIE CAPAG, SA & Ors*,[32] albeit of persuasive value, indicates to the contrary. The decision, which concerned the recognition and enforcement of a foreign arbitral award in India, stipulated that an arbitration agreement would inter alia be construed as 'international' if it was performed abroad.[33] The Supreme Court in *World Sport Group (Mauritius) Ltd v MSM Satellite (Singapore) PTE Ltd* has confirmed that the agreement to arbitrate does not violate sections 23 or 28 of the ICA which prohibits, as illegal and opposed to public policy, all contracts which restrict the right to a legal proceeding.[34] An arbitration agreement is separable and severable from the substantive provisions in the main contract, which stipulate the rights and obligations of the parties regarding performance.[35]

Section 53 of the ACA defines a foreign arbitral award which has been given under the 1927 Geneva Convention in a manner which is similar to section 48 discussed above. The foreign arbitral award must be made in a reciprocating territory and must be given under the parties' agreement in writing to settle their international commercial disputes by arbitration. Unlike the New York Convention, the provisions of the 1927 Geneva Convention limit recognition and enforcement to foreign arbitral awards 'rendered in proceedings "between persons who are subject to the jurisdiction of one of the High Contracting Parties"'.[36]

C. Foreign Arbitral Awards Given Following Reference by an Indian Court

In certain circumstances, a foreign arbitral award under the New York Convention or the 1927 Geneva Convention may be issued after an Indian court decides to refer the parties to an international commercial contract to arbitration in a reciprocating territory.[37] Sections 45 and 54 of the ACA empower the court to refer parties to arbitration when it has been 'seized of an action in a matter to which the parties have made an such an agreement' upon a request by one party. The court may, however, refrain from referring the parties when it finds that the arbitration agreement 'is null and void, inoperative or incapable of being performed'.[38] The court will therefore be empowered to refer the matter to arbitration even if the main contract is null and void.[39] This is because an arbitration agreement is separable from the rest of the contract.[40]

In *Shin-Etsu Chemical Co Ltd v Aksh Optifibre Ltd*, the Supreme Court clarified that the determination regarding the validity of the arbitration agreement must be based on a prima facie

[32] (n 29).

[33] ibid, headnote.

[34] Civil Appeal No 895 of 2014 [11], [31].

[35] *Reva Electric Car company Pvt Ltd v Green Mobil*, [2012] 2 SCC 93; *Enercon (India) Limited* (n 29) [79], [80]; and *World Sport Group (Mauritius)* (n 34) [23], [24] referring to the decision of the House of Lords in *Premium Nafta Products Ltd v Fili* [2007] UKHL 40. See also, K Hober and A Magnusson, 'The Special Status of Agreements to Arbitrate: The Separability Doctrine; Mandatory Stay of Litigation.' (May 2008) 2(1) *Dispute Resolution International* 56–74.

[36] See the Commentary to the New York Convention (n 11) 8 [4].

[37] See ss 45 and 54 of the ACA.

[38] ibid. See also, *Shin-Etsu Chemical Co Ltd v Aksh Optifibre Ltd* [2005] 7 SCC 234; *SMS Tea Estates (P) Ltd v Chandmari Tea Co. (P) Ltd* [2011] 14 SCC 66; and *World Sport Group (Mauritius)* (n 34) [23], [24] referring to the decision of the House of Lords in *Premium Nafta* (n 34).

[39] See the decision of the courts in *Reva Electric Car company Pvt Ltd* (n 35); *Enercon (India) Limited* (n 29) [79], [80]; and *World Sport Group (Mauritius)* (n 34) [23], [24].

[40] ibid.

examination, as opposed to a final finding.[41] In doing so, the court referred to the judicial practice in major jurisdictions such as France, Switzerland, Hong Kong, the UK and Ontario and thus frowned upon rendering a final finding on the validity of an international commercial arbitration agreement for a number of reasons.[42] The court indicated that a final finding on the validity of an international commercial arbitration agreement has the susceptibility of exposing it to the danger of elongated proceedings due to the need to record the necessary evidence. A final finding which has relied on affidavits (and not evidence) is considered to have been based on insufficient material.[43] The need to record evidence is, therefore, mandatory in a full-fledged hearing to eliminate the likelihood of fraud, coercion and other similar acts that may render the agreement null and void.[44] In a related vein, as we have seen, the principles of Indian private international law obligate a court to apply the proper law of the arbitration agreement, which is usually the same as the proper law of the contract,[45] to test its validity at the time of making a final finding.[46] A final finding on the validity of the arbitration agreement may therefore require proof of foreign law, based on in-depth evidence as opposed to affidavits.[47] The obligation to make a final finding would thus lead to 'enormous expenditures' and delays.[48]

Moreover, a final finding would be counter-productive of the principle of *res judicata* if that court was faced with a similar question regarding the validity of the arbitration agreement at the time of enforcement.[49]

The court's decision to refuse to refer the parties to arbitration is appealable to the Commercial Division of the High Court under section 50(1)(a) of the ACA.[50] At the same time, the court's decision that the international commercial arbitration agreement is valid is not appealable under section 50.[51] The decision of the Supreme Court in *World Sport Group (Mauritius) Ltd*[52] illustrates the circumstances in which an international commercial arbitration agreement would be considered as 'null and void inoperative or incapable of being performed'. The Court was seized of a dispute which arose after MSM had concluded an agreement with World Sport in which the latter agreed to relinquish to MSM media rights that it had initially acquired from the Board of Cricket Control (BCCI) to broadcast a cricket tournament.[53] The terms of the contract permitted MSM to re-acquire the rights which it had held over several years from BCCI (before the latter gave them to World Sport) to telecast the tournament.[54] The dispute arose when MSM sued World Sport before the Bombay High Court and alleged that the latter had relinquished rights which it did not have by fraudulent misrepresentation.[55] The chief issue before the Supreme Court was whether Indian law permitted the Judiciary to refer the matter to arbitration when

[41] (n 38).
[42] ibid 240 et seq.
[43] ibid 238.
[44] (2005) 7 SC 234.
[45] See the decision of the Supreme Court in *National Thermal Power Corporation v Singer Corporation* [1992] 3 SCC 551.
[46] *Shin-Etsu* (n 38) 238, 239.
[47] ibid.
[48] ibid.
[49] ibid 238.
[50] ibid. See also, ss 3A, 4, 7 and 10 of the Commercial Division and Commercial Appellate Division of High Courts Act 2015 [CCA] read along with ss 47 and 50 of the Arbitration and Conciliation (Amendment) Act 2015 [2015 Arbitration Act].
[51] ibid.
[52] (n 34).
[53] ibid.
[54] ibid.
[55] ibid.

the claim involved an allegation of fraud.[56] The Court stated that an arbitration agreement would be regarded as null and void when there was no consensus between the parties, for instance, when the consent was received by misrepresentation, coercion, fraud or undue influence.[57] In such circumstances, the arbitration agreement would be 'devoid of any legal effect'.[58] Likewise, an arbitration agreement would be considered as 'inoperative' when it has ceased to have an effect, for instance, when the time limit to refer the matter to a tribunal has passed or when there is already a court decision which operates as *res judicata* between the same parties on the same matter.[59] An agreement would be 'incapable of being performed' when it is not possible to set up an arbitral tribunal for some reason, such as when the arbitration clause is vaguely worded.[60] The Court, however, refused to hold that the arbitration agreement as vitiated by fraud because of the doctrine of separability which separates such clauses from the rest of the contract. Accordingly, the court referred the parties to arbitration.

It must be noted that the *mere enquiry* into allegations of fraud would not, however, render an arbitration agreement null and void, inoperative or incapable of being performed.[61] Instead:

> it is only in those cases where the court finds that there are serious allegations of fraud, which make a virtual case of criminal offence ... [that] it becomes necessary that such complex issues can be decided only by the civil court on the appreciation of evidence that needs to be produced.[62]

III. The Execution of Foreign Arbitral Awards in India

A. The Prohibition of the Annulment of an Award

Indian private international law prohibits an Indian court from annulling a foreign arbitral award under the New York Convention or the 1927 Geneva Convention. Instead, the ACA empowers the Indian courts to refuse to recognise or to enforce a foreign arbitral award that is given under the New York Convention or the 1927 Geneva Convention if it has violated any criteria indicated in sections 48 or 57 respectively. The Supreme Court in *Bharat Aluminium Co. v Kaiser Aluminium Technical Service Inc.* (popularly referred to as *BALCO*) stated that arbitral awards which have been made in another Contracting State would not be considered as 'domestic' under Indian procedural law.[63] For this reason, an award, which is otherwise valid under the law of the country where it was given, cannot be annulled by the Indian judiciary under section 34, if the court is not the juridical 'seat' of the agreement.[64] This is for the reason that section 34 is included in Part I of the ACA, whose regulation is limited to domestic arbitral awards.[65] Thus, only the

[56] ibid.
[57] ibid [27].
[58] Commentary to Art II(3) of the New York Convention (n 11) 70 [104].
[59] ibid [29], referring to Kronke, Nacimiento, et al (eds), *Recognition and Conferment of Foreign Arbitral Awards: A Global Commentary on the New York Convention* (Wolters Kluwer, 2010) 82.
[60] ibid [26].
[61] ibid [29].
[62] *Ameet Lalchand Shah & Ors v Rishab Enterb & Anr* SC Civ. Appeal No 4690 of 2018 arising out of SLP(C) No 16789 of 2017 [31].
[63] (2012) 9 SCC 552 [137]–[138], which overruled the earlier decisions in *National Thermal Power* (n 45); *Bhatia International v Bulk Trading SA* [2002] 4 SCC 105; and *Venture Global Engineering v Satyam Computer Services Ltd & Anr* [2008] 4 SCC 190.
[64] ibid.
[65] ibid.

court in the country which is the seat of the arbitration may annul the decision by applying the *lex loci arbirti*, ie, the law of the jurisdiction which is the seat of the arbitration.

Under the principles of Indian private international law, the 'seat' of the arbitration is juridical.[66] The 'seat' thus refers to the supervisory and exclusive jurisdiction of the courts over the arbitration process.[67] It must be distinguished from the 'venue' of arbitration.[68] The 'venue' refers to the physical place where the arbitration proceedings are conducted for administrative convenience.[69] The courts have clarified that, in the absence of any contrary indicia, the parties' choice of a juridical seat indicates their desire to apply the arbitration law of that country.[70] If the parties do not choose such juridical seat, the same may be selected by the arbitral tribunal.[71] The courts have accordingly held that the venue of arbitration would not assume the position of the juridical seat, except when the application of the closest connection test 'concomitantly' points towards the same.[72] By this principle, the venue of an arbitration may assume the position of a seat when the former is also the place of performance and the law of the venue is the proper law of the contract.[73]

The Arbitration and Conciliation (Amendment) Act 2015 (2015 Amendment Act) expressly prohibits an Indian court from setting aside or annulling any arbitral award arising out of an international commercial agreement even when it finds it 'vitiated by patent illegality appearing on the face of the decision'.[74] A foreign arbitral award cannot, therefore, be challenged on the merits of the dispute.[75]

The Supreme Court's ruling in *BALCO* was, nonetheless, briefly overruled in 2018, in the case of *Hardy Exploration*.[76] The Judiciary stated that an international commercial arbitral award which had its juridical seat outside India could be annulled under section 34 of the ACA, unless the parties had expressly or impliedly agreed to exclude Part I of the legislation.[77] The decision opened the gates for conflicting judgments on the validity of a foreign award which could be challenged concurrently under two legal systems, namely, the law of: (1) the country of the 'seat' of arbitration; and (2) India even when it was not the juridical seat. This led to problems in the enforcement of the foreign award.[78] The Indian position on the subject has since been restored by the Supreme Court's ruling in *BGS SGS Soma JV v NHPC Ltd*, which concerns the enforcement of foreign arbitral awards under the New York Convention. The Court confirmed that foreign arbitral awards could only be challenged within the parameters stipulated in section 48 of the ACA.[79]

[66] ibid 598.

[67] ibid.

[68] ibid; and *Reliance Industries Ltd v Union of India* [2014] 7 SCC 603; and *Indus Mobile Distribution Pvt. v Datawind Innovations Pvt. Ltd* Civil Appeal Nos 5370–5371 OF 2017. But see *Brahmani River Pellets v Kamachi Industries* Civil Appeal No 5850 of 2019 [19, 20], in which, the Supreme Court stated that the 'venue' may be assumed to be the juridical 'seat'.

[69] *BGS SGS Soma JV v NHPC Ltd* Civil Appeal No 9307 of 2019 [73]–[84].

[70] ibid [69], referring to *Roger Shashoua & Ors. v Mukesh Sharma* [2009] EWHC 957 (Comm); and *Enercon (India) Limited* (n 29).

[71] See s 20(3) of the ACA read along with the 246th Report of the Law Commission, Ministry of Law and Justice vide (Notification) F.No.A-60011/48/2010-Admn.III (LA); and *BGS SGS Soma* (n 69) [92].

[72] *Enercon (India)* (n 29) [65]; and *Union of India v Hardy Exploration and Production (India) Inc* Civil Appeal No 4628 OF 2018 [29], [33] [Hardy Exploration].

[73] *Enercon (India)* ibid, [112], [121].

[74] Section 34(2A) of the 2015 Arbitration Act.

[75] *BALCO* (n 63) [135]–[142], read along with Explanation 2 to s 48 of the 2015 Arbitration Act.

[76] (n 72).

[77] ibid [34], referring to *Bhatia International v Bulk Trading SA* [2002] 4 SCC 105.

[78] *BGS SGS Soma* (n 69) [94]–[96], referring to *BALCO* (n 63) [143], [154].

[79] ibid.

B. The Procedure for Execution

Every foreign arbitral award given under the New York Convention or the 1927 Geneva Convention is eligible for recognition and enforcement in India unless it contradicts the requirements of sections 48 or 57 of the ACA respectively.

The enforcement of a foreign award is 'as if' it is a decree of the court and is akin (but not equal) to the enforcement of a decree of a court.[80] A foreign arbitral award does not 'metamorphize into a decree [un]till the court is satisfied that it is enforceable'.[81] This is because the decree in the form of an award is passed by the arbitration tribunal, which lacks the power to enforce the decision.[82] An arbitral award is 'lifeless from the point of enforceability' 'until it is made a rule of the court and a judgment and consequential decree are passed' in India.[83] While the award usually binds only the parties, it may, in certain occasional circumstances bind third parties, for instance, when the latter have in their position as agents, assignees, representatives or successors of a party have claimed 'through or under' that party.[84] Unlike in the case of recognition and enforcement of foreign judgments in the Republic, Indian private international law does not require the determination of the tribunal's 'international jurisdiction' as a pre-requisite to determining the effectiveness of a foreign award in India. The procedure for the recognition and enforcement of foreign arbitral awards is therefore more straightforward.

Sections 46 and 55 of the ACA clarify that a foreign arbitral award which is capable of execution in India shall be treated as binding 'for all purposes on the persons as between whom it was made' when the foreign award creditor (ie the successful party) initiates a petition for the same before a civil court which would have had jurisdiction over the subject-matter if it was seized of the matter.[85] Indian law confers such jurisdiction over the Commercial Division of the High Court where the assets of the foreign-award debtor are located to enforce foreign awards that are sounded in money.[86] A foreign arbitral award may be recognised and enforced in all the forums where the assets of the foreign-award debtor are located.[87] In all other cases, the Commercial Division of the High Court where the foreign-award debtor resides or carries on business will have jurisdiction to enforce a foreign arbitral award if it is not sounding in money.[88]

It must be noted that the 1927 Geneva Convention, however, obligates the foreign award creditor to seek a declaration in the country where the award was granted before applying for its enforcement in another jurisdiction.[89] The New York Convention does not stipulate a similar requirement. In this manner, the process for recognition and enforcement of foreign arbitral awards under the New York Convention facilitates international trade and commerce by

[80] *Cheran Properties Ltd* (n 17) [11].

[81] *Cairn India Ltd & Ors v Government of India* O.M.P.(EFA)(COMM.) 15/2016 & I.A. Nos 20459/2014 & 3558/2015 29 [22] fn 2, referring to GB Born, *International Commercial Arbitration: International Arbitral Awards: vol III*, 2nd edn (Wolters Kluwer Law & Business, 2014), 2980, Chapter 22.03[A].

[82] *Cheran Properties Ltd* (n 17) [11]; and N Blackaby and C Partasides with A Redfern and M Hunter, *Redfern and Hunter on International Arbitration* 5th edn (Oxford University Press, 2009) 632.

[83] *Oil and Natural Gas Commission [ONGC] v Western Company of North America* [1987] SCR (1) 1024, 1043.

[84] See *Chloro Controls (I) Pvt. Ltd v Severn Trent Water Purification Inc* [2013] 1 SCC 641, 664; and *Cheran Properties Ltd* (n 17) [23–25].

[85] Explanation to Section 47 of the ACA.

[86] ibid; and the decision of the High Court of Delhi in *Union of India v Dabhol Power Co* IA No 6663/2003 Suit No 1268/2003. Also see RJ Bettauer, 'India and International Arbitration: The *Dabhol* Experience' (2009) 41 *George Washington International Law Review* 381.

[87] *Cairn India Ltd* (n 81) [8.1].

[88] ibid.

[89] See Commentary to Articles I, IV and V of the New York Convention (n 11) 17, 18, 97, 124.

eliminating the legal and technical bottlenecks caused by the process of double *exequatur*' that is applicable under the 1927 Convention.[90]

The limitation to file a petition for the recognition or the enforcement of a foreign arbitral award in India is within three years from the date that it became final and binding on the parties in the jurisdiction where it was made.[91] Sections 47 and 56 of the ACA, obligate the party seeking to recognise or enforce a foreign arbitral award in India to present the following documents in its petition. These are:

(1) the original award or a copy thereof duly authenticated in the manner required by the law of the country in which it was made;
(2) the original arbitration agreement or duly certified copy thereof; and
(3) such evidence as may be necessary to prove that the award is foreign.[92]

IV. Disqualification of a Foreign Arbitral Award from Recognition or Enforcement in India

There are limited grounds on which, a foreign arbitral award may be refused enforcement in India. As indicated above, the ACA prohibits the court from refusing to recognise or to enforce a foreign arbitral award, except if it violates one or more criteria indicated in sections 48 or 57 of legislation. This section discusses the grounds on which a foreign arbitral award may be refused recognition or enforcement under the New York Convention and the 1927 Geneva Convention.

A. Disqualification of Foreign Awards under the New York Convention

The New York Convention stipulates 'a "ceiling" or a maximum level of control', which Contracting States may exercise for the execution of foreign arbitral and arbitral agreements.[93] Accordingly, section 48 of the ACA which incorporates Article V of the New York Convention into Indian law permits a court to refuse the recognition or the enforcement of a foreign arbitral award if the award-debtor furnishes the court with the proof of one or more of the following:

(1) The parties subject to arbitration were under some incapacity under the law applicable to them; or, when the agreement is not valid under the law to which the parties have subjected it or, failing any indication thereon, under the law of the country where the award was made.[94]
(2) The foreign-award debtor was not given proper notice of the appointment of the arbitrator or, of the arbitration proceedings or, was otherwise unable to present his case.[95]
(3) The award deals with a difference or, contains decisions, which are outside the scope of the parties' agreement.[96]

[90] ibid.
[91] Article 137 of the Limitation Act 1963, Act No 36 of 1963.
[92] ibid; and *Glencore Grain Rotterdam B.V.* v *Shivnath Rai Harnarain (India) Co* C.S. (O.S.) 541 of 1998.
[93] Commentary to the New York Convention (n 11) 190 [5].
[94] Section 48(1)(a) of the ACA; and Art 5(1)(a) of the New York Convention.
[95] Section 48(1)(b) of the ACA; and Art 5(1)(b) of the New York Convention.
[96] Section 48(1)(c) of the ACA; and Art 5(1)(c) of the New York Convention.

(4) The composition of the arbitral tribunal or its procedure was not according to the agreement of the parties or the law of the country where it was held.[97]
(5) The award has not yet become binding on the parties, or has been set aside or suspended i) by a competent authority in the country, in which the award was made or, ii) under the law where the award was made.[98]

Each of these grounds has been discussed in detail below.

i. Defences Available to the Foreign Award Debtor

a. Incapacity of the Parties or the Invalidity of the Agreement

The term 'capacity' indicates 'the legal ability of a person to act and enter into an agreement in its own name and on its own behalf'.[99] There is no reported case where a foreign arbitral award has been refused enforcement due to the incapacity of the parties at the time of the conclusion of the arbitration agreement. However, the ACA empowers the court to refuse to give effect to a foreign arbitral award in India if the arbitration agreement has been concluded between parties who lacked the capacity to contract. The appropriate time to assess the capacity of the parties is the time of the conclusion of the contract. The capacity of the parties must be tested according to the law applicable to them.[100] As we have seen in the chapter on 'Applicable Law in Contractual Obligations', the law that will govern the capacity of the parties is different from the law that will govern most other parts of the contract, which includes the arbitration clause. The Supreme Court in *Technip SA v SMS Holding (Pvt) Ltd & Ors* indicated in an *obiter dictum* that the *lex loci domicilii* (the law of the domicile of the person) should govern the questions on the capacity of the parties, subject to the public policy of India.[101] Section 10 of the ICA authorises all persons who are above 18 years of age to conclude contracts. The fact that only one party lacked the capacity would suffice to invalidate the foreign arbitral award.[102] Thus, the law to test the capacity of the parties and the validity of the parties' agreement differs.

Similarly, the invalidity of the arbitration agreement 'under the law to which the parties have subjected it' will result in the failure of the foreign arbitral award to be recognised or enforced under Indian law. As we have seen in chapter 10 on 'Applicable Law in Contractual Obligations', the putative proper law of the contract will govern the question of the validity of the contract.[103] Therefore, if the parties have expressly chosen the governing law for their international commercial contract, then the validity of their arbitration agreement will be governed by that law. Suppose the parties have not expressly or impliedly chosen the law to govern their arbitration agreement.[104] In that case, the ACA empowers the courts to assess the validity of the same under 'the law of the country where the award was made'.[105]

[97] Section 48(1)(d) of the ACA; and Art 5(1)(d) of the New York Convention. Also see *BGS SGS Soma* (n 69) [35]; and *Hardy Exploration* (n 72) [15, 24].
[98] Section 48(1)(e) of the ACA; and Art 5(1)(e) of the New York Convention; and the decision of the Supreme Court in *BALCO* (n 63) [135]–[142].
[99] See the Commentary to the New York Convention (n 11) 135 [11].
[100] ibid 138 [19].
[101] See EA Fredericks, 'Contractual Capacity and the Conflict of Laws in Common Law Jurisdictions (Part 2): Australasia, North America, Asia and Africa' (2020) 41(1) *Obiter* 10, 31–32 referring to *Technip SA* [2005] 60 SCL 249 SC.
[102] See the Commentary to the New York Convention (n 11) 135 [9].
[103] See the decision of the Supreme Court in *National Thermal Power* (n 63) [6].
[104] See the Commentary to the New York Convention (n 11) 142 [31].
[105] ibid.

As indicated earlier, *Shin-Etsu*[106] clarified that the courts in India are merely empowered to make a prima facie finding on the validity of the arbitration agreement. It is, therefore, the arbitral tribunal which has the authority to render a final finding on the same.[107] Thus, the courts have held that 'all issues, including jurisdictional objections' should be decided by the arbitrator having regard to the principle of *kompetenz-kompetenz* which is applicable under Indian law.[108] However, just as the Indian court may decline to refer the parties to arbitration if it prima facie finds that the agreement is invalid for some reason (such as when the parties lacked the capacity to conclude the agreement or when the consent of the parties is not valid because it was obtained by fraud or deception the incapacity of the parties), it may refuse to recognise or enforce the foreign arbitral award for the same reason.[109]

b. Lack of Due Process

The lack of due process in the form of procedural irregularities will invalidity a foreign arbitral award in India.[110] Such irregularities must, however, be raised by the foreign award-debtor.[111] The court is prohibited from raising such issues on its own motion.[112] There is no reported case in which the courts have refused to recognise or enforce an award on this ground. Thus, there are high standards that the court will adopt before invalidating an award on this ground. A foreign arbitral award may, nonetheless, be invalidated if the party against whom it is sought has not been given proper notice of the arbitral proceedings or the appointment of the arbitrator. At the same time, there are no formal requirements as to the form or service of the notice.[113] The court will generally consider the conduct of the parties, as opposed to the technicalities of the service to assess whether the party was aware or ought to have been aware of the proceedings.[114] Similarly, the inability of the award-debtor to present its case by not being given an opportunity to be heard will empower the court to refuse to recognise or enforce a foreign award.[115]

c. Award Addresses a Dispute Outside Terms of Parties' Submission to Arbitration

A court may refuse to recognise or enforce a foreign arbitral award if it contains a decision which is outside the scope of the parties' agreement to arbitrate. Such an award will be conceived as patently illegal and against the public policy of India insofar as the decision of the arbitral tribunal contravenes the express terms of the parties' contract.[116] As the court in an *obiter dictum* in *Cairn India Ltd* illustrated, a foreign award will be construed as being outside the scope of

[106] (n 38).
[107] ibid 238 et seq.
[108] See the decision of the Supreme Court in *M/s Uttarakhand Purv Sainik Kalyan Nigam Ltd v Northern Coal Field Ltd* Special Leave Petition (C) No 11476 of 2018 [9.11]; and the decision of the Delhi High Court in *Kalyan Nigam Limited and Union of India v Shapoorji Pallonji & Co. Pvt. Ltd* ARB.P. 588/2019 [6].
[109] *Shin-Etsu* (n 38) 238 et seq; and the Commentary to the New York Convention (n 11) 134 [5].
[110] See the Commentary to the New York Convention, ibid 155 [1].
[111] ibid 155 [2].
[112] ibid.
[113] ibid 161 [22], [25].
[114] ibid 162 [26].
[115] see *Shri Lal Mahal Ltd v Progetto Grano Spa* (2014) 2 SCC; *ONGC Ltd v Saw Pipes Ltd* [2003] 5 SCC 705, 723–24 [31] *[Saw Pipes]*; and *Renusagar Power Co. Ltd v General Electric Co* [1994] Supp (1) SCC 644. Also see Commentary to the New York Convention, ibid 163 [31].
[116] *Cairn India Ltd* (n 81) 39 and 40 referring to the decisions of the Supreme Court in *Saw Pipes* (n 115); and *Renusagar Power Co* ibid 69.

the parties' agreement if the arbitral tribunal had awarded an amount which exceeded the sum agreed in the contract.[117]

Likewise, the tribunal's decision to decide the dispute *ex aequo et bono*, according to the principles of soft law or non-state law in the absence of an express indication or authorisation by the parties will be considered as patently illegal and a contravention of India's public policy. Such awards will, therefore, not be recognised or enforced in India if the foreign award-debtor furnishes proof to this effect.[118]

In *Prakash Steelage Ltd v Uzac SA*, the French arbitral tribunal applied the UNIDROIT Principles on International Commercial Contracts [PICC][119] to adjudicate a dispute on the sale of stainless steel between the respondent, Prakash Steelage Ltd (a company incorporated in India) and Uzuc SA (a company incorporated in Romania).[120] However, the parties had not chosen the PICC to govern their dispute and had instead, opposed its application.[121] The parties indicated their preference for being governed by the substantive laws of their country.[122] The tribunal decided the matter against the Prakash Steelage Ltd which was ordered to pay damages of €1 million for breach of its contractual obligations.[123] The Paris Court of Appeal refused to annul the decision of the tribunal which had decided according to soft law, even when the parties had not expressly agreed on the same.[124] The decision would be unenforceable in India if the foreign award debtor (namely, Prakash Steelage Ltd) furnishes proof to the court of the same.

d. Composition of Tribunal or Procedure followed is not According to Parties' Agreement or the Law of the Seat

As the Supreme Court in *Transocean Shipping Agency P. Ltd* has opined, the standard of proof for alleging that the composition of the arbitral tribunal was irregular and not according to the parties' agreement, is high.[125] There is no reported case in which the courts in India have refused to recognise or enforce a foreign award on this ground. The ground concerns a procedural irregularity in arbitration proceedings. For this reason, it prohibits a court to refuse to recognise or enforce an award unless the person against whom raises the allegation to this effect.[126] The requirement underscores the doctrine of party autonomy, insofar as it empowers the court to refuse to recognise or enforce a foreign arbitral award if the person against whom it is sought proves that the composition of the tribunal or its procedure violated the agreement of the parties.[127] The reference to the law of the country where the arbitration took place has a subsidiary role in assessing the validity of the foreign arbitral award. Therefore, the law of the country where the arbitration took place can only be referred to in the absence of an express or implied agreement between the parties on the composition of the tribunal.[128]

[117] *Cairn India Ltd* ibid.
[118] ibid.
[119] UNIDROIT, 'UNIDROIT Principles on International Commercial Contracts, 2016': www.unidroit.org/english/principles/contracts/principles2016/principles2016-e.pdf [PICC].
[120] Cour d'appel de Paris, 25 February 2020, n° 17/18001, available at https://translate.google.com/translate?hl=en&sl=fr&u=https://www.dalloz-actualite.fr/document/paris-pole-1-ch-1-25-fevr-2020-n-1718001&prev=search, accessed on 13 May 2020.
[121] ibid.
[122] ibid.
[123] ibid.
[124] ibid.
[125] *Transocean Shipping Agency* (n 25).
[126] See the Commentary to the New York Convention (n 11) 189 [2].
[127] ibid 191 [9].
[128] ibid 193 [15].

e. Award not Yet Binding, Set Aside or Suspended in the Seat or under the Law by which Award Made

In general, an award is considered to have become binding on the parties if it is no longer open to ordinary means of challenge through a review or an appeal.[129] As we have discussed above, a foreign arbitral award is presumed to be binding on the parties.[130] For this reason, the onus lies on the foreign award-debtor to prove that the award is not binding on the parties.[131] A foreign arbitral award which is not binding or has been set aside by the competent authority in the place in which it is made or under the law where it was made, is not eligible for recognition or enforcement in India. The expression 'competent authority' refers to the court(s) which have the jurisdiction to set aside the award.[132] In this respect, the Supreme Court in *BALCO* clarified that the expression 'the law of which the arbitral award was made' refers to the procedural law (and not the substantive law of the underlying contract) of the arbitration, if it differs from the 'seat' of arbitration.[133]

ii. Additional Factors

In certain circumstances, a court may *suo moto* refuse to recognise or enforce a foreign arbitral award under section 48(2) of the ACA. This may be the position in two scenarios.

a. Subject Matter of Award not Arbitrable under Indian Law

The parties' decision to settle a matter by arbitration when the dispute is not arbitrable under Indian law will result in the court's refusal to recognise or enforce such an award. There is no reported case in which the court has refused to recognise or enforce a foreign arbitral award on this ground. However, certain issues such as those arising in relation to family law and succession are not arbitrable under Indian law.

b. Award Contravenes Public Policy of India

Unlike the CPC which regulates the recognition and enforcement of foreign judgments in India, the ACA expressly empowers the court to refuse to execute a foreign arbitral award which violates the public policy of India. In this respect, the Supreme Court of India has been reported to refrain from adopting 'a transnational definition of the concept of public policy' on the ground that it is unworkable.[134] For this reason, the foreign arbitral award's violation of 'public policy' is assessed against domestic norms.[135] Judicial dicta clarify that the term 'public policy' refers to the public good or public interest and its interpretation differs from time to time.[136] A foreign arbitral award will therefore be considered as a violation of the public policy of India if its enforcement will adversely affect the administration of justice in the Republic.[137]

[129] ibid 201 [7].
[130] See s 44 of the ACA.
[131] See the Commentary to the New York Convention (n 11) 214 [13], [14].
[132] ibid 217, 218 [21].
[133] ibid 219 [24], referring to *BALCO* (n 63).
[134] See the Commentary to the New York Convention (n 11) 243 [14].
[135] ibid; and *Cairn India* (n 81) [8.1], [28.1], [29].
[136] see *Saw Pipes* (n 115) 723–724; and *Cairn India* ibid, [28.1].
[137] *Cairn India* ibid, [8.1], [28.1], [29].

The Explanation to section 48(2)(a) of the ACA which was introduced by the 2015 Amendment Act clarifies that the public policy of India will be considered to have been violated in four circumstances. These are when the foreign arbitral award is: (1) affected by fraud or corruption;[138] (2) contravenes the fundamental policy or the interests of the Republic;[139] (3) against justice or morality; or (4) patently illegal.[140] The Supreme Court has in a plethora of cases clarified that procedural defects, such as inadmissible evidence or rejecting evidence, would not vitiate a foreign award to prevent its enforceability in India, as these grounds are not considered a breach of the fundamental policy of Indian law.[141]

A foreign arbitral award which has not been given on the merits of the case would not be considered a contravention of the fundamental policy of India.[142] In a related vein, judicial dicta demonstrate that the courts in India have interpreted the term 'patently illegal' widely to prevent the provisions of the ACA from becoming 'nugatory'.[143] The illegality of a foreign arbitral award must, therefore, not be trivial and must go to the root of the decision and shock the conscience of the court.[144] For this reason, foreign arbitral awards, which have been given in violation of natural justice insofar as they have failed to provide the foreign award debtor with an opportunity to be heard, will be construed as being patently illegal and in contravention of the public policy of the Republic.[145] Likewise, foreign arbitral awards which have contravened substantive law in force in India will also be considered as patently illegal and opposed to public policy of India.[146]

B. Disqualification of Foreign Awards under the 1927 Geneva Convention

The ACA similarly empowers an India court to refuse to recognise or enforce a foreign arbitral award given under the 1927 Geneva Convention if it violates the requirements stipulated in section 57 of the statute. The grounds indicated therein resemble those provided in section 48 applicable for the recognition and enforcement of foreign awards under the New York Convention. The ACA permits a foreign award which is given under the 1927 Geneva Convention to be enforced if:

(1) it was made pursuant to the parties' agreement to arbitrate which is valid according to the law applicable to them;[147]
(2) the subject-matter was capable of settlement by arbitration;[148]

[138] cf the decision of the Supreme Court in *World Sport Group (Mauritius)* (n 34) [29], which clarifies that *mere allegations* into fraud would not render the award illegal.
[139] Also see Explanation 2 to s 48 of the 2015 Arbitration Act, which prohibits a foreign arbitral award to be reviewed on the merits of the decision while assessing if it is against the fundamental policy of India.
[140] See also, *Cairn India* (n 81) [8.1], [28.1], [29].
[141] See ibid; *Shri Lal Mahal* (n 115); *Saw Pipes* (n 115); *Renusagar Power Co.* (n 115); and *Vijay Karia & Ors v Prysmian Cavi E Sistemi SRL & Ors* [2020] SCC Online SC 177.
[142] *BALCO* (n 63) [135]–[142], read along with Explanation 2 to s 48 of the 2015 Arbitration Act.
[143] *Cairn India* (n 81) [28.1].
[144] ibid.
[145] See ibid; *Shri Lal Mahal* (n 115); *Saw Pipes* (n 115); *Renusagar Power Co* (n 115); and *Vijay Karia* (n 141).
[146] ibid.
[147] Section 57(1)(a) of the ACA.
[148] ibid, s 57(1)(b).

(3) it was made by the arbitral tribunal provided for in the submission or which has been constituted in a manner agreed upon by the parties according to the law governing the arbitration procedure;[149]
(4) it is final and binding in the country in which it was made;[150] and
(5) it is not opposed to the public policy or any law in force in India.[151]

Unlike section 48 which governs the recognition and enforcement of foreign arbitral awards made under the New York Convention, section 57 does not differentiate between the grounds on which a court may refuse to give effect to foreign awards on the application of a person against whom it is sought and on its own motion. The court may thus refuse to recognise or enforce a foreign award if it is satisfied that:

(1) the award has been annulled in the country in which it was made;[152]
(2) the foreign award debtor was not provided with a notice of the proceedings in sufficient time to enable him/her to present his/her case or was not represented properly if s/he was under a legal incapacity;[153] or
(3) the award does not deal with differences falling within the scope of the submission to arbitration, or it contains decisions that are beyond the scope of the arbitration agreement.[154]

V. Conclusion

In this chapter, we discussed the principles of Indian private international law on the recognition and enforcement of foreign arbitral awards. The mechanism to give effect to foreign arbitral awards is governed by the provisions of the ACA which gives effect to the provisions of the New York and the 1927 Geneva Conventions to which India is a signatory. It was seen that the determination of whether a foreign arbitral award is eligible for recognition or enforcement in India is strictly confined to the parameters stipulated in Part II of the ACA. Such arbitral awards cannot be annulled by an Indian court under the provisions of Part I of the ACA, the application of which is limited to domestic arbitral awards. Foreign arbitral awards which are found to be ineligible may be refused recognition and enforcement if and only if they satisfy one or other of the criteria in sections 48 and 57 of the ACA which govern awards which have been given under the New York and the 1927 Geneva Convention respectively.

It was seen that the grounds on which foreign arbitration awards made under the New York Convention or the 1927 Geneva Convention may be denied recognition or enforcement are similar. At the same time, the denial of the recognition and enforcement of foreign awards which are given under the New York Convention appears to be more stringent than that for awards which have been issued under the 1927 Geneva Convention. The former prohibits a court from refusing to give effect to a foreign award except if the person against whom it is given furnishes proof that the decision violates one or more of the grounds indicated therein. A court is therefore

[149] ibid, s 57(1)(c).
[150] ibid, s 57(1)(d).
[151] ibid, s 57(1)(e) read along with Explanation 1 and 2 to the section, which provides the criterion to assess the violation of the public policy of India.
[152] ibid, s57(2)(a).
[153] ibid, s 57(2)(b).
[154] ibid, s 57(2)(c).

prohibited from *suo moto* refusing to recognise or enforce a foreign arbitral award which is given under the New York Convention except if the subject-matter was not arbitrable under Indian law or if the award has contravened the public policy of India. In comparison, section 57 of the ACA, which stipulates the grounds on which an Indian court may refuse to recognise or enforce a foreign arbitral award given under the 1927 Geneva Convention, makes no similar distinction. Foreign arbitral awards which have been issued under the 1927 Geneva Convention may be refused recognition or enforcement if any of the indicia mentioned in section 57 are satisfied, irrespective of whether the party against whom it is rendered furnishes proof to that effect or the court *suo moto* decides to act.

PART VI

Final Remarks

14

Looking Forward

The previous chapters have examined the core issues and legal principles that govern jurisdiction, choice of law, and the enforcement of foreign judgments and arbitral awards in cross-border disputes before Indian courts. The analysis reveals that compared with other branches of municipal regulations, a systematic body of rules on private international law is absent in India.[1] Further, there has not been any detailed study on the origin and development of Indian private international law. The subject has often been either overlooked or little discussed by academics, advocates, judges, and legislatures. The legislative vacuum and lack of focus on the subject is not the result of an absence of legal disputes involving foreign elements. Legal, political, and historical reasons are attributed to this imbroglio.

In India, the domain of private international law had a quiet beginning starting with the British rule when disputes involving foreign elements came up before the courts. During the colonial era, various personal laws gave rise to a plethora of interpersonal conflicts of law. Since India was a federation between British India and Princely States with different legal systems, judgments from the Princely States were considered foreign decisions.[2] Thus, the genesis of private international law in originated during British rule and followed the English law narrative applied in the conflict of law cases.[3] During the early phases of British rule, most of the disputes in private international law touched upon issues such as marriage,[4] divorce,[5] property[6] and the recognition of judgments.[7] Disputes were addressed by resorting to common law principles operating in Britain.

The achievement of Independence had a discernible impact on the development of private international law. Interpersonal disputes, which operated as private international law disputes arising out of divergent personal laws, came to a standstill. The same pattern was witnessed in respect of disputes concerning Princely States. However, the phase immediately after Independence was a dull period for the progression of private international law. Disputes concerning domicile and citizenship dominated the period.[8] At the same time, one may question whether the issues of domicile that arose pertained to private international law or were simply constitutional matters.

The authors acknowledge the research assistance rendered by Upasna Agrawal: Alumnus, OPJGU; Smita Gupta: student RGNUL Patiala; Rohan Khatana: student, Symbiosis Law School, Noida; and Varnita Singh: student, GNLU, Gandhinagar.

[1] FE Noronha, *Private International Law in India* 2nd edn (Universal law Publishing, 2013) 26–27; P Diwan and P Diwan, *Private International Law: Indian and English* 4th (Deep Publishers, 1998) 59–60.

[2] Noronha, ibid.

[3] ibid 26–27.

[4] *Noor Jahan Begum v Eugene Tiscenko* AIR [1941] Cal 582.

[5] *Sophy Auerbach v Shivaprosad Agarwalla* AIR [1945] Cal 484.

[6] *United Arab Republic And Anr. v Mirza Ali Akbar Kashani* AIR [1962] Cal 387.

[7] *Panchapakesa Iyer and Ors. v K.M. Hussain Muhammad Rowther and Ors* AIR [1934] Mad 145.

[8] *Central Bank of India v Ram Narain* AIR [1955] 36; *Michael Antony Rodrigues v State of Bombay*, AIR [1956] 1 Bombay 729; *D.P. Joshi v State of Madhya Bharat* AIR [1955] 334; *Kedar Pandey v Narain Bikram Sah* AIR [1966] 160.

The exact parameters concerning the domain and scope of private international law remained a debatable topic. In the Indian scenario, disputes touching upon domicile were covered mostly as part of constitutional law.

Among the myriad disputes with a foreign element that the Indian judiciary decided, a plethora of these have revolved around aspects of jurisdiction and the recognition and enforcement of foreign judgments. Some of the questions included whether there were agreed principles that regulated the authority of domestic courts to adjudicate cross-border disputes with a foreign element. In a related vein, the blurring of international borders and the free flow of trade and commerce escalated the number of cases seeking the recognition and enforcement of foreign judgments. Although the legislature has attempted to codify the principles for the recognition and enforcement of foreign judgments, these have been far from perfect and, if anything, have only contributed to ambiguities in Indian law. Consequently, the courts have attempted to fill these gaps and clarify the circumstances in which a foreign judgment would possess extraterritorial effect in the Republic. In doing so, the courts have held firmly to the common law doctrine of obligation and the grounds on which a foreign judgment would be given effect in India are few and narrow.[9] At the same time, it may be said that the principles of Indian private international law on the recognition and enforcement of foreign judgments are not as predictable or certain as those for the recognition and enforcement of foreign arbitral awards. A chief contributing factor for this predictability in the law on the recognition and enforcement of foreign arbitral awards has been India's accession to the 1958 New York Convention – the provisions of which have been incorporated in Part II of the ACA.

That said, there has been a general tendency for the Indian courts to refer to the principles of common law whenever they have encountered disputes in private international law for which there were no existing principles in India. However, in the case of *Satya v Teja*,[10] while deciding on the validity and recognition of a foreign divorce, it was observed that the Indian legal system is free to deviate from the established notion of the common law and adopt the best practices from other jurisdictions or decide principles of their own.[11] This approach (of deviation) is seen in cases concerning intercountry child abduction. Over the years, the judiciary has developed a fleet of jurisprudence based on the overarching welfare of the child principle.[12] In this endeavour, the country has attempted to invoke the practices developed in other jurisdictions and has also spent conscious intellectual effort to generate a private international law system that responds to the socio-economic, cultural, and political interests and sensibilities of the legal system in India. At the same time, statutory efforts aimed at regulating intercountry child abduction have not been successful.

In due course, the exigencies of international trade in turn increased the cross-border disputes that have arisen in relation to international contracts and the question of the governing law assumed a pivotal role. As such, Indian courts have never been reluctant in accepting party autonomy in the choice of law since the pre-Independence era.[13] However, some earlier decisions

[9] See generally, S Khanderia, 'The Hague Judgments Project: Assessing its Plausible Benefits for the Development of the Indian Private International Law' [2019] *Commonwealth Law Bulletin* 452, 452–457 [Khanderia, *The Hague Judgments Project*].

[10] *Satya v Teja* AIR [1975] 105.

[11] ibid [8].

[12] *Sarita Sharma v Sushil Sharma* JT [2000] (2) SC 258; *Ruchi Majoo v Sanjeev Majoo* [2011] 6 SCC 479; *Surya Vadhan v State of Tamilnadu and Others* [2015] (5) SCC 450.

[13] S Khanderia and S Peari, 'Party Autonomy and the Choice of Law under Indian and Australian Private International Law' [2020] *Commonwealth Law Bulletin* 1, 8 [Khanderia and Peari, *Party Autonomy in India and Australia*].

of the Supreme Court, such as those in *Delhi Cloth and General Mills Co Ltd v Harnam Singh*[14] and *British India Steam Navigation Co Ltd v Shanmughavilas Cashew Industries*,[15] prohibited the choice of a neutral foreign law.[16] Accordingly, the courts merely permitted a choice of foreign law insofar as it bore some connection with the parties or their contract, thus forming the centre of gravity of the contract. The choice should have been of that law which forms the centre of gravity of the agreement, thus indicating a restrictive approach.[17] Parties could choose a foreign law by ensuring that factors such as the place of contracting (*locus contractus*), place of performance (*locus solutionis*), the forum (*lex fori*), the seat of arbitration, language, and currency were localised within that legal system.[18] The approach of the Supreme Court shifted to a broader concept of party autonomy existing at common law in *National Thermal Power Corporation* wherein the Court held that the parties' freedom to choose the governing law is only subject to being 'bona fide, legal and not opposed to overriding public policy'.[19] The subsequent decisions of the courts have continued to endorse the broader interpretation of the court.[20] The Supreme Court in *Modi Entertainment Network and Another v WSG Cricket PTE. Ltd* confirmed that the principles of Indian private international law permit the choice of any foreign law, including a neutral one.[21]

It is important to reiterate that, although judicial decisions have evolved the notion of party autonomy and have succeeded in creating certain predictable rules on choice of law and jurisdiction, the parameters of the phrase 'bona fide, legal and not opposed to public policy' continue to remain nebulous. The ICA does not contain provisions to regulate choice of law and choice of jurisdiction. Given increased commercial transactions, the contours of party autonomy should be clarified through statutory reform. Decisions of the Supreme Court have confirmed that party autonomy in the choice of law similarly extends to international commercial arbitration. The doctrine has been held as 'virtually the backbone' and 'one of the foundational pillars'.[22]

At the same time, the Indian courts have had limited experience in handling cross-border disputes in matters of tort. Thus far, the courts have merely had the opportunity to comment on governing law in non-contractual matters in two disputes.[23] In this regard, the approach of the judiciary has been conservative and the courts have continued to hold firmly to the obsolete doctrine of double actionability which has been discarded in most parts of the world. Moreover, existing dicta are merely of persuasive value, considering that none of these decisions have been seen by the Supreme Court. Therefore, the time is ripe for lawmakers in India to formulate coherent principles on the subject that take into account the legal developments across the globe. The trend of increased private international disputes is expected to grow further, with new areas of dispute ranging from cross-border torts and other non-commercial conflicts coming into its ambit. Pending legislation, it is suggested that the Supreme Court develops clear guidelines as regards the applicable law in non-contractual matters – while at the same time, discarding the redundant principle of 'double actionability' in the interests of justice.

[14] AIR [1955] SC 590 [37].

[15] [1990] 3 SCC 481

[16] S Khanderia, 'Indian Private International Law *vis-à-vis* Party Autonomy in the Choice of Law' (2018) 18(1) *Oxford University Commonwealth Law Journal* 1, 7–8 [Khanderia, *Party Autonomy*]; and S Khanderia, Practice does not Make Perfect: Rethinking the Doctrine of 'The Proper Law of the Contract' – A Case for the Indian Courts' (2020) 16(3) *Journal of Private International Law* 423, 426–428. [Khanderia, *Practice does not Make Perfect*].

[17] ibid.

[18] Khanderia, *Practice does not Make Perfect* (n 16) 426–428.

[19] [1992] 3 SCC 551.

[20] Khanderia, *Party Autonomy* (n 16) 11–12.

[21] [2003] 4 SCC 341.

[22] See *White Industries Australia Limited v Coal India Limited*, [2004] 2 Cal LJ 197 (CHC).

[23] See *Kotah Transport Ltd v Jhalawar Transport Services Ltd* AIR [1960] Raj 224; and *Sona Devi v Anil Kumar* [2011] 3 TAC 552.

Recent times have witnessed areas of judicial scrutiny that have posed conceptual and practical challenges to the understanding of traditional principles of private international law. In this regard, the development of the principles of private international law and its application in the realm of online transactions has been particularly challenging due to gaps in the rules on jurisdiction. For example, in 2017 *Godman to Tycoon – The Untold Story of Baba Ramdev* by Priyanka Pathak Narain, was published. The book garnered controversy because it contained defamatory material against yoga guru turned entrepreneur Swami Ramdev. The publisher and the author were sued by Swami Ramdev and the Delhi High Court found that the book contained material that was prima facie defamatory. The Court accordingly restrained the publication, distribution, and sale of the book until the defamatory material was removed from it.[24] The case is pending an appeal before the Supreme Court and as of now the ban is still operating. However, the plaintiffs (Ramdev and another) filed an original suit before the Delhi High Court alleging that the defendant intermediaries (Facebook and others) were disseminating videos and details which summarised the contents of the book, parts of which have been held as defamatory by the Court.[25] The Delhi High Court relied on the judgment of the EU Court of Justice (CJEU) in *Eva Glawischnig-Piesczek v Facebook Ireland Limited*[26] concerning online defamation, where the CJEU had held that the national courts of a Member State could order blocking of access to information on a worldwide basis. Reliance was also placed on the judgment in *Google v CNIL*,[27] where the CJEU left it to national courts to determine whether there was any legal requirement on a data controller to remove internet content on a global basis. The Delhi High Court ordered the defendants to take down, remove, block, restrict and disable access on a global basis, to all videos, weblinks and URs on a list annexed to the plaint. These had been uploaded from IP addresses within India. In the case of those uploaded from outside India, the defendants were directed to block access and disable them from being viewed on the Indian domain and ensure that users in India were unable to access the same. The Court held that, if the content were uploaded from India or were located in India, the Indian courts would have jurisdiction to pass worldwide injunctions.[28] The judgment sets a problematic precedent for future cases as the Court overlooked the fact that the scope of defamation and defamatory content varies from jurisdiction to jurisdiction. In particular, the Court imposed the standards of free speech and defamation applicable in India on other jurisdictions. There are countries where the threshold of free speech varies significantly from that in India. Also, the procedural and substantive aspects of the law governing defamation are different in various jurisdictions. For example, the onus of proving that disputed matter does not amount to defamation, falls entirely upon the defendant under English law. In contrast, the onus on the plaintiff in the US is high.[29] This would result in a conflict of laws.

A potentially significant area of judicial statements pertains to cross-border disputes in the context of the jurisdiction of the courts for transactions concluded online. A close examination of the existing dicta demonstrates that the Indian courts have relentlessly attempted to develop the principles of Indian private international law on jurisdiction to accommodate the changing realities as a result of increased internet-based trade and commerce. Accordingly, in *World Wrestling Entertainment v M/s Reshma Collection and others*,[30] the court decided to stretch the parameters

[24] *Swami Ramdev v Juggernaut Books* CM(M) 556/2018 & CM APPL. 19354/2018.

[25] *Swami Ramdev & Anr. v Facebook, Inc and Ors* CS (OS) 27/2019.

[26] ibid [69].

[27] ibid [64].

[28] ibid [88].

[29] MA Franklin and DJ Bussel, 'The Plaintiff's Burden in Defamation: Awareness and Falsity' (1984) 25 *William and Mary Law Review* 825.

[30] [2014] SCC OnLine Del 2031.

of section 20 of the CPC read along with the Copyright Act, which stipulate the grounds on which an Indian court may assume jurisdiction for contracts that have been concluded online. Consequently, the court stated that, in such disputes, every court within whose territory a website can be accessed would be eligible to adjudicate on the matter. The mere fact that the defendant did not reside within the court's territory would, thus, be irrelevant in determining the place where the cause of action arose in online transactions. In a related vein, in *Casio India Co. Limited v Ashita Tele Systems Pvt. Limited*, the court decided to assume jurisdiction in a passing-off action on the mere fact that the defendant's website was accessible in its territory, therefore rendering it eligible to adjudicate on the matter.[31] However, in disputes of a comparable nature, namely in the *Banyan Tree* case,[32] the court deviated from its earlier position. It stated that the mere fact that a website was accessible in its territory (New Delhi) would not suffice in conferring jurisdiction. Instead, the plaintiff must clearly demonstrate that the defendant had 'purposefully availed' itself of the court's jurisdiction by specifically targeting customers there to conclude commercial transactions through the website, thereby causing economic loss to the plaintiff. The court's dictum in *Banyan Tree* has continued to represent judicial opinion on the subject.

The interface between private international law and intellectual property has continued to remain a pivotal issue that has raised complex problems of legal policy. Disputes such as *Tyburn Productions v Conan Doyle*[33] have highlighted the complexity of balancing the territoriality engrained in IPRs with the possibility of multiple suits between the same parties. How will the Indian courts respond to these legal conundrums? The importance of answering these questions will only increase in the future.

In a related vein, the efforts of the Law Commission of India, which has played an active role in examining the principles of private international law, are noteworthy. The Law Commission's observations in its Report on the Law of Foreign Marriages,[34] its Report on the Law of Foreign Divorces;[35] its Report on Transnational Litigation, Conflict of Laws and the Law of Limitation;[36] and its Report on the Need to Accede to the Hague Convention on the Civil Aspects of International Child Abduction (1980)[37] deserve mention.

The increased discussion and case law reveal the slow progress in Indian private international law. Though the Indian private international law community is small, there is a growing interest in the study of private international law in India. It is important to stress that a systematic study of private international law will create the required political will and institutional support for its evolution. A systematic study becomes significant in an environment of growing international transactions in family and commercial matters. In this scenario of increasing case laws and developments, India can learn valuable lessons from Nepal, another developing country, which has taken the first step towards codifying its principles on private international law rules in its Civil Procedure Code.[38] Such rules can assist in providing clarity on jurisdiction, applicable law, and the recognition and enforcement of foreign judgments.

Predictable legal principles can create avenues for attracting litigation and arbitration. This, in turn, can lead to economic development and the strengthening of India's legal system.

[31] [2003] [27] PTC 265 (Del).

[32] *Banyan Tree Holding (P) Limited v A. Murali Krishna Reddy & Anr* 2009 SCC OnLine Del 3780.

[33] *Tyburn Productions v Conan Doyle* [1991] Ch 75.

[34] Law Commission of India, *The Law of Foreign Marriages* (Report No 23, 1962).

[35] Law Commission of India, *The Recognition of Foreign Divorces* (Report No 65, 1976).

[36] Law Commission of India, *Transnational Litigation – Conflict of Laws – Law of Limitation* (Report No 193, 2005).

[37] Law Commission of India, *Need to Accede to the Hague Convention on the Civil Aspects of International Child Abduction* (1980) (Report No 218, 2009).

[38] The National Civil (Code) Act, (Nepal) 2017 (2074).

However, along with clarity, it is also important to keep in mind that private international law is faced with mammoth challenges as a response to globalisation and increased individual movement and interactions. The fact that there is no reported case in which parties have expressly chosen the jurisdiction of Indian courts or the application of Indian law in civil and commercial matters, speaks volumes about the faith of the international community in this legal system.

At the international level, India's association with the HCCH has been slow and gradual. India only became a member of the HCCH in 2008. However, the country has been involved in international negotiations and became part of the effort of codification initiated by the HCCH. In particular, India has acceded to those Hague Conventions, which deal with procedural matters focused on enhancing cross-border legal cooperation. Prominent among them include the 1961 Convention Abolishing the Requirement of Legalisation for Foreign Public Documents (the Apostille Convention);[39] the 1965 Convention on the Service Abroad of Judicial and Extrajudicial Documents in Civil or Commercial Matters;[40] and the 1970 Hague Convention on the Taking of Evidence Abroad in Civil and Commercial Matters.[41] However, accession to these Conventions is not surprising as they concern legal co-operation, and it is convenient for jurisdictions to cooperate on these matters. Among the Hague Conventions relating to the welfare of the child, India has only acceded to the 1993 Convention on Protection of Children and Co-operation in Respect of Intercountry Adoption.[42] India has steadfastly opposed the Convention dealing with intercountry child abduction. One of the core objections which India has highlighted with regard to the convention is the absence of explicit mechanisms to protect women who flee with their children from the habitual residence due to domestic violence.[43] At the same time, the reason behind the Republic's resistance to other Hague Conventions, such as the HCCCA or the 2019 Judgments Convention, remains unknown. Existing dicta confirm that the principles of Indian private international law vis-à-vis choice of court and the acceptance of party autonomy complement the provisions of the HCCCA.[44] Thus, India would only benefit from accession to the HCCCA in the form of increased predictability and certainty. This would also be true for India's accession to the 2019 Hague Convention on the Recognition and Enforcement of Foreign Judgments in Civil and Commercial Matters.

At the same time, it is crucial that the legal principles consider mechanisms to balance the interests of weaker and more vulnerable parties. Legislative reforms must clearly identify and stipulate mechanisms to ascertain the contravention of public policy. In matters of family and succession, this will be all the more complex in a country like India where personal laws dominate the formulation of legal principles and result in resistance to reforms.

[39] Convention Abolishing the Requirement of Legalisation for Foreign Public Documents (5 October 1961) Status table, available at: www.hcch.net/en/instruments/conventions/status-table/?cid=41. The Convention facilitates the circulation of public documents executed in one signatory to the Convention to be accepted and given effect in another state party to the Convention.

[40] Convention of 15 November 1965 on the Service Abroad of Judicial and Extrajudicial Documents in Civil or Commercial Matters, Status Table, available at: www.hcch.net/en/instruments/conventions/status-table/?cid=17.

[41] Convention of 18 March 1970 on the Taking of Evidence Abroad in Civil or Commercial Matters, status table www.hcch.net/en/instruments/conventions/status-table/?cid=82.

[42] Convention on Protection of Children and Co-operation in Respect of Intercountry Adoption (29 May 1993).

[43] S Jolly, 'International Parental Child Abduction: An Explorative Analysis of Legal Standards and Judicial Interpretation in India' (2007) 31 *International Journal of Law, Policy and the Family* 20–40.

[44] See S Khanderia, 'The Hague Judgments Project: Assessing its Plausible Benefits for the Development of the Indian Private International Law' [2019] *Commonwealth Law Bulletin* 452, 462 et seq. [Khanderia, *The Hague Judgments Project*]; and S Khanderia, 'The Hague Convention on Choice of Court Agreements and the Enforcement of Forum-Selection Clauses in Indian Private International Law' (2019) 9(3) *International Journal of Private Law* 125, 128 et seq. [Khanderia, *The Hague Convention*].

At an international level, European and US scholars have dominated the study of private international law. Their scholarship inspired the codification of the rules in several areas of private international law by the HCCH. Hence, it has been argued that the development of private international law is comparable to that of public international law and has followed a Eurocentric approach, reflected in the rate of the accession of such nations to many of the Hague Conventions. Consequently, several Hague Conventions lack participation from developing nations. Thus, although Hague Conventions attempt to codify the principles of private international law in a manner that ensures a greater degree of legal certainty and predictability in cross-border transactions, it is essential that the sensibilities and concerns of non-western nations are considered especially in family matters. A uniform set of legal principles on the subject may not offer the solution. It is also highly questionable whether universal values exist in the choice of law. Therefore, it is equally crucial that efforts to codify principles contribute to the progress of private international laws in those countries lacking the legal infrastructure necessary to participate fully and effectively in global negotiations.

It is opined that private international law in India deserves to be systematically studied and researched for the current framework of private international law in the Republic to be improved. It is hoped that the current book will contribute to this endeavour.

BIBLIOGRAPHY

Articles

Agarwal, PK, 'The theory of characterization: a critical legal study perspective' (2015) 4(3) *Voice of Research* 45.

Alavi, H, 'A Step Forward in the Harmonisation of European Jurisdiction: Regulation Brussels I Recast' (2015) 8(2) *Baltic Journal of Law and Politics* 159.

Albornoz, MM, 'Choice of law in international contracts in Latin American legal systems' [2010] *Journal of Private International Law* 23.

Alexander, GS, 'The Application and Avoidance of Foreign Law in the Law of Conflicts: Variations on a Theme of Alexander Nekam' [1975] *Cornell Law Faculty Publications Paper* 260.

Allarousse, V, 'A Comparative Approach to the Conflict of Characterization in Private International Law' (1991) 23 *Case Western Reserve Journal of International Law* 479.

Allemès, F, 'The Problem of Renvoi in Private International Law' (1926) 12 *Transactions of the Grotius Society* 63.

Alston, P, 'The Best Interests Principle: Towards a Reconciliation of Culture and Human Rights' (1994) 8/1 *International Journal of Law Policy and the Family.*

Andrews, DM, 'Note, Non-Muslim Mothers V. Egyptian Muslim Fathers: The Conflict Between Religion and Law in International Child Custody Disputes and Abductions' (2000) 23 *Suffolk Transnational Law Review* 595.

Armstrong, CS, 'The Hague Convention on the Law Applicable to Traffic Accidents: Search for Uniformity Amidst Doctrinal Diversity' (1972) 11 *Columbian Journal of Transnational Law* 74.

Atkinson, J, 'The Meaning of "Habitual Residence" Under the Hague Convention on the Civil Aspects of International Child Abduction and The Hague Convention on the Protection of Children' (2011) 63 *Oklahoma Law Review* 4.

Baade, HW, 'Marriage and Divorce in American Conflicts Law: Governmental-Interests Analysis and the Restatement (Second)' (1972) 72 *Colum Law Review* 329.

Bailey, A, 'Reconceiving Surrogacy: Toward a Reproductive Justice Account of Indian Surrogacy' (2011) 26 *Hypatia: A Journal of Feminist Philosophy* 4.

Bala, N and Chamerland J, 'Family Violence and Proving "Grave Risk" for Cases Under the Hague Convention Article 13(b)' [2017] *Queen's University Legal Research Paper* 091/2017.

Ball, JP, 'Sovereign Immunity of Governmental Trading Entities' [1959] *Sydney Law Review* 143.

Bartholomew, GW, 'Polygamous Marriage' (1952) 15 *Modern Law Review* 35.

——, 'Recognition of Polygamous Marriages in Canada' (1961) 10 *International and Comparative Law Quarterly* 305.

Bates, LT, 'Remission and Transmission in American Conflict of Laws' (1931) 16 Cornell Law Quarterly 311.

Baty, T, 'Capacity and Form of Marriage in the Conflict of Laws' (1917) 26(6) *The Yale Law Journal* 444.

Baxi, U, 'Demosprudence versus Jurisprudence: The Indian Judicial Experience in the Context of Comparative Constitutional Studies' (2014) 14 *Macquarie Law Journal* 3.

Beaumont, P and Walker, L, 'Recognition and enforcement of Judgments in Civil and Commercial Matters in the Brussels I Recast and Some Lessons from it and the Recent Hague Conventions for the Hague Judgments Project' (2015) 11(1) *Journal of Private International Law* 31.

Beckett, WE, 'The Question of Classification in Private International Law' [1934] *British Yearbook of International Law* 55.

——, 'What is Private International Law' (1926) 7 *British Yearbook of International Law* 73.

Bernadet, B, 'Regulation 2201/2003 (Brussels II bis) on Recognition and Enforcement of Judgments in Matters of Parental Responsibility' (2012) 46/1 *Zbornik Radova* 239.

——, 'Surrogacy with Cross-Border Effects: Reality and Law' (2012) 46/4 *Zbornik Radova* 97.

Bernardini, P, 'Private Law and General Principles of Public International Law' (2016) 21 *Uniform Law Review* 184.

Bettauer, RJ, 'India and International Arbitration: The Dabhol Experience' (2009) 41 *George Washington International Law Review* 381.

Blair, M, 'International Application of the UCCJEA: Scruntinizing the Escape Clause' (2004) 38/3 *Family Law Quarterly.*

Bleimaier, JK, 'The Doctrine of Comity in Private International Law' (1979) 24 *Cath Law* 327.

Blom, J, 'Choice of Law Methods in the Private International Law of Contract' (1980) 18 *Canadian Yearbook of International Law* 161.

——, 'The Enforcement of Foreign Judgments: Morguard Goes Forth into the World' (1997) 28 *Canadian Business Law Journal* 373.

Blynn, EL, 'In Re: International Child Abduction v. Best Interests of the Child: Comity Should Control' (1986) 18/2 *University of Miami Inter-American Law Review*.

Bodzin, MI, 'International Parental Child Abduction: The Need for Recognition and Enforcement of Foreign Custody Decrees' (1988–1989) 3 *Emory Journal of International Dispute Resolution* 205.

Bonell, MJ, 'Soft Law and Party Autonomy: The case of the UNIDROIT Principles' (2005) 51 *Loy Law Review*.

——, 'The UNIDROIT Initiative for the Progressive Codification of International Trade Law' (1978) 27(2) *International and Comparative Law Quarterly* 413.

Bonomi, A, 'Rome I Regulation on the Law Applicable to Contractual Obligations' (2010) 10 *Yearbook of Private International Law* 165.

Boo, L, 'The Writing Requirement in Contemporary Practice: Is There Really a Need for Change' (2008) 2 *Dispute Resolution International* 75.

Bowen, DL, Hudson, VM and Nielsen, PL, 'State Fragility and Structural Gender Inequality in Family Law: An Empirical Investigation' (2015) 4 *Laws* 654.

Bowers, G, 'Brexit and the Implications for Tacit Choice of Law in the United Kingdom' (2018) 39(3) *Obiter* 727.

Bozin-Odhiambo, D, 'Re-examining Habitual Residence as the Sole Connecting Factor in Hague Convention Child Abduction Cases' (2012) 3/1 *Family Law Review*.

Brand, RA, 'Community Competence for Matters of Judicial Cooperation at the Hague Conference on Private International Law: A View from the United States' (2002) 21 *Journal of Law and Commerce* 191.

Brankle, N, 'Gay Rights in India: Matter of Naz Foundation Decision' (2015)15 *Chicago-Kent Journal of International & Comparative Law* 1.

Briggs, A, 'Crossing the River by Feeling the Stones: Rethinking the Law on Foreign Judgments' (2004) 8 *Singapore Yearbook of Private International Law* 1.

——, 'Polygamous Marriages and English Domiciliaries'(1983) 32 *The International and Comparative Law Quarterly* 737.

——, 'In praise and defence of Renvoi' (1998) 47(4) *International & Comparative Law Quarterly* 877.

——, 'Foreign Judgments and Human Rights' (2005) 121 *LQR* 185.

——, 'Recognition of Foreign Judgments: A Matter of Obligation' (2013) 129 *LQR* 87.

Briggs, EW, "Renvoi' in the Succession of Tangibles: A False Issue Based on Faulty Analysis' (1954) 64 *Yale Law Journal* 195.

Browne, NL, 'Relevance and Fairness: Protecting the Rights of Domestic Violence Victims and Left-Behind Fathers Under the Hague Convention on International Child Abduction' (2011) 60/5 *Duke Law Journal*.

Bruch, CS, 'Religious Law, Secular Practices, and Children's Human Rights in Child Abduction Cases under the Hague Child Abduction Convention' (2000–2001) 33/1 *New York University Journal of International Law and Politics* 49.

——, 'The Hague Child Abduction Convention: Past Accomplishments, Future Challenges' (1999) 1/1-2 *European Journal of Law Reform* 97.

——, 'The Unmet Needs of Domestic Violence Victims and Their Children in Hague Child Abduction Convention Cases' (2004) 38/3 *Family Law Quarterly*.

Burpee, AL, 'Momma Drama: A Study of How Canada's National Regulation of Surrogacy Compares to Australia's Independent State Regulation of Surrogacy' (2009) 37 *Georgia Journal of International and Comparative Law* 305.

Calliess, GF, 'Value-added Norms, Local Litigation and Global Enforcement: Why the Brussels Philosophy Failed in the Hague' (2004) 5 *German Law Journal* 1490.

Campbell, H, 'Domicile of Choice' (1918) 3 *International Law Notes* 68.

Candeub, A and Kuykendall, M, 'Modernising Marriage' (2010) 44 *University of Michigan Journal of Law Reform* 765.

Carbone, J, 'Legal Applications of the "Best Interest of the Child" Standard: Judicial Rationalization or a Measure of Institutional Competence?' (2014) 134 *Official Journal of the American Academy of Pediatrics* 2.

Caroline, LG, 'International Child Abduction and the Hague Convention: Emerging Practice and Interpretation of the Discretionary Exception' (1990) 25/2 *Texas International Law Journal*.

Carroll, L, 'Recognition of polygamous marriages in English Matrimonial Law: The statutory reversal of "Hyde v Hyde" in 1972' [1984] *Institute of Muslim Minority Affairs Journal* 5:1 81.

Carruthers, J, 'Party Autonomy In The Legal Regulation Of Adult Relationships: What Place For Party Choice In Private International Law?' (2012) 61 *The International and Comparative Law Quarterly* 881.

Carruthers, JM, 'Substance and Procedure in the Conflict of Laws: A continuing debate in relation to damages' (2004) 53(3) *International and Comparative Law Quarterly* 691.

Carswell, RD, 'The Doctrine of Vested Rights in Private International Law' (1959) 8 *International and Comparative Law Quarterly* 268.

Carter, PB, 'The Role of Public Policy in English Private International Law' (1993) 42 *ICLQ* 1.

Cassels, J, 'The Uncertain Promise of Law: Lessons from Bhopal' (1991) 29 *Osgoode Hall Law Journal* 1.

Castel, JG, 'Procedure and the Conflict of Laws' (1970) 16 *McGill Law Journal* 603.

Chappell Jr, RH, 'Lex Loci Delicti and Babcock v. Jackson' (1966) 7 *William and Mary Law Review* 249.

Chen, W and Goldstein, G, 'The Asian Principles of Private International Law: objectives, contents, structure and selected topics on choice of law' [2017] *Journal of Private International Law* 13:2.

Cheshire, GC, 'Nationality and Domicile in Swedish Private International Law' (1951) 4 *International Law Quarterly* 39.

Childress, DE III, 'Comity as Conflict: Resituating International Comity as Conflict of Laws' (2010) 44 *University of California Davis Law Review* 12.

Chittale, YS, 'First Decision of Supreme Court Involving Conflict of Law' (1956) 5 *American Journal of Comparative Law* 629.

——, 'India: First Decision of Supreme Court Involving Conflict of Laws; Law Applicable to Debt' (1956) 5(4) *The American Journal of Comparative Law* 629, 631.

Chng, K, 'A Theoretical Perspective of the Public Policy Doctrine in the Conflict of Laws' (2018) 14(1) *Journal of Private International Law* 130.

Choisne, MEM, 'Juridical Solutions in the U.S.A. for Parental Kidnapping in Child Custody Cases' (1990) 24 *Revista Juridicaal De La Universidad Interamerican De* 309.

Chong, A, 'Moving towards harmonisation in the recognition and enforcement of foreign judgment rules in Asia' (2020) 16(1) *Journal of Private International Law* 31.

——, 'The Public Policy and Mandatory Rules of Third Countries in International Contracts' (2006) 2(1) *Journal of Private International Law* 27.

——, 'Transnational Public Policy in Civil and Commercial Matters' (2012) 128 *LQR* 88.

Clarkson, LS, 'What Effect Does European Private International Law on Cross-border Divorce Have on National Family Laws and International Obligations of the Member States?' (2019) 5 *Athens Journal of Law* 435.

Cook, WW, *'The Logical and Legal Bases of the Conflict of Laws'* (1924) 33 (5) *Yale Law Journal* 457.

Cormack, JM, 'Renvoi, Characterization, Localization and Preliminary Question in the Conflict of Laws: A Study of Problems Involved in Determining Whether or Not the Forum Should Follow Its Own Choice of a Conflict-of-Laws Principle' (1940) 14 *Southern California Law Review* 221.

Costa, M, 'Polygamous Marriages in the Conflict of Laws' (1966) 44 *Canadian Bar Review* 293.

Covell, T, 'Bhopal Disaster Litigation: It's Not over Yet, The' (1991) *16 North Carolina Journal of International Law and commercial Regulation* 279.

Cowen, Z, 'A Note on Potentially Polygamous Marriages' (1963) 12 *The International and Comparative Law Quarterly* 1407.

Cox, B, 'Same Sex marriage and Choice of law: if we Marry in Hawai, Are we still married when we get home' [1994] *Wisconsin Law Review* 1065.

——, 'Same-Sex Marriage and the Public Policy Exception in Choice-of-Law: Does It Really Exist?', in Symposium Issue on 'Federalism Revisited: Extraterritorial Recognition of Same-Sex Marriage' (1996) 16 *Quinnipiac Law Review* 61.

Crawford, EB, 'The Adjective and the Noun: Title and Right to Sue in International Private Law' [2000] *JR* 347.

Cuniberti, G, 'Beyond Contract – The Case of Default Arbitration in International Commercial Disputes' (2009) 32(2) *Fordham International Law Journal* 417.

Currie, B, 'The Constitution and the Choice of Law: Governmental Interests and the Judicial Function' (1958) 26 *University of Chicago Law Review* 9.

Curry, A, 'The Uniform Premarital Agreement Act and its Variations throughout the States' (2010) 23 *Journal Of The American Academy Of Matrimonial Lawyers* 355.

Danny, JB, 'Remarks on the 1980 Hague Convention on the Civil Aspects of International Child Abduction' (2000–2001) 33 *New York University Journal of International Law and Politics* 1.

Dantanarayana, R and Wilson, J, 'Child Custody and 'Enforcement' of Foreign Child Custody Orders in Sri Lanka' (2017) 10/1 *Family Law Update* 11.

Dave, D, 'Practical Perspectives on Recognition and Enforcement in a Modern World: A Review of Most Common Grounds for Refusing Enforcement including Public Policy' (2008) *2 Dispute Resolution International* 133.

Davies, L, 'The Influence of Huber's De Conflictu Legum on English Private International Law' (1937) 18 *British Yearbook of International Law* 49.

Davies, M, 'Renvoi and Presumptions about Foreign Law: Neilson v Overseas Projects Corporation of Victoria Ltd' (2006) 30(1) *Melbourne University law Review* 8.

De Araujo, N and Guedes de C Saldanha, F, 'Recent developments and current trends on Brazilian private international law concerning international contracts' [2013] *Panorama of Brazilian Law* 73.

De Verneuil Smith, P et al, 'Reflections on *Owusu*: The Radical Decision in *Ferrexpo*' [2015] *Journal of Private International Law* 389.

DeHart, GF, 'The Relationship between the 1980 Child Abduction Convention and the 1996 Protection Convention' (2000) 33 *New York University Journal of International Law and Politics* 1.

Di Robilant, A, 'Genealogies of Soft Law' (2006) 54 *The American Journal of Comparative Law* 3.

Dicey, AV, 'Chetti v Chetti' (1909) 25 *Law Quarterly Review* 202.

Dickinson, A, 'Further Thoughts on Foreign Torts – *Boys v. Chaplin* Explained? (*Red Sea v. Bouygues*)' [1994] *Lloyd's Maritime and Comparative Law Quarterly* 463.

Dimitry, T, 'The Conversion of a Polygamous Union into a Monogamous Marriage' (1968) 17 *International and Comparative law Quarterly* 721.

Dorosin, M, 'You Must Go Home Again: Friedrich v. Friedrich, the Hague Convention and the International Child Abduction Remedies Act' (1993) 18/3 *North Carolina Journal of International Law and Commercial Regulation.*

Drobac, A, 'For the Sake of the Children: Court Consideration of Religion in Child Custody Cases' (1998) 50 *Stanford Law Review* 5.

Droz, GAL and Dyer, A, 'The Hague Conference and the Main Issues of Private International Law for the Eighties' (1981) 3/1 *Northwestern Journal of International Law and Business.*

Duncan, WR, 'The Domicile of Married Women' (1976–1977) 1 *Dublin University law Journal* 38.

Dyer, A, 'The Hague Convention on the Civil Aspects of International Child Abduction-towards Global Cooperation: It's successes and Failures' (1993) 93 *International Journal of Children's Rights* 1.

EGL, 'Polygamy and the Conflict of Laws' (1923) 32 *Yale Law Journal 1* 471.

E von Overbeck, A, 'Renvoi in the Institute of International Law' (1963) 12 *American Journal of Comparative Law* 544.

Edwards, CHC, 'Private International Law' (1966) 2 *Man Law Journal* 109.

Eekelaar, J, 'The Interests of the Child and the Child's Wishes: The Role of Dynamic Self-Determinism' (1994) 8 *International Journal of Law Policy and the Family* 1.

Einhorn, T, 'Same -Sex Family Unions in Israeli law' (2008) 4(2) *Utrecht Law Review* 222.

Ertman, MM, 'Race Treason: The Untold Story of America's Ban on Polygamy' (2010) 19 *Columbia Journal of Gender and Law* 287.

Eskridge Jr, WN, 'A History of same Sex Marriage' (1993) 79 *Va Law Review* 1419.

Esplugues, CA, 'Legal recognition of polygamous Marriages' (1984) 17 *Comparative and International Law Journal of Southern Africa* 302.

Estin, A, 'Marriage and Divorce Conflicts in the International Perspective' (2017) 27 *Duke Journal Of Comparative & International Law* 502.

Falconbridge, D, 'Characterization in the Conflict of Laws', (2005) *Law Quarterly Review* 2, 2.

—— 'Characterization in the Conflict of Laws' (1937) 53 *Law Quarterly Review* 235, 236.

Fallon, S, 'Justice for All: American Muslims, Sharia Law, and Maintaining Comity with American Jurisprudence' (2013) 36 *Boston College International and Comparative Law Review-European Law* 153.

Farrelly, MJ, 'Basis of Private International Law' (1893) 9 *Law Quarterly Review* 242.

Fawcett JJ, 'Evasion of Law and Mandatory Rules in Private International Law' (1990) 49(1) *The Cambridge Law Journal* 44.

—— 'Law Commission Working Paper No. 88: The law of Domicile' (1986) 49(2) *The Modern Law Review* 225.

—— 'Non-exclusive Jurisdiction Agreements in Private International Law' [2001] *Lloyd's Maritime & Commercial Law Quarterly.*

Fentiman, R, 'Domicile Revisited' (1991) 50(3) *Cambridge Law Journal* 445.

—— 'The Validity of Marriage and the Proper Law' (1985) 44 *Cambridge Law Journal* 256.

Fenton-Glynn, C, 'Review Article: Human Rights and Private International Law: Regulating International Surrogacy' (2014) 10/1 *Journal of Private International Law* 157.

Fincham, D, 'Rejecting Renvoi for Movable Cultural Property: The Islamic Republic of Iran v. Denyse Berend' (2007) 14 *International Journal of Cultural Property* 111.

Fischer, H, 'The Convention on the Law Applicable to Traffic Accidents' (1971) 9 *Canadian Yearbook of Int'l Law* 189.

FitzGerald, SV, 'Indian and Far Eastern Cases on the Conflict of Laws, 1934' (1935) *Journal of Comparative Legislation and International Law* 17, 4.

Frank, RJ, 'Note, American and International Responses to International Child Abductions' (1984) 16 *New York University Journal of International Law and Policy.*

Fredericks, EA and Neels, JL, 'The proper law of a documentary letter of credit: Part 1' [2003] *South African Mercantile Law Journal* 63.

Fredericks, EA, 'Contractual Capacity and the Conflict of Laws in Common Law Jurisdictions (Part 2): Australasia, North America, Asia and Africa' (2020) 41(1) *Obiter* 10.

Gabriel, HD, *The Advantages of Soft Law in International Commercial Law: The Role of UNIDROIT, UNCITRAL, and the Hague Conference*' (2009) 34 *Brook Journal of International Law* 658.

Gaertner, V, 'European Choice of Law Rules in Divorce (Rome III): An Examination of the Possible Connecting Factors in Divorce Matters against the Backgrounds of Private International Law Developments' (2006) 2 *Journal of Private International Law* 99.

Garman, JJ, 'International Law and Children's Human Rights: International, Constitutional, and Political conflicts Blocking Passage of the Convention on the Rights of the Child' (2007) 41 *Valparaiso University Law Review* 2.

Geistfeld, MA, 'A Roadmap for Autonomous Vehicles: State Tort Liability, Autonomous Insurance, and Federal Safety Regulation' (2017) 105 *California Law Review* 1611.

George, JP and Teller, AK, 'Conflict of Laws' (2004) 57 *SMU Law Review* 719.

Ghosal, AK, 'Federalism in the Indian Constitution' (1953) 14(4) *The Indian Journal of Political Science* 317.

Ghosh A, and Kar, P, 'Pre-Nuptial Agreements In India: An Analysis Of Law And Society' (2019) 12 *National University of Juridical Sciences Law Review* 2.

Ghosh, A and Khaitan, N, 'A Womb of One's Own: Privacy and Reproductive Rights' (2017) 52 *Engage, Economic and Political Weekly* 42.

Gill, J, 'The Definition of Award under the New York Convention' (2008) 2 *Dispute Resolution International* 114.

Gillen, NP, 'Practical Perspectives: Obstacles to Arbitration in the Developing World' (2008) 2 *Dispute Resolution International* 143.

Glenn, HP, 'Comment: The Conflict of Laws – the 1976 Hague Convention on Marriage and Matrimonial Property Regimes' (1977) 55 *Canadian Bar Review* 586.

Goodman, J and Talpis, J, 'Beals v Saldana and the Enforcement of Foreign Judgments in Canada' (2004) 40 *Canadian Business Law Journal* 227.

Goodrich and Herbert, F, 'Divorce Problems in the Conflict of Laws' (1923) *Texas Law Review* 2.

Gössl, Lilian S, 'Open Issues in European International Family Law: Sahyouni, 'Private Divorces' and Islamic Law Under the Rome III Regulation' (2017) *The European Legal Forum*.

Govindraj, VC, 'Foreign Arbitral Awards and Foreign Judgments Based on Such Awards' (1964) 13 *Tnt. Camp. L.Q.* 1465

Gray, A, 'The rise of Renvoi in Australia: creating the theoretical framework' (2007) 30(1) *University of New South Wales Law Journal* 103.

Griggs, L, 'A Radical Solution for Solving the Liability Conundrum of autonomous Vehicles' (2017) 25 *Competition and Consumer Law Journal* 151.

Griswold, E, 'Renvoi Revisited' (1938) 51 *Harvard Law Review* 1165.

Guezand, P and Lahlou, Y, 'The Brussels I BIS Regulation: Has Shown Some Progress but Can Do Better' (2016) 2 *International Business Law Journal* 195.

Hans van loon, 'The Hague Conference on Private International Law' (2007) 2(2) *Hague Justice Journal* 1.

Harder, S, 'The Effects of Recognised Judgments in Civil and Commercial Matters' (2013) 62(2) *International and Comparative Law Quarterly* 441.

Hartley, TCK, 'The Domicile and Matrimonial Proceedings Act 1973' (1974) 37 *Modern Law Review* 179.

Hausmann, R, 'Pleading and Proof of Foreign Law – a Comparative Analysis' [2008] *The European Legal Forum* 1.

Hay, P, 'The Use and Determination of Foreign Law in Civil Litigation in the United States' (2014) 62 *The American Journal of Comparative Law* 213.

Heaton, J, 'Striving for Substantive Gender Equality in Family Law: Selected Issues' (2005) 21 *South African Journal on Human Rights* 547.

Ho, HL, 'Policies underlying the Enforcement of Foreign Commercial Judgments' (1997) 46 *International and Comparative Law Quarterly* 443.

Hober, Kaj, and Magnusson, A, 'The Special Status of Agreements to Arbitrate: The Separability Doctrine; Mandatory Stay of Litigation' (2008) 2 *Dispute Resolution International* 1.

Hofheimer, A, 'Gestational Surrogacy: Unsettling State Parentage Law and Surrogacy Policy' (1991) 19 *N.Y.U. Review of Law & Social Change* 3.

Hogan, J, 'International Law – Sovereign Immunity' [1961] *University of Miami Law Review* 450.

Holder, WE, 'Public Policy and National Preferences: The Exclusion of Foreign Law in English Private International Law' (1968) 17 *International and Comparative Law Quarterly* 926.

Hughes, 'Judicial Method and the Problem in Ogden v. Ogden' (1928) 44 *Law Quarterly Review* 217.

Huo, Z, 'An imperfect improvement: the new conflict of laws act of the People's Republic of China' [2011] *International and Comparative Law Quarterly* 1065.

Hutchinson, A, 'Domicile of Origin and Domicile of Choice' (1977) *New Law Journal* 879.

István Nagy, C, 'The Rome II Regulation and Traffic Accidents: Uniform Conflict Rules with Some Room for Forum Shopping – How so?' (2010) 6(1) *Journal of Private International Law* 93.

Iyer, A, 'Domicile and Habitual Residence' (1985) 6 *Singapore Law Review* 115.

Jaffey, JE, 'The English Proper Law Doctrine and the EEC Convention' (1984) 33 *International and Comparative Law Quarterly* 531.

Jagota, R and Chanana, P, 'Executability and Enforceability of Foreign Judgments and Decrees in India: An Analysis of Judicial Trends' (2016) 7 *Indian Journal of Law & Justice* 78.

Jagota, R, 'Executability & Enforceability of Foreign Judgments and Decrees inIndia: An Analysis of Judicial Trends' (2015) *Indian Journal of Law & Justice* 15.

James, RD, 'Polygamy and Capacity to Marry' (1979) 42 *The Modern Law Review* 533.

Janis, MW, 'The Recognition and Enforcement of Foreign Law: The Antelope's Penal Law Exception' (1986) 112 *Faculty Articles and Papers* 303.

Jhambholkar, L, 'Conflict of Laws', (July-September 1991) 33 *Journal of the Indian Law Institute* 434.

——, 'Recognition Of Foreign Divorce Decrees In India: A Case For Contextual Interpretation' (1991) 33 *Journal of the Indian Law Institute* 432.

——, 'Domestic Violence and the Hague Abduction Convention: The Indian Perspective' (2017) 57 *Indian Journal of International Law.*

Joel, NA, 'Religious and Legal Pluralism in Global Comparative Perspective' (2011) 25 *Emory International Law Review* 967.

Johnson, TA, 'The Hague Child Abduction Convention: Diminishing Returns and Little to Celebrate for Americans' (2000) 33/1 *New York University Journal of International Law and Politics.*

Jolly, S and Vohra, R, 'Recognition of Foreign Same Sex Marriage In India A Legal Exploratory Analysis' (2017) 59 *Journal of Indian Law Institute* 302.

Jolly, S, 'International Parental Child Abduction: An Explorative Analysis of Legal Standards and Judicial Interpretation in India' (2007) 31 *International Journal of Law, Policy and the Family* 20.

——, 'Surrogacy and Family Ties: A Comparative Analysis of Indian and Japanese Legal Framework' (2010) 2 *University of Legal Studies Journal.*

Juenger, FK, 'Contract Choice of Law in the Americas' (1997) 45 *American Journal of Comparative Law* 195.

——, 'The Inter-American Convention on the Law Applicable to International Contracts: Some Highlights and Comparisons' (1994) 42 *The American Journal of Comparative Law* 381.

——, 'Private International Law or International Private Law' (1994) 5 *King's College Law Journal* 45.

Jurčys, P, 'Applicable law to intellectual property infringements in Japan: Alternative lex loci protectionis principle' [2010] *International Review of Law, Computers & Technology* 24:2.

Kahn-Freund, O, 'Reflections on Public Policy in the English Conflict of Laws' (1953) 39 *Transactions of the Grotius Society* 39.

Karsten, IGF, 'The Recognition of Divorces and Legal Separations Act 1971' (1972) 35 *MLR* 299.

Kenny, D, 'Re Flightlease: The 'Real and Substantial Connection' Test for Recognition and Enforcement of Foreign Judgments Fails to Take Flight I Ireland' (2014) 63 *International and Comparative Law Quarterly* 197.

Kessedjian, C, 'The Permanent Bureau, Hague Conference on Private International Law: Preliminary Document No 7 – International Jurisdiction and Foreign Judgments in Civil and Commercial Matters' (1997).

Khaitan, T, 'Koushal v Naz: Judges Vote to Recriminalise Homosexuality' (2015) 78 *MLR* 672.

Khanderia, S and Peari, S, 'Party Autonomy and the Choice of Law under Indian and Australian Private International Law' [2020] *Commonwealth Law Bulletin* 1.

Khanderia, S, 'Indian Private International Law *vis-à-vis* Party Autonomy in the Choice of Law' (2018) 18(1) *Oxford University Commonwealth Law Journal* 1.

——, 'International Approaches as Plausible Solutions to Resolve the Battle of Forms under the Indian Law of Contract' (2019) 8 *Global Journal of Comparative Law* 1.

——, 'The Hague Convention on Choice of Court Agreements and the Enforcement of Forum-Selection Clauses in Indian Private International Law' (2019) 9(3) International *Journal of Private Law* 125.

——, 'The Hague Conference on Private International Law's Proposed Draft Text on the Recognition and Enforcement of Foreign Judgments: Should South Africa Endorse it?' (2019) 63(3) *Journal of African Law* 413.

——, 'The Hague Judgments Project: Assessing its Plausible Benefits for the Development of Indian Private International Law' [2019] *Commonwealth Law Bulletin* 452.

——, 'Practice does not make Perfect: Rethinking the Doctrine of 'The Proper Law of the Contract' – A Case for the Indian Courts' (2020) 16(3) *Journal of Private International Law* 423.

——, 'The Ascertainment of the Applicable Law in the Absence of Choice in India and South Africa: A Shared Future in the BRICS' [2020] *Oxford University Commonwealth Law Journal.*

Kieran, W, 'Polygamous Marriages and Potentially Polygamous Marriages in Irish Law: A Critical Reappraisal' (2013) 36 *Dublin University Law Journal* 249.

Kincaid, P, 'Rationalising Contract Choice of Law Rules' (1993) 8(1) *Ottago Law Review* 93.

Kindregan Jr, CP and White, D, 'International Fertility Tourism: The Potential for Stateless Children in Cross-Border Commercial Surrogacy Arrangements' (2013) 36/3 *Suffolk Transnational Law Review* 527.

Kirshner, SN, 'Selling a Miracle: Surrogacy through International Borders: Exploration of Ukrainian Surrogacy' (2015) 14/1 *Journal of International Business and Law* 77.

Knop, K, Michaels, R and Riles, A, 'From Multiculturalism to Technique: Feminism, Culture, and the Conflict of Laws Style' (2012) 64(3) *Cornell Law Faculty Publications* 1307.

Kohm, LM, 'Tracing the Foundations of the Best Interest of the Child Standard in American Jurisprudence' (2007–2008) 337/10 *Journal of Law and Family Studies.*

Koppleman, A, 'Against Blanket Interstate Non-recognition of Same-Sex Marriage' (2005) 17(1) *Yale Journal of Law & Feminism Symposium* 205.

——, 'Same-Sex Marriage, Choice of Law, and Public Policy' (1997–1998) 76 *Texas Law Review* 921.

Kramer, L, 'Return of the Renvoi' (1991) 66 *New York University Law Review* 979.

——, 'Same-Sex Marriage, Conflict of Laws, and the Unconstitutional Public Policy Exception'(1997) 106 *Yale Law Journal* 1965.

Krvavac, M, 'The Hague Convention on the Law Applicable to Traffic Accidents and Rome II Regulation' (2018) 79 *Collection of Papers, Faculty of Law* 141.

Kuhn, AK, 'Doctrines of Private International Law in England and America Contrasted with those of Continental Europe' (1912) 12(1) *Columbia Law Review* 44.

Kumar, AP, Inder, D and Sharma, N, 'Surrogacy and Women's Right to health in India: Issues and Perspectives' (2013) 57 *Indian Journal of Public Health* 2.

Lakshmanan, AC, 'International Child Abduction – Parental Removal' (2008) 48 *Indian Journal of International Law* 427.

Lamont, R, 'Habitual Residence and Brussells IIbis: Developing Concepts for European Private International Family Law' (2007) 3/2 *Journal of Private International Law.*

Larry, AJ, 'Parental Kidnapping Prevention Act of 1980 – An End to Child Snatching, The Note' (1981) 8/2 *Journal of Legislation* 357.

Leflar, RA, 'Choice-Influencing Considerations In Conflicts of Law' (1996) 41 *New York University Law Review* 26.

Leflar RA, 'Extrastate Enforcement of Penal and Governmental Claims' (1932) 46 *Harvard Law Review* 193.

Liang, J, 'Statutory restrictions on party autonomy in China's private international law of contract: how far does the 2010 codification go?' [2012] *Journal of Private International Law* 77.

Lorenzen, EG, 'Huber's De Conflictu Legum' (1919) 13 *Illinois Law Review* 375.

——, 'The *Renvoi* Theory and the Application of Foreign Law' (1910) 10 (4) *Columbia Law Review* 327.

——, 'The Renvoi Doctrine in the Conflict of Laws: Meaning of "the Law of the Country' (1917) 27 *Yale Law Journal* 510.

——, 'The Theory of Qualifications and the Conflict of Laws' (1920) 20 *Columbia Law Review* 246.

——, 'The Characterisation, Classification, or Characterisation Problem in the Conflict of Laws' (1941) 50 *Yale Law Journal* 743.

Lutz-Christian, Wolff, 'Hong Kong's Conflict of Contract Laws: Quo Vadis?' (2010) 6(2) *Journal of Private International Law* 465.

Maddaugh, PD, 'Validity of Marriage and the Conflict of Laws: A Critique of the Present Anglo-American Position' (1973) 23(2) *The University of Toronto Law Journal* 117.

Mahmood, T, 'Religion, Lw, and Judiciary in Modern India' [2006] *Birmingham Young Law Review* 755.

Maidment, S, 'The Legal Effect of Religious Divorces' (1974) 37 *Modern Law Review* 611.

Malhotra, A and Malhotra R, 'Divorce Nullity and Related Matters under the Hindu Marriage Act 1955' (2005) *International Survey of Family Law* 275.

Manning, WD, Longmore MA and Giordano PC, 'The Changing Institution of Marriage: Adolescents' Expectations to Cohabit and to Marry' (2007) 69 *Journal of Marriage and Family* 559.

Marie, MC, 'Hague Convention on the Civil Aspects of International Child Abduction: An Analysis of its Efficacy' (1990-1991) 6/2 *Connecticut Journal of International Law.*

Marshall, BA and Keyes M, 'Australia's Accession to the Hague Convention on Choice of Court Agreements' (2017) 41 *Melbourne University Law Review* 246.

Marshall BA, 'Reconsidering the Proper Law of the Contract' (2012) 13 *Melbourne Journal of International Law* 505.

Martin, J and Hunter, H, 'The UNCITRAL Model Law' (1985) *13 International Business Law* 399.

Maxwell, L, 'The Disparity in Treatment of International Custody Disputes in American Courts: A Post-September 11th Analysis' (2005) 17/1 *Pace International Law Review.*

Mc Comish, J, 'Pleading and Proving Foreign Law in Australia' (2007) 31(2) *Melbourne University Law Review* 400.

McEleavy, PE, 'Brussels II *bis*: Matrimonial Matters, Parental Responsibility, Child Abduction and Mutual Recognition' (2004) 53/2 *The International and Comparative Law Quarterly* 511.

——, 'The Brussels II Regulation: How the European Community Has Moved into Family Law' (2002) 51 *The International and Comparative Law Quarterly* 883.

——, 'Regression and Reform in the Law of Domicile' (2007) 56(2) *International and Comparative Law Quarterly* 453.

——, 'Current Developments: Private International Law' (2011) 60 *International and Comparative Law Quarterly* 1065.

McVeigh, R and Maria-Elena, DD, 'Voting to Ban Same-Sex Marriage: Interests, Values, and Communities' (2009) 74 *American Sociological Review* 891.

Mehren, A and Nadelmann, KH, 'The Draft Convention on Recognition of Divorces and Legal Separations' (1968)16(4) *American Journal of Comparative Law* 580.

Mehren, A, 'Conflict of Laws in a Federal System: Some Perspectives' (1969) 18(3) *International and Comparative Law Quarterly* 681.

——, 'Drafting a Convention on International Jurisdiction and the Effects of Foreign Judgments Acceptable Worldwide: Can the Hague Convention Project Succeed' (2001) 49 *American Journal of Comparative Law* 191.

Mehren ATV, 'Enforcing Judgments Abroad: Reflections on the Design of Recognition Conventions' (1998) 24 *Brooklyn Journal of International Law* 17.

Meidanis, H, 'Public Policy and Ordre Public in the Private International Law of the EU: Traditional Positions and Modern Trends' (2005) 30(1) *European Law Review* 95.

Menendez, AE, 'Road Traffic Accidents: From the Hague Convention of 4 May 1971 to Regulation (EC) No 864/2007 (Rome II)' (2007) 7 *Anuario Espanol Derecho Int'l Priv* 505.

Mills, A, 'The Dimensions of Public Policy in Private International Law' (2008) 4(2) *Journal of Private International Law* 201.

——, 'The Hague Choice of Court Convention and Cross-Border Commercial Dispute Resolution in Australia And the Asia-Pacific' (2017) 18(1) *Melbourne Journal of International Law* 1.

Min, Xu et al., 'The Fourth Industrial Revolution: Opportunities and Challenges' (2018) 9(2) *International Journal of Financial Research* 90, 93.

Ming-Sho-Hu, 'Taiwan's Road to Marriage Equality: Politics of Legalizing Same-sex Marriage, China Quarterly' [2019] *Issue* 238.

Moreno Rodrigues, JA and Albornoz, MM, 'Reflections on the Mexico City Convention in the Context of the Preparation of the Future Hague Instrument on International Contracts' [2011] *Journal of Private International Law* 491.

Morris, JHC, 'The Proper Law of a Contract: A Reply' (1950) 3 *International Law Quarterly* 197

——, 'The Proper Law of Tort' (1951) *Harvard Law Review* 881.

——, 'The Recognition of Polygamous Marriages in English Law'(1953) 66 *Harvard Law Review* 961.

——, 'The Scope of the Carriage of Goods by Sea Act 1971' (1979) 95 *Law Quarterly Review* 59, 66.

Murphy, K, 'The Traditional View of Public Policy and Ordre Public in Private International Law' (1981) 11(3) *Georgia Journal of International and Comparative Law* 591

Mustafa, H, 'Wednesbury, Proportionality and Judicial Review' (2015) 2 *LUMS Law Journal* 1.

Nadelmann, KH, 'Private International Law Lord Fraser and the Savigny (Guthrie) and Bar (Gillespie) Editions' (1971) 20 *International and Comparative law Journal* 213.

Nakdai, L, 'It's 10 P.M., Do You Know Where Your Children are?: The Hague Convention on the Civil Aspects of International Child Abduction' (2002) 40/2 *Family Court Review an Interdisciplinary Journal.*

Nanda, VP, 'For Whom the Bell Tolls in the Aftermath of the Bhopal Tragedy: Reflections on Forum Non Conveniens and Alternative Methods of Resolving the Bhopal Dispute' (1987) 15 *Denver Journal of International Law and Policy* 235.

Nariman, FS, 'India and International Arbitration' (2009) 41 *George Washington International Law Review* 367.

Narrain, S, 'Lost in Appeal: The Downward Spiral from Naz to Koushal' (2013) 6 *NUJS Law Review* 575.

Neels, JL and Fredericks EA, 'Tacit choice of law in the Hague Principles on Choice of Law in International contracts' [2011] *De Jure* 101.

——, 'The Nature, Objective and Purposes of the Hague Principles on Choice of Law in International Contracts' (2014) 15 *Yearbook of Private International Law* 45.

——, 'The Role of the Hague Principles on Choice of Law in International Commercial Contracts in Indian and South African Private International Law' (2017) 22 *Uniform Law Review / Revue de droit uniforme* 443.

Neill, O and Allison, R, 'Recognition of Same-Sex Marriage in the European Community: The European Court of Justice's Ability to Dictate Social Policy' (2004) 37(1) *Cornell International law Journal* 200.

Nishitani, Y, 'Party Autonomy in Contemporary Private International Law – The Hague Principles on Choice of Law and East Asia' (2016) 59 *Japanese Yearbook of International Law* 300.

Novicoff, ML, 'Blocking and Clawing Back in the Name of Public Policy: The United Kingdom's Protection of Private Economic Interests against Adverse Foreign Adjudication' (1985-1986) 7 *Northwestern Journal of International Law and Business* 12.

Nussbaum, A, 'Rise and Decline of the Law-of-Nations Doctrine in the Conflict of Laws' (1942) 42 *Columbia Law Review* 189.
——, 'The Problem of Proving Foreign Law' (1941) 50 *Yale Law Journal* 1018.
——, 'Treaties on Commercial Arbitration – A Test of International Private-Law Legislation' (1942) 56 *Harvard Law Review* 219.
Nwagbara, C, 'Recognition of Polygamous Marriages under the English Law' (2014) 26 *Journal of Law, Policy and Globalization* 13
Okoli, C and Ariste, G, 'The operation of the escape clauses in the Rome Convention and Rome I Regulation' (2012) 8 *Journal of Private International Law* 513.
Ong, DSL, 'Parental Child Abduction in Singapore: The Experience of a Non-Convention Country' (2007) 21/2 *International Journal of Law, Policy and the Family* 220.
Panagopoulos, G, 'Substance and Procedure in Private International Law' (2005) 1(1) *Journal of Private International Law* 6.
Pandey, AK and Santhalia, R, 'Inter-Country Abductions and Private International Law' (2010) 3 *NUJS Law Review* 2.
Parashar, A, 'Welfare of Child in Family Laws – India and Australia' (2003) 1 *NALSAR Law Review* 1.
Park, WW, 'Non-Signatories and the New York Convention' (2008) 2 *Dispute Resolution International* 84.
Parker, S, 'The Best Interests of the Child – Principles and Problems' (1994) 8/1 *International Journal of Law Policy and the Family.*
Pascal, RA, 'Characterization as an Approach to the Conflict of Laws' (1940) 2 *Louisiana Law Review* 715.
Paul, JR, 'The Transformation of International Comity' (2008) 71 *Law & Contemp Probs* 19.
Peiris, GL, 'Wednesbury Unreasonableness: The Expanding Canvas' (1987) 46 *Cambridge Law Journal* 53.
Pfund, PH, 'The Project of the Hague Conference on Private International Law to Prepare a Convention on Jurisdiction and the Recognition/Enforcement of Judgments in Civil and Commercial Matters' (1998) 24(1) *Brooklyn Journal of International Law* 7.
Pitel, S, 'Enforcement of Foreign Judgments: Where Morguard Stands after Beals' (2004) 40 *Canadian Business Law Journal* 189.
Pradhan, S and Patnaik, R, 'Internet and Society: Latest Developments in Cyberspace' (2018) 6(2*) Nirma University Law Journal* 21, 30.
Probert, R, 'Hyde v Hyde: Defining or Defending Marriage' (2007) 19 *Child and Family Law Quarterly* 322.
Qisheng, He, 'The EU conflict of laws communitarization and the modernization of Chinese private international law' [2012] *Rabels Zeitschrift für ausländisches und Internationales Privatrecht / The Rabel Journal of Comparative and International Private Law* 47.
Quillen, B, 'The New Face of International Child Abduction: Domestic-Violence Victims and Their Treatment Under the Hague Convention on the Civil Aspects of International Child Abduction' (2014) 49 *Texas International Law Journal* 3.
Raeburn, W, 'The Open Offer Formula and the Renvoi in Private International Law' (1948) 25 *British Year Book of International Law* 211.
Raghavan, 'Foreign Judgment and Foreign Awards Enforcement in India' *Supreme Court Review* 37 (1965).
Raiteri, M, 'Citizenship as a Connecting Factor in Private International Law for Family Matters' (2014) 10 *Journal of Private International Law* 309, 312.
Rajagopalan, S, 'Bhopal Gas Tragedy: Paternalism and Filicide' (2014) 5 *Journal of Indian Law and Society* 201.
Rajamannar, PV, 'The Future of Private International Law in India' (1952) 1 *Indian Yearbook of Int'l Affairs* 20.
Rama Rao, TS, 'Conflict Of Laws In India' (1958) 2 *Jahrg H* 2259.
——, 'Private Inter- national Law in India' (1955) 3 *The Indian Yearbook of Int'l Affairs* 219.
——, 'Conflict of Laws in the Indian Tax System' (1959) 8 *Indian Yearbook of Int'I Affairs* 215.
Rao, TS, 'Some Recent Developments And 'Non-Developments' In Indian Private International Law' (1985)27(4) *Journal of the Indian Law Institute* 558
Ramachandran, VG, 'Conflict of Laws as to Contracts' (1970) 12 *Journal of Indian Law Institute* 269.
Rana, P, 'Distant Silences and Default Judgments: Access to Justice for Transnationally Abandoned Women in India' (2014) 1 *Indian Journal of Public Law and Policy* 122.
Ravichandran, N, 'Legal Recognition of Same-Sex Relationships in India' (2014) 5 *Journal of Indian Law and Society* 95.
Redding, JA, 'Dignity, Legal Pluralism, and Same-Sex Marriage' [2010] *Brooklyn Law Review* 791.
Reed, A, 'Essential Validity of Marriage: The Application of Interest Analysis and Depecage to Anglo-American Choice of Law Rules' (2000) 20 *New York Law School Journal of International and Comparative Law* 387.
Reese, WLM, 'Does domicile bear a single meaning?' (1955) 55(5) *Columbia Law Review* 589.
——, 'Marriage in American Conflict of Laws' (1977) 26 *International and Comparative Law Quarterly* 952.
——, 'The Hague Convention on Celebration and Recognition of the Validity of Marriages' (1979) 20 *Virginia Journal of International Law* 25.

Remus, T, 'Revival of Rabel's Transnational Characterisation for Rules of Conflict: Some Answers in a European Convention' (2017) *International Business law Journal* 439.
Restin, AL, 'Marriage and Divorce Conflicts in International Perspective' (2017) *Duke Journal of Comparative & International Law* 485.
Rivers, DR, 'Comment, The Hague International Child Abduction Convention and The International Child Abduction Remedies Act: Closing Doors to the Parent Abductor' (1989) 2 *Global Business and Development Law Journal* 2.
Rogerson, P, 'Private International Law-Jurisdiction' (2010) 69(3) *The Cambridge Law Journal* 452.
——, 'Habitual Residence: The New Domicile' (2000) *49 International and Comparative Law Journal* 86.
Roodt, C, 'Recognition and Enforcement of Foreign Judgments: Still a Hobson's Choice among Competing Theories?' (2005) 38(1) *The Comparative and International Law Journal of Southern Africa* 15.
Rosenblum, D, 'Loving Gender Balance: Reframing Identity-Based Inequality Remedies' (2008) 76 *Fordham Law Rev* 2873.
Rühl, G, 'The Protection of Weaker Parties in the Private International Law of the European Union: A Portrait of Inconsistency and Truancy' (2014) *Journal of Private International Law* 335.
——, 'The Protection of Weaker Parties in the Private International Law of the European Union: A Portrait of Inconsistency and Truancy' (2014) *Journal of Private International Law* 335.
Rutten, S, 'Recognition of Divorce by Repudiation (talaq) in France, Germany and the Netherlands' (2004) 11 *MJ* 3, 263.
Saijwani, V, 'Personal Laws of Divorce in India with a Comment on Chaudry v. Chaudry' (1989) 11 *Women's Rights Law Reporter* 41.
Saxena, P, Mishra, P and Malik, S, 'Surrogacy: Ethical and Legal Issues' (2012) 37/4 *Indian Journal of Community Medicine*
Schawlowski, D 'The Islamic Mahr in German and in English Courts' (2010-11)16 *YIME* 148.
Scharffs, BG and Disparte, S, 'Comparative Models For Transitioning From Religious to Civil Marriage Systems' (2010) 12(2) *Journal of Law and Family Studies* 409.
Scherpe, JM, 'The Legal Recognition of Same Sex Couples in Europe and the Role of the European Court of Human Rights' (2010) 10 *Equal Rights Review* 83.
Schmitthoff, CM, 'Conflict avoidance in theory and Practice' (1956) 21(3) *Law and Contemporary Problems* 430.
——, 'Doctrine of the Proper Law of the Contract in the English Conflict of Laws' (1940) 28 *The Georgetown Law Journal* 447.
——, 'Validity of Marriage and the Conflict of Laws'(1940) 56 *Law Quarterly Review* 514.
Schnitzer-Reese, EA, 'International Child Abduction to Non-Hague Convention Countries: The Need for an International Family Court' (2004) 2 *Northwestern Journal International Human Rights* 1.
Schoenfeld, BN, 'Federalism in India' (1959) 20 (1) *The Indian Journal of Political Science* 52–62, 52.
Schwab, K, 'The Fourth Industrial Revolution' [2016] *World Economic Forum* 7.
Scott, ES, 'A World Without Marriage' (2007) 41 *Family Law Quarterly* 537.
Serban-Alexandru, S, 'The Decline and Upswing of Renvoi in the Private International Law of the European Union' [2017] *Conf Int'l Dr* 180.
Shah P, 'Attitudes to polygamy in English law' [2003] *International & Comparative Law Quarterly* 52(2).
——, 'In Pursuit of the Pagans: Muslim Law in the English Context' (2013) 45(1) *Journal of Legal Pluralism & Unofficial Law* 58.
Sharma, KM, 'Civil Law in India' (1969) 1 *Washington University Law Quarterly* 1.
Shava, M, 'Choice of Law and the Doctrine of Renvoi in Israeli Law – A Comparative Commentary' (2000) 15 *Tel Aviv University Stud. Law* 123.
Siberman, L, 'Hague Convention on International Child Abduction: A Brief Overview and Case Law Analysis' (1994) 28/1 *Family Law Quarterly.*
——, 'Hague International Child Abduction Convention: A Progress Report' (1994) 57/3 *Law and Contemporary Problems.*
——, 'Interpreting the Hague Abduction Convention: In Search of a Global Jurisprudence' (2005) 38/4 *UC Davis Law Review.*
——, 'Same Sex Marriage: Refining the Conflict of laws Analysis'(2005) 153 *University of Pennsylvania Law Review* 2195.
Siddiqui, TR, 'Interpretation of Islamic Marriage Contracts by American Courts' (2007) 41 *Family Law Quarterly* 3.
Silberberg, H, 'The Recognition and Enforcement of Foreign Judgments in South Africa' [1977] *Institute of Foreign and Comparative Law, UNISA, Pretoria.*
Singh, RK, 'Law of Dower (Mahr) in India' (2010) 12(1) *Journal of Islamic Law and Culture* 58.
Sinha, MK, 'The Bhopal Gas Leak Disaster Case: Union Carbide Corporation etc v Union of India etc' (1992) 1 *Asia Pacific Law Review* 118.
Smart, P, 'Interest Analysis, False Conflicts, and the Essential Validity of Marriage' (1985) 14 *Anglo-American Law Review* 225.

Smearman, CA, 'Second Wives' Club: Mapping the Impact of Polygamy in U.S. Immigration Law' (2009) 27 *Berkley Journal of International Law* 382.

Smith, B, 'The Proposed Hague Convention on Jurisdiction, Recognition and Enforcement of Judgments' (1999) 12(2) *Revue Québécoise de Droit International* 73.

Smith, JAC, 'Eastern Marriages in English Law' (1952) 1 *International and Comparative Law Quarterly* 801.

Solimine, ME, 'The Impact of *Babcock v. Jackson*: An Empirical Note' (1993) 56 *Albany Law Review* 773.

Sommerich, OC and Busch, B, 'Expert Witness and the Proof of Foreign Law' (1953) 38 *Cornell Law Review* 125.

Sorieul, R, 'The Influence of the New York Convention on the UNCITRAL Model Law on International Commercial Arbitration' (2008) 2 *Dispute Resolution International* 1.

Southard, W, 'The Reciprocity Rule and the Enforcement of Foreign Judgments' (1977) 16 *Columbia Journal of Transnational Law* 327.

Soysa, SD, 'Custody Disputes between Parents and Third Parties- An Evaluation of the Sri Lankan Law' [1985] *University of Colombo Review* 123.

Spiro, E, 'The Incidence of Jurisdiction in the Recognition and Enforcement of Foreign Judgments' [1978] *Acta Juridica* 59.

——, 'The Evolution of the Closest (Most Significant) Connection in the Conflict of Laws' (1990) 53.

Sprankling, JG and Lanyi, GR, 'Pleading and Proof of Foreign Law in American Courts' (1983) 19 *Stanford Journal of International Law* 3.

Stein, SB, 'Choice of Law and the Doctrine of Renvoi' (1971) 17 *Mc Gill Law journal* 582.

Stern, WB, 'Foreign Law in the Courts: Judicial Notice and Proof' (1957) *45 California Law Review* 23.

Stevenson, JR, 'The Relationship of Private International Law to Public International Law' (1952) 52 *Columbia Law Review* 562.

Stone, DM, 'The English Concept of Domicile' (1954) 17 *MLR* 244.

Stone, P, 'The Concept of Habitual Residence in Private International Law' (2000) 29 *Anglo-American Law Review* 342.

Strebel, FD, 'The Enforcement of Foreign Judgements and Foreign Public Law' (1999) 21 *Loyola of Los Angeles International and Comparative Law Journal* 55.

Subramanian, N, 'Legal Change and Gender Inequality: Changes in Muslim Family Law in India' (2008) 33 *Law and Social Inquiry* 631.

Subramanian, S, 'The Indian Supreme Court Ruling in Koushal v. Naz: Judicial Deference or Judicial Abdication' (2015) 47 *George Washington International law Review* 711.

Sykes, EI, 'The Essential Validity of Marriage' (1955) 4 *International and Comparative Law Quarterly* 159.

Symeonides, SC, 'Rome II and Torts Conflicts: A Missed Opportunity' (2008) 56(1) *American Journal of Comparative Law* 173.

Szászy, S, 'The Basic Connecting Factor in International Cases in the Domain of Civil Procedure' (1966) 15(2) 436

TJB, 'The Impact of Babcock v. Jackson on Conflict of Laws' (1966) 52(2) *Virginia Law* 302.

Takahashi, K, 'A major reform of Japanese private international law' [2006] *Journal of Private International Law* 311.

Tebbe, N, 'Religion and Marriage Equality Statutes' [2015] *Harvard Law & Policy Review* 25.

Teitz, LE, 'The Hague Choice of Court Convention: Validating Party Autonomy and Providing an Alternative to Arbitration' (2005) 53(3) *American Journal of Comparative Law* 543.

Tercier, P, 'The 1927 Geneva Convention and the ICC Reform Proposals' (2008) 2 *Dispute Resolution International* 19.

Thaorey, P, 'Informational Privacy: Legal Introspection In India' (2019)2 *Indian Law Institute Law Review* 160.

Thompson, EL and Yunus FS, 'Choice Of Laws Or Choice Of Culture: How Western Nations Treat The Islamic Marriage Contracts In Domestic Court'(2007) 25 *Wisconsin International Law Journal Volume* 361, 385.

Timmer, LJE, 'Abolition of Exequatur under the Brussels I Regulation: Ill Conceived and Premature' (2013) 9 *Journal of Private International Law* 129.

Trapnell, EM, 'Uniform Child Custody Jurisdiction Act' (1978) 12 *University of Richmond Law Review* 4.

Trimmings, K and Beaumont, PR, 'Article 20 of the 1980 Hague Abduction Convention' (2014) 9/1 *The Journal of Comparative Law.*

Tsang, KF, 'Double Actionability: An Outdated Rule in Modern Times' (2017) 86 *University of Missouri-Kansas City Law Review* 73.

Tu, G and Xu, M, 'Contractual conflicts in the People's Republic of China: the applicable law in the absence of choice' (2011) *Journal of Private International Law* 179.

Unger, J, 'The Place of Classification in Private International Law' (1937) 19 *Bell Yard: Journal of the Law Society's School of Law* 3.

Vanita, R, 'Same-Sex Weddings, Hindu Traditions, and Modern India' [2009] *Feminist Review* 91.

VenkataRao, R, SubhaRao (eds), 'A Public Disclosure on Privacy – An Analysis of Justice K.S. Puttaswamy v. UOI' [2018] *NLSIU Bangalore* 1.

Vivatyaraphol, T, 'Back to Basics: Determining a Child's Habitual Residence in International Child Abduction Cases Under the Hague Convention' (2009) 77/6 *Fordham Law Review.*

Vondracek, O, 'Art. 4 of the Roman Convention on the Law Applicable to Civil and Commercial Obligations: A Fruitful Compromise: Analysis of the Rules of the Law of Characteristic Performance and the Property Law of Contract' (2007) 8 *Common Law Review* 32.

Wachtell, SR, 'The Proof of Foreign Law in American Courts' (1935) 69 *US L. Rev.* 526

Wade, J, 'The English Concept of domicile: A Re-evaluation' (1974) 21(3) *Netherlands International Law Review* 265.

Wade, JA, 'Capacity to Marry: Choice of Law Rules and Polygamous Marriages' (1973) 22 *International and Comparative Law Quarterly* 571.

Walsh, K, 'Polygamous Marriages and Potentially Polygamous Marriages in Irish Law: A Critical Reappraisal (2013) 36 *Dublin University Law Journal* 249.

Walsh, MR and Savard, SW, 'International Child Abduction and the Hague Convention' (2006) 6 *Barry Law Review* 29.

Wardle, LD, 'International Marriage and Divorce Regulation and Recognition: A Survey (1995) 29(3) *Front de libération du Québec* 507.

Wardle, LD, 'Marriage and Religious Liberty: Comparative Law Problems and Conflict of Laws Solutions' (2010) 12 *Journal of Law and Family Studies* 315.

Watt, HM, 'Party Autonomy' in international contracts: from the makings of a myth to requirements of global governance' [2010] *European Review of Contract Law* 1.

Webb, PRH and Auburn FN, 'New Zealand Conflicts of Laws: A Bird's Eye View: Essays in Honour of John Humphrey Carlile Morris' (1977) 26 *British Institute of International and Comparative Law* 971.

Weinburg, L, 'The Federal-State Conflict of Laws: Actual Conflicts' (1992) 70 *Texas Law Review* 1743.

Weiner, MH, 'International Child Abduction and the Escape from Domestic Violence' (2000) 69/2 *Fordham Law Review* 609.

Weiner, MH, 'Using Article 20' (2004) 38/3 *Family Law Quarterly.*

Williams, SH, 'Technological Opacity, Predictability, and Self-Driving Cars' (2016) 38 *Cardozo Law Review* 121.

Woestehoff, K, 'The Drafting Process for a Hague Convention on Jurisdiction and Judgments with Special Consideration of Intellectual Property and E-Commerce' [2005] *LLM Theses and Essays*, Paper No. 54.

Wolff, M, 'The Choice of Law by the Parties in International Contracts' (1937) 49 *Juridical Review* 110.

Work, TS, 'India Satisfies Its Jones for Arbitration: New Arbitration Law in India' (1997) 10 *Transnat'l Law* 217.

Yamaguchi, S and Lindhorst, T, 'Domestic Violence and the Implementation of the Hague Convention on the Civil Aspects of International Child Abduction: Japan and US Policy' (2016) 17/4 *Journal of International Women's Studies.*

Yee, WW, 'The Exclusion of Foreign Law: Public Policy in Choice of Law Process' (1995) 16 *Singapore Law Review* 286.

Yntema, HE, 'The Historic Bases of Private International Law' (1953) 2 *American Journal of Comparative Law* 297, 305–08

Yntema HE, 'The Objectives of Private International Law' (1957) 35 *Canadian Bar Review* 721.

Yoko, K, 'A Haven for International Child Abduction: Will the Hague Convention Shape Japanese Family Law?' (2015) 46 *California Western International Law Journal* 1.

Zhang, Y and Van Hook, J, 'Marital Dissolution Among Interracial Couples' (2009) 71/1 *Journal of Marriage and Family.*

Zohar, G, 'Habitual Residence: An Alternative to the Common Law Concept of Domicile' (2009) 9 *Whittier Journal of Child and Family Advocacy* 169.

Books

Abdullah, N, *Private International Law of Afghanistan* 6th edn (Saed, 2016).

Agarwal, KB and Singh, V, *Private International Law in India* (Kluwer Law International, 2010).

Ahmed, A, Mohammedan Law 25th edn (Central Law Agency, 2012).

Akhtar, N, *Family Law on Divorce and Judicial Separation* (Deep and Deep Publications, 2003).

Andrews, LB, *Between Strangers: Surrogate Mothers, Expectant Fathers, & Brave New Babies* (Harper & Row, 1989).

Augenhofer, S, *Unfair Competition and Acts Restricting Free Competition: Commentary on the European Rules of the Conflict of Laws* (Calliess eds).

Bate, JP, *Notes On the Doctrine of Renvoi in Private International Law* (Stevens and Sons, 1904).

Beale, JH, *A Treatise on the Conflict of Laws* vol 1 (Baker Woorhis & Co, 1935).

Beaumont, PR and McEleavy, P, *Antons Private International law* 3rd edn (W. Green, 2011).

——, *The Hague Convention on International Child Abduction* (Oxford University Press, 1999).

Bhadbhade, N, *Pollock and Mulla on the Indian Contract and Specific Relief Acts: Volume 1* 14th edn (Lexis Nexis Publications, 2014).

Blackaby, N and Partasides, C with Redfern, A and Hunter, M, *Redfern and Hunter on International Arbitration* 5th edn (Oxford University Press, 2009).
Bonell, MJ, *An International Restatement of Contract Law: The UNIDROIT Principles of International Commercial Contracts* (Transnational Publishers, 2005).
Bonvillain, N, *Women And Men: Cultural Constructs Of Gender* (Prentice Hall, 2001).
Briggs, A, *Dicey, Morris and Collins on the Conflict of Laws* vol 2, 15th edn (Sweet and Maxwell, 2015).
——, *Private International Law in Myanmar* (Oxford University Press, 2015).
——, *The Conflict of Laws* 4th edn (Oxford University Press, 2019).
Carr, C, *Unlocking Medical Law and Ethics* 2nd edn (Routledge, 2015).
Cheshire, GC, *Private International Law* 2nd edn (Oxford University Press, 1938).
——, Private International Law 6th edn (Clarendon Press, 1961).
Clarkson, CMV and Hill, J, *The Conflict of Laws* (Oxford University Press, 2006).
——, *The Conflict of Laws* 4th edn (Oxford University Press, 2011).
Collier, JG, *Conflict of Laws* 3rd edn (Cambridge University Press, 2001).
Collins, L, Morse, CGJ, McClean, D, *Dicey, Morris & Collins on the Conflict of Laws* 14th edn (Sweet and Maxwell, 2006).
Currie, B, *Selected Essays on the Conflict of Laws* (Duke University Press, 1963).
Davies et al., *Nygh's Conflict of Laws in Australia* 9th edn (LexisNexis Butterworths, 2020).
Davies, Bell and Brereton (eds) *Nygh's Conflict of Laws in Australia* 8th edn (Lexis Nexis, 2010).
DeMarco, D, *Biotechnology and the Assault on Parenthood* (Ignatius Press, 1991).
Desai, SA and Mulla, DF, *Mulla Hindu Law* 21st edn (Lexis Nexis, 2013).
Dicey, A, *A Digest of the Law of England with Reference to the Conflict of Laws* (Stevens and Sons, 1896).
Dicey, A, Morris, J and Collins, J (eds), *Dicey and Morris on the Conflict of Laws* 11th edn (Sweet and Maxwell, 1987).
Diwan, P and Diwan, P, *Private International Law: Indian and English* 4th edn (Deep Publishers, 1998).
Durantaye, K, *Infringement of Intellectual Property: Commentary on the European Rules of the Conflict of Laws* (Calliess eds).
Edwards, AB (Updated by E Kahn), 'Conflict of Laws', in WA Joubert, *The Law of South Africa* vol 2, part 2, 2nd edn (2003).
Falconbridge, JD, *Essays On The Conflicts Of Laws* (Canada Law Book Company, 1947).
——, *Essays on the Conflict of Laws* 2nd edn (Canada Law Book Company, 1954).
——, *Essays on the Conflicts of Laws* 2nd edn (Cambridge University Press, 2009).
Fawcett, J, Carruthers, JM and North, P, *Cheshire, North and Fawcett: Private International Law* 14 edn (Oxford University Press, 2008).
Fentiman, R, *Foreign Law in English Courts* (Oxford University Press, 1998).
Forsyth, C, *Private International Law – The Modern Roman-Dutch Law Including the Jurisdiction of the High Courts* 5th edn (Juta Publications, 2012).
Fournier, P, *Muslim Marriage in Western Courts: Lost in Transplantation* (Routledge, 2016).
Fredericks, E, *Contractual Capacity and the Conflict of Laws in Common Law Jurisdictions (Part 2): Australasia, North America, Asia and Africa* (Forthcoming, 2019).
Garbolino, D, *International Child Custody Cases: Handling Hague Convention Cases in US Courts* 3rd edn (The National Judicial College, 2000).
Garnett, R, *Substance and Procedure in Private International Law* (Oxford University Press, 2012).
Gerber, P and O'Byrne, K, *Surrogacy, Law and Human Rights* 1st edn (Routledge, 2016).
Glendhill, A, *The Republic of India: The Development of Its Laws and Constitution* (Greenwood, 2013).
Govindaraj, VC, *The Conflict of Laws in India: Inter-Territorial and Inter-Personal Conflict* 2nd edn (Oxford University Press, 2019).
Graveson, RH, *Conflict of Laws* 7th edn (Sweet and Maxwell, 1974).
Gupta, A, *This Alien Legacy: The Origins of 'Sodomy' Laws in British Colonialism, Human Rights Watch* (New York, 2008).
Hein, J, *Environmental Damage: Commentary on the European Rules of the Conflict of Laws* (Calliess eds).
——, *Rome Regulations: Commentary on the European Rules of the Conflict of Laws* (Calliess eds).
Hibbert, *WN, International Private Law or Conflict of Laws* (University of London Press, 1918).
Higgins, R and others, *Oppenheim's International Law* 8th edn (Longmans, Green and Co, 1955).
Hill, D, *Private International Law* (Edinburgh University Press, 2014).
Huber, U, *De Conflictu Legum in Diversis Imperiis* (reprinted in Friedrich Carl Von Savigny, *A Treatise on the Conflict of Laws* 2nd edn (translated by Guthrie Rothman Reprints, 1972).
Jain, MP, *Indian Constitutional law* 8th edn (Lexis Nexis, 2018).
——, *Outlines Of Indian Legal And Constitutional History* 7th edn (Lexis Nexis, 2014).
Johnson, WS, *Time to Embrace: Same-Gender Relationships in Religion Law and Politics* 2ndedn (Wm B Eerdmans Publishing Co, 2006).

Leflar, RA, *American Conflicts Law* 3rd edn (Indiana Polis, 1977).
Lorenzen, EG, *Selected Articles on the Conflict of Laws* (Yale University Press, 1947).
Magnus, U, Mankowski, P, *Brussels II bis Regulation* (Walter de Gruyter, 2012).
Mahmood, T, *Statute Law Relating To Muslims In India: A Study In Islamic And Constitutional Perspectives* 1st edn (Institute of Objective Studies, 1995).
Menski, W, *Modern Indian Family law* (Routledge, 2013).
Mills, A, *Party Autonomy in Private International Law* (Cambridge University Press, 2018).
Morris, JHC, *The Conflict of Laws* 2nd edn (Stevens and Sons, 1980).
Mortenson, R et al., *Private International Law in Australia* 3rd edn (Lexis Nexis, 2011).
Nelson, RA, *Indian Penal Code* 9th edn (S. K. Sarvaria, 2003).
Niekerk, V and Schulze, C, *The South African Law of International Trade: Selected Topics* (Saga Legal Publications Pretoria, 2016).
Noronha, FE, *Private International Law in India: Adequacy of Principles in Comparison with Common Law and Civil Law Systems* (Universal Law Publishers, 2010).
——, *Private International Law in India* 2nd edn (Universal law Publishing, 2013).
North, P and Fawcett, JJ, *Cheshire and North's Private International Law* 13th edn (Oxford University Press, 2006).
North, PM, *Essays in Private International Law* (Clarendon Press, 1993).
Nussbaum, A, *Principles of Private International Law* (Oxford University Press, 1945).
Nygh, PE, *Autonomy in International Contracts* (Clarendon Press, 1999).
O'Brien, J, *Conflict of Laws* 2nd edn (Cavendish Publishing Company, 1999).
Okoli, CSA, *Place of Performance: A Comparative Analysis* (Hart Publishing, 2020).
Oppong, R, Private International Law in Commonwealth Africa (Cambridge University Press, 2013).
Paisson, L, *Marriage in Comparative Conflict of Laws: Substantive Conditions* (Brill, 1981).
Peari, S, *The Foundation of Choice of Law: Choice and Equality* (Oxford University Press, 2018).
Pitel, S et al., *Private International Law in Common Law Canada: Cases, Texts and Materials* 4th edn (Emond Publishing, 2016).
Pregat, AB, *Same Sex Relationships and Israeli Law, in Same Sex Couples - Comparative Insights on Marriage and Cohabitation* (Springer, 2015).
Rabel, E, *The Conflict of Laws: A Comparative Study* vol 1, 2nd edn (Ann Arbor: The University of Michigan Press, 1958).
Robertson, H, *Characterization in the Conflict of Laws* (Harvard University Press, 1940).
Rödl, *Industrial Action: Commentary on the European Rules of the Conflict of Laws* (Calliess eds).
Rogers, WVH, *Winfield & Jolowicz on Tort* 18th edn (Sweet & Maxwell, 2010).
Rogerson, P, *Collier's Conflict of Laws* 4th edn (Cambridge University Press, 2016).
Rozée, V and Unisa, S, *Assisted Reproductive Technologies in the Global South and North* 1st edn (Routledge, 2016).
Saha, TK, *Textbook on Legal Methods, Legal Systems and Research* (Universal Law Publishers, 2010).
Sapre, A, *Ratanlal & Dhirajlal: The Law of Torts* 28th edn (Lexis Nexis, 2018).
Sarcevic, P, *Yearbook of Private International Law* vol 6 (European Law Publishers, 2015).
Savigny, FKV, 'Private International Law and the Retrospective Operation of Statutes: A Treatise on the Conflict of Laws and the Limits of Their Operation in Respect of Place and Time' cited in J Fawcett, JM Carruthers and P North, *Cheshire, North and Fawcett: Private International Law* 14 edn (Oxford University Press, 2008).
——, *System of Modern Roman Law* (Hyperion Press, 1867).
——, *Treatise on the Conflict of Laws* 2nd edn (Gutherie translation, 1880).
Saxena, PP, *Family Law Lectures: Family Law* 3rd edn (Lexis Nexis, 2011).
Schacht, J, *The Origins of Muhammadan Jurisprudence* (Oxford University Press, 1950).
Schmid, C and Pinkel, T, 'Article 5 Rome II' in Calliess (ed) *Rome Regulations: Commentary on the European Rules of the Conflict of Laws* (Wolters Kluwer, 2015).
Schulze, C, *On Jurisdiction and the Recognition and Enforcement of Foreign Money Judgments* (University of South Africa Press, 2005).
Schuz, R, *The Hague Child Abduction Convention: A Critical Analysis* 1st edn (Hart Publishing, 2013).
Setalvad, AM, *Conflict of Laws* (Lexis Nexis, 2009).
Sharma, K, *Family Law Lectures: Family Law* 4th edn (Lexis Nexis, 2015).
——, *Fiscal Federalism and Indian Constitution* (Satyam law International, 2017).
Shetreet, S and Chodosh, H, *Uniform Civil Code for India: Proposed Blueprint for Scholarly Discourse* (Oxford University Press, 2015).
Shukla, VN, *Constitution of India* 12th edn (Eastern Book Co, 2013).
Simmonds, KR, '*Contemporary Problems in the Conflict of Laws*' *Essays in Honour of John Humphrey & Carlile Morris* (Springer, 1978).

Singh, A, *Law of Contract and Specific Relief* 12th edn (Eastern Book Company, 2013).
Singh, MP, *Indian Federalism: An introduction* 1st edn (National Book Trust, 2011).
Singh, SS, *Unification of Divorce Laws in India* (Deep and Deep Publishers, 1993).
Snyder, RC, *Gay Marriage and Democracy: Equality for All* (Rowman & Littlefield, 2006).
Steinbock, B, *Legal and Ethical Issues in Human Reproduction* (Ashgate, 2002).
Symeneoids, S, *American Private International law* (Kluwer Law International law, 2008).
——, *Codifying Choice of Law Around the World: An International Comparative Analysis* (Oxford University Press, 2014).
Takwani, CK, *Civil Procedure with Limitation Act 1963* 8th edn (Eastern Book Company, 2017).
Tiburcio, C and Dolinger, J, *Private International Law in Brazil* 2nd edn (Wolters Kluwer, 2017).
Trimmings, K, Torremans, P, Mills, A, Grusic, U and Heinze, C, *Cheshire, North, and Fawcett: Private International Law* 15th edn (Oxford University Press, 2017).
Tulibacka, M, *Product Liability Law in Transition: A Central European Perspective* (Ashgate Publishers, 2009).
Venkatachalaih, MN, *Halsburys Laws of India - Evidence* 2nd edn (Lexis Nexis, 2019).
Walker, J, *Halsbury's Laws of Canada: Conflict of Laws* (Lexis Nexis, 2011).
——, *Halsbury's Laws of Canada: Conflict of Laws* (Lexis Nexis, 2016)
Westermack, E, *A Short History of Marriage* (Literary Licensing, 2013).
Westlake, J, *A Treatise on Private International Law with Principal Reference to Its Practice in England* (William Maxwell & Son, 1890).
Wolff, M, *Private International Law* 2nd edn (Oxford Clarendon Press, 1950).
Young, PD, *Religion Sex and Politics: Christian Churches and Same-Sex Marriage in Canada* (Black Point NS: Fernwood Publishing, 2012).

Chapters in Books

Ahmad, F, 'The Problem with Personal Laws in India' in S Choudhry and J Herring (eds), *The Cambridge Companion to Comparative Family Law* (Cambridge University Press, 2019) 225–253.
Ali, K, 'Marriage in Classical Islamic Jurisprudence: A Survey of Doctrines' in F Vogel and A Quraishi (eds), *The Islamic Marriage Contract: Case Studies in Islamic Family Law* (HUP, 2008).
Ali, S, 'Inter-country Child Abductions, – Pakistan Legal Response' in SR Garimella and S Jolly (eds), *Private International Law: South Asian States' Practice* (Springer, 2016).
Allan, S, 'The Surrogate in Commercial Surrogacy: Legal and Ethical Considerations' in P Gerber and K O'Byrne (eds), *Surrogacy, Law and Human Rights* (Routledge, 2016).
Anand, P, 'India' in J Stewart (ed), *Family Law: Jurisdictional Comparisons* (Sweet and Maxwell, 2011).
Bailey, M, Baines, B, Amani, B and Kaufman A, 'Expanding Recognition of Foreign Polygamous Marriages: Policy Implications for Canada' in A Campbell (eds), *Polygamy in Canada' Legal and Social Implications for Women and Children A Collection of Policy Research Reports* (The Alberta Civil Liberties Research Centre, 2005).
Baxi, U, 'Conflict of Laws' in *Annual Survey of Indian Law 1967 and 1968* (Indian Law Institute).
Currie, B, 'Notes on Methods and Objectives in the Conflict of Laws' in *Selected Essays on the Conflict of Laws* (Duke University Press, 1963).
Droux, J, 'A League of its Own? The League of Nations' Child Welfare Committee (1919-1936) and International Monitoring of Child Welfare Policies' in R García, MD Rodogno and L Kozma (eds), *The League of Nations' Work on Social Issues: Visions, Endeavours and Experiments* 89-103 (United Nations, 2016).
Dutta, A, 'Domicile, habitual residence and establishment' in J Basedow and others (eds), *Encyclopaedia of Private International Law* (Edward Elgar Publishing, 2017).
Fentiman, R, 'The Significance of Close Connection' in J Ahern and W Binchy (eds), *The Rome II Regulation on the Law Applicable to Non-Contractual Obligations: A New Litigation Regime* (Martinus Nijhoff Publishers, 2009).
Franzina, P, *The Evolving role of Nationality in Private International law*, in S Forlati and A Annoni (eds), *The Changing Role of Nationality in International Law* (Routledge, 2013).
Gardiner, J, 'Same-sex Marriage - A Worldwide Trend?' in P Gerber and A Sifris (eds), *Current Trends in the Regulation of Same-sex Relationships* (Federation Press, 2011).
Garimella, SR, 'India' in A Reyes (ed), *Recognition and Enforcement of Judgments in Civil and Commercial Matters* (Hart Publishing, 2019).
Graziano, TK, 'Freedom to Choose the Applicable Law in Tort – Articles 14 and 4(3) of the Rome II Regulation' in J Ahern and W Binchy (eds), *The Rome II Regulation on the Law Applicable to Non-Contractual Obligations: A New Litigation Regime* (Martinus Nijhoff Publishers, 2009).

Hossain, S, 'Cross Boder Divorce Regime in Bangldesh' in SR Garimella and S Jolly (eds) *Private International Law: South Asian State Practice* (Springer, 2017).

J, von Hein, 'Article 4 and Traffic Accidents' in J Ahern and W Binchy (eds), *The Rome II Regulation on the Law Applicable to Non-Contractual Obligations: A New Litigation Regime* (Martinus Nijhoff Publishers, 2009).

Jhambolkar, L, 'Conflict of Laws', in SK Verma and Kusum (eds), *Fifty Years of the Supreme Court of India: Its Grasp* (Indian Law Institute, 2000).

Jolly, S, 'Cross Border Surrogacy: Indian State Practice' in S Jolly and SR Garimella (eds), *Private International Law: South Asian States' Practice* (Springer, 2017).

Magnus, U, 'Article 4 Rome I Regulation: The Applicable Law in the Absence of Choice' in Ferrari and Leible (eds), *Rome I Regulation. The Law Applicable to Contractual Obligations in Europe* (Sellier European Law Publishers 2009).

Malhotra, A and Malhotra, R, 'India' in E Sutherland (ed), *The Future of Child and Family Law: International Predictions* (Cambridge University Press, 2012).

Mills, A, 'The Application of Multiple Laws under the Rome II Regulation' in J Ahern and W Binchy (eds), *The Rome II Regulation on the Law Applicable to Non-Contractual Obligations: A New Litigation Regime* (Martinus Nijhoff Publishers, 2009).

Neels, JL, 'Choice of forum and tacit choice of law: The Supreme Court of India and the Hague Principles on Choice of Law in International Commercial Contracts (an appeal for an inclusive comparative approach to private international law)' in UNIDROIT (ed) *Eppur si muove: The Age of Uniform Law. Essays in Honour of Michael Joachim Bonell to celebrate his 70th birthday* (2016).

——, 'Indian perspectives on the Hague Principles' in D Girsberger, TK Graziano and JL Neels (eds), *Choice of Law in International Commercial Contracts. Global Perspectives on the Hague Principles* (Oxford University Press, 2021) (Forthcoming).

Nimushakavi, V, 'Cross-Border Divorce Decrees – Recognition in India and Public Policy Considerations' in SR Garimella and S Jolly (eds) *Private International Law: South Asian State Practice* (Springer, 2017).

Pathirana, K, 'Cross Border Divorce: Sri-lankan Practice', in S Ramani and S Jolly (eds), *Private International Law* (Springer, 2017).

Shah, P, 'Distorting Minority laws, Religious and European Minority legal Systems' in P Shah and Marie-Claire Foblets (eds) *Family, Religion and Law: Cultural Encounters in Europe* (Routledge, 2015).

Sharma, M, 'Inter-Country Child Abduction: Indian Legal Response' in SR Garimella and S Jolly (eds), *Private International Law: South Asian States' Practice* (Springer, 2017).

Singh, K, 'Child Custody Cases in the context of International Migration' in P Rajni and P Uberoi (eds), *Marriage, Migration and Gender* (SAGE Publications, 2008).

Skelton, A, 'International Children's Rights Law: Complaints and Remedies' in U Kilkelly and T Liefaard (eds), *International Human Rights of Children* (Springer, 2019).

Stone, P, 'Product Liability under the Rome II Regulation' in J Ahern and W Binchy (eds), *The Rome II Regulation on the Law Applicable to Non-Contractual Obligations: A New Litigation Regime* (Martinus Nijhoff Publishers, 2009).

Trimmings, K and Beaumont, P, 'General Report on Surrogacy' in K Trimmings and P Beaumont (eds), *International Surrogacy Arrangements: Regulation at the International Level* (Hart Publishing, 2013).

Wafer, J, 'Muhammad And Male Homosexuality' in SO Murray and W Roscoe (eds), *Islamic Homosexualities: Culture, History, And Literature* (NYU Press, 1997).

Wijeyeskera, R, 'Inter-country Child Abduction – Sri Lankan Legal Response' in SR Garimella and S Jolly (eds), *Private International Law: South Asian States' Practice* (Springer, 2016).

Other Resources

'Surrogate Baby Born in India Arrives in Japan' *Hindustan Times* (3 November 2008) www.hindustantimes.com/world/surrogate-baby-born-in-india-arrives-in-japan/story-clfjpEmKM0wORsHNmwG7CP.html.

'The Parentage/Surrogacy Project' (Hague Conference on Private International Law) www.hcch.net/en/projects/legislative-projects/parentage-surrogacy.

Asian Principles for the Recognition and Enforcement of Foreign Judgments 2020, Asian Business Law Institute, available at https://info.sal.org.sg/abli/ebooks/recognition-enforcement-foreign-judgments/.

Bogsch, A, *The First Hundred Years of the Berne Convention for the Protection of Literary and Artistic Works* in *Berne Convention Centenary* (International Bureau of Intellectual Property, 1986).

Central Adoption Resource Authority, 'Eligibility Criteria for Prospective Adoptive Parents' (*CARA, Ministry of Women & Child Development*) http://cara.nic.in/Parents/eg_ri.html.

Complete Constitutional Justice' (2015) 2015 Int'l Surv Fam L 121.

Council on General Affairs and Policy of the Conference, 'Conclusion and Recommendations adopted by the Council on General Affairs and Policy of the Conference' (*Hague Conference on Private International Law*, 7–9 April 2010) https://assets.hcch.net/upload/wop/genaff2010concl_e.pdf.

Directorate General for Internal Policies, 'Cross-border Parental Child Abduction in the European Union' (*European Parliament*, 2015) 87 www.europarl.europa.eu/RegData/etudes/STUD/2015/510012/IPOL_STU(2015)510012_EN.pdf.

Divorce and Separation in India, Premchand Dommaraju, Population and Development Review Vol 42, No 2 (June 2016).

Duncan, W, *Purpose of the Malta Process* (The Judges' Newsletter, 2010) https://assets.hcch.net/docs/8a903d75-7364-47bf-85e0-dc777d602277.pdf.

Emon, AM and Khaliq, U, *Private International Law, Islamic Law, and Cross-Border Child Abduction A Historico-Legal Analysis* (Anver M. Emon, 2016) www.anveremon.com/projects/hague-abduction-convention-.pdf.

Ergas Y, *The Transnationalization of Everyday Life: Cross-Border Reproductive Surrogacy, Human Rights and the Re-Visioning of International Law* (Deconstructing and Reconstructing 'Mother' Workshop, Columbia University, 12 March 2012) 20 http://claradoc.gpa.free.fr/doc/444.pdf.

Federal Law Gazette, Part 111 Classification number 100-1.

Garbolino, JD, *The Impact of the Brussels II Regulation on Hague Convention Proceedings in the European Union* (Federal Judicial Center, March 2016) www.fjc.gov/sites/default/files/2016/Impact%20of%20Brussels%20II_0.pdf.

Gupta, MD, 'WCD Ministry Undecided on Child Abduction Meet in Hague', *Hindustan Times* (4 February 2017) www.hindustantimes.com/india-news/wcd-ministry-undecided-on-child-abduction-meet-in-hague/story-tVysBbSqOkcjepx85LM1SJ.html.

Hague Conference on Private International Law 'Overview of the Judgments Project' www.hcch.net/en/projects/legislative-projects/judgments 3 and 17.

Hague Conference on Private International Law, 'Other connected parties' https://www.hcch.net/en/states/other-connected-parties.

Hoff, PM, *The Uniform Child-Custody Jurisdiction and Enforcement Act* (National Criminal Justice Reference Service, December 2001) www.ncjrs.gov/pdffiles1/ojjdp/189181.pdf.

Ireland: Supreme Court, *H.A.H. v. S.A.A. and Others*, 12 December 2017, available at www.refworld.org/docid/5a2fb7814.html.

Jaising, I, 'Hague Convention on Child Abduction: India Must not Sign this Flawed Arrangement', *Hindustan Times* (20 October 2017) www.hindustantimes.com/opinion/hague-convention-on-child-abduction-india-must-not-sign-this-flawed-arrangement/story-ChZzhDAjzqZI6aVVcVlRlK.html.

Jyoti, D, 'Plea in Kerala High Court seeks recognition for same-sex marriages', *Hindustan Times* (28 January 2020), available at www.hindustantimes.com/india-news/plea-in-kerala-hc-seeks-recognition-for-same-sex-marriages/story-usG9x12oM4urkZPQK99aHP.html.

Law no 2015-925 of 29 July 2015 on the reform of the right of asylum, www.legifrance.gouv.fr/eli/loi/2015/7/29/INTX1412525L/jo.

Lowe, N and Stephens, V, *A Statistical Analysis of Applications Made in 2008 under the Hague Convention of 25 October 1980 on the Civil Aspects of International Child Abduction* (HCCH Permanent Bureau and the International Centre for Missing and Exploited Children, February 2018) https://assets.hcch.net/docs/d0b285f1-5f59-41a6-ad83-8b5cf7a784ce.pdf.

Lowe, N, *A Statistical Analysis of Applications made in 2008 under the Hague Convention of 25 October 1980 on the Civil Aspects of International Child Abduction* (Hague Conference on Private International Law, May 2011) www.hcch.net/en/publications-and-studies/details4/?pid=5421&dtid=32.

Morgan, LW, *Grave Risk of Harm Under Article 13(b) of the Hague Convention on International Child Abduction: What Constitutes a War?* (Family Law Reader, July 2002) www.famlawconsult.com/archive/reader200207.html.

Nair, S, 'Inter-Country Child Abduction: Govt Panel against Hague Treaty', *Indian Express* (9 May 2018) https://indianexpress.com/article/india/inter-country-child-abduction-govt-panel-against-hague-treaty-5169074/.

Palattiyil, G, Blyth, E, Sidhva, D and Balakrishnan, G, *Globalization and Cross-Border Reproductive Services: Ethical Implications of Surrogacy in India for Social Work*' [2010] 53/5 International Social Work https://journals.sagepub.com/doi/abs/10.1177/0020872810372157#articleCitationDownloadContainer.

Permanent Bureau & Co-Reporters, Hague Conference on Private International Law: Summary of the Outcome of the Discussion in Commission II of the First Part of the Diplomatic Conference (6–20 June 2001).

Permanent Bureau, 'A Preliminary Report on the Issues Arising from International Surrogacy Arrangements' (*Hague Conference on Private International Law*, March 2012) https://assets.hcch.net/docs/d4ff8ecd-f747-46da-86c3-61074e9b17fe.pdf.

Permanent Bureau, 'Conclusions And Recommendations And Report Of The Special Commission On The Practical Operation Of The 1993 Hague Intercountry Adoption Convention' (*Hague Conference on Private International Law*, 17–25 June 2010) https://assets.hcch.net/upload/wop/adop2010_rpt_en.pdf.

Permanent Bureau, 'Domestic and family Violence and the Article 13 "grave risk" Exception in the operation of the Hague Convention of 25 October 1980 on the Civil Aspects of International Child Abduction: A Reflection Paper' (*Hague Conference on Private International Law*, May 2011) https://assets.hcch.net/docs/ce5327cd-aa2c-4341-b94e-6be57062d1c6.pdf.

Permanent Bureau, 'Hague Conference on Private International Law, Domestic and Family Violence and the Article 13 "Grave Risk" in the Operation of the Hague Convention of 25 October 1980 on the Civil Aspects of International Child Abduction: A Reflection Paper' (*HCCH*, May 2011) https://assets.hcch.net/upload/wop/abduct2011pd09e.pdf.

Permanent Bureau, 'Hague Conference on Private International Law, Report of the Third Special Commission meeting to review the operation of the Hague Convention on the Civil Aspects of International Child Abduction' (*HCCH*, 17–21 March 1997).

Permanent Bureau, 'Private International Law Issues Surrounding the Status of Children, Including Issues Arising from International Surrogacy Arrangements, (*Hague Conference on Private International Law*, March 2011) www.hcch.net/upload/wop/genaff20llpdlle.pdf.

Permanent Bureau, 'The Seventh Meeting of the Special Commission on the Practical Operation of the 1980 Hague Child Abduction Convention and the 1996 Hague Child Protection Convention, October 2017' (*HCCH*, 3 June 2017) https://assets.hcch.net/docs/0a0532b7-d580-4e53-8c25-7edab2a94284.pdf.

Permanent Bureau, Hague Conference on Private International Law: Preliminary Document No. 16 – Some Reflections on the Present State of Negotiations on the Judgments Project in the Context of the Future Work Programme of the Conference (2002).

Pinky Saxena, 'Hindu Law' [2011] 47 Annual Survey of Indian law http://14.139.60.114:8080/jspui/bitstream/123456789/4177/1/019_2011_Hindu%20Law.pdf.

Points, K, *Commercial Surrogacy And Fertility Tourism In India: The Case of Baby Manji* (The Kenan Institute for Ethics at Duke University) 6 https://kenan.ethics.duke.edu/wp-content/uploads/2018/01/BabyManji_Case2015.pdf.

Press Information Bureau, 'National Commission for Protection of Child Rights (NCPCR) to Constitute 'Mediation Cell' for cases of Child Custody Dispute in NRI Marital Discord' (*Press Information Bureau*, 1 August 2019) https://pib.gov.in/newsite/PrintRelease.aspx?relid=181332.

Robinson, G, *United States: Maryland High Court Holds Islamic "Talaq" Divorce Unconstitutional* (2008), Global Legal Monitor, www.loc.gov/law/foreign-news/article/united-states-maryland-high-court-holds-islamic-talaq-divorce-unconstitutional/.

Sharma, KA, *Limping Marriages and Holidays Wives* in Critiquing, Nationalism, Transnationalism, and Indian Diaspora www.drkavitasharma.org/pdf/Limping%20Marriages%20and%20Holiday%20Wives.pdf.

Singh, K and Rajput, P, *Laws Relating to NRI Marriages and their Impact on Women*, http://ncwapps.nic.in/ExpertCommitteePDFFiles/EC_NRIMarriages.pdf.

The official text of the 1927 Protocol may be accessed in the League of Nations, '*Treaty Series*' vol 92, 301, https://treaties.un.org/doc/Publication/UNTS/LON/Volume%2092/v92.pdf.

Turhan, Z and Helena, M, *Brussels II Bis: The Right of the Child to Be Heard in International Proceedings* [2015] 70/11-12.

United Nations Commission on Trade Law, https://uncitral.un.org/en/about.

Reports

246 Report of the Law Commission, Ministry of Law and Justice vide (Notification) F.No.A-60011/48/2010-Admn.III (LA).

Australian Law Reform Commission Report, 'Choice of Law' Report No 58.

Bellet, P and Goldman, B, 'Explanatory Report on the 1970 Hague Divorce Convention'.

Commission Decision of 22 December 2008 on the request from the United Kingdom to accept Regulation (EC) No 593/2008 of the European Parliament and the Council on the law applicable to contractual obligations (Rome I) (notified under document number C(2008) 8554).

Council on General Affairs and Policy, 'Report of the Experts' Group on the Parentage/Surrogacy Project (meeting from 29 October to 1 November 2019)' (*Hague Conference on Private International Law*, March 2020).

Dogauchi, M and Hartley, T, The Permanent Bureau: Hague Conference on Private International Law – Preliminary Document No. 26, Preliminary Draft Convention on Exclusive Choice of Court Agreements, Explanatory Report (December 2004).

Final Report to the Study on Intellectual Property and the Conflict of Laws, ETD/99/B-3000/E/16 (18 April 2000).

Giuliano, M and Lagarde, P, (1980) *Report on the Convention on the law applicable to contractual obligations* [1980] OJ C282/1, 23.

Hague Conference on Private International Law, 'Commentary on the Hague Principles on Choice of Law in International Contracts' (approved 15 March 2015).

Hague Conference On Private International Law, Explanatory Report On The 1978 Marriage Convention 291 (1978) Draft Convention adopted by the Thirteenth Session and Explanatory Report by Ake Malmström.

Hague Conference on Private International Law, Judgments Convention: Revised Preliminary Explanatory Report (Note 10 of May 2018).

Hartley, T and Dogauchi, M, (HCCH Publications 2007) 'Explanatory Report on the 2005 Hague Convention on Choice of Court Agreements'.

HCCA, 'Convention of 2 July 2019 on the Recognition and Enforcement of Foreign Judgments in Civil or Commercial Matters: Explanatory Report' (2020).

HCCH, 'Note on Article 1(1) of the 2016 Preliminary Draft Convention and the Term 'Civil or Commercial Matters', Preliminary Document No 4 of December 2016 for the attention of the Special Commission of February 2017 on the Recognition and Enforcement of Foreign Judgments.

Justice Rajesh Bindal Committee, 'Report of Justice Rajesh Bindal Committee to Examine Vol. I and The Civil Aspects of International Child Abduction Bill, 2016 and The Protection of Children (Inter-Country Removal and Retention) Bill, 2016' (*Chandigarh Judicial Academy*, 21 April 2018).

Law Commission of India, *Need to accede to the Hague Convention on the Civil Aspects of International Child Abduction (1980)* (Law Com No 218, 2009).

Law Commission of India, *Reforms in Guardianship and Custody Laws in India (2015)* (Law Com No 257, 2015).

Law Commission of India, *The Guardians and Wards Act, 1890 and Certain Provisions of the Hindu Minority and Guardianship Act, 1956 (1980)* (Law Com No 83, 1980).

Law Commission of India, *The Limitation Act, 1963* (Law Com No 89, 1983).

Law Commission, and Scottish Law Commission, *Private International Law: Choice of Law Rules in Marriage* (Com No 165; Scot Law Com No 105, 1987).

Law Commission, *Indian Penal Code,* (Law Commission Report No 42, 1971).

Law Commission, *Irretrievable Breakdown of Marriage – Another Ground for Divorce* (Law Com No 217, 2009).

Law Commission, *Laws on Registration of Marriage and Divorce – A Proposal for Consolidation and Reform* (Law Com No 211, 2008).

Law Commission, *Marital Property Agreements* (Law Com CP No 198, 2011).

Law Commission, *Need for Family Law Legislations for Non-resident Indians* (Law Com No 219, 2009).

Law Commission, *The Law of Domicile* (Law Com No 88, 1986).

Law Commission, *The Recognition of Foreign Divorces Decrees in India* (Law Commission Report No 65, 1976).

Malmstrom, A, *Explanatory Report* on 1978 Hague Convention on Celebration and Recognition of the Validity of Marriages.

Nygh, P and Pocar, F, Hague Conference on Private International Law: Preliminary Document No. 11 – Preliminary Draft Convention on Jurisdiction and Foreign Judgments in Civil and Commercial Matters (2000).

Perez-Vera, E, 'Explanatory Report by Elisa Perez-Vera' (*HCCH* 1981).

Schulz, A, 'The Future Convention on Exclusive Choice of Court Agreements and Arbitration Parallel Proceedings and Possible Treaty Conflicts: In Particular with ICSID and the New York Convention on the Recognition and Enforcement of Foreign Arbitral Awards' Preliminary Document No 32 of June 2005, Permanent Bureau, Hague Conference on Private International Law.

Scottish Law Commission, *Private International Law: The Law of Domicile* (Scot Law Com No 63, 1985).

Select Committee, 'Report Of The Select Committee On The Surrogacy (Regulation) Bill, 2019 Presented to the Rajya Sabha' (*PRS*, 5 February 2020).

Villasenor, J, 'Products Liability and Driverless Cars: Issues and Guiding Principles for Legislation' (2014) Report: Brookings Institution 11.

GLOSSARY

animus manendi et revertendi	The intention of remaining; to acquire a domicile a person must have an abode in one place with the intention of remaining there
animus non revertendi	The intention of not returning
ashirvad	Literally, 'blessings'. An essential ceremony for a Parsi marriage
Bikram Sambat (BS)	Nepalese calendar
bona fide	In good faith
brutum fulmen	A judgment or decision that is void and has no legal effect at all
culpa in contrahendo	The parties' standard of conduct in pre-contractual dealings
dehors	To be outside the scope of (something)
dépeçage	The right of the parties to an international contract to select different laws to govern parts of the contract that are separable from one another
dower (*mehr*)	Money or property which the wife is entitled to receive from the husband in consideration of marriage. There are two kinds of dower or *mehr*: (1) prompt *muajjal* dower payable at the time of marriage; and (2) deferred *muajjal* dower payable either on the dissolution of the marriage or on the happening of a specified event
ex aequo et bono	According to what is right and good
ex parte	A court decision or order made without the appearance of the opposite party
favor matrimonii	Law that favours the recognition of marriage
forum rei sitae	The court within whose jurisdiction immovable property is situated
Jains	Adherent of Jainism, an ancient Indian religion
jura novit curia	The court knows the law
khula	A procedure through which a woman can divorce her husband in Islam, by returning the dower (*mehr*) or something else that she received from her husband

Kompetenz-Kompetenz	The power of the arbitral tribunal to rule on its own power
lakh	100,000 units
laissez-faire	The concept that businesses should be at a liberty to develop without government control
lex causae	The law of the cause
lex fori	The law of the forum
lex loci arbirti	The law of the jurisdiction that is the seat of the arbitration
lex loci celebrationis	The law of the place of celebration of marriage
lex loci *contractus*	The law of the place of the conclusion of a contract
lex loci damni	The law of the place where damage occurred
lex loci delicti commissi	The law of the place where a wrong was committed or occurred
lex loci domicilii	The law of the domicile of the person
lex patriae	The law of the nationality of the person
lex loci protectionis	The law of the place where the intellectual property right is protected
lex situs	The law of the jurisdiction where property is situated
lex loci solutionis	The place of the performance of the contract
lex mercatoria	Commercial law as chiefly developed by the international business community. It is based on customary practices and the general principles of law
lex specialis	Special rules
Lok Sabha	Lower House of the Indian Parliament
mala fides	Bad faith
mubarat	Type of Islamic divorce in which the husband and wife mutually consent to be freed from their married state
Muluki Dewani (Samhita) Ain	Nepalese expression – *Muluki* (Country) *Dewani* (Civil) *Samhita* (Codification) *Ain* (Act) – the Nepal Civil Code
Muluki Dewani Kariyabidhi (Samhita) Ain	Nepalese expression – *Muluki* (Country) *Dewani* (Civil) *Kariyabidhi* (Procedural) *Samhita* (Codification) *Ain* (Act) – the Nepal Civil Procedure Code
negotiorum gestio	Claiming payment for the voluntary management of the affairs of another
Parsis	Member of a group of followers in India of the Iranian prophet Zoroaster

Rajya Sabha	Upper House of the Indian Parliament
raison d'être	Reason or justification for existence
res judicata	A matter that has already been adjudicated by a competent authority and cannot be pursued again by the same parties
res sub judice	A matter that is pending a decision or judgment
sapindas	The term *sapindas* is unique to Hindu law. Two persons are *sapindas* if they have a common ancestor
Sikhs	Sikhism is a monotheistic religion which originated in the Punjab region of India
sharia	Islamic religious law that regulates the life of Muslims
sine qua non	Without which something will not be possible
situs	The location of something (usually property)
stare decisis	The doctrine of precedent that obligates the courts to follow the previous decisions of a similar nature
suo moto	Action taken by the court on its own motion
talaq	Islamic word for divorce
Taka	Bangladesh currency
ubi jus ibi remedium	Where there is a right, there is a remedy
ultra vires	Beyond a person's legal power or authority
void ab initio	Invalid from the beginning

INDEX

Note: Alphabetical arrangement is word-by-word, where a group of letters followed by a space is filed before the same group of letters followed by a letter, eg 'social morality' will appear before 'socialist'. In determining alphabetical arrangement, initial articles and prepositions are ignored.